Bambang SM Praptomo practised law in Indonesia from 1985 to 2010, and is now retired. After graduating B.A. in English Teaching from the State Institute for the Teaching Profession and Pedagogy in Surabaya, East Java, Indonesia, he obtained a law degree from the University of Indonesia, Jakarta, in 1985, and a Master's degree in philosophy from the University of Indonesia, Jakarta, in 2004.

Published by ARLON PUBLISHING

an imprint of Oxford Legal Publishing Limited

www.arlonpublishing.co.uk

OXFORD

"Publishers of Intelligent Books for Intelligent Readers" © 2017

ARLON PUBLISHING

focuses on and aims to further study and knowledge in

all dimension and fields of legal studies.

ARLON
PUBLISHING

Published in the United Kingdom by ARLON PUBLISHING

Oxford Legal Publishing Limited is registered in England as No.10898419

at the following address:

Clarendon House
52 Cornmarket Street
Oxford OX1 3HJ
United Kingdom

All correspondence should be addressed to contact@arlonpublishing.co.uk

British Library Cataloguing in Publication Data

Data Available

Bambang SM Praptomo is the author of this work.

ISBN: 978-1-912142-25-5

TRANSFORMATIONAL GENERATIVE LAW

Rule of Law and Legal Determination viewed through Chomskyan theory: A structural dimension of evolutionary law

Bambang SM Praptomo

ARLON
PUBLISHING

OXFORD

Table of Contents

TABLE OF CASES

TRANSFORMATIONAL GENERATIVE LAW

Rule of Law and Legal Determination viewed through Chomskyan theory: A structural dimension of evolutionary law

CHAPTER I

Underlying Theories

I.1. SOME SIGNIFICANT NOTIONS IN CHOMSKYAN THEORY

***

Like Leibniz, Humboldt (1836) reiterated the Platonistic view that, for the individual, learning is largely a matter of *Wiedererzeugung*, that is, of drawing out what is innate in the mind.[1] However, the empiricist holds that language is essentially an adventitious construct, taught by "conditioning" (Skinner or Quine) or by drill and explicit explanation (Wittgenstein), or built up by elementary 'data-processing' procedures (as modern linguist typically maintains), but in any event, relatively independent in its structure of any innate mental faculties. The empiricist speculatively assumes that only the procedures and mechanisms for the acquisition of knowledge constitute an innate property of the mind.[2] Rudolf Carnap explored logical epistemology based on the logical system as constructed by Alfred North Whitehead and Bertrand Russell in *Principia Mathematica* for the consideration of issues as to the acquisition of knowledge. In his *Der Logische Aufbau der Welt* (henceforth *Aufbau*), Carnap is explicitly concerned with the task of creating a *Konstitutionssystem*, or 'constructional system,' which contains a set of basic elements and a set of basic relations which, taken together, constitute the basis of the whole system, with the consequence that all other objects ('*Gegenstanden*') in the system are ultimately defined in terms of this basis. Carnap's distinctive kind of logical epistemology exerts a profound influence upon American philosophers during the 1940s and 1950s.[3] Carnap was one of the most prominent members of the Vienna Circle whose desire was to provide a secure foundation for the sciences, the rejection of metaphysics, and the utilization of logical analysis for the purposes of philosophical enquiry. The *Aufbau* came to be viewed as one of the seminal texts of logical positivism.[4] He says that a change in approach occurred when I recognized, under the influence of the Gestalt psychology of Wertheimer and Köhler that the customary method of analyzing material things into separate sense-

1 Noam Chomsky, Aspects of the Theory of Syntax, (Cambridge, MA: MIT Press, 1965), p. 51.

2 Ibid., [footnote omitted].

3 Marcus Tomalin, 'Goodman, Quine, and Chomsky: from a grammatical point of view', in Lingua 113 (2003), pp. 1223-1253 (p. 1225).

4 Ibid., p. 1224.

data was inadequate – that an instantaneous visual field and perhaps even an instantaneous total experience is given as a unit, while the allegedly simple sense-data are the result of a process of abstraction. Therefore, I took as elements total instantaneous experience rather than single sense-data. I developed a method called 'quasi-analysis', which leads, on the basis of the similarity-relation among experiences, to the logical construction of those entities which are usually conceived as components. On the basis of a certain primitive relation among experiences, the method of quasi-analysis leads step by step to the various sensory domains-first to the visual domain, then to the positions in the visual field, the colors, and their similarity system, the temporal order, and the like.[5] The 'similarity-relation' referred to above constituted the only extralogical relation incorporated in the basis of the system.[6] From this single extralogical primitive, Carnap was able to derive more complex relations such as 'part-similarity', 'part-identity' and so on. Assuming this minimal basis, Carnap proceeds to construct larger objects by means of definition [called 'explicit']. If, however, a concept is introduced that cannot be specified by means of explicit definition, then a process of implicit definition is required, which permits ascension to a new constructional level.[7] Consequently, the various constructional levels (which are ultimately determined by the extralogical basis) largerly determine the structure of the system created.[8]

Constructional system theory has influenced the initial Transformational Generative Grammar (TGG) formalism. Nelson Goodman and Williard Van Orman Quine were instrumental in enabling concepts derived from the theory of construction systems to be directly involved in the development of TGG.[9] The research project undertaken by Goodman and Leonard (and, eventually, Quine) was directly inspired by the *Aufbau*. In his 1963 essay '*The Significance of Der Logische Aufbau der Welt,*' Goodman articulated a robust defence of logical epistemology and believed that 'simplicity' and 'economy' were crucial aspects of system construction.[10] A constructional system possessing a simpler, more economical, basis was preferable to an alternative system that utilized a more complex basis.[11] Quine focuses on the notion of theory-internal simplicity and distinguishes

---

5 Ibid., p. 1226, quoting P.A. Schilpp, 'The Philosophy of Rudolf Carnap', (La Salla:. The Open Court, 1963), pp. 16-17.

6 Ibid., p. 1227, referring to R. Carnap (1928), 'The Logical Structure of the World: Pseudoproblems in Philosophy', translation by R.A. George, (London: Routledge & Kegan Paul, 1967) (reprint), p. 127.

7 Ibid., referring to Carnap (1928/1967), Ibid., 65ff.

8 Ibid.

9 Ibid., p. 1224.

10 Ibid., p. 1229, 1230.

11 Ibid., p. 1230.

consistently between the 'economy of practical expressions', which is merely a notational convenience, and 'economy in grammar and vocabulary', which actively simplifies theoretical discourse.[12] The former concerns 'apparent', while the latter 'real'. Carnap, Goodman and Quine agree that the language must be nominalistic, i.e, its terms must not refer to abstract entities but only to observable objects or events. The main motivation for a nominalistic approach to constructional system theory is the belief that, by rejecting abstract entities, the infamous paradoxes that had bedeviled all attempts to place mathematics on a secure foundation in the early 20th century might be avoided.[13] Consequently, Goodman and Quine make a clear distinction between platonistic logic (i.e., logic that admits abstract entities such as classes) and nominalistic logic (i.e., logic that does not admit abstract entities), outlining some of the strategies that must be employed in order to convert platonistic statements into nominalistic statements.

Bloomfield's writings were on conditioned response to stimuli – what behaviorism is about, and his care was not to suggest forms or paradigms to the informant, but rather to arrange situations in which forms, including members of paradigms, might naturally be spoken.[14] It is a recognition that all people are suggestible, and that language users have an unconscious capacity to adapt to one another's usage from which the linguist-informant relationship is not immune. This caveat can be phrased in terms of cognitive psychology or indeed in terms of any psychology that recognizes human suggestibility.[15] As to psychological consideration, Chomsky (1951)[16] is no more than the observation that in an 'analytic grammar' (which he would later call a generative grammar, that is, one going from more general elements to more particular by potentially recursive steps) the context of an element is introduced at the same time as the element itself. He holds

12 Ibid., p. 1231, citing W.V.O.Quine, 'From a Logical Point of View', (Cambridge, MA: Harvard University Press, 1953), p. 26.

13 Ibid., pp. 1233-1234, referring to Schilpp (1963), supra note 5, p. 79.

14 Bruce E. Nevin, 'More Concerning the Roots of Transformational Generative Grammar', in Historiographia Linguistics xxxvi:2/3 (2009), pp. 461-481(p. 463). That this notion of linear causation of behavior by the environment is an absurdity, and the astonishment that we should feel at how long it was seriously entertained, is a subject for another place. In brief, behaviorism offers an account of the coercive induction of goals or purposes, something which as a matter of principled commitment it could not recognize as either fact or theoretical construct.

15 Ibid.

16 Ibid., p. 464, referring to [Avram] Noam Chomsky, 'Morphophonemics of Modern Hebrew', A Thesis In Linguistics Presented to the Faculty of the Graduate School of the University of Pennsylvania in partial fulfillment of the requirements for the degree of Masters of Arts, 1951, 1979b, in the collection of the Van Pelt Library at the University of Pennsylvania, p. 8.

that one cannot really understand what a noun phrase is except in the contextual frame provided by other phrases, or until it is presented against the background of the sentence of which it is a part. But this is what has been called an analytic process. This consideration seems to have some relevance, at least on the higher levels of analysis, but, generally speaking, I do not know how much (if any) weight is to be attributed to it.

Chomsky (1951)[17] refers to distributional analysis (by which he says that the elements and their combinations are identified) as a 'process of discovery'. The algorithmic bent of Generative Grammar is his core interest. Chomsky (1957) defines syntax as the study of principles and processes by which sentences are constructed in particular languages.[18] Notice that the phrase 'principles and processes' in the definition suggest a cognitive or mental activity, since for him a grammar mirrors the behavior of the speaker who can produce or understand an indefinite number of sentences. On the whole, the mentalistic outlook of generative grammar has continued to be hugely influential throughout linguistic and cognitive neuroscience.[19] According to Chomsky (1965), a language acquisition device is an intrinsic property, and the language-acquisition device is only one component of the total system of intellectual structures that can be applied to problem solving and concept formation; in other words, the *faculté de langage* is only one of the faculties of the mind. The problem of mapping the intrinsic cognitive capacities of an organism and identifying the systems of belief and the organization of behavior that it can readily attain should be central to experimental psychology.[20] However, so far attentions are directed to tasks that are extrinsic [not intrinsic] to an organism's cognitive capacities. And, some incidental information about the effect of intrinsic cognitive structure and intrinsic organization of behavior on what is learned has rarely been the focus of serious attention (outside of ethiology). In the Logical Structure of Linguistic Theory (LSLT), formulated in 1973, published in 1975, Chomsky says that Goodman's ongoing critique of induction seemed to point in a rather different direction, suggesting the inadequacy in principle of inductive approaches. Quine's critique of logical empiricism also gave some reason to believe that this line of inquiry might be a plausible one. Quine argued that the principles of scientific theory are confronted with experience as a systematic complex, with adjustments possible at various points, governed by such factors a general simplicity.

---

17 Ibid., p. 465, referring to Chomsky (1951/1979b), Ibid.

18 Noam Chomsky, Syntactic Structures, (The Hague: Mouton Publishers, 1957), p. 11, 15.

19 Ray Jackendoff, 'Précis of Foundations of Language: Brain, Meaning, Grammar, Evolution', in BEHAVIORAL AND BRAIN SCIENCE (2003) 26, pp. 651-707 (p. 652).

20 Chomsky (1965), supra note 1, pp. 56-57.

Perhaps, then, analogous considerations hold for the fundamental problem of linguistic theory.[21] Chomsky acknowledged (1975) that it was he who sought mechanical discovery procedures. [22] When he gave up on automated linguistic analysis, then since it was supposed (following Piaget) that the cognitive capacities of adult linguist cannot be ascribed to infants and children, he assigned the role of human insight to an innate language organ in children, and to linguistic intuitions in adults, the latter arising out of the former by the process of language acquisition (as distinct from language learning).

***

Among the significant notions in Chomskyan theory are *performance* and *competence*. The first methodological assumption that Transformational Generative Grammar (TGG) makes is that grammatical knowledge can be studied independently from others. TGG focuses on grammatical *competence* (e.g., the knowledge that certain forms have certain meanings, etc.), and more precisely on the mentally represented system (ultimately physically represented system) that characterizes this knowledge, termed *grammar*. Grammars therefore constitute the basic objects of inquiry within this framework.[23] *Performance* refers to the kinds of language that are actually produced and heard. *Competence*, by contrast, refers to what we know about our language; it is unimpeded by factors that might muddy the waters of performance. For example, the first time we read this really long complicated sentence "Who did Bill say Frank claimed that Mary seems to have been likely to have kissed?", we might have the initial unacceptability of the sentence because of a performance problem. But then when we thought about it and stared at it a bit, we saw that the sentence was actually a fairly standard grammatical sentence of English. What we did was to access our competence in (or knowledge of) English grammar. Understanding spoken conversational language and being able to judge the well-formedness of a sentence, seem to actually be different skills corresponding roughly to performance and competence.[24]

---

21 Iwo Iwanov, 'Linguistics and the formal sciences: The origins of generative grammar by Marcus Tomalin, in SIL Electronic Book Review 2011-003, referring to N. Chomsky, 'The Logical Structure of Linguistic Theory', (New York: Plenum Press, 1975) [Publication of a further revision of Chomsky 1955/56], p. 33.

22 Nevin (2009), supra note 17, p. 465, referring to Chomsky (1955/56), Ibid., p. 30, 33.

23 Youssef Aoun and Dominique Sportiche, 'Transformational Generative Grammar and the Study of Language', in GLOW Newsletter 5, September 1980.

24 Carnie, A., Syntax-Generative Introduction-Part I: Preliminaries: Generative Grammar, 3rd ed.,(Chichester, UK: Wiley-Blackwell, A John Wiley & Sons Publication, 2013), p. 17.

The study of *competence* is on speaker's functional-knowledge of language, the study of *performance* is on the actual processes (viewed computationally or neutrally) taking place in the mind/brain that put this functional-knowledge to use in speaking and understanding sentences.[25] A basic claim of the Chomsky 1965 version of generative grammar was that in addition to the surface form of sentences, that is, the form we hear, there is another level of syntactic structure, called Deep Structure, which expresses underlying syntactic regularities of sentences. For example, a passive sentence like "The bear was chased by the lion" has a Deep Structure in which the noun phrases are in the order of the corresponding active "The lion chased the bear".[26] There is a fundamental distinction between *competence* (the speaker-hearer's knowledge of his language) and *performance* (the actual use of language in concrete situations). Performance is a direct reflection of competence only under the idealization of linguistic theory which is concerned primarily with an ideal speaker-listener, in a completely homogeneous speech-community, who knows its language perfectly and is unaffected by such grammatically irrelevant conditions as memory limitations, distractions, shifts of attention and interest, and errors (random or characteristic) in applying his knowledge of the language in actual performance.[27]

There are some suggestive observations concerning the role of superficial aspect of sentence structure on performance in determining acceptability (that is, their role in limiting performance).[28] The theory of performance is the theory of language use. No doubt, a reasonable model of language use will incorporate, as a basic component, the generative grammar that expresses the speaker-hearer's knowledge of the language; but this generative grammar does not, in itself, prescribe the character of functioning of a perceptual model or a model of speech production.[29] The theory of performance, outside of phonetics, have come from studies of performance models that incorporate generative grammars of specific kinds – that is, from studies that have been based on assumptions about underlying competence.[30] In general, it seems that the study of performance models incorporating generative grammar may be a fruitful study; furthermore, it is difficult to imagine any other basis on which a theory of performance might develop. [31] It is the descriptivist limitation-in-principle

25 Jackendoff (2003), supra note 19, p. 652, referring to Chomsky (1965), supra note 21.

26 Ibid., p. 654, referring to Chomsky (1965), Ibid.

27 Chomsky (1965), Ibid., p. 3, 4.

28 Ibid., p. 13.

29 Ibid., p. 9.

30 Ibid., p. 10.

31 Ibid., p. 15.

to classification and organization of data, to 'extracting patterns' from a corpus of observed speech, to describing 'speech habit' or 'habit structures', insofar as these may exist, etc, that precludes the development of a theory of actual performance.

Schwartz (1993) defines performance as behavior based on competence. Linguistic behavior based on this knowledge is termed learned linguistic behavior.[32] Humboldtian conception of underlying competence is a system of generative processes (*see* Chomsky 1964).[33] A theory of linguistic competence is supposed to simply define the permissible structures in the language, without saying how those structures are produced in real time. However, a competence theory ought to lend itself to being embedded in a theory of proceesing, that we ought to be able to say how the functional-knowledge that constitutes the competence theory is actually put to use. There turns out to be an inherent structural reason why competence has to be isolated from performance in the syntacocentric view of language.[34] A grammar of a language purports to be a description of the ideal speaker-hearer's intrinsic competence. If the grammar is, furthermore, perfectly explicit – in other words, if it does not rely on the intelligence of the understanding reader but rather provides an explicit analysis of his contribution – we may (somewhat redundantly) call it a *generative grammar*. A fully adequate grammar must assign to each of an infinite range of sentences a structural description indicating how this sentence is understood by the ideal speaker-hearer.[35]

The study of performance includes the concept of acceptability, whereas the study of competence includes 'grammaticalness'. Like acceptability, grammaticalness is, no doubt, a matter of degree (*cf.* Chomsky, 1955, 1957, 1961), but the scales of grammaticalness and acceptability do not coincide. Grammaticalness is only one of many factors that interact to determine acceptability. The study of performance could profitably begin with an investigation of the acceptability of the simplest formal structures in grammatical sentences. The most obvious formal property of utterances is their bracketing into constituents of various types, that is, the "tree structure" associated with them.[36] Putman argues that the set of sentences of a natural language acceptable to a speaker under performance conditions is recursive rather than an argument about the set of sentences specified as

32 B.D. Schwartz, 'On explicit and negative data effecting and affecting competence and linguistic behavior', in Studies in Second Language Acquisition, 15, 1993, pp. 147-163.

33 Chomsky (1965), supra note 31, p. 4.

34 Jackendoff (2003), supra note 26, pp. 662-663.

35 Chomsky (1965), supra note 33, p. 4, 5.

36 Ibid., p. 11, 12.

grammatical by the speaker's competence.[37] The notions of performance and competence in linguistics as above stated have led the present author to identify similar notions in law, which will be addressed in Chapters III and V in light of Chapter II of this book.

***

There are two ways to go about writing grammatical rules. One is to tell people how they *should* speak (this is of course the domain of English teachers and copy-editors); we call these kinds of rules *prescriptive rules* (as they prescribe how people should speak according to some standards). The other approach is to write rules that describe how people *actually* speak, whether or not they are speaking 'correctly'. These are called *descriptive* rules.[38] Generative Grammar claims to be a theory of cognitive psychology, so it is reasonable to ask whether formal rules *really* exist in the brain / mind of speaker. Obviously, the rules *per se* don't exist in our brains, but they do model the external behavior of the mind.[39] Generative grammar has aimed at being an explanatory theory. Furthermore, a central tenet of generative grammar, especially clear in the work of Chomsky since the mid-1970s (e.g. Chomsky 1973), has been the idea that a single theory can serve simultaneously as a descriptive theory and as an explanatory theory. Explanatory theories (or theoretical frameworks) are theories about why language are the way they are.[40] Such a view follows from Chomsky's idea about innateness: if one believes that languages are the way they are because of our innate linguistic knowledge, then a theory about that innate linguistic knowledge will simultaneously serve as a theory about what languages are like and as a theory about why they are that way.[41] The central principle to Chomskyan generative grammar is that explanation ought to be built into description. The idea that explanation can be built into description and hence descriptions of what languages are like can establish explanations for why they are that way.[42] Chomsky[43] says that the grammar defines the relation 'the deep

37 P. Stanley Peters, Jr and R.W. Ritchie, 'On the Generative Power of Transformational Grammars,' in INFORMATION SCIENCES 6, 49-83(1973), p. 82, referring to Chomsky (1965), Ibid., pp. 3-4, 10-15.

38 Carnie (2013), supra note 25, p. 9.

39 Ibid., p. 9.

40 Matthew S. Dryer, 'Descriptive Theories, Explanatory Theories, and Basic Linguistic Theory', in Felix Ameka, Alan Dench & Nicholas Evans (eds), in Catching Language: Issues in Grammar Writing,(2006), pp. 207-234, § 1.

41 Ibid.

42 Ibid., § 4.1.

43 Francis Jeffry Pelletier, 'The generative power of rule orderings in formal grammars', in Linguistics 18 (1980), pp. 17-72 (p. 25), referring to Chomsky (1965), supra note 37, p. 141.

structure M underlies the well-formed surface structure M' of the sentence S and derivately, it defines the notions 'M is a deep structure', 'M is a well-formed surface structure', 'S is a well-formed sentence', and many others (such as 'S is structurally ambiguous', 'S and S are paraphrases', 'S is a deviant sentence formed by violating rule R or condition C').[44]

One major aspect of Chomsky's povital work 'LSLT' (Logical Structure of Linguistic Theory) is the focus on so-called evaluation procedures. Put crudely, an evaluation procedure helps us decide which grammar of a given set of possible grammars is more adequate, that is, which corresponds best to a given linguistic corpus.[45] Having given up on discovery of language structure, Chomsky takes for granted a population of diverse putative structures, and his aim is to 'discover' which is correct. He attacks the notion of discovering language structures and rejects the feasibility of such discovery procedures. He suggests that immediate constituent analysis as described by Wells and by Harris is a practical procedure for discovering the constituents of a language. Methodologically, immediate constituent analysis depends upon native speaker judgments of successive bisections into paired constituents.[46] The syntactic component of a generative grammar is the rules that specify the well-formed strings of minimal syntactically functioning units (*formatives*) and assign structural information of various kinds both to these strings and to strings that deviate from well-formedness in certain respects.[47]

Descriptive theories (or theoretical frameworks) are theories about what languages are like. They are theories about what tools we need in order to provide adequate description of individual languages.[48] A theory of visual perception would attempt to account for what a person actually sees and the mechanisms that determine this rather than his statements about what he sees and why, though these statements may provide useful, in fact, compelling evidence for such a theory.[49] Descriptive order is unarguably of a different logical type, however, from structural order (rule ordering is 'meta' to the rules that are ordered, which in turn are 'meta' to the 'actual sequence' in the output of the rules), and while structural order is invariant under different analyses (with the well-understood exception of Harrisian long components, which have no relevance for Chomsky), descriptive order may change sharply under different analyses. The descriptive order of rules

44 Ibid., referring to Chomsky (1965), Ibid., pp. 140-141.

45 Iwanov (2011), supra note 21.

46 Nevin (2009), supra note 22, n.9, referring to Chomsky (1975), supra note 22, p. 80, 116, 177 n.13, 139, 149 n.21, 171.

47 Chomsky (1965}, supra note 44, p. 3.

48 Dryer (2006), supra note 40.

49 Chomsky (1965), supra note 47, pp. 8-9.

are radically changed while still accounting for the same 'actual sequences' of linguistic elements.[50]

Notions similar to the notions of prescriptivity and descriptivity as above mentioned exist in jurisprudence. In jurisprudence, legal doctrinal writers and jurists talk about descriptive jurisprudence and prescriptive jurisprudence, and the law itself is descriptive and at the same time prescriptive in its existence. The notions of descriptivity and prescriptivity in cognitive science, epistemology and philsophy as underlying the composition of this book will be addressed in Chapter I.2, and similar notions in law will be addressed through Chapters II to V, specifically in Chapters II, III, IV.4, V.1.6, V.1.7, V.3, V.4 and V.5.

***

A language must contain a finite list of words and a set of rules (or grammar) that collectively describe or 'generate' the sentences of the language.[51] Rules of grammar in the sense of generative grammar are unconscious principles that play a role in the production and understanding of sentences.[52] Within traditional linguistic theory, furthermore, all languages have essentially their 'creative' aspect, so all languages provide the means for expressing indefinitely many thoughts and for reacting appropriately in an indefinite range of new situations (for references, *cf.* Chomsky, 1964, forthcoming). A universal grammar accommodates the creative aspect of language use and expresses the deep-seated regularities which are universal.[53]

It was well understood that linguistic processes are in some sense 'creative', however, it is possible to attempt an explicit formulation of the 'creative' processes of language only upon the development of how a language can (in Humboldt's words) 'make infinite use of finite means' in the last 30 years prior to 1965, in the course of studies in the foundations of mathematics. Then, the full-scale study of generative grammar is no longer technically hindered. A generative grammar means simply a system of rules that in some explicit and well-defined way assign structural descriptions to sentences. It is mostly mental processes with which generative grammar will be dealing. A generative grammar attempts to specify what the speaker actually knows, not what he may report about his knowledge.[54] A generative grammar is not a model for a speaker or a hearer. It attempts to characterize in the most neutral possible terms

50 Nevin (2009), supra note 46, p. 473, referring to Chomsky (1951/1979b), supra note 17.

51 Jackendoff (2003), supra note 34, p. 652.

52 Ibid., referring to N. Chomsky (1965), supra note 49.

53 Chomsky (1965), Ibid., p. 6.

54 Ibid., p. 8.

the knowledge of the language that provides the basis for actual use of language by a speaker-hearer. When we speak of a grammar as generating a sentence with a certain structural description, we can mean simply that the grammar assigns this structural description to the sentence.[55] The term 'generate' is familiar in the sense intended [here] in logic, particularly in Post's theory of combinational systems. Furthermore, 'generate' seems to be the most appropriate translation for Humboldt's term *erzeugen*, which he frequently uses, it seems, in essentially the sense as intended. This use of the term 'generate' is well established both in logic and in the tradition of linguistic theory.[56] Humboldt holds that since the natural inclination to language is universal to man, and since all men must carry the key to the understanding of all languages in their minds, it follows automatically that the form of all languages must be fundamentally identical and must always achieve a common objective. The variety among languages can lie only in the media and the limits permitted the attainment of the objectives.[57] So, like Chomsky, Humboldt[58] supposes that there is a Universal Grammar, a feature of the mind, which constrains the form that languages may have. He expresses the notion of Universal Grammar from the perspective of language variability. He links limits on language variability to a universal ability he sees in human psychology to acquire a language.

Generative grammar purports to describe the issue of competence. A generative grammar must be a system of rule that can iterate to generate an indefinitely large number of structures. This system can be analyzed into the tree major components of a generative grammar: the syntactic, phonological, and semantic components.[59] The phonological component of a grammar determines the phonetic form of a sentence generated by the syntactic rules. That is, it relates a structure generated by the syntactic component to a phonetically represented signal. The semantic component determines the semantic interpretation of a sentence. That is, it relates a structure generated by the syntactic component to a certain semantic representation. Both the phonetical and semantic components are therefore purely interpretive. The syntactic component of a grammar must specify, for each sentence, a *deep structure* that determines its semantic interpretation and a *surface structure* that determines its phonetic interpretation. The

55 Ibid., p. 9.

56 Ibid.

57 Kyle Johnson, 'Introduction to Transformational Grammar', University of Massachusetts at Amherst, Fall 2004, p. 4, referring to Wilhelm von Humboldt, 1836, "Űber die verschiedenheit des menschlichen sprachbaues und ihren einfluss auf die geistige entwickelung des menschengeschlechts," Berlin: Royal Academy of Sciences of Berlin.

58 Ibid., p. 5.

59 Chomsky (1965), supra note 56, pp. 15-16 [footnote omitted].

first of these is interpreted by the semantic component; the second by the phonologically component.[60] The *base* of the syntactic component is a system of rule that generate a highly restricted (perhaps finite) set of *basic strings*, each with an associated structural description called a *base Phrase-marker*. These base Phrase-markers are the elementary units of which deep structures are constituted. Underlying each sentence of the language there is a sequence of base Phrase-markers, each generated by the base of the syntactic component. Chomsky refers to this sequence as the *basis* of the sentence that it underlies. In addition to its base, the syntactic component of a generative grammar contains a *transformational* subcomponent. This is concerned with generating a sentence, with its surface structure, from its base. Since the base generates only a restricted set of base Phrase-markers, most sentences will have a sequence of such objects as an underlying basis. Among the sentences with a single base Phrase-marker as basis, we can delimit a proper subset called 'kernel sentence'. These are sentences of a particularly simple sort that involve a minimum transformational apparatus in their generation. The basic strings underlie kernel sentences. The basic string and base Phrase-markers do, it seems, play a distinctive and crucial role in language use. Chomsky makes the tacit simplifying (and contrary-to-fact) assumption that the underlying basic string is the sentence, the base Phrase-marker is the surface structure as well as the deep structure.[61] Phrase-markers are represented as trees to aid the reader's intuition, and Phrase-markers are represented as label bracketing for technical convenience.[62]

The underlying thesis of generative grammar is that sentences are generated by a subconscious set of procedures (like computer programs), being part of our minds (or of our cognitive abilities). The goal of syntactic theory is to model these procedures. In generative grammar, the means for modeling these procedures is through a set of formal grammatical rules. These rules tell you the order in which to put your words. This is the kind of information encoded in generative rules. These rules are thought to generate the sentences of a language, hence the name *generative* grammar.[63]

Chomsky states that each possible grammar should assign a structural description to each 'possible sentence', and that for certain possible grammar-sentence pairs the structural description will indicate that the sentence deviates from well-formedness, further will state the respect in which the sentence deviates from well-formedness.[64] There should

60 Ibid., p. 16 [footnote omitted].
61 Ibid., pp. 17-18.
62 Peters & Ritchie (1973), supra note 37, p. 50.
63 Carnie (2013), supra note 38, p. 6.
64 Peters & Ritchie (1973), supra note 62, fn.12.

be an algorithm to determine for an arbitrary possible grammar and an arbitrary string over the terminal vocabulary what structural descriptions the grammar assigns to the string, if any, as well as whether the grammar generates the string at all.[65] Harris acknowledges the diversity of heuristics, hunches, criteria and distributional methods that linguists use to wrestle their data into a coherent and useful description; the purpose of his 'methods' was to verify that findings, however reached, retain a valid relation to the fundamental data of native speaker judgments.[66] This grounding in primary data is in contrast to Chomsky's framing of validation procedures in terms of adjudicating among a purported huge number of alternative grammars, except that linguists in practice have already followed their informal criteria to converge on one or a few alternatives, so that there is no 'huge number' from which to choose. It is brute force computer algorithms that generate many ramifying alternatives, reasonable or not, for logical adjudication.[67] Chomsky adapted for his formulation of immediate constitutent analysis as Phrase Structure Grammar, and the source of the new familiar, and as it were, trademarked, terms 'generate' and 'generative'. Especially relevant is Seuren's identification (p. 100) of 'the algorithmic character of [...] generative grammar'.[68] Seuren contends that a formal calculus is an algorithmically organized system allowing for derivations to be carried out solely on the strength of the symbols used and their arrangement with regard to each other.[69] In other words, a calculus that is formal in the mathematical sense generates an 'object language' which is necessarily itself 'formal' in the linguistic sense. Seuren inexplicably continues to ascribe the formal treatment of language to positivism and behaviorism.[70] As John Goldsmith says, "Generative grammar is, more than it is anything else, a plea for the case that an insightful theory of language can be best on algorithmic explanation"[71].

---

65 Ibid., p. 71, referring to Chomsky (1965), supra note 60, pp. 31-32, fn.18.

66 Nevin (2009), supra note 50, p. 466. These are of two kinds. Judgments of contrast are based on substitutability, a distributional criterion, and Harris's criterion for transformation was the preservation of relative acceptability from one subset of sentences to another (where each is the set of satisfiers of a sentence form, that is, a sequence of form-class variables and constants).

67 Ibid.

68 Ibid., p. 462 [accompanying text omitted].

69 Ibid., p. 470, referring to Pieter Seuren, 'Concerning the Roots of Transformational Generative Grammar', in Historiographia Linguistica 36 (2009), pp. 97-115 [Review article on Tomalin 2008], p. 111.

70 Ibid.

71 Ibid., p. 462, referring to John Goldsmith, 'From Algorithm to Generative Grammar and Back Again', in Paper delivered to the Chicago Linguistic Society, 2004, (available at http: // hum..uchicago.edu/~ jagoldsm/Webpage), p. 1. Perhaps including even Chomsky, in his introduction to LSLT (Chomsky [1975],

As several times stated that generativity sometimes refers to the infinite use of finite means and to a grammar's ability to generate the set of grammatical sentences.[72] And the distinction between strong and weak generative capacity of a grammar has been characterized by Chomsky (1965:60): "Given a theory of language structure, we can distinguish *weak generative capacity* from its *strong generative capacity* in the following way. Let us say that a grammar weakly generates a set of sentences and that it strongly generates a set of structural descriptions (recall that each structural description uniquely specifies a sentence, but not necessarily conversely). The study of strong generative capacity is related to the study of descriptive adequacy. A grammar is descriptively adequate if it strongly generates the correct set of structural descriptions. A theory [of grammar] is descriptively adequate if its strong generative capacity includes the system of structural descriptions for each language."[73] Wall's interpretation of 'strong generative capacity' seems to include derivational history, that, nearly all the work on formal grammars deals exclusively with the sets of strings they generate (called the *weak generative capacity* of the grammar) and little has been said about the kinds of structural descriptions (constituent-structure trees) assigned to the grammatical strings (strong generative capacity).[74] A natural language grammar must, of course, not only generate the correct set of string, but it must also specify correct structural descriptions – 'correct' in the sense that they agree with the speaker's intuitions in marking a sentence as n–ways ambiguous, marking two sentences as paraphrases of each other, specifying the grammatical relations that hold between parts of a sentence etc. Pelletier argues since weak generative capacity is properly included in strong generative capacity, this makes no real difference when one is investigating strong generative capacity.[75] However, Pelletier does wish to emphasize the sometimes-neglected point that some overall properties of a grammar cannot be included in its weak generative capacity (such as relations between deep structure and surface structure), and any such properties shall be treated here as part of the grammar's strong

supra note 22, fn.16), although, like everything that he has to say about his mentor, this reference is grudging and equivocal. Footnote 16 is on the statement that "The notion 'generative grammar' [...] was never clearly developed."

72 Charles Kemp, Aaron Bernstein and Joshua B. Tenenbaum, 'A Generative Theory of Similarity,' in Conference Paper - proceedings of the Twenty-Seventh Annual Conference of the Cognitive Science Society 27(27), 2005 – cloudfront. escholarship.org.

73 Pelletier (1980), supra note 44, p. 60.

74 Ibid., p. 26, referring to R. Wall, 'Mathematical Linguistics,' in W.O. Dingwall (ed.), in A Survey of Linguistic Science, 1971, (College Park: University of Maryland Press), pp. 683-712.

75 Ibid. [accompanying text omitted].

generative capacity.[76] It is not implausible to have the notion of strong generative capacity in law, but the relation between deep structure and surface structure being considered as generative capacity is what this book seeks to identify or reveal in law, especially in legal reasoning, which will be addressed in Chapter IV.10.

***

According to the theory of transformational grammar, only certain kinds of formal operations on strings can appear in grammar – operations that, furthermore, have no a priori justification. What might in general be considered "elementary operations" on strings do not qualify as grammatical transformation at all, while many of the operations that do qualify are far from elementary, in any general sense. Specifically, grammatical transformations are necessarily "structure-dependent" in that they manipulate substrings only in terms of their assignment to categories.[77] In transformational grammar, the surface structure is determined by repeated application of certain formal operations called "grammatical transformation" to objects of a more elementary sort. The Immediate Constituent analysis (labeled bracketing) of an actual string of formatives may be adequate as an account of surface structure, but is certainly not adequate as an account of deep structure which is constituted of elementary objects.[78]

Seuren conflates morphophonemics with transformations, even making the unusual claim that Bloomfield, in his *Language* of 1933, also had 'transformations' (p. 108) because he reconstructed base forms from which he derived alternants by morphophonemic rules. Neither Harris nor Chomsky would call such derivations transformational. According to Seuren, Harris, 'with Chomsky following', borrowed the notion of transformation from 'the mathematical-logic literature ....[b]ut instead of treating transformation as a logical entailment relation [...] they transformed transformations into procedures ensuring syntactic well-formedness.[79] Contrary to Seuren's assumption, Harris's notion of transformation did not originate with Carnap and the logicians. It is a straightforward application of set theory and linear algebra to the data of language, as he plainly stated in (Harris 2002:5-6) and elsewhere.[80] The concept of transformation (linear mapping) in abstract algebra applies in a straightforward way to mapping from subset to subset within the set of sentences. This is obvious to a mathematician, if not to the average linguist. The mapping of transformation is established when

76 Ibid.

77 Chomsky (1965), supra note 65, p. 55.

78 Ibid., p. 17.

79 Nevin (2009), supra note 71, p. 472, referring to Seuren (2009), supra note 69, p. 108, 109.

80 Ibid., p. 474 [accompanying text omitted].

there is a 1-1 correspondence between the members of the two subsets, and a property of any member of one set holds for the corresponding member of the other. The criteria property for transformation is 'acceptability or normal discourse-neighborhood' (Harris 1968: 195).[81] Chomsky had stated that in LSLT, transformations are understood in a very different sense; it probably would have been preferable to select a different terminology instead of adapting Harris's in this rather different context.[82] In the event, Chomsky has dropped the term and his subsequent reformulations of theory have invented new terminology for what continue to be Carnap-style transformation rules applied to abstract representations of structure.[83] Chomsky has applied the mechanics of Post production systems (Post 1943) to a somewhat simplified form of the immediate constituent analysis of Bloomfield, which is based on psychological intuitions of divisibility, but certainly not to the more subtle word-expansion grammar of Harris (1942), which is based on substitution tests (a distributional basis that is 'mentalistic' insofar as it is grounded in native speaker judgment). [84] He subsequently applied 'deformations' to this pre-baked formalism so as to represent transformations, a property of language revealed to him by Harris, and took off thence in his own direction.[85] The introduction of the *transformational* component to syntactic description is meant to overcome the weakness of the immediate constituent (IC) analysis: for the IC model fails to see, for example, the inherent relation between active and passive sentences (p. 6).

It was Chomsky who replaced these set-theoretic and algebraic concept with Carnap's notion of 'transformation rule'. Doing so is more or less inevitable, given his insistence on representing the internal structure of sentences by phrase-structure trees, and it is a necessary presupposition for 'recasting' transformations as operations on those abstract structures.[86] Harris's transformations are a property of language, Chomsky's are a formal device for representing that property (more or less) by rules that 'enrich' a phrase-structure grammar. Rules of grammar may be widely variant in form, as a matter of notation and metagrammatical superstructure (and indeed have widely varied in the history of Generative Grammar), but transformations in the algebraic sense are variable only insofar as language varies, changes, and evolves. For Harris's and Chomsky's notions of transformation, Seuren says, "predicate-argument relations remained constant through transformations". For Harris, the preservation of

81 Ibid. [accompanying text and footnote omitted].

82 Ibid., p. 476, referring to Chomsky (1975), supra note 71, p. 43.

83 Ibid.

84 Ibid., p. 477 [footnote omitted].

85 Ibid. [accompanying text omitted].

86 Ibid., p. 475 [accompanying text omitted].

'predicate-argument relations' is an outcome of applying the distributional criterion for transformation (preservation of relative acceptability, or of context for full acceptability), whereas when transformations are defined as deformation of abstract structures, it is the properties of those structures, such as 'predicate-argument relations,' which are criteria.[87]

A transformational grammar contains two components: a base component (consisting of a phrase structure grammar) and a transformational component (consisting of a finite ordered set of grammatical transformations). Furthermore, transformations are defined to apply cyclically in derivations converting step by step a phrase-marker generated by the base into a derived phrase-marker. If the latter contains no occurrences of a special sentence boundary symbol, it is a surface structure and the phrase-marker initiating the derivation is a deep structure underlying it. A transformational grammar then generates as its language the set of all strings which have a surface-phrase-marker.[88] For Chomsky, according to Tomalin, transformations cause a change in the order of elements in existing sentences (*cf.* p. 168 – Tomalin's book). These sentences have been formed by the application of, for example, phrase structure rules.[89] Transformational rules map one representation to another, typically by way of relocating constituents. Interestingly, it appears that all such rules are 'structure dependent'. That is, they make reference to the relative structural positions of the moved thing and the position it is moved to. They don't, for example, make reference to points in a string on the basis of their position relative to some numerical count of formatives.[90] Chomsky proposes that the appropriate form for the rules of a natural language is a context-free phrase structure grammar supplemented by transformational rules.[91] Peters and Ritchie[92] define a transformation as the mapping induced on an n-term structural condition by an n-term transformation mapping. The transformational mapping is a composition of four elementary rules (deletion, substitution, left-adjunction, and right-adjunction) and must satisfy 'the principle of recoverability of deletion' (roughly: one can delete some non-terminal of a string if there is a copy of it somewhere still left in the structural change, and one can delete a specified terminal symbol).

---

87 Ibid., p. 476.

88 Peters & Ritchie (1973), supra note 65, p. 50.

89 Iwanov (2011), supra note 45.

90 Johnson (2004), supra note 57, p. 4.

91 Jackendoff (2003), supra note 52, p. 652, referring to Chomsky (1957), supra note 18.

92 Pelletier (1980), supra note 76, p. 27, referring to Peters & Ritchie (1973), supra note 37, section 2.

It was alleged[93] the fact that people can classify arbitrary strings as being grammatical or ungrammatical shows that natural languages must be recursive sets, and not arbitrary recursively enumarable sets. Thus transformational grammar is too powerful a theory, and must be restricted in some way to generate only recursive sets. Putman (1961) made various suggestions about constraining the theory of transformational grammar so that the class of languages it generates is some subset of the recursively enumarable languages.[94] One method would be to demand that no transformational rules ever yield an output shorter than its input. Another method would be to establish two upper limits x and v on any transformational grammar so that at most x terminal symbols can be deleted by any one transformation and at most v such transformation can be applied in any derivation. Such restrictions amount to constraining the class of languages generated to being recursive.

Transformativity and generativity similar to those in Chomskyan theory occur in law. Theories of transformativity and generativity in cognitive science, epistemology and philosophy will be discussed in Chapter I.3 in light of which transformativity and generativity in legal reasoning [in law] will be addressed in Chapter IV.10 of this book.

I.2. DESCRIPTIVITY, NORMATIVITY AND PRESCRIPTIVITY

I.2.1. OVERVIEW

***

Philosophy of mind is the area of philosophy which strives for comprehensive and systematic understanding of that which thinks and experiences, namely the mind. Philosophic arguments advance and enrich psychology, while facts and lessons from psychology make philosophy of mind more coherent and trustworthy. One means whereby philosophers and psychologist give and receive assistance is formal interdisciplinary activity. One currently popular form of interdisciplinary activity of relevance to the philosophy of mind is known as cognitive science. Cognitive science engages philosophers, psychologists, neuroscientists, computer scientists and others, all devoted to how best to understand intelligent thought and behavior and the cognitive

93 Ibid., p. 29. The earliest of these sorts of criticism appears to be Putman (1961), but they have become quite common in the intervening years.

94 Ibid., p. 31, referring to H. Putman, "Some issues in the theory of grammar", 1961, reprinted in G. Harmon (ed.), "On Noam Chomsky (1974), 80-103," Garden City: Anchor Books.

aspects of mind. These include features such as reasoning, perception and memory, among others.[95] It is consciousness that captures object into knowledge. In saying that consciousness states appear like something from the inside, we mean that these states not only are there in subjects, but that they possess a specific quality or *like-thisness* to them. The qualitative like-thisnesses of conscious experience ('qualia' or 'phenomenal qualia') are there in subjects, we do not mean that if a brain surgeon took off the top of our skull and peered into our brain while we savored coconut milk, they would see sweet qualia. We mean that qualia are interior with a type of interiority that is different from the way that our neurons are inside our head. Qualia are inside in the sense that there is something it is like to experience sweet tastes, and there is no obvious reasons to think that this inside something can be open to public inspection.[96]

Like Plato, Aristotle devotes an entire treatise, the *Posterior Analytics*, to the theory of knowledge, or *episteme*, and his project is a theory of *understanding*.[97] Aristotle's conception of *episteme* involves a grasp not just of a single isolated proposition, but of the whole causal and inferential network of propositions that lie behind it.[98] According to Aristotle, intellectual virtues are theoretical wisdom, science (*episteme*), intuitive understanding (*nous*), practical wisdom and craft expertise [Book VI]. 'Theoretical wisdom produces happiness by being a part of virtue' (Aristotle, 1144a3-6), and that 'practical wisdom looks to the development of theoretical wisdom, and issues command for its sake' (Aristotle, 1145a8-11).[99] Practical reasoning presupposes there is some goal to be accomplished. Aristotle says 'Virtue makes the goal right, practical wisdom (makes) the things leading to it' (Artistotle, 1144a7-8). Aristotle made a division into two types of knowledge: Techne, which can be interpreted as knowledge for production; and Phronesis, which can be interpreted as knowledge for value rational action. In the beginning of the 'Nicomachean Ethics', it is written that every art and every inquiry, and similarly every action

---

95 George Graham, Philosophy of Mind, an introduction, second edition, (Malden, MA, USA & Oxford OXD 1JF, UK: Blackwell Publisher, 1998), p. 7.

96 Ibid., p. 201.

97 Robert Pasnau, 'Epistemology Idealized,' 6, in Mind, Vol. 122, Issue 488 (2013), pp. 987-1021, advanced publication 12 February 2014.

98 Ibid., p. 10. This is not to say that no one ever will, or ever has achieved the ideal. Indeed, Aristotle takes the striking view that philosophy has in the past 'probably often been developed as far as possible and then perished' (Meta. XII.8, 1074b10-11; see also Politics VII.10.1329b25-35). But this reflects not so much any particular optimism regarding past cultures, but only his insight into the implications of maintaining, as he does, that the world's past history is infinite.

99 Richard Kraut, 'Aristotle's Ethics', in Stanford Encyclopedia of Philosophy, first published Tuesday, May 1, 2001; substantive revision Monday, March 29, 2010, pp. 15-16.

and pursuit, is thought to aim at some good; and for this reason the good has rightly been declared to be that at which all things aim. But a certain difference is found among ends; some are activities; others are products apart from the activities that produce them.[100] Albert the Great remarks of *scientia* (= *episteme*) that 'this is the end and the most perfect and the sole unconditionally desirable thing among the logical sciences'.[101] And when Thomas Aquinas comes to analyze Aristotle's definition of '*episteme*' (71b10), he begins with the remark that 'to have *scientia* of something is to cognize it perfectly. From this principle he derives the various features of the definition: that what is known in this way must be necessary, and that it must be grasped through a grasp of its cause.[102]

Descartes holds onto the general framework of an epistemic ideal as which theoretical inquiry should aim.[103] He then immediately remarks, in discussing this rule, that 'All *scientia* is certain and evident cognition.' He adds that we reject all such merely probable cognitions and resolve to believe only what is perfectly cognized and what cannot be doubted. The two best-known of Descartes's conception of scientia are his *infallibilism*, that such beliefs must be certain and indubitable, and his *foundationalism*, that such beliefs must be supported by a foundation of beliefs that are themselves certain and indubitable. To these two characteristics we might add a third, his *internalism*, which is to say that the possession of certain, foundationally-structured beliefs does not yield *scientia* unless the believer grasps the reasons that show beyond doubt the truth of the beliefs.[104]

Popper's thesis is to combat conventionalists. His theory "fallibilism" retains the inductive picture of laws of nature (as general statements of correlations among phenomena) and evidence (as particular statements of correlations among observables). Evidence is valuable, he proposes, only if it tends to falsify general statements. A distinction is made between empirical and non-empirical hypotheses. Empirical hyphoteses are those which could be falsified by emphirical evidence and therefore scientific, but those which 'could not be falsified by any kind of test are regarded as non-empirical or metaphysical'. 'Possibility of being falsified' is central in his scientific philosophy, and only hypotheses that increase the degree of

100 Goran Goldkuhl, 'The grounding of usable knowledge: An inquiry in the epistemology of action knowledge', in Paper accepted to HSS99 (Högskolor och Samhälle i Samverkan), Falun, March 16-18, 1999, p. 2, referring to Aristotle. 'Nicomachean Ethics,' in McKeon R (ed. 1947), Introduction to Aristotle, Modern Library, (New York: McGraw-Hill).

101 Pasnau (2013/2014), supra note 97, p. 12, referring to Albert the Great, Analytica posteriora 1.1.1 (ed. Jammy, vol.1).

102 Ibid. [footnote omitted].

103 Ibid., p. 15 [accompanying text and footnote omitted].

104 Ibid., pp. 15, 16-17.

falsibility should be admitted. The principles of logic followed by Popper is within the deductive picture of law of nature.[105] Popper's concern is to achieve agreement between a theory and observational evidence. In the event there is falsifying evidence against consequences of a theory, to save the theory is possible, based on the logic of theoretical scope as determined by inductivism, by rejecting the evidence outright or by accounting for it through adding auxiliary hypothesis or modifying the rules of correspondence which link the axioms of the theory to statement of empirical determined magnitudes.[106] In his theory, logical relations exist only between falsifying evidence and hyphotheses, but not between favorable evidence and hypotheses. Consequently, general existential statements and particular probability statements, which are the very type of empirical statements for many thinkers, are to be demoted from scientific status, whereas it is in existential statements that most of the permanent advances of science are preserved, against a background of shifting hypotheses.[107]

As to very characteristic of a phenomenalist point of view, George Berkeley draws some conclusions that in short, the Law of Nature simply describes the succession of phenomena, and is reduced to general rules, by means of which we may make very probable conjectures about our further experiences. As he argues 'The *fire* which I see is not the cause of the pain I suffer upon my approaching it, but the mark that forewarns me of it'. For Berkeley [and Patricius] there is no distinction between things as they are and things as they seem, and, for both, the proper of science is the Babylonian task of formulating the rules of succession of common experiences.[108] Rom Harré declares that scientific explanation consists in finding or imagining plausible generative mechanism for the patterns amongst events, for the structures of things, for the generation, growth, decay, or extinction of things and materials, for changes within persisting things and materials. According to Harré, one criterion of the appropriateness of analogical links embedded in a theory is the generation of existential hypothesis from the theory. If no existential hypothesis are suggested by a theory, then the theory does not advance our understanding of the underlying mechanism of natural process.[109] Larry Laudan's [compromise] position is that the philosophy of science contains both a descriptive element and a normative

105 Rom Harré, The Philosophy of Science, second edition, (Oxford-New York: Oxford University Press, 1985), pp. 48-49; John Losee, A Historical Introduction to the Philosophy of Science, second edition, (Oxford-New York: Oxford University Press, 1972, 1980), pp. 170-171.

106 Losee (1972/1980), Ibid.

107 Harre (1985), supra note 105, pp. 50-52.

108 Ibid., p. 72.

109 Losee (1972/1980), supra note 106, p. 145, referring to Rom Harré, 'The Principles of Scientific Thinking', (London: Macmillan, 1970), p. 125.

element. It is descriptive with respect to the standard cases selected, but normative with respect to other historical episodes. The adequacy of Laudan's model depends on the choice of standard cases. Of course, our beliefs about standard cases may change. The preferred intuitions about scientific rationality serve as standard cases, judgments about which provide a point of comparison for all other judgments about scientific rationality. Standards of rationality themselves are subject to historical development.[110]

All knowledge in social practices is not made explicit or linguistically codified. Much knowledge works in the background of consciousness and directs attention and action. Such knowledge is often labeled *tacit knowledge*. Knowledge of this character does not always remain tacit. It can be explicit through articulation and reconstruction.[111] Knowledge in social practice can be improved through reconstruction, evaluation and justifying practical knowledge.[112] There are essentially two approaches to the theory of knowledge. The first conceives of epistemology as primarily *prescriptive* or *normative*. Epistemology does not begin by looking at how we actually know, but instead tells us how we ought to know. It does not begin by assuming the existence of actual knowledge, but instead places all of our knowledge in 'square quotes' until a norm of justification can be found a priori and a process of global justification can be carried out. Only after such a global justification is carried out can we make use of scientific discoveries about what actual knowledge 'looks. like.[113]

The sets of useful knowledge [above mentioned] can be partitioned into two subsets: one is the knowledge that catalogs natural phenomena and regularities ('knowledge of what'), called *propositional knowledge*. The other is the knowledge that prescribes certain actions that constitute the manipulation of natural phenomena for human material needs ('production'), called *prescriptive knowledge*. Propositional knowledge also contains practical informal knowledge about nature such as the properties of materials, heat, motion, plants and animals; an intuitive grasp of basic mechanics (including the six 'basic machines' of classical antiquity: the lever, pulley, screw, balance, wedge and wheel): regularities of ocean current and the weather: and folk wisdoms in the "an-apple-a-day-keens-the-doctor-away" tradition. Prescriptive knowledge has the form

110 Ibid., pp. 213-214.

111 Goldkuhl (1999), supra note 100, p. 1, referring to M. Polanyi, 'Personal knowledge', 1958, (London: Routledge & Kegan Paul, B. Rolf, 1995), Profession, tradition och tyst kunskap, Nya Doxa, Nora.

112 Ibid.

113 Alexander Tabarrok, "If You're So Rich .. In The Economic Approach to Epistemology', in Reason Papers, A Journal of Interdisciplinary Normative Study, Issue No. 19, Fall 1994, pp. 146-159 (p. 146).

of techniques or instructions: the archtypical technique is recipe, which instructs one how to prepare a certain dish. In principle, all techniques are such sets, although vastly more complex and often full with nested do-loops, if-then statements and so on. It is the technique, not the artefact, that is the fundamental unit of analysis in evolutionary accounts of technology. They are sets of executable instructions or recipes for how to manipulate nature. When these instructions are carried out in practice, we call it *production*, and then they are no longer knowledge but action.[114] As to how to ground action knowledge, a distinction is made between *empirical external theoretical* and *internal* grounding. The empirical grounding has to do with the effectiveness of the application of knowledge. External theoretical grounding relates the action knowledge to other knowledge of theoretical character. One part of this is the grounding of the action knowledge in general explanatory theories. Internal grounding means an investigation of internal warrants (as e.g. values and categories) and internal cohesion of the knowledge.[115]

Descriptive epistemologies can be construed as competitors to traditional normative epistemologies. On this view, both are trying to address the same concerns and offering competing solutions. A standard objection to such approaches is that descriptive accounts are not adequate to do justice to the prescriptive elements of normative methodologies. The extent to which an evolutionary approach contributes to the resolution of traditional epistemological and philosophical problems is a function of which approach one adopts (*cf.* Dretske 1971, Bradie 1986, Ruse 1986, Radnitsky and Bartley 1987, Kim 1988). However, descriptive epistemology might also be seen as a successor discipline to traditional epistemology. On this reading, descriptive epistemology does not address the questions of traditional epistemology because it deems them irrelevant or unanswerable or uninteresting. Many defenders of naturalized epistemologies fall into this camp (*e.g.* Munz 1993). Campbell views that descriptive epistemology might be seen as complementary to traditional epistemology. On this analysis, the function of the evolutionary approach is to provide a descriptive account of knowing mechanisms while leaving the prescriptive aspects of epistemology to more traditional approach.[116]

The Standard Analytic Epistemology (SAE) has its prescriptive

---

114 Joel Mokyr, 'The Knowledge Society: Theoretical and Historical Underpinnings', Department of Economics and History, in part of Joel Mokyr's The Gift of Athena: Historical Origins of the Knowledge Economy (Princetown: Princetwon University Press, 2002), p. 2.

115 Goldkuhl (1999), supra note 112, p. 1.

116 Michael Bradie and William Harms, 'Evolutionary Epistemology', in Stanford Encyclopedia of Philosophy, first published Thursday, January 11, 2001, substantive revision Thursday, January 5, 2012, § 1.3.

and descriptive dimensions. The descriptive core of SAE, as argued by Bishop and Trout, is a theory that captures the considered epistemic judgments of philosophers. Some proponents of SAE believe that those judgments are best captured by a coherentist theory, other believe that they are best captured by a foundationalist theory, others believe that they are best captured by a reliabilist theory. What is idiosyncratic about a full-fledged naturalistic theory of epistemology is that its core, its starting-point, is an empirical theory. If this characterization has merit, then [we have argued that] the major theories of SAE are examples of naturalized epistemology.[117] The stasis requirement is meant to tell us what counts as evidence for the theories of SAE. The stasis requirement is an extraordinary conservative principle. Why does philosophical practice embody the stasis requirement? It is not a requirement that protects theories of SAE (e.g., reliabilism, coherentism, foundationalism) from negative evidence. The stasis requirement tells us something about the nature of the theories of SAE: They are meant to account for "our" considered epistemic judgments.[118] SAE will again be touched in Chapter I.2.4.1.

I.2.2. DESCRIPTIVITY

***

True descriptive theory can be empirically ascertained, meaning it is verified if it corresponds with reality (the facts); falsified if it does not correspond with reality.[119] A full descriptive accounts of truth and justification both demand a theory of meaning. Until a sign has meaning, it cannot be true or false. Moreover, determining the meaning of justificatory claims may provide a descriptive theory of justification. Presumably, what makes a claim of justification true is the basis of that justification.[120] No descriptive discipline could describe the whole of reality in all its details. Isolated factual conditions [as such] do not explain anything. Every descriptive theory must confine attention to those aspects of reality it deems relevant. In itself it is simply a fact that some aspects or details are relevant, while others are not. Someone assigns a

---

117 Michael Bishop and J.D. Trout, 'The Pathologies of Standard Analytic Epistemology', in NOUS 39.4 (2005), pp. 696-714, § 2.3.

118 Ibid., § 2.1.

119 Nandi, V., 'Model of Neutral-Inclusivity–Book of Instruments–About What is, can and should be, Nonpropositional and Propositional Reality - The Normativeness of "Purely Descriptive"Theorizing', (Amsterdam: Stichting Foundation, 1986). §3.2.3.

120 Bradie & Harms (2016), supra note 116, § 2.4.

higher value to a theory or description which describes a relevant state of affairs than to an irrelevant theory or description, although both theories or descriptions are true. He is then said to demand a true theory or description to be relevant, and to reject irrelevant, factual theories or descriptions.[121] As a consequence of this significant emphasis on observational, the descriptive approach to argumentation stresses the pragmatical dimension of argumentation, following the philosophical and linguistical works of John L. Austin, H.P. Grice and John Searle. The idea behind this emphasis is well introduced by French philosophy. Michel Foucault, for instance, defines 'enunciation' (enonce) as the basic element of discourse, as opposed to proposition, which is a logical and epistemological element. An enunciation for Foucault is an undivided combination of four functions that define together a legitimate domain of discourse: the subject-speaker, the range of reference, the conceptual field that accompanies the enunciation, and the generating rules of the enunciation. The act of enunciation (enunciation) is, Foucault maintains, the concrete event, in speech, writing, metaphor and so on. In this way, Foucault describes a complex pragmatical situation.[122]

The descriptive approach is not just another theory of reason and rationality, but a decision as to the proper dependence relation between argumentation and rationality. In other words, arguments are not to be evaluated according to some given *a priori* concept of rationality, but things that exhibit and presuppose some given reality of rational practice. Introducing the descriptive approach in this way shows that one of the motives to such an approach is mainly epistemological and it is well represented in Toulmin's earlier works, *Human Unserstanding* (1972) and *Knowing and Acting* (1976).[123] Many researchers in argumentation value the descriptive approach because they feel it enjoys the advantages of the empirical study. This feeling exists since the focus is usually on the conceptual study of argumentation, which shows important results in constructing the empiricist translation that yields a general definition of the concept of rationality. This translation yields a definition much acclaimed since it gives the translation in terms of some observable argumentative practices.[124] The primary goal of the descriptive approach to argumentation is to reinstate the adequacy of the theory as a descriptive

121 Nandi (1986), supra note 119.

122 Menashe Schwed, 'Descriptive theories of argumentation as part of Quine's project of "naturalized" epistemology', (May 17, 2001), in OSSA Conference Archieve, Paper 104, University of Windsor Scholarship – OSSA Conference Archive – OSSA 4, p. 2.

123 Ibid., p. 3, referring to Toulmin's earlier works, 'Human Unserstanding' (1972) and 'Knowing and Acting,' (1976).

124 Ibid, p. 6.

theory based on observation of the social reality.[125]

There is an axiom that there would indeed be solely one true, factual theory corresponding with reality as a 'unified whole'. Strictly speaking, only the true theory's correspondence with reality is a fact, whereas in the case of false theories there is no fact, or the 'fact' is a privative one.[126] The suggestion is that there would be only one true descriptive of factual discipline.[127] The goal of descriptive approach to argumentation is to be observational rather than evaluative or critical. [128] There is the view that the statements of the theory are true or false, and that many of the entities referred to in a theory do exist. They are as much in the real world as are human beings, houses, stones, stars, and so on. This view Harré calls 'realism'. Now a realist does not maintain that every hypothetical entity exists, nor does he maintain that every statement in a theory is to come up for instant judgment as either true or false. All he needs to maintain is that some hypothetical entities are real, and that since some theoretical statements have been judged true or false, other such statements can, in principle, come under that sort of judgment.[129] To make the realist position clear, the concepts of *reference* and *demonstration* need be introduced. Nouns, for instance, can appear in phrases whose function is to enable us to refer to things, whether or not they are present. Referring to entities is, then, something we do with words. Since words can be understood in isolation from the entities that they are used to talk about, verbal reference can be made to things whether or not the things can be observed or presently shown to us, provided we can understand the meanings of the words used to make reference. 'Demonstration', and its close relative 'indication', are typically acts performed with or by gesture, in which an entity is pointed out. An entity cannot be indicated in its absence, only in its presence. A typical indicating gesture is that of pointing. To be able to indicate something is the final, incontrovertible proof of its existence. It should be clear that we can refer to many things we cannot indicate, but that if we can demonstrate a thing to which we have previously made reference, on this or other occasions, then we have proved that thing exists.[130]

Historical relativism reduces the philosophy of science to a descriptive survey of actual practice.[131] W. Dilthey brought to philosophical reflection the great problem of the intelligibility of the historical [as such],

---

125 Ibid.

126 Nandi (1986), supra note 119.

127 Ibid.

128 Schwed (2001), supra note 125, p. 1, 2.

129 Harré (1985), supra note 108, p. 90.

130 Ibid., pp. 90-91.

131 Losee (1972, 1980), supra note 110, p. 218.

he was inclined by a second cultural fact to search for the key to a solution, not on the side of ontology, but in the reform of epistemology itself. The second fundamental cultural fact thus alluded to is represented by the rise of positivism as a philosophy, if by that we understand, in very general terms, the demand that the model of all intelligibility be taken from the sort of empirical explanation current in the domain of the natural sciences. It seems that the only way of rendering justice to historical knowledge was to give it a scientific dimension.[132] The great opposition throughout Dilthey's work was the opposition between the *explanation of nature* and the *understanding of history*. It is in the sphere of psychology that he searches for the distinctive feature of understanding. Every human sciences – and by that Dilthey means every modality of the knowledge of man which implies a historical relation – presupposes a primordial capacity to transpose oneself into the mental life of others. For in natural knowledge, man grasps only phenomena distinct from himself, the fundamental 'thingness' of which escapes him. In the human order, man knows man; however alien another man may be to us, he is not alien in the same sense of an unknowable physical thing. The difference of status between natural things and the mind dictates the difference of status between explanation and understanding. Man is not radically alien to man, because he offers signs of his own existence. To understand these signs is to understand man. It is as activity, as free will, as initiative and enterprise that man seeks to understand himself. This is what the positivist school completely ignores: the difference in principle between the mental world and the physical world.[133] By *interconnection* the life of others can be discerned and identified in its manifestation. Knowledge of others is possible because life produces forms, externalizes itself in stable configurations; feelings, evaluations and volitions tend to sediment themselves in a structured *acquisition* [acquis] which is offered to others for deciphering.[134] After 1900, Dilthey relied upon Husserl to give consistency to the notion of interconnection. During the same period, Husserl established that mental life is characterized by intentionality, that is, by the property of intending an identifiable meaning. Mental life itself cannot be grasped, but we can grasp what it intends, the objective and identical correlate in which mental life surpasses itself. The passage from understanding, defined primarily in terms of the capacity to transpose oneself into another, to interpretation, in the precise sense of understanding the expressions of life fixed by writing, posed a double problem. On the one hand, hermeneutics completed interpretative psychology by adding to it a

---

132 John B. Thompson, Paul Ricouer Hermeneutics and the human sciences, essays on language, action and interpretation, edited, translated and introduced by John B. Thompson, editions de la Maison des Sciences de l'Homme – Paris, (Cambridge University Press, 1981), pp. 48-49.

133 Ibid., pp. 49-50.

134 Ibid., p. 50.

supplementary stage; on the other hand, interpretative psychology turned hermeneutics in a psychological direction.[135] Hermeneutics comprises something specific: it seeks to reproduce an interconnection, a structured totality, by drawing support from a category of signs which have been fixed by writing or by any other process of inscription equivalent to writing. So it is no longer possible to grasp the mental life of others in its immediate expressions; rather it is necessary to reproduce it, to reconstruct it, by interpreting objectified signs. This *Nachbidden* [reproducing] requires distinct rules, since the expressions are embedded in objects of a peculiar nature. As with Schleiermacher, it is philology – the explanation of texts – which provides the scientific stage of understanding.[136]

***

We distinguish between two different branches of Methodological Naturalism: the Quinean ('Replacement Naturalism') and the Goldmanesque ('Normative Naturalism'). Goldman's paradigm of Normative Naturalism has dominated philosophical research in the area of law, though it is Quine's notion of Replacement Naturalism that bears most immediate on Legal Realism.[137] According to Replacement Naturalist, the goal of theorizing is description or explanation; according to Normative Naturalists, the goal is regulation of practice through the promulgation of norms or standards.[138] Quine attacks the Cartesian or Carnapian programs which seek to determine what is justified in an absolute sense – the sense that a belief is justified if it is indubitable. Also both of these programs are prescriptive in nature, their success would lead directly to a type of formula which could be applied to any belief to determine whether it is justified or not. Quine breaks the Cartesian program into the 'conceptual' and 'doctrinal' parts. [Leaving this confusing notation aside] the 'conceptual' side amounts to the normative (prescriptive) idea of what knowledge (or more precisely justification) is. In other words, the Cartesian seeks to find a set of rules which can be used to determine whether a given belief is justified or not, by reducing the belief in question to foundational beliefs. The 'doctrinal' part attempts to show

135 Ibid.

136 Ibid., p. 51.

137 Brian Leiter, 'Rethinking Legal Realism: Toward a Naturalized Jurisprudence', in 76 Texas Law Review 267 (1997), p. 290. See e.g., Phillip Kitcher, 'The Naturalist Return,' in 101 PHIL. REV. 53 (1992) (surveying recent literature).

138 Ibid., pp. 290-91. Notice that this latter goal is not peculiar to Normative Naturalism – it is equally well the goal of traditional epistemology, from Descartes to the early Carnap. The methods employed to realize this goal distinguish the Normative Naturalist from the traditional epistemologist. See ALVIN I. 'GOLDMAN, EPISTEMOLOGY AND COGNITION' (1986), pp. 6-9 (contrasting scientific approaches to cognition with historical epistemology).

that a given belief is in fact justified because it does meet the condition that it can be deduced from some foundational justified beliefs. Quine's argument relies upon the fact that the Cartesian program fails in its goal of finding anything of substance which is in fact justified. This is mostly due to a lack of foundationally justified beliefs and the strength of justification required for inference.[139] Quine argues that because these types of traditional epistemology have failed in their goals concerning justification, epistemology itself should be replaced with a 'naturalized' version. For Quine the term 'naturalized' is akin to the term 'scientific'. He in effect would like to turn epistemology into a natural science – complete with hypotheses, observations and conclusions. In naturalized epistemology the subject of the hypotheses, observations and conclusions is the human being himself. Instead of looking at a person's beliefs and asking 'are those beliefs justified?' Quine looks at the person and asks simply 'what caused those beliefs?'[140]

Gettier's stunning refutation of the traditional justified-true-belief account of knowledge is also an influence on the empirical basing of epistemology.[141] This stimulated accounts according to which the knowing character of a belief was separated from its normative, justificatory background. Justified belief was often replaced by appropriately caused belief,[142] or belief which is counterfactually (and thus nomically) related to the situation described in its content.[143] This brought even *knowledge* closer to empirical study. Psychologists may have no account of epistemic justification, but they do deal in the etiology of belief. Another influence is the ascendancy of cognitive psychology. Any dynamic scientific movement draws philosophical attention. But the cognitivists promise answers to questions which epistemologists were just about to ask.[144]

Quine shows in his work that although he favors the empiricist tradition, this tradition does not refute in any sense the skeptical argument as long as the 'external' position is a legitimate one from the epistemological point of view. This is his naturalization move against skepticism. This move

139 Shawn O'Niel, 'Quine's Naturalization and Kim's Response, in PL370, 3-5, Fall 2004, p. 3.

140 Ibid.

141 Ron Amundson, 'The Epistemological Status of a Naturalized Epistemology', (1981), in Inquiry 26, pp. 333-44, Part I, referring to Edmund Gettier, 'Is Justified True Belief Knowledge?' Analysis, Vol. 23 (1963), pp. 121-3.

142 Ibid., referring to Alvin I. Goldman, 'A Causal Theory of Knowledge', reprinted in George S. Pappas and Maeshall Swain (Eds.), Essays on Knowledge and Justification (Itacha: Cornell University Press, 1978).

143 Ibid., citing F.I. Dretske, 'Conclusive Reasons', reprinted in Pappas and Swain ed., id.

144 Ibid.

is to insist upon maintaining an internal position within the boundaries of a theory and at the same time to reject the skeptical move from the external position as a kind of extremism (Quine's naturalized epistemology). From the viewpoint of naturalized argumentation, there is no sense of investigating rationality and our conceptual resources in argumentation by placing ourselves outside their actual use, namely the 'external' position, since there is no such detached position from which such a philosophical inquiry can be conducted.[145] There is the information or knowledge gathered from the actual practices of argumentation, collected from an 'internal' point of view of the theory. From the 'internal' position, questions about what we know about arguments are answered by appealing to other things of the same sort that are already known from the 'internal' position. It is a kind of knowledge from 'within' the theory or argumentation. There is also the 'external' point of view which skepcticism questions the epistemic status of the knowledge claimed by the theory from its 'external position'. It is the traditional move of skepticism, where it withdraws or detaches itself from the body of knowledge. Only from the detached philosophical viewpoint is it possible to face the whole body of knowledge and evaluate it. This move is 'external' since it is taken from the 'outside' of the theory and, consequently, shifts the focus from the things believed within the theory to reasons to believe.[146] For the skeptical challenge to be launched, skepticism needs to point out that the knowledge in the area of argumentation is something that arises from the 'internal' position. The reason is that the particular cases of knowledge within the area of argumentation seem unproblematic only from the 'internal' position, like the everyday and simple practices or cases of argumentation. However, these cases are only seemingly unproblematic because they are investigated from within the area of argumentation and from within a theory. What seems to be true within a theory describing everyday practices of argumentation is found after an 'external' investigation to be open to doubt, in fact not to express something we know about the essence of argumentation.[147]

Quine encourages us to draw our metaphysics and epistemology from the successes of our best science and his influence is from the science onto the philosophy.[148] According to Quine's 'naturalized epistemology', the descriptive approach rests on the rejection of the normative standpoint

145 Schwed (2001), supra note 128, pp. 6-7, referring to W.v.O. Quine, 'Epistemology Naturalized', in Ontological Relativity and Other Essays, (New York: Columbia University Press, 1969), pp. 69-90.

146 Ibid., p. 5.

147 Ibid., pp. 5-6.

148 Peter Lipton (reviewer), 'Philosophy of Science Today, Oxford University Press, 2003', in Peter Clark and Katherine Hawley (eds.), in Notre Dame Philosophical Reviews ISSN: 1538-161 (2015) .

and, thus rests on the denial of any 'external' position so essential to the skeptical arguments. Any normative standpoint contains a move of *imposing* something from the outside and thus, opens the way to the skeptical argument. A statement would be regarded as descriptive or normative not because of its meaning or by determining which experience counts as evidence for or against such a statement. Instead, experience counts for or against the entire body of statements that constitutes a theory in a holistic manner, and little that is systematic can be said about the meaning of particular statements of the theory. Quine's skeptical holism with the radical relativism eliminates the possibility to maintain a clear distinction between descriptive and normative statements. Consequently, as the normative/descriptive distinction is unattainable, thus so is the idea that normative theories have a status radically distinct from that of descriptive ones. The only thing left is some gradualness between two points. Thus, one argumentative theory is more normative or descriptive than another theory, but not purely normative or descriptive. Theories that tend to the more descriptive end of the descriptive/normative continuity focus on analyzing the actual argumentative discourse and the whole practice that wraps such pieces of discourse. Theories that tend more to the normative end focus on the requirement for sound argument and enable the evaluation and criticism of actual argumentative discourse. Consequently, the descriptive approach to argumentation collapses into the normative one.[149]

According to Naturalism, a satisfactory theory of adjudication must be continuous with empirical inquiry in the natural and social sciences.[150] We can now generalize Quine's point as follows. Let us say that a Replacement Naturalist in any branch of philosophy holds that, for any pair of relata that might stand in a justificatory relation – e.g., evidence and theory – reasons and belief, legal reason and judicial decision – if no normative account of the relation is possible, then the only theoretically fruitful account is the descriptive/explanatory account given by the relevant science of that domain.[151] Naturalism in philosophy is always first

149 Schwed (2001), supra note 147, p. 8, referring to W.v.O. Quine, 'Pursuit of Truth' (Cambridge, MA.: Harvard University Press, 1990).

150 Leiter (1997), supra note 138, p. 285. For some representative statements of the "naturalistic" position in philosophy, see Daniel Dennett, Foreword to RUTH GARREIT MILLIKAN, 'LANGUAGE, THOUGHT, AND OTHER BIOLOGICAL CATEGORIES' pp. ix-x (1984) and Peter Railton, 'Naturalism and Prescriptivity', in FOUNDATIONS OF MORAL AND POLITICAL PHILOSOPHY 155-63 (Ellen Frankel Paul et al. eds. 1990), Railton calls this view "methodological" naturalism. Ibid, pp. 155, 155-57.

151 Ibid., p. 293. One might, of course, hold that the descriptive account just gives us all there is to justification: so, e.g., describing the causal history of a belief may be all there is justifying that belief. See the discussion in Jerry Fodor, 'Encounters with Trees', in LONDON REV. BOOKS, Apr. 20, 1995. The possibility,

a methodological view to the effect that philosophical theorizing should be continuous with empirical inquiry in the sciences.[152] The naturalism, following Quine, rejects the idea that there could be a 'first philosophy', a philosophical solution to problems that proceeds a priori, that is, prior to any experience.[153] Instead, the philosophical naturalist demands continuity with the natural and social sciences in one or both of the following ways: what Leiter calls 'Results Continuity' and 'Methods Continuity'.[154] Results Continuity requires that the claims of philosophical theories be supported by the results of successful sciences. Epistemologists like Alvin Goldman look to the results of psychology and cognitive sciences to find out how the human cognitive apparatus really works; only with that information in hand, argues Goldman, can the epistemologist construct norms for how humans ought to form beliefs.[155] Methods Continuity demands only that philosophical theories emulate the methods of inquiry and styles of explanation characteristic of successful sciences.[156]

The central enterprise of epistemology on Quine's view is to understand the relation between our theories of the world and the evidence (i.e., sensory input) on which they are based.[157] Quine's replacement thesis is "the view that epistemological questions may be replaced by psychological questions".[158] Quine proposes: "[e]pistemology, or something like it, simply falls into place as a chapter of psychology and hence of natural sciences. It studies a natural phenomena, viz., a physical human subject.

---

however, has no bearing on the project here.

152 Ibid., p. 289. The failure of philosophers to solve the so-called "demarcation problem" – e.g., the problem of what demarcates genuine science from pseudo-science – does not – as far as Leiter can see, doom this definition of naturalism, just as the "paradox of the heap" does not doom our ability to distinguish heaps from single grains – even if, in both cases, there are fuzzy borderline cases.

153 Ibid. It bears emphasizing here that most contemporary naturalists do not go as far as Quine in repudiating the idea of a "first philosophy" (nor in embracing his austere physicalism – see e.g., CHRISTOPHER HOOKWAY, 'QUINE: LANGUAGE, EXPERIENCE AND REALITY' 124 (1988). While all would concur with Quine that philosophy cannot be exclusively an a prior discipline, most naturalists still think there is significant work for conceptual analysis to do. A classic example is GOLDMAN (1986), supra note 138.

154 Ibid.

155 Ibid. See GOLDMAN (1986), supra note 153.

156 Ibid. Such a view does not suppose the methodological[ly] unity of the various sciences; so as not to be empty, it does require that the methods of the sciences not be so various as to encompass all possible methodological postures.

157 Ibid., p. 291.

158 Ibid., p. 292, quoting Hilary Kornblith, 'Introduction: What Is Naturalistic Epistemology?,' in NATURALIZING EPISTEMOLOGY 4 (Hilary Kornblith ed. 2d. ed.1994), p. 4.

This human subject is accorded a certain experimentally controlled input-certain patterns of irradiation in assorted frequencies, for instance – and in the fullness of time the subject delivers as output a description of the three-dimensional external world and its history. The relation between the meager input and the torrential output is a relation that we are prompted to study for somewhat the same reasons that always prompted epistemology; namely, in order to see how evidence relates to theory, and in what ways one's theory of nature transcend any available evidence".[159] Quine holds that the central concern of epistemology is the theory-evidence relationship; if the foundationalist story about this relationship is a failure, then that leaves only one story worth telling about this relationship, namely, the story told by "a purely descriptive, causal-nomological science of human cognition.[160] The science of human cognition replaces armchair epistemology: we naturalize epistemology by turning over its central question – the relationship between theory and evidence – to the relevant empirical science.[161]

Descriptive knowledge is a natural phenomenon. By and large, we have it. The task of epistemology is not to elaborate a set of tests or criteria to identify knowledge, rather, these tests and criteria are created by the inquirers themselves within the context of enquiry and are embodied tacitly in the process of enquiry itself.[162] On this account epistemology's task is not purely descriptive, especially if 'pure' description means simply 'gazing' on knowledge without any presupposition or theoretical constructs. Nor is it descriptive as opposed to practical. Indeed, the ultimate aim of epistemology is not contemplative but practical. Like medicine, which articulates and codifies norms of health which are implicit in actual healthy bodies, epistemology seeks to articulate and then to codify norms of rationality which are immanent in actual knowledge. These norms can then be used to pursue knowledge in a more self-conscious and effective manner. But it should always be kept in mind that these tools of art are based upon and complete the work of nature. They thus depend upon the prior existence and intelligibility of natural knowledge. On this model, philosophy is not the hanging judge of the sciences, but rather a midwife for knowledge.[163]

***

Various pragmatists, naturalists, evolutionary epistemologists and phenomenologists have advocated an approach to knowledge that is primarily descriptive. This approach assumes (overtly or covertly) that

159 Ibid., quoting Quine (1969), supra note 145, pp. 75-76.

160 Ibid., referring to Jaegwon Kim, 'What's "Naturalized Epistemology"?', in 2 PHIL. PERSPECT. (1988), p. 388.

161 Ibid., pp. 292-293.

162 Tabarrok (1994), supra note 113, pp. 146-147.

163 Ibid., p. 147.

the problem of knowledge is not whether we have it or not, but rather what the knowledge that we do have is like.[164] Of psychology, Quine knew only behaviorism, and the normative role he assigned to a naturalized epistemology could be no more than an instrumental, calculating device. We can do better now because psychology is better. We have Ameliorative Psychology.[165] Ameliorative Psychology with its naturalistic approach will be again touched in Chapter I.2.4.1. Earlier epistemologists tried to do two tasks within one theory – both to explain human belief causally and to justify human beliefs as knowledge. We may address the descriptive problem free of the burden of the normative and foundationalist issues. This is much of the point of Quine's influential epistemology naturalized.[166]

An explanation of behavior, on Skinner's view, must involve the deducibility of a behavior (or behavior-probability) from prior observable conditions. This is an epistemological principle, guiding Skinner's scientific endeavor. A behaviorist has empirical reason to reject a casualist view of explanation. Unobserved causes are neither stimuli nor responses, and so (according to the behaviorist) play no role in human behavior. This is an implication of *substantive* behaviorist theory. Skinner is aware of the dual aspect of the cognitive scientist. He is conscious of developing an empirically validated epistemology. Moreover, *he has succeeded.* The epistemological account of explanation as deduction from observed events is supported by substantive behaviorist theory. Skinner's anti-causalist views on explanation are not mere armchair prejudice; they have empirical support. Casualist explanation would require cognitive capacities which (behaviorist) psychology has discovered scientists not to possess.[167] Postivist explanation rules out cognitive theory in favor of behaviorist theory, which returns the favor by ruling out causalist explanation in favor of positivist explanation. The issue is then 'whether the epistemology determined the theory or the theory determined the epistemology'.[168] Positivists believe that reality is stable and can be observed and described from an objective viewpoint (Levin, 1988), i.e., without interfering with the phenomena being studied. They contend that phenomena should be isolated and that observations should be repeatable. This often involves manipulations of reality with variations in only a single independent variable so as to identify regularities in, and to form relationships between, some of the constituent elements of the social world. Predictions can be made on the basis of the previously observed and

---

164 Ibid., pp. 146-147.

165 Bishop & Trout (2005), supra note 117, § 3.

166 Amundson (1981), supra note 144, Part I, referring to Quine (1969), supra note 159.

167 Ibid., Part III.

168 Ibid.

explained realities and their inter-relationships.[169] Positivist contends that only factual knowledge from observation is trustworthy. Only things which can be directly observed [or measured] are considered by positivists as valid for scientific attention. Positivistic knowledge is also culturally dependent since culture can affect interpretation of observantion.

Contemporary epistemologists show strong interest in relating epistemologytothesubstantivediscoveriesofpsychology.Thisinterestresults from several influences. One important influence is many epistemologists' loss of the Cartesian ambition to provide an epistemological foundation for non-philosophical (including science) knowledge. There is a part of classical epistemological task, namely, to simply describe human epistemic processes. The other part was to show that these processes are rational, and that they do lead to knowledge.[170] Both epistemologists and psychologists are interested in the conditions under which and the processes by which beliefs are formed, and the susceptibility of humans to perceptual illusion and conceptual confusion. Ron Amundson refers to the areas shared by epistemologists and psychologists as descriptive epistemology, in contrast with the (mostly) normative issues which are philosophy's alone.[171]

Descriptive social knowledge refers to social facts or explanatory categories, such as 'reasons for action' in terms of a person's intention. Descriptive social knowledge encompasses subjective preferences, hopes, interests, expectations or feelings as well as knowledge about consequences of actions for others, self and the relationship between self and other; finally knowledge about strategies that serve to achieve certain goals.[172] Descriptive theories describes phenomena, behaviors, events or objects, as they are and enlights the understanding thereof. A descriptive theory seeks to support the process of thought by providing consistent and appropriate terminology. According to Tabarok,[173] one of the chief benefits of the descriptive approach is that it is open to being informed by the discoveries of the social and natural sciences. Each new discovery is an opportunity for further reflection on and understanding of the nature of knowledge. Whereas the prescriptive epistemologists must suspend all scientific knowledge in scare quotes until the task of epistemology has been

169 Davison, R.M.,'An Action Research Perspective of Group Support Systes: How to Improve Meetings in Hong Kong,' Chapter Three, in a Ph.D.Thesis, City University of Hong Kong, 1998, pp. 3-1– 3-2.

170 Amundson (1981), supra note 166, Part I.

171 Ibid., Part I.

172 Monika Keller and Wolfgang Edelstein, 'The Development of Socio-Moral Meaning Making: Domains, Categories, and Perspective-Taking', 5, in W.M. Kurtines & J.L. Gewirtz (Eds.), (Hillsdale, NJ: Erlbaum, 1991), in Handbook of moral behavior and development: Vol. 2, Research, pp. 89-114.

173 Tabarrok (1994), supra note 161, p. 149.

completed, the descriptive epistemologists can accept the discoveries of the sciences as *prima facie* paradigm cases of genuine knowledge.

***

Postmodernism is understood as a philosophical position to the effect that there is no objective truth, that objective knowledge of the world is impossible, that there are no 'essences', that the era of 'metanarratives' (in Lyotard's famous phrase) is past.[174] Postmodernist's arguments take two forms: what we may call the 'Disappointed Absolutist' argument (to borrow from Han's apt term for a similar view to The Concept of Law [HART, at 135]), and the 'Flesh & Blood' argument. The Disappointed Absolutist argument runs as follows: Assuming some impossibly high standard for what will count as 'justification', 'objectivity', or 'semantic determinacy', it turns out that no beliefs are justified, that no claim about the world are objective, and that no texts have determinate meanings (*See* HART, *ibid*, - noting that skepticism about legal rules often stems from the adoption of an unattainable standard for what is to count as a rule). The problem with this argument, which leads almost all philosophers to dissent from it, is that it never queries whether the underlying standard of justification, objectivity, or semantic determinacy is sensible or plausible, or whether it is what we really mean when we talk about justification or objectivity or determinacy.[175] Some philosophers dissent for a slightly different reason; they think the high standard of justification or of objectivity can be met.[176] Postmodernist literature never evinces even an awareness of these argument.[177] The Flesh & Blood argument runs this way: since, as knowers, we cannot escape our human situation – we cannot transcend – as it were, our flesh and blood (not to mention our race, our gender, our class, etc.) – we can never have objective knowledge of the world.[178] To some extent, this argument piggy-backs on the Disappointed Absolutist argument. Yet it also introduces a new element, an explanation for why we cannot meet the high standards the latter argument presupposes: because we are always

174 Leiter (1997), supra note 162, n.93. See JEAN-FRANCOIS LYOTARD, 'THE POSTMODERN CONDmON', pp. xxiii-xxiv (Geoff Bennington & Brian Massumi trans. 1984).

175 Ibid. See e.g., JOHN M. ELLIS, 'AGAINST DECONSTRUCTION' 77-79 (1989); JAMES S. FISHKIN, 'BEYOND SUBJECTIVE MORALITY' 129 (1984); HILARY PUTMAN, 'REASON, TRUTH AND HISTORY' 160-68 (1981); Judith Jarvis Thomson, 'Moral Objectivity', in GILBERT HARMAN & JUDITH JARVIS THOMSON, 'MORAL RELATIVISM AND MORAL OBJECTIVITY' 65, 154 (1996).

176 Ibid. See e.g., PANAYOT BUTCHVAROV, 'SKEPTICISM IN ETHICS' 3-10 (1989).

177 Ibid.

178 Ibid. See e.g. STANLEY FISH, 'DOING WHAT COMES NATURALLY' 1, 5-6 (1989).

'situated'. The mistake of this argument to draw a false inference from the fact (is it an objective fact?) of our being 'situated' to the conclusion is that we cannot transcend our situation. There is certainly not a philosopher alive today who would deny that, as knowers, our beliefs about the world are shaped by our 'situation': our particular cultural and historical moment, the particular traditions that inform our sensibility and judgment, the theoretical paradigms that determine how the world appears to us, and the natural and bodily endowment that make us who we are. Almost all of this is banal in the post-Kantian philosophical universe; and even in the pre-Kantian one, it has its adherents, like Hume.[179] This notwithstanding Steven Winter's wildly mistaken claim that Hume was guilty of an "emphasis on Reason as a transcendent faculty.[180]

Even if we are situated – as no one denies – it may still be possible to have objective knowledge of a strong objective world. This is precisely what post-Kantian and post-Quinean philosophers like Richard Boyd, Philip Kitcher, and Peter Railton have been arguing for the last twenty years. Perhaps they are wrong. But if they are, it is not because they do not recognize the banal fact that we are 'situated'; rather, it is because their arguments for how we overcome the limits of our situation are wrong. But, once again, the postmodernist literature is blissfully unaware that there could even be such arguments.[181] In any event, it is safe to say that outside of parts of academic culture in the humanities, social sciences, and law, postmodernism (in the philosophical sense described above) has been almost completely irrelevant. Recent years, in fact, have witnessed a proliferation of essentialist theories about human beings and other naturalistic 'metanarratives'. Peter Kramer's best-seller is typical of the real *zeitgeist*. "Our culture is caught in a frenzy of biological materialism", observes Kramer, "The] impressive, close-up view of the power of biology over an unexpectedly broad spectrum of human behavior [provided by psychopharmacological drugs like Prozac] .....ha[s] done a good deal to move my assumption about how people are constituted in the direction of the contemporary *zeitgeist*".[182] Postmodernists would do well to heed Neitzsche's methodological proclamation that "the basic text of homo natura must again be recognized: To translate man back into nature. ** to see to it that man henceforth stands before man as even today, hardened in the discipline of science. Why did we choose this insane task? Or, putting it differently: why have knowledge at all?[183]

179 Ibid.

180 Ibid., referring to Steven L. Winter, 'Bull Durham and the Uses of Theory', in 42 STAN. L. REV. (1990), p. 639, 658.

181 Ibid.

182 Ibid., referring to PETER D. KRAMER, 'LISTENING TO PROZAC', p. xiii, xv (1993).

183 Ibid., referring to FRIEDRICH NIETZSCHE, 'BEYOND GOOD AND EVIL',

***

Let's go back to descriptivity and talk about descriptive decision making. The purpose of descriptive decision analysis is to develop models of decision making which provide valid descriptions of actual decision making behavior. Such models can be evaluated on predictive ability, face validity, psychological insights into choice behavior, enhancement of understanding of cognitive processes, elegance, parsimony, etc. Much behavioral decision research has focused on identifying deviation of people's actual judgments or choices from those which would result from normative models.[184] The close ties between normative and descriptive theories can easily be seen when we consider a scientist conducting an experiment. Theories of theoretical rationality are concerned with how we achieve the goal of acquiring correct beliefs about the world. To explain the observed behavior, for example, randomization of subjects, it seems natural to invoke normative theories of how experiments should be conducted. The reason why normative theories work as descriptive explanation here is that we understand the scientist as a rational, goal-oriented person. Every reasoning, in contrast, is rarely guided by explicit methodological knowledge. Nevertheless, people's beliefs also have a normative force. People view themselves as motivated by reasons, and strive for optimality to achieve their goals. They distinguish between true and false beliefs; knowing they may err, they revise their beliefs and accept correction.[185]

The growing interest in cognitive mechanism is the result of two sets of findings: the changes in judgments that occur as a function of changes in the way a task is presented,[186] and the observation that people use simplifying heuristics to deal complex judgment tasks. These findings are interconnected; many demonstrations of task-dependent results, such as the effect of the 'framing' of a task on judgments[187] show that the invariance

---

pp. 161-62 (Walter Kaufmann trans., 1966).{ On Nietzsche's naturalism, see Brian Leiter, 'Nietzsche and Aestheticism,' in 30 J. HIST. PHIL. (1992), pp. 275, 278-80; Brian Leiter, 'the Paradox of Fatalism and Self-Creation in Nietzsche', in WILLING AND NOTHINGNESS: SCHOPENHAUER AS NIETZSCHE'S EDUCATOR {Christopher Janaway ed. Fortcoming 1998}).

184 L. Robin KELLER, 'The role of generalized utility theories in descriptive, prescriptive, and normative decision analysis', in North-Holland Information and Decision Technologies 15 (1989), pp. 259 – 271 (pp. 259-260).

185 Michael R. Waldmann, 'Neurath's ship: The constitutive relation between normative and descriptive theories of rationality', in BEHAVIORAL AND BRAIN SCIENCES (2011) 34:5, p. 273.

186 Gordon F. Pitz & Natalie J. Sachs, 'Judgment and Decision: Theory and Application', in Ann Rev. Psychol. 1984. 35, pp. 139-63 (p. 145), referring to J.W. Payne, 'Contingent decision behavior', in Psychol. Bull. 92 (1982), pp. 382-402.

187 Ibid., referring to A. Tversky & D. Kahneman, 'The framing of decisions

demanded by prescriptive models is not present. What is significant for a cognitive psychologist is that the *context* in which a judgment is made affects that judgment. Many variables other than those to which a person is asked to respond can be shown to affect the judgment: the thematic background,[188] the number of alternative choices given to or provided by a subject,[189] the availability of irrelevant references,[190] and the kind of judgment required.[191] None of this is surpising, of course. The results emphasize how significant are factors that affect the salience of task features, and how important is the encoding of a problem and its representation prior to an attempted solution.[192] A review of findings in this area led by Payne has reached a conclusion.[193] The conclusion is that an understanding of psychological mechanism is emerging that relies on a 'time-dependent' or process analysis of judgment or decision making (JDM) tasks, and which involves a 'contingent mixture' of several decision processes.

Studies of heuristic and task-dependent judgment processes generally adopt one of two perspectives that reflect different views of the automaticity of the processes. Some authors, notably Kahneman & Tversky (1982a), have drawn an analogy between judgmental heuristics and perceptual processes. They suggest that errors, biases, and context-dependent judgments are the result of cognitive mechanism of which subjects are largely unaware.[194] An alternative view is that strategies of judgment are under a person's deliberate control. This view is implied in studies that use process tracing techniques to examine strategies. Several studies have examined information search patterns to infer the

---

and the psychology of choice', in Science 211(1981), pp. 453-58, 1981.

188 Ibid., referring to H.J. Einhorn & R.M. Hogarth, 'A theory of diagnostic inference: II. Judging causality', Cent. Decis. Res., Grad. Sch. Bus., Univ. Chicago, 1982b.

189 Ibid., referring to Einhorn & Hogarth (1982b), Ibid.; A. Koriat, S. Lichtenstein & B. Fischhoff, 'Reasons for confidence', in J. Exp. Psychol: Hum. Learn. Mem. 6 (1980), pp. 107-118.

190 Ibid., referring to T. Gilovich, 'Seeing the past in the present. The effect of associations to familiar events on judgments and decisions', in J. Pers. Soc. Psychol. 40 (1981), pp. 797-808.

191 Ibid., referring to J.C. Hershey & P.J.H. Schoemaker, 'Equivalence judgments that are not equivalent: Probability vs. certainty equivalence methods in utility measurement', Cent. Decis., Grad. Sch. Bus., Univ. Chicago, 1983.

192 Ibid., referring to R.A. Griggs & S.E. Newstead), 'The role of problem structure in a deductive reasoning task', in J. Exp. Psychol: Learn. Mem. Cognit. 8 (1982), pp. 297-307.

193 Ibid., pp. 145-146, referring to Payne (1982), supra note 186, pp. 382-402.

194 Ibid., p. 146, referring to Tversky and Kahneman (1981), supra note 187, pp. 453-458.

underlying strategy.[195] Both automatic, perception-like heuristics and more deliberate information processing strategies are involved in most judgment or decision making tasks. So far neither has been the subject of formal model or systematic body or research as have, say, expected utility theory or information integration theory. Process tracing studies have been successful in describing strategies, but generally not in predicting their use.[196] Theories of judgmental heuristics have often been ad hoc; Wallsten points out that much of the literature consists only of a catalog of biases.[197] Such an approach is obviously limited in explanatory power unless it includes a statement of the principles that govern the use of each heuristic. One of the most widely used concepts in heuristics theory is representativeness.[198]

If a general theory of judgment or decision making is to be found, it would be helpful to establish a compendium of basic cognitive mechanism involved in judgment or decision making tasks. A sequential process that passes through stages might be assummed to exist. We recognize that it is a recursive activity, at each stage there may be subsidiary decisions to be made. When a problem is presented, salient features are identified, other information is reviewed from memory, and a meaningful organization of this information is created. The various sources of information are evaluated and integrated, and a judgment or choice is generated.[199] The description of a problem includes many features arranged in complex patterns. Before a person can respond he must encode the information and develop a representations for the problem. One way of describing the representation is as a 'mental model' that relates the problem to other knowledge.[200] In building the mental model there are many issues left uncertain by the problem statement, uncertainties that must be either resolved or represented in the model in some way. These uncertainties include the

---

195 Ibid. See e.g., J.A. Herstein,'Keeping the voter's limits in mind: A cognitive process analysis of decision making in voting', in J. Pers. Soc. Psychol.40 (1981), pp. 843-61; H. Montgomery & T. Adelbratt, 'Gambling decisions and information about expected value,' in Oregon. Behav. Hum. Perform. 29 (1982), pp. 39-57; H. Shaklee & B. Fischhoff, 'Strategies of information search in causal analysis,' in Mem. Cognit. 10 (1982), pp. 520-30.

196 Ibid., referring to N.M. Klein, 'Utility and decision strategies: A second look at the rational decision maker', in Organ. Behav. Hum. Perform. 31 (1983), pp. 1-25.

197 Ibid., referring to T.S. Wallsten, 'The theoretical status of judgmental heuristics. In Decisions Making Under Uncertainty,' in R.W. Scholz (ed.), Amsterdam: North Holland, 1983, In press.

198 Ibid.

199 Ibid., p. 147.

200 Ibid., referring to P.N. Johnson-Laird, 'Mental models in cognitive science. In Perspectives on Gognitive Science, ed. D.A. Norman', (Hillsdale NJ: Erlbaum, 1981), pp. 147-191.

unpredictability of future events, together with such less obvious unknown factors as one's likely feelings after a choice has been made.[201] The way in which these uncertainties are represented in the mental model has marked effect on the subsequent judgment. The nature of this effect is dependent in part on the way a problem statement is worded[202] and in part on the idiosyncratic perspective adopted by the decision maker; the result is not always easy to predict.[203]

The perspective adopted by Berkeley & Humphrey suggests that judgments and decisions occur as response to uncertainty; the initial statement of a problem leaves many questions unanswered, and a person's subsequent behavior is a reflection of efforts to remove or cope with the uncertainty.[204] To resolve uncertainty, information is retrieved from memory and used to fill in missing details of the mental model. For example, while the hypotheses to be evaluated or the options to be considered are sometimes defined as part of the problem, in many cases they too are unknown and must be generated before a decision can be made. Because recall is constructive rather than reproductive, the use of information is guided by the model itself in an interactive way. There are numerous sources of information that are likely to have different effects on construction of the model. As to decision-making model, prospect theory is a descriptive account of risky choice. In this context, Tversky and Kahneman distinguishes two phases in the choice process: a phase of framing and editing, followed by a phase of evaluation.[205] The first phase consists of a preliminary analysis of the decision problem, which frames the effective acts, contigencies of the decision maker. Additional operations that are performed prior to evaluation include cancellation of common components and the elimination of options that are seen to be dominated by others. In the second phase, the framed prospects are evaluated, and the prospect of highest value is selected. The theory distinguishes two ways of choosing between prospects: by detecting that one dominates another or by

201 Ibid., referring to D. Berkeley & P. Humphreys, 'Structuring decision problems and the bias heuristic', in Acta Psychol. 50 (1982), pp. 201-52.

202 Ibid., pp. 147-148, referring to Tversky and Kahneman (1981), supra note 194, pp. 453-458; P. Slovic, B. Fischhoff and S. Lichtenstein,'Response mode, framing, and information processing effects in risk assessment. In New Directions for Methodology of Social and Behavioral Science: Question Framing and Response Consistency', in. R. Hogarth (ed.), (San Francisco: Jossey-Bass, 1982), pp. 21-36.

203 Ibid., p. 148, referring to B. Fischhoff, 'Predicting frames', in J. Exp. Psychol: Learn, Mem. Cognit. 9 (1983), pp. 103-116.

204 Ibid., referring to Berkeley and Humphreys (1982), supra note 201, pp. 201-252.

205 Amos Tversky and Daniel Kahneman, 'Rational Choice and the Framing of Decisions', in The Journal of Business, Vol. 59, No. 2, Part 2: The Behavioral Foundations of Economic Theory, (Oct, 1986), pp. S251-S278 (p.S257).

comparing their values. As to uncertainty in decision making, Kahneman and Tversky distinguish between external (environmentally determined) and internal (knowledge based) uncertainty, and between uncertainty based on event frequencies and uncertainty based on reasoned argument. The use of event frequencies is perhaps best understood and appears to be easiest to deal with. Assuming that events are equally salient, information retrieved from memory can be used accurately to assess relative frequencies, and tasks that demand the direct use of this information are performed more accurately than tasks that require frequencies to be translated into, say, probability judgments.[206] The more information is given directly or retrieved from memory, the less uncertainty the person feels, but there is often an unwarranted increase in confidence as additional information becomes available.[207]

No account of the judgment or decision making process is complete unless it speaks to the representation of the problem; the representation in turn depends on how prior experience is incorporated into the mental model created for the problem. In the study of deductive inference it is well known that the conclusions drawn from a set of premises are generally consistent with a person's experience, but not necessarily with the principles of deductive logic. The logic of choice, Tversky and Kahneman have found, does not provide an adequate foundation for a descriptive theory of decision making. The deviation of actual behavior from the normative model are too widespread to be ignored, too systematic to be dismissed as random error, and too fundamental to be accommodated by relaxing the normative system. A descriptive model of choice accounts for preferences that are anomolous in the normative theory.[208] If an abstract problem can be formulated in terms that are consistent with experience, the person responds appropriately.[209] Thus, a critical variable in the successful application of an abstract principle is whether the wording of the problem

---

206 Pitz & Sachs (1984), supra note 204, p. 148, referring to D. Kahneman & A. Tversky (1982b),' Variants of uncertainty'. See D. Kahneman, P. Slovic & A. Tversky, 'Judgment Under Uncertainty: Heuristics and Biases, (Cambridge: Cambridge Univ. Press., 1982), pp. 509-20; W.C. Howell & S.P. Kerkar, 'A test of task influences in uncertainty measurement', in Organ. Behav. Hum. Perfor. 30 (1982), pp. 365-390.

207 Ibid., referring to B. Fischhoff & D. MacGregor, 'Subjective confidence in forecasts', in J. Forecasting 1 (1982), pp. 155-172.

208 Tversky & Kahneman (1986), supra note 205, p.S252.; Pitz & Sachs (1984), Ibid., referring to P.N. Johnson-Laird & P.C. Watson, 'Thinking', (Cambridge: Cambridge Univ. Press, eds. 1997).

209 Pitz & Sachs (1984), Ibid., referring to J.R. Cox & R.A. Griggs, 'The effects of experience on performance in Watson's selection task', in Mem. Cognit. 10 (1982), pp. 496-502.

leads to a representation that is consistent with the principle.[210] Kahneman & Tversky draw similar conclusions concerning inductive inference: "human reasoning cannot be adequately described in terms of content-independent formal rules".[211] A full understanding of the judgment process depends on how experience is organized. To obtain a complete specification of a person's knowledge is an overwhelming task, but there may be certain prototypical situations that are widely recognized;[212] it may be possible to define general principles of judgment for these prototypes.[213] In some situations, representiveness is determined by the similarity of a hypothetical process (e.g., a possible disease) to observed outcomes (e.g. symptoms exhibited by a patient), or by the perception of a causal relationship between process and outcomes. For some problems the perception of representativeness is mediated by judgments of similarity, for example, the similarity of a personality description to a general stereotype. It has proved as difficult to define similarity satisfactorily as it is to define representativeness. One traditional approach is to use multidimensional geometric models in which the proximity of two items in space determines their perceived similarity.[214] Tversky & Gati propose a feature-based model in which similarity depends on a linear combination of common and distinctive features.[215] For the most part their model applies to tasks that require direct perceptual judgments, using stimuli such as simple schematic figures. It is presumably easier to define relevant features for schematic figures that it is for complex decision problem. Nevertheless, these theoretical development may be the first steps toward a general characterization of judgments based on perceived similarity.

A model of similarity judgment must consider not just single features or dimensions, but also patterns of co-occuring features. For example, Bar-Hillel[216] suggests that the judged likelihood of a sample is determined by the similarity of configural patterns in the sample (e.g. the configuration of test scores for a sample of students) to a prototypical

---

210 Ibid., p. 149, referring to Griggs and. Newstead (1982), supra note 192, pp. 297-307.

211 Ibid., referring to D. Kahneman & A. Tversky, 'On the study of statistical intuitions', 1982a. See Kahneman, Slovic and Tversky (1982), supra note 206, pp. 493-508.

212 Ibid., referring to N. Cantor, W. Mischel & J.C. Schwartz, 'A prototype analysis of psychological situations', in Cogn. Psychol. 14 (1982), pp. 45-77.

213 Ibid.

214 Ibid.

215 Ibid., referring to A. Tversky & I. Gati, 'Similarity, separability, and the triangle inequity', in Psychol. Rev. 89 (1982), pp. 123-154.

216 Ibid., p. 150, referring to M. Bar-Hillel, 'What features make samples seem representative?' in J. Exp. Psychol: Hum. Percept. Perform. 6 (1980), pp. 578-89.

sample. Studies of concept learning and categorization suggest that a person abstracts information about pattern of common events, so that the similarity of an event to a prototype depends on whether a pattern has occurred frequently for that prototype.[217] There is much in common between judgments of category membership and judgments of representativeness. Like other judgments, covariation is evaluated in the context of a more general mental model. For example, Pitz, Englert, Haxby and Leung suggest that frequency judgments in a complex environment are mediated by hypotheses about the structure of the problem; changes in judgment occur only if information disconfirms a current hypothesis.[218] Perception of covariation are jointly dependent on observed information and prior assumptions about the problem setting; there is an interaction between the judged frequency of co-occurrence and knowledge of causal connections between events.[219] Abelson has argued that abstract generalizations of cause-effect relationships, or scripts, mediate the perception of covariation among events. As to causality, Rehder and Hastie (2001) found that common cause and common effect features were weighed more heavily than features under a wide variety of conditions, and have suggested that features are more heavily weighed to the extent they are involved in many causal relationships regardless of whether they play the role of causes and effects: a proposal which may be referred to as the relational centrality hypothesis.[220] Einhorn and Hogarth have conducted a detailed study based on the hypothesis that the perception of a causal relationship between events is a function of several 'cues to causality' that might be present.[221] They assume that cues such as temporal order, contiguity in space, and similarity, combine additively to determine the strength of an impression of causality. The perception of causality, like covariation, is a dynamic process. When people can select information relevant to a causal hypothesis, they seek

217 Ibid. See e.g., B. Hayes-Roth & F. Hayes-Roth, 'Concept learning and the recognition and classification of exemplars', in J. Verb. Learn. Verb. Behav. 16 (1977), p. 321-338.

218 Ibid., referring to G.F. Pitz, J.A. Englert, K. Haxby & L.S. Leung, 'Learning conditional frequencies in a probability learning task', in Acta Psychol. 47 (1981), pp. 229-243.

219 Ibid., referring to L. Adelman, 'The influence of formal, substantive, and contextual task properties on the relative effectiveness of feedback in multiple-cue probability tasks', in Organ. Behav. Perform. 27 (1981), pp. 423-442; D.L. Jennings, M. Amabile & L. Ross (1982),'Informal covariation assessment: Data-based versus theory-based judgments'. See Kahneman, Slovic and Tversky (1982), supra note 211, pp. 211-230; R.P. Abelson, 'Psychological status of the script concept', in Am. Psychol. 36 (1981), pp. 715-729.

220 Bob Rehder, 'Categorization as causal reasoning,' in Cognitive Science 27 (2003) 709-748 (Cognitive Science Society, Inc, Elsevier) ["2003a"], p. 741.

221 Pitz & Sachs (1984), supra note 219, p. 150, referring to Einhorn & Hogarth (1982b), supra note 189.

mostly to confirm their current hypothesis rather than explore others.[222] Einhorn and Hogarth emphasize that judgments of causality depend on the context in which judgments take place; two events may be seen as causally connected in one context but not in another.[223] In addition, an important determinant of perceived causation is the absence of other explanations for the phenomenon. The basic level category maximizes within category similarity relative to between-category similarity, suggesting that there exists an optimal level of detail for descriptive and inferential tasks.[224]

Complex problems are characterized by conflict, either in the inferences to be drawn from the information or in the decision maker's preferences for outcomes. To resolve the conflict it is necessary either to eliminate all but a subset of mutually consistent features or to integrate the conflicting information to produce a complete judgment. Linear models of information integration, especially those that presume the existence of an averaging process, imply that integration occurs by averaging the values assigned to each feature according to their relative weight. The ubiquity of the averaging process is one of the most interesting findings to emerge from the information integration literature.[225] Weights are often considered to be a function of the salience of problem features.[226] The most productive account of weights is that which shows relationships between estimated weights and other behaviors. Birnbaum and Stegner have demonstrated that estimates derived from a configural weight averaging model are predictive of a person's judgments in a different context.[227] An averaging process is a compensatory integration mechanism in which a judgment represents a tradeoff among conflicting evaluations. In most cases the averaging process is assumed to be automatic and not subject to deliberate control or verbal report. The concept of an autonomous compensatory tradeoff process appears in several explanations of judgments processes: Einhorn and Hogarth refer to such a process in the evaluation of diagnostic evidence

---

222 Ibid., referring to Shaklee & Fischhoff (1982), supra note 195, pp. 520-530.

223 Ibid., referring to Einhorn & Hogarth (1982b), supra note 221.

224 Ibid., p. 151.

225 Ibid., referring to L.L. Lopes, 'Procedural debiasing', Tech. Rep. No. 15, Wis. Hum. Inf. Process Program, Madison, 1982a; J. Shanteau & G.F. Nagy, 'Information integration in person perception: Theory and application. In Progress in Person Perception', M. Cook (ed.), (London: Metheun, 1982).

226 Ibid., referring to J.C. Shanteau & C.H. Ptacek (1983), 'Role and implication of averaging processes in advertising', in Advertising and Consumer Psychology, ed. L. Percy, A. Woodside, New York: Lexington. In press.

227 Ibid., p. 152, referring to M.H. Birnbaum & S.E. Stegner, 'Measuring the importance of cues in judgment for individuals: Subjective theories of IQ as a function of heredity and environment', in J. Exp. Soc. Psychol. 17 (1981), pp. 159-182.

and in judgments of causality.[228] Cost-benefit theories of strategy selection suggest that a tradeoff exists between cognitive efforts and judgmental accuracy. The problem with theories that assume a tradeoff mechanism is that they are hard to distinguish from noncompensatory, feature selection processes. Simply demonstrating that judgments of, say, causal connection are related to several different cues does not show that the cues combine in a compensatory fashion.[229] Whatever information processing occurs as part of the judgment or decision making process, the only observable behavior is a response – usually a judgment or a choice. Information processing theorists, however, have taken as their major concern the strategies that people use in acquiring and using information.[230] By examining verbal protocols, it has been possible to examine overt behavior that precedes the final judgment or choice. From the protocols one can trace the sequence of operations involved in information acquisition and make inferences about the way the information is used.[231] Most theories assumes that evaluations of the information are translated into a response by procedures that are independent of the evaluation process. Functional measurement theory[232] and Birnbaum's methods of scale free model testing[233] are two methods for separating the judgment process from the evaluation process. Within an information processing framework the most common account of the response process relies on the concept of 'anchoring and adjustment': an anchor point is selected that serves as a starting point for the response; it is then adjusted in a direction and by an amount determined by other features of the problem. Einhorn and Hogarth propose that anchoring and adjustment is a significant part of the inference process.[234]

***

Before an analysis of a problem can be implemented, it is necessary to define the elements of the problem and the structural interrelationships

---

228 Ibid., referring to H.J. Einhorn & R.M. Hogarth, 'A theory of diagnostic inference: I. Imagination and the psychophysics of evidence', Cent. Deeds. Res., Grad, Sch. Bus., Univ. Chicago, 1982a; Einhorn & Hogarth (1982b), supra note 223.

229 Ibid.

230 Ibid., pp. 152-153.

231 Ibid., p. 153. See e.g., N.M. Klein, 'Utility and decision strategies: A second look at the rational decision maker', in Organ. Behav. Hum. Perform. 31 (1983), pp. 1-25.

232 Ibid., referring to N.H. Anderson, 'Functional measurement and psychophysical judgment', in Psychol. Rev. 77 (1970), pp. 153-170.

233 Ibid., referring to M.H. Birnbaum 'Controversies in psychological measurement', in Social Attitudes and Psychological Measurement', (Hillsdale,NJ: Erlbaum,1982), pp. 401-485.

234 Ibid., referring to Einhorn & Hogarth (1982a), supra note 228.

among them. Several authors have pointed out how critical the problem structure is to the decision aiding process. In a description of a career decision aid, for example, Wooler suggests that its most useful contribution may be in helping a person understand the interrelationships and conflicts among elements of the problem.[235] To be successful, the structure must represent both the external features of the problem and the knowledge and values of the decision maker. If the structure is completely task-determined it can be built into the decision aid prior to its use. Nevertheless, even if the structure can be predefined, it may still be more helpful to have the decision maker generate the structure.[236] The best approach to generating a problem structure is likely to be one based on a theoretical model of the structure of knowledge.[237] Pitz, Sachs and Heerboth discussed a number of methods for using a decision maker's description of problem elements to help the person recognize details of the structure, based on assumption about the organization of the underlying knowledge.[238] Different methods may serve different purposes, depending on the way that the knowledge is to be used. Pearl, Kim and Fiske found that a goal-directed approach proved best for encouraging a person to generate more options, while a decision tree structure was most successful in helping a person to recognize the best action.[239]

Descriptivity in cognitive science, epistemology and philosophy as above discussed illuminates the notion of descriptivity in jurisprudence, includingdescriptivityinjudicial-decisionmaking. Descriptivejurisprudence will be sketched out in Chapter II.1, in which positivist and realist legal schools put forward their arguments to support their descriptive theses in jurisprudence. They describe the law as it really is and refuse intervention in form of evaluation according to what the law ought to be, for scientific pretention. Descriptive judicial decision making has been argued by realist writers and critical legal writers in jurisprudence, which will also be briefly discussed in Chapters IV.4 & V.1.1. of this book.

---

235 Ibid., p. 155, referring to S. Wooler, 'A decisional for structuring and evaluating career options', in J. Oper. Res. 33 (1982), pp. 343-351.

236 Ibid., referring to N.J. Sachs & G.F. Pitz, 'Choosing the best method of contraception: Application of decision analysis to contraceptive counseling and selection', South Ill. Univ. , Carbondale, 1981.

237 Ibid., pp. 155-156, referring to P.C. Humphreys, S. Wooler & L.D. Phillips, 'Structuring decisions: The role of structuring heuristics', Tech. Rep. 80:I, Decis. Anal. Unit. Brunel Univ., Uxbridge, England, 1980.

238 Ibid., p. 156, referring to G.F. Pitz, N.J. Sachs & J. Heerboth, 'Procedures for eliciting choices in the analysis of individual decision,' in Organ. Behav. Hum. Perform. 26 (1980b), pp. 396-408.

239 Ibid., referring to J. Pearl, J. Kim and R. Fiske, 'Goal-directed decision structuring systems', Tech. Rep., CLA-ENG-81-21, Cogn. Syst. Lab., Univ. Calif., Los Angeles, 1981.

I.2.3. NORMATIVITY

***

There are theories of mind which emphasize self-control. A popular contemporary approach is to treat human conduct as the outcome of actors following rules. Rules can be broken and unsatisfactory rules can be changed. If one believes that one's patterns of action are determined by rules rather than by 'mechanistic' process described in laws of nature one gains greater control over one's life. Belief in such a theory will tend to enhance human powers. In the case of physical sciences we can often distinguish between the moral issues that come up in the course of the pursuit of scientific knowledge (vivisection) and those that are involved in the practical application of that knowledge (germ warfare). In sociological studies, if it is true that human societies are in part a product of the social theories and historical beliefs held by their citizens then society is not an independent reality that can be thought of as standing wholly outside a science of society. Belief about the physical world can influence human psychology.[240]

Franz Bretano holds that aboutness is exclusively a feature of mental phenomena, and that nothing which is both mental and possesses aboutness is physical. He certainly seems to have proven that there are mental phenomena which are not physical and that mind (with aboutness) is not brain (without aboutness).[241] Understanding mentally exists in human mind, and the mind is discursive. On the foundation of the discursive mind model lays a thesis of the cognitive system's discursive organization. This thesis is that a number of relatively autonomic, holistic modules of representation exist in our mind, of which every one is linked to a specific social context, which is present in one's socialization history.[242] Different modules contain specific cognitive-affective resources, shaped by different ways of giving meaning to personal experience. These patterns of naming and weighing experience are developed within the relationships with significant others, important groups or influential social background. The essential assumptions of the discursive mind model are about the modularity of cognitive system, about the social origin of an individual's knowledge and about the specificity of a person's knowledge structures for a social context.[243] The first assumption – about the modular character

240 Harre (1985), supra note 105, pp. 188-189.

241 Graham (1993/1998), supra note 95, pp. 152, 155.

242 Katarzyna Stemplewska-Zakowics, Dorota Kobylinska, Hubert Suszek and Bartosz Szymczyk, 'Exploration in the Discursive Mind: Theoretical Model', in International Journal for Dialogical Science, Fall, 2010, Vol. 4, pp. 81-94 (p. 82).

243 Hubert Suszek, Dorota Kobylinska, Katarzyna Stemplewska-Zakowics and

of the cognitive system – refers to widely accepted nowadays schematic organization of cognitive structure. The second assumption concerning the social origin of one's knowledge is one of the cornerstone of the social-cognitive approach to personality[244] and the social cognition approach.[245] As may be reckoned, the contemporary trends tend to consider the impact of the phenomena and processes, that are intersubjective in their nature, increasingly more. They all draw a coherent vision of human as someone[246] who is shaped by relationships with others and is being consistently engaged in the social process or meaning creating.[247] The third assumption does not play a key role in mainstream theories; however it is present in the concept of social constructivism and discursive psychology. Rom Harre's theory of positioning is the most important of these concepts[248] (Harre & Gillet 1994; Hare & van Langenhove 1999) as well as the influential ideas of Kenneth Gergen.[249]

Harre and Gillet present individuals as agents who skillfully use cultural and discursive resources to accomplish their intentions. Cultural context and discursive position constrain individuals, but individuals also choose how to respond to their situations.[250] Harre and Gillet developed 'discursive psychology' in which all experience is mediated in order to overcome mind-body dualism. They argue that the mediators are not semi-permanent mental entities, but discursive practices and cultural context. They move away from mythical mental entities (p. 40), because

---

Bartosz Szymczyk, 'Exploration in the Discursive Mind: Research', in International Journal for Dialogical Science, Fall, 2010, Vol. 4, pp. 95-122 (p. 82, 96).

244 Stemplewska-Zakowics, et al. (2010), supra note 242, p. 83, referring to A. Bandura, 'A social cognitive theory of personality', in L. Pervin & O. John (eds.), Handbook of Personality (New York: Guilford Publication, 1999), 2nd ed., pp. 154-196; D. Cervone & L.A. Pervin, 'Personality: Theory and research', 10th ed., (New York: John Wiley and Sons, 2008).

245 Ibid., referring to J. Forgas, 'Social cognition: Perspectives on everyday understanding', (London: Academic Press, 1981); J. P. Forgas & K. D. Williams, 'The social self', (New York: Psychology Press, 2002).

246 Ibid. See E.T. Higgins, 'Social cognition: Learning about what matters in the social world', in European Journal of Social Psychology, 30 (2000), pp. 3-39.

247 Ibid.

248 Ibid., referring to R. Harre & G. Gillet, 'The discursive mind', (London: Sage, 1994); R. Harre & L. van Langenhove, 'Positioning theory: Moral contexts of intentional action', (Oxford, UK: Blackwell, 1999).

249 Ibid., referring to Kenneth Gergen, 'The saturated self. Dilemmas of identity in contemporary life', (New York: basic Books, 1991).

250 Stanton Wortham, 'Reviews of Rom Harre and Grant Gillet, The Discursive Mind, and James P. Gee, The Social Mind', in University of Pennsylvania – Scholarly Commons, Graduate School of Education, GSE Publications, 6-1-1997, reprinted from Theory and Psychology, Volume 7, Issue 3 June 1997, pp. 422-424.

such entities do not really explain anything. As later Wittgenstein argues, having a copy of the world in one's head does nothing to explain how we actually think and act, and leads to a regress of representations.[251] Harre distinguishes between *instruments*, which are all sorts of detectors and measuring devices, and *apparatus*, which are devices that isolate parts of the world to be studied. Instruments are *causally* related to the rest of the world because the interaction between instruments and world gives quantitative or qualitative information about the latter. Apparatuses help scientists isolate aspects of a complex reality. In addition, they create working models of natural processes. According to Harre, apparatus are *conceptually* related to the world because, by drawing analogies, we *reason* from what happens in the laboratory to how things might be in nature.[252] As to experimental apparatus Harre introduces the notion of *intensive design*.[253] By this notion, he aims at an account of the method of induction that would fit actual scientific practices. He rejects the traditional idea of 'induction by enumeration'. To the contrary, the stories illustrate that researchers often prove their point by a few or just one exemplar. Results established on a few examples are taken to be typical and generalized to all the members of the same species, and in some cases, even to other species including human beings.

Attitudes and emotions come into existence in the performance of actions (Harre and Gillet, p. 22). Memories are in the telling (Gee, p. 60). The report of a memory is not reproduction of a representation but instead a socioculturally located event. This does not mean that memories, judgments and emotional displays emerge *de novo* every time without constraints. Cultural context and discursive practices as well as individuals' physical and mental states provide *resources* that people use to accomplish their judgments, displays and other actions.[254]

As already mentioned before, Rom Harre's theory of positioning is the most important of the social and discursive theory (Harre and Gillet, 1994, Harre and van Langenhove, 1999). The specific structural basis of these theories can be dwelt upon. Because they reject experimental methodology and traditional psychological notions such as cognitive representation, there is also nothing strange in the fact that these theories do not offer any precise models of the architecture of the mind, directly from which some specific, testable hypothesis could be drawn.[255] Preliminary evidence for the

251 Ibid.

252 Mieke Boon, 'Tales of Experimentation', Book Review of Rom Harre, Pavlov's Dogs and Schrodinger's Cat: Scenes from the living laboratory', (Oxford University Press, 2009), in Metascience, 20:159-163 – Oxford.

253 Ibid.

254 Wortham (1997), supra note 250.

255 Stemplewska-Zakowics, et al. (2010), supra note 249, p. 83, referring to

hypothesis, that the mind is dialogically structured and that each I-position [each representation module] is represented in a separate representation module, might be shaped in a particular social context. A growing body of research investigates various aspects of the dialogical self theory and the concept of positioning.[256] The notion of I-position comes from a notion of the voice proposed by Bakhtin (1984) who is commonly referred to in the discursive and dialogical approach. The voice was understood by Bakhtin as a "talking personality".[257] The problem of stability vs. variability is essential for the whole personality psychology. Referring to personality, the model of relational mind assumes that the personal dispositions of a person are variable not only between different situations, but mostly between social contexts.[258] One of the possible applications of the discursive mind model is the field of stereotype and prejudices. Despite the fact that this field had an abundance of relevant theoretical concepts and a great deal of empirical data, the discursive mind model can offer new insights. If we assume that each of the I-positions within a person has its own cognitive-affective resources, it may happen that one of the positions is biased towards a certain group and perceives it in a stereotypical way, whilst the other I-position of the same person is free of such prejudice.[259]

Greenwald (1982) has postulated the existence of subsystems as part of the 'personalysis' conception of inner multiplicity. This conception depicts the mind as an informational system consisting of many relatively independent subsystems. Each subsystem carries an expanded knowledge volume and can influence the behavior of a person in its own domain. Greenwald does not determine which specific subsystems can be distinguished, so it is not conflicting with his concept to assume that these subsystems can be the I-positions or voices in Harre's theory.[260] According to the discursive mind model, I-positions are relatively autonomic modules of cognitive system which consist of script-like structure combining personal knowledge and socially shared knowledge. These structures are activated in certain conditions (automatically or intentionally) and henceforth – up till when the next I-position is activated – determine the range of processable information and the specific rules of this processing.

Harre & Gillet (1994), supra note 248.

256 Suszek et.al. (2010), supra note 243, p. 95.

257 Ibid., p. 101, referring to M.M. Bakhtin, 'Problem of Dostoevsky's poetic', in C. Emerson, Ed., & Trans (Minneapolis: University of Minneapolis Press, 1984).

258 Ibid., p. 101.

259 Ibid., p. 87.

260 Stemplewska-Zakowics et.al.(2010), supra note 255, p. 88, referring to A.G. Greenwald., 'Is anyone in charge? Personalysis vs. the principle of personal unity', in J. Suls (ed.), Psychological perspective on the self (Vol. 1) (Hillsdale, NJ: Erlbaum, 1982), pp. 151-181.

The process of taking up a certain I-position is called positioning (Harre and van Langenhove, Hermans, 1996, 2000) and it is essential in the discursive mind model, because it is crucial for the whole chain of events which happens afterwards.[261]

It can be agreed, that the thesis about the specificity of the knowledge structures for the social context was not found false. A successful replication would bring new light to the nature of stereotypes and reinforce the point of view according to which they are a result of the social negotiation process of giving names and a part of a shared reality (*see* Higgins, 2000).[262] This would mean that a given stereotype is stored in the mind only in a certain module of representation, which contains content developed in a specific social context.[263]

***

Before continuing the discussion on cultural/social discursive theories, we now switch first to inferentialism from which normativity can [also] be identified. The large theoretical, explanatory and strategic commitments that have shaped and motivated Anglo-American philosophy of the twentieth century includes empiricism, naturalism, representionalism, semantic-atomism, formalism about logic and instrumentalism about the norms of practical rationality(31), Robert Brandom resolutely follows the Anglo-American tradition 'pursuing a recognizable successor project'of what traditionally was thought of as an 'analysis of meaning'.[264] Brandom thinks of language as a tool that permits us 'to endorse in what we say what before we could endorse only in what we did'(153). The general idea here is that as exemplars of Homo sapien we are agents taking our environment in our actions to be a certain way. Taking for granted in what we do that our environment is a certain way is what we share with animals, *sentient* creatures like us. A *santient*'s behavior, which implies awareness of his environment as being a certain way, might be reinforced by the success of his unfloding life. But reinforcement is not the same as endorsement.[265] Santient agents are aware in the sense of being awake, and are capable of responding in a reliable, differential way to relevant inputs. The reliable pattern of the behavior of merely santient agents is not normative, however:

261 Ibid., p. 89.

262 Suszek et al. (2010), supra note 259, pp. 99-100. See E.T. Higgins, 'Social cognition: Learning about what matters in the social world', in European Journal of Social Psychology, 30 (2000), pp. 3-39.

263 Ibid., p. 100.

264 Jan Bransen, 'Normativity as the Key to Objectivity – An exploration of Robert Brandom's Articulating Reasons,' 4, in Inquiry, Vol. 45(3), 2000, pp. 373-392.

265 Ibid., p. 6.

it is merely regular, not rule-governed. The stickleback's treatment of the other animal as a trespasser and the person's treatment of the door as the proper way to leave the room can quite harmlessly be thought of as beliefs, albeit, perhaps, mindless beliefs.[266] They are intentional, but not in a fully conceptual way. They are not endorsements, not taking for which the agent accepts responsibility (for example in the face of opposition). It is in this respect significant that a stickle quite accidently 'discover' the boundary of his territory in virtue of a draw between his anger and his fear, a fear that grows in response to the growing anger of the animal he is chasing off.[267] The stickleback doesn't endorse his anger or his fear, but is moved by them. We, exemplars of Homo sapien, respond differently. We live in an essentially social world; we face an environment populated by similar creatures who are in the habit of holding one another responsible for the way they take their environment to be. Responsibility is the key here, as we could have learned, according to Brandom, from one of Kant's fundamental insights (163). Our responses display understanding; they display our appreciation of the distinction between correct and incorrect ways we take our environment to be, between ways of acting that can and that cannot be endorsed.[268]

'Inferentialism' is Brandom's term of art for his account of the nature of the conceptual, the nature of meaning, content and awareness, the nature of what makes us exemplars of Homo sapien. Inferentialism is basically the claim that meaning (i.e., conceptual content) should not be analyzed in terms of *reference* but in terms of *inference*. The fact that a statement means something, that it has intentional import, that it says something about something, that it employs conceptual content is a fact we should not try to understand in terms of referential relations between the statement and some other state of affairs, but in terms of relations between the statement and other statements. The role of assertion, as Brandom calls 'the game of giving and asking reasons', should be analyzed in terms of inferential relations between an assertion and other assertions. Assertions bear inferential relations to one another in two directions: they are the consequents of certain antecedents (.....stream) and are antecedents of certain consequents (.... stream). Brandom is a rationalist who claims that the discursive practice of asserting, inferring and justifying is fundamental to the very possibility of talking and therefore thinking. He builds upon a

266 Ibid., p. 7. The striking phrase "mindless beliefs" is coined by Josefa Toribio, 'Semantic Responsibility,' in Philosophical Explorations 5(1), 2002, p. 49.

267 Ibid. Being at a loss between these opposing emotions, the stickleback digs into the sand. Cf. R.J. Wootton, 'A functional biology of Sticklebacks', (London: Croom Helm, 1984).

268 Ibid., pp. 6-7.

set of ideas he attributes to Sellars, primarily among them the idea that conceptual content *is* just inferential role. And inferential role, being essentially a normative matter, is cashed out in terms of commitments (and crucially entitlements). Inferential relations form a pattern, revealing what follows from the applicability of a concept, and what it follows from. One can think 'downstream' from antecedents to consequents, and 'upstream' from consequents to antecedents. Brandom thinks of the conceptual as an essentially linguistic affairs including intentional states, and of intentional content as a matter of inferences sapien creatures can handle, both mentally, in virtue of endorsement in what they do, and linguistically, in virtue of commitments entailed in what they say.[269] In Bransen's words, inferentialism provides a conception of human understanding.[270] Inferentialsm's promise is to overcome the one-sidedness of the empiricist, rationalist and sociohistoric traditions [of the schools of thought] by proposing to analyze the phrase *growth of understanding* in terms of becoming better in the game of asking and giving reasons.

Brandom's appropriation is of Sellar's famous attack on the Myth of the Given. We might naively think of a perceptual state as primarily an awareness, a receptive state, a state of being affected in a certain way, a state with a certain qualitative 'feel'. But even if we were to concentrate on a perceptual state as merely an awareness, it would probably only academically speaking be possible to think of this affectedness as completely detached from another essential feature of perceptual states: that it is an observational report.[271] Sellars' central thought comes in right here, according to Brandom, by stressing that the role of an observational report *with conceptual content* is not a matter of arousing feeling or motivating the agent, but consists essentially in committing the agent to endorsing inferential relations.[272] The perceptual state of a concept-using creature is essentially a normative state: it is a discursive entry transition. Observing a sunset over there in the conceptual mode, is a matter of being committed

269 Ibid., p. 2, 8.

270 Ibid., p. 3.

271 Ibid., p. 9.

272 Ibid., p. 10. For Brandom, an important aspect of Sellars' central thought is the radical way in which it frustrates attempts to discern similarities between the perceptual states of merely sentient and those of sapient creatures. All we can really say about both kinds of creatures are capable of responding in a reliable differential way to relevant inputs. The rest – i.e., that we talk about perceptual states as receptive, affective states, as observational reports, and as motivating the agent's behavior – is merely metaphorical anthropomorphizing. Brandom's insistence on the distinction between sentient and sapient creatures, and his claim that in human experience it is norms "all the way down', uncover problems in the context of the cognitive development of children that deserve serious attention [following text omitted].

to certain discursive inferences. The fact that the perceptual state is a receptive, or affective state just means that it is an *entry* transition: by being in this state one enters the game of giving and asking for reasons with a specific 'deontic score'. Three consequences should be noted: (i) the meaning of the perceptual state is not one captured by its referring to its object; (ii) inferentialism does not mean that the conceptual content of the perceptual state is inferred from a preceding sensation; (iii) the distinction between the perceptual states on concept-users and non-concept-users is a matter of normativity, of the concept-user's responsibility to endorse the inferential relations he is committed to by being in the perceptual state he is in.[273] The discursive practice of giving and asking for reasons is analyzed by Brandom[274] in terms of his favorite idioms as 'deontic scorekeeping' (81). A speech act means whatever it means in terms of its inferential role, i.e., in terms of how it changes the 'deontic score', how it changes the commitments (and entitlements) one undertakes, acknowledges and attributes.

An important feature of Brandom's inferentialist picture of Homo sapien is the analogy he seeks to exploit between perception as a discursive entry transition and action as a discursive exit transition. For Brandom, neither sensations nor desires have an important role to play as allegedly raw feels that mediate between mind and world. Sensations are mere abstractions. They would remain of perceptual states, if one were to succeed in thinking away their role as observational reports. But one cannot succeed in thinking this role away in case one thinks of the perceptual states of concept-users. On Brandom's view it is not desires but intention that we basically need in order to explain actions. Desires do not function as premise in a practical reasoning, but rather make explicit the inferential commitment endorsed in the intention that produces the action (89). Practical reasoning is an explicit normative affairs involving two types of discursive commitments – the cognitive (acknowledged in belief) and the practical (acknowledged in intention). The full depth of the analogy between perception and action can best be elucidated by quoting Brandom: "Observation (a discursive *entry* transition) depends on reliable dispositions to respond differentially to states of affairs of various kinds by acknowledging certain sorts of commitments, that is, by adopting deontic attitudes and so changing the score. Action (a discursive *exit* transition) depends on reliable dispositions to respond differentially to the acknowledging of certain sorts of commitments, the adoption of deontic attitudes and consequent change of score, by bringing about various kinds of states of affairs"(83). Practical reasoning takes these cognitive and practical commitments – beliefs (i.e., true-takings) and intentions (i.e., true-makings) – into account, and Brandom spends some time on the idea

273 Ibid.

274 Ibid., p. 8.

of material inferences to argue against Humean suspicions that inferences involving merely these two types of commitments are enthymemes (i.e., are inferences that make use of a hidden premise). Material inferences are valid not because of their logical form, but because of their content.[275] "I want to stay dry" is not a crucial premise needed to explain the act of opening my umbrella, but is merely making explicit as an avowal the commitment endorsed in the intention and already made explicit in the act. The upshot of this story that living the life of a Homo sapien, i.e., having experiences with conceptual content, is a matter of being committed to playing the game of giving and asking for reasons. Commitments are normative statuses, attitudes to conceptual contents one acknowledges, attributes and undertakes in an essentially social context.[276]

***

Normativity has to do with discursiveness, meaning pattern and behavior shaping in psychology. Within this context, explicit knowledge, of which one is aware, is nothing more than a tip of the iceberg. Every piece of such knowledge is wrapped with the representation of personal experience stemming from the social context, in which it was acquired – interpersonal relationships, participation in a group, being a member of a certain community. The record of experience forms the personal implicit knowledge – theoretically, it can be accessible to the subject's awareness. However, more often it remains below the threshold of his or her conscious awareness – engaged in processing information about an object of knowledge, of which one is aware.[277] Relating to information processing, Van Dijk's thesis might be considered. Van Dijk (1989, 2008, 2009) describes two types of mental model needed to explain text processing: the text model and the context model.[278] The former is a representation of the data being currently processed whereas the latter is an overriding script-like structure, which represents the social situation (the subjective meaning of it) in which a particular act of information processing takes place. Context models continuously shape and control the text models' activity, therefore the developing discourse maintains its suitability over changing conditions.

---

275 Ibid., p. 11.

276 Ibid., p. 12.

277 Stemplewska-Zakowics et.al. (2010), supra note 261, p. 88.

278 Ibid., p. 83, referring to T.A.van Dijk, 'Social cognition and discourse', in H. Giles & R.P. Robinson (eds.), in Handbook of social psychology and language, (Chichester, UK: Wiley, 1989), pp. 163-183; T.A. van Dijk, 'Discourse and context. A sociological approach' (Cambridge, UK: Cambridge University Press, 2008); T.A van Dijk, 'Critical discourse studies; A sociocognitive approach', in Ruth Wodal & Michael Meyer (eds.), in Methods of critical discourse analysis (London: Sage, 2009), pp. 63-85

The sociocultural approach proposed by James Wertsch (1991) can be considered another interesting attempt of filling the interaction-cognition gap. His "tool-kit" metaphor views the mind as a collection of discursively constructed instruments for understanding reality and acting on it. The dialogical self theory put forward by Hubert Hermans (1996, 1999) and Hermans and Kempen (1993) shares the main assumptions of the Wertsch's conception: however it goes further in describing the internal activity of a discursively structured mind.[279] According to the cultural/discursive paradigm the phenomena are patterns of meanings, a flux every moment of which is modulating and transforming as meanings shift and change. The analytical and explanatory models are discourses, treated dialogically, and systems of implicit and explicit rules, cultural conventions and normatively disciplined practices. These are essential features of the formation and maintenance of persons as selves.[280] Looked at from a wider perspective adopting the cultural/discursive paradigm involves abandoning the use of causal concepts in psychology in favor of concepts drawn from linguistic interactions as models for psychology generally. Instead of trying to show that a sequence of events are linked causally, that is a prior event or state as the necessary and sufficient condition to the coming to be of the subsequent event or state, we should see patterns of thought, feeling, acting and perceiving as linked semantically. It is the meaning of a prior act or experience that leads on the subsequent act, thought or feeling as a contribution to a meaningful sequence. The meaning patterns of conversations, the dialogical shaping of human behavior, according to Hermans & Hermans-Konopka (2010), provide the best models for a scientific psychology.[281]

Wittgenstein's popular hunch is that 'meaning is use'.[282] Three

279 Ibid., referring to James V. Wertsch, 'Voices of the mind. A sociocultural approach to mediated action', (Cambridge, MA: Harvard University Press, 1991); H.J.M. Hermans, 'Voicing the self: from information processing to dialogical interchange', in Psychological Bulletin, 19, 1 (1996), pp. 31-50; H.J.M. Hermans, 'the polyphony of the mind: A multivoiced and dialogical self', in J. Rowan & M. Cooper (eds.), The plural self, Multiplicity in everyday life, (London: Sage, 1999), pp. 107-131; H.J.M. Hermans and H.J.G. Kempen, 'The dilaogical self: Meaning as movement', (San Diego, CA: Academic Press, 1993).

280 Rom Harre, 'Psychology's Recovery of its Proper Projects and Methods – Editorial', in Europe's Journal of Psychology, 2012, Vol. 8(3), pp. 315-320, referring to H.J.M. Hermans & A. Hermans-Konopka, 'Dialogical self theory: Positioning and counter-positioning in a globalizing society', (Cambridge: Cambridge University Press, 2010).

281 Ibid., referring to Hermans & Hermans-Konopka (2010), Ibid.

282 Ibid., referring to L. Wittgenstein, 'Philosophical Investigation', (Oxford: Blackwell, 2001, Original work published in 1953); R. Harre and M.A. Tissaw, 'Wittgenstein And Psychology: A Practical Guide', (Aldershot: Ashgate, 2005).

Wittgenstein insights are most important: (1) the private language arguments – symbols are essentially social; (2) the rejection of age old but vicious dichotomies such 'mind and body' and developing alternatives, such as 'private/public', 'individual/social' to frame psychological investigations; (3) the idea of fields of family resemblance, in which we take account of the content dependence of the meanings of key terms such 'intention', 'remembering', 'grief' and so on, rather than artificially inventing a common meaning and seeking in vain for a suitable referent.

***

The causal analysis has been championed by Jerry Fodor, Fred Dretske and several other philosophers. Some materialists offer links with biology and other natural sciences. Some use the related languages of co-variation and counter-factual dependence rather than concepts of causation. Some introduce notions of proto-Intentionality ('Intentionality' supposedly of a less robust sort than Brentano Intentionality) and to try to construct a physicalistic analysis of Intentionality from a causal or co-variational analyses of proto-Intentionality.[283] In crudest form, according to the causal analysis something physically internal to the brain is about some object when the object causes that internal activity. For instance, believing that Uncle Roderick is bald means being in a brain state or process produced by Roderick and his bald pate. Since Roderick's ss causes the brain activity, the activity is about the uncle. One virtue of using the concept of causality in analysis of aboutness is causality respects the asymmetry of aboutness. Causality – like aboutness (and unlike resemblance) – is asymmetrical. If A causes B, B does not cause A. If flipping the light switch causes the illumination of the room, the illumination does not cause the flip. Analogously: just because X is about Y does not mean that Y is about X. Just because Carl's belief is about his uncle, does not mean that his uncle is about Carls' belief.[284]

The most serious unfulfilled project for the materialist causal analysis of aboutness is to provide a satisfactory account of misrepresentation. In whatever detail materialists formulate the account, the objection can always be raised: It does not explain the difference between representation and misrepresentation: between true belief and false belief; between accurate photo and inaccurate photo. Some causal theorists try to counter-reply to the charge that appeal to causality cannot account for misrepresentation by distinguishing two major causal axes along which representation/ misrepresentation can occur. They take as their primary target the idea that misrepresentation does not have the same cause as representation. Misrepresentation occurs along an improper

283 Graham (1993/1998), supra note 241, p. 158.

284 Ibid., p. 159.

or wayward axis, whereas representation occurs along a proper axis. One reason why causality provides an appealing account of aboutness for the materialist is that materialists take causality to be part of the sticks and stones – or better: cement and glue – of the physical world: to be part of the material processes of the world. If causation is physical and aboutness can be analyzed in terms of causation, then aboutness, at bottom, is physical. Another reason is that objects or stimuli in the physical world often make causal contribution to Intentionality states or conditions. What things are seen, felt, or heard in visual, tactile, and auditory perception is determined in part by causal contribution, and such causal contribution as made by seen, felt, or heard objects is relevant perceptual experiences. Causal contribution is one thing, Intentionality another.[285] This is all about consciousness, and the concept of consciousness rests at the foundation of the causal explanation of human behavior. Causality has its descriptive and normative dimensions.[286] If related to moral, consciousness plays a moral role. A number of philosophers contend that all and only conscious creatures morally count. William James writes: "Neither moral relations nor moral law can swing *in vacuo*. Their only habitat can be a mind which feels them". Peter Singer says that the only acceptable limit to our moral concern is the point at which there is no awareness .....no conscious preference, and hence no capacity to experience. James and Singer believe that the fact that a creature is conscious means that it counts, morally. Conscious creatures possess moral standing.[287]

***

Bransen elaborates on the central idea of inferentialism, but a couple of important implications follow immediately. Firstly, inferentialsm is a resolute holistic semantic: "one cannot have any concept unless one has *many* concepts"(15). Secondly, inferentialism is an essentially normative theory: inferential relations are to be understood in terms of *endorsements*, *commitments* and *entitlements*. These normative statuses, as Brandom calls them, are the building blocks of meaning. And thirdly, the context in which these inferential relations can exist as normative statuses is the essentially social game of asking and giving reasons; commitments, endorsements and entitlements are attributed, acknowledged and undertaken.[288] Endorsements are a natural starting-point for Brandom's picture of Homo sapien, accommodating his thesis that it is normativity 'all the way down'.[289]

285 Ibid., p. 159, 160, 161.

286 Ibid., p. 202.

287 Ibid., p. 203, referring to William James, 'Essays in Pragmatism', in. A. Castell (ed.), (New York: Hafner, 1948), p. 69; Peter Singer, 'The significance of animal suffering', in Behavioral and Brain Sciences, 13 (1990), p. 12.

288 Bransen (2000), supra note 276, p. 3.

289 Ibid., p. 6. Cf. Robert Brandom, 'Making It Explicit', (Cambridge, MA.:

Endorsements and commitments are matters of responsibility that imply a normative context of justification. Commitments imply norms, and one of the most important but easily underestimated consequences of there being norms is that some of one's attitudes and actions deserve approval. Norms are of course binding, and as such they constrain one's options. Commitments clearly carry this connotation of being constraints. But it is important to emphasize that this is the reverse side of a significant liberating effect of normativity: that one's responses can be correct, that one can have entitlements. The game of giving and asking for reasons presupposes that there *are* reasons, and as such as one can be asked for reasons, one can *give* reasons; one can spread one's entitlements.[290]

The idealism of Brandom's Hegelian approach is just a matter of recognizing that there cannot be normativity without entitlements. Brandom defends reliabilism and argues for the existence of entitlements in particular, essentially social circumstances. The obvious strength of reliabilism is that reliabilism on this account offers a clear understanding of entitlements as features of a social environment. Entitlements are created within the social context by inferences from attributions to endorsements. Brandom argues that the rules of the game of giving and asking for reasons precisely make the game the fascinating game it is, a game that turns us into concept-using exemplars of Homo sapien, because the rules of inference that define it create two distinct normative statuses: commitments and entitlements.[291] It is the normative pragmatics out of the pragmatist philosophical tradition and the logical inferentialist approach to linguistic analysis out of the analytic tradition, which Brandom has developed.[292] This is his contribution to the philosophy of language, where he holds that language is as 'the social practices that distinguish us as rational, indeed logical, concept-mongering creatures' (thus giving us priority to pragmatic rather than semantic or syntax), so Brandom has his deontic scorekeeping account of social norms, showing his concept of objectivity.

Observing the above theoretical elaborations by Harre, Gillet and Brandom, it might be concluded that normativity is a concept in Homo Sapien's mind, and the basic ingredients of normativity are commitment, endorsement, responsibility and discursivesness. Normativity is the core of norms, or normativity causes norms, which in jurisprudence appears to be the rule [including principle] of law. The notion of normativity in law is addressed in descriptive and prescriptive [or normative] jurisprudence, and this will be laid out in Chapter II. Within prescriptive [or normative]

Harvard University Press, 1994), pp. 625ff.

290 Ibid., p. 13.

291 Ibid., pp. 13-14, 16.

292 Ibid., p. 5, referring to Brandom (1994), supra note 289, p.xi.

jurisprudence, legal doctrinal writers and jurists contend that norm prescribes action, and this normativity is any where inherent in law.

I.2.4. PRESCRIPTIVITY

I.2.4.1. ANALYTICAL VIEW OF PRESCRIPTIVITY

***

A teleological view of nature is the basis of Aristotle's physics and ethics. He based his physics primarily on observation of nature; and his assumption was that the behavior of inanimate matter is similar to the behavior of living things. He used the world 'natural' to describe 'behavior that is in keeping with something's natural ends'.[293] The teleology of life is the anchor of Dilthey's later generalization of the concept of hermeneutics, in which his work has elected a fusion between the concept of dynamism and that of structure: life appears as a dynamism which structures itself. Acquired meaning, present values and distant goals constantly structure the dynamic of life, according to the three temporal dimensions of past, present and future.[294] Stephen Toulmin points out that most important in the history of science have been changes in 'Ideals of Natural Order'.[295] Ideals of Natural Order are standards of regularity which mark off for us those happenings in the world around us which do require explanation by contrasting them with 'the natural course of events' – that is, those events which do not.[296] Toulmin suggests that it is the recognition of anomalies which leads to the creation of new ideals of natural orders. Given a competition between ideals of natural orders, it is the 'fittest' that survive, 'fitness' being a matter of conceptual integration [and fertility].

As mentioned in Chapter I.2.2, historical relativism reduces the philosophy of science to a descriptive survey of actual practice. But merely record of actual practice is to abandon the search for evaluative standards. Surely a philosopher of science ought to be concerned to distinguish science from non-science and 'good science' from 'bad science'. A viable philosophy of science must achieve relevance of the history and practice of science without becoming absorbed in the history of science or the sociology of

293 Charles Siegel, Ethics, What We Still Know After a Skeptical Age, (Berkeley, California: Preservation Institute, 2009), pp. 17-18.

294 Thompson (1981), supra note 132, p. 52.

295 Losee (1972/1980), supra note 110, p. 200, referring to Stephen Toulmin, 'Foresight and Understanding', (New York: Harper Torel Books, 1961), p. 112.

296 Ibid., p. 199, referring to Toulmin (1961), Ibid., p. 79.

science.[297] Traditional epistemology is often said as normative epistemology or prescriptive epistemology. As already mentioned in Chapter I.2.1, both prescriptive epistemology and descriptive epistemology can be also viewed as complementary to each other (Campbell's view).[298] Traditional epistemology which is prescriptive can be construed as a predecessor of descriptive epistemology.[299] Traditional epistemologies can also be construed as competitors to descriptive epistemologies. On this view, both are trying to address the same concerns and offering competing solutions. A standard objection to such approaches is that descriptive accounts are not adequate to do justice to the prescriptive elements of normative methodologies. The extent to which an evolutionary approach contributes to the resolution of traditional epistemological and philosophical problems is a function of which approach one adopts (*cf.* Dretske 1971, Bradie 1986, Ruse 1986, Radnitsky and Bartley 1987, Kim 1988).[300]

One of the distinctions concerns descriptive versus prescriptive approaches to epistemology and the growth of human knowledge. Traditionally, epistemology has been construed as a normative project whose aim is to clarify and defend conceptions of knowledge, foundations, evidential warrant and justification. Writers contend that epistemology, properly understood, is a normative discipline.[301] The difference between the normative and the descriptive approaches to argumentation is an epistemological one that draws from the philosophical discussion of rationality and theory of reason, as Schwed has noted.[302] The difference stems from the question whether the criteria for valuation are imposed on, or just extracted by way of empirical observation from actual argumentative discourse. However, this fundamental difference is not to be sought in the history of argumentation studies and especially not in its criticism of formal logic. The difference should rather be sought in the philosophical roots of such a goal, since its roots are deep in the general empiricist tradition.

Alvin Goldman explicitly endorses the claim that the concept of epistemic justification is a normative concept, and denies for that reason that he is proposing a meaning analysis of epistemic justification. Rather he proposes to identify the non-normative (necessary and sufficient) conditions upon which epistemic justification supervenes.[303] Goldman

---

297 Ibid., p. 218.

298 Bradie & Harms (2016), supra note 116, § 1.3.

299 Id., § 1.3. See e.g., Peter Munz, 'Philosophical Darwinism: On the Origin of Knowledge by Means of Natural Selection', (London: Routledge, 1993).

300 Ibid.

301 Ibid.

302 Schwed (2001), supra note 128, pp. 1-2.

303 Alvin Goldman, "What is Justified Belief?" in George Pappas (ed,),

argues that "traditional epistemology has a strong evaluative normative strain".[304] Richard Rorty says that [t]he holism of Wilfrid Sellars and Quine is a product of their commitment to the thesis that justification is not a matter of a special relation between ideas (or words) and objects, but of conversation, of social practice. [W]e understand knowledge when we understand the social justification of belief.[305] But this gets Quine wrong in an important respect, for it makes it sound like Quine has some positive view about justification, namely that it consists in 'social practice'. However, Quine's point, as Leiter[306] reads him, is that there's nothing to 'understand [about] knowledge' at all, if 'understanding knowledge' means understanding justification. If we could have told the foundationalist story about justification, that would have been interesting, but we can't, thinks Quine, so justification simply drops out of the picture as a topic for fruitful theoretical inquiry. Someone might do the descriptive sociology and map the 'social justification of belief' as we find it, but that wouldn't shed special light on justification. Quine's preferred alternative is to study the evidence-theory relation as a matter of empirical psychology – again, not as a way of analyzing 'justification', but as a way of understanding 'knowledge', i.e., the 'theories' we construct on the basis of meager evindence.

***

There is a form that prescription from philosophers of science may take, different from methodological advice and ethical guidance. The philosophical work may impinge directly on the content of a particular scientific theory. This form of philosophical intervention has been in Lawrence Sklar's development of his conception of what it is to give a philosophical interpretation of a foundational theory in physics. It is the anomaly-resolution model of philosophical interpretation, which is also natural because so much philosophical activity is driven by puzzles, so the model fits into a broader conception of the epistemology of philosophy. At the same time, most philosophy of science does in fact draw on the positive content of our best scientific theories and upon exemplary scientific practices, rather than upon the weak points of science, and to use such success stories to defend a philosophical claim need involve no pernicious circularity.[307] Harre argues that the aim of philosophy of science

---

Justification and Knowledge, (Dordrecht: Reidel, 1979), pp. 1-23; Goldman (1986), supra note 138.

304 Leiter (1997), supra note 138, n.120, referring to.Goldman (1986), id., pp. 3, 2-3.

305 Ibid., n.121, referring to RICHARD RORTY, PHILOSOPHY AND THE MIRROR OF NATURE passim (1979), p. 170.

306 Ibid.

307 Lipton (2015), supra note 148.

is to elucidate the principles assumed in science.[308] These will be found through studies of logic, metaphysics and epistemology. But the philosophy of science must be related to what scientists actually do, and how they actually think. Ideal forms of reasoning, ideals of truth and objectivity, and ideal systems of concepts will be unfolded. Some of the principles that have been proposed in earlier philosophies of science and have been followed by other generations of scientists will be criticized. We shall be 'checking out' philosophical thinking by reference to the actual practice of science, because we must not formulate ideals in our theory of science which are incompatible with any important scientific practice.

The major contemporary theories of Standard Analytic Expistemology (SAE) as already mentioned in Chapter I.2.1 includes versions of foundationalism (Chisholm 1981, Polloct 1974), coherentism (Bonjour 1985, Lehrer 1974), reliabilism (Dretske 1981, Goldman 1986) and contextualism (DeRose 1995, Lewis 1996). Most proponents of SAE agree that a thoroughgoing naturalism in epistemology can't work. It is supposed that a naturalistic theory of epistemology takes as its core, as its starting-point, an empirical theory. The standard argument against naturalistic approaches to epistemology is that empirical theories are essentially descriptive, while epistemology is essentially prescriptive, and a descriptive theory cannot yield normative, evaluative prescriptions. In short, naturalistic theories cannot overcome the is-ought divide.[309] Proponents of SAE might hold that we can connect the descriptive results of SAE with normative prescriptions by noting that normative epistemic claims are a priori. It is natural to suppose that figuring out the truth about epistemology will involve the close analysis of our epistemic concepts. To characterize SAE as a descriptive endeavor (as you have done) might be correct, but it is misleading. The theories of SAE aim to describe an essentially normative concept, and that's why SAE is normative. To put it crudely, discovering conceptual truth involves the accurate description of (the 'content' or the extension of) concepts. So discovering conceptual truths about the epistemological involves the accurate description of epistemological concepts (their content of their extension). And this is precisely what SAE does. And so even though this endeavor is descriptive (it involves describing our concepts), it nonetheless yields normative, a priori prescriptions. It tells us what it really is for a belief to be justified, and so what we ought to believe.[310]

Ameliorative Psychology as mentioned in Chapter I.2.2 is on the attractions of some of the empirical science that is devoted to passing

308 Harré (1985), supra note 130, p. 29.

309 Bishop & Trout (2005), supra note 117, the opening paragraph.

310 Ibid., § 2.4.

normative judgments and prescribing new and better ways to reason. It is an empirical inquiry (or, rather, a set of empirical inquiries) that aims to give positive advice about how we can reason better. It includes work in psychology, statistics, machine learning and Artificial Intelligence. A significant part of Ameliorative Psychology is known as 'predictive modeling' and it includes discussion of models such as linear models, multiple regression formulas, neural networks, naïve Bayes classifiers, Markov Chain Monte Carlo algorithms, decision three models and support vector machines. It also includes significant parts of more traditional psychology, including the well-known heuristics and biases program launched by the groundbreaking research of Kahneman and Tversky (Kahneman, Slovic, and Tversky 1982).[311] Bishop and Trout argues that the core of our naturalistic epistemological theory consists of the descriptive findings of Ameliorative Psychology.[312] But Ameliorative Psychology is also deeply normative in the sense that it makes (implicitly or explicitly) evaluative 'ought' claims that are intended to guide people's reasoning. Epistemic prescriptions are an essential feature of Ameliorative Psychology.

The standard approach to epistemology taken by most analytic philosophers begins with a theory that aims to describe their considered epistemic judgments. From that descriptive core, they infer (with rather too little support) that this theory yields correct epistemic prescriptions. The alternative approach begins with Ameliorative Psychology, which investigates and often discovers new ways to reason better about issues of practical significance. Bishop & Trout's claim that certain parts of psychology are essentially normative will strike many as surprising (or perhaps outrageous). But they are not the first to notice this. Quine's initial failure to discuss the normative, reason-guiding potential of psychology made it easy for proponents of SAE to reject Quine's naturalism. But in some of his later writings, Quine noted the normative impetus of psychology: Naturalization of epistemology does not jettison the normative and settle for the indiscriminate description of ongoing procedures. For me normative epistemology is a branch of engineering. It is the technology of truth-seeking, or, in a more cautiously epistemological term, prediction.[313]

Bishop and Trout contend that the central theories of foundationalism, coherentism, reliabilism and contextualism are structurally analogous to the naturalistic approach Ameliorative Psychology. They have at their core a descriptive theory, and from that descriptive theory, proponents of SAE

311 Ibid., § 1.

312 Ibid.

313 Ibid., § 3, referring to W.V.O. Quine, 'Reply to Morton White', in Lewis Hahn and P. Schiipp (eds.) ,The Philosophy of W.V. Quine, (La Salle, IL: Open Court, 1986), pp. 664-665.

draw normative epistemological prescriptions.[314] For most proponents of SAE, the primary goal of epistemology is to provide an account of knowledge and epistemic justification. In the case of SAE, what would it be for an account of justification to be successful? In a typically clear and careful article, Jaegwon Kim identifies a number of criteria that any account of justification must meet in order to succeed. The most important of these success conditions is what we call the stasis requirements: Although some philosophers have been willing to swallow skepticism just because what we regard as correct criteria of justified belief are seen to lead inexorably to the conclusion that none, or very few, of our beliefs are justified, the usual presumption is that our answer to the first question should leave our epistemic situation largely unchanged. That is to say, it is expected to turn out that according to the criteria of justified belief we come to accept, we know, or are justified in believing, pretty much what we reflectively think we know or are entitled to believe.[315] Bishop and Trout have noted that this requirement – that the right account of justification leave our epistemic situation largely unchanged – is profoundly conservative.[316] In particular, it is extraordinary that SAE should have built right into it a requirement that makes it virtually impossible that a successful epistemological theory would force us to radically alter our epistemic judgments.

Micheal Williams argues that the normative nature of epistemology makes it possible to fully 'naturalize' it: [Epistemic claims] depends on meeting certain norms or standards which define, not what you <u>do</u> do, but what you <u>must</u> or <u>ought</u> to do. To characterize someone's claim as expressing or not expressing knowledge is to pass judgment on it. Epistemic judgments are thus a particular kind of value-judgment. It is far from obvious that investigations with such a strongly normative component can be fully 'naturalized'.[317] Williams's argument applies equally to the theories of SAE: When it comes to epistemic judgments, the theories of SAE define (or at least attempt to define) what we '<u>do</u> do', not what we '<u>must</u> or <u>ought</u> to do'.[318] Richard Feldman maintains that psychology and philosophy must at best co-exist, because psychology can't ask or answer the distinctive normative questions epistemology sets for itself: The original epistemological questions seem to be perfectly good questions, well worthy of our attention. It is difficult to see, then, why the availability of this other field of study [psychology], concerning how we reason, is a

314 Ibid., § 2.

315 Ibid., § 2.1, referring to Kim (1988), supra note 160, p. 382.

316 Ibid.

317 Ibid., § 2.3, referring to Michael Williams, 'Problem of Knowledge: A Critical Introduction to Epistemology', (New York: Oxford University Press, 2001), p. 11.

318 Ibid., § 2.3.

suitable replacement for the evaluative questions that are at the heart of epistemology.[319] [The proponent of SAE is replacing normative questions about how to evaluate reason and belief with descriptive questions about how proponents of SAE evaluate reason and belief.[320]]

Lawrence BonJour argues that any epistemology subsumed by psychology does not have the resources to evaluate, positively or negatively, : "beliefs about alleged occult phenonema of various sorts, such as astrological or phrenological beliefs. For just as naturalized epistemology can say nothing positive about the justification of science or common sense, and is thus impotent in the face of skepticism, so also it can say nothing distinctively negative about the justification of these less reputable sorts of belief".[321] Any theory of SAE that accurately describes how a certain group of people make certain evaluative judgments 'can say nothing positive about the justification of science or common sense, and is thus impotent in the face of skepticism, so also it can say nothing distinctively negative about the justification of' disreputable beliefs. Of course, such a theory might tell us how some people evaluate those beliefs. But that's not the same as actually evaluating those beliefs.[322] Here is one of many proponents of SAE who take on Quinean naturalism in epistemology. [T]he most extreme version of naturalism in epistemology eschews normativity altogether, seeking to replace traditional epistemology (with its concern with justification, rationality, reasonability, and their normative colleagues) by descriptive psychology; this seems to be Quine's suggestion.[323] Reflective equilibrium is a reasonably popular view among analytic philosophers and it is plausible to suppose that the methods of SAE are geared toward capturing our judgments in reflective equilibrium.[324] Proponents of SAE will not typically suggest that they are trying to provide an account of their naïve epistemic judgments, but of their considered epistemic judgments. There may be many ways to spell out what it is for our judgments to be considered, but a standard approach would appeal to reflective equilibrium.[325] Nelson Goodman introduced reflective equilibrium as a process that involves aligning our judgments about particular instances with our judgments

---

319 Ibid., § 2.3, referring to Richard Feldman, 'Epistemology', (Upper Saddle River, NJ: Prentice-Hall, 2003), p. 168.

320 Ibid., § 2.3.

321 Ibid., referring to Laurence BonJour, 'Epistemology: Classic Problems and Contemporary Responses', (Lanham, MD: Rowman and Littlefield, 2002/2010), p. 244.

322 Ibid.

323 Ibid., referring to Alvin Plantinga, 'Warrant and Proper Function', (New York: Oxford University Press, 1993), p. 45 [footnote omitted].

324 Ibid., § 2.1.

325 Ibid.

about general principles. The process of justification is the delicate one of making mutual adjustment between rules and accepted inferences; and in the argument achieved lies the only justification needed for either.[326] Narrow reflective equilibrium is the process of bringing our normative judgments about particular cases into line with our general normative prescriptions and vice versa. Wide reflective equilibrium, according to Bishop and Trout quoting Rawls and Daniels, differs from narrow reflective equilibrium by including our best theories in the mix.[327] So wide reflective equilibrium is the process of bringing into alignment our best theories as well as our normative judgments about particular cases and our general normative prescriptions.

Responding to Quine's naturalized epistemology, Kim argues that the field of epistemology must be essentially normative, it must prescribe conditions for justification (or knowledge) and thereby determine which beliefs are justified (or can be considered knowledge). To some extent all of the epistemological programs to date have dealt with justification of some sort. The word epistemology itself is defined as the study of the nature of knowledge – in practice epistemology is the study of a validation or justification of a body of knowledge claims. Epistemology is the study of justification of knowledge claims, not necessarily a study which defines knowledge in terms of justification for the knower (which is the case for the Cartesian and Carnapian programs). According to Kim, naturalized epistemology has no bearing on the study of epistemology at all, it is only concerned with causal relationships, not validation of knowledge claims.[328] Plantinga has effectively reminded us the etymology of the word 'justification' certainly suggests that we are dealing with a value term.[329] Ayer described knowledge as true belief where one had the right to be sure. The concept of justification is normative.[330] Richard Foley rejects the 'standard interpretation of Quine's view', – roughly, my interpretation is the text-calling attention instead to places where Quine affirms a normative role even for his naturalized epistemology.[331] While Foley correctly recognizes

326 Ibid., referring to Nelson Goodman, 'Fact5, Fiction, and Forecast', (Indianapolis, IN: The Bobbs-Merrill Co., Inc., 1965), p. 64.

327 Ibid., § 2.1, referring to John Rawls, 'Theory of Justice', (Cambridge, MA: The Belknap Press of Harvard University Press, 1971); Norman Daniels, "Wide reflective equilibrium and theory acceptance in ethics", in Journal of Philosophy, 76 (1979), pp. 256-282.

328 O'Niel (2004), supra note 139.

329 Alvin Plantinga, "Justification in the 20th Century", in Enrique Villandeva (ed.), Philosophical Issues 2, Rationality in Epistemology, (Atascadero, California: Ridgeview Publishing Co., 1992), pp. 43-78.

330 A.J. Ayer, The Problem of Knowledge, (Edinburgh: Penguin, 1956).

331 Leiter (1997), supra note 304, n.120, referring to Richard Foley, 'Quine and Naturalized Epistemology', in 19 MIDWEST STUD. PHIL. 246 (1994), pp.

that for Quine these norms admit of no a priori justification, he seems to think this is trivial, since (1) the norms Quine favors are ones we could almost never give up anyway; and (2) Quine identifies them, according to Foley, from the "armchair" rather than empirically.[332] Foely holds that normative judgments all assess the efficacy of achieving goals and ends.[333] In a sense all normative judgments are species of judgments concerning practical rationality. There are different kinds of normative judgments concerning what we ought to do and what we ought to belief because there are different goals or ends that we are concerned to emphasize. Foley suggests restricting the relevant epistemic goal to that of now believing what is true and now avoiding belief in what is false.

The prescriptive approach to epistemology is connected to a particular model of the nature of philosophy and its relationship to the sciences, culture and practice. In this view, epistemology issues judgments which determine the knowledge status of other disciplines. Philosophy is seen as a sort of hanging judge, requiring the sciences etc., to queue up to face judgment under philosophically legislated norms of method. Those sciences which measure up to these demarcation criteria are judged to be True, those that are not are forever banished to the realm of scare quotes.[334] Prescriptive knowledge, Keller and Edelstein say, refers to actions that are allowed, prohibited, responsible, or irresponsible in view of normative standards, such as moral or conventional standards.[335] This type of knowledge refers to shared or intersubjectively valid norms or values according to which the members of a group, or people in general, ought to orient their behavior. These norms provide persons not only with 'reasons for action' in the sense of descriptive social cognition, but with 'good' or 'prima facie' and morally justified reasons (Ross 1963) and with evaluative standards according to which actions or persons are judged in cases of complying with or violating norms. From the validity claims of these norms individuals derive the knowledge that certain intentions and the means used to pursue them are responsible or irresponsible.

Action knowledge means knowledge used to govern human action. One can describe this as rules for action or prescriptions for action. A prescriptive statement does not only consist of a reference to a certain

---

246-250.

332 Ibid., n.120, referring to Foley (1994), Ibid., pp. 253-59. Foley's provocative paper, according to Leiter, underestimates how much of a break this really is from the tradition, and overestimates how much normative epistemology Quine really offers.

333 Richard Foley, The Theory of Epistemic Rationality, (Cambridge, MA : Harvard University Press, 1987), p. 8.

334 Tabarrok (1994), supra note 164, p. 146.

335 Keller & Edelstein, (1991), supra note 172, p. 5.

kind of act. It includes also a reference to a goal which is assumed to be attained when performing this kind of act.[336] A prescriptive statement will also often include some reference to situations and other action conditions of importance.[337] The epistemological character of this kind of action knowledge is prescriptions for actions in order to reach certain goals. This is how the *instrumental rationality* and the *rationality of choice* are applied. There is a clear relation to causality. If action is performed (=cause) then the desired goal is reached (=effect). If the prescriptive statement expresses what *ought* to be done, a causal statement (if cause then effect) is no expression of *ought*, but describes what *is*; a state of affairs.[338]

Some philosophers sympathetic to free will reject the externalist explanation assumption. They argue that at least some decisions or actions cannot be sufficiently explained by reference to circumstances altogether outside themselves. Explanatory externalism is incorrect. Explanation of decision and action is possible, but externalist explanation is not comprehensive. At least, some choices and actions partly are self-explaining or have sufficient explanations partly within themselves. One common theme in internalist arguments is that ultimate control is limited and structured by the background abilities, history, and environment of the free or dual powerful person.[339] An explanatory statement can be transformed into a prescriptive one. *Is* is however used as a basis for derivation into *ought*. It is not possible to derive *ought* from *is* directly. It is necessary to state what is *desired* (part of *ought*) and this is distinguished from what *is*. If one knows what is desired then it is possible to derive *ought* from *is* and the stated goal. What is desired is not possible to express just with reference to causes and effects. Desires and goals are always what people want to achieve. To summarize: Is + want = ought.[340] Explanatory statements together with formulated goals can be converted to prescriptive statement. This shows a clear epistemological relationship between prescriptive and explanatory statements. Prescriptive statements can thus be grounded in

---

336 Goldkuhl (1999), supra note 115, p. 5, referring to Goran Goldkuhl, 'Välgrundad metodutveckling', VITA Höstseminarium 1993, IDA, Linköping University.

337 Ibid., p. 5, referring to C. Argyris & D. Schön, 'Organizational learning II – theory, method and practice', in Addison-Wesley, Reading, 1996.

338 Ibid.

339 Graham (1993/1998), supra note 283, p. 186. The array of versions of explanatory internalism is varied. Versions go by different names including 'free willism', 'libertarianism', 'the theory of self-determination', and 'agency theory.' Each version bears a distinct theoretical load. Profession of agency theory, for example, requires distinguishing between two different types of causation or causal explanation: event causation and agent causation. The theory of self-determination directs attention to considerations of selfhood and personal identity.

340 Goldkuhl (1999), supra note 338, p. 6.

explanations of theoretical character. Explanatory grounding is a kind of theoretical grounding and only indirectly related to empirical observations. Explanatory grounding means that action rules and other action knowledge are justified in general explanatory theories, which often are on a more abstract level than the action knowledge itself. Such explanatory theories require empirical confirmation to be worth serving as a warrant. Such explanatory statements can be on a more abstract level and must therefore be derived and translated to a more concrete level of prescriptive statements.[341] A prescribed action (as it is part of the prescriptive statement) is seen as an *action rule*. It describes the type of action suggested to be performed. Concerning explanatory statement, truth is the main validity claim to be raised. But a prescription is not true or false. It is more or less useful. Thus, *usefulness* is the key validity claim for prescription. A vindicated efficiency of a prescription is of course open to empirical reviews and can thus be transformed into issues of truth. Goldkuhl contends that the main validity claim of prescriptive action knowledge is usefulness.[342]

***

Interpretivists contend that only through the subjective interpretation of and intervention in reality can reality be fully understood. The study of phenomena in their natural environment is key to the interpretivist philosophy, together with the acknowledgement that scientists cannot avoid affecting those phenomena they study. They admit that there may be many interpretations of reality, but maintain that these interpretations are in themselves a part of the scientific knowledge they are pursuing.[343] Recognizing the lack of objectivity sometimes associated with interpretivist research methods, we adopt a positivist [quantitative] approach to the development of our key research instrument.[344] We believe that all methods are valuable if used properly, that research can include elements of both the positivist and interpretivist approaches, if managed carefully.[345]

Pragmatic approaches focus mainly on prescriptive knowledge and emphasize problem solving. Pragmatists believe that positivistic value-free knowledge and normative value knowledge are to be interdependent. Workability or appropriateness for the problem at hand is the central pragmatic criterion for judgment. Test for workability is primary test for reliability of prescriptive knowledge. Epistemic evaluation is often appropriately prescriptive in character because believers are capable of exercising some kind of control – call it doxastic control – over the way

341 Ibid., p. 10.
342 Ibid., p. 6.
343 Davison (1998), supra note 169, p. 3-2.
344 Ibid., p. 3-4.
345 Ibid., p. 3-3.

in which they regulate their beliefs. Evaluation with respect to epistemic standards – and, in particular, with respect to standards of epistemic rationality or justification – is often naturally interpreted as instructing or directing its target to reason in certain ways and not others.[346] The mechanism of doxastic control is just the mechanism via which a believer's conception of ideal belief regulation is coupled to the ways in which she actually regulates her beliefs.[347] As to belief, Nolfi's argument is in relation to doxastic control.[348] An account of doxastic control will have to spell out the way in which a believer's judgments about how she ought to believe are *coupled* to the way in which she actually believes.

If the fact that a believer exercises doxastic control is to explain why a believer is appropriately subject to prescriptive epistemic evaluation, it follows that exercising doxastic control must involve being such that the way in which one actually forms, revises, or sustains one's beliefs is somehow the product of or regulated by one's own conception of ideal belief formation, maintenance, and revision.[349] In Nolfi's reading,[350] doxastic control is that which ensures that a believer is capable of responding to, following, or taking up and putting into practice instructions, directions, or advice regarding how she ought to regulate her beliefs. If a believer lacks the capacity to exercise doxastic control, then she is not appropriately subject to evaluation with respect to standards of epistemic rationality or justification that is genuinely prescriptive in character. And the fact that we typically exercise doxastic control explains why we are typically appropriate targets of prescriptive epistemic evaluation.

***

The relevance of the distinction between prescriptive and descriptive obligations, and the related fundamental problem that norms do not have truth values, is not only theoretical and conceptual, but it has important practical implications for normative multi-agent systems. Contending this, Aucher, Boella and van der Torre give an example, assuming that you ask the librarian of your university to get a journal paper available

346 Kate Nolfi, 'Why Is Epistemic Evaluation Prescriptive?', Special Issue on the Nature of Belief, edited by Susanna Siegel, in Inquiry: An Interdisciplinary Journal of Philosophy 57(1) (2014), pp. 97-121.

347 Ibid., p. 21.

348 Ibid., p. 11.

349 Ibid. Nolfi assumes here that a believer's conception of ideal belief regulation is, at least in paradigmatic cases constituted by her normative judgments about how she ought to believe, and can be given voice by her intentions to regulate her beliefs in certain specific ways.

350 Ibid., p. 3.

on the Springer web-site.[351] The library has a list of journals published by Springer containing the journals for which the library has free access (either a journal of this list is on open access or the university subscribed to it). This list is updated every month but the librarian did not check it for some time, and so he does not know if the requested journal is on the list, although he should have known it. He then logs on the journal and tries to download the paper. We consider two kinds of events corresponding to two different uses of obligations. Descriptive use: The Springer web-site informs the librarian that he should not pay to download any paper of this journal. As a result, the librarian now knows that this journal was on the list of journals for which the library has free access. Prescriptive use: The Springer web-site refuses to download the file. However, after the librarian makes a new contract with Springer, the web-site declares that he should not pay to download any paper of this journal since for the contract the journal is now on free of charge for the library.

Alchourrön and Bulygin distinguish between norm and normative proposition. Normative proposition is descriptive, whereas norm is prescriptive. In descriptive sense, the sentence 'it is obligatory to keep [on the] right on the streets' is a description of the fact that a certain normative system contains an obligation to keep [on the] right on the streets. In prescriptive sense, the statement is the obligation of traffic law itself.[352] Alchourrön and Bulygin discussed the possibility of a logic of norms, which they distinguish from the logic of normative propositions.[353] Alchourrön explains the distinction with the following box metaphor.[354] According to him, we may depict the difference between the descriptive meaning (normative propositions) and the prescriptive meaning (norm) of deontic sentences by means of thinking the obligatory sets as well as the permitted sets as different boxes ready to be filled. When the authority ∞ uses a deontic sentence prescriptively to norm an action, his activity belongs to the same *category as putting something into a box.* When ∞, or someone else, uses the deontic sentence descriptively, his activity belongs to the same category

351 Guillaume Aucher, Guido Boella and Leendert van der Torre, 'Prescriptive and Descriptive Obligations in Dynamic Epistemic Deontic Logic', AICOL – AI Approaches to the Complexity of Legal Systems – 2009, Dec 2009, Rotterdam, Netherlands, in LNAI 6237 (2010), pp. 150-161 (p. 151).

352 Ibid., p. 150, referring to C. Alchourrön, 'Philosophical foundations of deontic logic and the logic of defeasible conditionals,' in : J, J. Meyer & R. Wieringa (eds.), Deontic Logic in Computer Science Normative System Specification, (Chichester: John Wiley & Sons, 1993), pp. 43-84; C.F. Alchourrön & E. Bulygin, 'The suppressive conception of norms', in R. Hilpinan (ed.) 'New studies in deontic logic', (Dordrecht: D. Reidel, 1981), pp. 95-124.

353 Ibid., p. 158, referring to Alchourrön (1993), Ibid.; Alchourrön & Bulygin (1981), Ibid.

354 Ibid., p. 58, referring to Alchourrön (1993), Ibid.

as *making a picture of* ∞ *putting something into a box.* A proposition is like a picture of reality, so to assert a proposition is like making a picture of reality. On the other hand, to issue (enact) a norm is like putting something in a box. It is a way of creating something, of building a part of reality (the normative qualification of an action) with the purpose that the addressees have the option to perform the authorized actions while performing the commanded actions.

***

There is some certain degree that the so called 'Expected Utility (EU) theory' might help judicial decision makers in judicial decision making. A judgment or decision making task is characterized either by *uncertainty* of information or outcome, or by a concern for a person's *preferences,* or both. Unlike other tasks, [they may exist] no criterion for determining whether a single choice or judgment is correct, since the response is based in part on personal opinions or preferences. It is possible, however, to impose a mathematical or logical structure on the task that defines the *consistency* of a set of responses. The prescriptions for consistent behavior are generally derived from formal probability theory and from Expected Utility (EU) theory, a prescriptive model of choice founded on axioms proposed by von Neumann & Morgenstern (1947).[355] Analogous difficulties arise with the Neumann-Morgenstern definition.[356] It can be shown that if an individual's choices between risky prospects satisfy certain postulates, then there exist utility numbers corresponding to the alternatives in such a way that his decisions can be interpreted as maximizing expected utility. Rawls holds that the individual person chooses as if he were guided by the mathematical expectation of these utility numbers; and these assignments of utility are unique up to a positive linear transformation.[357] It is not maintained that the individual himself uses an assignment of utilities in making his decisions. These numbers do not guide his choices, nor do they provide a first-person procedure of deliberation. Rather, given that a person's preferences among prospect fulfill certain conditions, the observing mathematician can, theoretically at least, compute numbers that describe these preferences as maximizing expected utility in the sense defined.

Broome (1991) interprets utilities as measuring comparison of objective betterness and worseness, rather than personal preferences. There is nothing in the formalism of expected utility theory that requires

355 Pitz & Sachs (1984), supra note 239, p. 140.

356 Rawls (1971), supra note 327, p. 322. For an account of this, see Baumol, 'Theory and Operations Analysis', pp. 512-528; Luce and Raiffa, 'Games and Decisions', pp. 12-38.

357 Ibid., p. 522.

us to use subjective rather than objective values.[358] Those who interpret utilities in terms of personal preference face a special challenge: the so-called *problem of interpersonal utility comparisons*.[359] Expected utility is well suited as a prescriptive model for decision making under risk. First, its strong normative appeal has made it popular among decision analysts. Second, the required analysis is straightforward, assuming all required information on alternative actions, states, probabilities, and outcomes are available. Third, multiattribute utility models exist [Keeny], so a more accurate description of problem attributes is possible. Fourth, many applications have already been successfully carried out, so the theory has been field tested.[360] Schoemaker (1982), in a review of EU theory, concludes that the theory has been and continues to be productive. In spite of its limitations from both the prescriptive and descriptive perspectives, much of the research would not have resulted without the existence of EU theory in the first place.[361] As such, the model has yielded deeper insights and more refined questions, both descriptively and normatively. The interaction of prescriptive and descriptive theory through multiattribute formulations of decision problems promises to increase further its prescriptive value (e.g., Kunreuther & Schoemaker 1981), as well as its descriptive power.

A primary problem with expected utility as a prescriptive decision analysis technique is *assessment of the utility function*. Assessed functions can often vary systematically with the response method.[362] Another assessment problem is the discrepancies between preferences when elicited with paired comparison and direct rating methods. This discrepancy is called the *preference reversal phenomenon*.[363] Another issue in prescriptive decision analysis is determining how far to aid a decision maker in restructuring the problem and the relevant preferences. If a person's subjective probability of an injury when not wearing seat belts

358 Rachael Briggs, 'Normative Theories of Rational Choice: Expected Utility', in Stanford Encyclopedia of Philosophy, first published Friday, August 8, 2014, § 1.2.

359 Ibid.

360 Keller (1989), supra note 184, p. 263. Multiattribute utility models, referring to Ralph L. Keeny and Howard Raiffa, 'Decisions with Multiple Objectives: Preferences and Value Tradeoffs', (New York: John Wiley, 1976).

361 Pitz & Sachs (1984), supra note 355, pp. 143-144, referring to P.J.H. Schoemaker, 'The expected utility model: Its variants, purposes, evidence and limitations', in J. Econ. Lit. 20 (1982), pp. 29-63.

362 Keller (1989), supra note 360, p. 263.

363 Ibid., referring to Sarah Lichtenstein & Paul Slovic, 'Reversals of preference between bids and choices in gambling decisions', in J. Exp. Psych., 89 (1) (1971), pp. 46-55; David M. Grether & Charles P. Plott, 'Economic theory of choice and the preference reversal phenomenon', in Amer, Econ. Rev. 69 (4) (1979), pp. 623-638.

is too low, seat belts might not be worn when they 'should' be, based on the objective probability of injury. In this case, an analyst may wish to point out objective probability information. Similarly, a person may violate principles required by expected utility. An analyst is confronted with deciding how far to push a person to conform with expected utility before allowing the person to violate these principles and use a generalized utility model for guiding choices.[364]

***

The current state of theory in judgment and decision making represents a blend of formal prescriptive approaches and models based on hypothetical cognitive mechanism. The influence of prescriptive decision theory has been strong, although it may in the past have served to keep the study of decision making separate from other topics in psychology. Basic concepts of decision theory have been used in other areas to account for behavior ranging from signal detection (Green & Swets 1966) to word recognition (Atkinson & Juola 1973). Prescriptive models apparently have been more successful in describing these simpler, automatic processes than in describing judgments that require thoughtful deliberation.[365] As in the case of, say, word recognition, a prescriptive model may find its most suitable application in describing automatic, non-deliberate processes.[366]

Prescriptive decision theory provides a set of rules for combining beliefs (probabilities) and preferences (utilities) in order to select an option. The theoretical distinction between beliefs and preferences has been one of the most significant of decision theory's contributions to the study of behavior. In evaluating formal decision theory as a foundation for descriptive models, it is helpful to keep this distinction in mind. For example, it is possible in principle to validate a statement of belief but not a preference or value judgment. Because a prediction of future events can be verified, the probability theory component of formal decision theory has rather more prescriptive force than assumption about the structure of a person's value system.[367] There is no criterion other than personal judgment that can determine the validity of the prescriptive model (Einhorn & Hogarth 1981).[368] The final test of an understanding of judgment and

---

364 Ibid.

365 Pitz & Sachs (1984), supra note 361, p. 141, referring to D.M. Green & J.A. Swets, 'Signal Detection Theory and Psychophysics', (New York: Wiley, 1966); R.C. Atkinson & J.F. Juola, 'Factors influencing speed and accuracy of word recognition', in Attention and Performance, S. Kornblum (ed.), Vol. 4 (New York: Academic, 1973).

366 Ibid., p. 143.

367 Ibid., p. 142.

368 Ibid., referring to H.J. Einhorn & R.M. Hogarth, 'Behavioral decision

decision processes, according to Pitz and Sachs, is to develop procedures for helping people make important decisions.[369] The existence of biases and errors in unaided judgments is part of the motivation for aiding the judgment process; the assumption is that aided judgments are less subject to error. The aid is based on a prescriptive formulation that decomposes the problem into its separate elements and presumably helps the decision maker to overcome the limitations of unaided judgments. Thus the development of decision aids requires an understanding of the processes involved in performing the task, together with a suitable prescriptive theory that can serve as a normative formulation for the problem.

I.2.4.2. ETHICS AND ITS PRESCRIPTIVITY

I.2.4.2.1. MORAL, THE GOOD AND RIGHTNESS

In fact, no idea in Western civilization has been more consistently linked to ethics and morality than the idea of justice. From the *Republic*, written by the ancient Greek philosopher Plato, to *A Theory of Justice*, written by the late Harvard philosopher John Rawls, every major work on ethics has held that justice is part of the central core of morality.[370] In moral philosophy in the *Republic,* Plato described the Idea of the Good as being to the intelligible realm. To achieve the knowledge of the Idea of the Good, human beings need extra-ordinarily sustained intellectual and moral effort, and the intellect constitutes the highest part of the soul above the merely sensible and physical.[371] Plato says that the good is known through reason. Training in sciences and metaphysics is required for a full understanding of our good.[372] In Plato's early dialogues, virtue is 'nothing but a kind of knowledge' and 'vice is nothing but a lack of knowledge'. Plato argues that justice is desireable both in itself and for the sake of its result (Plato's Book II, at 357d-358a).[373] Plato's central insight[374] is that moral thinking must be integrated with our emotion and appetites. In Book II of the *Republic,* we are told that the best type of good is one that is desirable both in itself and

---

theory: Processes of judgment and Choice', in Ann. Rev. Psychol, 32 (1981), pp. 53-88.

369 Ibid., p. 155.

370 Manuel Velasquez, Claire Andre, Thomas S.J. Shanks and Michael J. Meyer, 'Justice and Fairness', in Issues in Ethics V# N2 (Spring 1990), p. 1.

371 Richard Tarnas, The Passion of the Western Mind, Understanding the Ideas That Have Shaped Our World View, (New York: Ballantine Books, 1993), pp. 41-43.

372 Kraut (2014), supra note 99, p. 1.

373 Ibid., p. 7, 9 . See Plato's Book II, pp. 357d-358a.

374 Ibid., p. 7.

for the sake of its result, and justice is to be placed in this category and is to be sought for its own sake. Therefore, the highest kind of good must be one that is not desirable for the sake of anything else.

Aristotle first studied ethical virtue in general, then moved to particular ethical virtues (temperance, justice, courage, and so on), and finally arrived at consideration of intellectual virtues (practical wisdom, theoretical wisdom, etc). He made a distinction between two kinds of virtue (Aristotle, 1103a1-10); virtues of mind or intellect which pertain to the part of the soul that engages in reasoning, and ethical virtues which pertain to the part of the soul that cannot itself reason but is nonetheless capable of following reasons. There are two kinds of intellectual virtues: those that pertain to 'theoretical reasoning' and those that pertain to 'practical thinking' (Aristotle, 1139a3-8).[375] Proper appreciation of the way in which goods such as friendship, pleasure, virtue, honor and wealth fit together as a whole is needed for a good life. Practice and learning general rules are the ways of acquiring practical wisdom or the way of applying general understanding to particular cases.[376] Aristotle's writings in the *Nicomachean Ethics* and the *Eudemian Ethics* begins with happiness (*eudaimonia*) as topic of discussion, and turns to virtue (*arête*) and 'the character traits that human beings need in order to live at its best'. His search for the good is a search for the highest good, presumably having three characteristics: 'it is desireable for itself', 'it is not desireable for the sake of some other good', and 'all other goods are desireable for its sake'. *Eudaimon* ('happiness' or 'living well') is the highest goal, and all are subordinate goals (health, wealth and other resources). Men seek such subordinate goals because 'they promote well-being,' 'not because they are what well-being consists in'. Aristotle holds the *ergon* ('function' 'task' 'work') of human being consists 'in activity of the rational part of the soul in accordance with virtue'(Aristotle, 1097b22-1098a20). Our capacity to guide ourselves by using reason gives us the potential to live a better life. 'Using reason well over the course of a full life' is what happiness consists in. The highest good is virtuous activity.[377] A happy life, according to Aristotle, must include pleasure, and there are other pleasures besides those of the senses. In Book X he says that pleasure is 'a good but not the good', but in Book VII he strongly suggests that 'the pleasure of contemplation is the good'. Aristotle's conclusion[378] was that 'intellectual contemplation and, to a lesser extent, moral virtue are the most important human activities'.

375 Ibid., p. 8. See Plato.

376 Ibid., p. 1.

377 Ibid., p. 2, 3, 4, 5.

378 Siegel (2009), supra note 293, p. 18; Kraut (2014), Ibid., p. 23.

The stoics and Aristotle had a similar position, as to what virtues are, that 'the virtues are means to natural goods'. But the goals of their ethical theories are different. Tranquility of life is the main goal of the stoics' ethical theory; and the main goal is to be achieved by proving that 'people have complete control over their capability to live a good life'. The stoics claim that 'virtue is the only good'. The completely virtuous wise man lives a supremely good life in whatever situations.[379] Virtues, for Aristotle as for Aquinas, are 'habits that allow our reason to harness or control our passions' in order our natural ends of human life can be achieved.[380] The cardinal virtues clarifies that: 'temperance involves reason's ability to control excessive appetites'; 'fortitude involves reason's ability to act despite emotions such as fear or disappointment'; 'justice involves reason's ability to control our impulse toward selfishness in our relations with others'; and 'prudence involves being governed by reason generally, rather than acting immediately on passion'. Virtues are means to natural goods and are also good in themselves. Aquinas used 'reason and observation of human nature' as the basis of his fundamental ethical idea that virtues are habits that allow us to fully actualize our capabilities and therefore allow human nature to flourish.

Talking of the goodness/reasonableness or badness/ unreasonableness of an action or reason from the agent's internal perspective is ambiguous. It may suggest two things, which Graham calls the 'judgmentalist' and 'holist' appraoches to the matter.[381] [The judgmentalist approach takes as its premise that an action to be reasonable (internally) must be judged reasonable by the agent. It concentrates on the agent's calculation]. The holist approach, in contrast, factors the agent's judgment as just one among many factors in discovering whether an action is reasonable from the agent's point of view. It focuses instead on the richness, complexity, and often unconscious elements in the agent's perspective. It acknowledges that people sometimes know themselves (their own reasons) too insufficiently to identify their better reasons. All internal factors must receive their due place if we are to call an action unreasonable from the agent's point of view.

Internal rationality is agent-centered. It concerns the agent's own attitude. Aristotle imagines a standard of internal rationality imposed by the agent in calculation and deliberation. But agent's points of view are multi-dimensional, complex, and sometimes ambiguous. Sometimes, especially in cases of self-doubt or failures of self-knowledge, the so called 'better' judgment is incompatible with what matters most to a person; it

---

379 Siegel (2009), Ibid., pp. 19-20.

380 Ibid., pp. 22-23.

381 Graham (1993,1998), supra note 339, pp. 134-135.

raises from less than the internally best reasons. On this broader conception of internal rationality – which Graham calls *fidelity to the agent's overall internal perspective* – none of us make all and only those calculations of better which in fact are (subjectively) better and which faithfully reflect our total point of view. If behavior runs against the grain of one's most inclusive or personally important reasons, then, admittedly, it is unreasonable (internally) to knowingly act in such a fashion. However, if behavior runs merely against the grain of one's own self-assessment, then this may be reasonable if the assessment fails to reflect subjectively more important considerations.[382] This has to do with contincence which consists in abiding by one's better conscious judgment. If continence is a virtue or admirable feature of rational agency, the corresponding vice may be that of weakness of will or 'incontinence'.[383] A strong-willed agent is someone who acts in terms of their better conscious judgment, that is, in terms of what they judge to be their best reasons. Even if it seems to outsiders as if they are unrestrained and uncontrolled, they are self-possessed and self-controlled. They are concerned with their reasons for action; they listen to the dictates of their deliberation; [and, finally, they hold fast to those dictates]. They do what they decide that they should do.[384] A weak-willed or incontinent agent is someone who acts against his or her better conscious judgment; they knowingly fail to abide by the dictates of deliberation. Graham[385] argues that in certain situations incontinence may actually be more reasonable than continence, internally. If incontinence is a vice it is a defeasible vice, which means that even if it is usually or typically unreasonable, people can be incontinent for subjectively good reason. Aristotle says that whereas the continent person seems to be the same as one who abides by his rational calculation; ...the incontinent person seems to be the same as the one who abandons it (*Nichomachean Ethics*, 1145b10-11). The argument may be reconstructed as follows: "Internally good reasons are reasons consciously judged good by the agent. Incontinent agents knowingly act against reasons which they judge good. Hence, incontinence is subjectively unreasonable". Aristotle operates with what may be called a *consistency* with *conscious judgment* model of subjective reasonableness. His idea is that an action is reasonable, subjectively, just when it is consistent with the agent's judgment of the goodness or reasonableness of his reason.

***

382 Ibid., pp. 133-134.

383 Ibid., p. 131. In talking of continence and incontinence, Graham trusts readers will not be misled by vision of enuresis. He wants to make clear which fish he is trying to fry: 'incontinence' and 'continence' are technical terms of philosopher's art.

384 Ibid.

385 Ibid., pp. 131-132.

Scientific discoveries, beginning with the physics of Galileo and Newton, had an effect on philosophers in trying to explain nature based on the new science. In the seventeenth century, the classical teleological view of nature, based on final causes, began to be abandoned by philosophers 'in favor of the new physics, based solely on prior causes'. Ethical theories were developed by philosophers based on the new science and reason.[386] Ethical theories developed by empiricists are based on 'observations of people's actual moral judgments' and of 'the motivations behind the judgments'. Early empiricists assumed that 'moral sentiments were the same everywhere', and philosophers just had to analyze 'these common moral sentiments'.[387]

In the seventeenth century, Thomas Hobbes developed 'the first important modern empiricist ethical theory'. The theory is on the basis of the idea that 'people seek pleasure and avoid pain'. He explained human behavior based on the physics of his time. Motion of matter outside of our bodies affects our senses, which causes motion of matter inside our bodies, which causes our feelings of appetite or aversion, which causes us to seek or to avoid things around us. Our behavior is based on this chain of physical causes. Spinoza in his ethical philosophy held that good and evil were related to human pleasure and pain. Good and evil are relative concepts, nothing is intrinsically good or bad except relative to particular individual. His mathematical and logical approach to metaphysics, and therefore ethics, concluded that emotion is formed from inadequate understanding.[388] It was Leibniz who first spelled out a utilitarian decision procedure: "In comparing the moral qualities of actions... we are led by our moral sense of virtue to judge thus; that in equal degrees of happiness, expected to proceed from the action, the virtue is in proportion to the number of persons to whom the happiness shall extend (and here the dignity, or moral importance of persons, may compensate numbers); and, in equal numbers, the virtue is the quantity of the happiness, or natural good; or that the virtue is in a compound ratio of the quantity of good, and number of enjoyers.... so that that action is best, which procures the greatest happiness for the greatest numbers; and that worst, which, in like manner, occasions misery" (R, 283-4).[389] Anthony Ashley Cooper, the 3rd Earl of Shaftesbury, is generally thought to have been the one of the earliest 'moral sense' theorists, holding that we possess a kind of 'inner eye' that allows us to make moral discriminations. This seems to have been an innate sense

386 Siegel (2009), supra note 378, p. 23.

387 Ibid., p. 25.

388 Ibid., pp. 25-27.

389 Julia Driver, 'The History of Utilitarianism', in Stanford Encyclopedia of Philosophy, first published Friday, March 27, 2009, p. 5; Joachim Hruschka, 'The Greatest Happiness Principle and Other Early German Anticipations of Utilitarian Theory', in Utilitas, 3 (1991), pp. 165-77.

of right and wrong, or moral beauty and deformity. In Shaftesbury's view, the virtuous person is one who contributes to the good of the whole. He held that in judging someone virtuous or good in a moral sense we need to perceive that person's impact on the systems of which he is a part.[390] David Hume claims that moral judgments are based on feelings of benevolence, wishing to do good, toward others. If classical ethical theories subordinate passions to reason, Hume subordinates reason to passion. Hume says that, when it comes to determining how we should act, reason is, and ought only to be, the slave of the passions, and can never pretend to any other office than to serve and obey them.[391] A motive for action is given by emotions, not by reason. It is our emotions which give us 'a motive for acting by telling us what is good or bad'. Reason can only tell us 'the most effective means of getting what is good and avoiding what is bad'. According to Hume, humans have 'complex motives', including 'feelings of self-love' and 'feelings of benevolence'; and 'moral language is based on the feelings of benevolence'. But he admits that he cannot give a reason why people follow moral emotions rather than self-interest emotions, because he believes that we cannot derive normative conclusions from factual observations, and therefore we cannot derive 'ought statements' from 'is statements'.[392] Hobbes says 'people want the good life for themselves', and Hume says that 'they want it for society as a whole', but both believe 'the good life consists of economic prosperity, pleasure and respectability'. This sort of ethics seemed tenable in a society like the Britain of that time, where people generally had the same idea of the good life and were parochial enough to believe that people in all places and at all times felt very much as they did.[393] Hume was in favor of a naturalistic view of human nature and a reliance on our sympathetic engagement with others.[394] Francis Hutcheson was very much interested in virtue evaluation. He also adopted the moral sense approach[395]. However, he emphasized on action choice and the importance of moral deliberation to action choice. Scarre has noted that 'the picture which emerges from Hutcheson's discussion is that the moral sense causes us to look with favor on actions which benefits others and disfavor those which harm them.

Jeremy Bentham's '*An Introduction to the Principles of Morals and Legislation* (1789)' is a presentation of an ethical theory that actions are

390 Driver (2014), Ibid., p. 3.

391 Siegel (2009), supra note 388, p. 27, referring to Hume, 'Treatise of Human Nature', Book 2, Part 3, Section 3.

392 Ibid., pp. 27-29.

393 Ibid., pp. 29-30.

394 Driver (2014), supra note 390, p. 3.

395 Ibid., pp. 5-6, referring to Geoffrey Scarre, 'Utilitarianmism', (London: Routledge, 1996), pp. 53-54.

right insofar as they produce happiness or prevent sufferings, and is an explanation of a political theory that the purpose of civil or criminal laws is to maximize the amount of happiness which may be enjoyed by society. He has rejected the notion that the law of reason is a sufficient principle of morality. The law of reason and the law of nature are only theoretical of speculative principles and cannot be practically applied to every moral situation. Bentham defined ethics as the art of producing the greatest possible amount of happiness for oneself and for others; and ethics is both the art of fulfilling one's duty to oneself and the art of fulfilling one's duty to others.[396] For Bentham,[397] what made some laws bad was their lack of utility, their tendency to lead to unhappiness and misery without accomplishing happiness. If a law or an action does not do any good, then it isn't any good. He also promulgated the principle of utility as the standard of right action on the part of governments and individuals. Actions are approved when they are such as to promote happiness, and disapproved of when they have a tendency to cause unhappiness. He focused on act-evaluation, not on character evaluation, therefore he shifted from the intrinsic to the instrumental approach, where actions are wrong in virtue of their effect or consequence, thus instrumentally wrong.

J. S. Mill has held that intellectual pleasures are of a higher, better sort than the ones that are merely sensual. It is better to be Socrates 'dissatisfied' than a fool 'satisfied'. Intellectual pleasure will score more highly than the sensual ones along several parameters, and this could give us reason to prefer those pleasure, but it is a quantitative not a qualitative reason, on Bentham's view. Mill continued to argue that people desire happiness, and that the general happiness is 'a good to the aggregate of all persons'. Like Bentham, Mill sought to use utilitarianism to inform law and social policy. Natural features of human psychology such as conscience and a sense of justice underwrite motivation. The sense of justice, for example, results from very natural impulses, and part of this sense involves a desire to punish those who have harmed others, and this desire in turn ...is a spontaneous outgrowth from two sentiments, both in the highest degree natural ...; the impulse of self defense and the feeling of sympathy... (Chapter 5, *Utilitarianism*). The justification must be separate issue. The feeling is there naturally, but it is our 'enlarged' sense, our capacity to include the welfare of others into our consideration, and make intelligent decisions, that gives it the right normative force.[398] Moral considerability, according to Utilitarians, is a matter of having one's interests factored into calculus to determine which action minimizes the bad and maximizes the

396 Ibid., referring to Jeremy Bentham, 'An Introduction to the Principles of Morals and Legislation', (1789), (Amherst : Prometheus Books, 1988), p. 1 & 310.

397 Ibid., pp. 6-9.

398 Ibid., pp. 10-12.

good.[399] Henry Sidgwick thought that good could be analyzed as what ought to be desired.[400] He regarded the good as consisting in some consciousness, and he was concerned with developing an account of the different methods of Ethics he had found implicit in common moral reasoning.[401] These methods are intuition based morality and utilitarianism. A simple reliance on intuition, for example, cannot resolve fundamental conflicts between values or rules, such as Truth and Justice that may conflict. The rules which seem to be a fundamental part of common sense morality are often vague and underdescribed, and applying them will actually require appeal to something theoretically more basic, that is utilitarianism. Absolute interpretations of rules seem highly counter-intuitive, and yet we need some justification for any exceptions, provided by utilitarianism. His view is that utilitarianism directs us to make the number enjoying it as great as possible.

***

The highest degree of moral status ['Full Moral Status'] is understood to involve: (i) a very stringent moral presumption against interferring with the being in various ways – destroying the being, experimenting upon it, directly causing its suffering, etc.; (ii) a strong, but not necessarily stringent, reason to aid; and (iii) a strong reason to treat fairly.[402] A being has the highest degree of moral status if and only if the being has very sophisticated cognitive capacities, which might be intellectual or emotional. However, some could lower the standards by holding that if the relevant cognitive capacities were rudimentary enough, even severely cognitively impaired human beings would qualify. Such an account might appeal to the capacity to experience pleasure or pain (sentience), to have interests or basic emotions, or the capacity for consciousness.[403] Some views attempt to ground strong moral reasons not to interfere, and perhaps also to aid and treat fairly, by appeal to not only sophisticated cognitive capacities but also to special relationships (these are therefore disjunctive accounts). On such accounts, specific agents must not interfere with an individual or must respect that individual's right in virtue of being in a relationship with that individual. On one popular version, the relevant relationship is being a fellow member of a community, where the community is composed of all

---

399 Agnieszka Jaworska and Julie Tennenbaum, 'The Ground of Moral Status', in Stanford Encyclopedia of Philosohy, first published Thursday, March 14, 2013, the beginning part.

400 Phillip Stratton-Lake, 'Intuitionism in Ethics', in Stanford Encyclopedia of Philosophy, first published Monday, December 15, 2014, § 2.3.

401 Driver (2014), supra note 394, pp. 13-15.

402 Jaworska & Tennenbaum (2013), supra note 399, § 2.

403 Ibid., § 4.1, 4.3.

those of the same biological species.[404] There are also authors focusing on non-species relationships not as a sufficient ground for moral status but as an enhancer of moral status. Suppose, for example, that having a well-being, sentience, or consciousness is sufficient for some moral status (e.g., weak rights not to be harmed and to be aided); the status is full (e.g., the rights are at full strength) when, for example, the individual is in a specific relationship with a moral agent, where the relationship is that of co-belonging to a community.[405] Some philosophers have attempted to ground the moral status of an entity on features that do not connect with interests in any way. One such feature is not being designed by anyone to fulfill any purpose, which some philosophers hold as a ground for being treated as an end and not a mere means and thus having at least some degree of moral status.[406]

Historically, the most famous sophisticated intellectual capacities account was given by Immanuel Kant, according to whom, moral reasons are categorical. Categorical reasons are ones that apply to us independently of what we care about.[407] Kant views that autonomy or the capacity to set ends via practical reasoning, must be respected and ground the dignity of all rational beings. Such autonomy or capacity is unconditionally valuable and the ultimate condition of value of everything else.[408] Kant upon completing his Grounding for the Metaphysics of Morals, recognized that, now it is an essential principle of all use of our reason to push its knowledge to a consciousness of its necessity (for without necessity there would be no rational knowledge). But there is an equally essential restriction of the same reason that it cannot have insight into the necessity either of what is or what does happen or of what should happen, unless there is presupposed a condition under which it is or does happen or should happen. In this way, however, the satisfaction of reason is only further and further postponed by the continual inquiry after the condition. Reason, therefore, restlessly seeks the unconditionally necessary and sees itself compelled to assume this without having any means of making such necessity concievable; reason is happy enough if only it can find a concept

404 Ibid., § 4.5, referring to R. Nozick, 'Do Animals Have Rights?' in his Socratic Puzzles (Cambridge, MA: Harvard University Press, 1997), pp. 303-310; (possible) T.M. Scanlon, 'What We Owe to Each Other', (Cambridge. MA: Harvard University Press, 1998), p. 185.

405 Ibid., § 4.5.

406 Ibid., § 4.6, referring to A. Brennan, 'The Moral Standing of Natural Objects', in Environmental Ethics, 6 (1984), pp. 35-56 (pp. 55-56); E. Katz, 'Nature as Subjects: Human Obligation and Natural Community', (Lanham, MD: Rowman & Littlefield,1997), pp. 129-131.

407 Stratton-Lake (2014), supra note 400, § 2.3.

408 Jaworska & Tennenbaum (2013), supra note 406, § 4.1 and 5.

which is compatible with the assumption. And so even though we do not indeed grasp the practical unconditioned necessity of the moral imperative, we do nevertheless grasp its inconcievability. This is all that can be fairly asked of a philosophy which strives in its principles to reach the very limit of human reason.[409] The rationalists develop their ethical theory based on reason, and they do not derive normative statements as to value from fact. Kant, like Hume, holds that the 'ought' and the 'is' are totally separate, there is no link between them. So, they say we cannot derive values from facts, therefore Kant's ethical theory is based entirely on reason. According to Kant, there is a faculty of 'practical reason that tells us what is right and wrong', which is different from the faculty of 'pure reason that tells us what is true and false.'[410] Under practical reason, the moral autonomy or freedom of human beings depends on their ability to behave according to laws that are given to them by the proper exercise of that reason. This contrasted with earlier forms of morality, which depended on religious understanding and interpretation, or nature for their substance.[411] Kant says reason itself (*Vernunt*) has natural ends, the solution to the metaphysical problems, especially the discovery of the foundations of morality (26).[412] Rationalists try to base ethics on 'direct, rational knowledge that some things are good and others are bad'. Siegel argues that they fail because their principles tend to be showing the absence of thought (vacuous).[413] They do not say enough to tell us what a good life is, and because they cannot answer someone who disagrees and claims to have different direct rational knowledge of different moral principles.

Some intuitionists allow that goodness can be defined in terms of rightness (Sidgwick and Ewing) or rightness in terms of goodness (early Moore). Ewing thinks that to be good is to be the object of a fitting pro-attitude. Scanlon has argued that goodness is to be understood as something's having properties that give us reason to have a pro-attitude towards it.[414] The simplicity of moral properties, such as rightness and goodness, and our ideas of them, was important for early intuitionists such as Price, as he accepts the empiricist doctrine that simple ideas cannot be

---

409 Ari Kohen, 'The Problem of Secular Sacredness: Ronald Dworkin, Michael Perry, and Human Rights Foundationalism', Paper 37, in Journal of Human Rights 5 (2006), pp. 235-256 (pp. 241-242), referring to Immanuel Kant, 'Grounding for the Metaphysics of Morals', trans. James W. Ellington, (Indianapolis: Hackett Publishing Company, 1993), pp. 61-62.

410 Siegel (2009), supra note 393, pp. 33-34.

411 Ibid., p. 24.

412 Ibid., p. 26.

413 Ibid., p. 24.

414 Stratton-Lake (2014), supra note 407, § 2.3, quoting A.C. Ewing, 'The Definition of Good', (London: Routledge, 1947); Sanclon (1998), supra note 404.

invented but must be acquired by immediate intuition, as all simple ideas must 'be ascribed to some power of *immediate* perception in the human mind, i.e., either sensibility or the understanding'. Consequently, the ideas of right and wrong must be immediate perceptions of either sensibility of the understanding. What we see is that Price concedes that certain feelings may attend our apprehension of right and wrong, but these impression are merely the consequence of our perception of right and wrong. They are not what is perceived. The ideas of right and wrong are simple and natural, in Price's view, since he allows that there are simple ideas of natural properties, and that some of these, such as causality and equality, are grasped by the understanding rather than sensibility.[415] G.E Moore has laid most stress on the non-natural nature of moral properties, though his focus was on goodness rather than rightness. He denies a natural property as one that can exist by itself in time and not merely as a property of some natural objects. The idea is then that natural properties, such as the pleasantness or squareness of an object, can exist independently of that object, whereas the goodness of a good thing cannot exist independently of that thing.[416] Moore introduced the term "*naturalistic fallacy*" in his book *Principia Ethica*, written in 1903. His project in the book is to analyze the concept of good. The result of his analysis is that good is simple, indefinable and unanalyzable. Defining the concept of 'good' is as impossible as defining "yellow". Yellow is a simple concept. It is simple in that it cannot be defined in terms of any other concept (for instance green). Yellow is yellow, that is as far as one can get when trying to define it. Just so with good. Good cannot be defined or analyzed. To do so, to define good as anything other than itself is, therefore, to commit the "naturalistic fallacy". Moore argues that good is a basic ethical concept from which all other ethical concepts must be dervied. He distinguishes good from what has good. Good is the predicate good (a simple concept), but what has good is that which posseses the predicate good. Thus while one cannot define what good is, one can say which particular things are good.[417] Moore agreed to promote the good, but believed that the good included far more than what could be reduced to pleasure. One of Moore's important contribution in the theory of utilitarianism was to put forward an 'organic unity' or 'organic whole' view of value. 'Organic' is used to denote the fact that a whole has an intrinsic value different in the amount from the sum of the values of its parts... (PE,

415 Ibid., § 2.1, quoting Richard Price (1758), 'A Review of the Principle Questions in Morals', in The British Moralists 1650-1800, II, D.D. Raphael (ed.) (Oxford: Clarendon Press, 1968), pp. 131-198 (pp. 141, 144-145).

416 Ibid., quoting G.E. Moore, 'Principia Ethica', in T. Baldwin (ed), (Cambridge: Cambridge University Press, 1903/1993a), p. 93.

417 Julia Tanner, 'The Naturalistic Fallacy,' University of Durham', in Richmond Journal of Philosophy 13 (Autumn 2006), referring to G.E. Moore (1993a), Ibid., p. 55, 58, 60 [back].

36). For example, an arm may have no value at all separated from the body, but have a great deal of value attached to the body, and even increase the value of the body. In the section of *Principa Ethica* on the Ideal, the principle of organic unity comes into play in noting that when persons experience pleasure through perception of something beautiful (which involves a positive emotion in the face of a recognition of an appropriate object, an emotive and cognitive set of elements), the experience of the beauty is better when the object of the experience, the beautiful object, actually exists. The idea was that experiencing beauty has a small positive value, existence of beauty has a small positive value, but combining them has a great deal of value (PE, 189 ff.). A true belief in the reality of an object greatly increases the value of many valuable wholes (199).[418]

Intuitively the intuitionists seem right. Empirical investigation can tell us many things about the world, but it does not seem that it can tell whether certain acts are right or wrong, good or bad. This is not to say that our moral views are not revisable in the light of empirical findings. Moore's open question argument can be regarded as giving form to this intuition.[419] If the moral property of being good, for instance, could be defined in wholly psychological, biological, or sociological terms, then moral truths would turn out to be either psychological, biological or sociological truths, which could then be discovered by empirical research by the appropriate science. But, he argues, all such definitions must fail, for it is always an open question whether the thing that has the relevant empirical property is good.

Armed with an account of the main conviction of common-sense morality, William D. Ross attacked ideal utilitarianism and Kantianism.[420] His basic complaint about his rivals is that each, in a different way, 'over-simplifies the moral life' (FE 189). Both Kant and ideal utilitarianism fail to capture some salient element of the 'main moral convictions of the plain man' (RG 2021n1). Ross contends that Kant oversimplifies the moral life in a number of distinct ways. First, Kant is wrong to think that 'the rightness or wrongness of an individual act can be inferred with certainty from its falling or not falling under a rule capable of being universalized' (FE 189; KT 25). Second, Kant is wrong to think that there is only one motive that has value, and that the moral life consists in a contest between one element which alone has worth [*i.e.*, the good will] and a multitude of others which have none; the truth is rather that it is a struggle between a multiplicity of desires having various degrees of worth (FE 206; KT 3, 18,93). Third, Kant is wrong to think that moral rules have 'absolute authority admitting of no

418 Driver (2014), supra note 401, pp. 15-16.

419 Stratton-Lake (2014), supra note 416, § 2.1.

420 Anthony Skelton, 'William David Ross', in Stanford Encyclopedia of Philosophy, first published Tuesday, August 12, 2010, substantive revision Tuesday, June 19, 2012, § 4.2 – The Good.

exception' (FE 313, 134, 173; KT 24, 95).

John Dewey's ethical philosophy is that 'end' should not limit 'growth'. The Greeks replaced traditional morality with rational morality, in which their notion of the good life could limit progress. Criticizing the Greeks, Dewey says "reason as a substitute for custom was under the obligation of supplying objects and laws as fixed as those of, custom had been".[421] He posits "Moral goods and ends exist only when something has to be done",[422] so that ethics should be redefined as practical work to solve problems : experimental logic when carried into morals makes every quality that is judged to be good as it contributes to amelioration of existing ills.... When physics, chemistry, biology, medicine, contribute to the detection of concrete human woes and to the development of plans for remedying them, they become moral; they become parts of the apparatus of moral inquiry of science. ... Natural science...becomes in itself humanistic in quality. It is something to be pursued not in a technical and specialized way for what it is called truth for its own sake, but with the sense of its social bearing. It is technical only in the sense that it provides the technique of social and moral engineering.[423] Dewey's conclusion is that reason, always an honorific term in ethics, becomes actualized in the methods by which .. intelligent plans of improvement are worked out.[424] But, reason can say nothing about the purpose of these improvements, about whether they are directed at a worthwhile end: "the process of growth, improvement and progress, rather than the static outcome and result, becomes the significant thing.. Growth itself is the only moral 'end".[425] 'Fixed ends' would get in the way of endless 'growth', improvement and progress.[426] Dewey threw away any limits to progress.

H.A. Prichard maintains that all systems of ethics are attempts to justify and explain preconceived feelings of obligation and intuitions about how one ought to act, and claims that moral philosophy is simply an attempt to prove and rationalize preexisting intuitions about what constitutes right and wrong.[427] The most commonly endorsed method of moral inquiry among contemporary moral philosophers is the method described by John

421 Siegel (2009), supra note 413, p. 68, quoting John Dewey, 'Reconstruction in Philosophy', (New York : New American Library, Mentor Books, 1950), p. 131.

422 Ibid., quoting Dewey (1950), Ibid., p. 136.

423 Ibid., referring to Dewey (1950), Ibid., pp. 138-139.

424 Ibid., referring to Dewey (1950), Ibid., p. 140.

425 Ibid., p. 69, referring to Dewey (1950), Ibid., p. 141.

426 Ibid.

427 Eric Chaffee, 'Always Do the Right Thing: Ethical Intuitionism and Legal Compliance', March 10, 2008, in Washington University Law Review, Commentaries, Current Issue : Vol. 89:6, referring to H.A. Prichard, 'Does Moral Philosophy Rest on a Mistake?' in 21 Mind 21 (1912), pp. 21-22.

Rawl[428] under the label 'reflective equilibrium', as already mentioned before. According to the method of reflective equilibrium, we begin with a set of moral intuitions about particular cases, filter out those that are the obvious products of distorting influences, and then seek to unify the remaining intuitions under a set of more general principles. We seek principles that both imply and explain our particular judgments. But the match between principles and intuitions will inevitably be very imperfect in the first instance. A candidate principle may imply a great many of our intuitions and yet have some implications that conflict with other intuitions. In that case we may modify or even abandon the principle; but, if the principle has considerable explanatory power with respect to a wide range of intuitions and cannot be modified without significant sacrifice of this power, we may instead decide to reject the recalcitrant or disobedient intuitions. In this way we make reciprocal adjustments between intuitions and principles until our beliefs at various levels of generality are all brought into a state of harmony, or reflective equilibrium.

Huemer's own positive view is moderately complex. In a lengthy chapter on practical reason he considers a well-known argument in support of non-cognitivism which appeals to a broadly Humean conception of motivation. Huemer's solution, as McNaughton understands it, is to reject the Humean account of normative reasons, and to abandon the claim that only desires can motivate, while retaining moral belief internalism – the view that moral beliefs can be inherently motivational.[429] If Hume and the ethicists following him believed that we just as obviously cannot come to conclusions about what ought to be based on premises about what is, because these are two different types of relation or affirmation, Siegel has proven that ethics and logic are compatible, where ethical inference is drawn through syllogism. Reason tells ethics about the good.[430] Siegel distinguishes between 'ought statements' aiming at some arbitrarily chosen end ('Conditional Imperatives') and 'ought statements' that aim at some natural end ('Natural Imperatives'), in which syllogism is applicable. An example of a syllogism in conditional imperatives is: - Your goal is to walk to the library, - The library is three blocks straight ahead; In order to walk to the library, you ought to walk three blocks straight ahead. An example of natural imperatives is: - The function of the lungs is to supply the body with oxygen; - Exercise increases the ability of the lungs to supply the body with

428 Jeff McMahan, 'Moral Intuition', Chapter 5 in The Blackwell Guide to Ethical Theory,' second edition, edited by Hugh LaFollette and Ingmar Persson, (Blackwell Publishing Ltd, 2013).

429 David McNaughton, 'Michael Huemer, Ethical Intuitionism', (Palgrave: Macmillan, 2006), in Notre Dame Philosophical Review, 2016, College of Arts and Letters, Notre Dame, IN 46556.

430 Siegel (2009], supra note 426, pp. 40-45.

oxygen: - For your lungs to supply your body with oxygen well, you ought to exercise.

In Siegel's contention, empiricism fails to develop ethical theories because they cannot move from 'is statement' to 'ought statements'. Rationalists base ethics purely on reason, without observing human nature, as Kant points out that we have a separate faculty of practical reason that sees moral truths, and Moore says that we have a direct intuitive knowledge of the human good that is independent of our observation of human nature.[431] Siegel says that we will see that both empiricism and rationalism fail to develop ethical theories. As a result, there is no widely accepted modern tradition of moral philosophy that replaced the widely accepted classical tradition of natural ethics.[432] According to Siegel, modern philosophers failed to develop ethical theories based on the new science and reason precisely because of their rejection to the teleological view of nature.[433] Ignoring final causes gives no basis for the most obvious evaluative conclusions.[434] The history of moral philosophy since the seventeenth century is the story of a series of failed attempts to get around this problem, as Alasdair MacIntyre has shown. Siegel shows that 'ought statements' can be derived from teleological 'is statements', by pointing out examples in history. The normative conclusion that 'women ought to be allowed to develop their natural capabilities to become fully educated or to manage their own business' can be derived from the factual premise that 'it has been proven that women had these natural capabilities'. The normative conclusion that 'people ought to have freedom of conscience and freedom of thought in order to let them develop their capability' can be derived from the factual premise that 'since classical Greece people began believe that we have the capability of using our conscience and our reason to decide what is right and wrong'. These historical examples show that different factual premises lead to different normative conclusions. He says there is no logical problem that stands in the way of deriving values from the facts about human nature. A teleological 'is statement' can imply an 'ought statement', and statements about human capabilities can imply "ought statements" because they involve implicit teleology.[435] Siegel holds that arguing from non-teleological 'is-statements' to 'ought-statements', or, deriving 'ought statements' from 'is statements' about what has actually happened in the past, is fallacy, like what believers in evolutionary progress and in economic

431 Ibid., p. 32, 33, 34, 38.

432 Ibid., p. 24.

433 Ibid., referring to Alasdair MacIntyre, 'After Virtue' (Notre Dame, Indiana: University of Notre Dame Press, 1981).

434 Ibid., p. 23.

435 Ibid., pp. 46-47.

progress did.[436] We can only derive 'ought statements' from teleological 'is statements' which describe function or purpose, providing 'the standard that let us decide which impulse and which economic institutions are good'.

Siegel suggests a more modest ethical approach for the sake of ethical clarity. The more modest approach to ethical theory is to focus on the idea that we live a good life by developing and using our natural capabilities as fully as possible, setting aside theories about the nature of the entire universe and about the nature of our knowledge, which we do not understand. Since we clearly understand the telos of each human capability, using this approach we can establish some fundamental points very clearly. The theory of natural ethics is, perhaps, clear enough that we will not discover one day that it is good to be sick and bad to be healthy or that it is good to be ignorant and bad to be knowledgeable. Ethics can become an established clear body of knowledge only if we can take a more modest approach that disentangles it from vague theories about the nature of the universe and of human knowledge.[437] In Siegel's words, presumably, this sort of drift could continue. Society as a whole drifts because we do not have any reasoned public discussion of the good life.[438] Moral relativism follow economists who believe in the moral philosophy called 'preference utilitarianism' and who do not give people any guidance that will help them make wise choices. Technologies such as genetic engineering and mood-echancing 'designer drugs' threaten to manipulate people far more dramatically than we have ever been manipulated in the past, changing what it means to be human. It is dangerous to continue our usual policy of moral drift, of letting the economy and technology develop in their own terms rather than harnessing them to some idea of the good life. Siegel concludes that the most likely alternative to moral drift is natural ethics: the idea that we live a good life by developing and using our natural capabilities as fully as possible. Let's look at the sort of future that natural ethics could bring by humanizing the economy, by humanizing technology and by promoting respect for nature.

To close the discussion on moral, the good and rightness, we can quote Harre that justifying an activity may be done by reference to its consequences and/or to its intrinsic value. For instance, our attitude to science might be based on an assessment of the improvement in public health that would come about as a consequence of applying scientific discoveries in everyday life.[439] As to the good and the right, the right is

436 Ibid., p. 53.
437 Ibid., pp. 59-60.
438 Ibid., pp. 70-72.
439 Harré (1985), supra note 240, pp. 184-185.

rational. However, being rational is not only cognitively mechanical, but also moral; but being moral is not only cognitively mechanical, but also intuitional.

I.2.4.2.2. MORAL PRESCRIPTIVITY

All as already mentioned in Chapter I.2.4.2.1 above are on moral and the good and rightness, indicating prescriptivity. Normative approaches consider that intrinsic values (good or bad) knowable and emphasize on intrinsic values to produce prescriptive knowledge. Objective normative approaches refer to the position that the desirability of an outcome can be known based on experience or logic. Objective normativists accept that value knowledge is sometimes essential for statements about what should be done to accomplish specific goals or objectives. Any discipline that deals with public policy must use normative value judgments. Objective theories, then, are supposed to track what objective value is. In this way, we can see how such theories would provide an answer to our normative questions: if there are indeed objective values, and if objective theories capture them, then we would have good reason to take the recommendations of these theories.[440] Richard Mervyn Hare's moral theory starts with prescriptivism, which is the view that moral and other value judgments are typically prescriptive.[441] To call a judgment prescriptive is to say that it is used to prescribe action, that is, to perform some speech act in a large group that includes comanding, advising, encouraging, discouraging, and so on, with respect to some particular action or kind of action.

In ethics, consequentialists hold that the rightness or wrongness of an act is determined by the moral goodness or badness of its consequences. Some consequentialists, such as Railton, interpret this to mean that we ought to do whatever will in fact have the best consequences.[442] Jackson argues that the right act is the one with the greatest expected moral value, not the one that will in fact yield the best consequences.[443] As Jackson

440 Valerie Tiberius and Alicia Hall, 'Normative theory and psychological research: Hedonism, eudaimonism and why it matters', Author Posting, (Taylor & Francis, 2010), in The Journal of Positive Psychology, Volume 5 Issue 3, May 2010, p. 12.

441 Walter Sinnot-Armstrong, R.M. Hare (1919 -,The Language of Moral, (Oxford: Clarendon Press, 1952), p. 326.

442 Briggs (2014), supra note 359, § 4.3. See i.e., Railton (1984).

443 Ibid., referring to F. Jackson, 'Decision-theoretic consequentialism and the nearest and dearest objection', in Ethics, 101 (1991), pp. 461-482.

notes, the expected moral value of an act depends on which probability function we work with. He argues that, while every probability function is associated with an 'ought', the 'ought' that matters most to action is the one associated with the decision-maker's degree's of belief at the time of action. Other authors claim priority for other 'oughts'. Mason favors the probability function that is most reasonable for the agent to adopt in response to her evidence, given her epistemic limitations,[444] while Oddie and Menzies favor the objective chance function as a measure of objective rightness.[445]

The principal purposes that normative ethical theories serve is to articulate and advocate an ethical code, i.e., to provide justifiable and reliable principles to determine what is moral (and immoral) behavior. In the most basic sense, theories are abstract conceptual constructs that attempt to describe and explain certain phenomena. Normative ethical theories then represent systematic attempts to describe and explain moral or ethical phenomena. As theories, all normative ethical theories share certain conceptual and structural characteristics. To be precise, in normative ethical theories it is possible to isolate a tripartite structure that comprises a moral standard, general moral principles and particular moral principles and judgments.[446] Moral standards represent the most fundamental and general principles that underlie normative ethical theories. A moral standard provides the criteria that generate moral principles and moral judgments, i.e., it specifies what characteristics all moral actions must possess.[447] Consider the utilitarian moral standard: *Actions are moral to the degree that their consequences produce the most happiness.* This represents neither a general moral principle nor a specified moral judgment, rather it determines what characteristics these principles and judgment must possess. General moral principles are principles that focus on general action classes, i.e., that claim that all actions in a certain class are either moral or immoral. The principle 'It is immoral to act with the direct intention to kill a human being' is a general moral principle since it asserts that all actions that include such intention are immoral. Particular moral principles and judgments represent the final level in normative ethical theories. These principles and judgments focus on more specific action classes or on specific actions. Moral principles and judgments use

444 Ibid., § 4.3, referring to E. Mason, 'Objectivism and Prospectivism About Rightness', in Journal of Ethics and Social Philosophy, 7 (2013), pp. 1-21.

445 Ibid., referring to Oddies & Menzies (1992).

446 M.H. Dixon, 'Normative Ethical Theories, A Closer Examination', Ohio Northern University, www2.onu.edu/~m~dixon/handouts/ethical theories.html., p. 1, referring to C.E. Harris, 'Applying Moral Theories,' 3rd Edition, (Belmont, CA: Wadsworth, 1997). John Stuart Mill discusses a quite similar tripartite structure in Utilitarianism.

447 Ibid., referring to C.E. Harris (1997), Ibid., pp. 61-62.

the concepts ‘good’ and ‘right’ (and their opposites) to describe certain actions.[448]

The two main concepts of ethics are those of the right and the good; the concept of a morally worthy person is, according to Rawls, derived from them. The structure of an ethical theory is, then, largely determined by how it defines and connects these two basic notions. Now it seems that the simplest way of relating them is taken by teleological theories: the good is defined independently from the right, and then the rights is defined as that which maximizes the good.[449] Teleological theories have a deep intuitive appeal since they seem to embody the idea of rationality. It is natural to think that rationality is maximizing something and that in morals it must be maximizing the good. Teleological doctrines differ, pretty clearly, according to how the conception of the good is specified. If the good is defined as pleasure, we have hedonism; if as happiness, eudaimonism, and so on. The principle of utility in its classical form as defining the good as the satisfaction of desire, or perhaps better, as the satisfaction of rational desire. [For just as] it is rational for one man to maximize the fulfillment of his system of desires[, it is right for a society to maximize the net balance of satisfaction taken over all of its members].[450] According to Rawls, moral personality is characterized by two capacities: one for a conception of the good, the other for a sense of justice.[451] When realized, the first is expressed by a rational plan of life, the second by a regulative desire to act upon certain principles of rights. Thus a moral person is a subject with ends he has chosen, and his fundamental preference is for conditions that enable him to frame a mode of life that expresses his nature as a free and equal rational being as fully as circumstances permit. Now the unity of the person is manifest in the coherence of his plan, this unity being founded on the higher-order desire to follow, in ways consistent with his sense of right and justice, the principles of rational choice. A person shapes his aims gradually only.

Whether knowledge about ethics and ethical principles is due to experience, reason or some combination, all issues which serve to separate normative ethical theories pose it is possible to these theories as either deontological, teleological or relativistic. Deontological normative ethical theories focus on moral obligations and duties (i.e., what is right) rather than on an action’s end or consequences (i.e., what is good). These are duties that one must observe and represent actions that are either moral or immoral in

448 Ibid.

449 Rawls (1971), supra note 356, p. 24. Here Rawls adopts W.K. Frankena’s definition of teleological theories in Ethics (Englewood Cliffs, N.J. : Prentice Hall, Inc. 1963), p. 13.

450 Ibid., p. 24-26.

451 Ibid., p. 561.

themselves.[452] Deontological ethics stresses that reason intuition or moral sense reveals what is right, i.e., what is right is obvious and undeniable. This knowledge presents to us rules that are moral obligations, i.e., that represent actions that are *in themselves* moral or immoral.[453] Teleological normative ethical theories focus on moral value or goodness rather than on moral duties or obligations. These theories argue that an action's consequences (what is good) rather than on moral obligations (what is right), and appeal to human nature and experience to determine what the good is. Teleological theories base the insistence that all individuals receive equal and impartial considerations in our moral actions on the fundamental principle that all individuals are equal and so have an equal right to their own interests and happiness. Since an action's consequences are an empirical matter, teleological theories argue that experience, rather than reason, determines what is good. Reason role in teleological theories is more as a means to manipulate knowledge than as knowledge's sources.[454] Relativistic normative ethical theories include theories that have dramatic differences and that represent radical approaches to ethics. Moral relativism is the philosophical position that there is no absolute or universal good or right and so there is no absolute or universal moral principles. Ethical egoism argues that moral behavior is relative to the individual, i.e., what is moral to one individual might be immoral to other individuals. What is moral then is what the individual believes to be moral. Cultural relativism, in contrast, argues that moral behavior is relative to cultures, i.e., what is moral in one culture might be immoral in other cultures. What is moral then is what each culture believes to be moral.[455] Ethical theories represent the attempt to systematize ethical knowledge in the same manner that scientific theories attempt to systemize empirical knowledge. The more comprehensive ethical theories will include both metaethical and normative components and should provide answers to certain crucial questions. These questions also provide the means to determine whether particular theories are deontological, teleological or relativistic.[456] Ethics or the philosophy of moral prescribes the good and justice, [whereas certainty is much mechanically prescribed by normativity].

452 Dixon, supra note 448, p. 5, referring to Milton D. Hunnesx, 'Chronological and Thematic Charts of Philosophies and Philosophers', (Grand Rapids, MI: Academic Books, 1986), p. 25.

453 Ibid., p. 7 [footnote omitted].

454 Ibid., p. 7, 8, 9 [footnote omitted].

455 Ibid., p. 9.

456 Ibid., p. 10.

I.2.4.3. OTHER DISCIPLINES' PRESCRIPTIONS

***

Ever since the appearance of social sciences as separate domains of inquiry in the late 19th century, an interplay has occurred between movements for greater specialization on the one hand and efforts at interdisciplinary integration on the other hand.[457] Aguste Comte, one of the founders of modern social sciences, envisaged a unified social science. In the middle of 19th century he expressed a concern that specialization in human thought, while permitting a felicitous development of the spirit of detail otherwise impossible ....spontaneously tends ......to snuff out the spirit of togetherness, or at least to undermine it profoundly.[458] Interdisciplinarity as it is generally understood today was originated in mid-1920's in the US. During that time the US Social Science Research Council in one of its programmes mentioned its desire to promote research which brings in more than one discipline.[459] In 1930's, Otto Neurath at the University of Chicago initiated an impressive effort to prepare an *International Encyclopedia of Unified Science.* Despite these efforts, a painful fact of reality was stated by R.S. Lynd in 1939: The failure of the social sciences to think through and to integrate their several responsibilities for the common problem of relating the analysis of parts to the analysis of the whole constitutes one of the major lags crippling their utility as human tools of knowledge.[460] At the academic level, it has been argued at least since the 1940's that a fuller understanding of social phenomena requires the cooperation of specialists in different intellectual disciplines, making use of the light that each can throw on the others' analyses.[461] Multi-disciplinary research projects reports

---

457 Raymond C. Miller, 'Varieties of Interdisciplinary Approaches in the Social Science: A 1981 Overview', in Issues in Intergrative Studies No. 1 (1982), pp. 1-37 (p. 1), referring to Bert Hoselitz, 'Reader's Guide to the Social Sciences', (New York: Free Press, 1959), pp. 15-16.

458 Ibid., p. 3. Quoted in William Kapp, 'Toward a Science of Man in Society: A Positive Approach to the Integration of Social Knowledge', (The Hague, Netherlands: Martinus Nijhoff, 1961), p. 60.

459 Kristine Medne and Tatjana Muravska, 'Interdisciplinary: Dilemas within the Theory, Methodology and Practice,' in Interdisciplinary in Social Sciences: Does It Provide Answers to Current Challenges in Higher Education and Research?, edited by Tatjana Muravska & Zaneta Ozolina (Riga: University of Latvia Press, 2011), p. 68, referring to J.T. Klein, 'A Conceptual Vocabulary of Interdisciplinary Science," in P. Weingart & N. Stehr, Practicing Interdisciplinarity, (Toronto: University of Toronto Press, 2000), pp. 19-25.

460 Miller (1982), supra note 458, p. 3. Quoted in Kapp (1961), supra noted 458, p. 3.

461 David Hulme and John Toye, 'The case for cross-disciplinary social science research on poverty, inequality and well-being,' in Journal of Development

with a chapter from each of the participating disciplinary specialists show little evidence of communication between them.[462]

Since 1945, a number of new multi- and interdisciplinary fields have evolved. Among them are political science, social sociology, criminology, biotechnology, molecular biology, information science, cultural studies and urban studies.[463] The social movements of the sixties spawned several new interdisciplines which are still in existence. Moreover, the prevalent vocationalism of the seventies has shifted attention from the theoretical to the applied fields of study, which are by necessity interdisciplinary in nature.[464] During the 1970's there was a great desire for "progress" and "growth" and interdisciplinary research was mostly perceived as a tool rather than a concept. Industrialized nations started to allocate increased financial resources for interdisciplinary research in areas of economic competitiveness, specifically, engineering and manufacturing, computer science, medicine and biotechnology.[465] In the early 1990's interdisciplinary approach was associated most of all with the strategic research.[466]

Looking back at the evolution of interdisciplinarity from the beginning of the 20th century to the present, one can say that interdisciplinary approach in the last century was fuelled by social sciences, expansion of the problem oriented research, as well as the need for applied knowledge. At the same time, the consistent governmental support for interdisciplinary research and education has formed a widespread view within the scientific community that the concept of interdisciplinarity is mainly promoted by policy-makers, rather than by the interest of academic and scientific community.[467] The present-day complexity, volatility and diversity of the globalized world, present changes and ever-new challenges to higher education and research. In this context, V.B. Mansila concludes, that a deep understanding of contemporary life requires an interdisciplinary approach. There is growing need for the involvement of express of different disciplines to handle the complex issues in contemporary society and carry out interdisciplinary research related to various topical problems while the higher education needs a new approach that can give students

---

Studies, 2006 – Taylors & Francis, p. 25. See Julian Huxley's discussion of the social sciences in UNESCO: its Purpose and its Philosophy, Paris, UNESCO, 1946, 44-7.

462 Miller (1982), supra note 460, p. 6.

463 Medne & Muravska (2011), supra note 459, p. 69.

464 Miller (1982), supra note 462, p. 67.

465 Medne & Muravska (2011), supra note 463, p. 69, referring to J.T. Klein, 'Interdisciplinarity and complexity: an evolving relationship', in E:CO Special Double Issue, Vol. 6 Nos. 1-2:4 (2004).

466 Ibid.

467 Ibid.

generic knowledge, wide outlook, professional skills and competences.[468] Each profession has a vocabulary, specialized knowledge and techniques, and behavior peculiar to the group, which sets it apart from other professions. Otherwise there would not be a profession. The physician has his bag, his 'pathology –diagnosis-treatment' jargon, his illegible prescription handwriting, and a whole battery of chemical, electrical and mechanical devices to achieve his purposes. The social worker has usually a psychoanalytical vocabulary, his 'case conference' and his control of relief money and living arrangements, as tools. It is so with each profession. It would seem that the first step in achieving interprofessional cooperation would be to seek areas of agreement and common vocabularies.[469]

Very recently, economists and social psychologists have begun to work together and in the future psychology may well demand greater attention. And every social science draws on philosophy, in one way or another, in search of answers to its specific ontological, epistemological, methodological and conceptual problems.[470] Some sociologists indeed seem to have greater intellectual affinity with researchers 'outside' their subject area than with others inside it. As an illustration, positivist and critical realist sociologists working (in the same department) on social capital and poverty may find they rarely communicate. The positivists may, however, find their work closely related to econometricians social networks, while the critical realists will find a close affinity to researchers within human geography.[471] Knowledge-based experts have common intellectual interests and aims, and a shared understanding and acceptance of the methods by which their sort of knowledge is successfully created. This is in contrast with the definition by Haas (1992: 1-37), who stresses shared faith in the application of knowledge to policy, thus allowing an epistemic community to encompass members from a variety of disciplines.[472] There are general reasons arising from the splintering of theoretical and applied knowledge, for believing that the adoption of a more cross-disciplinary research strategy would strengthen the coherence and social relevance of the results that researchers generate.[473]

---

468 Ibid., p. 67, referring to V.B. Mansila (2004).

469 Dorothy McCuskey and Winifred Jensen Conaway, 'The Interdisciplinary Approach', in Educational Leadership, Spring Conference, Region III ASCD (The Woodner Hotel, Washington, D.C., April 23, 1995), p. 396, 398.

470 Hulme & Toye (2006), supra note 461, pp. 4-5.

471 Ibid., p. 21.

472 Ibid., p. 22, referring to P. Hass, ' Introduction: epistemic communities and international policy coordination', in International Organization, Vol. 46, No. 1, 1992, Winter (1-37).

473 Ibid., p. 3.

***

Cross-disciplinary research can be seen as having two main variants: interdisciplinary and multidisciplinary approaches. The term 'interdisciplinary' is the older, dating from the 1920's. It was used then mainly in the context of the natural sciences, although the idea also affected the social sciences. Interdisciplinary research often implied a belief that those who practiced it could create new research fields as a result. This promise was more likely to be fulfilled in the natural sciences than in the social sciences, for the different axes of cohesion in the latter. The term was slow to gain currency, and it was only from the 1960's that it began to make much impact.[474] Interdisciplinarity is relatively more challenging to social scientists and is likely to take them out of their intellectual conform zones. It requires that an individual (or more likely a group drawn from two or more disciplines) seek to integrate the concepts and methodologies of different disciplines from the outset of a research project. This is demanding (intellectually and in terms of finance and researcher time), as each discipline has to learn about the logic of other disciplines and to strive to integrate these logics without compromising the standards of rigour of its own discipline.[475]

Cross-disciplinary group, according to Raymond Miller, consists of persons trained in different fields of knowledge (disciplines) with different concepts, methods, and data and terms organized into a common effort on a common problem with continuous inter-communication among the participants from the different disciplines ...interaction may range from simple communication of ideas to the mutual integration of organizing concepts, methodology, procedures, epistemology, terminology, data, and organization of research and education in a fairly large field.[476] Probably the most readily recognized cross-disciplinary approach is the hybrids. These involve the combining of parts of two existing, related disciplines to form interstitial new cross-disciplines which attempt to bridge perceived gaps between disciplines. Well known examples include social

474 Ibid., p. 23-24. Historically, development studies has played a major role within Anglophone social sciences in promoting crossdisciplinary research. A. Abbot, 'Chaos of Disciplines', (Chicago: University of Chicago Press, 2001), p. 33, observes that '[t]he 1960s, by contrast [to earlier decades] proved an interdisciplinary bonanza, as the modernization paradigm swept development studies in anthropology, sociology, economics and political science. Enormous multidisciplinary teams took on major problems ....population, area studies, agriculture, development.'

475 Ibid., p. 27.

476 Miller (1982), supra note 464, p. 8.

psychology, economic anthropology, political sociology, biogeography, culture and personality, economic history, and so on. There is the cross-disciplinary approaches which Miller has labeled grant synthesis. The grand synthesizers are scholars who argue that interdisciplinarity correctly refers to the systematic integration of all disciplinary structures. They seem to envisage a merging-together of all the scientific disciplines that deal with the same material field, i.e., human behavior. Unfortunately, even though these disciplines may superficially share some attributes, the difference between them are formidable. They do not naturally tend to converge even when brought together in close interaction, because their frames of reference, their languages, their respective world views are fundamentally incommensurable. Each term, each proposition is inextricably embedded in the make-sense pattern of the discipline. There is really no feasible way to add up all the disciplinary components and produce a coherent whole.[477]

Ravi Kanbur's definition are as follows: cross-disciplinarity is a generic term referring to any analysis or policy recommendation based substantively on analysis and method of more than one discipline; interdisciplinarity refers to research that attempts a deep integration of two or more disciplinary approaches from the beginning and throughout an active research exercise; and, multidisciplinarity refers to work in which individual discipline-based researchers (or teams) do their best, within their disciplinary confines, to examine an issue and subsequently collaborate to develop together an overall analytical synthesis and conclusions.[478]

***

Interdisciplinarity is integration of knowledge, concepts or techniques of several disciplines that helps to create new knowledge or a deeper understanding.[479] The knowledge, concepts, methods and approaches of several disciplines that are compared, combined and applied in such a manner resulted in deeper understanding of a problem. Interdisciplinarity has dual nature, instrumental and cognitive. Instrumental interdisciplinarity is a process, i.e., a way to solve, analyze or explore complex issues such as socio-economic problems. One can say that in this case the interdisciplinary approach turns disciplines and subjects into instruments

---

477 Ibid., p. 11.

478 Hulme & Toye (2006), supra note .475, pp. 24-25, citing Ravi Kanbur (2002), 'Economics, social science and development', in World Development 30(3) (2002), pp. 477-486 (p. 483).

479 Medne & Muravska (2011), supra note 468, p. 70, referring to Seipel (2005).

to explore a topic, problem or idea.[480] Cognitive interdisciplinarity is the organization of a discipline and creation on new knowledge.[481] A crossing of frontiers of academic disciplines and the creation of new disciplines are seen as the ultimate and at the same time the most controversial form of interdisciplinarity.[482] Harvard University Faculfty staff, for example, defines interdisciplinary understanding as the capacity to integrate knowledge and modes of thinking in two or more disciplines to produce a cognitive advancement – e.g., explaining a phenomenon, solving a problem, creating a product, raising a new question – in ways that would have been unlikely through single disciplinary means.[483] There is no single specific definition for interdisciplinarity; researchers indicate that it is difficult to find a common definition that would embrace the various manifestations of interdisciplinary approach. The most frequent expressed descriptions of interdisciplinarity are the following: the use and combination of different knowledge and skills, the application of a number of methods in problem-solving, a problem-oriented approach and etc. Interdisciplinary approach involves combination and integration of theories and methodologies of various disciplines. Its characteristic feature is the crossing and revision of borders of the disciplines.[484]

***

The multi-disciplinary approach involves the simple act of juxtaposing several disciplines. Each discipline does 'his own thing' in his own universe of discourse. Consequently, communication is poor, and whatever breadth having been achieved remains superficial.[485] The multidisciplinary approach fully recognizes the existence of autonomous disciplines; it draws on the knowledge of several disciplines and each of them provides a

480 Ibid., p. 70, referring to J.T. Klein, 'A Platform for a Shared Discourse in Interdisciplinary Education,' in Journal of Social Science Education, Vol. 5, No. 2 (2006).

481 Ibid., referring to E. Shove & P. Wouters, 'Interactive agenda setting in the social sciences – Interdisciplinarity, in Discussion paper' (2004), available at http://www.lancs.ac.uk.

482 Ibid., referring to M. Davidson, 'Bones of Contention: Using Self and Story in the Quest to Professionalize Higher Education, An Interdisciplinary Approach', in Teaching in Higher Education, 9/3/2004, pp. 299-310.

483 Ibid., p. 71, referring to V.B. Mansilla, 'Asessing Student Work at Disciplinary Crossroads', Harvard Graduate School of Education, in Magazine Change (2005), vol.37, Issue 1.

484 Ibid., p. 70-71.

485 Miller (1982), supra note 477, p. 6.

different perspective on a problem or issue. In multidisciplinary analysis, every discipline makes a contribution to the overall understanding of an issue, but in a primary additive fashion.[486] Multidisciplinary approach is the lowest degree of integration. It is not conceptually different from disciplinary approach. In multidisciplinary approach, one can describe as collaboration between disciplinary approaches, without exceeding the disciplinary borders, their theoretical and methodological frames and without changing them.[487] In the case of multidisciplinary approach, each discipline considers the problem from its perspective (Seipel, 2005).[488] This approach confronts the disciplines, applies their accumulated knowledge and methods, thus contributing to the study of the specific problem.[489]

D.C. Danisor shows that the purpose of law identifies itself with the reason of law (*ratio legis*) which is also called "the spirit of the law", and it is formulated in a preamble or in an express disposition of the text itself [although this procedure is kind of rare].[490] This attracts attention in a justified manner that in order to better interpret a text it is essential to clearly notice this law reason, to admit, for instance, which are the interests that the law tends to protect, which are the abuses which it wants to stop, which is the political or social result that it tends to realize, etc.[491]

***

In addition to multi-disciplinary and cross-disciplinary approaches, there is the third major category of Miller's classification schema, which is the trans-disciplinary approach. Trans-disciplinary approaches are articulated conceptual frameworks which claim to transcend the narrow scope of disciplinary world views and metaphorically encompass the several parts

486 Medne & Muravska (2011), supra note 484, pp. 70-71.

487 Ibid., p. 70, referring to U.M. Holm & M. Liinason, 'Research Report on the European Union, Disciplinary Boundaries between the Social Sciences and Humanities', in Comparative Report on Interdisciplinary, European Commission's project "Changing Knowledge and Disciplinary Boundaries Through Integrative Research Methods in the Social Sciences and Humanities", The University of Goteborg, 2005.

488 Ibid., quoting Siepel (2005), supra note 479.

489 Ibid.

490 Lucian-Sorin Stănescu, 'The Teleological Interpretation and the Discovery of the Constitution's Efficiency Meanings,' in Fiat Iustitia No. 1/2014, p. 230, referring to D.C. Danisor, I. Dogaru & Gh. Danisor, 'Teoria generală a dreptului,' (Bucharest: C.H. Beck, 2006), p. 396.

491 Ibid., p. 231, referring to Danisor, et.al, Ibid.

of the material field which are handled separately by the individual specialized disciplines. These overarching thought models are holistic in intent. They propose to reorganize the knowledge structure in the social sciences (and in some cases, other fields of inquiry as well). Though some supporters of trans-disciplinary approaches suggest that their favorable conceptual framework should actually replace existing disciplinary approaches, others see them as alternatives or as providers of coherence for cross-disciplinary efforts.[492] Trans-disciplinary approaches include general systems, structuralism and Marxism, phenomenology, policy sciences, evolution, sociology, etc.[493] Thus, according to Miller, there are three major approaches to interdisciplinary social sciences – multi, cross and trans-disciplinary. Multi-disciplinary approaches are limited to the juxtaposing of disciplines – usually generated by the need to deal with some social problem. Cross-disciplinary approaches involve an effort of connecting and combining across disciplinary boundaries. Miller suggests seven categories of cross-disciplinary activity: topical focus, professional preparation, life-experience perspective, shared components, cross-cutting organizing principles or concepts, hybrids and grand synthesis. Trans-disciplinary approaches involve overarching non-discipline-bound thought models, such as general systems, structuralism, Marxism and sociobiology.[494]

A conceptual structure followed by structuralists sees the basic social science disciplines nor as sociology, economics and political science, but as communication, transaction, and organization, approached through a base in system analysis.[495] Structuralism, [as] another major transdisciplinary approach, shares some assumptions with general systems. These assumptions include the relatedness of all things, their organization into levels of isomorphic structure with laws of transformation, structures (or systems) manifesting homeostatic self-regulation and holism. But structuralists do not deal primarily with the empirical observables of systems, nor do they believe that the participants in them are necessarily aware of the latent structures which are influencing them. Structuralists look for the underlying formal structures, the deep structures, which they believe reflect the basic cognitive, biologically derived from structure of human thought. They see these structures as binary oppositions, at times with mediators, such as hot-cold, me-other, raw-cooked, life-death, etc.[496]

492 Miller (1982), supra note 485, p. 11.

493 Ibid., p. 12.

494 Ibid., pp. 15-16.

495 Ibid., p. 13, referring to Alfred Kuhn, 'Unified Social Science', (Homewood, Illinois: Dorsey Press, 1975), p.vi.

496 Ibid.

The unconscious activity of the mind consists in imposing forms upon content, and if these forms are fundamentally the same for all minds – ancient or modern, primitive or civilized (as they study of the symbolic function, as expressed in language, so strikingly indicates) – it is necessary and sufficient to grasp the unconscious structure underlying each institution and each custom in order to obtain a principle of interpretation valid for other institutions and other customs.[497] According to Gardner, the structuralist position threatens the behaviorist and functionalist views which currently dominate Anglo-American social sciences, for not only does it rely on innate mental structures and non-historical, universal similarities but it also "finds no need to posit 'needs for' or 'functions of" structure.[498] The most important part and test of the structuralist method in Deetz's view is the effort 'to take logical permutations from a formulated structural unity and find empirical instances in widely varying situations which fulfill these possibilities'.[499] Piaget, on several occasions, has suggested that structural analysis will provide the basis for eventual interdisciplinary integration. Structuralism, especially the Levi Strauss variety, has come under heavy attack from many quarters, including proponents of competing trans-disciplinary approaches such as Marxism. Marxism and structuralism differ in their starting premises, Marxism giving pre-eminence to the material force of production in the formation of human societies, including its symbolic manifestations, whereas structuralists look for the deep structure in the human mind as influencing the eventual form of human customs and institutions.[500]

Sociobiology as a proponent of trans-disciplinarity is the application of the principles of natural selection and evolutionist biology to the study of animal social behavior. The major spokesmen for sociobiology consider it [sociobiology] the 'new synthesis'. The only way forward is to study human nature as part of the natural sciences, in an attempt to integrate the natural sciences with the social sciences and humanities.[501] No paradigm approaches natural selection in its ability to explain a wide range of behavior phenomena among animals and none offers equivalent promise of cutting a clean swath through the morass of data and theory currently surrounding

497 Ibid., p. 14, referring to Levi Strauss as quoted in Jean Piaget, 'Stucturalism', (New York: Harper & Row, 1971), pp. 110-111.

498 Ibid., referring to Howard Gardner, 'The Quest for Mind', (New York: Random House, 1974), p. 221.

499 Ibid., referring to Stanley Deetz, 'Structuralism: A Summary of its Assumptions and Conceptual Bases,' in Review of Social Theory, April 1973, p. 163.

500 Ibid., referring to Gardner (1974), supra note 498, pp. 222-223.

501 Ibid., p. 15, referring Edward O. Wilson, 'On Human Nature', (New York: Bantam Books, 1979), p. 7.

research on human behavior.[502] Though there were analogies to biological evolution, the basic thrust was cultural evolution as an adaptive form of behavior to a changing environment. The environment was primarily changed by increases in knowledge, accumulating energy control, and improvements in the technology of production. Cross-disciplinary efforts were undertaken, and some suggested the increased usage of evolution as a holistic concept for handling the increasing data dealing with the question of how societies change.[503]

Interdisciplinarity, mutlidisciplinarity and/or trans-disciplinarity account the notion that a discipline may see what other disciplines see when viewing common issues. Prescriptions between disciplines may appear through interdisciplinarity, mutlidisciplianrity and/or trans-disciplinarity. The notion(s) of [interdisciplinary, mutlidisciplianry and/or trans-disciplinary] prescriptivity is(are) also existent in law under prescriptive jurisprudence which will be discussed in Chapter II.2, in which legal doctrinal writers and jurists argue that the descriptive aspect of law alone is not sufficient to portray the law completely. Legal prescriptivists hold that law is prescriptive in addition to being descriptive.

I.2.5. BETWEEN DESCRIPTIVITY AND NORMATIVITY

***

Both descriptive and normative theories (and also speculative or statistical, modal ones) need be coherent in order to be valid, and both depend on a number of axioms which must be accepted without proof. But – it has been contended – which descriptive theory is 'true' can be empirically ascertained: it is verified if it corresponds with reality (the facts); falsified if it does not correspond with reality.[504] Normative, ethical or moral theories – it is then contended – cannot be empirically verified or falsified. But this in itself is a trivial truth simply following from what *empirical* means: *capable of being verified or falsified by observation or experiment.* The underlying suggestion is though, that there would be only one true descriptive of factual discipline, whereas all coherent, normative theories would or could be equally 'valid' however contradictory among themselves. [In four steps (below)] it can be demonstrated that this kind of factualization

502 Ibid., referring to David P. Barash, 'Evolution as a Paradigm for Behavior,' in Michael Gregory et.al. eds., Sociobiology and Human Nature, (San Franscisco: Jossey-Bass, 1978), p. 32.

503 Ibid., referring to Claude S. Phillips, Jr., 'The Revival of Cultural Evolution in Social Science Theory,' in The Journal of Developing Areas, Vol. 5, No. 3, April 1971, p. 338.

504 Nandi (1986), supra note 121.

is in complete error, and that every so-called purely descriptive form of theorizing depends as much on norms or normative choices as an adequate normative discipline.[505]

First, based on the axiom that there would indeed be solely one true, factual theory corresponding with reality as a 'unified whole', and that all other coherent, factual are descriptive theories, and all incoherent ones are false. This, then, would be a fact and ....not more than that! (Strictly speaking, only the true theory's correspondence with reality is a fact, whereas in the case of false theories there is no fact, or the 'fact' is a privative one). It is definitely not a fact that an utterance or a complex of utterance ought to be true or ought not to be false: this is a norm – a norm of correspondence to be precise. Thus, as soon as someone assignes a higher value to a theory which has been verified because it has been verified, or which has never been falsified because it has never been falsified, he is involved in a normative act or an act expressive of (the belief in) a norm (if it is not to be a mere question of personal preference). The suggestion, however implicit, that a true theory or truth is superior to a false theory of falsehood requires or presupposes a normative principle of truth. [Hence, those who stress the need of empirical verfification or falsification, and who reject untrue, factual or descriptive theories must also reject any and every normative theory that does not recognize a principle of truth(fulness) even though that normative theory might be coherent].[506]

Secondly, no descriptive discipline could describe the whole of reality in all its details, and certainly covering law models do not do that. (Isolated factual conditions as such do not explain anything). Every descriptive theory must confine attention to those aspects of reality it deems relevant. In itself it is simply a fact that some aspects or details are relevant, while others are not. But as soon as someone assigns a higher value to a theory or description which describes a relevant state of affairs than to an irrelevant theory or description, although both theories or descriptions are true, he is involved in a normative act or an act expressive of (the belief in) a norm (if it is not to be a mere question of personal preference). The inherent suggestion is that a relevant description or relevance is superior to an irrelevant description or irrelevance, and this requires or presupposes a normative principle of relevance. [Hence, those who demand a true theory or description to be relevant, and who reject irrelevant, factual theories or descriptions must also reject any and every normative theory that does not recognize a principle of relevance even though that normative theory might be coherent and recognize a principle of truth].[507]

---

505 Ibid.

506 Ibid.

507 Ibid.

Thirdly, something is only relevant with respect to a certain entity looked upon as a goal, objective or value to be aimed at. To treat an entity (a certain point of a scale, or a certain predicate of a calena, say) as a goal or objectives is a normative act or an act expressive of (the belief in) a norm (if it is not to be a mere question of personal preference again). This requires or presupposes a normative principle which determines what the one or more goals are (or should be) with respect to which something is relevant or not. [Hence, those who demand a true theory or description to be relevant with respect to one or more particular goals, and who reject factual theories or descriptions irrelevant to this goal or these goals must also reject any and every normative theory that does not recognize a principle furnishing at least this particular goal(s), even though that normative theory might be coherent and recognize a principle of truth and one of relevance].[508]

The fourth step is that of two true theories or descriptions which are both relevant with respect to the same goal(s), the simpler theory or description is superior to an unnecessarily complicated theory or description. It may not always be clear which theory or description is simpler in practice but *simpler* is to be understood as *requiring a smaller number of primitive notions and axioms or principles*. Applying this same principle of parsimony to normative theorizing means that a coherent normative theory which recognizes a principle of truth, a principle of relevance and two or more principles furnishing its goals must be rejected too if another coherent normative theory which recognizes a principle of truth and a principle of relevance has only one principle furnishing the same or the same and even more acceptable goals. It does in no way follow from this what that goal should be, or that there is one ultimate goal. It does follow, however, that the original factualist claim that all coherent normative theories would or could be equally 'valid', independently of the existence and adoption of descriptive theories, cannot be sustained.[509]

The conclusion of the four steps above is that descriptive theory or description requires or presupposes normative principles. The distinction between the factual and the normative spheres, between fact and value, becomes blurred more and more when not considering facts and norms as objectives given in themselves, but when considering thought about facts and norms, that is, factual and normative beliefs or disciplines. [Facts and norms may be entirely independent of each other], in our theorizing on facts and norms, the normative principle of factual thought may not differ from those of normative thought at all.[510]

508 Ibid.
509 Ibid.
510 Ibid.

Waldmann claims that in psychological theories of rationality there is an intrinsically constitutive relation between normative and descriptive theories.[511] Normative theories provide idealized descriptive accounts of rational agents. Waldmann exemplifies the claim from the domain of theoretical and from practical rationality. However, he argues that we need to resist the temptation to collapse descriptive theories with any specific normative theory.[512] Theories of theoretical rationality are concerned with how we achieve the goal of acquiring correct beliefs about the world. The close ties between normative and descriptive theories can easily be seen when we consider a scientist conducting an experiment. To explain the observed behavior, for example, randomization of subjects, it seems natural to invoke normative theories of how experiments should be conducted. The reason why normative theories work as descriptive explanation here is that we understand the scientist as a rational, goal-oriented person. Every reasoning is, in contrast, rarely guided by explicit methodological knowledge. Nevertheless, people's beliefs also have a normative force. People view themselves as motivated by reasons, and strive for optimality to achieve their goals. They distinguish between true and false beliefs; knowing they may err, they revise their beliefs and accept correction.[513] A natural place to look for candidate explanation is normative theories of causal inference. In fact, virtually all currently competing theories of causal reasoning can be structured according to the preferred normative account motivating the theory (Waldmann & Hagmayer, in press). Causal reasoning cannot be modeled without some normative theory that tells us what causal judgments are.[514]

Moral reasoning, which belongs to the domain of practical rationality, is another example of the constitutive relation between normative and descriptive theories. When we request moral judgments from subjects we do not want to learn about their preferences, wants or inhibitions; rather, we want them to provide a normative evaluation of whether an act is right or wrong. Again we conceive of subjects as rational agents who offer us responses to normative requests.[515]

As already mentioned before, the difference between normative and descriptive approaches should be sought in the philosophical roots of goal, since its roots are deep in the general empiricist tradition,[516] consequently the discriptive approach to reasoning stresses the pragmatical dimension

511 Waldmann (2011), supra note 185, p. 273, referring to Sphon (2002).

512 Ibid, p. 123.

513 Ibid.

514 Ibid.

515 Ibid.

516 Schwed (2001), supra note 302, p. 1, 2.

of argumentation,[517] therefore, arguments are not to be evaluated based on some given a priory concept of rationality, but things that exhibit and presuppose some given reality of rational practice.[518] Since arguments are viewed from within a theory, skepticists question the epistemic status of knowledge.[519] What seems to be true within a theory regarding everyday reasoning is doubtful from external viewpoint.[520] Skepticists are traditionally more toward the outside of the theory concerned, as a result, they shift the focus from the things believed within the theory to reason to believe.[521]

To value the descriptive approach causes the advantage of empirical study, because the focus is usually on the conceptual study of argumentation, showing important results in constructing the empiricist translation yielding a general definition of the concept of rationality.[522] To value a description or fact means to impose norm or prescription on the description or fact, and this imposition indicates that there is relationship between descriptivity and normativity. [To the present author,] in line with this, many legal doctrinal writers and jurists argue that norm prescribes action.

I.2.6. PRESCRIPTIVITY TO FILL THE GAP BETWEEN NORMATIVITY AND DESCRIPTIVITY.

One might object to a strict delineation between scientific and normative systems. Norms certainly apply to the construction of scientific systems of the world (such as the norm that truth ought to be sought after, that systems of beliefs that do not accurately describe the world ought to be rejected, etc). Normative inquiry might inform science as to the proper goals of scientific pursuit. Similarly, science might inform ethics with regard to predictability consequences of actions, perhaps, or it might supply crucial information for the evaluation of observable states.[523] Whether or not prescriptivity is distinct from normativity, or, prescriptivity includes normativity or vice versa, since both prescriptivity and normativity prescribe action and many writers often refer to the same thing when elaborating prescriptivity and normativity, the position taken by this book is that normativity is originally and purely internal, and prescriptivity comes from the external into the

517 Ibid., p. 2.

518 Ibid., p. 3.

519 Ibid., p. 5.

520 Ibid., pp. 5-6.

521 Ibid., p. 5.

522 Ibid., p. 6.

523 Dale Dorsey, 'A Coherence Theory of Truth in Ethics,' in Philosophical Studies (2006) 127, pp. 493-523 (p. 495).

internal. In this position, the present author follows a thesis of cognitive science researchers or doctrinal writers (Budge, Keller, Brown, Pitz & Sachs, and Waldmann) that prescriptivity fills or bridges the gap between descriptivity and normativity.

Quine's naturalized epistemology throws out any sense of justification of beliefs, focusing on merely the environmental causes of such beliefs. As such, it lacks the normative or prescriptive element found in traditional epistemology. Natularized epistemology does not address what the rules are for justification, or whether any belief is justified. However, both traditional epistemology and naturalized epistemology look at the relationship between input (sense data) and output (beliefs) in a person. Traditional epistemology looks at the relationship in an evidential or justificatory light.[524] The evidential light has to do with descriptivity, and the justificatory light with prescriptivity.

Amundson argues that we reinterpret, but not abandon, the attempt to base descriptive epistemology on substantive cognitive theory. Philosophers who are today involved in showing the implications for realist epistemology of current cognitive psychology should be seen as articulating a paradigm. They are not performing the historically unique task of empirically justifying an epistemology. Such empirically supported epistemologies are common in the history of the cognitive sciences. Perhaps today's cognitivists/realists are articulating the *right* paradigm. Amundson believes that there is a true descriptive epistemology, and true theory of cognition, and that the two are mutually endorsing.[525] Descriptive knowledge comprises observational facts, empirical regularities, theories and hypotheses. Prescriptive knowledge builds on design product knowledge including characteristics of artefacts, e.g., idea, concept, style or behavior and design process knowledge including technological norms and rules, determining how to achieve an included outcome in a particular situation.[526] Kuechler and Vaishnavi say that descriptive theories originate from natural science and social science which serve as an input to design science by 'suggest(ing) novel techniques or approaches to information systems (IS) design problem', and that prescriptive theories are theories which give explicit prescription of 'how to do something'.[527] Lopes has shown that

524 O'Niel (2004), supra note 139.

525 Amundson (1981), supra note 141, Part V.

526 Oliver GaB, Norbert Koppenhagen, Harald Bregel, Alexander Madche and Benjamin Muller, 'Anatomy of Knowledge Bases used in Design Science Research,' in A Literature Review, in ADFA, p. 1,2011), § 2, referring to J Irvan, 'A paradigmatic analysis of information systems as a design science,' in Scandinavian Journal of Information Systems 19(2) (2007), pp. 39-64.

527 Ibid., referring to B. Kuechler & V. Vaishnavi, 'Theory development in design science research: anatomy of a research project,' in European Journal of

judgments can be made more consistent with prescriptive principles if one can identify the process by which the judgments are produced.[528] Relating to this, the coherence of probability assessments, i.e. the consistency of a set of judgments with the axioms of probability theory, is also a matter for concern when using decision aids.

Referring to Budge, Keller[529] has written that *prescriptive decision analysis* bridges the gap between descriptive observations of the way people do make choices and the normative guidelines for how they should make choices: it prescribes techniques for aiding decision making. Prescriptive decision analysis can be called decision engineering, since analysts are designing techniques to aid decision makers in making better decisions. Analysts must meet design specifications (normative goals), based on descriptive constraints of human judgmental abilities. Prescriptive decision analysis should be judged with a more holistic focus than that used in evaluating normative decision analysis. As Budge says, researchers should avoid the tendency to test a theory 'to destruction' by sequentially examining separate properties of the theory. Instead, the same theoretical structure should combine logical and ethical considerations with descriptive facts. The whole theory, rather than isolated axioms, should be the unit of analysis. Thus, the existence of appropriate and easily implemented methods for assessing preferences and a feasible analysis procedure will be just as important as logical coherence when a theory is used for prescriptive purposes. In addition, a prescriptive theory should take into account descriptive research to adjust for biased judgments of preferences, probabilities, or problem structure received from decision makers. Such a theory should also be designed to operate on the set of data available. For example, good choices should be prescribed even if data on alternative actions or states of nature are incomplete.

Brown expands the conception of 'prescriptive' to include developing decision making aids for more realistic decision environments. Normative models often assume the decision maker has complete knowledge of all the alternative actions, states of nature, payoffs and probabilities at a single point in time, at which the decision (or set of contingent, sequential decision plans) will be made. A broader conception of the modeling environment may lead, for example, to a focus on better problem structuring or to

---

Information Systems 17(5) (2008), pp. 489-504.

528 Pitz & Sachs (1984), supra note 355, p. 157. See L.L. Lopes, 'Procedural debiasing,' in Tech. Rep. No. 15, Wis. Hum. Inf. Process. Program, Madison (1982a).

529 Keller (1989), supra note 360, p. 260. See Ian Budge, 'Benthamism as a 'positive' rational choice theory of democracy: Does it work?' In: Lincoln Allison, ed., The Utilitarian Response: Essays on the Contemporary Viability of Utilitarianism as a Political Philosophy (Sage, London, forthcoming), chapter X.

models allowing sequential restructuring of the problem.[530] One reason for the concern with prescriptive models is that they provide guidelines for aiding the decision process. Errors of judgment suggest ways in which performance might be improved, especially if one understands why errors occurred.[531]

I.3. TRANSFORMATIONAL GENERATIVE THEORY, A SORT OF

I.3.1. SIMILARITY

***

Similarity-matching or similarity-mapping between two objects under various theories is outlined in this book in order to see some models of similarity matching. Those theories are on similarity-matching between domains and/or concepts. Concept learning has traditionally been studied in the context of relatively unstructured objects that can be described as collections of features. A number of successful accounts of concept learning can be viewed in terms of probabilistic models defined over different ways to represent structure in feature sets, such as prototypes, exemplars, or logical rules.[532] The probabilistic program approach can be seen as a generalization of approaches to generative representations of concepts.[533] We think it more likely that the notion of similarity is ultimately grounded in the world, and it evolved for the purpose of comparing real-world

530 Ibid., referring to Rex Brown, 'Toward a prescriptive science and technology of decision-making', in Ann. Operat. Res.19 (1989).

531 Pitz & Sachs (1984), supra note 528, p. 140.

532 Andreas Stuhlmuller, Joshua B. Tenenbaum and Noah D. Goodman, 'Learning Structured Generative Concepts', in Proceedings of the Annual Meeting of the Cognitive Science Society, 32(32)-2010, cloudfront.escholarship.org., referring to J.R. Anderson, 'The adaptive character of thought', (Hillsdale, NJ: Lawrence Erlbaum Associates, 1990); M. Oaksford & N. Chater, 'Rational models of cognition', (Oxford: Oxford University Press, 1998); L. Shi, N. Feldman & T.L. Griffiths, 'Performing bayesian inference with exemplar models', Proceedings of the 30th Annual Conference of the Cognitive Science Society (2008), pp. 745-750; N.D. Goodman, J.B. Tenenbaum, J. Feldman & T.L. Griffiths, 'A rational analysis of rule-based concept learning', in Cognitive Science, 32(1) (2008), pp. 108-154.

533 Ibid., referring to Kemp, et.al., (2005), supra note 73; B. Rehder & S. Kim, 'How causal knowledge affects classification: A generative theory of categorization', in Journal of Experimental Psychology: Learning, Memory, and Cognition (2006); J. Feldman,'The structure of perceptual categories,' in Journal of Mathematical Psychology (1997).

objects. If so, then knowledge about what kinds of objects are likely to exist should be deeply bound up with the notion of similarity. More commonly, subjects are shown a pair of objects and asked to rate the similarity of the pair.[534] Definitions of similarity are tied to a particular application or a form of knowledge representation. Similarity is a fundamental and widely used concept. Similarity measures have been proposed, such as information content (Resnik, 1995b), mutual information (Hindle, 1990), distance-based measurement (Lee *et al.*, 1989; Rada *et al.*, 1989), and features contrast model (Tversky,1977).[535] Intuitionally, the similarity between two objects is related to their commonality. The more commonality they share, the more similar they are. Also, the similarity between two objects is related to the differences between them. The more difference they have, the less similar they are. The similarity between two objects is measured by the ratio between the amount of information needed to state the commonality of the objects and the information needed to fully describe what the objects are.[536] Extensive psychological research has examined the way people compare pairs of items to determine their similarity. Mounting evidence suggests that the similarity of two complex items depends on the degree of match between their component objects (common and distinctive *attributes*) and on the degree of match between the *relations* among the component objects.[537]

The concept of similarity also plays a crucial but less direct role in the case of pattern and form recognition. It is frequently assumed that the greater the similarity between a pair of stimuli, the more likely one will be confused with the other in a recognition task.[538] The two stimuli are linked by using a distance-based similarity measure to predict the confusions in recognition experiments.[539] It is now widely suspected, however, that

---

534 Kemp et. al., (2005), Ibid.

535 Dekang Lin, 'An Information-Theoric Definition of Similarity", in a research partly supported by NSERC Research Grant OGP121338, lcml.1998.

536 Ibid.

537 Dedre Gentner and Arthur B. Markman, 'Analogy – Watershed or Waterloo? Structural alignment and the development of connectionist models of analogy,'(1993), in a work sponsored by ONR grant BNS-87-20301, Neural Information Processing Systems Foundation/NIPS, Inc., 1987-2018, p. 856.

538 F. Gregory Ashby and Nancy A. Perrin, 'Toward a Unified Theory of Similarity and Recognition', in Psychological Review 1988, Vol. 95, No. 1, pp. 124-150, p. 124. See, e.g., R.D. Luce, 'Detection and recognition', in R.D. Luce, R.R. Bush & E. Galanter (Eds.), in Handbook of mathematical psychology Vol. 1 (New York: Wiley, 1963), pp. 103-190; R.N. Sephard, 'Attention and the metric structure of the stimulus space', in Journal of Mathematical Psychology, I (1964), pp. 54-87; A. Tversky & I. Gati, 'Similarity, separability, and the triangle inequality,' in Psychological Review, 89 (1982), pp. 123-154.

539 Ibid., referring to I.B. Appelman & M.S. Mayzner, 'Application of geometric models to letter recognition: Distance and density', in Journal of Experimental

standard distance-based similarity measures do not provide an adequate account of perceived similarity.[540] Similarity varies across different context, and to understand the identification-categorization relationship is significantly dependent upon the manner in which similarity varies across different contexts. Although similarity is not invariant, it is presumed to change in constrained and systematic ways.[541] Concerning similarity matching, Shepard proposed that metric space be utilized to model internal representations for almost any stimulus including concept. We rarely encounter the exact same situation twice. There is always some change in the environment. This incremental change is the crucial elements – the more similar the new environment is to something we already know, the more we will respond in a similar way.[542] The similarity parameters, in Shepard's original formulation,[543] were given an explicit interpretation in terms of distance in a psychological space.

Psychology: General, 111(1982), pp. 60-100; D.J. Getty, J.B. Swets & J.A. Swets, 'Use of perceptual dimensions in signal identification', in R.S. Nickerson (Ed.), Attention and performance Vol. 8 (Hillsdale, NJ; Erlbaum, 1980), pp. 361-380; D.J. Getty, J.B. Swets & J.A. Swets, 'On the prediction of confusion matrices from similarity judgments', in Perception & Psychophysics, 26 (1979), pp. 1-19; L.H. Nakatani, 'Confusion-choice model for multidimensional psychophysics', in Journal of Mathematical Psychology, 9 (1972), pp. 104-127; R.M. Nosofsky, 'Choice, similarity, and the context of classification', in Journal of Experimental Psychology: Learning, Memory and Cognition, 10 (1984), pp. 299-309; R.M. Nosofsky, 'Overall similarity and the identification of separable-dimension stimuli: A choice model analysis', in Perception & Psychophysics, 38 (1985b), pp. 415-432; R.M. Nosofsky, 'Attention, similarity, and the identification-organization relationships', in Journal of Experimental Psychology: General, 115 (1986), pp. 39-57; R.N. Shepard, 'Stimulus and response generalization: A stochastic model relating generalization to distance in psychological space', in Psychometrika, 22 (1957), pp. 325-345; R.N. Shepard, 'Stimulus and response generalization: Tests of a model relating generalization to distance in psychological space', in Journal of Experimental Psychology, 55 (1958b), pp. 509-523.

540 Ibid. See, e.g., C.L. Krumhansl, 'Concerning the applicability of geometric models to similarity data: The interrelationship between similarity and spatial density', in Psychological Review, 85 (1978), pp. 445-463; A. Tversky, 'Features of similarity', in Psychological Review, 84 (1977), pp. 327-352.

541 Nosofsky (1986), supra note 539, p. 39. See e.g., Tversky (1977), Ibid.; A. Tversky & I. Gati, 'Studies of similarities', in E. Rosch & B.B. Lloyd (eds.), Cognition and categorization, (Hillsdale, NJ: Erlbaum, 1978).

542 Jose Quesada, 'Human Similarity theories for the semantic web', Similarity theories, (1987), in CEUR Workshop Vol-419, paper-7,CEUR Workshop Org., Proceedings of the 1st International Conference 2008, quoting R.N. Shepard 'Toward a universal law of generalization for psychological science,' Science 237 (1987), pp. 1317-1323 (pp. 3-4).

543 Nosofsky (1986), supra note 541, p. 40, referring to Shepard (1957), supra note 540.

***

Similarity is central to categorization, since categorization by virtue of generalization is a function of similarity.[544] People can distinguish different forms of knowledge that they need in order to gain expertise: declarative knowledge, routines and procedures, recognition of familiar patterns, perceptual discrimination skills, and mental models. People build a larger repertoire of patterns and prototypes, learn how to categorize new items, change categories and re-define the patterns and prototype as they gain new experience.[545] The importance of categorization was emphasized by Bruner, Goodnow and Austin in their 1956 classic, *A Study of Thinking*. The process of categorization classifies discriminably different things into groups, and such different things are thereby rendered equivalent. Similar principles may underlie subjects' identification and categorization of multidimensional stimuli.[546]

There are at least three views of the origins of categories. In *linguistic* view, a linguistic label provides a cue that a category exists, and people proceed to learn to identify it. This is the view at least implicit in most experimental research on categorization. In *feature overlap* view, people notice that a number of objects overlap substantially and proceed to form a category to include these items.[547] There is experimental research[548] to show that people can learn categories in the absence of category labeling. Common experience also says this is true. In *similar function* view, people notice that a number of objects serve similar functions and proceed to form a category to include them.[549] It involves distinguishing the features of an object into those that are functional (e.g., it can be used for sitting) and those that are not (e.g., it has four legs). These three views need not be in opposition. They are all special cases of the predictive nature of categories.

---

544 Ibid., p. 39, referring to Shepard (1987), supra note 542.

545 Gary Klein and Holly C. Baxter, 'Interservice/Industry Training, and education Conference', in Paper No. 2500, (I/ITSEC), 2006, Klein Associates, A Division of Applied Research Associates, Inc., Fairborn, OH 45324-6362, p. 3.

546 Nosofsky (1986), supra note 544, referring to J.S. Bruner, J.J. Goodnow & G.A. Austin, 'A study of thinking', (New York: Wiley, 1956).

547 John R. Anderson, 'The Adaptive Nature of Human Categorization,' in Psychological Review 1991, Vol. 98, No. 3, pp. 409-429, pp. 410-411. This seems essentially the position of Rosch (Rosch, Mervis, Gray, Johnson & Boyes-Braem, 1976) - Basic objects in natural categories, in Cognitive Psychology, 7, pp. 573-605. - and closest to Anderson's position.

548 Ibid., p. 411. See e.g., L.S. Fried & K.J. Holyoak, 'Induction of category distributions: A framework for classification learning', in Journal of Experimental Psychology: Learning, Memory, and Cognition, 10 (1984), pp. 234-257.

549 Ibid., referring to K.E. Nelson, 'Concept, word, and sentence: Interrelations in acquisition and development,' in Psychological Review, 81 (1974), pp. 267-285.

Categorization is justified by the observation that objects tend to cluster in terms of their attributes, be these physical features, linguistic labels, functions, or whatever.[550] The context theory proposed by Medin and Schaffer (1978) has provided good fits to data in numerous classification experiments.[551] The theory assumes, essentially, that subjects' classification of a given stimulus is determined on the basis of its similarity to the stored category exemplars.[552] Prototype model of categorization is among the most well-known findings in categorization investigation. In the prototype model, categorization decisions are based on the similarity of objects to the abstracted central tendency or prototype of a set of category exemplars.[553] A category prototype is sometimes classified more accurately than the actual category exemplars.[554] This type of result is not necessarily inconsistent with an exemplar model.[555] A category prototype would be expected to be fairly similar to almost all the category exemplars.[556]

Shepard, Hovland and Jenkins showed that confusion errors in an

---

550 Ibid.

551 Nosofsky (1984), supra note 539, p. 104, referring to D.L. Medin, 'Structural principles in categorization', in T.J. Tighe & B.E. Shepp (Eds.), Perception, cognition, and development: International analysis (Hillsdale, NJ.; Erlbaum, 1983), pp. 203-230; D.L. Medin, M.W. Altom, S.M. Edelson & D. Freko, 'Correlated symptoms and simulated medical classification', in Journal of Experimental Psychology: Learning, Memory, and Cognition, 8 (1982), pp. 37-50; D.L. Medin, G.I. Dewey & T.D. Murphy, 'Relationships between item and category learning: Evidence that abstraction is not automatic', in Journal of Experimental Psychology: Learning, Memory, and Cognition, 9 (1983), p. 607-625; D.L. Medin & M.M. Schaffer, 'Context theory of classification learning', in Psychological Review, 85 (1978), p. 207-238; D.L. Medin & E.E. Smith, 'Strategies and classification learning', in Journal of Experimental Psychology: Human Learning and Memory, 7 (1981), pp. 241-253.

552 Ibid., referring to Medin & Schafter (1978), Ibid.

553 Nosofsky (1986), supra note 546, p. 55. See e.g., M.I. Posner & S.W. Keele, 'On the genesis of abstract ideas', in Journal of Experimental Psychology, 77 (1968), pp. 353-363; M.I. Posner & S.W. Keele, 'Retention of abstract ideas', in Journal of Experimental Psychology, 83 (1970), pp. 304-308; E. Rosch, 'On the internal structure of perceptual and semantic categories', in T.E. Moore (ed.), Cognitive development and the acquisition of language (New York: Academic Press, 1973); E. Rosch, C. Simpson & R.S. Miller, 'Structural basis of typicality effects', in Journal of Experimental Psychology: Human Perception and Performance, 2 (1976), pp. 491-502.

554 Ibid.

555 Ibid., referring to D.L.Hintzman & G.Ludlam, 'Differential forgetting of prototypes and old instances: Simulation by an exemplar-based classification model', in Memory & Cognition, 8 (1980), pp. 378-382; Medin & Schaffer (1978), supra note 552.

556 Ibid.

identification task, which presumably gave an indication of interstimulus similarity relations, could not be used directly to generate successful categorization predictions. Shepard, Hovland and Jenkins rejected an exemplar-based generalization model for predicting categorization performance from identification performance. As an alternative, they suggested that subjects learned to attend selectively to the relevant stimulus dimensions in a given categorization problem and formulated rules about how values on these dimensions interact.[557] Shepard did an analysis of how training on one stimulus generalizes to other stimuli as a function of similarity. He conceived of the organism's tendency to generalize as a function of the probability that the two stimuli were in the same 'consequential region' where this could be read as a category. In Shepard's view a consequential region was some subset of a multidimensional region. The probability that the test stimulus and the original stimulus were in the same consequential region was a function of the distance between the two and the systems' prior (expressed as a probability density) about the size of the consequential region.[558] Shepard's analysis was basically Bayesian. He assumed that consequential regions were regions of uniform probability of a stimulus. He showed that, given this assumption of a uniform distribution, one gets close approximations to exponential generalization gradients over a wide variety of prior assumptions about possible distributions of size of the uniform interval, assuming all positions are equally likely.[559] A likely category member is one that maintains the expected pattern of correlations between causally related features, to be exhibited by a population of category members generated by a causal network.[560] Objects that are likely to have been generated by a category's causal model are considered to be good category members, and those unlikely to be generated are poor category members.[561]

---

557 Ibid., p. 53, referring to R.N. Shepard, C.I. Hovland & H.M. Jenkins, 'Learning and memorization of classifications', in Psychological Monographs, 75 (1961), (13, Whole No. 517).

558 Anderson (1991), supra note 550, p. 422, referring to Shepard (1987), supra note 542.

559 Ibid., p. 423, referring to R.N. Shepard, 'A law of generalization and connectionist learning', in Plenary address to the Cognitive Science Society,Ann Arbor, MI,1989, August 18.

560 Bob Rehder and Jay B. Martin, 'Towards A Generative Model of Causal Cycles', in: Kokinov,B., Karmiloff-Smith,A., Nersessian N.J (eds.), European Perspectives on Cognitive Science ISBN 978-954-535-660-5, (New Bulgarian University Press, 2011).

561 Bob Rehder and Shin Woo Kim, 'Causal Status and Coherence in Causal-Based Categorization', in Journal of Experimnetal Psychology: Learning, Memory, and Cognition 2010, Vol. 36, No.5, pp. 1171-1206 (pp. 1174-1175), referring to S.A. Sloman & D.A. Lagnado, 'Do we "do"?' in Cognitive Science, 29 (2005), pp. 5-39 ; M.R. Waldman & K.J. Holyoak, 'Predictive and diagnostic learning within causal

***

Traditionally, psychological distance is associated with perceived dissimilarity and thus dissimilarity has become an important concept in the area.[562] The most common approach represents the perceptual effects of stimuli as points in a multidimensional metric space and assumes that judgments of the perceived similarity of two stimuli are inversely related to the distance between their perceptual representation.[563] This class of models, known as the geometric models of similarity, is contained within the larger class of multidimensional scaling (MDS) models. MDS models assume the same sort of stimulus representation but do not necessarily require the perceptual space to be metric. An alternative approach, proposed by Micko and yielding similar results, represents stimuli as vectors in a multidimensional space.[564] Metric spaces have problems as a model for how humans represent similarities; Tversky has pointed out that violations of the three assumptions of metric models (minimality, symmetry and the triangle inequality) are empirically observed. Minimality might mean all identical objects seem equally similar.[565] Similarity can be represented in a metric space, since metric distance in an Euclidean space is, of course, symmetric. Regarding the triangle inequality axiom, if an object is similar to each of the two other objects, the two objects must be at least fairly similar to each other.[566]

---

models: Asymmetries in cue competition', in Journal of Experimental Psychology: General (1992), pp. 121, 222-236.

562 Ashby & Perrin (1988), supra note 540, p. 124.

563 Ibid., p. 125. See e.g., M.I. Davison, 'Multidimensional scaling'(New York: Wiley, 1983); J.B. Kruskal, 'Multidimensional scaling by optimizing goodness of fit to a nonmetric hypothesis', in Psychometrika, 29 (1964a), pp. 1-27; J.B. Kruskal, 'Nonmetric multidimensional scaling: A numerical method', in Psychometrika, 29 (1964b), pp. 115-129; R.N. Shepard, 'The analysis of proximities: Multidimensional scaling with an unknown distance function I', in Psychometrika, 27 (1962a), pp. 125-140; R.N. Shepard,' The analysis of proximities: Multidimensional scaling with an unknown distance function II', in Psychometrika, 27 (1962b), pp. 219-246; W.S. Togerson, 'Theory and methods of scaling', (New York: Wiley, 1958).

564 Ibid., referring to H.C.Micko, 'The "halo" method for multidimensional ratio scaling', in Psychometrika, 35 (1970), pp. 199-227; H.C.Micko &G. Fischer, 'Spatial model for multidimensional scaling', in Journal of Mathematical Psychology, 7 (1970), pp. 8-43; H. Eisler, 'Similarity in the continuum of heaviness with some theoretical and methodological considerations', in Scandinavian Journal of Psychology, I(1960), pp. 69-81; G. Ekman, 'A direct method for multidimensional ratio scaling,' in Psychometrika, 28(1963), pp. 33-41; G.Ekman & R.Lindman,'M ultidimensional ratio scaling and multidimensional scaling', in Reports from the Psychology Laboratories, The University of Stockholm,1961 (Rep. No. 103).

565 Quesada (1987/2008), supra note 542, p. 5, referring to Tversky (1977), supra note 540.

566 Ibid., p. 6, referring to Krumhansl (1978), supra note 540.

In the simple and weighted Euclidean models, the dimensions are assumed to be perceived independently.[567] The weighted Euclidean model was generated to allow for perceptual dependencies by Tucker (1972) and Carroll and Chang (1972); see also Carroll & Wish, 1974. Their idea (see also Tanner, 1956) was that the degree of perceptual dependence should be related to the angle between dimensions (see Ashby & Townsend, 1986), and so the resulting model known as the general Euclidean model.[568] MDS models have been hierarchically defined. For simplicity, we focus on the two-dimensional case and the Euclidean metric. One of the assumptions of the simple Euclidean MDS model is that the psychological space is the same for all subjects. Horan and Caroll & Chang introduced the weighted Euclidean model which assumes that subjects share the same psychological space but that each individual stresses the dimensions differently.[569]

***

A research has assumed that a classifier's belief about feature configurations is derived from first-hand observation. Murphy and Medin noted that the relative weighing of a feature (as well as the relative importance of common and distinctive features) varies with the stimulus context and task, [570] so that there is no unique answer to the question of how similar is one object to another.[571] Relating to the form of the salience function or

567 Ashby & Perrin (1988), supra note 564, p. 125, referring to D.H. Krantz & A. Tversky, 'Similarity of rectangles: An analysis of subjective similarity', in Journal of Mathematical Psychology, 12 (1975), pp. 4-34.

568 Ibid., pp. 124-125, referring to Krantz & Tversky (1975), Ibid.; L.R. Tucker, 'Relations between multidimensional scaling and three-mode factor analysis', in Psychometrika, 37 (1972), pp. 3-28; J.D. Carroll & J.J. Chang, 'IDOSCAL (individual differences in orientation scaling): A generalization of INDSCAL allowing IDIOsyncratic reference systems as well as analytic approximation to INDSCAL,' in Paper presented at the meeting of the Psychometric Society, Princeton, NJ, March 1972; J.D. Carroll & M. Wish, 'Models and methods for three-way multidimensional scaling', in D.H. Kratnz, R.C. Atkinson, R.D. Luce & P. Suppes (Eds.), in Contemporary developments in mathematical psychology, Vol. II (New York: Freeman, 1974), pp. 57-105; W.P. Tanner, 'Theory of recognition', in Journal of the Acoustical Society of America, 28 (1956), pp. 882-888; F.G. Ashby & J.T. Townsend, 'Varieties of perceptual independence', in Psychological Review, 93 (1986), pp. 154-179.

569 Ibid., p. 125, referring to C.B. Horan, 'Multidimensional scaling: Combining observations when individuals have different perceptual structures,' in Psychometrika, 34 (1969), pp. 139-165; J.D. Carroll & J.J. Chang (1970), 'Analysis of individual differences in multidimensional scaling via an N-way generalization of "Eckart-Young" decomposition', in Psychometrika, 35 (1970), pp. 283-319.

570 Quesada (1987/2008), supra note 566, pp. 3-4, referring to R.N. Shepard (1987), supra note 558, pp. 3-4.

571 Rehder & Kim (2010), supra note 561, p. 1176. See e.g., B. Hayes-Roth & F.

the nature of the relevant features, Tversky and Gati have identified three ordinal properties in the case in which stimuli features can be indentified and experimentally manipulated. The ordinal properties characterize what is called a 'monotone proximity structure'. If an axiom or property is ordinal, then it holds for judged dissimilarity if and only if it holds for perceived dissimilarity (assuming, as usual, a monotone relation between the two). Ordinal properties can therefore be tested directly. For example, symmetry is an ordinal property.[572] It is not difficult to show that the feature-contrast model predicts consistency and transitivity, and if feature saliency is an increasing function of the number of features, then it also predicts dominance. Therefore, a large class of feature-contrast models are monotone proximity structures.[573] In general, we expect the feature-contrast model to predict an increase in similarity with the number of features a pair of stimuli have in common and a decrease with the number of distinct features. However, the model is exceedingly general. Feature salience is an elusive term that may be only weakly related to the number of relevant features.[574] Similarly, the process of identifying features may be problematic. For example, Tversky and Gati used the term *features* to describe any property, characteristic, or aspect of objects that are relevant to the task under study.[575]

The generative framework of Kemp, Bernstein and Tanenbaum should help to explain how similarity judgments are guided by intuitive theories. [576] They develop a formal theory of similarity and compare it to the featural account[577] which suggests that the similarity of two objects is a function of their common and distinctive features, and the transformational account which suggests that similarity depends on the number of operations required to transform one object into the other. Picking up the features critical for similarity comparison may be assisted by generative

Hayes-Roth, 'Concept learning and the recognition and classification of examples', in Journal of Verbal Learning and Verbal Behavior, 16 (1997), pp. 321-338; Medin & Schaffer (1978), supra note 556; J.S. Reitman & G.H. Bower (1973), 'Storage and later recognition of exemplars of concepts', in Cognitive Psychology, 4 (1973), pp. 194-206.

572 Ashby & Perrin (1988)], supra note 569, pp. 126-127, referring to Tversky & Gati (1982), supra note 539; I. Gati & A. Tversky, 'Representation of qualitative and quantitative dimensions', in Journal of Experimental Psychology: Human Perception and Perfomance 8 (1982), pp. 325-340.

573 Ibid., p. 127.

574 Ibid., p. 126.

575 Ibid., referring to Tversky & Gati (1982), supra note 572, p. 126.

576 Kemp et al. (2005), supra note 534, referring to Ulrike Hahn, Nick Chater and Lucy B. Richardson, 'Similarity as transformation', in Cognition 87 (2003), pp. 1-32.

577 Ibid., referring to Tversky (1977), supra note 540.

process.[578] Interfeature causal relations are represented as probabilistic causal mechanisms in the generative model.[579] Kemp, Bernstein and Tennenbaum believe that the featural model, [the transformational model and their generative model] offer precisely the same expressive power.[580] The featural model can capture an arbitrary dataset perfectly if we have complete freedom to choose the features, and so can the other models if we have complete freedom to choose the transformations or generative processes. It follows that all of the models can mimic each other – given a particular choice of features for the featural model, for example, there will be transformations and generative processes that allow the other models to make exactly the same prediction.

Building on causal-model theory (Sloman & Lagnado, 2005; Waldman & Holyoak, 1992), the generative model offered by Rehder and Rehder & Kim assumes that inter-feature causal relations are represented as probabilistic causal mechanism and that classifiers consider whether an object is likely to have been produced or generated by those causal mechanism.[581] When features of categories are linked by causal relations, two different effects on classification judgments have been documented. The first, the *causal status* effect, is that features that appear earlier in a causal network (and thus are more 'causal') are weighed more heavily in classification than less causal features. The second, the *coherence effect*, is that good category members are those whose combination of features make sense in light of causal laws (*e.g.*, cause and effect feature both present and both absent).[582]

***

Many real world object concepts are richly structured, defined in terms of features connected in systems of relations, parts and subparts at multiple scales of abstraction, and even recursive embedding.[583] Bloom's (1956) taxonomy includes a component of synthesis – building a structure or pattern from diverse elements; and putting parts together to form a whole, with emphasis on creating a new meaning or structure.[584] Besides objects, examples of structured concepts can be found in language (e.g., the mutually

---

578 Ibid .

579 Rehder & Martin (2011), supra note 560.

580 Kemp et. al (2005), supra note 578.

581 Rehder & Kim (2010)], supra note 561, pp. 1174-1175, quoting Sloman & Lagnado (2005), supra note 561; Waldman & Holyoak (1992), supra note 561.

582 Bob Rehder and Shin Woo Kim, 'The Role of Coherence in Causal-Based Categorization', Department of Psychology, New York University, 2008, p. 285.

583 Stuhlmuller at al. (2010), supra note 532, referring to A. Markman, 'Knowledge representation', (1999).

584 Klien & Baxter (2006), supra note 545, p. 4.

recursive system of phrase types in a grammar), in the representation of events (e.g. a soccer match with its fixed subparts), and processes (e.g. the recipe for making a pancake with steps at different levels of abstraction). Each example of a structured concept itself has internal structure which makes it potentially very informative. The regularities underlying structured concepts can often be expressed with instructions for *generating* the examples. Stuhlmuller, Tenenbaum and Goodman describe an approach to representing structured concepts – more typical of the complexity of real world categories – using probabilistic generative processes.[585]

There is evidence that similarity involves structured pattern matching. The central idea underlying structured pattern matching is that similarity involves an alignment of relational structure.[586] Similarity also involves structured pattern completion. People's predictions were determined not just by the local information, but by whether it was connected to matching information. Thus, pattern completion is structure-sensitive.[587] Comparing the same item with different things can highlight different aspects of the item. When an item takes part in many comparisons, it may be interpreted differently in each comparison. Comparison is flexible.[588] Comparisons of a single pair of items may yield multiple interpretations. Even a single comparison can yield more than one distinct interpretation. This situation may arise when the items are richly represented, with many different clusters of knowledge. It can also arise when the comparison permits more than one alignment, as when the similarities of the objects in an item suggest different correspondences than do the relational similarities (i.e., components are cross-mapped.)[589] The findings in the research by Gertner & Markman[590] suggest that comparisons of both perceptual and conceptual materials involve structural alignment. Further, structural alignment promotes structure sensitive pattern completion. Finally, comparisons allow for multiple interpretations of a single item in different comparisons or multiple interpretations of a single comparison. Any model of human cognition that involves comparison must exhibit these properties.

Some researchers argued that neither spatial models nor discrete

---

585 Stuhlmuller at al. (2010), supra note 583.

586 Gentner & Markman (1987-2018), supra note 537, p. 856.

587 Ibid., pp. 856-858.

588 Ibid., p. 858. See B.A.Spellman & K.J. Holyoak, 'If Saddam is Hitler then who is George Bush? Analogical mapping between systems of social roles,' in Journal of Personality and Social Psychology, 62(6) (1992), pp. 913-933.

589 Ibid., p. 859, referring to D. Gentner & C. Toupin, 'Systematicity and surface similarity in the development of analogy', in Cognitive Science, 10 (1986), pp. 277-300.

590 Ibid., p. 860.

set theoretic models are well suited to model human representation. In several experiments humans show evidence of using structured representation rather than a collection of coordinates or features.[591] The structural matching theory assumes that mental representation consists of hierarchical systems that encode objects, attributes of objects, relations between objects, and relations. Structure mapping models are then the closed to the data structures that the semantic web uses.[592] The details on how the matching is done vary with the different models; The structure mapping engine SME was the original; it works by forcing one-to-one mapping.[593] That is, it limits any element in one representation to corresponding to at most one element in the other representation. SIAM (Similarity, Interactive, Activation, and Mapping) is a spreading activation model; it consists of a network of nodes that represent all possible feature-to-feature, object-to-object, and role-to-role correspondence between compared stimuli.[594] The activation of a particular node indicates the strength of the correspondence it represents. SIAM treats one-to-one mapping as a soft constraint. Structured representations gain some of their power from the ability to create increasingly complex representations of a situation by embedding relations in other relations and creating higher-order relation structure. These higher-order structures can encode important psychological elements like causal relations and implications.[595] Structure-mapping theory therefore makes some substantive predictions about tasks that involve comparison.[596] Tasks that require the identification of specific differences should be easier for two similar representations than for two disparate ones because full alignment is required for the determination of such differences. In contrast, tasks that require only overall match, such as determining whether two images are identical, can often be completed by means of a heuristic based on the quantity of local matches. This heuristic

591 Quesada (1987/2008), supra note 566, p. 7. See, R.L. Goldstone,'The Role of Similarity in Categorization-Providing a Groundwork', in Cognition 52(1994), pp. 125-157; R.L. Goldstone, 'Similarity,' in Wilson, R.A., Keil, F.C. (eds.): MIT encyclopedia of the cognitive sciences (Cambridge, MA: MIT Press, 1999), pp. 763-765; A.B.Markman & D.Gentner, 'Structural Alignment During Similarity Comparisons,' in Cognitive Psychol 25 (1993), pp. 431-467.

592 Ibid., pp. 7-8, referring to Markman (1999), supra note 583, p. 13.

593 Ibid., p. 9, referring to B. Falkenhainer, K. Forbus, D. Gentner, 'The Structure-Mapping Engine: Algorithm, and Examples', in Artif. Intell. 41 (1989), pp. 1-63.

594 Ibid., referring to R.L. Goldstone, 'Similarity, Interactive Activation, and Mapping', in J. Exp. Psychol.-Learn.Mem.Cogn. 20 (1994), pp. 3-27.

595 Ibid., referring to Markman (1999), supra note 592.

596 Andrew Lovett, Eyal Sagi and Dedre Gentner, 'Analogy as a mechanism of comparison', in the Spatial Intelligence and Learning Center (SILC), Conference Paper 2007, referring to D.Gentner & A.B. Markman, 'Structural alignment during similarity comparisons,' in Cognitive Psychology, 25 (1993), pp. 431-467.

will generate faster 'different' judgments when the representations are very different than when they are quite similar.[597] Featural and transformational models generally assume that systems are analogous to the extent that there is a structure-preserving one-to-one map between their elements.[598] The generative approach, however, allows analogous systems to have very different numbers of elements, as long as they appear to have been produced by the same process.[599]

***

Kemp, Bernstein and Tenenbaum have suggested how similarity judgment applies to domains ranging from the simple (feature vectors) to the complex (graphs and other structured objects). They are optimistic that their framework will help explain how similarity judgments are guided by sophisticated theoretical knowledge.[600] Kemp, Bernstein and Tenenbaum propose that similarity judgments are inferences about generative process, and that two objects appear similar when they are likely to have been generated by the same process. They present a formal model based on this idea, and suggest that it may be particularly useful for explaining high-level judgments of similarity.[601] Kemp, Bernstein and Tenenbaum in their paper offer a generative theory of similarity, a notion often invoked by models of high-level cognition. As already said, they argue that two objects are similar to the extent that they seem to have been generated by the same underlying process. The literature on similarity covers settings that extend from the comparison of simple stimuli like colored patches to the comparison of highly-structured objects like narratives. The generative approach is relevant to the entire spectrum of applications, but they are particularly interested in high-level similarity. In particular, they are interested in how similarity judgments draw on *intuitive theories*, or systems of rich conceptual knowledge in Murphy & Medin (1985).[602] Kemp, Bernstein and Tenenbaum suggest that high-level similarity is well explained by the generative approach. High-level judgments are likely to rely on intuitive theories, and intuitive theories often specify exactly the kind of information needed by the generative approach: information about the causal histories of objects.[603]

---

597 Ibid.

598 Kemp et al. (2005), supra note 578, referring to D. Gentner, 'Structure-mapping: A theoretical framework for analogy', in Cognitive Science, 7 (1983), pp. 155-170.

599 Ibid.

600 Ibid.

601 Ibid.

602 Ibid.

603 Ibid.

Similarity of two entities requires operations to transform an entity so as to be identical to another. The idea of similarity as transformation is promising in that it is very general and seems able to solve some of the previous theories problems.[604] The representational distortion theory of Hahn and Chater uses a measure of transformation called Kolmogorov complexity.[605] The main assertion of the theory is that representations that can be generated by a short program are simple, and the ones that require longer programs are more complex. The degree to which two representations are similar is determined by how many instructions must be followed to transform one into another. The minimality assumption is also implemented in this approach. Kolmogorov complexity deals with structured representations, feature representations and continuous representations if needed. Of course, feature theories can argue that each of the transformations proposed can be added as a feature without leaving the feature approach. However, adding higher order relationships as features makes evident one of the weak points of feature theories; anything can be a feature.[606] Kolmogorov complexity has a natural application as a measure of similarity between representations, A and B. The simplest measure is the length of the shortest program which takes A as input, and produces B as output – that is, the length of the shortest program that 'distorts' one representation into the other. Two entirely unrelated representations will be maximally dissimilar – because there will be no efficient way of transforming one into the other. Indeed, in this case, the most efficient transformation will simply involve deleting the first representation, and reconstructing the second from scratch – because there is no shared information between the objects that can be exploit.[607]

Transformational distance models could be more general [than Tversky's contrast model]. This view is shared by Hahn and Chater: "..indeed, the [Kolmogorov complexity] model can be viewed as a generalization of

---

604 Quesada (1987/2008), supra note 595, p. 10. See e.g., N. Chater, 'Cognitive Science – The logic of human learning', in Nature 407 (2000), pp. 572-573; N. Chater, 'The search for simplicity: A fundamental cognitive principle?' in Q. J. Exp. Psychol. Sect. A-Hum. Exp. Psychol 52 (1999), pp. 273-302; E.M. Pothos & N. Chater, 'A simplicity principle in unsupervised human categorization', in Cognitive Science 26 (2002), pp. 303-343; E. Pothos & N. Chater, 'Categorization by simplicity minimum description length approach to unsupervised clustering', in: Hahn, U. Ramscar, M (eds.): Similarity and categorization (Oxford: Oxford University Press, 2001); S. Dennis, 'A memory-based theory of verbal cognition', in Cognitive Science 29 (2005), pp. 145-193.

605 Ibid., referring to U. Hahn & N. Chater, 'Concepts and similarity', in: Lamberts, K. Shanks, D. (eds.): Knowledge, concepts, and categories (Cambridge, MA: MIT Press, 1997); Hahn et. al., (2003), supra note 576.

606 Ibid., p. 11.

607 Hahn et. al.(2003), supra note 605, p. 3.

the feature and spatial model of similarity, to the extent that similar sets of features (nearby points in space) correspond to short program".[608] Hahn, Chater and Richardson propose that similarity is determined by the transformation distance between representations: entities which are perceived to be similar have representations which are readily transformed into one another, whereas transforming between dissimilar entities requires many transformations. They introduce a family of transformation-based accounts of similarity, called 'Representational Distortion' (RD), as a specific example of a transformational approach to similarity.[609] According to RD, the similarity between two entities is a function of the 'complexity' required to 'distort' or 'transform' the representation of one into the representation of the other. The simpler the transformation distorting one representation to the other, the more similar they are assumed to be[610][the term to distort here means to easily conclude that the two objects compared are similar because similarities between them are adequate]. RD should be thus viewed as a general framework for understanding similarity, not as a specific psychological model. RD theory tries to provide a framework for understanding similarity-based processes in the spirit of rational analysis,[611] providing a derivation of the Shepard (1987) Universal Law of Generalization.[612] It also aims to provide an explanation for the utility of similarity in inference – why it makes sense, for example, to categorize items on the basis of the categories of similar items.[613]

One direction for future research aiming at detailed transformational account is to attempt to specify particular sets of transformations that are typically used in particular domains. Specifically, such research should attempt to use more extensively insights from work on transformational theories of perception[614] to tie down the set of transformations appropriate

608 Quesada (1987/2008), supra note 606, p. 11, referring to Hahn & Chater (1997), supra note 605, p. 71-71.

609 Hahn et al., (2003), supra note 607, p. 1.

610 Ibid., p. 2.

611 Ibid., p. 4, e.g., Anderson (1990), supra note 532.

612 Ibid., referring to N. Chater & P.M.B. Vitanyi, 'Generalizing the universal law of generalization', 2002, submitted for publication; N. Chater, P.M.B. Vitanyi & N. Stewart (in press), 'Universal generalization and universal inter-item confusability, Behavioral and Brain Sciences.

613 Ibid., referring to N. Chater & U. Hahn, 'Representational distortion, similarity, and the universal law of generalization', in Paper - Proceedings of the Interdisciplinary Workshop on Similarity and Categorization, SimCat97, pp. 31-36, Edinburg: Department of Artificial Intelligence, University of Edinburg, 1997.

614 Ibid., p. 28, referring to S.E. Palmer, 'Symmetry, transformation, and the structure of perceptual systems', in J. Beck (ed.), Organization and representation in perception, (Hillsdale, NJ: Erlbaum, 1982), pp. 95-144; S.E. Palmer, 'The psychology of perceptual organization: a transformational approach', in J. Beck.

in explaining similarity judgments concerning simple perceptual stimuli (object). Another important issue in this context is highlighted by the philosopher Goldman. Goldman (1986) pre-figures the notion of similarity as transformation in his work on providing a 'naturalized' (i.e., psychological) epistemology. He raises the empirical question of whether there is a finite set of such transformations or whether the set of cognitively salient transformations is potentially unbounded. Goldman also suggests that the lawfulness of human similarity judgments might be furthered by an inherent *preference ranking* for transformations, which comes into play where multiple transformational sequences could link the same stimulus pair[615] [the same stimuli pair here is two cases to be compared].

In three experiments, Hahn, Chater and Richardson have provided first evidence for the general claim that the similarity between two objects is determined by transformational relationships. These results present a challenge for other accounts of similarity, based on feature comparison or spatial distance, and they indicate that similarity can be explained in terms of transformation merits further theoretical and empirical investigation.[616] The transformational approach holds that s1 is similar to s2 if s1 can be readily transformed into s2. People assume that every transformation is reversible – if there is a transformation mapping s1 into s2, there must also be a transformation mapping s2 into s1. Intuitively, the process tends to generate small variations on the chosen prototype, where the permissible variations depends on the set of transformation. The transformation distance is between s1 and s2.[617]

The researches and identification above mentioned have shown that similarity-matching is generative. In addition to being generative, similarity-matching is also simultaneously transformational. Similarity [or similarity-matching] is therefore generative-transformational.

B.Hope & A. Rosenfeld (eds.), Human and machine vision, (New York: Academic Press 1983), pp. 269-339); S.E. Palmer, 'Goodness, gestalt, groups, and Garner: local symmetry subgroups as a theory of figural goodness', in G.R. Lockhead & J.R. Pomerantz, The perception of structure: essays in honor of Wendall R. Garner, (Washington, DC: American Psychological Association, 1991), pp. 23-39; R.N. Shepard, 'Psychological complementarity', in M. Kubovy & J.R. Pomerantz (eds.), Perceptual Organization, (Hillsdale, NJ: Erlbaum, 1981), pp. 279-341.

615 Ibid., referring to A.I. Goldman, 'Epistemology and cognition', (Cambridge, MA: Harvard University Press, 1986).

616 Ibid., pp. 28-29.

617 Kemp et al. (2005), supra note 603.

I.3.2. ANALOGY

***

Causes and the necessary mechanism responsible for regularities and patterns among phenomena are necessarily to be found, thought out, imagined and to be the subject of hypotheses. Not knowing the mechanisms underlying the processes we are studying, we have to imagine them, and they must be plausible, reasonable, and possible mechanisms. To achieve this we proceed by the method of analogy, supposing that they are like something about which we already know a good deal, and upon the basis of our knowledge of which we can imagine similar mechanisms at work behind the phenomena we are investigating.[618] An analogy is a relationship between two entities, processes, or what you will, which allows inferences to be made about one of the things, usually that about which we know least, on the basis of what we know about the other. If two things are alike in some respects we can reasonably expect them to be alike in other respects, though there may be still others in which they are unlike. In general between any two things there will be some likenesses and some unlikenesses. The art of using analogy is to balance up what we know of the likenesses against the unlikenesses between two things, and then on the basis of this balance make an inference as to what is called the neutral analogy, that about which we do not know.[619] Harre says that analogy exploits similarity. Similarities between two situations are in the heart of analogy. An analogy is a comparison between two objects or systems of objects, that highlights respects in which they are thought to be similar. Analogical reasoning is any type of thinking that relies on an analogy. Historically, analogical reasoning has played an important, but sometimes mysterious, role in a wide range of problem-solving context.[620]

An early version of the deductivist approach is exemplified by Aristotle's analysis of the argument from *paradeigma* or example. On this analysis, an analogical argument between a source situation to a target situation begins with the assumption of positive analogy between the situations, as well as the additional information within the source situation. The analogy proceeds via the generalization to the conclusion. Some recent analyses follow Aristotle in treating analogical arguments as reliant upon extra (sometimes tacit) premises, typically drawn from background knowledge. Davies and Russel[621] introduce a version that relies upon what

618 Harré (1985), supra note 308, pp. 171-172.

619 Ibid., p. 172.

620 Paul Bartha, 'Analogy and Analogical Reasoning', in Stanford Encyclopedia of Philosophy,' first published Tuesday, June 25, 2013, the beginning part.

621 Ibid., § 4.1.

they call determination rules. In contrast to the Aristotelian analysis via the generalization, a determination rule does not trivialize the analogical argument. Only by combining the rule with information about the source situation we can derive the value of the target situation.

Aristotle's theory provides us with four important and influential criteria for the evaluation of analogical arguments: a) The strength of an analogy depends upon the number of similarities; b) Similarity reduces to identical properties and relations; c) Good analogies derive from underlying common causes or general law; and d) A good analogical argument need not pre-suppose acquaintance with the underlying universal (generalization). These four principles form the core of *common-sense model* for evaluation analogical arguments.[622] Most theories of analogy agree with Aristotle and Hume on this general point. Disagreement relates to the appropriate way of measuring overall similarity. Some theories assign greatest weight to *material analogy*, which refers to shared, and typically observable features. Others give prominence to *formal analogy*, emphasizing high-level structural correspondence.[623] According to Rom Harré, one criterion of the appropriateness of analogical links embedded in a theory is the generation of existential hypothesis from the theory. If no existential hypothesis are suggested by a theory, then the theory does not advance our understanding of the underlying mechanism of natural process. As already mentioned before, Harré has declared that scientific explanation consists in finding or imagining plausible generative mechanism for the patterns amongst events, for the structures of things, for the generation, growth, decay, or extinction of things and materials, for changes within persisting things and materials.[624]

Some philosophers have attempted to portray and justify analogical reasoning in terms of some simpler inductive pattern. The problem of providing a general justification for analogies reduces to the problem of justifying that simpler inference pattern. There have been three moderately popular versions of this strategy.[625] The first treats analogical reasoning as generalization from a single case. Cartwright argues that we can sometimes generalize from a single careful experiment, where we have sufficient control of the materials and our knowledge of the requisite background assumptions is secure.[626] The second strategy treats analogical

622 Ibid., § 3.2

623 Ibid., § 3.2.

624 Losee (1972, 1980), supra note 295, p. 145, referring to Rom Harré, 'The Principles of Scientific Thinking', (London: Macmillan, 1970), p. 125.

625 Bartha (2013), supra note 623, § 4.2.

626 Ibid., referring to N.Cartwright, 'Aristotelian Natures and the Modern Experimental Method,' in Inference Explanation and Other Frustrations, J.Earman ed, Berkeley, 1992, p. 51.

reasoning as a kind of sampling argument. The simplest versions of the sampling argument is due to Mill. An argument from analogy, he writes, is 'a competition between the known points of agreement and the known points of difference'. Argument of A and B in 9 out of 10 properties implies a probability of 0.9 that B will posses any other property of A: 'we can reasonably expect resemblance in the same proportion'.[627] A third type of inductive justification recognizes the argument from analogy as a distinctive form, but treats its past successes as evidence for future success. Steiner suggests that many of the analogies that played a major role in early twentieth-century physics count as 'Pythagorean'. A 'Pythagorean' analogy is one founded on purely mathematical similarities that have no known physical basis at the time it is proposed.[628] However, Liston suggests that, dispite the mystery, physicists are entitled to use Pythagorean analogies on the basis of induction from past successes.[629] [The scientist] can admit that no one knows how [Pythagorean] reasoning works and argue that the very fact that similar strategies have worked well in the past is already reasoned enough to continue pursuing them hoping for success in the present instance.

In a simple quasi-formal characterization, an analogical argument is as follows. An analogy is between a source situation/domain and a target situation/domain. A situation or domain is a set of objects, properties, relations and functions, together with a set of accepted statements about those objects, properties, relations and functions. More formally, a situation or domain consists of a set of objects and an interpreted set of statements about them. The statements need not belong to a first-order language, but to keep things simple, any formalization employed here will be first-order. Formally, the analogy between the source situation and the target situation is a one-to-one mapping between objects, properties, relations and functions in the two situations. Not all of the items in the source situation and the target situation need to be placed in correspondence. Commonly, the analogy only identifies correspondence between a selected set of items. In practice, we specify an analogy simply by indicating the most significant similarities (and sometimes differences).[630]

---

627 Ibid., referring to J.S. Mill, 'A System of Logic', (London, Longmans-Green, 1843/1930), p. 367.

628 Ibid., referring to M. Steiner, 'The Application of Mathematics to Natural Science', in Journal of Philosophy 86 (1989), pp. 449-480; M. Steiner, 'The Applicability of Mathematics as a Philosophical Problem', (Cambridge, MA: Harvard University Press, 1998).

629 Ibid., referring to M. Liston, 'Critical Discussion of Mark Steiner's The Applicability of Mathematics as a Philosophical Problem', in Philosophia Mathematica, 3(8) (2000), pp. 190-207 (p. 200).

630 Ibid., § 2.2.

Commonsene gives the criteria for evaluation analogical arguments. Some of the most important ones are: 1) The more similarities between two situation, the stronger the analogy; 2) The more difference, the weaker the analogy; 3) The greater the extent of our ignorance about the two situations, the weaker the analogy; 4) The weaker the conclusion, the more plausible the analogy; 5) Analogy involving causal relations are more plausible than those not involving causal relations; 6) Structural analogies are stronger than those based on superficial similarities; 7) The relevance of the similarities and differences to the conclusion (i.e., the hypothetical analogy) must be taken into account; and 8) Multiple analogies supporting the same conclusion make argument stronger. These principles can be helpful, but are frequently too vague to provide much insight.[631]

***

Many people propose formal criteria for evaluating analogies based on overall structural similarity (the structure-mapping theory). Analogical inferences emerge as a consequence of identifying the 'best mapping'. The goodness of an analogical argument is based on the goodness of the associated analogy mapping, and the goodness of the analogy mapping is given by metric that indicates how closely it approximates isomorphism. The most influential structuralist theory has been Gentner's structure-mapping theory, implemented in a program called the *structure-mapping engine* (SME) as mentioned in Chapter I.3.1. He asserts that analogies are about relations, rather than simple features. No matter what kind of knowledge (causal models, plans, stories, etc.), it is the structural properties (i.e., the interrelationships between the facts) that determine the content of an analogy.[632] In order to clarify this thesis, Gentner introduces a distinction between *properties*, or monadic predicates, and *relations*, and further distinguishes among different *orders* of relations and functions, defined inductively.[633] The best mapping is determined by systematicity: the extent to which it places higher-order relations and items that are nested in higher-order relations, in correspondence. Properties and functions are unimportant, unless they are part of a relational network. In sum: systematicity can be a rough indicator of a plausible analogical

631 Ibid., § 3.1.

632 Ibid., § 3.4, referring to Falkenhainer et al,.(1989/90), supra note 593, p. 3.

633 Ibid.,§ 3.4, referring to D. Gentner, 'Structure-Mapping: A Theoretical Framework for Analogy,' in Cognitive Science 7 (1983), Bolt Beranek and Newman Inc. pp. 155-70.

argument, and this explains why the structure-mapping approach enjoys a measure of success. But systematicity does not magically produce or explain the plausibility of an analogical argument. When we reason by analogy, we must determine which features of both situations are relevant and *how* they relate to the analogical conclusion.

Contemporary 'structural mapping' theories employ a restricted version: each structural similarity between two situations contributes to the overall measure of similarity, and hence to the strength of the analogical argument.[634] The analogy 'A T is (like) a B' defines a mapping from B to T, T will be called the *target*, since it is the domain being explicated. B will be called the *base*, since it is the domain that serves as a source of knowledge.[635] An analogy can be mapped from base to target.[636] Relations have priority over object-attributes in analogy. However, not all relations are equally likely to be preserved. Part of our understanding about analogy is that it conveys a system of connected knowledge, not a mere assortment of independent facts. Such a system can be represented by an interconnected predicate structure in which higher-order predicates enforce connections among lower-order predicates.[637] The *structure-mapping theory* has its central claim that analogy is characterized by the mapping of relations between objects, rather than attributes of objects, from base to target; and, further, that the particular relations mapped are those that are dominated by higher-order relations that belong to the mapping (the *systematicity* claim).[638] Relational structure may influence the assignment of meaning to spatial representations when assignments, or mappings, are based on correspondence between objects, relations between them, and relations between relations. The relation structure hypothesis predicts that in the interpretation of spatial representations, conceptual elements are mapped to spatial elements, conceptual relations are mapped to spatial relations, and higher-order conceptual relations are mapped to higher-order spatial relations.[639] Quoting Markman and Gentner (1993), Gattis mentions that relational similarity also influences the second step in analogical reasoning, mapping aspects of the two concepts together.[640] An analogy or metaphor may be based on a mapping

634 Ibid., § 2.3.

635 Gentner (1983), supra note 633, p. 157.

636 Ibid., p. 159.

637 Ibid., p. 162.

638 Ibid., p. 168.

639 Merideth Gattis, 'Mapping relational structure in spatial reasoning,' in Cognitive Science 28 (2004), pp. 589-610, Elsevier, p. 592.

640 Ibid., p. 592, referring to A.B.Markman &D.Gentner,'Splitting the differences: A structural alignment view of similarity,' in Journal of Memory and Language 32 (1993), pp. 517-535.

between the relation between objects (sometimes called a relational mapping or relational match).

Lovett, Sagi and Gentner suggest that the theories of analogical thinking are useful not only in explaining creativity and problem solving, but also as a tool for understanding the processes underlying comparison, both conceptual and perceptual.[641] Specifically, they will suggest that one such theory of analogies, Structure-mapping Theory can be used to describe not only the processes of analogical reasoning but also those involved in comparison.[642] According to Structure-mapping Theory, analogies are understood via process of *structural alignment*. The alignment of two representations is assumed to proceed via a local-to-global process that begins by placing identical elements (attributes and relations that exist in both representations) into potential correspondences. These correspondences form an initial set of *local matches*. These local matches are coalesced into structurally consistent connected clusters (called *kernels*), which are merged together to form one or a few structurally consistent global interpretations. This global alignment facilitates the generation of analogical inferences, but also reveals structural commonalities between the two representations as well as *alignable differences*.[643] Therefore this process can be used for the identification of specific differences between representations as well as for the generation of analogical inferences.[644] Furthermore, the more similar the two representations are, the easier the alignment process becomes resulting in the faster identification of specific differences. However, in cases where identification of specific differences is not required, such as when making simple judgments of 'same' or 'different', it is possible to shortcut this process by employing a simple heuristic.[645]

641 Lovett, et al.(2007), supra note 596, referring to Gentner & Markman (1997).

642 Ibid., referring to Falkenhainer et al., (1989), supra note 632; Gentner (1983), supra note 636; D. Gentner, 'Why we're so smart,' in D. Gentner and S. Goldin-Meadow (eds.), Language in mind: Advances in the study of language and cognition, (Cambridge, MA: MIT Press, 2003), pp. 195-235; Gentner & Markman (1993), supra note 596; D. Gentner & A.B. Markman,'Structural alignment in comparison: No difference without similarity', in Psychological Science, 5 (1994), pp. 152-158; Markman & Gentner (1993), supra note 640.

643 Ibid.

644 Ibid., referring to D. Gentner & V. Gunn, 'Structural alignment facilities the noticing of differences', in Memory and Cognition 29 (2001), pp. 565-577; Gentner & Markman (1994), supra note 642; Markman & Gentner (1993), supra note 640; A.B. Markman & D. Gentner, 'Commonalities and differences in similarity comparison', in Memory & Cognition, 24 (1996), pp. 235-249.

645 Ibid., referring to A.B. Markman & D. Gentner, 'Nonintentional similarity processing', in R. Hassin, J.A. Bargh and J.S. Uleman (Eds.), The new unconscious, (New York: Oxford University Press, 2005), pp. 107-137.

Basically, according to Lovett, Sagi and Gentner the lower the number of initial local matches, the more likely it is that the two things differ.[646] Moreover, in order for two things to be identical, a minimum number of local matches is required – specifically, there need to be enough local matches so that the resulting mapping might cover all of the representations.

Pattern recognition is central to cognition. At the perceptual level, we notice key features of the world (like symmetry), recognize objects in front of us and identify the letters on a printed page. At a higher level, we recognize problems we have solved before and determine similarities – including analogical similarities – between new situations and old ones.[647]

***

In Norton's broad sense, however, 'material analogy' simply refers to similarities rooted in factual knowledge of the source and target domains (objects).[648] Mary Hesse has suggested that to use an analogy in science often claim that two types of relations hold between an analogue and a system to be explained. The first is similarity relations between the properties of the analogue and the properties of the system to be explained. The second is causal relations or functional relations which hold both for the analogue and for the system to be explained.[649] For Hesse, an acceptable analogical argument must include 'observable' or 'pre-theoric' similarities between situations, which she refers to as *material analogy*. These are horizontal relationships of similarity between properties of objects in the source and the target. She also requires that the hypothetical analogy, the feature transferred to the target situation, be *causally related* to the positive analogy, where accepted propositions in a source situation and corresponding accepted propositions in a target situation represent accepted (or known) similarities. In her words, the essential requirements for a good argument from analogy is 'a tendency to co-occurance', i.e., a causal relationship. Hesse's final requirement is that the essential properties and causal relations of the source situation have not been shown to be part of the negative analogy, where there are accepted (or known) differences in the source and target situations.[650] Hesse's (1966) theory is scientific. She introduced useful terminology based on the *tabular representation*, in

646 Ibid.

647 Gentner & Markman (1987-2018), supra note 537, p. 855.

648 Bartha (2013), supra note 634 § 3.3.

649 Losee (1972, 1980), supra note 624, p. 142.

650 Bartha (2013), supra note 648, § 3.3, referring to M. B. Hesse, 'Models and Analogies in Science', (Notre-Dame: University of Notre-Dame Press, 1966).

which the *horizontal relations* in an analogy are the relation of similarity (and difference) in the mapping between domains (such as the earth and Mars), while the *vertical relations* are those between the objects, relations and properties within each domain. The correspondence (similarity) between earth's having a moon and Mars' having moons is a horizontal relation; the causal relation between having a moon and supporting life is a vertical relation within the source domain (with the possibility of a distinct such relation existing in the target as well).[651] Hesse's theory of material analogy has shown that analogy generates the insight of the target situation by matching the similarities between the source situation and the target situation based on the already known insight of the source situation.

On learning by analogy and constraint transfer, Winston (1981) details: 1/ a natural language interface translates English sentences describing a precedent and a problem into links in a semantic net; 2/ a matcher determines a correspondence between the parts of the precedent and the problem; 3/ an analogizer determines if the questioned link in the problem is supported by the given links in the problem, and to do this, the analogizer transfers the CAUSE links supplied by the precedent onto the problem; and 4/ a rule generator constructs an if-then rule to capture that portion of the causal structure in the precedent that is ferreted out by the problem. The *then* part of the if-then rule comes from the questioned link in the problem. The *if* parts come from links identified by the transferred CUASE structure.[652] In more complicated situations, no single precedent can supply enough causal structure. Consequently, several precedents must be strung together. A new precedent is sought whenever there is a path in the transferred CAUSE structure that does not lead to an already established link in the problem.[653]

Like Gentner, Holyoak and Thagard regard the heart of analogical reasoning as analogy mapping, and they stress the importance of systematicity, which they refer to as a structural constraint. Unlike Gentner, they acknowledge two additional types of constraints. *Pragmatic* constraints take into account the goals and purposes of the agent, recognizing that 'the purpose will guide selection' of relevant similarities. Semantic constraint represent estimates of the degree to which people regard source and target items as being alike, rather like Hesse's feature similarities.[654] Winston, Binford, Katz and Lowry argue that the novelty

651 Ibid., referring to Hesse (1966), Ibid.

652 Patrick H. Winston, Thomas O. Binford, Boris Katz and Michael Lowry, 'Learning Physical Descriptions from Functional Definitions, Examples and Precedents,' in AAAI-83 Proceedings, 1983, pp. 433-434.

653 Ibid. p. 434.

654 Bartha (2013), supra note 650, § 3.5.1, referring to K. Holyoak & P. Thagard, 'Analogical Mapping by Constraint Satisfaction', in Cognitive Science13

of this constraint-satisfaction model is that these structural, semantic and pragmatic constraints are implemented not as rigid rules, but rather as 'pressures' supporting or inhibiting potential pairwise correspondence. The model is implemented in a connectionist program called ACME (Analogical Constraint Mapping Engine), which assigns an initial activation value to each possible pairing between elements in the source and target situations (based on semantic and pragmatic constraints), and then runs through cycles that update the activation values based on overall coherence (structural constraints).[655] The 'light' version of a theory for good analogical reasoning from the constraint-satisfaction model is as follows: structural, semantic and pragmatic constraints contribute to the overall *coherence* of an analogy, and the best analogy are those that maximize coherence (*cf.* Thagrad 1989).

***

Studies of analogy in scientific learning and in reasoning have emphasized the importance of shared complex representation structures.[656] Recent work

---

(1989), pp. 295-355; K. Holyoak & P. Thagard, 'Mental Leap: Analogy in Creative Thought', (Cambridge, MA: MIT Press, 1995).

655 Ibid.

656 Gertner (1983), supra note 638, p. 166, referring to J. Clement, 'Analogy generation in scientific problem solving', in Paper - Proceedings of the Third Annual Meeting of the Cognitive Science Society, 1981; J. Clement, 'Spontaneous analogies in problem solving: The progressive construction of mental models', in Paper presented at the meeting of the American Education Research Association, New York, 1982; A.M. Collins & D. Gentner, 'Constructing runnable mental models', in preparation; Hesse (1966), supra note 650; J.R. Hobbs, 'Metaphor, metaphor schemata, and selective inferencing', (SRI Technical Note 204), Menlo Park, CA. SRI International. Artificial Intelligence Center, December 1979; R.R. Hoffman, 'Metaphor in science,' in R.P. Honeck & R.R. Hoffman (Eds.), The psycholinguistics of figurative language (Hillsdale, NJ: Lawrence Erlbaum Associates, 1980); J. Moore & A. Newell, 'How can Merlin understand?' in L. Gregg (ed.), Knowledge and cognition, (Potomac, MA: Lawrence Erlbaum Associates, 1973); R. Oppenheimer, 'Analogy in science', in Paper presented at the 63rd Annual Meeting of the American Psychological Association, San Francisco, September 1955; G. Polya, 'Mathematics and plausible reasoning', Vol.1 (Princeton, NJ: Princeton University Press, 1973); M.S. Riley, 'Representation and the acquisition of problem-solving skill in basic in basic electricity/electronics', in Paper presented at the Computer-based Instructional Systems and Simulation meeting, Carnegie-Mellon University, January 1981; D.E. Rumelhart & D.A. Norman, 'Analogical process in learning,' in J.R. Anderson (Ed.), Cognitive skills and their acquisition, (Hillsdale, NJ: Lawrence Erlbaum Associates, 1981); L. Steels, 'An applicable view of object

in cognitive science has begun to explore more powerful representational schemes. The Merlin system[657] featured a mechanism for "viewing x as y"[658] which involved explicit comparisons of the shared and non-shared predicates of two situations. Winston, using a propositional representation system, has simulated the process of matching a current situation with a previously stored precedent and using the similarity match to justify importing inferences from the precedent to the current situation.[659] Further, in recent work he has investigated importance-dominated matching; here the match between old and new situations is performed by counting only those predicates that occur in causal chains.[660] In Gentner's view this requirement is somewhat more restrictive than the structure-mapping principle that participation in any higher-order chain results in preferential mapping.[661] However, it has the similar effect of focusing the matcher on systematic relational structures rather than on haphazard resemblance between situation. One valuable aspect of Winston's work is his modeling of the process of abstracting general rules from the analogical matches.

Analogies are widely recognized as playing an important *heuristic* role, as aids to discovery. They have been employed, in a wide variety of settings and with considerable success, to generate insight and to formulate possible solutions to problems.[662] From what has been sketched above, it can be concluded that analogy is generative. Rom Harré holds analogy is generative,[663] and Hesse does too.[664] Analogy exploits similarity. Since similarity has been identified as transformational by cognitive science

---

oriented programming,' (MIT A.I. Memo No. 15) (Cambridge, MA: Massachusetts Institute of Technology, March 1982); A. Stevens, A. Collins & S.E. Goldin, 'Misconceptions in student's understanding,' in Journal of Man-Machine Studies, 1979, 11, pp. 145-156; K. VanLehn & J.S. Brown, 'Planning nets: A representation for formalizing analogies and semantic models of procedural skills', in R.E. Snow, P.A. Federico & W.E. Montague (eds.), Aptitude, learning and instruction: Cognitive process analyses, (Hillsdale, NJ: Lawrence Erlbaum Associates, 1980).

657 Ibid., referring to Moore & Newell (1973), Ibid.

658 Ibid. See, also Steel (1982), supra note 656.

659 Ibid., referring to P.H. Winston, 'Learning and reasoning by analogy,' in CACM, 1980, 23, No.12.; P.H. Winston, 'Learning new principles from precedents and exercise,' in MIT Artificial Intelligence Memo No. 632 (Cambridge, MA: Massachusetts Institute of Technology, May 1981).

660 Ibid.

661 Ibid., pp. 166-167.

662 Bartha (2013), supra note 655, § 1.

663 Losee (1972, 1980), supra note 649, p. 145, referring to Harré (1970), supra note 624, p. 125.

664 Bartha (2013), supra note 662, § 3.3, referring to Hesse (1966), supra note 656.

researchers in the previous sub-chapter, analogy which exploits similarity is also transformational, in addition to being generative. Therefore, analogy [and similarity] is[are] generative-transformational.

I.3.3. CONSISTENCY

That consistency had been coherent relation was followed by some early versions of coherence theory. The consistency of a proposition with a certain set is the coherence of such a proposition with the set.[665] Consistency is a necessary condition for coherence.[666] Early consistency theories failed to yield a general account of the mechanisms by which attitudes are formed and decisions are made. However, over the past decade the principles underlying consistency theories have been revived in the form of connectionist models of constraint satisfaction. Constraint satisfaction mechanisms can cause coherence shifts, thereby transforming ambiguous inputs into coherent decisions.[667]

The most influential theories of cognitive consistency had appeared in the 1950s, including Osgood and Tennenbaum's (1955) congruity theory, Festinger's (1957) cognitive dissonance theory, and Heider's (1958) balance theory.[668] Tennenbaum summarized the position as follows: The reasoning behind [the consistent position] relates to the organism's presumed need to apprehend and comprehend things and events about him. In monitoring, processing and interpreting information from the environment, some degree of consistency and equilibrium is seen as essential for reasons of parsimony and economy of effort, as well as to allow for the predictability of, and hence adaptability to, subsequent encounters......most assume a universal value for the organism in his having a stable predictable view of his environment.[669]

---

665 James O. Young, 'The Coherence Theory of Truth', in Stanford Encyclopedia of Philosophy, first published Tuesday, September 3, 1996; substantive revision Wednesday, March 27, 2013.

666 Jonathan Dancy, An Introduction to Contemporary Epistemology, Justification, Coherence Theories, (Basil Blackwell, 1985), p. 110.

667 Dan Simon & Keith J. Holyoak, 'Structural Dynamics of Cognition: From Consistency Theories to Constraint Satisfaction', in Personality and Social Psychology Review, 2002, Vol. 6, pp. 283-294 (p. 283).

668 Anthony G. Greenwald, Lauire A. Rudman, Brian A. Nosek, Mahzarin R. Banaji, Shelly D. Farnham and Deborah S. Mellot, 'A Unified Theory of Implicit Attitudes, Stereotypes, Self-Esteem, and Self-Concept', in Psychological Review, 2002, Vol. 109, No. 1, pp. 3-25 (p. 3).

669 Simon & Holyoak (2002), supra note 667, p. 285, referring to P. Tennenbaum, 'Summary: Is anything special about consistency?' in R.P. Abelson, E. Aronson, W.J. McGuire, T.M. Newcomb, M.J. Rosenberg & P.H. Tennenbaum (eds.), Theories of cognitive consistency: A sourcebook, (Chicago: Rand MacNally,

Festinger's cognitive dissonance theory grew to be dominant.[670] The theory drew attention to the dramatic problem of understanding cognitive change following 'forced compliance'. Dissonance research revealed that human beings could be manipulated into telling lies[671] insulting other people,[672] and eating grasshoppers.[673] And human beings would also subsequently change their attitudes to believe the lie they told, to derogate the victim of their insult, and to develop a liking for the taste of grasshoppers. Heider's balance theory was attacked to some certain extent by the progress of cognitive dissonance research.[674] Dissonance researchers claimed that dissonance theory had made its strongest and clearest predictions when the dissonance was as a part of violation of consistent, stable, competent and moral self-concept.[675] Even though dissonance theory was built on a seemingly rational foundation of cognitive consistency, its interpretation of forced compliance was counterintuitive and puzzling.[676] Researchers have attacked dissonance theory because of its excessive response in nature,[677] and because of its manifestation becoming an inconsistency theory.[678] Heider(1960) holds that states of 'order and coherence' are established by mutual interdependency among elements of thought, and the phenomenon of the mutual interdependency was a principal characteristic of structural

---

1968), pp. 343-346.

670 Ibid., referring to L. Festinger, 'A theory of cognitive dissonance', (Stanford, CA: Stanford University Press, 1957).

671 Ibid., referring to L. Festinger & J.M. Carlsmith, 'Cognitive consequence of forced compliance', in Journal of Abnormal and Social Psychology, 58 (1959), pp. 203-210; Greenwald et al.,(2002), supra note 668, p. 3.

672 Ibid., referring to K.E. Davis & E.E. Jones, 'Changes in interpersonal perception as a means of reducing cognitive dissonance', in Journal of Abnormal and Social Psychology, 61 (1960), pp. 402-410.

673 Ibid., referring to P.G. Zimbardo, M. Weisenberg, I. Firestone & B. Levy, 'Communicator effectiveness in producing public conformity and private attitude change', in Journal of Personality, 33 (1965), pp. 233-255.

674 Ibid., referring to Festinger (1957), supra note 670, pp. 7-8.

675 Ibid., referring to E. Aronson, 'Dissonance theory, progress and problems', in R.P. Abelson, E. Aronson, W.J. McGuire, T.M. Newcomb, M.J. Rosenberg & P.H. Tennenbaum (eds.), Theories of cognitive consistency: A sourcebook, (Chicago: Rand MacNally, 1968), pp. 5-27.

676 Greenwald et al. (2002), supra note 668, p. 3.

677 Simon & Holyoak (2002), supra note 675, p. 284, referring to M.J. Rosenberg & C.I. Hovland, 'Cognitive, affective, and behavioral components of attitudes', in M.J. Rosenberg, C.I. Hovland, W.J. McGuire, R.P. Abelson & J.W. Brehm (eds.), Attitude organization and change: An analysis of consistency among attitude components, (New Heaven, CT: Yale University Press, 1960), pp. 1-14.

678 Ibid., referring to J.E. Singer, 'Motivation for consistency,' in S. Feldman (ed.), Cognitive consistency: Motivational antecedents and behavior cosequents, (New York: Academic Press, 1966), pp. 47-73.

dynamics.[679] Elements that 'go together' tend to form stable structures, whereas inconsistent elements generate forces that operate toward the reinstitution of stability.[680] He explained: These conceptions, symmetry, consonance, balance and simplicity, are, of course, implied in that idea with which Gestalt theory started and which always was central to it, namely, the idea of a 'good' figure. This model implies a number of different entities with certain properties and standing in certain relations, which make up a constellation of factors tending toward a standard state.[681] Heider has later suggested, the tendency toward consistency implicitly brings the various pieces in human cognition into consonance. [682] The tendency should not just be considered to merely repair disturbances of coherence. McGuire contends that consistency maximization is significant.[683] According to McGuire, chains of human reasoning are in a 'loose-link' network. Remote elements of the system are gradually touched by consistency-driven forces through the related links, and this process gradually changes the network's activation toward a higher state of coherence.[684] McGuire highlighted the expectation that consistency theories would provide the basis for a general psychology of inference: The end was a description on how people think in the broadest sense of the term.[685] By using the assumed psychological necessity for maintaining a highly structured, highly consistent belief system, I hoped to do no less than construct and test a psychology of inference, that is, a depiction of the manner and extent to which one idea leads to another psychologically.

In 1960s, consistency theories were reformulated with the advent of connectionist theories of cognition, and in particular, constraint satisfaction

679 Ibid., p. 283, referring to F. Heider, 'Attitudes and cognitive organization', in Journal of Psychology, 21 (1946), pp. 107-112 (p. 175).

680 Ibid., referring to F. Heider, 'The gestalt theory of motivation', in M.R. Jones (ed.), Nebraska symposium on motivation, Vol. 8, (Lincoln: University of Nebraska Press, 1960), pp. 145-172.

681 Ibid., referring to F. Heider (1960), Ibid., p. 68.

682 Ibid., p. 284, referring to F. Heider, 'On balance and attribution', in P.W. Holland & S. Leinhardt (eds.), Perspectives on social network research, (New York: Academic Press, 1979), pp. 11-23.

683 Ibid., referring to W.J. McGuire, 'Theory of the structure of human thought', in M.J. Rosenberg, C.I. Hovland, W.J. McGuire, R.P. Abelson & J.W. Brehm (eds.), Attitude organization and change: An analysis of consistency among attitude components, (New Heaven, CT: Yale University Press, 1068), pp. 1-14.

684 Ibid., p. 285, referring to W.J. McGuire, 'A syllogistic analysis of cognitive relationships', in M.J. Rosenberg, C.I. Hovland, W.J. McGuire, R.P. Abelson & J.W. Brehm (eds.), Attitude organization and change: An analysis of consistency among attitude components, (New Heaven, CT: Yale University Press, 1960), pp. 65-111.

685 Ibid., p. 283, referring to McGuire (1968), supra note 683, pp. 140-141.

mechanisms. In models of this type, complex tasks are performed by networks in which the decision variables are interconnected by excitatory and inhibitory links representing positive and negative relations among the variables. Constraint satisfaction models operate by applying a relaxation algorithm that settles the network into a stable state in which the asymptotic activation levels of the units define a set of highly activated variables. Bidirectional activation enables units that mutually support each other via excitatory connections (i.e., those that 'go together') to become highly active, and collectively inhibit their rivals. The bidirectional influence between related units play a critical role in allowing the system to impose a coherent interpretation on the overall situation. Connectionist constraint-satisfaction models were first applied to lower-level cognitive processes, notably letter and word perception.[686] Holyoak & Thagard (1989) and Spellman & Holyoak (1992) have noted that models based on similar algorithm were later applied to a variety of higher-level cognitive process, including analogical mapping.[687]

Prominent consistency researchers argued that consistency attainment should be deemed as proactively making sense of the world. Heider (1979) argues that the tendency toward balanced states is based on the desire to have our cognitive food prepared so that it is easy to swallow, to assimilate.[688] Abelson describes the cognitive function as motivated by the need to 'organize the information stored by the individual in a way that is likely to be useful to him, directly or indirectly, for effective or behavioral purposes'.[689] Pepitone has claimed that the pressure to reduce inconsistency follow from the fact that consistent structures 'are simpler to maintain than distinctions, discrepancies and contradictions', so inconsistency is to be reduced.[690] K.W. Back emphasized the effectiveness of cognitive processing as a necessary means for survival: Consistency makes it possible for the organism to structure the world in an economical way to react to facts

686 Ibid., p. 285, referring to J.L. McClelland & D.E. Rumelhart, 'An interactive activation model of context effects in letter perception: Part 1: An account of basic findings', in Psychological Review, 88 (1981), pp. 375-407.

687 Ibid., referring to K.J. Holyoak & P. Thagard, 'Analogical mapping by constraint satisfaction', in Cognitive Science, 13 (1989), pp. 295-355; Spellman & Holyoak (1992).

688 Ibid., p. 284, referring to Heider (1979), supra note 682, p. 16.

689 Ibid., referring to E. Aronson, 'Psychological implication', in R.P. Abelson, E. Aronson, W.J. McGuire, T.M. Newcomb, M.J. Rosenberg & P.H. Tennenbaum (eds.), Theories of cognitive consistency:A sourcebook, (Chicago: Rand MacNally, 1968), pp. 112-139 (p. 133).

690 Ibid., referring to A. Pepitone, 'Some conceptual and empirical problems of consistency models,' in S. Feldman (Ed.), Cognitive consistency: Motivisional antecedents and behavior consequents, (New York: Academic Press, 1966), pp. 257-297.

which are connected in a consistent way.[691] A conclusion has been drawn by Simon and Holyoak from those arguments by prominent researchers.[692] Simon and Holyoak concluded that consistency attainment should be deemed as proactively making sense of the world.

I.3.4. COHERENCE

I.3.4.1. COHERENCE THEORY

***

Early versions of the coherence theory were associated with idealism. It is the versions taking the metaphysical routes to coherentism. Walker (1989) attributes coherentism to Spinoza, Kant, Fichte and Hegel. Idealists are led to a coherence theory of truth by their metaphysical position. From the idealists' perspective, reality is something like a collection of beliefs. The truth of a belief can only consist in its coherence with other beliefs, not in correspondence with something which is not a belief.[693] Another route to coherentism is epistemological. Coherence with a set of beliefs may constitute the test of truth but that truth consists in correspondence to objective facts.[694] Another epistemological argument for coherentism is based on the view that we cannot 'get outside' our set of beliefs and compare propositions to objective facts.[695] This argument, like Blanshard's, depends on a coherence theory of justification. We can only know that a proposition coheres with a set of beliefs. We can never know that a proposition corresponds to reality.[696] In Dancy's words, relation between beliefs is crucially asymmetrical; there is an asymmetrical distinction between evidence and theory under which evidence confirms and disconfirms theory in a way in which theory cannot confirm or disconfirm evidence.[697] Foundationalism offers such a structure

691 Ibid., pp. 284-285, quoting K.W. Back, 'Equilibrium as motivation: Between pleasure and enjoyment', in R.P. Abelson, E. Aronson, W.J. McGuire, T.M. Newcomb, M.J. Rosenberg & P.H. Tennenbaum (eds.), Theories of cognitive consistency: A sourcebook, (Chicago: Rand MacNally, 1968), pp. 311-318.

692 Ibid., p. 284.

693 Young (2013), supra note 665, § 2.1.

694 Ibid., § 2.2., referring to B. Blanshard, 'The Nature of Thought', (London: George Allen and Unwin, 1939).

695 Ibid., referring to C. Hempel, 'On the Logical Positivits, Theory of Truth,' Analysis, 2 (1935), pp. 49-59; O. Neurath, 'Philosophical Paper' 1913-46, in Robert S. Cohen and Marie Neurath (eds.), (Dordrecht and Boston: D. Reidel, 1983).

696 Ibid.

697 Dancy (1985), supra note 666, p. 110.

in its assertion that the direction of justification is all one-way. The notion of inference itself is asymmetrical. It is possible to infer B from A without being able to infer A from B.

All coherentists agree that consistency is a necessary condition for coherence. F. Bradley added that a coherent set should be complete or comprehensive in some sense.[698] The notion of coherence, on which a more completely holistic theory is based, is intended to be symmetrical.[699] Led by W.V.O. Quine's powerful argument,[700] coherence and holistic theories of knowledge and justification predominance in current Anglo-American philosophical circles, and foundational empiricist theories are becoming weaker.[701] Coherence theories deny that knowledge has the linear structure that foundationalist theories assert. Coherence theories of knowledge,[702] justification,[703] perception,[704] truth,[705] and ethics,[706] to name a few, have been a powerful, and perhaps the predominant, force in modern philosophy.[707] The fundamental idea of coherentism is simple enough, according to which there is no way for conceptual, propositional

698 Ibid., referring to A.C. Ewing, 'Idealism: A Critical Survey', (London: Methuen, 1934), quoting F.Bradley, 'Essays on Truth and Reality', (Oxford: Clarendon Press,1914), pp. 202-203.

699 Ibid.

700 Kenneth J. Kress, 'Legal Reasoning and Coherence Theories: Dworkin's Rights Thesis, Retroactivity, and the Linear Order of Decisions', in 72 Cal. L. Rev. 369 (1984), p. 369, referring to W.V.O. QUINE, 'Two Dogmas of Empiricism', in FROM A LOGICAL POINT OF VIEW 20 (2d rev.ed. 1980) ["Quine 1980a"]; W.V.O. QUINE, 'On What There Is', FROM A LOGICAL POINT OF VIEW I (2d rev. ed. 1980) ["Quine 1980b"]; W.V.O. QUINE, 'WORD AND OBJECT' (1960).

701 Ibid. See, e.g., G. HARMAN, 'THOUGHT' (1973); M. WILLIAMS, 'GROUNDLESS BELIEF' (rev. ed. 1977); Harman, 'The Inference to the Best Explanation', in 74 PHIL. REV. 88 (1965).

702 Ibid., p. 370, referring to Harman (1965), Ibid.

703 Ibid., referring to QUINE (1980a), supra note 700; QUINE (1980b), supra note 700; QUINE (1960), supra note 700.

704 Ibid., referring to Chisholm, 'On the Nature of Empirical Evidence', in R. Chisholm & R. Swartz eds., EMPIRICAL KNOWLEDGE: READINGS FROM CONTEMPORARY SOURCES 224, 1973.

705 Ibid. See generally BLANSHARD (1939) supra note 694; N. RESCHER, 'THE COHERENCE THEORY OF TRUTH' (1973); Dauer, 'In Defense of the Coherence Theory of Truth,' in 11 J.PHIL., 791 (1974).

706 Ibid., referring to RAWLS (1971), supra note 449; John Rawls, 'Outline of a Decision Procedure for Ethics', in 60 PHIL. REV. 177 (1951); see also R. DWORKIN, 'TAKING RIGHTS SERIOUSLY' 159-60 (rev. ed. 1978) – But see p. 353 (denying that the reflective equilibrium coherence theory provides a satisfactory account of private moral reasoning).

707 Ibid.

beliefs to be justified by appeal to non-conceptual, non-propositional sensory experience. Beliefs can only be justified by other beliefs. The sole basis for epistemic justification is relations among beliefs, rather than between beliefs and something external. More specifically, it is alleged, what justifies beliefs is the way they fit together: the fact that they *cohere* with each other.[708] Laurence BonJour mentions that although consistency is a requirement for coherence, mere consistency is not by itself enough for any serious degree of coherence, and it seems plausible to suppose that all of the aspects or ingredients of the relations among beliefs can be viewed as inferential relation.[709] The members of a coherent system of beliefs stand in fairly pervasive inferential relations of this sort to each other, with the degree of coherence depending on the degree to which this is so, that is, on the number and strength of these inferential connections.

***

Descarte's basic epistemological approach is foundationalist in character: it views justification and knowledge as ultimately derivatives from a set of basic or foundational elements whose justification does not depend in turn on that of anything else. For Descarte, as for many foundationalists, the foundation for knowledge and justification consists of (i) a person's immediate awareness of his or her own conscious states of mind, together with (ii) his or her a priori grasp of self-evidently true propositions. Beliefs deriving from these two sources require no further justification, whereas beliefs about most or all other matters, and especially beliefs concerning objects and occurrences in the material world, require justification or reasons that ultimately appeal, whether directly or indirectly, to immediate experience and a priori insight.[710]

If we take coherence as criterion both of truth and of justification, we have a good chance of being able to see there is an enormous advantage in having theories of truth and justification that fit each other. The theory of truth ought to fit the epistemology and not be allowed to ride independent of it.[711] Dancy thinks that in this way coherentism makes a virtue of necessity. In the absence of fixed points and the lack of any clues about where revision should start, our belief-set is merely provisional. Revisions will be called for, and the need to revise may occur anywhere. This is a form of fallibilism. Coherentists welcome it and claim that their approach reveals the strength

708 BonJour (2002/2010), supra note 321, p. 187.
709 Ibid., p. 188.
710 Ibid., p. 177 [footnote omitted].
711 Dancy (1985), supra note 699, p. 117.

of fallibilism; fallibilism is not an unfortunate defect but an essential part of the epistemological enterprise, the drive continually to revise in the search for greater coherence.[712] Rescher holds that coherence directs attention away from the individual's struggle to construct his own epistemology; instead it gives a sense to the notion of knowledge as a social phenomenon, something that can be shared and which can increase by means of that sharing. In this respect they don't diverge from the tradition except in failing to insist that the initial data are restricted to basic facts about one's own sensory states. However, the testimony of others can be used more or less immediately to increase the coherence of one's own belief-set, and one can think of oneself as a collaborator, even as one more likely to learn from others than to contribute to the sum total of knowledge (a sort of epistemological modesty).[713] Colin McGinn argues that coherentists are committed to the view that, for example, 'snow falls from the sky' is true iff the belief that snow falls from the sky coheres with other beliefs.[714] Now it follows from this and the redundancy biconditional (*p* is true iff *p*) that snow falls from the sky iff the belief that snow falls from the sky coheres with other beliefs. It appears then the coherence theorist is committed to the view that snow could not fall from the sky unless the belief that snow falls from the sky coheres with other beliefs. From this it follows that how things are depends on what is believed about them. This seems strange to McGinn since snow could fall from the sky even if there were no belief about snow, or anything else. The linking of how things are and how they are believed have led McGinn to say that coherentists are committed to idealism, this being the view that how things are mind-dependent.

Coherence is supposed to be primarily a property of *a group* or *system* of beliefs (though presumably a sufficiently complicated individual belief could be incoherent within itself). Proponents of coherence speak of beliefs agreeing with each other of fitting together or 'dovetailing' with each other.[715] Part of what is required here is logical consistency: beliefs that are logically inconsistent with each other plainly do not fit together or agree to any extent at all.[716] Coherentists, according to Dancy, would claim that this holistic theory fits our actual practice far better than the more restrictive foundationalist account.[717] We do not always preserve the observational at

712 Ibid., p. 118.

713 Ibid., p. 119, referring to N. Rescher, 'The Coherence Theory of Truth', (Oxford: Oxford University Press, 1973), p. 332.

714 Young (2013), supra note 693, § 4, referring to Colin McGinn,'The Truth about Truth', in Richard Schantz (ed.), What is Truth?, (Berlin:Walter de Gruyter, 2002), pp. 194-204 (p. 195).

715 BonJour (2002/2010), supra note 710, p. 187 [footnote omitted].

716 Ibid.

717 Dancy (1985), supra note 713, p. 118.

the expense of the theoretical. Equally, we do support our observational beliefs by appeal to our theoretical ones. So there is no theoretical need to accept the asymmetries, and our practice reveals that we don't do so anyway.

***

The coherence theory of truth holds that a proposition is true iff it is a member of a coherent set. Classical coherentists held that truth was a matter of degree. The theory defines truth for members of sets. Propositions cannot be coherent [but proposition sets can be coherent], in the required sense, and sets cannot be called true unless they are members of larger sets.[718] A coherence theory of truth states that the truth of any (true) proposition consists in its coherence with some specified set of propositions. The truth conditions of propositions consist in other propositions. In contrast, the correspondence theory states that the truth conditions of propositions are not (in general) propositions, but rather objective features of the world. Although the coherence and correspondence theories are fundamentally opposed in this way, they both present (in contrast to deflationary theories of truth) a substantive conception of truth. That is, the coherence and correspondence theories both hold that truth is a property of propositions that can be analyzed in terms of the sorts of truth - conditions propositions have, and the relations stand in to these conditions.[719]

Bradley ascribes to the 'data of perception' or the 'sense-world' an asymmetrical role in the individual's epistemology.[720] Material *comes from* the sense-world, and without that world knowledge could not *begin*. And it has a continuing role, both in our need continually to return to previous 'data of perception' and in our need to make sense of the continuing flow of new sensory life. Bradley is willing to accept that the sense-world plays a special role in epistemology, but he is unwilling to accept that that special role emerges in the sort of asymmetry which characterizes foundationalism.[721] Bradley holds that experience provides data (genetic asymmetry), but that the question whether something which appears as datum should remain as accepted fact is one which is not even partially determined by its origin as datum. Data stand for acceptance into our world in the same way and by the same criteria as does any other

718 Ibid, p. 113.

719 Young (2013), supra note 714, preliminary overview.

720 Dancy (1985), supra note 716, p. 123, referring to Bradley (1914), supra note 698, p. 209.

721 Ibid, pp. 123-124, referring to Bradley (1914), id., p. 210.

propositions. The test in each case is what he calls 'system', or in other words the question whether the coherence of our world is increased by their admission as accepted fact. In this respect there is no asymmetry; all propositions (in the sense, as it were, of proposals) that are justified receive a justification of exactly the same sort.

More than one coherent set of propositions means plurality, and this objection to the coherence theory of truth (the plurality objection) is standard. Blanshard argues that the plurality objection fails to appreciate the empiricist character of his coherentism. For he takes it, as do other coherentists such as Bradley, that there is only one coherent set, and this set is distinguished from all rivals by being empirically grounded. This is so, according to Bradley, because of the very aim of thought and enquiry, which is to discover the most systematic ordering of our experience.[722] Responding to Bradley's contend as above mentioned that a coherent set should be complete or comprehensive in some sense being intended to be symmetrical, coherence requires consistency and completeness, the notion of entailments appeared because consistency and completeness were not enough; they did not capture the feeling that a coherent set stuck together or fitted together in a special way. To capture this, classical coherentists use the notion of entailment (*p* entails *q* iff, given *p*, *q must* be true).[723] According to traditional entailment, '*p* entails *q*' is understood atomistically, as a feature of the individual meanings of *p* and *q*; given the meaning of *p* and that of *q*, if *p* is true then *q* must be, and this indepedently of considerations be elsewhere in the system. Blanshard's understanding of entailment is not the traditional one. For him, entailment only occurs within a system; and since the system determines the meanings of *p* and *q*, it determines the strength of the link between *p* and *q*. So as the system grows, that link can become stronger.[724] There is anyway an obvious intuitive link between entailment, as Blanshard sees it, and explanation.[725] To explain *q* by appeal to *p* is to show why *q* should be true, given *p*. The explanation works to the extent that it shows that, given *p*, *q* must be true. Explanation thus reveals entailment, in Balnshard's sense. And like entailment, explanation should be viewed holistically rather than atomistically.

The notion of mutual entailment as the central element in a coherent set, as Blanshard uses it, is symmetrical enough. Coherentists want to give a sense to the notion that as one's belief-set grows, it improves (we

722 Ibid., p. 114, referring to Blanshard (1939), supra note 705; Bradley (1914), Ibid., p. 210.

723 Ibid., p. 110.

724 Ibid., p. 112.

725 Ibid.

hope); it becomes more coherent. Since we are never likely to achieve a complete coherent set, the definition of coherence in terms of entailment has the consequence that nobody's beliefs are actually coherent at all.[726] Blanshard wrote that in a fully coherent system, no proposition would be arbitrary, every proposition would be entailed by the others jointly and even singly, no proposition would stand outside the system.[727] The objects which are linked by the relation of mutual explanation in a coherent set in the coherence theory of truth are propositions.[728] Several other authors have defended coherence theories that emphasize the importance of explanatory relations.[729] On the account of the coherent as the mutually explanatory, it seems that the requirement of completeness can be quietly dropped, because the need for completeness is already accounted for by the search for a higher degree of mutual explanatories, and because there is no really clear notion of completeness available here. Coherence is a property of a set of beliefs, not of the members. The set is coherent to the extent that the members are mutually explanatory and consistent.[730] What Blanshard, Bradley and those coherentists say is that the enterprise is to start from the data of experience and to construct a set of beliefs around those data which will order the data in the most systematic (coherent) way. So the set of beliefs which we do construct *must* be empirically grounded, and this grounding in the data of experience guarantees that there will be only one set which constitutes 'the most systematic ordering',[731] [In this sense, degree of truth may mean the degree of truth according to the most systematic ordering]. The alternative account of coherence, offered by Lehrer [and Sellars], defines a coherent set as one which is consistent, complete and mutually explanatory.[732] Therefore, the idea here will be that, as the set increases in size, we can hope that each member of it is better explained by the rest, explanations can improve in quality; this accounts for the growth of justifiction. And the notion of mutual explanation is clearly symmetrical, in the required sense.

726 Ibid., p. 111.

727 Ibid., pp. 110-101, quoting Blanshard (1939), vol.2, pp. 265-266, supra note 722.

728 Ibid., p. 117.

729 Erik J. Olsson, 'Coherentist Theories of Epistemic Justification' in Stanford Encyclopedia of Philosophy, first published on Tuesday, November 11, 2003; substantive revision on Thursday, November 15, 2012, § 4. See e.g., William Lycan, 'Judgment and Justification', (New York: Cambridge University Press, 1988); William Lycan, 'Explanation Rebuttals (Coherentism Defended Again)', in The Southern Journal of Philosophy, 50 (1) (2012), pp. 5-20.

730 Dancy (1985), supra note 728, pp. 111-112.

731 Ibid., p. 114, referring to Blanshard (1939), supra note 727; Bradley (1914), supra note 722.

732 Ibid., p. 111, referring to Lehrer (1974); Sellar (1973).

Most, if not all, influential coherence theorists assign some beliefs that are close to experience a special role, whether they are called 'supposed facts asserted' (Lewis, 1946), 'truth-candidates' (Nicolas Rescher, 1973), 'cognitively spontaneous beliefs' (BonJour, 1985)[733] or something else. These theories may be more fruitfully classified as versions of *weak foundationalism* than as pure coherence theories. Weak foundationalists typically hold that coherence is incapable of justifying beliefs from scratch, it can provide justification for beliefs that already have some initial, perhaps miniscule, degree of warrant, e.g., for observational beliefs.[734] Rescher has pointed out that a proposition is a truth-candidate if it is potentially true, so that there is something that speaks in its favor.[735] Rescher's truth-candidates are obviously related to Lewis's 'supposed facts asserted'. In both cases, the propositions of interest are *prima facie* rather than *bona fide* truths. The purpose of Rescher's investigation (1973) is not to investigate the possibility of *defining* truth in terms of coherence but to find a truth *criterion*, a systematic procedure for selecting from a set of conflicting and even contradictory truth-candidates those elements which it is rational to accept as *bona fide* truths.[736] Common to any coherence theory of truth is the problem of characterizing what exactly coherence is supposed to be. As Richard Kirkham puts the matter: The term 'coherence' as used by coherence theories has never been very precisely defined. The most we can say by way of a general definition is that a set of two or more beliefs are said to cohere if and only if (1) each member of the set is consistent with any subset of the others and (2) each is implied (inductively if not deductively) by all of the others taken as premises or, according to some coherence theories, each is implied by *each* of the others individually.[737] Philosophers argue that the theory of coherence of truth is manifestly false, because no matter how tight our account of coherence is we shall have to admit that there may be more than one coherent set of propositions. Nothing in the notion of coherence,

---

733 Olsson (2012), supra note 729, § 1, referring to C.I. Lewis, 'An Analysis of Knowledge and Valuation', (LaSalle: Open Court, 1946); N. Rescher, 'The Coherence Theory of Truth', (Oxford: Oxford University Press, 1973) ["Rescher 1973a"]; L. BonJour, 'The Structure of Empirical Knowledge', (Cambridge, Mass: Harvard University Press, 1985).

734 Ibid.

735 Ibid., § 4, referring to Rescher, 'Cognitive Systematization', (Oxford: Blackwell, 1973) ["1973b"].

736 Ibid, referring to Rescher (1973b) Ibid.; Rescher, 'Cognitive Systematization', (Oxford: Blackwell, 1979).

737 Dale Dorsey, 'A Coherence Theory of Truth in Ethics' in Philosophical Studies (2006) 127, pp. 493-523, (p. 498), referring to Richard L. Kirkham, 'Theories of Truth: A Crucial Introduction', (Cambridge, MA: MIT Press, 1992), p. 104.

as defined, gives us any right to say that there is a unique most coherent set. But it is obviously the case that there can be at most one complete set of truth. So truth cannot be defined in terms of coherence alone.[738]

***

The coherence theory of justification holds that a belief is justified to the extent to which the belief-set of which it is a member is coherent. Each belief is to be evaluated by appeal to the role it plays in the belief-set. If the coherence of the set would be increased by abandoning the belief and perhaps by replacing it by its opposite, the belief is not justified. If the set is more coherent with this belief as a member rather than with any alternative, the belief is justified.[739]

By a traditional account of coherence we will mean one which construes coherence as a relation of mutual support, consistency or agreement among given data (propositions, beliefs, memories, testimonies etc). According to Ewing, a coherent set is characterized partly by consistency and partly by the property that every belief in the set follows logically from the others taken together.[740] Thus, a set, if consistent, is highly coherent on this view because each element follows by logical deduction from the rest in concert. Ewing suggested that it would be sufficient that each member of a coherent set be entailed by all the rest.[741] While Ewing's definition is admirably precise, it defines coherence too narrowly. Few sets that occur naturally in everyday life satisfy this austere part of his definition: the requirement that each element follow logically from the rest when combined.[742] Lewis's definition of coherence or 'congruence', can be seen as a refinement and improvement of Ewing's basic idea. As Lewis defines the term, a set of 'supposed facts asserted' is coherent (congruent) just in case every element in the set is supported by all the other elements taken together, whereby 'support' is understood not in logical terms but in a weak probabilistic sense. Lewis's work is seminal of *weak foundationalism*, and the work has given us precise and sophisticated definitions of coherence as well as detailed studies of the relationship between coherence and truth

---

738 Dancy (1985), supra note 732, p. 113, referring to Russell, 'On the Nature of Truth', in Paper - Proceedings of the Aristotelian Society, 7 (1907), pp. 228-249.

739 Ibid., p. 116.

740 Olsson (2012), supra note 736, § 3, referring to Ewing (1934), supra note 698.

741 Dancy (1985), supra note 739, p. 111, referring to Ewing (1934), Ibid.

742 Olsson (2012, supra note 740, §3, referring to Ewing (1934), Ibid.

(probability), culminating in some potentially disturbing impossibility results that shed doubt on the possibility of defining coherence in a way that makes it indicative of truth.[743] Lewis allows that individual reports need not be very credible considered in isolation for coherence to have a positive effect. He is firmly committed to the view that their credibility must not be nil. He writes that [i]f ...there were no initial presumption attaching to the mnemically presented ....then no extent of congruity with other such items would give rise to any eventual credibility. In other words, if a belief system is completely isolated from the world, then no justification will ensue from observing the coherence of its elements.[744] Like in the coherence theory of truth, in the coherence theory of justification the objects which are linked by the relation of mutual explanation in a coherent set are also propositions. So when we talk of the justification of *a*'s belief that *p* we are asking whether the proposition *p* forms, with other propositions which *a* believes, a promisingly coherent set. If it does, the truth of *p* is explained by appeal to the truth of those others.[745] Lehrer has a different approach.[746] He suggests that what needs to be explained is not the truth of *p* but rather the fact that *a* believes that *p*. So in this respect our theory of truth fits our theory of justification.

Coherentism has its basis in epistemology[747] and ramification into ontology,[748] but has also become popular in ethical theory,[749] and

---

743 Ibid., referring to Lewis (1946), supra note 733.

744 Ibid., § 5, referring to Lewis (1946), Ibid.

745 Dancy (1985), supra note 741, p. 117.

746 Ibid., referring to Lehrer (1974), supra note 732.

747 Jaap Hage, 'Three Kinds of Coherentism', in Michal Araszkiewics & Jaromir Savelka (eds), in Coherence: Insight from Philosophy, Jurisprudence and Artificial Intelligence (Dodrecht: Springer, 2003), p. 1, referring to Laurence BonJour,' The Structure of Empirical Knowledge', (Cambridge, MA: Harvard University Press, 1985); Keith Lehrer, 'Coherentism', lemma in Jonathan Dancy and Ernest Sosa (eds.), A Companion to Epistemology, (Oxford: Blackwell, 1992), pp. 67-70; Keith Lehrer, 'Theory of Konwledge', 2nd edition, (Boulder: Westview Press, 2000); Paul Thagard and Karsten Verbeurgt, 'Coherence as Constraint Satisfaction', in Cognitive Science 22 (1998), pp. 1-24; Paul Thagard, 'Coherence in Thought and Action', (Cambridge, MA: MIT Press, 2000); Jonathan Kvanvig, 'Coherentist Theories of Epistemic Justification', in Edward N. Zalta (ed.), in Stanford Encyclopedia of Philosophy (Summer 2011 Edition).

748 Ibid., referring to Rescher (1973a), supra note 733; James O. Young, 'The Coherence Theory of Truth', in Edward N. Zalta (ed.), in Stanford Encyclopedia of Philosophy (Fall 2008 Edition).

749 Ibid., referring to John Rawl, "Theory of Justice, (Oxford: Oxford University Press, 1972); Norman Daniels, 'Reflective Equilibrium', in Edward N. Zalta (ed.), in Stanford Encyclopedia of Philosophy (Spring 2011 Edition).

in jurisprudence.[750] BonJour has contended that, in the philosophy of knowledge, coherent beliefs are beliefs that are mutually supportive in an overall context of justification. Coherent beliefs exist in a web, where complex interrelationships hold the beliefs together in a justificatory 'package'.[751] The coherence theory of justification rides on a particular common sense intuition: when we gather information from less than fully reliable sources, then the more coherent the story that materializes is, the more confident we may be, *ceteris paribus*. Within the context of information gathering from certain types of sources, coherence is a property of stories which plays a confidence boosting role.[752] In apparent agreement with Lewis, BonJour writes: " [a]s long as we are confident that the reports of the various witnesses are genuinely independent of each other, a high enough degree of coherence among them will eventually dictate the hypothesis of truth telling as the only available explanation of their agreement". However, BonJour proceeds to reject Lewis's point about the need for positive antecedent credibility: "[w]hat Lewis does not see, however, is that his own [witness] example shows quite convincingly that no antecedent degree of warrant or credibility is required".[753] Lewis's claim is that coherence will not have any confidence boosting power unless the sources are initially somewhat credible. But, BonJour is proposing that coherence can play this role even if there is no antecedent degree of warrant, so long as the witnesses are delivering their reports independently.

According to Lehrer, coherence is a relation of 'fitting together with', rather than, say, a relation of 'being inferable from': [i]f it is more reasonable for me to accept one of [several] conflicting claims than the other on the basis of my acceptance system..., then that claim fits better or coheres better

750 Ibid., referring to Neil MacCormick, 'Legal Reasoning and Legal Theory', (Oxford Univesity Press, 1978); Neil MacCormick, 'Rhetoric and the Rule of Law', (Oxford University Press, 2005); Ronald Dworkin, 'Law's Empire', (London: Fontana, 1986); Aleksander Peczenik, 'On Law and Reason' 2nd edition, (Dordrecht: Springer, 2008); Amalia Amaya, 'Formal Models of Coherence and Legal Epistemology', in Artificial Intelligence and Law 15 (2007), pp. 429-447.

751 Anthony Ford, 'Robust Coherence: An Approach to Multi-agent Experience-based Planning', U.S. Air Force Research Laboratory, 525 Brooks Road, Rome NY, 13441, Association for the Advancement of Artificial Intelligence, 2009, p. 26, referring to L. BonJour, 'The Coherence Theory of Empirical Knowledge', in Philosophical Studies, 30 (5) (1976), pp. 281-312.

752 Stephen Hartmann and Luc Bovens, 'A Probabilistic Theory of the Coherence of an Information Set', in a research supported by a grant of the National Science Foundation, Science and Technology Studies (SES 00-80580) and grants of the Transcoop Program and of the Feodor Lynen Program of the Alexander von Humboldt Foundation, Hartman & Bovens 2001, p. 195.

753 Olsson (2012), supra note 744, § 5, referring to BonJour (1985), supra note 747, p. 148.

with my acceptance system, and so ...[a] belief may be completely justified for a person because of some relation of the belief to a system to which it belongs, the way it coheres with the system, just as a nose may be beautiful because of some relation of the nose to a face, the way it fits with the face.[754] In Lehrer's view, "[c]oherence ..is not a global feature of the system (1997, 31), nor does it depend on global features of the system". Lehrer employs the concept of coherence in his definition of justification, in turn is a chief ingredient in his complex post-Gettier definition of knowledge. According to Lehrer, a person is justified in accepting a proposition just in case that proposition coheres with the relevant part of her cognitive system. For Lehrer, the relevant part is the acceptance system of the person, consisting of reports to the effect that the subject accepts this and that.[755] In later works, Lehrer has emphasized the importance of coherence with a more complex cognitive entity which he calls the 'evaluation system'.

Since, as stated before, coherentists want to give a sense to the notion that as one's belief-set grows, it improves (we hope); it becomes more coherent and we are never likely to achieve a complete coherent set and therefore the definition of coherence in terms of entailment has the consequence that nobody's beliefs are actually coherent at all, so if we are to have a coherence theory of justification, we need to give a good sense to the idea that justification can grow.[756] So a belief can be true without being justified and can be justified without being true, on the coherence account [this is the link as questioned above]. Justification can grow, but as it grows it need not be approaching truth. Of course as a belief-set grows and becomes more coherent, we have more and more reason to suppose that its members are true. But they may not be true; indeed it is always quite probable that further expansion will require revision somewhere. What is the link here between justification and truth? A belief-set with reasonable coherence, Dancy holds, will make each of its members justified.[757] But that does not mean that they are all true. It may be that the belief-set cannot be further expanded; that after a while the addition of further beliefs, however it may be done, always continues to decrease the coherence of the growing whole. In that case the members of the set are not all true, because they cannot all be members of a genuinely coherent whole. But they are still justified.

---

754 Ibid., § 4, referring to K. Lehrer, 'Justification, Coherence and Knowledge,' in Erkenntnis, 50 (1997), pp. 243-257.

755 Ibid., referring to K. Lehrer, 'Theory of Knowledge' 1st edition, (Boulder: Westview Press, 1990); See e.g., Lehrer (2000), supra note 747; K. Lehrer, 'Coherence, Circularity and Consistency: Lehrer Replies', in E. J. Olsson (ed.), The Epistemology of Keith Lehrer, (Dordrecht: Kluwer, 2003), pp. 309-356.

756 Dancy (1985), supra note 746, p. 111.

757 Ibid., p. 116.

***

In Thagard and Verbeurgt (1998), coherence is described as a set of constraints between elements in a system of beliefs.[758] Determining a maximally coherent set of beliefs consists of sorting elements into the appropriate set, accepted or rejected, based on their constraints. This approach requires the establishment of both positive and negative constraints based on how the elements in the system are related to each other. Positive constrained elements are either both accepted or both rejected. The two elements that are positively constrained must be sorted into the same set. Certain relations between beliefs can be characterized as coherent, while others denote incoherence. Elements that are related by a coherent relation are positively constrained (belong in the same set), while elements related by an incoherent relation are negatively constrained (belong in different sets). Each of these constraints has a strength value, which indicates how much that constraint contributes to the overall coherence of the system. This system attempts to maximize constraint satisfaction based on the strength of the constraints, which means that not all constraints need to be met, just as many as provide the highest total contribution to coherence.

Thagard considers a strong emphasis on explanatory relations between beliefs. Like Rescher, Thagard takes the fundamental problem to be which elements of a given set of typically conflicting claims that have the status of *prima facie* truths to single out as acceptable. However, where Rescher proposes to base the choice of acceptable truths on considerations of plausibility, Thagard suggests the use of explanatory coherence for that purpose.[759] According to Thagard, *prima facie* truths can cohere (fit together) or 'incohere' (resist fitting together).[760] The first type of relation includes relations of explanation and deduction, whereas the second type includes various types of incompatibility, such as logical inconsistency. If two propositions cohere, this gives rise to a positive constraint. If they incohere, the result is a negative constraint. A positive constraint between two propositions can be satisfied either by accepting both or by rejecting both. By contrast, satisfying a negative constraint means accepting one proposition while rejecting the other. A 'coherence problem' is one of dividing the initial set of propositions into those that are accepted and those that are rejected in such a way that most constraints are satisfied.

758 Ford (2009), supra note 751, pp. 26-27, referring to Thagard & Verbeurgt (1998), supra note 747, p. 22 (1).

759 Olsson (2012) supra note 755, § 4, referring to Thagard (2000), supra note 747; Rescher (1973a), supra note 733.

760 Ibid., referring to Thagrad 2000, id. [footnote 759].

Coherence can also be used to determine the appropriate actions and goals in a situation, an approach called *deliberative coherence*. The goal of this approach is to form a plan, consisting of actions and goals. This system is populated with facilitation and incompatibility relations that allow the set of possible actions and goals to be pruned using coherence. In deliberative coherence, the acceptability of factual beliefs influences the relations in the systems.[761] The central feature of constraint satisfaction mechanism is that the mental model will reconfigure itself until the constraint settle at a point of maximal coherence. Coherence, the state at which similarly linked variables are similarly activated, occurs when the variables that support the emerging decision are strongly endorsed and those supporting the alternative are dismissed, rejected, or ignored. In complex decisions, the initial mental representation of the task is naturally incoherent. Constraint satisfaction processes force the task variables to change toward a better fit with the gradually emerging state of coherence.[762] This reversed induction gives coherence-based reasoning its bidirectional character: while the strength of supporting variables determines the conclusion, the variables themselves are transformed by the cognitive process so as to provide considerably stronger support for conclusion.[763]

---

761 Ford (2009), supra note 758, p. 27, referring to P. Thagard & E. Milligram, 'Inference to the best plan: A coherence theory of decision', in A. Ram & D. Leake (ed.), Goal-driven Learning, 1995, pp. 439-454.

762 Dan Simon, 'A Third View of the Black Box: Cognitive Coherence in Legal Decision Making', in The University of Chicago Law Review (2004) 71:511, p. 522. The phenomenon of reversed induction and structural reconfiguration are the hallmarks of Gestalt psychology. Gestalt psychologist Max Wertheimer explains "one has a feeling how successive parts should follow one another; one knows what a 'good continuation' is; how 'inner coherence' is to be achieved, etc.; one recognizes a resultant 'good Gestalt" simply by its own "inner necessity". Max Wertheimer, 'Laws in Organization of Perceptual Forms', in Willis D. Ellis, ed, A Source Book of Gestalt Psychology 71, 83 (Routledge, 1955). Constraint satisfaction theory has been dubbed a "new kind of Gestalt theory." Stephen E. Palmer, 'Gestalt Psychology Redux,' in Peter Baumgartner and Sabine Payr, eds, Speaking Minds: Interviews with Twenty Eminent Cognitive Scientists 160 (Princeton 1995). See also Keith J. Holyoak, 'Problem Solving', in Edward E. Smith and Daniel N. Osherson, eds., 3 An Invitation to Cognitive Science; Thinking 267, 289-90 (MIT 2d ed 1995) (discussing similarities between the concepts of constraint satisfaction and Gestalt Theory). The Gestaltian roots of connectionism have also been discussed in Simon and Holyoak, in 6 Personality & Soch Psych Rev., pp. 283-285.

763 Ibid. Another way to appreciate how coherence-based reasoning differs from conventional theories of cognition is to consider how it breaks with the prevalent understanding of the relationship between the two building blocks of cognitive psychology — representation and computation. At the core of cognitive psychology is the general idea that mental activity is the product of applying a procedure, computation, or manipulation to a state of affairs represented in the mind. In general terms, all cognitive processing entails the dual function of

Coherence-based reasoning presumes a connectionist architecture of mental representations, which can be likened to an intricate electrical network. As to connectionist representations, all mental processing starts with mental representation of the task.[764] Decisions are made within certain problem spaces that contain and delimit the representation of the task variables, that is, all the factors that are to be included in the decision at hand. The representations of the variables are called *mental models* of the decision task.[765] In the connectionist architecture, each variable is represented in

---

representation and computation. The latter component is best understood as a form of making an inference or judgment, whereas the former concerns mentally representing the variables. The dominant theories of cognitive psychology presume separability of the two components, as do most theories of decision making and legal reasoning. These theories assume invariance and exogeneity of mental representations. That means (1) that the representations of the task variables do not change during the performance of the task, at least not in any systematic manner; and (2) that the representations of the task variables are determined by factors such as background knowledge, personal preference, cultural conventions, and the like, which are external and antecedent to the decision-making task itself. Coherence-based reasoning demonstrates the mental representations are not entirely invariant or exogenous to the process of making decisions, and suggests that representational shifts are central to decision-making process itself.

764 Ibid., p. 520. In order to perform any mental operation, the variables involved in the task must first be represented somehow in the mind. Put succinctly, "[a]ll that you know about the world and your only basis for acting on the world is found in your mental representations. "Ronald T. Kellog, Cognitive Psychology 8 (Sage 2d ed 2003). See also Lawrence W. Barsalou, 'Cogntive Psychology': An Overview for Cognitive Scientists 55 (Lawrence Erlbaum, 1992). Representation should not be understood as entailing conscious recognition. In Dennett's terms, it need not be in one's "speech centre." See D.C. Dennett, 'Content and Consciousness' 118-19 (Humanities 1969).

765 Ibid. The exact nature of mental representations is a topic of intense debate between advocates of two general approaches: connectionist models and symbolic systems. For review of the debate, see Keith J. Holyoak and John E. Hummel, 'The Proper Treatment of Symbols in a Connectionist Architecture', in Eric Dietrich and Arthur B. Markman, eds., Cognitive Dynamics: Conceptual and Representational Change in Humans and Machines 229, 229-31, (Lawrence Erlbaum, 2000); Gary F. Marcus, 'The Algebraic Mind: Integrating Connectionism and Cognitive Science', 1-4(MIT 2001). The research reported in the Article [on the footnote] is consistent with a hybrid conception of representation, called symbolic connectionism. See Keith J. Holyoak, 'Symbolic Connectionism: Toward Third-Generation Theories of Expertise', in K. Anders Ericsson and Jacqui Smith, eds., Toward a General Theory of Expertise: Prospects and Limits 301, (Cambridge, 1991); Holyoak and Hummel, 'Proper Treatment of Symbols' pp. 232-259 (articulating the theoretical position for a network-like structure of symbolic knowledge). Symbolic connectionist networks do not define variables at the neuron level. As Holyoak and Spellman explain, systematic reasoning requires symbolic representations without which links between elements would be incapable of defining meaningful relationships.

the mind as a unit, which is then connected through the network to all the other units.[766] The initial representation of a mental task is determined foremost by the rich and detailed store of background knowledge about one's physical, social, and conceptual worlds.[767] The mental model of a complex decision task contains a myriad of variables that point in more than one direction and thus do not all fit into a coherent mental model. One subset of variables [a, a, ...a] supports conclusion A, and the other subset [b, b, ...b] supports the opposite conclusion B.[768] With regard to constraint satisfaction, in all but easy cases, neither subset of variables dominates the other. Since each variable has some bearing on the task, it can be said to impose a *constraint* on the network.[769] Connectionist system processes mental tasks through a non-conscious process in which the mentally represented variables interact with one another like an electrical network. Activation spreads throughout the mental model.[770] In Simon's view, each

---

See Keith J. Holyoak and Barbara A. Spellman, 'Thinking,' in 44 Ann Rev Psych 265, 270-72 (1993). Representations are thus constructed by high-level conceptual building blocks that share some of the symbolic properties of more traditional cognitive architectures. See Stephen J. Read, Eric J. Vanman and Lynn C. Miller, 'Connectionsm, Parallel Constraint Satisfaction Processes, and Gestalt Principles: (Re)Introducing Cognitive Dynamics to Social Psychology,' in 1 Personality & Soch Psych Rev 26, 32 (1997).

766 Ibid., pp. 520-521. The principal characteristic of connectionist representations is the level of activation of the elements. The level of activation stands for the degree of the respective variable's strength, or acceptability. Elements are connected to other elements by links, which can be either positive (supportive) or negative (inhibitory). Coherent relationships are denoted by positive links; inconsistent relationship are donated by negative links. Links also vary in degree: where the association between the respective variables is strong, the link is said to carry much weight. The seminal work on constraint satisfaction theories is David Rumelhart and James McCelland, eds., 1 'Parallel Distributed Processing: Explorations in the Microstructure of Cognition' (MIT 1986). For introductions to connectionism, see Thagard, 'Coherence in Thought and Action,' pp. 1-13 (explaining the importance of coherence as a concept in philosophy and psychology): William Bechtel and Adele Abrahamsen, 'Connectionism and the Mind: An Introduction to Parallel Processing in Networks', (Basil Blackwell, 1991). For an excellent review of the field, see Read, Vanman, and Miller, in 1 Personality & Soc Psych Rev 26, 27-32.

767 Ibid., p. 521. For a review of representations of knowledge, see Markman, 'Knowledge Representation,' pp. 1-26. See also Stephen J. Read, 'Constructing Causal Scenarios: A Knowledge Structure Approach to Causal Reasoning', in 52 J Personality & Soc Psych 288 (1987).

768 Ibid.

769 Ibid. Each constraint is a function of the respective element's level of activation and the weight of its links. Each variable is said to constitute a soft constraint. See Bechtel and Abrahamsen (1991), supra note 766, pp. 58-60.

770 Ibid. Positively linked elements excite one another, while negatively linked

and every constraint influences, and is influenced by, the entire network, so that every processing cycle results in a slightly modified mental model.[771] Over time, unsupported variables or those suppressed by other variables degrade and even die out, while those that are mutually supported gain strength.

Coherence has been explained in terms of logical and conceptual relations,[772] explanatory relations,[773] constraint satisfaction,[774] or has been described as a 'seat of the pants feel'.[775] The search for a criterion for coherence can amongst others be explained by the intuition that although a set of justified beliefs must be logically consistent, mere consistency does not provide a ground for assuming that the beliefs are justified. There must be something 'more', and this 'more' is dubbed (given a nick name) coherence.

I.3.4.2. COHERENCE IN TERMS OF CAUSAL KNOWLEDGE

More recent accounts emphasize the role of abstract conceptual, mostly causal knowledge as an integral part of category representation.[776] People

---

ones inhibit each other. The induced activation of any pair of linked elements depends on their relative initial levels of activation and on the weight and sign of the link that connects them. Highly activated elements strongly affects others and are resistant to external influence; weakly activated elements hardly affect others and are sensitive to external activations.

771 Ibid.

772 Hage (2003), supra note 750, p. 6, referring to Peczenik (2008), supra note 750, section 4.1.

773 Ibid., referring to Lehrer (2000), supra note 755, pp. 100-103.

774 Ibid., referring to Thagard (2000), supra note 747; Michal Araszkiewicz (2010), 'Balancing of Legal Principles and Constraint Satisfaction', in R.G.F. Winkels (ed.), Legal Knowledge and Information Systems, (Proceedings of the Jurix 2010 conference), (Amsterdam: IOS Press, 2010), pp. 7-15; Amalia Amaya, 'Legal Justification by Optimal Coherence', in Ratio Juris 24 (2011), pp. 304-329.

775 Ibid., referring to Hilary Putman, 'Reason, Truth and History', (Cambridge: Cambridge University Press, 1981), pp. 132-133.

776 Ralf Mayrhofer and Anselm Rothe, 'Causal Status meets Coherence: The Explanatory Role of Causal Models in Categorization', in N.Miyake, D.Peebles & RP Cooper(eds), Proceedings of the 34th Annual Conference of Cognitive Science Society (pp. 743-748)2012, Austin,TX., p. 743. See G.L. Murphy & D.L. Medin,'The role of theories in conceptual coherence', in Psychological Review, 92 (1985), pp. 289-316; B. Rehder, 'Causal-based classification: A review', in B. Ross (Ed.), The Psychology of Learning and Motivation (52) (2010), pp. 39-116; B. Rehder & R. Hastie, 'Causal knowledge and categories: The effects of causal beliefs on

often represent knowledge about how strongly and why features are correlated with each other within a category.[777] This kind of causal knowledge underlying category concepts can be formalized in causal graphic models or Bayes nets.[778] Whereas the causal status effect is defined with respect to the weight of individual features, the coherence effect arises from the impact of feature interactions.[779] According to the coherence hypothesis, exemplars whose feature configurations are most coherent with the category's causal model are seen as the best members. Causal models, therefore, provide us with information about which features should go together in an exemplar.[780] One possibility is that the causal classification processes and the traditional similarity-based processes operate side-by-side; each makes an independent contribution to the ultimate categorization decision.[781] Imagine a billiard table. The cue ball rolls across the felt and strikes the 8-ball, launching the 8-ball. Most observers will report seeing the cue ball *cause* the 8-ball to move. Hume (1739) argues that impressions of causality are mere fabrications of a sophisticated mind. The impression of causality is a learned nexus from the first to second ball, based on repeated observations of the conjunction of the two motions, their spatio-temporal contiguity, and the temporal priority of the one motion relative to the other.[782] Kant (1788) argued that causality was an innate and fundamental category of cognition; Piaget (1971) made it an integral part of his theory of development; and

---

categorization, induction, and similarity', in JEP: General 130 (2001), pp. 323-360; Sloman et al.,'Feature centrality and conceptual coherence', in Cognitive Science, 22 (1998), pp. 189-228.

777 Ibid., referring to Ahn et. al., 'Effect of theory-based feature correlations on typicality judgments', in Memory & Cognition 30 (2002), pp. 107-118; Murphy & Medin (1985), Ibid.

778 Ibid. See Rehder (2003a), supra note 220; Bob Rehder, 'A causal-model theory of conceptual representation and categorization,' in JEP:LMC, 29 (2003) ["2003b"], pp. 1141-1159; M.R. Waldmann, K.J. Holyoak and A. Fratianne, 'Causal knowledge and the acquisition of category structure', in JEP : General, 124 (1995), pp. 181-206.

779 Ibid., p. 744, referring to B. Rehder (2010), supra note 777. .

780 Ibid., p. 744, referring to Rehder (2003b), supra note 778; Rehder (2010), Ibid.

781 Rehder (2003a), supra note 778, p. 740, referring to E.J. Wisniewski & D.L. Medin, 'On the interaction of theory and data in concept learning', in Cognitive Science, 18 (1994), pp. 221-282.

782 John K. Kruschke and Michael M. Fragassi, 'The perception of causality: Feature binding in interacting objects', in a research was supported in part by NIMH FIRST Award 1-R29-MH51572-01 to Kruschke, and by an Indiana University Cognitive Science Program Summer Research Fellowship to Fragassi - access to the lab at U.C. Berkeley for this research in 1986-87, referring to David Hume, 'A treaties of human nature' (1739), (Oxford, England: Oxford University Press, Republished 1980).

more recently Leyton (1992) has argued that the extraction of causality is at the core of perception and cognition.[783]

Since Hume the traditional analysis of causal relations has been that they are indistinguishable from the symmetric relation of correlation. This tradition has largely continued in modern cognitive psychology. For example, the study of causal reasoning and attribution has often assumed that the perception of causality is no more than the perception of correlation under special conditions, namely, temporal precedence (causes must not follow their effects in time), spatial contiguity, and certain assumptions regarding the default background conditions against which causal induction take place.[784] One model that has been offered as an account of the causal status effect is a *dependency model* of Sloman, Love and Ahn (1998).[785] According to the dependency model, features are more important to category membership (i.e., are more *conceptual central*) to the extent they have more *dependents*, that is, features that depend on them (directly or indirectly). A causal relation is an example of a dependency relation in which the effect depends on its cause. [The notion of causal relation then continue to the concept of causal history. To go to the concept of causal history, the starting may be 'stilumus']. In traditional Kolmogorov/Chaitin complexity, to conceive of a 'most-compact' description for a stimulus is possible, given a particular language of description. Further, 'description' in traditional Kolmogorov/Chaitin complexity refers only to the current state of the stimulus.[786] Leyton's

783 Ibid., referring to I. Kant, 'Critique of pure reason' (1788), translated by N.K. Smith (1965), (New York: St. Martin's Press, 1965); J. Piaget, 'Les Explications Causales', Presses Universitaires de France, Paris, 1971, translation by D. & M. Miles, Understanding Causality, (New York: Norton, 1974); L. Leyton, 'Simmetry, Causality, Mind' (Cambridge, MA: MIT Press, 1992).

784 Rehder (2003b), supra note 780, p. 735. See. e.g. P.W. Cheng & L.R. Novick, 'A probabilitistic contrast model of causal induction', in Journal of Personality and Social Psychology, 58 (1990), pp. 545-567; P.W. Cheng & L.R. Novick, 'Causes versus enabling conditions', in Cognition, 40 (1991), pp. 83-120; P.W. Cheng & L.R. Novick, 'Covariation in natural causes induction', in Psychological Review, 99 (1992), pp. 365-382; H.H. Kelly, 'The process of causal attribution', in American Psychologist, 28 (1973), pp. 107-128; M.W. Schustack & R.J. Sternberg, 'Evaluation of evidence in causal inference,' in Journal of Experimental Psychology: General, 110 (1981), pp. 101-120.

785 Bob Rehder and Shin Woo Kim, 'Causal Status and Coherence in Causal-Based Categorization', in Journal of Experimental Psychology: Learning, Memory, and Cognition, 2010, Vol. 36, No. 5, 1171-1206 (p. 1174), referring to Sloman et al., (1998), supra note 776.

786 Monika Krishan, 'Review of Symmetry, Causality, Mind, Michael Leyton, Cambridge, Massachusetts: MIT Press, 1992, 630 pages,' action editor: Stefan Wermter, in Book review/Cognitive Systems Research 8 (2007):131-133, ScienceDirect, Elsevier.

'representation' includes references to previous states of the stimulus that may or may not be available for inspection in the present.[787] Leyton[788] holds that a stimulus is designed by a series of operations that act to give the stimulus its present form. Every stimulus object is perceived to originate in a state of least distinguishability i.e., one that is maximally homogeneous. The associated set of operations then transform the featureless 'original' into something with greater differentiability, with increasing definition at each stage. To the mind, a stimulus is not a static object, frozen in time but rather that it comes with a past, a past that is inferred from the current form of the stimulus. The mind extracts, from the shape of an object, information about the forces that lead to its being just so. Leyton's suggestion is that the mind, in the process of forming a representation of a stimulus object, attempts to uncover the *history* of the object, as it were. Since representation involves tracing the stimulus object's history in terms of the various processes that caused the stimulus to be what it is, the result is a *causal* history of the stimulus [causal history plays an important role in knowledge formation]. Humans have always been fascinated by the widespread existence of symmetry in nature. The Gestaltists were some of the first to suggest that the mind is sensitive to regularities occurring in the environment. However, Leyton proposes that symmetry detection is not an end in itself but serves to delineate the causal trajectory of the stimulus. The particular operation that takes the stimulus past into the stimulus present is assumed to have acted along the directions of these symmetry axes. The path from the present to the past involves increasing the symmetry present in the stimulus by removing existing asymmetries at each stage of the process.

***

Causal reasoning cannot be divorced from causal theory-based categorization, insofar as a concept itself is represented as a causal structure. That is, at some level, the concept itself consists of the category features and the interrelations among those features.[789] Rehder was able to assess not just feature weights but also feature *interactions*, that is, how important certain *combinations* of features are to category membership.[790]

787 Ibid.

788 Ibid., referring to Leyton (1992), supra note 783.

789 Jennelle E. Yopchick and Nancy S. Kim, 'The influence of causal information on judgments of treatment efficacy', in Memory & Cognition 2009, 37 (1), pp. 29-41 (doi:10.3758/MC.37.1.29), p. 30, referring to Murphy & Medin (1985), supra note 777.

790 Bob Rehder and Shin Woo Kim, 'The Role of Coherence in Causal-Based Categorization', Department of Psychology, New York University, 6 Washington Place, New York, NY 10003 USA, 2008, p. 286, referring to Rehder (2003b), supra note 784.

Apparently, good category members are those that manifest the complex pattern of correlations one expects to be generated by a causal network. This sensitivity to coherence has been found in numerous studies,[791] including those testing other causal networks.[792]

The causal relationships between the features of a concept have been found to affect categorization judgments. Robust evidence for a *coherence effect* shows that exemplars inconsistent with a category's causal laws are judged less likely to be category members.[793] Consistent evidence for a *root cause effect* proves that the presence of the root cause strongly affects judgments of category membership likelihood. This effect may be orthogonal to the coherence effect; both may occur simultaneously and contribute to the overall categorization judgment. Both evidence for a *coherent effect* and that for a *root cause effect* suggest that the importance people place on root causes in categorization judgments is due to their generative nature. As the root cause ultimately gives rise (directly or indirectly) to all the other features of the concept, it is perceived as the most generative feature in the concept and, consequently, important to the concept.[794]

***

Previous studies (e.g., Rehder, 2003b) may have exaggerated coherence effects and minimized the causal status effect by use of the word 'normal' to describe atypical feature values.[795] Previous research has shown that causal knowledge influences the classification of objects. In fact, research has established a number of robust empirical generalizations regarding how the importance of a feature changes as a function of its position in a network of causal relationships.[796] A feature will become more important

791 Ibid., referring to J. Marsh and W. Ahn, 'The role of causal status versus inter-feature links in feature weighting', in R. Sun & N. Miyake (eds.), in Paper - Proceedings of the 28th Annual Conference of the Cognitive Science Society, 2006, pp. 561-566.

792 Ibid., referring to Rehder & Hastie (2001), supra note 776; Rehder (2003a), supra note 781; B. Rehder and S. Kim, 'How causal knowledge affects classification: A generative theory of categorization', in Journal of Experimental Psychology: Learning, Memory, and Cognition, 32 (2006), pp. 659-683.

793 Yopchick & Kim (2009), supra note 789, p. 30, quoting Rehder (2003a), Ibid.

794 Ibid. See e.g., Ahn et. al., 'Causal status as a determinant of feature centrality', in Cognitive Psychology, 41 (2000), pp. 361-416; Rehder & Kim (2006), supra note 792.

795 Rehder & Kim (2008), supra note 790, p. 285, referring to Marsh & Ahn (2006), supra note 791.

796 Rehder (2003b), supra note 784, p. 710, referring to W. Ahn, 'Why are different features central for natural kinds and artifacts? The role of causal status

to the extent it has many causes.[797] According to causal-model theory, people's intuitive theories about categories of objects consist of a model of the category in which both a category's feature and the causal mechanism among those features are explicitly represented.[798] The results of Rehder's research on Categorization as causal reasoning 2003 support the claim that people have a representation of the causal mechanism that link category features, and that they categorize by evaluating whether an object's features were likely to have been generated by those mechanism. That is, people have models of the world that lead them to expect a certain distribution of features in category members, and consider exemplars good category members to the extent they manifest those expectations. A key assumption of causal-model theory is that the presence of causal knowledge changes one's expectations regarding not only individual features, but also the entire combination of features that a category member is likely to display.[799] This result was predicted on the grounds that a primary role of theoretical knowledge is to determine how well the features of an object relate to, cohere with, one another. Rehder (2003a, b) and Rehder & Kim (2006, 2010) have revealed a certain correlation between coherence, category and causality.[800] They have demonstrated *coherence effects* in which good category members are those that exhibit the pattern of interfeature correlations one expects to be generated by causal relations.

Ahn (1998) and Ahn, Kim, Lassaline and Dennis (2000) suggested that features would be more heavily weighted to the extent they were more causal, that is, more deeply embedded in a network of causal relationships. Sloman, Love and Ahn (1998) have proposed that features that are 'depended on' are less 'mutable' (and hence more important to

---

in determining feature centrality,' in Cognition, 69 (1998), pp. 135-178; Ahn et.al., (2000), supra note 794; Rehder, in press; Sloman et al., (1998), supra note 785.

797 Ibid., referring to Rehder & Hastie (2001), supra note 792.

798 Ibid., p. 711. See e.g., B.C. Malt & E.E. Smith, 'Correlated properties in natural categories', in Journal of Verbal Learning and Verbal Behavior, 23 (1984), pp. 250-269; Ahn et. al. (2002), supra note 777; Rehder in press, supra note 796; Rehder & Hastie (2001), Ibid. [footnote 797]; E.J. Wisniewski, 'Prior knowledge and functionally relevant features in concept learning', in Journal of Experimental Psychology: Learning, Memory, and Cognition, 21 (1995), pp. 449-468; B. Rehder & B.H. Ross (2001), 'Abstract coherent categories', in Journal of Experimental Psychology: Learning, Memory, and Cognition, 27(2001), pp. 1261-1275.

799 Ibid., pp. 734-735.

800 Bob Rehder and Jay B. Martin, 'Towards A Generative Model of Causal Cycles', in: Kokinov, B., Karmiloff-Smith, A., Nersessian N.J., (eds.), European Perspectives on Cognitive Science, (New Bulgarian University Press, 2011), referring to Rehder (2003a, b), supra note 793 & 778; Rehder & Kim (2006, 2010), supra note 792.

category membership) than those that are not,[801] where a cause-effect link is an example of a dependency relation in which the effect depends on the cause.[802] According to Mayrhofer and Rothe, only those feature combinations matter that are relevant with respect to the underlying causal mechanisms, because it is the mechanism but not regularity that has explanatory value.[803] When causal mechanisms are established in terms of typical features, the causal model serves as an explanation why the category's prototype or prototypical exemplar (i.e., all features present) is as it is. Since the presence vs. absence of the cause feature modulates the positive influence of the effect features, we expect membership rating that – in the aggregate – exhibit a strong causal status effect.[804] Rehder contends that, according to causal-model theory, people's causal models of categories influence their classification behavior by leading them to expect certain distributions of features in category members. Specifically, a to-be-classified object is considered a category member to the extent that its features were likely to have been generated by the category's causal law, such that combinations of features that are likely to be produced by a category's causal mechanisms are viewed as good category members and those unlikely to be produced by those mechanism are viewed as poor category members.[805] As a result, causal-model theory will assign a low degree of category membership to objects that have many broken feature correlations (i.e., cases where causes are present and effects are absent or vice versa). Objects that have many preserved correlations (i.e., causes and effects both present or both absent) will receive a higher degree of category membership because it is just such objects that are likely to be generated by causal law.

When features of categories are linked by causal relations, two different effects on classification judgments have been documented. The first, the *causal status* effect, is that features that appear earlier in a causal network (and thus are more 'causal') are weighed more heavily in classification than less causal features. The second, the *coherence effect*, is that good category members are those whose combination of features make sense in light of causal laws (e.g., cause and effect feature both

801 Rehder (2003b), supra note 799, pp. 740-741, referring to Sloman et al., (1998), supra note 785.

802 Ibid., referring to Ahn (1998), supra note 796; Ahn et. al., (2000), supra note 796.

803 Mayrhofer & Rothe (2012), supra note 780, p. 45. See F.C. Keil, 'Explanation and understanding', in Annual Review of Psychology, 57 (2006), pp. 227-254 (for an overview).

804 Ibid.

805 Rehder (2003b), supra note 802, p. 712.

present and both absent).[806] Some researchers propose that causal knowledge determines the individual feature weights in categorization judgments,[807] whereas others, however emphasize the role of feature combinations and whether those are coherent with the statistical regularities imposed by the category's causal model. [808]

A *causal status effect* occurs when features that are causes are more important to category membership than their effects. As said before, features that appear earlier in a category's causal network (and thus are 'more' causal) carry greater weight in categorization decisions. The presence of a causal status effect does not imply that features' causal status is the sole factor determining their categorization weight.[809] According to causal status hypothesis, features that are causally more central (i.e., that have more dependents in the causal model or that appear earlier in a causal chain) have greater influence in categorization decisions when other perceptual (e.g., salience) or statistical (e.g., cue validity) properties of the material are held constant or controlled for.[810] The causal status of a feature is, therefore, an important determinant of its decision weight. Conceptually, the causal status effect has been linked to psychological essentialism.[811] Hence, people believe in things having essences that make them the objects they are. An essence, then, is the (unobservable) root cause for the surface features that can be observed in category members.[812] Features that have a high causal status might be seen as most diagnostic for an object's essence and, therefore, category membership.[813]

I.3.4.3. COHERENCE EFFECT

A coherence effect occurs when combinations of features that are consistent with causal law provide additional evidence of category membership.[814] The

806 Rehder & Kim (2008), supra note 790, p. 285.

807 Mayrhofer & Rothe, supra note 804, p. 747. See Ahn et al., (2000), supra note 802, for causal status hypothesis.

808 Ibid. See e.g., Rehder (2003a), supra note 793; Rehder (2003b), supra note 796; Rehder & Kim (2010), supra note 785, for coherence hypothesis.

809 Rehder & Kim (2010), Ibid., p. 1171.

810 Mayrhofer & Rothe (2012), supra note 807, p. 744. See Ahn et al. (2000), supra note 807.

811 Ibid., referring to Ahn et al. (2000), Ibid.

812 Ibid., referring to S.A. Gelman & H.M. Wellman, 'Insides and essences: Early understandings of the nonobvious', in Cognition, 38 (1991), pp. 213-244.

813 Ibid. See e.g., Ahn et al. (2000), supra note 811; Gelman & Wellman (1991), Ibid; See also Rehder & Kim (2010), supra note 809.

814 Rehder & Kim (2010), Ibid., p. 1171.

method deployed by Rehder and Kim (2006) allows for an assessment of not only feature weights but also feature *interactions*, that is, how important certain *combinations* of features are for forming good category members. In fact, research has established that participants are quite sensitive to whether potential category members exhibit not just the right features considered individually but also the right combination of features, a phenomenon known as the coherent effect.[815] Coherence has been shown to affect every category-based judgment in which it has been assessed. Coherence affects category-based induction, with more coherent items supporting stronger induction.[816] Coherence also affects categorization even when feature relations are neither explicitly causal nor provided as part of the experiment.[817] In other words, coherence is one of the most important manifestations of knowledge-based (or 'theory-based') categories.[818]

It is noteworthy that coherence effects not only run deep, they also run wide; they can spread from one case to the next. Coherence spread from a verdict, through the common issue to another following verdict, and reached as far as causing shifts in other variables in that case.[819] According to Mayrhofer and Rothe, causal knowledge is important in categorization because it provides people with explanatory links such that they can make sense of presented exemplar.[820] Thus, categorization is seen as inference to the best explanation. They derived at least two possible explanatory roles of causal models; First, a causal model can serve as explanation why prototypical exemplar is as it is. Second, a causal model can also serve as explanation why a category member might deviate from the prototypical exemplar. Mayrhofer and Rothe found a causal-status effect in the first case and a coherence effect in the latter one, suggesting both are faces of the same coin.

Since as has been laid out above that consistency is the requirement for coherence, consistency and coherence form a path or paths along the corridor of which classification or categorization may appear or be identified. Coherence, especially coherence within a category as a coherent set, constraints human mind in order to be consistent and to avoid [anomalous] arbitrariness in decision-making therefore leads to the pursuit of predictability and certainty.

---

815 Ibid., p. 1173, referring to Rehder & Kim (2006), supra note 792.

816 Rehder & Kim (2008), supra note 790, p. 285. [See] e.g., A.L. Patalano & B.H. Ross, 'The role of category coherence in experience-based prediction', in Psychonomic Bulletin & Review, 14 (2007), pp. 629-634; B. Rehder & R. Hastie, 'Category coherence and category-based property induction', in Cognition, 91 (2004), pp. 113-153.

817 Ibid., referring to Wisniewski (1995), supra note 798.

818 Ibid.

819 Simon (2004), supra note 762, p. 537.

820 Mayrhofer & Rothe (2012), supra note 813, p. 748.

I.3.5. GENERATIVITY AND TRANSFORMATIVITY THROUGH SIMILARITY, ANALOGY AND COHERENCE

This sub-chapter is the conclusion of Chapter I.3. As has already been shown in Sub-chapter I.3.1 above that similarity is generative-transformational. The philosopher Alvin Goldman pre-figures the notion of similarity as transformation in naturalized epistemology.[821] Hahn, Chater and Richardson propose that similarity is determined by the transformation distance between representations: entities which are perceived to be similar have representations which are readily transformed into one another, whereas transforming between dissimilar entities requires many transformations.[822] Similarity judgments are inferences about generative process, and that two objects appear similar when they are likely to have been generated by the same process.[823] A generative theory of similarity is a notion often invoked by models of high-level cognition. Two objects are similar to the extent that they seem to have been generated by the same underlying process. The generative approach is relevant to the entire spectrum of applications, but they are particularly interested in high-level similarity.[824] Keil discusses the case of an animal that is born a skunk, then undergoes surgery that leaves it looking exactly like a raccoon. Since the animal is generated in the same way as a skunk (born of skunk parents), people conclude that it remains a skunk, no matter how it appears on the surface.[825] These examples suggest that the generative approach may be broadly useful in explaining high-level similarity judgments.[826]

Similarity evolved for the purpose of comparing real-world objects. If so, then knowledge about what kinds of objects are likely to exist should be deeply bound up with the notion of similarity. This prediction task is of practical importance. In this matter, generative processes help pick up the features critical for the similarity comparison.[827] The generative approach is uniquely well-suited to explaining high-level similarity judgments. Intuitive theories often specify exactly the kind of information needed by the generative approach: information about the causal histories of objects.[828] Similarity judgments are inferences about generative processes.

821 Hahn et al.(2003), supra note 607, p. 28, referring to Goldman (1986), supra note 615.

822 Ibid., p. 1.

823 Kemp et al. (2005), supra note 617.

824 Ibid.

825 Ibid., referring to F.C. Keil, 'Concepts, kinds, and cognitive development', (Cambridge, MA: MIT Press, 1989).

826 Ibid.

827 Ibid.

828 Ibid.

The generative processes have been simpler than the processes that appear in people's intuitive theories.[829] The generative framework should help to explain how similarity judgments are guided by intuitive theories. A formal theory of similarity had been developed and compared to the transformational account which suggests that similarity depends on the number of operations required to transform one object into the other.[830] In several cases the assessment of similarity relies on inference about generative processes. Suppose we are shown a prototype object and asked to predict what similar objects might exist in the world. One of the predictions is that objects are produced by small perturbations of the process that generated the prototype. By definition, an object produced by a small perturbation of an existing generative process will have a plausible causal history.[831]

The transformational approach holds that s1 is similar to s2 if s1 can be readily transformed into s2. People assume that every transformation is reversible – if there is a transformation mapping s1 into s2, there must also be a transformation mapping s2 into s1. Intuitively, the process tends to generate small variations on the chosen prototype, where the permissible variations depends on the set of transformation. The transformation distance is between s1 and s2.[832] From the researches and approaches as above mentioned, it has been proven that similarity is transformational and generative. The notion of transformational generative similarity will be combined with analogy and coherence in order to indentify further transformational generative notion for the purpose of this writing.

Sub-chapter I.3.2. has identified that analogy is generative-transformational. Hesse's theory of material analogy has shown that analogy generates the insight of the target situation by matching the similarities between the source situation and the target situation based on the already known insight of the source situation.[833] As already mentioned before, analogies are widely recognized as playing an important *heuristic* role, as aids to discovery. They have been employed, in a wide variety of settings and with considerable success, to generate insight and to formulate possible solutions to problems.[834] Rom Harré holds analogy

829 Ibid.

830 Ibid., referring to Hahn et al. (2003), supra note 821.

831 Ibid.

832 Ibid.

833 Bartha (2013), supra note 650, § 3.3, referring to Hesse (1966), supra note 650.

834 Ibid., § 2.

is generative,[835] and so does Hesse.[836] According to Kemp, Bernstein and Tenenbaum, analogies form one special family of comparisons between relational systems, and the generative approach offers a view of analogy that is intriguingly different from [other] previous approaches.[837] Featural and transformational models generally assume that systems are analogous to the extent that there is a structure-preserving one-to-one map between their elements.[838] The generative approach, however, allows analogous systems to have very different numbers of elements, as long as they appear to have been produced by the same process.[839] Analogy is adopted by the generative approach.

Sub-chapter I.3.3. has been on consistency as condition of coherence. Prominent consistency researchers argued that consistency attainment should be deemed as proactively making sense of the world. In explaining consistency, Heider says that conceptions, symmetry, consonance, balance and simplicity, are, of course, implied in that idea with which Gestalt theory started and which always was central to it, namely, the idea of a 'good' figure. This model implies a number of different entities with certain properties and standing in certain relations, which make up a constellation of factors tending toward a standard state.[840] Elements that 'go together' in states of 'order and coherenece' tend to form stable structures.[841] Pepitone claimed that the pressure to reduce inconsistency follow from the fact that consistent structures 'are simpler to maintain than distinctions, discrepancies and contradictions',[842] so inconsistency is to be reduced.[843] K.W. Back contended that consistency makes it possible for the organism to structure the world in an economical way to react to facts which are connected in a consistent way.[844] From those arguments by prominent researchers, Simon and Holyoak have drawn a conclusion.[845] They have

835 Losee (1972, 1980), supra note 624, p. 145, referring to Harré (1970), supra note 624, p. 125.

836 Bartha (2013), supra note 833, § 3.3, referring to Hesse (1966), supra note 833.

837 Kemp et al. (2005), supra note 832, referring to C. Kemp, T.L. Griffiths and J.B. Tennembaum, 'Discovering latent classes in relational data,' in AI Memo 2004-019, MIT.

838 Ibid., referring to Gentner (1983), supra note 633.

839 Ibid.

840 Simon & Holyoak (2002), supra note 667, p. 283, referring to Heider (1960), supra note 680, p. 68.

841 Ibid., referring to Heider (1960), Ibid.

842 Ibid., p. 284, referring to Pepitone (1966), supra note 690.

843 Ibid., quoting Pepitone (1966), Ibid.

844 Ibid., pp. 284-285, referring to Back (1968), supra note 691.

845 Ibid., p. 284.

concluded that consistency attainment should be deemed as proactively making sense of the world.

Coherence as discussed in sub-chapter I.3.4 above has been proven generative-transformational. Bayesian model is also generative, when such a model uses the likelihood under the true generative process to judge category membership. The full Bayesian model, which maintains uncertainty over generating concepts, can make different predictions in certain cases.[846] A generative Bayesian model uses the likelihood under the true generative process to judge category membership. Therefore, judging category membership through coherence is generative in nature [in category's causal model in terms of causal relation as well as category membership].[847] Rehder and Martin say that one important advantage of the generative model is that it provides a straightforward account of coherence effects[848]. A population of category members generated by a causal network should exhibit the expected pattern of correlations between causally related features. Thus a likely category member is one that maintains those correlations.

Applications of the generative approach can also be found in generative theories of categorization.[849] The generative model is a model on causal knowledge and classification.[850] The generative model (Rehder & Kim, 2010) assumes that objects will be considered good category members to the extent they maintain correlation that are expected on the basis of causal relation.[851] Rehder & Kim (2010) showed that the generative model predicts the observed sensitivity of the causal status effect to causal strength. Specifically, if a causal link is deterministic, then an effect should be at least as prevalent among category members as its cause (and more prevalent when the effect has additional causes), and thus the cause can be less important to category membership decisions than the effect.[852] A generative model offered by Rehder, 2003a, 2003b, Rehder & Kim 2006 is as an account of causal knowledge and classification.[853] Building on

846 Stuhlmuller et al. (2010), supra note 532.

847 Ibid.

848 Rehder & Martin (2011), supra note 800.

849 Kemp et al. (2005), supra note 839, referring to J.R.Anderson, 'The adaptive nature of human categorization', in Psychological Review, 98(3) (1991), pp. 409-429; Feldman (1997), supra note 534; Rehder (2003b), supra note 805.

850 Rehder & Kim (2010), supra note 785, p. 1174, referring to Rehder (2003a), supra note 781; Rehder (2003b), Ibid.; Rehder & Kim (2006), supra note 792.

851 Ibid., p. 1176.

852 Rehder & Martin (2011), supra note 848, referring to Rehder & Kim (2010), Ibid.

853 Rehder & Kim (2010), supra note 850, p. 1174, referring to Rehder (2003a), supra note 850; Rehder (2003b), supra note 850; Rehder & Kim (2006), supra

causal-model theory (Sloman & Lagnado, 2005; Waldman & Holyoak, 1992), the generative model assumes that interfeature causal relations are represented as probabilistic causal mechanism and that classifiers consider whether an object is likely to have been produced or generated by those causal mechamism. Objects that are likely to have been generated by a category's causal model are considered to be good category members, and those unlikely to be generated are poor category members.[854] An account of *coherence effects* and correct predictions regarding the strength of causal links is an advantage of the generative model.[855] When features of categories are linked by causal relations, the *coherence effect* is that good category members are those whose combination of features make sense in light of causal laws (*e.g.*, cause and effect feature both present and both absent).[856] A population of category members generated by a causal network should exhibit the expected pattern of correlations between causally related features. Thus a likely category member is one that maintains those correlations, so a straightforward account of coherent effect is in the generative model.[857] Rehder and Martin propose an extension to the generative model that addresses causal cycles.[858] Importantly, this proposal builds on the basic insight provided by Kim, Luhman, Pierce and Ryan (2009) regarding the "unfolding" of causal cycles one time step. However, their account will enjoy the advantages of the generative model, including an account of coherence effects and correct predictions regarding the strength of causal links.

The generative model of Kemp, Bernstein and Tenenbaum and the transformational model offer precisely the same expressive power. The two models can mimic each other – given a particular choice of the transformation for the transformation model, there will be generative processes that allow the generative model to make exactly the same prediction.[859] Even though the generative model of Kemp, Bernstein and Tenenbaum is different from or might be broader in scope than Chomskyan generative theory, both express the notion of generativity.

In conclusion of the researches and identification as above described, similarity, analogy, consistency and coherence synergically cause generative-transformational processes. This generative-transformational process [or one similar to this] in legal reasoning will be addressed [and identified] in

---

note 850.

854 Ibid., pp. 1174-1175, referring to Sloman & Lagnado (2005), supra note 561; Waldman & Holyoak (1992), supra note 561.

855 Rehder & Martin (2011), supra note 848.

856 Rehder & Kim (2008), supra note 790, p. 285.

857 Rehder & Martin (2011), supra note 855.

858 Ibid.

859 Kemp et al. (2005), supra note 849.

Chapter IV, and this identification is the focus of this book which makes effort to declare that legal reasoning is generative-transformational or that there is transformational-generative law.

CHAPTER II

Descriptive and Prescriptive Jurisprudence

II.1. DESCRIPTIVE JURISPRUDENCE

II.1.1. OVERVIEW

Following Chomskyan theory in which prescriptivity and descriptivity are existent in grammar, the present author sketches out in this book the existence of descriptivity and prescriptivity in law, as already expressly or implicitly argued by many legal doctrinal writers. Descriptive jurisprudence seems to vary from positivist, historical, sociological and athropological viewpoints to realist viewpoints, including behavioristic, sociological and Scandinavian wings, whereas some doctrinal writers such as Fuller and Finnis include the description of normative dimension of law in their writings.

Descriptive legal philosophers are concerned with the boundaries between the things of the world which are law and those which are not. They try to provide an account of the few essential features that something in the world has to have in order to count as an example or instantiation of law. Theorists try to discover the necessary features that all laws have in common, the features in virtue of which they are all laws. In trying to articulate those features, they bring to the fore what is already found in practice. To articulate those features does not aim to change the practice; rather, it tries to describe what the practice, prior to and regardless of the theorists' analysis, is, without morally evaluating it.[1] Some look at the world and see order and patterns; others look at the same world and see multiplicity, diversity and difference.[2] Hart has concluded that in spite of many variations in different cultures and in different times, [law] has taken the same general form and structure.[3] Twinning sees a 'great juristic

1 Danny Priel, 'The Boundaries of Law and the Purpose of Legal Philosophy,' in Law and Philosphy, 2008/09, p. 3.

2 Danny Priel, 'Two Models of General Jurisprudence' (2013), in Comparative Research in Law & Political Economy, Research Paper No. 39/2013, p. 1. Cf AW Brian Simpson, 'Reflection on The Concept of Law', (OUP, 2011), p. 125. This is Simpson's gloss on the famous distinction between the fox and the hedgehogs.

3 Ibid., p. 2, referring to HLA Hart, 'The Concept of Law', 3rd ed., (OUP, 2012), p. 240; also David Hume, 'Dialogues on Natural Religion', (OUP, 1993), p. 113.

bazaar': colorful, diverse and filled with different legal specimens suffused with local culture. The legal world is more varied and plentiful than other legal theorists have described it, and that any attempt to capture all its manifestations in a single, fairly unified account is hopeless.[4] Twinning's overall 'message is anti-reductionist: it emphasis the complexity of legal phenomenon and warns against simplistic, exaggerated, false, meaningless, superficial and ethnocentric generalizations about law in the world as whole.[5] Though distinct, this [prescriptive] idea seems to be a piece with Twinning's descriptivism: just as we should not impose our categories on legal phenomenon, just as we should not try to theorize them in a way that could be seen to impose upon them our cultural biases, so we should abandon the idea (and ideal) of law that applies to all.[6] The entire enterprise of descriptive jurisprudence is concerned with the need to be able to separate law from non-law. The dilemma of descriptive general jurisprudence is either to adopt question-begging criteria for the category of law, or to abandon all criteria. Hart was caught on the first of this dilemma; Twinning, on the second.[7]

In order to be able to give a descriptive account of the "nature" of law the philosopher must give an account that will cover only those things that are laws. If she includes within her 'sample' things that are not laws or excludes some things that are laws, the account will be incorrect.[8] Dworkin often says that his theory is a better account of existing practice [called 'law']. But suppose it were proven conclusively that this is not the case, none of the significant elements of his theory (e.g., that law is an interpretive practice, that judges should engage in some kind of moral reasoning etc.) would be undermined in the slightest, he could simply respond: 'that's too bad; let us change our practice then.[9] Marmor contends that descriptive law 'does not purport to justify or legitimize any aspect of its subject matter' and that it is 'morally neutral', i.e., that it need not take a stance on any particular moral or political issues, nor is it committed to any moral or political evaluations.[10] Marmor distinghuises between describing an

4 Ibid., p. 2, referring to William Twinning, 'Globalization and Legal Scholarship,' Butterworths, 2000, p. 19.

5 Ibid., p. 2, referring to Twinning (2000), Ibid.

6 Ibid., p. 9.

7 Ibid., p. 7.

8 Danny Priel, 'Evaluating Descriptive Jurisprudence', (2007), in American Journal of Jurisprudence: Vol. 52: Iss. 1, Article 6, p. 146.

9 Ibid., p. 147 [accompanying text omitted].

10 Ibid., p. 139, referring to Andrei Marmor, 'Legal Positivism: Still Descriptive and Moral Neutral', in Oxford Journal of Legal Studies 26 (2006) 683. Priel is not sure how independent the two alleged features of legal positivism are. As Marmor defines the terms any theory that is morally neutral will also be descriptive (though

evaluative attitude and making an evaluative judgment,[11] adopting the same view that Hart neatly summarized when he said that '[d]escription may still be a description, even when what is described is an evaluation'.[12] Nance's definition of law best reflects the purpose of neutrality and objectivity, a desire not to prejudge the normative and empirical connection to be developed, as well as a modesty, born of experience, with regard to our ability to cut to the heart of the matter by a simple definitional exercise.[13] In Priel's view, a rough and ready definition of descriptive jurisprudence is that it is concerned with giving us an account what law is, or it is sometimes put, that it is concerned with law's 'nature' or 'essence'.[14] In giving such an account the theorist refrains from making judgments about the practice or suggesting any changes to it. He or she only aims to describe what the practice, or the most important features of it, happen to be.

II.1.2. LEGAL POSITIVIST

Positive philosophy which had appeared in classical times made greater progress in more recent times. Bentham propounded that the law should be viewed from its utility standpoint, and the test of utility (greatest resultant happiness for the greatest number) should be the only method for law improvement in the reform of English law in nineteenth century, rather than accepting slavishly some innate metaphysical, moral, or Natural law, because such a slavish acceptance was a great hindrance to that task.[15] Bentham's analysis as to happiness and sufferings was known as *'felicific calculus'*.[16] Using Bentham's idea as a basis, John Austin in his *Analytical*

---

the opposite is not true).

11 Ibid., p. 149, referring to Marmor (2006), Ibid., pp. 701-702.

12 Ibid., p. 149, referring to Hart (2012), supra note 862, p. 244.

13 Dale A. Nance, 'Legal Theory and the Pivotal Role of the Concept of Coercion', in University of Colorado Law Review, Volume 57, Number 1, Fall 1985, pp. 6-7. A similar point is emphasized by Professor Nonet and Selznick in distinguishing between "weak definitions" and the "strong theories" which are to be built thereon. See P. NONET & P. SELZNICK,'LAW AND SOCIETY IN TRANSITION: TOWARD RESPONSIVE LAW' 8-18 (1978).

14 Priel (2008/2009), supra note 860, pp. 1-2.

15 Jeremy M. Miller, 'The Science of Law: The Maturing of Jurisprudence into Fundamental Principles in Fairness', 1985, in Western State University Law Review, Volume 13, Spring 1986, Number 2, p. 374, referring to Jeremy Bentham, 'An Introduction to the Principles of Morals and Legislation', in Approaches to Ethics, 2nd ed., 1969, pp. 307-308 [Jeremy Bentham, 'An Introduction to the Principles of Morals and Legislation ch. IV (1892)', and 'The Theory of legislation' (Ogden ed. 1932)].

16 Edwin W. Patterson, Law in Scientific Age, (New York and London: Columbia University Press, 1963), pp. 49-50.

Jurisprudence holds that the true essence of law is 'the command of the sovereign by sanction'. Law was simply that which was in the lawbooks or otherwise ordered by the government.[17] Austin's remarkable contribution in legal theory was 'a change' from 'the concept of just law' to 'the concept of law as the sovereign's command' and to clearly state that law and power are closely related.[18] Among legal positivist philosophers of *Allgemeine Recthslehre* were Adolf Merkel, Binding, Bierling, Thon, Bergbohm, and Vanni. *Allgemeine Recthslehre* was 'a critical revision of the elements common to different branches of jurisprudence'.[19] Those legal thinkers attempted generalization of certain restricted data of a transitory historical period or of a specific matter only, they did not attempt a universal synthesis.[20] Del Vechhio says that the school's concept is usually 'a generic data or sign of a number of particular things', not 'the idea of a substance common to them and belonging objectively to all the species'.[21]

Positivism is primarily a conceptual theory about the nature of law.[22] Conceptual viewpoint is generally formalistic. 'Formalism' is committed to the descriptive claim that judges respond primarily - indeed, perhaps exclusively - to the rational demands of the applicable rules of law and modes of legal reasoning.[23] The Formalist's descriptive claim is that judges are (primarily) rule-responsive.[24] Formalism is a claim about how judges do – and ought to – decide cases.[25] Positivism is a general scientific orientation the influence of which on the definition of law is one which emphasizes

---

17 Vilhelm Aubert, In Search of Law, Sociological Approaches to Law, (Oxford: Martin Robertson, 1983), p. 9; Miller (1985), supra note 874, p. 374, referring to G. Christie, 'Austin, The Province of Jurisprudence Determined', in Jurisprudence, ed. 1973 ["Christie 1973a"], pp. 471-474.

18 Ibid.

19 Giorgio Del Vechhio, 'The Concept of Nature and the Principle of Law', in his "The Formal Basis of Law" (1908), (Boston: Boston Printing Co., 1914, reprinted by Fred B. Rothman & Sons, 1969), pp. 110-111, referring to Merkel's article "Ueber das Verhaltnis der Rechtsphilosophie zur 'positiven' Rechtswissenschaft und zum allgemenine Theil derselben."

20 Ibid.

21 Ibid., pp. 112-113, referring to Petrone, 'La fase recentissima della Filosofia del diritto in Germania,' p. 139.

22 Leiter (1997), supra note 161, n.158.

23 Ibid., p. 278 [accompanying text omitted].

24 Ibid. "Formalism" can also name a normative view, to the effect that judges ought to be primarily rule- and legal-reason-responsive. Theories of adjudication, of course, typically make both descriptive and normative claims. See Brian Leiter, 'Heidegger and the Theory of Adjudication', in 106 YALE L.J. 253 (1996) ["1996b"], pp. 255-258.

25 Ibid., n.158.

predictivism even with regard to social science methodology.[26] Nothing of a prescriptive character then follows – certainly not, for example, any right to rule or obligation (*prima facie* or all things considered) to obey the law.[27] The positivists are descriptive writers. The descriptive theorist aims to give an account of law as an existing legal practice.[28] The touchstone of positivism is the distinction between description and prescription, in large part of a rejection of classical teleological metaphysics.[29] In the context of jurisprudence, this is manifested as an insistence upon a distinction between 'analytical jurisprudence' and 'normative jurisprudence', the former being concerned with the analysis of the concepts and structures of 'law as it is', the latter being concerned with evaluative criticism of law.[30]

Austin argues there exists a determinate group of persons, the sovereign, the general commands of which are habitually obeyed by others in the community and which is not in the habit of obeying anyone else.[31] He might nevertheless reject the gunman's action as an instance of legal phenomena, since the gunman is not the sovereign in the society.[32] Even though Austin does speak of 'superiority' and 'inferiority' as implicit in commands, he clarifies that the relationship involved must be understood in terms of power, rather than authority.[33] This manifests Austin's positivistic effort to define law in wholly non-evaluative terms.[34] Kelsen writes: "[A] theory of law must begin by defining its objective matter, and then proceeds ....to arrive at a definition of law, it is convenient to start from the usage of

---

26 Nance (1985), supra note 872, p. 21.

27 Ibid., p. 23 [accompanying text and footnote omitted].

28 Priel (2008/2009), supra note 873, p. 20.

29 Nance (1985), supra note 885, p. 10. See H.L.A. HART, 'THE CONCEPT OF LAW' (1961), p. 180 et. seq. See also J. FINNIS, 'NATURAL LAW AND NATURAL RIGHTS' (1980), Ch. II.

30 Ibid., p. 11. See e.g., J. MURPHY & J. COLEMAN, 'THE PHILOSOPHY OF LAW,' (1984), p. I, 22. Aside from the separation of analytical jurisprudence from normative jurisprudence, the identification of the essential features of positivism is extremely problematic. Many philosophers regard the unifying theme of analytical positivism to be the insistence upon having a purely formal test for determining the legal validity of a given rule, i.e., a test which is independent of the content of the rule. For example: "Whatever X says is the law is the law." Thus, X is said to posit the law. As a reaction to classical natural law, there is also a demand for a test which is independent of divine sanction (vt: Z, X # God) and of authority inherent in other non-human sources (viz., X # Nature). See generally Murphy & Coleman (1984). Ibid., pp. 13-38.

31 Ibid., referring to J. AUSTIN, 'THE PROVINCE OF JURISPRUDENCE DETERMINED,' (H.L.A. Hart ed. 1954) (first published in 1832).

32 Ibid., pp. 11-12.

33 Ibid., pp. 11, referring to Austin (1954), supra note, 890, pp. 24-25.

34 Ibid.

language, that is, to determine the meaning of the word 'law' as equivalent to the German word *Recht*, French *driot*, Italian *diritto*.[35] Our task will be to examine whether the social phenomena described by these words have common characteristics by which they may be distinguished from similar phenomena, and whether these characteristics are significant enough to serve as elements for a concept of social-scientific cognition.[36] Kelsen arrives at two features of law which are characteristic and significant: (1) these 'objects' are systems of norms for human behavior (*i.e.*, 'social orders'); and (2) they are coercive. This means that such orders react against certain events regarded as undesirable because detrimental to society, especially against human behavior of this kind, with a coercive act.[37] A requirement of effectiveness ('by and large') of the system arises from (i) Kelsen's claim[38] that one cannot have a 'system' of norms without a basic norm with reference to which the validity of the other norms is determined and which itself is simply 'presupposed', together with (ii) his claim that an ineffective norm cannot be presupposed. It is not explained why a norm which is not 'lastingly effective' is not presupposed. This appears to be an empirical claim about the behavior of 'norm presupposing'.

Building upon Kelsen, Hart[39] develops his theory that the distinctive feature of law is its combination of primary and secondary rules, the latter including (in particular) a 'rule of recognition' analogous in some ways to Kelsen's basic norms.[40] In doing so, Hart utilizes an important set of methodological categories, when a social group has certain rules of conduct, this fact affords an opportunity for many closely related yet different kinds of assertion; for it is possible to be concerned with the rules, either merely as an observer who does not himself accept them, or as a member of the group which accepts and uses them as guides to conduct. We may call these respectively the 'external' and the 'internal' points of view. Statements made from the external point of view may themselves be of different kinds. Hart still believes that law should be made, described and should

---

35 Ibid., p. 14 [footnotes omitted].

36 Ibid., pp. 13-14, referring to Kelsen (1967), infra note 896, pp. 30-31.

37 Hans Kelsen, Pure Theory of Law, translation from the Second (Revised and Enlarged) German Edition by Max Knight, (Berkeley, Los Angeles, London: University of California Press, 1967), p. 33.

38 Nance (1985), supra note 888, pp. 14-15, referring to Kelsen (1967), Ibid., § 34. See also Kelsen (1967), Ibid., p. 31.

39 Ibid., p. 16, referring to Hart (1961), supra note 888, pp. 86-87.

40 Ibid., referring to Hart (1961), Ibid., V-VI. By a "primary rule" Hart means a rule directed to all individuals in the social group indicating how the individuals should or should not act in various circumstances. "Secondary rules" are rules about the primary rules, about how the latter can be authoritatively identified, changed to specific cases. Hart (1961), Ibid., pp. 89-95.

develop by 'use of the utilitarian formula working through Positivism'.[41] Law, according to Hart's definition, is as approximately the acceptance by the people of the soverign and thus of the rules promulgated by that sovereign. He wrote that bad law was law. Hart grounded his account of law in an analysis of a *practice*. Practices for Hart are rule-governed activities accompanied by a certain attitude of 'acceptance', and it is in the idea of law as a kind of practice that Hart thought to have found the key to the science of jurisprudence.[42] Hart thought that philosophical *method* of introspection and conceptual analysis could answer this question better than any 'external' observation of the kind practiced by sociologists. Hart opted for 'descriptive jurisprudence' because he was (mild) moral sceptic and also because of his non-institutional conception or morality.[43] A major defect in much of the earlier theory, according to Hart, is its tendency to opt for the third point of view, which Hart calls the 'extreme external point of view', and is exemplified by attempts to characterize 'legal obligation' as referring to no more than a prediction of the behavior of officials.[44] Hart eschews the behaviorist 'extreme external point of view', presumably in favor of a 'theoretical' approach which entails a *non-extreme* external point of view.[45] Much of jurisprudence takes its basic building block to be rules, more precisely, norm.[46]

Alexy distinguishes between the observer's perspective and participant's perspective.[47] After offering a definition of law ('from

---

41 Miller (1985/1986), supra note 874, p. 392, referring to G. Christie, 'A Note on the Work of H.L.A Hart', in Jurisprudence 637-638 (G. Christie, ed. 1973) ["Christie 1973c"]; H.L.A. Hart, 'Utilitarianism and Natural Rights,' in 53 TUL. L.Rev. 3 (1979).

42 Priel (2013), supra note 861, p. 5.

43 Ibid., p. 6.

44 Nance (1985), supra note 897, p. 16, referring to Hart (1961), supra note 899, pp. 79-88. See, e.g., Holmes, 'Path of the Law,' in 10 HARV. L. REV. 457, (1897), p. 461.

45 Ibid., p. 22. See Hill, 'Legal Validity and Legal Obligation,' in 80 YALE L. J. (1970), pp. 54-58, esp. 57 n.45.

46 Roy Kreitner, 'Biographing Realist Jurisprudence', in Law & Social Inquiry, Vol. 35, Issue 3, pp. 765-791, Summer 2010, p. 778 [accompanying text and footnote omitted].

47 John Finnis, 'Law as Fact and as Reason for Action: A Response to Robert Alexy's on Law's "Ideal Dimension', in American Journal of Jurisprudence 59 (2014), Oxford Legal Studies Research Paper No. 21/2014, Notre Dame Law School Legal Studies Research Paper No. 1418, p. 2, referring to Robert Alexy, 'The Argument from Injustice: A Reply to Legal Positivism', (Oxford: Oxford University Press, 2002, 27). This book is a translation by Stanley L. Paulson and Bonnie Litchewski Paulson of Begriff und Geltung des Rechts (Freiburg im Breisgau: Verlag Herder, 1992); the translation of the title would be 'The Concept and the

the participant's perspective'), does Alexy introduce the idea of law's 'dimensions', by remarking that legal systems or individual legal norms that fail to satisfy their own 'claim to correctness' are 'legally defective', and that 'that is an expression of the fact that there is necessarily an ideal dimension to the law'.[48] It is illuminated too by Alexy's 2013 article: "...the observer is confined to social facts...". That is not to say that his considerations cannot include considerations about what the participants whom he observes think the law ought to be. One might term such considerations about what persons think the law ought to be 'indirect' or 'third-person' considerations by contrast to the direct and first-person considerations of the participant. All this implies that *from the standpoint of an observer, only the real dimension of law is of interest*.[49] Although the last statement does not logically commit Alexy to holding that law's real dimension consists of all those aspects of law, and of the law, that can be identified and affirmed from the observer's perspective.[50] Alexy conceives that the observer's point of view is really so inclusive. These observers can not only report all the criteria of decision that courts and lawyers actually use in some society, but can apply these established criteria to facts not yet considered by any lawyers or courts.[51] Alexy says "...the observer is free to contest any moral duty to obey or to apply law ...". But one who contests (or affirms) moral duties is not doing so *qua* observer; whether or not he is strictly a participant in the legal system discussed, he thereby abandons the descriptive for the

---

Validity of Law or Laws.'

48 Ibid., referring to Alexy (2002), Ibid., p. 127.

49 Ibid., p. 3, referring to Am J Juris, pp. 103-104 (emphasis added). Alexy goes on: "For this reason, from the standpoint of an observer, positivism with one exception is correct. "He thinks that an exception needs to be made because the positivist will – erroneously – count as a legal system even systems that make no "claim to correctness." But as the example of Raz shows, self-styled positivists may well agree with Alexy that a system that makes no claim to correctness (Richtigkeit: as Raz would say, to legitimacy) is not legal, and would regard this agreement neither as carrying them out of the observer's perspective nor as introducing into law an "ideal dimension," since the claim is not the less real for being mistaken. (Raz holds that the claim, though conceptually necessary for a system to be legal, is generally false, as it stands, since in moral truth, he thinks, there is no general moral obligation, even prima facie, to obey the law; and Alexy for his part rightly says, in 'The Argument from Injustice' p. 34, that a system that makes such a claim may yet be "without a doubt unjust in the extreme").

50 Ibid.

51 Ibid., p. 5. But here Finnis prioritizes some over others of Alexy's statements about the observer: the statement in "An Answer to Joseph Raz" p. 46 that: "The observer, qua observer, can only describe the practice of the Constitutional Court and the debate on which the Court is engaged. He cannot engage in argument on the question of which answer is legally correct. As soon as he does that, he ceases to be an observer and becomes a participant."

normative, the descriptive for the practical; he addresses not the world as it is but the world as it ought to be (so far as the moral choices, or types of moral choice, under discussion could affect it). What Alexy says about participation in legal argument applies *a fortiori* to participation in moral argument, about law or anything else.[52] An observer's purely descriptive legal theory cannot participate in an inquiry about the relation between 'the principle of justice' and the principle of certainty; for such an inquiry is a moral inquiry about the requirements of justice in situations where the justice-based presumption that legal obligations entails moral obligations is defeated by the injustice inherent in a (purported) legal rule and the obligation it purports to impose.[53] Alexy's article structures legal theory around 'the dual nature of law'.[54] His thesis that law has both an ideal and a real dimension, and his use of 'conceptual analysis' and (not the same thing) conceptual 'construction' to expound law's ideal dimension.

Finnis agrees with Hart that legal systems are constituted by various facts about the behavior and attitudes of officials and that the legal theorist's task is to explain these patterns. But to this Finnis adds an important proviso: we cannot fully understand these social facts without understanding "their objective, their value, their significance or importance, as *conceived by the people who performed them, engaged in them, etc.*"[55] In short, we cannot fully understand a society's legal practices without accounting for the participants' understanding of the point or purpose of those practices. There is, however, no universal or even general agreement about the point or purpose of law. Societies can and do vary greatly in their conceptions of this point or purpose.[56] Finnis has not seen Alexy challenging Hart's thesis that, since participants (say judges) may have any of many viewpoints besides a moral viewpoint, the specifically legal point of view is precisely – or corresponds precise to – the viewpoint of an observer who, like Alexy's observer, *understands* all the items that any participant regards as established law (all the rules cognizable by reference to an officially accepted rule of recognition, together with any principles accepted in

---

52 Ibid., n.17 [accompanying text omitted].

53 Ibid., p. 21 [footnote omitted].

54 Ibid., p. 1,3, referring to Robert Alexy, 'Some Reflections on the Ideal Dimension of Law and on the Legal Philosophy of John Finnis,' in Am J Juris 58 (2013), pp. 97-110 (p. 97) (Abstract).

55 Alex Langlinais and Brian Leiter, 'The Methodology of Legal Philosophy', to appear in T. Gendler et al. (eds.), The Oxford Handbook of Philosophical Methodology, draft of October 26, 2012, p. 14, referring to John Finnis, 'Natural Law and Natural Rights', 2nd edition, (Oxford: OUP, 2011), p. 3 (emphasis added); John Finnis (2003), 'Law and What I Trully Should Decide', in The American Journal of Jurisprudence 48 (2003), pp. 107-129 (p. 118).

56 Ibid., p. 14, referring to Finnis (2011), Ibid., p. 4.

official practice).[57] It is right to try to understand law from the perspective of participants in the reaching of decision (choices) about whether and what laws to make, to recognize, to apply and to comply with; and Finnis agrees that this perspective on the law is primary, and the observer's secondary (and indeed derivative). But Alexy's method of explaining law from the participant's perspective differs widely from Finnis's. Alexy's method is conceived primarily[58] as *conceptual analysis* or a search for conceptual necessities. Finnis's method is not a matter of conceptual analysis, but rather of understanding how basic human ends – needs and goods – and appropriate means come together in a critically justified understanding – concept – of law. That is to say: this process of critical practical reflection – not to be confused with the 'construction' and adoption of an 'expedient' concept[59] -- proceeds by way of articulating and testing substantive claims about what practical reason(ableness) requires of anyone and everyone, requirements that include a *need for law* as a characteristically indispensable means to securing the common good of justice and peace, by coordination achieved by way of authority of an appropriately rule of lawkind.[60] Once laws are in place, the practice of thinking and acting more or less in accord with them can be observed (perceived and described). So there can be an observer's perspective on actual or past laws. But this perspective has little or no theoretical significance, since its criterion of

---

57 Finnis (2014), supra note 906/913, p. 5.

58 Ibid., p. 6. Alexy's The Argument from Injustice, pp. 20-23, 40, 42, 62 appears to Finnis to hold that there are also "normative arguments or considerations of expediency [Zweckmassigkeit] (22) concerning the concepts to be adopted in theorizing about, and defining, law; but these are envisaged as supplementary to the tracing (where possible) of conceptually necessary connections and definitions (23). Zweckmassigkeit might also be translated as purposiveness, or usefulness. Note: the conception of normativity and of "normative necessity" articulated p. 21 n.40 is extremely voluntaristic: "that something is normatively necessary means nothing other than that it is commanded [geboten]." But Finnis should leave this voluntarism out of account.

59 Ibid. One part of Alexy's work does something apparently similar, insofar as it consists in "expedient or adequate [zweckmassige oder adaquate] concept formation that is justified by normative arguments" about the Radbruch formula, the debate about which, "there is widespread agreement today," "cannot be decided on the basis of analytical or conceptual arguments alone: "The Argument from Injustice, 40. But these normative arguments are not about so much about the moral need for law, and law's consequent essential or central-case features, but rather about whether or not it is expedient or inexpedient to adopt a boundary-line between the legally valid and the legally invalid by reference to injustice or at least severe or intolerable injustice. This sort of devising of a conceptual boundary on normative grounds treats as quasi-central – because conceptual, at least in its product – what Finnis regards (NLNR 351) as "a subordinate theorem."

60 Ibid.

correctness (accuracy, truth) is consistency with the describable facts of opinion, language and practice in some *particular* time(s) and place(s). Accounts of laws and legal systems from a purely descriptive viewpoint lack generality or theoretical character. Any aspiration to provide a descriptive *general* account, or theory, will be dependent, for its accomplishment, on adopting some participant's viewpoint as the criterion for selection and formation of concepts with which to give the account, or state the theory. The only participant's viewpoint that it is philosophically justifiable to adopt is the reasonable (and thus morally sound) participant's.[61] Finnis argues that Alexy's distinction between the observer's and participant's perspectives is a better way into legal theory or philosophy, which is properly neither analysis nor construction on concepts, but a practical (albeit abstract, 'theoretical') exploration of human needs and appropriate responses to them, responses to be articulated in concepts of law (and of related means of securing human goods and rights) that philosophical/theoretical reflection seeks to improve.[62]

II.1.3. HISTORICAL JURISPRUDENCE

The basic tenet of the historical school of jurisprudence is that law in its essence is not something imposed on a community from above or from without, but is an inherent part of its ongoing life, an emanation of the spirit of the people.[63] The historical school of law believed that the lesson of history and societal customs should, in large part, shape the texture of the law. 'History could teach what basic principles should foremost be included in the legal system'.[64] F.C.von Savigny's historical jurisprudence has structured the law in terms of autonomous concepts. It is possible to present the tenets of the historical school in a strait-forward practical form. Law is part of the culture of society. Different peoples have different laws just as they have different styles of clothing and different favorite foods. Legal enactments can nudge the culture in one direction or another, but if the culture rejects them firmly enough they will fail of their purpose.[65]

---

61 Ibid., p. 12.

62 Ibid., p. 1.

63 Robert E. Rodes, Jr., 'On the Historical School of Jurisprudence', in 49 The American Journal of Jurisprudence 2004, Notre Dame Law School – Legal Studies Research Paper No. 06-31, p. 165.

64 Miller (1985/1986), supra note 900, p. 375, quoting C. Conway, 'Jurisprudence', 1971, p. 2 ; and, B. Cardozo, 'The Nature of the Judicial Process,'1979, pp. 51-97.

65 Rodes (2004), supra note 922, p. 69. See Constance Baker Motley, 'Twenty Years Later', The Continuing Challenge (Evanston, III, Integrated Educ. Assoc., 1975), p. 11.

Economic and social development affect both what law is needed and what law is possible: consider the effect of women's liberation on alimony. Historical experience affects moral judgment and with it the willingness to accept this or that form of legal restraints.[66]

Against the analytical jurisprudence according to which law is as command and the conviction there is a practical law of nature or reason, the historical school insists that the law of a particular people emerges, and ought to emerge, from the unique historical experience of that people. It emerges also, if we are to take the *Volksgeist* seriously, from unique spiritual qualities of that people – qualities originally formed, no doubt, by their historical experience, but freestanding at any given point of time.[67] The hypothesis of an invisible and intangible lawmaker in the German historical school is 'the spirit of the people' or *Volksgeist*. The people, Savigny says, respect much more "what has not a visible and tangible origin" than "what has been made before our eyes by men of our own kind".[68] Savigny tried to prove that the Roman law was customary law. In maintaining that customary law is created by the spirit of the people and preferable to statutory law, he tried to sustain the authority of the Roman law, which at his time was positive law in Germany.[69] Savigny contends that law has a twofold life; first, as a part of the aggregate existence of the community, which it does not cease to be; and secondly, as a distinct branch of knowledge in the hands of the jurists.[70] Savigny did not see any inconsistency in anchoring law in the culture of the people and then assigning exclusive stewardship over it to specialized experts. As Reimann explains: "Culture [to Savigny] was not the totality of habits of a people, but the characteristics of its intellectual life. When this life grew more sophisticated over time, the ideas of intellectual elites in their respective fields shaped it more and more. In respect to law, therefore, the jurists represented the nation as a culture".[71]

66 Ibid. [footnote omitted].

67 Ibid., pp. 169-170.

68 Hans Kelsen, What is Justice?- Justice, Law, and Politics in the Mirror of Science, collected Essays by Hans Kelsen, (Berkeley and Los Angeles: University of California Press, 1957), p. 299, referring to F.C. von Savigny, 'Vom Beruf unserer Zeit fur Gesetzgebung und Rechtswissenschaft, third edition, (Heidelberg: 1840), p. 43.

69 Ibid.

70 Lewis A. Grossman, 'From Savigny through Sir Henry Maine': Roscoe Pound's Flawed Portrait of James Coolidge Carter's Historical Jurisprudence, American University, in WCL Research Paper No. 2009-21, p. 8, referring to Savigny (1831), infra note 932, p. 28.

71 Ibid., p. 8, 33, citing James C. Carter, 'The Proposed Codification of Our Common Law', in New York: Evening Post Job Printing Office, 1884, p. 88; Mathias Reimann, 'Nineteenth-Century German Legal Science', in Boston College Law Review 31 (1990), pp. 854-855.

In later works, Savigny was to use the term *Volkgeist*, spirit of the people, to designate what he regarded as the source of law.[72] Savigny's assertion is that "the common consciousness of the people is the peculiar seat of law".[73] Relating to the assertion, the grassroots are not immune to the rise and fall of attitudes and ideas in history, but they are less receptive to sudden radical change than either intellectuals or power wielders are. Adherence to a *Volksgeist*, therefore, can curb the enthusiasm of legislators for putting new ideas into practice simply because they have the power to do so.[74] The historical school proposes rather to make incremental improvements on the basis of an understanding of the ongoing historical process of which we are a part: [T]he subserviency of the present to the past will manifest itself even when the present is purposely opposed to the past. There is consequently no mode of avoiding this overruling influence of the existing matter; it will be injurious to us as long as we ignorantly submit to it; but beneficial if we oppose to it a vivid creative energy – obtain the mastery over it by a thorough grounding in history, and thus appropriate to ourselves the whole intellectual wealth of preceding generations.[75] Savigny is renowned largerly for his opposition to codification. He led the battle against Anton Frederich Justus Thibaut's 1814 proposal to codify German law. Savigny asserted that law was developed 'by internal silently-operating powers, not by the arbitrary will of a law giver'.[76] According to Savigny, there was an organic connection of law with the being and character of the people. For law, as for language, there is no moment of absolute cessation; it is subject to the same movement and development as every other popular tendency; and this very development remains under the same law of inward necessity, as in its earliest stages. Law grows with the growth, and strengthens with the strength of the people, and finally dies away as the nation loses its nationality.[77]

Savigny combined the historical of his jurisprudence with a commitment to building a coherent, logically-ordered system of law. In Reiman's words, "Once the leading principles had been found, the historical work had been done .... The legal scientists could then begin to build a truly

72 Rodes (2004), supra note 924, p. 166, referring to Friedrich Karl von Savigny, ' System des heutigen Romischen Rechts, vol. 1 (Berlin, Viet, 1840), 14 [accompanyng text and footnotes omitted].

73 Grossman (2009), supra note 929, p. 6, referring to F.C. von Savigny, 'Of the Vocation of Our Age for Legislation and Jurisprudence', Abraham Hayward trans. (London: Littlewood, [1831], p. 28.

74 Rodes (2004), supra note 931, p. 172.

75 Ibid., p. 167, referring to Savigny (1831), supra note 932, pp. 132-133.

76 Grossman (2009), supra note 932, p. 5, 6, referring to Savigny (1831), Ibid., p. 30.

77 Ibid., p. 6, referring to Savigny (1831), Ibid, p. 27.

scientific system with these principles".[78] In other words, Savigny believed that conceptual system-building was a critical aspect of legal science. Indeed, he thought it became the most important task of all once jurists obtained a certain level of historical knowledge.[79] Savigny thought that historically-derived principles could logically generate the rules for modern cases. He was also convinced that jurists, in some hard-to-define way, ensured that the law continued to reflect the organic evolution of these principles.[80] For many of Savigny's followers in the German historical school, the systematic ascpect of his jurisprudence was far more influential than the historical component. They almost entirely neglected the facet of Savigny's project dedicated to identifying legal principles through historical work.[81] The tenets of the historical school provide a useful rhetoric for anyone who wants to set up a customary way of doing things against the powers of arbitrary benevolence or mindless rationality.[82]

***

Sir Henry Maine contrasted primitive and non-western societies, in which 'the great bulk of men derive their rules of life from the customs of their village or city', with modern society, in which the Sovereign is ever more actively legislating on principles of his own, while local custom and idea are ever hastening to decay.[83] Maine seemed to speak sympathetically of codification and to criticize the manner in which a rule of English law has first to be disentangled from the recorded facts of adjudged printed precedents, then thrown into a form of words varying with the taste precision, and knowledge of the particular judge and then applied to the circumstances of the case for adjudication.[84] Maine maintained that legal

78 Ibid., p. 9, referring to Mathias Reimann, 'Historical School Against Codification: Savigny, Carter and the Defeat of the New York Civil Code', in American Journal of Comparative Law 37 (1989), p. 854.

79 Ibid.

80 Ibid., p. 10, citing Reimann (1990), supra note 930, p. 854; Whitman, 'The Legacy of Roman Law', (Princeton: Princeton Univ. Press, 1990), pp. 109-110, 117-120.

81 Ibid.

82 Rodes (2004), supra note 934, p. 172.

83 Grossman (2009), supra note 940, p. 13, referring to Henry Maine, 'Lectures on the Early History of Institutions (A Sequel to 'Ancient Law')', (New York: Holt, 1888, the English edition was published in 1875), p. 392.

84 Ibid., p. 14, referring to Henry Maine, 'Ancient Law: Its Connection with the Early History of Society, and its Relation to Modern Ideas', (London: John Murray, 1861), p. 14.

scholars had to take into account all aspects of social reality, including the customs and opinions of the people. He says: " ... [I]t is its history, the entire mass of its historical antecedents, which in each community determines how the Sovereign *shall* exercise or forbear from exercising his irresistible coercive power. All that constitutes this – the whole enormous aggregate of opinions, sentiments, beliefs, superstitions, and prejudices, of ideas of all kinds, hereditary and acquired, some produced by institutions and some by the constitution of human nature – is rejected by the Analytical Jurists".[85]

When Carter set forth his customary theory of law for the first time, he included a footnote citing Savigny – although this was apparently the only instance in which he ever mentioned that work in print: All well concieved efforts to make, or to declare, law, are therefore, efforts to apply [the] public, or, as we have styled it, national standard of justice to human conduct. This national standard .. is the final result of the moral and intellectual life and culture of a nation, the product of all the influences, public and private, which tend to cultivate and develop men's conceptions of what is just, expedient and useful, and which is unconsciously perceived and felt by every individual member of society by reason of the fact that he is such a member, and exposed to the like influences with his fellows.[86] Carter, as Grossman explored, evinced minimal interest in the logical arrangement of law, and he objected to deciding cases by deduction from general rules, because he thought such an approach generated unjust results. Carter maintains that judges should refer directly to societal customs as well as to judicial precedents.[87] If Savigny considered legal science mostly as a logical system and thus as an indispensible [sic] prerequisite for codification, for Carter legal science was a certain empirical method which made codification nonsensical.[88] Savigny links the law to the 'common consciousness of the people' or *Volkgeist*, and believes that the link demands that law's development be controlled by academic jurists rather than legislators. Carter equates the law to the 'social standard of justice' or 'custom', and maintains that the customary roots of the court-centered common law made it superior to codes and statutes.[89]

Pound characterizes Historical Jurisprudence as follows: 1) They consider the past rather than the present law; 2) They regard the law as

85 Ibid., p. 17-18, referring to Maine (1888), supra note 942, p. 360.

86 Ibid., p. 6,7, referring to Carter (1884), supra note 930, p. 41, citing Savigny (1831), supra note 932 [accompanying text omitted].

87 Ibid., p. 11, citing Lewis A. Grossman, 'Langdell Upside-Down', in Yale Journal of Law and the Humanities 19 (2007), pp. 190-193.

88 Ibid., p. 12, citing Reimann (1989), supra note 937, p. 105.

89 Ibid., referring to Roscoe Pound, 'Review of Law: Its Origin, Growth and Function by James Coolidge Carter', in Political Science Quarterly 24 (1909), p. 319.

something that is not and in the long run cannot be made consciously; 3) They see chiefly the social pressure behind legal rules. To them, sanction is to be found in the habits of obedience, displeasure of one's fellowmen [sic], public sentiment and opinion, or the social standard of justice; 4) Their type of law is custom, or those customary modes of decision that make up a body of juristic tradition or case law; and 5) As a rule, their philosophical views have been Hegelian.[90] Pound has indentified that the method of German Historical School is philosophical (indeed often metaphysical) and historian, and that of English Historical School is comparative and historical. Savigny was the intellectual father of the former group, and Sir Henry Maine was the most esteemed member of the latter.[91]

II.1.4. SOCIOLOGICAL JURISPRUDENCE

Positivism flourished and there is no eternal principles in positivits' definitions of law. Positivism was later followed by its offshoots, the historian school of law, sociological school of law and Jurimetric school. The sociological school of jurisprudence view that the most important factor in law is 'the balancing of competing social interests and the principles of sociology theory' in order to make the law mostly suitable for cultures.[92] Rudolf von Ihering says that the law is as a means to mediate those various interests. The law functions a means to solve social problems. The societal development can be achieved through a reform of law.[93] From the beginning Ihering possessed a lively sense of the nature of relations of life and their commerce, and the way, in which legal rules operate on them. His purpose was to show their practical bearings, to unify them under a single point of observation, and to disclose in them at the same time the terminal point of civil protection of private legal interests (not 'conceptionally necessary' interests but actual interests conforming to relative ends). Ihering with a preference for theories yields not to conceptual but to casuistic proof. The results achieved by casuistic reasoning concerning the interests involved in a legal proposition furnish the chief measure of legal judgment, even as against the *'lex lata'*, for he will not admit its conflict with purpose without cogent ground. He therefore delights to start with these interests, and examines to find whether the protective mantle of the

90 Ibid., p. 22, referring to Roscoe Pound, 'The Ideal and the Actual in Law – Forty Years After', in George Washington Law Review 1 (1933), pp. 599-600.

91 Ibid., p. 12.

92 Aubert (1983), supra note 877, p. 9, referring to Conway (1971), supra note 925, pp. 17-18; Benjamin Cardozo, 'The Nature of the Judicial Process', 1979, pp. 51-97; R. Pound, 'An Introduction to the Philosophy of Law', 1978, pp. 25-47.

93 Ibid.

law is adequate to safeguard them.[94] In the fourth volume of the 'Geist', Ihering defines rights as interests protected by the State; the standpoint of power substitutes for conformable purpose; and the will theory is expressly overthrown. Different aspects of rights are treated in a superior manner.[95] According to Ihering, the coincident purposes of individuals create social purpose which generates law. The postulate of a quiescent, logically unified system of concepts which constantly and systematically embraces the world of practical interests, would be consistent with this interpretation.[96] Ehrlich distinguishes between statute law and living law. The living law is 'the factual conventional practice in the society'. The true source of law is social practice, and the practice is then stated in formal statutes and decisions. Any laws not sourced from social practice would lack of social validity so they would not be fair and should not be valid. Weber argues that law evolution parallel with social evolution, from an irrational formal and substantive stage to a rational stage. He put forward a government model in which 'the bureaucracy should be accompanied by a law order of rational rules'. Durkheim's theory of law evolution views that law moves from the laws of primitive societies united by mechanical solidarity to the laws of complex societies whose cohesion is based on organic solidarity, with an emphasis on the distribution of works in the societies and a system of complementary distribution.[97] Weber and Hoebel define law in terms of public institutionalized enforcement of norms.[98]

As to the notion 'law as the *intersection* of coercion and the use of rules', one finds partial confirmation of that notion and the use of rules 'in anthropological and sociological definitions, such as Weber's definition of law'. An order will be called *law* if it is externally guaranteed by the probability that coercion (physical or psychological) to bring about conformity or to avenge violation will be applied by a *staff* of people holding themselves specially ready for that purpose.[99] One may characterize the satisfaction of both (the employment of coercion and the use of rules)

94 Adolf Merkel, Appendix I - Rudolf von Ihering Law as A Means to An End, translated from the German by Isaac Husik, translated and reprinted from Ihering's "Jahrbucher fur Dogmatik des heutigen Romische' und Deutschen Privatrechts,' Bd. Xxxii, N.F. xx (Jena, Gustav Fisher, 1893), pp. 432-433.

95 Ibid., pp. 440-441.

96 Ibid., p. 452.

97 Aubert (1983), supra note 951, p. 9.

98 Brian Z. Tamanaha, 'Understanding Legal Pluralism: Past to Present, Local to Global', in Sydney Law Review,Vol. 30, 375 (2008) ["2008a"], p. 392. See, Brian Z. Tamanaha, 'An Analytical Map of Social Scientific Approaches to the Concept of Law', in (1995)15 Oxford Journal of Legal Studies, pp. 506-508 (describing Weber's and Hoebel's approaches).

99 Nance (1985), supra note 904, n.163. See, e.g., M. WEBER, 'LAW AND ECONOMY IN SOCIETY 5' (M. Rheinstein ed. 1954).

sufficient conditions as generating a category of *paradigmatic*, though not necessarily optimal, legal phenomena: viz., 'law as the intersection of coercion and the use of rules'.[100] And with such a characterization, it would also make sense to say that coercion is a (logically) necessary feature of (paradigmatic cases of) law, the claim that law is in some definitional way required to employ coercion.[101]

Pound's theory of interests lies at the conceptual core of sociological jurisprudence. He consistently promulgated three types of interests: the individual, the public and the social.[102] Pound regards social interests as empirical entities because they are to be found only in society; more to the point, they are to be found in the law and legal processes of society.[103] Social interests, then, are not abstract presuppositions derived from such determinist sources as theological doctrine, the philosophical ideas about human nature, or the social psychological classification of instincts. Through a painstaking and thorough analysis of hundreds of legal documents, Pound inventories the social interests which have been asserted in 'civilized society' and which must be legally recognized and secured in order to maintain that society. He then proposes six broad categories of social interests and their subcategories. The six general interests are the social interests in the general security, the social interests in the security of social institutions, the social interests in the general morals, the social interests in the conservation of social resources, the social interests in general progress, and the social interests in the individual life. Because Pound's notion of social interests evolved through many years, Trevino has developed a composite description and defined social interests very generally at the prevalent claims, demands, desires, or expectations which human beings collectively seek to satisfy and which society must recognize and protect through the law. [104] Because the law protects them, they are given the status of legal rights. To put it slightly differently, a right is a legally protected social interests.

To say that law is socially constructed is to say that "legal facts" are certain kinds of social constructs.[105] Unlike physical facts, these kinds of

100 Ibid., p. 41, referring to Hart (1961), supra note 903, Cbs. V-VI.

101 Ibid. [accompanying text omitted].

102 A. Javier Trevino, 'The Influence of Sociology on American Jurisprudence: From Oliver Wendell Holmes to Critical Legal Studies', in Mid-American Review of Sociology, 1994, Vol XVIII, No. 1 & 2, pp. 23-46.

103 Ibid.

104 Ibid.

105 Langlinais & Leiter (2012), supra note 915, p. 5. Langlinais and Leiter are using slightly different terminology than John Searle. They use "social construct" to refer to aspects of reality that are constituted by human beliefs and attitudes; they use "social contract" as it is usually used in the jurisprudential literature to refer to those beliefs and actions of officials of a legal system that are constitutive

social constructs are realizable only in the context of human institutions. It is, thus, a hallmark of social constructs that they exist if and only if a society collectively recognizes them as existing.[106] That is to say, these kinds of social constructs are constituted and sustained by a kind of collective agreement – at least, in the case of law, an 'agreement' among those Hart calls 'officials' of the system.[107]

II.1.5. LEGAL REALIST

The impact of thinking upon wishing which, in the development of a science, follows the break-down of its visionary projects, and marks the end of its specifically utopian period, is commonly called realism. Representing the reaction against the wish-dreams of the initial stage, realism is liable to assume a critical and somewhat cynical aspect. In the field of thought, it places its emphasis on the acceptance of facts and on the analysis of their causes and consequences. It tends to depreciate the role of purpose and to maintain, explicitly or implicitly, that the function of thinking is to study a sequence of events on which it is powerless to influence or alter.[108] Jes Bjarup thinks that attempts have been made to actually change the science of current law into a socio-psychological discipline.[109] According to him, there is indeed room for such a science.[110] John Post, for example, explains that metaphysical (or ontological) naturalism is the view that "everything is composed of natural entities .....whose properties determine all the properties of whatever it is that exists, and that methodological naturalism is the view that acceptable methods of justification and explanation are

---

of law.

106 Ibid., pp. 5-6, with reference to John Searle (1995),'The Construction of Social Reality', (New York: The Free Press), pp. 32-34, 52-53.

107 Ibid.

108 Alejandro Lorite Escorihuela, 'Alf Ross: Towards a Realist Critique and Reconstruction of International Law', in EJIL (2003), Vol. 14 No. 4, 703-766, p. 704. 'In Sweden, they ask, "What can God do that man cannot?" And they answer, "Pull a bald old man's hair...." If legal science could understand the deeper meaning of this "joke," it would throw out every legal theory so far conceived. 'Lundstedt, 'La part de responsabilite de la science juridique dans le destin des peoples,' in Introduction à l'ètude du droit compare: Recueil d'ètudes en l'honneur d'Edouard Lambert (1938) 26.

109 Jorgen Dalberg-Larsen, Alf Ross and the Sociology of Law, (Stockholm Institute for Scandinavian Law, 1957-2010), p. 40, referring to Jes Bjarup, Alf Ross' realistic retslœre, Jes Bjarup & Jorgen Dalberg-Larsen, 'Retsbegreb, retsanvendelse og retsvidenskab, Bogformidlingens Forlag,' in Arhus 1993, pp. 31-58, especially pp. 43-44.

110 Ibid.

continous, in some sense, with those in science".[111] Ontological naturalism is thus a thesis about the nature of that which exists: there are only natural entities, whereas methodological naturalism requires that philosophical theorizing be continous with the science.[112] Armstrong takes (ontological) naturalism to be 'the doctrine that reality consists of nothing but a single all-embracing spatio-temporal system'.[113] Brian Leiter[114] says: "S-naturalism in philosophy is either the (ontololgical) view that the only things that exist are *natural* or *physical* things; or the (semantic) view that a suitable philosophical analysis of any concept must show it to be amenable to empirical inquiry. /.../. In the semantic sense, S-naturalism which is just the view that predicates must be analyzable in terms that admit of empirical inquiry: so, e.g., a semantic S-naturalist might claim that 'morally good' can be analyzed in terms of characteristics like 'maximizing human well-being' that admit of empirical inquiry by psychology and physiology (assuming that well-being is a complex psycho-physical state)".

II.1.5.1. BEHAVIORIST [PSYCHO-REALIST] WING

Christopher Langdell believes there is a science of law. If the written opinions of appellate courts are keenly observed and analyzed, 'the basic or fundamental recurrent legal principles could and would be discovered', Langdell uses Francis Bacon's approach, but more specific to using appellate courts' opinions only as analyzed in order to discover fundamental recurrent legal principles. As a derivative of Langdell's system, the American legal realism appeared, with Oliver Wendell Holmes, Jerome Frank, Benjamin Cardoso and Karl Llewellyn as their exponents.[115] Justice Holmes wrote that the law was *'just a prediction'* of what courts

---

111 Torben Spaak, 'Karl Olivecrona's Legal Philosophy: a Critical Appraisal', 8, (Uppsala:lustus forlag,2009), in Ratio Juris 24(2)(2011): 156-193, referring to John F. Post, 'Naturalism', In The Cambridge Dictionary of Philosophy. 2nd ed. (Robert Audi Ed.), pp. 596-597, (Cambridge: Cambridge University Press, 1999). See, Steven J. Wagner & Richard Warner, 'Introduction. In Naturalism, A Critical Appraisal. in. Steven J. Wagner & Richard Warner Eds., (Indiana: University of Notre Dame Press, 1993), pp. 1-21 (p. 12).

112 Ibid., pp. 8-9.

113 Ibid., p. 9, n.17, referring to D.M. Armstrong, 'Naturalism, Materialsm and First Philosophy', in Philosophia 8 (1978), pp. 261-276 (p. 261).

114 Ibid., p. 12, referring to Brian Leiter, 'Naturalism in Legal Philosophy', in Stanford Internet Encyclopedia of Philosophy (Fall 2002 Edition), Edward N. Zalta ed., pp. 1-16 (p. 3).

115 Miller (1985/1986), supra note 923, p. 375, referring to Jerome Frank, 'Courts on Trial' (1973), p. 226.

would do in the future, because 'there were no timeless qualities in rules'. Rules depended on judges how they would use them. Judges bent the rules to make them do what they wished. A law could say anything as what the judges wished. 'The closer one examined judicial opinions the more one saw not rules, but the judge, himself'. Law, according to Holmes, was not linked to a Natural Law morality, not linked with logic, but instead linked with the behavior of judges.[116] Holmes argues 'the life of the law has not been logic; it has been experience'.[117] He says that the man of science in the law is not merely a bookworm. To a microscopic eye for detail he must unite an insight which tells him what details are significant. *Not every maker of exact investigation counts, but only he who directs his investigation to a crucial point.*[118] Holmes once said, "We need to think things and not words". He held that "One mark of a great lawyer is that he sees the application of broadest rules".[119] You may recall his amusing story about the Vermont Justice of the Peace who was asked to adjudicate the issue arising between two farmers regarding the alleged destruction of a butter churn. In the words of Justice Holmes: "the Justice (of the Peace) took time to consider and then said that he had looked through the statutes and could find nothing about churns, and gave judgment for the defendant".[120] Restating the familiar words of Holmes . it is not the first use but the tiresome repetition of inadequate catchwords which I am observing.[121] Are we not somewhat surfeited with such hackneyed words in the new semantic vocabulary as 'behavior', 'background' and 'function'. Background has been so frequently used that we are beginning to lose sight of the fact that legal problems involve foreground as well. Every opinion, even every act, of the judiciary is explained in terms of judicial 'behavior'.[122]

Justice Frank argued that rules were illusory and amorphous, logic in law was artificial, and the finding facts, alone, mattered. Juridical discretion by judges was emphasized as a good thing. The greater the appearance of logic, the less justice, and likely, the more of a 'cover up' was

116 Ibid., referring to Christie (1973a), supra note 876, pp. 694, 648-663, 649, 652-657; 10 Harv. L. Rev. 457 (1897), pp. 459-464.

117 Ibid., pp. 379-383, referring to Oliver W. Holmes, 'The Common Law 5', (1963).

118 Walter B. Kennedy, 'A Review of Legal Realism', in 9 Fordhan Law Review 362 (1940), p. 364, referring to HOLMES, 'COLLECTED LEGAL PAPERS (1920)' 224. Italics inserted.

119 Ibid., p. 367, referring to Holmes (1920), Ibid.

120 Ibid., p. 367, referring to Homes (1920), Ibid.

121 Ibid., p. 371, referring to Bent, 'Justice Oliver Wendell Holmes' (1923), pp. 197-203.

122 Ibid., referring to F. Cohen, 'Transcendental Nonsense and the Functional Approach', in (1935) 35 Col. L. Rev. 833.

going on (regarding the judge trying to cover his bias). Justice and fairness are the most important aspect to law.[123] Frank concentrated his attention predominantly on the fact-finding process in the trial courts. He detached himself from any of the other legal realists by labeling them 'rule skeptics' and pronouncing himself a 'fact skeptic'.[124] He devoted his main scholastic energies to an analysis of the innumerable sources of error which may enter into a determination of the facts by a trial court. There may be "perjured witnesses, coached witnesses, biased witnesses, witnesses mistaken in their observation of the facts as to which they testify or in their memory of their observations, missing or dead witnesses, missing or destroyed documents, crooked lawyers, stupid lawyers, stupid jurors, perjured jurors, inattentive jurors, trial judges who are stupid or bigoted and biased or 'fixed' or inattentive to the testimony.[125] Many of these factors, he says, and above all the impenetrable and unique personality of the judge make every lawsuit in which conflicting oral testimony is presented a highly subjective affairs. According to Frank, the judge (or jury) has a 'virtually uncontrolled and virtually uncontrollable fact discretion' or 'sovereignty',[126] i.e., the power to choose which witnesses' stories are to be accepted as correct. Frank maintains that the objective legal norms are in many instances frustrated and nullified by the 'secret, unconscious, private, idiosyncratic norms' applied in the fact finding process by trial judges or jurors.[127] No rule can be the right rule, he states, if it is applied to the 'wrong facts', to unreal or mistaken facts.[128] The legal rules, whether judge-made or statute-made, and the social policies the rules embody, are at the mercy of the personal subjective reactions of trial judges or juries.[129] Thus Frank concludes that the judges often play havoc with the precedent system, with the consequence that the uniformity and stability which the rules may seem to supply at first blush are frequently rendered illusory and chimerical in practice.[130]

The Realists are 'anti-foundationalists' about judicial decisions in

---

123 Miller (1985/1986), supra note 974, p. 390, referring to G. Christie, 'Frank, Law and the Modern Mind' in Jurisprudence, ed. 1973 ["1973b"], p. 713.

124 Edgar Bodenheimer, 'A Decade of Jurisprudence in the United States of America: 1946-1959', in Natural Law Forum 1958, Paper 27, p. 51.

125 Ibid., referring to Frank, 'Modern and Ancient Legal Pragmatism', in 25 Notre Dame Lawyer (1950), p. 207, 254.

126 Ibid., referring to Frank, 'Short of Sickness and Death: A Study of Moral Responsibility in Legal Criticism', in 26 New York University Law Review 545 (1951), p. 584.

127 Ibid., p. 52, referring to Frank (1951), Ibid., p. 582.

128 Ibid., referring to Frank, 'Courts on Trial,' 1949 ["1949a"], p. 33.

129 Ibid., referring to Frank, 'Modern and Ancient Legal Pragmatism',(1949) ["1949b"], p. 327; cf. also 375.

130 Ibid., referring to Frank (1949b), id., p. 230, 328.

the sense that they deny that the legal reasons justify a unique decision: the legal reasons typically underdetermine the decision (at least in most cases actually litigated through the stage of appellate review). More precisely, the Realists claim that the law is rationally indeterminate in the sense that the class of legal reasons – i.e., the class of legitimate reasons a judge may offer for a decision – does not provide a justification for a unique outcome.[131] Just as sensory input does not justify a unique scientific theory, so legal reasons do not justify a unique decision. The Realists also take the second step that Quine [in his naturalized epistemology] takes: replacement. According to the Realist indeterminacy thesis, legal reasons underdetermine judicial decisions, meaning that the foundationalist enterprise of theory of adjudication is impossible.[132] According to the behaviorist, all human behavior can be explained in terms of the pairings of certain responses to certain stimuli: no reference to mental states – beliefs, desires, etc – is required. The Realists hold that it is primarily the underlying facts of the case, rather than the rules of law, that 'trigger' the response. Frank's own view is that 'the Stimuli affecting the judge x the Personality of the judge = Decisions', while the 'conventional theory' holds that 'Rule x Facts = Decision'.[133]

Ronald Dworkin claims that according to Realism, judges actually decide cases according to their own political or moral tastes, and then chose an appropriate legal rule as a rationalization.[134] Judge Jon Newman of the Second Circuit asserts that Realists believe that the judge simply selects the result that best comports with personal values and then enlists, sometimes brutally, whatever doctrines arguably support the result.[135] John Hart Ely says the Realist 'discovered' that judges were human and therefore were likely in a variety of legal contexts consciously or unconsciously to slip their personal value into their legal reasoning.[136] Steven Burton remarks that it is often 'claimed, in legal realist fashion, that judges decide whatever they want to decide when the law is unclear (and it is often or always unclear)'.[137]

131 Leiter (1997), supra note 884, p. 295. That the Realists think the law is "indeterminate" is, of course, quite familiar. On some of the problems about how to formulate the Realist view about indeterminacy, see Brian Leiter, 'Legal Indeterminacy,' in ILEGAL THEORY 481 (1995).

132 Ibid.

133 Ibid., pp. 278-79.

134 Ibid., p. 267, referring to Dworkin, 'Taking Rights Seriously', (London: Duckworth, 1977), p. 3.

135 Ibid., p. 268, quoting Jon O. Newman, 'Between Legal Realism and Neutral Principles: The Legitimacy of Institutional Values', in 72 CAL. L. REV. 200 (1984), p. 203.

136 Ibid., referring to JOHN HART ELY, 'DEMOCRACY AND DISTRUST: A THEORY OF JUDICIAL REVIEW', (1980), p. 44.

137 Ibid., referring to STEVEN J. BURTON, 'JUDGING IN GOOD FAITH',

Fred Schauer describes Realists as holding that legal decision-makers are largely unconstrained by forces external to their own decision-making preference.[138] The Frank-Hutcheson 'hunch' theory of judicial decision is that we explain the decision in terms of the 'hunch', and we explain the 'hunch' psychoanalytically (at least for Frank).[139] And Robert Satter, a Connecticut trial judge, says in a recent popular work that Realists assert that a judge exercises unbridled discretion in making decisions; he works backward from conclusion to principles and uses principles only to rationalize his conclusion. [Realists] consider the judge's values all-important.[140]

***

A psychology of jurisprudence would describe and explain the phenomenology of law, socialization into the law, and socialization by the law. Insofar as the behavioral effects of the law are symbolic,[141] there is a delicate interplay among these topics; the law both reflects and sustains the norms of the community. Therefore, the law should "work" best when positive and intuitive laws are congruent.[142] Contempary psycholegal research at Nebraska Program is similar in content to the agenda that Pound established early in the 20th century for sociological jurisprudence: to discover 'the actual social effects of legal institutions and legal doctrines',[143]

(1992), p. 43.

138 Ibid., referring to FREDERICK SCHAUER, 'PLAYING BY THE RULES', (1991), p. 191.

139 Ibid., p. 301.

140 Ibid., p. 268, referring to ROBERT SATTER, 'DOING JUSTICE: A TRIAL JUDGE AT WORK', (1990), p. 64.

141 Gary B. Melton, 'Realism in Psychology and Humanism in Law: Psycholegal Studies at Nebraska', in Nebraska Law Review, Vol. 69:251,1990 ["1990a"], p. 262. Melton argues that the law's most acute effects on behavior occur through its function as a moral educator. Melton & Saks, 'The Law as an Instrument of Socialization and Social Structure,' in 33 NEB. SYMP. ON MOTIVATION: THE LAW AS A BEHAVIOR INSTRUMENT (1985), pp. 251-268. The law is a system of social cues that guide the behavior of those who are motivated to adhere to community norms – most people – irrespective of the carrots or sticks that the law promises to provide: "Law teaches the moral and social norms of the community and, in a sense, announces, reiterates, and indeed ritualizes the myths and themes of the culture." Melton & Saks (1985), Ibid., p. 251.

142 Ibid.

143 Ibid., p. 264, referring to Roscoe Pound, 'The Scope and Purpose of Sociological Jurisprudence', in 25 HARV. L. REV. (1912), p. 513.

to determine 'means of making legal rules effective',[144] and to develop an approach to legal decision making that will result in 'reasonable and just solutions of individual cases'.[145] Michael Perlin offers a rich integration of cognitive and social psychology in an attempt to understand the factors affecting mental health law. His work fits within the continuing tradition in law and social sciences of study of the behavior of judges and other legal decision makers, including the electorate, as an effort to describe the law in action, apart from the abstract principles of the books.[146] Perlin sheds particular light on the psychological forces that may push jurist toward 'irrational' decisions based on social assumptions directly contrary to empirical research on the insanity defense.[147] The Legal Realists revealed Legal Formalism to be a sham, a 'style of reasoning'[148] masking personal and policy preferences. They deployed a new theory of how courts and judges worked. Realist theoreticians, riding off boldly in many directions, called for a commitment to the social scientific study of how courts worked, a behavioral or psychological explanation of the way the legal system functioned, a skepticism about the received wisdom of legal principles and rules – particularly those that claimed to cover every case – and a passionate belief in replacing an impersonal, formalistic legal structure with one conforming to a functional reality.[149] As one of particular trends of modern realism, psychologism, according to Walter Kennedy, is much more than a particular type of psychological theory. Under the catch-all title, he includes the current tendencies to account for judicial decisions, wholly or in part, in terms of personal impulses, economic factors, hunches, or institutional compulsives; and in corresponding degree to dismiss or minimize the authority of law, the exercise of reason and the impartiality of the judicial process.[150] Evidence is [at hand] to prove that realists are beginning to invoke the aid of pseudo-psychologism in the interpretation of judicial opinion. One form of psychologism is appearing wherein the judges are confidentially informed that external stimuli control their decisions even when they are not aware of these sub-vocal factors.[151] Judges

144 Ibid., referring to Pound (1912), id., p. 514.

145 Ibid., p. 265, referring to Pound (1912), id., p. 515.

146 Ibid., p. 267 [accompanying text omitted].

147 Ibid., p. 268.

148 N.E.H. Hull, 'Reconstructing the Origins of Realistic Jurisprudence: A Prequel to the Llewellyn-Pound Exchange over Legal Realism', in Duke Law Journal, Vol. 1989:1302, p. 1303, referring to K. Llewellyn, 'The Common Law Tradition: Deciding Appeals', (1960).

149 Ibid. [accompanying text omitted].

150 Kennedy (1940), supra note 977, p. 369.

151 Ibid., p. 370, referring to Yntema, 'The Horn Book Method and the Conflict of Laws', in (1928) 37 Yale L. J. 463; Oliphant, 'A Return to Stare Decisis' in (1928) 14 A.B.A.J, 159; Moore, 'Legal and Institutional Methods Applied to the Debiting

are acting behaviorwise even when they do not say so; they are *doing* the right thing a lot of times when they are not *saying* the words. Under this system it is possible for the juristic surgeon to probe beneath the surface of any judicial opinion and to pull forth latent reasons for the decision.[152]

The Realist, on Hart's reading, gives us a 'Predictive Theory' of law, according to which by the concept 'law', we just mean a prediction of what the court will do.[153] According to the Predictive Theory, a judge who sets out to discover the 'law' on some issue upon which she must render a decision is really just trying to discover what she will do, since the 'law' is equivalent to a prediction of what she will do.[154] In contrast to the Formalists, the Realists, then, share a commitment to the view that in deciding cases, judges respond primarily to the stimulus of the facts of the case.[155] If the Formalists' descriptive claim as saying that judges are (primarily) rule-responsive, the Realists claim that judges are (primarily) fact-responsive.[156] The Realists rejected formalism as an adequate descriptive theory of adjudication, and this has no bearing on whether or not they were positivists.[157]

II.1.5.2. SOCIOLOGICAL WING

Sociological Wing of Realism could propose that responsiveness to reasons itself requires explanation, it is just that the relevant explanation is sociological in character, not psychological.[158] The Core Claim of Legal Realism consists of the following descriptive thesis about judicial decision-making: judges respond primarily to the stimulus of facts.[159] So, judges

of Direct Discounts', in (1931) 40 Yale L.J. 1219.

152 Ibid. For example, see Nelles, Commonwealth v. Hunt (1932), in 32 Col. L. Rev. 1151. Cf. Pound, 'Economic Interpretation and the Law of Torts,' in 53 Harv. L. Rev. (1940), p. 365.

153 Leiter (1997), supra note 999, p. 270.

154 Ibid. The abbreviated discussion in the text is borrowed from Brian Leiter, 'Legal Realism', in A COMPANION TO PHILOSOPHY OF LAW AND LEGAL THEORY, pp. 261, 262-63 (Dennis Patterson ed., 1996) ["1996a"].

155 Ibid., p. 277.

156 Ibid., p. 278."Formalism" can also name a normative view, to the effect that judges ought to be primarily rule- and legal-reason-responsive. Theories of adjudication, of course, typically make both descriptive and normative claims. See Leiter (1996b), supra note 883, pp. 253, 255-58.

157 Ibid., n.158. See generally Leiter (1996a), supra note 1013.

158 Ibid., p. 301.

159 Ibid., p. 275. Proper emphasis must be put on the word "primarily": no Realist (except perhaps Underhill Moore) claimed that rules never mattered to the

reach decisions based on what they think would be fair on the facts of the case, rather than on the basis of the applicable rules of law.[160] Karl Llewellyn introduced 'Formal Style' and 'Grand Style' as two predominant 'styles' in the law.[161] The 'Formal Style' is the belief that law is 'pure logic and the rigid application of *stare decisis*'. The 'Grand Style' is the method of law, in which 'precedent has validity and is a guide only, and later judges has discretion or 'leeway' in applying them. Recourse is taken, most importantly, to the 'flavor' of the entire system of law and to social needs. 'Situation senses', a kind of ethics is used. The 'Formal Style' is not an accurate or an appropriate description of law, and the 'Grand Style' was the right one. Llewellyn argues 'the law, as its primary goal, is justice or fairness'. Oliphant says that courts respond to the stimulus of the facts in concrete cases before them rather than to the stimulus of over-general and outworn abstraction in opinions and treaties.[162] Judge Hutcheson admits that the vital, motivating impulse for the decision is an intuitive sense of what is right or wrong.[163] Similarly, Jerome Frank cited 'a great American judge', Chancellor Kent, who confessed that "..he first made himself 'master of the facts'. Then (he wrote) I saw where justice lay, and the moral sense decided the court half the time; I then sat down to search the authorities ....but I almost always found principles suited to my view

---

course of decision. See Leiter (1996a), supra note 1016, p. 268; The only Realist who would deny this would have been Underhill Moore, who took behaviorism in psychology more seriously than other Realists. For the behaviorist, of course, the mind is a black box, no to be invoked in explaining behavior. Thus, reasons are only relevant as certain types of (aural, visual) stimuli, but are not relevant in virtue of their rational content or meaning! "A proposition of law," says Moore, "is nothing more than a sensible object which may arouse a drive and cue response." Underhill Moore & Charles C. Callahan, 'Law and Learning Theory: A Study in Legal Control,' in 53 YALE L.J. (1943), p. 1, 3. For the behaviorist, then, responsiveness to reasons really means nothing more than seeking out the lawful correlation between the stimuli that constitute the input (e.g. facts, laws, reasons, etc.) and the cognitive output (e.g., a judicial opinion). This, of course, was precisely Moore's program, under the heading of the institutional method. For further discussion, See Leiter (1996a), Ibid., p. 268. Since most of the Realists, happily, were not orthodox behaviorists, the notion of being responsive to reason - legal or nonlegal - is compatible with their work.

160 Ibid. [accompanying text omitted].

161 Miller (1985/1986), supra note 974, p. 390, referring to Karl Llewellyn, 'The Common Law Tradition : Deciding Appeal', in Jurisprudence, 981, 999, 1002-3 (G. Christie, ed. 1973).

162 Leiter (1997), supra note 1019, p. 276, referring to Oliphant (1928), supra note 1010, p. 71, 75.

163 Ibid., referring to Joseph C. Hutcheson, Jr., 'The Judgment Intuitive: The Function and the "Hunch" in Judicial Decision', in 14 CORNELL L. Q. 274 (1929), p. 285.

of the case".[164] Precisely the same view of what judges really do when they decide cases is presupposed in Llewellyn's advice to lawyers that, while they must provide the court 'a technical ladder' justifying the result, what the lawyer must really do is 'on the facts'....persuade the court your case is sound.[165] Max Radin, in keeping with the Core Claim, suggested that the decision of a judge was determined by 'a type situation that has somehow been early called up in his mind'.[166] Judges are fact-responsive, and the facts, for Radin and Llewellyn, present themselves in ways that reflect what we might call the 'sociological' profile of the judge.[167] Roberto Unger's remark, drawing on the work of Talcott Parsons: "Many things besides law may fit into the category of normative order, for example, a society's religion and art. To the extent that law can be differentiated from these other aspects or normative order, it is distinguished by its primary emphasis on externally observable behavior and on the use of secular sanctions to penalize or redress deviant conduct".[168]

Recent accounts of realism tend to focus on ways to rescue realism from an extreme vision about indeterminacy in adjudication. Brian

---

164 Ibid. These quotations may be usefully compared with the following apt summary of Frank's view: "[H]ow do judges decide cases? To Frank, they begin with the desired conclusion and search for premises to substantiate it. Oriented to achieving certain results, judges rationalize their decisions by finding facts and selecting rules that justify the desired conclusion. By manipulating those facts and rules, judges enjoy unfettered discretion. But what persuades judges to reach one conclusion rather than another? .... Most important, according to Frank, are the "uniquely individual factors" that are the product of the judge's "entire life-history." Frank reveled in unfettered discretion .... ROBERT JEROME GLENNON, 'THE ICONOCLAST AS REFORMER: JEROME FRANK'S IMPACTION AMERICAN LAW' 44-45 (1985) (quoting JEROME FRANK, 'LAW AND THE MODERN MIND. 106', 115 (1930) (emphasis in original). Note, in particular, the prominent place given to the themes of Judicial Volition and Judicial Idiosyncrasy in this capsule summary of Frank's view. But as Leiter argues, it is not clear that even Frank views judges as "unfettered." Notice that this means the emphasis on the theme of Judicial Volition is really mistaken even in the case of Frank: for Frank, judicial decisions are determined, so that, in reality, there is no room for judicial choice. It is just that both judges themselves, and we as observers of their behavior, will find it hard, if not impossible, to identify the determinants. For that, the hard work of Freudian psychoanalysis is required.

165 Ibid. See, for example, Llewellyn's seminal discussion of the "strict" and "loose" views of precedents, in Karl Llewellyn, 'Remarks of the Theory of Appellate Decision and the Rules or Canons About How Statutes Are to Be Construed', in 3 VAND. L. REV. (1950), p. 76 (accompanying text omitted).

166 Ibid., p. 277, referring to Max Radin, 'The Theory of Judicial Decision: Or How Judges Think', in II A.B.A.J. 357 (1925), p. 362.

167 Ibid.

168 Nance (1985), supra note 960, n.102.

Tamanaha's (2009) account, for example, pursues this rescue project by claiming that most of the realists' insights were commonplace in the legal literature long before the realists wrote and that the critique was (and is) part and parcel of all conventional jurisprudence. On this view, the realists produced nothing distinctive and merely articulated conventional wisdom that, when properly tempered, should always inform views of adjudication. More sympathetic accounts of realism's innovation, such as those of Brian Leiter (1997) and Hanoch Dagan (2007), similarly concentrate on ways to characterize the realist critique of adjudication as pragmatic correctives to inadequate images of how judges actually decide.[169]

Realism's innovation might be related to Quine's steps in his naturalized epistemology. In viewing legal realism, Leiter holds, as to Quine's first step which is anti-foundationalism, [it is argued that] theory of adjudication is concerned not with the relationship between 'evidence' and 'scientific theory', but rather with the justificatory relationship between 'legal reasons' (the input, as it were) and judicial decision (the output). Theory of adjudication tries to tell judges how they ought to decide cases, i.e., it seeks to 'ground' judicial decisionmaking in reasons that require unique outcomes.[170] As to Quine's second step of replacement on which the Realist contend that the foundationalist enterprise of theory of adjudication is impossible, why not replace, then, the 'sterile' foundational program of justifying one legal outcome on the basis of the applicable legal reasons with a descriptive and explanatory account of what input – i.e., what combination of facts and reasons – produces what output – i.e., what judicial decision?[171] To give such an account is just to vindicate the Core Claim of Realism. As Underhill Moore puts it: "This study lies within the province of jurisprudence. It also lies within the field of behavioristic psychology. It places the province within the field".[172] Notice how closely this echoes Quine's idea that, epistemology ...simply falls into place as a chapter of psychology.[173] As already mentioned

169 Kreitner (2010), supra note 905, p. 785.

170 Leiter (1997), supra note 1026, p. 295 [accompanying text omitted].

171 Ibid. Such a naturalized jurisprudence would be in tension with most of modern legal philosophy, which follows H.L.A. Hart in accepting a hermeneutic model for understanding the social world. See, e.g., Stephen R. Perry, 'Interpretation and Methodology in Legal Theory,' in LAW AND INTERPRETATION 97 (Andrei Marmor ed. 1995). According to this model, we do not look for lawful regularities in the external behavior of social actors; rather, to understand social actors we must adopt their "internal" point of view and understand, for example, what their reasons mean to them. See Marmor (1995), Ibid, pp. 102-112. We can understand the Realists as contesting whether such an approach is really more explanatory and predictively fruitful than their non-hermeneutic approach to the social world.

172 Ibid., quoting Moore & Callahan (1943), supra note 1018, p. 1.

173 Ibid., pp. 295-296, referring to W.v.O. Quine, 'Epistemology Naturealized,' in Ontological Relativity and Other Essays, (New York: Columbia University Press,

before, according to Sociological Wing of Realism, the relevant explanation required in the context of responsiveness to reasons is sociological in character, not psychological.[174] Judges respond primarily to the stimulus of facts,[175] and judges reach decisions based on what they think would be fair on the facts of the case, rather than on the basis of the applicable rules of law.[176]

Quine shows in his work that although he favors the empiricist tradition, this tradition does not refute in any sense the skeptical argument as long as the 'external' position is a legitimate one from the epistemological point of view. This is his naturalization move against skepticism. This move is to insist upon maintaining an internal position within the boundaries of a theory and at the same time to reject the skeptical move from the external position as a kind of extremism (Quine's naturalized epistemology). From the viewpoint of naturalized argumentation, there is no sense of investigating rationality and our conceptual resources in argumentation by placing ourselves outside their actual use, namely the 'external' position, since there is no such detached position from which such a philosophical inquiry can be conducted.[177] Quine's skeptical holism with the radical relativism eliminates the possibility to maintain a clear distinction between descriptive and normative statements. As already mentioned before in Chapter I.2.2, as the normative/descriptive distinction is unattainable, thus so is the idea that normative theories have a status radically distinct from that of descriptive ones. The only thing left is some gradualness between two points. Thus, one argumentative theory is more normative or descriptive than another theory, but not purely normative or descriptive. Theories that tend to the more descriptive end of the descriptive/normative continuity focus on analyzing the actual argumentative discourse and the whole practice that wraps such pieces of discourse. Theories that tend more to the normative end focus on the requirement for sound argument and enable the evaluation and criticism of actual argumentative discourse. Consequently, the descriptive approach to argumentation collapses into the normative one.[178] We can now generalize Quine's point as follows. Let us say that a Replacement Naturalist in any branch of philosophy holds that .. for any pair of relata that might stand in a justificatory relation – e.g., evidence and theory – reasons and belief, legal reason and judicial

---

1969), pp. 69-80 (p. 82).

174 Ibid., p. 301.

175 Ibid., p. 275 [accompanying text omitted].

176 Ibid. [accompanying text omitted].

177 Schwed (2001), supra note 515, p. 6, 7, referring to Quine (1969), supra note 1032.

178 Ibid., p. 8, referring to W.v.O. Quine, 'Pursuit of Truth. Cambridge', (Cambridge, MA.: Harvard University Press, 1990).

decision – if no normative account of the relation is possible, then the only theoretically fruitful account is the descriptive/explanatory account given by the relevant science of that domain.[179]

According to what Leiter calls the 'Received View', Legal Realism is fundamentally: (1) a descriptive theory about the nature of judicial decision, according to which, (2) judges exercise unfettered discretion, in order, (3) to reach results based on their personal tastes and values, which (4) they then rationalize after-the-fact with appropriate legal rules and reasons. Like much 'conventional wisdom', the Received View of Realism has an element of truth: the core of Realism is, indeed, a certain sort of descriptive claim about how judges decide cases, according to which judges rationalize, after the fact, decisions reached on other grounds.[180] Two aspects of the Received View of Realism are at issue, the claim of 'judicial Volition', i.e., that judges exercise unfettered choice in picking a result and the claim of 'judicial Indiosyncrasy', i.e., that judges make this choice in light of personal or idiosyncratic tastes and values. In its extreme, Frankified form, the theses of Judicial Volition and Judicial Indiosyncrasy lead to the conclusion that judicial decision is utterly unpredictable, as it is never possible to isolate the significant indiosyncratic facts about the individual judge that influence his essentially unconstrained choice of outcome.[181] Leiter argues that it is quite misleading to think of Realism as committed to the claim that judges exercise 'unfettered' discretion,[182] or that they make choices based on 'personal' values and tastes, as in the 'Frankification' of Realism.[183] Realists – Karl Llewellyn, Jerome Frank, Underhill Moore, Felix Cohen, Leon Green,

179 Leiter (1997), supra note 1021, p. 293. One might, of course, hold that the descriptive account just gives us all there is to justification: so, e.g., describing the causal history of a belief may be all there is justifying that belief. See the discussion in Jerry Fodor, 'Encounters with Trees,' in LONDON REV. BOOKS, Apr. 20, 1995. The possibility, however, has no bearing on the project here.

180 Ibid., p. 268.

181 Ibid., p. 279. This is a key theme in FRANK (1930), supra note 1023, p. 111. Of course, it is possible that we could formulate good predictive theories even in the absence of knowledge about the causes of decision. Knowledge of deterministic causation guarantees prediction, but plainly the inverse does not hold. Yet Frank seems to assume – with at least good epistemic reason – that absent knowledge of what causes judges to decide as they do.

182 Ibid., p. 268. Use "unfettered" in Schauer's sense of being "unconstrained by forces external to their own decision-making preferences" - SCHAUER (1991), supra note 997, p. 191.

183 Ibid., p. 269. Some writers are even explicit about this identification. See e.g., ANTHONY T. KRONMAN, 'THE LOST LAWYER: FAILING IDEALS OF THE LEGAL PROFESSION', (1993), pp. 186-209. For an unself-conscious "Frankification" of Realism, see LAURA KALMAN, 'LEGAL REALISM AT YALE 1927-1960', (1986), pp. 6-8.

Herman Oliphant, Walter Wheeler Cook and Max Radin, among others – endorse the following descriptive claim about adjudication: in deciding cases, judges respond primarily to the stimulus of the facts. The Received View can then be seen as simply one interpretation of certain aspects of what Leiter calls this 'Core Claim' of Realism.[184] Where decision is based on unfettered choice, then there is no way to predict decision: what gives us an anchor for prediction is precisely the presence of fetters.[185] When the 'fetters' upon decision are idiosyncratic, the key to prediction will remain epistemologically opaque.[186]

We can now see the contour of the interpretation of the Core Claim that is needed to distinguish it from the Received View. First, choice of decision must, in fact, be sufficiently fettered that prediction is possible. And second, these fetters upon choices must not consist in idiosyncratic facts about individual judges, but rather must be of sufficient generality or commonality to be both accessible and to permit formulating general scientific laws of the kind that make prediction possible.[187] It is natural to construe realism as offering something like an 'inference to the best explanation':[188] given the actual existence of regular patterns of decision (which we Realist identify), the best explanation for the existence of such regularities must be that judges share certain features that channel their decisions into these patterns. The Realists tend to draw their best examples of the Core Claim from the realm of commercial law (rather, say, than constitutional law). Typically, the Realists argue that what judges decide on the facts in such cases falls into one of two patterns: either (1) judges enforce the norms of the prevailing commercial culture; or (2) they try to reach the decision that is socio-economically best under the circumstances.[189] Oliphant illustrates both ways in which decisions track the underlying facts of cases: [A]ll the cases holding the promises invalid are found to be cases of employees' promises not to compete with

184 Ibid. See, KRONMAN (1993), Ibid., subpart II(A).

185 Ibid., p. 280. There are really two senses of "fetters" at issue here. The Received View claims that the Realists believe there are no fetters on (at least many appellate) judicial decisions in the sense of fetters in the form of legal reasons. All the Realists do, in fact, accept this part of the Received View, so understood. What they reject, however, is the claim that there aren't fetters in the form of causal determinants of these decisions; thus, most Realists reject the image of judges as having unbounded volition in deciding cases - precisely the image that many writers infer from the Received View. For clarification on these issues, Leiter is indebted to Steven Burton.

186 Ibid. [accompanying text omitted].

187 Ibid., pp. 280-81.

188 Ibid., p. 281, referring to Gilbert H. Hannan, 'The Inference to the Best Explanation', in 74 PHIL. REV. 88 (1965), p. 88.

189 Ibid.

their employers after a term of employment. Contemporary guild [i.e., labor union] regulations not noticed in the opinions made their holding eminently sound. All the cases holding the promises valid were cases of promises by those selling a business and promising not to compete with the purchasers. Contemporary economic reality made these holdings eminently sound.[190] Underhill Moore's idea was this: identify the normal behavior for any 'institution' (e.g., commercial banking); then identify and demarcate deviations from this norm quantitatively, and try to identify the point at which deviation from the norm will cause a judicial decision that corrects the deviation from the norm (e.g., how far a bank must depart from normal check-cashing practice before a court will decide against the bank in a suit brought by the customer). The goal is predictive formula: deviation of degree x from '[i]nstitutional behavior – i.e., behavior which frequently, repeatedly, usually occurs'[191] - will cause courts to act. Thus, says Moore: "..the semblance of causal relation between future and past decisions is the result of the relation of both to a third variable, the relevant institutions in the locality of the court".[192] Llewellyn notes that the rules seems to have been rather harshly applied in a series of cases where the buyers simply may not have known at the time of rejection of other defects or where the seller could not have cured anyway. But a careful study of the facts of these cases revealed that in each case where the rule seemed harshly applied, what had really happened was that the market had fallen, and the buyer was looking to escape the contract. The court in each case, being sensitive to commerce or to decency,[193] applied the unrelated rule about rejection to frustrate the buyer's attempt to escape the contract. Thus the commercial norm-buyers ought to honor their commitments even under changed market conditions – is enforced by the courts through a seemingly harsh application of an unrelated rule concerning rejection. It is these 'background facts, those of mercantile practice, those of the situation-type'[194] that determine the course of decision.[195] In the context of commercial disputes, some of the Realists claim that what judges try to do is enforce the norms of commercial practice: the norms of commercial practice provides reasons for deciding rather than another ['legal reasons' in terms

---

190 Ibid., referring to Oliphant (1928), supra note 1010, p. 159.

191 Ibid., p. 282, citing Underhill Moore & Theodore Hope, Jr., 'An Institutional Approach to the Law of Commercial Banking,' in 38 YALE L.J. (1929), p. 707.

192 Ibid., referring to Underhill Moore & Gilbert Sussman, 'Legal and Institutional Methods Applied to the Debiting of Direct Discounts – VI. The Decisions, the Institutions, and the Degree of Deviation,' in 40 YALE L.J. 1219 (1931), p. 1219.

193 Ibid., referring to Karl Llewellyn, 'Some Realism About Realism – Responding to Dean Pound', in 44 HARV. L. REV. (1931), p. 124.

194 Ibid., referring to Llewellyn (1931), id., p. 126.

195 Ibid.

foundationalism].[196] If the anti foundationalist legal reasons are considered true, why think we should replace them with 'naturalistic' ones, i.e., with descriptive accounts of what 'inputs' causes what 'outputs'? A Realist has at least four possible responses.[197] First, to give a causal explanation of decisions in terms of reasons does require taking the normative force of the reasons qua reasons seriously.[198] So to give a causal explanation of the decision, as the naturalist wants to do, we must attend to the rationality of the reasons. Where reasons rationalize a decision determinately, why think there is a need for a naturalized explanation, even if one could be given? This suggests the need for a second, more promising, response. Second: If we are going to invoke instutitions about whether naturalistic explanations that do not invoke reasons as causes are more or less useful - or 'fruitful' or 'needed' - than rationalizing explanations, then surely it is an open empirical question which sorts of explanations we should prefer. The Realist might concede, then, that we could understand judicial decisions in terms of responsiveness to nonlegal reasons, but only [responsiveness] to relevant psycho-social facts about judges represents the more fruitful way to go. Third: The most likely response for the Realist to make – and, indeed, the most plausible – is to claim that even the nonlegal reasons, e.g., reasons of 'policy' or of 'morality' – are rationally indeterminate: just as the legal reasons underdetermine the decision, so, too, do the nonlegal reasons. If these considerations are correct, then any explanation of the decision in terms solely of reasons, legal or nonlegal, will necessarily be incomplete. The Realist goal is to locate and articulate the real cause of the decision which requires going beyond the domain of reasons. Fourth, persons respond to the reasons they do for considerations of efficiency or empathetic engagement with the experiences of actual individuals.[199]

The idea that judges decide based, for example, on how they feel about the particular parties or the lawyers [idiosyncrasy] termed 'fireside equities', may sometimes influence judges, but what more typically determines the course of decision is the 'situation-type', i.e., the general pattern of behavior exemplified by the particular facts of the disputed transaction,[200] and what would constitute normal or socio-economically

196 Ibid., p. 298. [As noted earlier], this descriptive claim informed Llewellyn's drafting work on Article 2 of the UCC. [other references omitted].

197 Ibid. The discussion that follows is indebted to fruitful debates on these issues with Jules Coleman, Joseph Raz, and Scott Shapiro.

198 Ibid. For the seminal discussion, see Donald Davidson, 'Actions, Reasons, and Causes', in 60 J.PHIL (1963), p. 685, reprinted in ESSAYS ON ACTIONS AND EVENTS (1980).

199 Ibid., pp. 298-300.

200 Ibid., p. 283. This becomes clear in the sort of instructional materials Realists prepared, which were organized not around doctrinal categories, but

desirable behavior in the relevant commercial context.[201] Judges would enforce the norms of commercial culture as applied to the underlying facts of the case, because, to the best explanation we can infer, there must be features of the 'sociological' (as opposed to the idiosyncratic physiological) profile of the judges that explains the predictable uniformity in their decisions. By dubbing the profile 'sociological', Leiter means to be inclusive, rather than exclusive: the idea is that judges instantiate general characteristics, rather than idiosyncratic ones. What these general characteristics are may be illuminated by sociology, or social psychology, or anthropology.[202] Echoing, but modifying Frank, Llewellyn argued that the place to begin is with the fact that the men of our appellate bench are human beings. And one of the more obvious and obstinate facts about human beings is that they operate in and respond to traditions. Tradition grips them, shapes them, limits them, guides them. To a man of sociology or psychology....this needs no argument.....[203] Radin suggested that the standard transactions with their regulatory incidents are familiar ones to him [the judge] because of his experience as a citizen and a lawyer.[204] Felix Cohen, by contrast, simply lamented that at present no publication [exists] showing the political, economic, and professional background and activities of our various judges,[205] presumably because such a publication would identify the relevant 'social' determinants of decision.[206] Thus, if the

---

rather around factual scenarios or "situation type." For example, Leon Green's torts casebook was originally organized not by the typical doctrinal categories (e.g. negligence, intentional torts, strict liability), but rather by the situation types in which harms occur: e.g., Surgical Operations (Chapter 2), Keeping of Animals (Chapter 3), manufacturers, Dealers (Chapter 5), Builders, Contractors, Workmen (Chapter 6), Traffic and Transportation (Chapter 9). LEON GREEN, 'THE JUDICIAL PROCESS IN TORT CASES,' pp. ix-x (1931). For Green, the Realist, there was no law of torts per se, but rather a regime of tort rules for "surgical operations," another for "manufacturers," etc. For a similar approach to a different area of law, see CHARLES ALAN WRIGHT, 'CASES ON REMEDIES', (1955) (dividing the subject not by type of remedy, but by type of injury). A related view of law (notably contract law) has been taken up more recently in transaction cost economics. See, e.g., OLIVER E. WILLIAMSON, 'REVISING LEGAL REALISM: THE LAW, ECONOMICS, AND ORGANIZATION PERSPECTIVES', (University of Cal. Berkley Program in Law and Econ. Working Paper No. 95-12, 1996, pp. 13-16.

201 Ibid.

202 Ibid., p. 283 and n.79.

203 Ibid., p. 284, referring to Llewellyn (1931), supra note 1052, p. 53.

204 Ibid., referring to Radin (1925), supra note 1025, p. 358.

205 Ibid., referring to Cohen (1935), supra note 981, p. 809, 846.

206 Ibid. "A truly realistic theory of judicial decisions," says Cohen, "must conceive every decision as something more than an expression of individual personality, as .....even more importantly a product of social determinants...."

Sociological Wing of Realism - Llewellyn, Moore, Oliphant, Cohen, Radin, among others – is correct, then Judicial decisions are causally determined by the relevant psycho-social facts about judges, and at the same time judicial decisions fall into predictable patterns because these psycho-social facts about judges – their professionalization experiences, their backgrounds, etc – are not idiosyncratic, but characteristics of significant portions of the judiciary.[207]

What is required for a 'naturalized' jurisprudence is that we seek methodological continuity with the natural and social sciences. Folk theories plainly satisfy this demand: they seek causal explanations for these decisions, inasmuch as they understand 'reasons' as 'causes'; and they look for regular, law-like-ideally lawful-patterns of decision. That lawyers posses workable, if informal, folk theories of judicial decision serves to vindicate and instantiate Realism's naturalistic program.[208]

II.1.5.3. SCANDINAVIAN REALIST

Uppsala philosophers, led by Axel Hagerström and Adolf Phalen, maintain that (i) conceptual analysis is a central philosophical task, (ii) subjectivism (conceived as the view that the object of a person's consciousness exists only in this consciousness) is false, (iii) metaphysics (conceived as the view that there is a reality beyond the world of time and space) is false, even pernicious, and (iv) there are no objective values.[209] As far as the Scandinavians are concerned, they unanimously rely on the ontology and epistemology of Hagerström,[210] which in philosophical lingo we might call, respectively, external realism[211] and empirism. External realism might

---

Cohen (1935), Ibid., p. 843. The notion is taken up at length in the extensive political science literature on judicial decision-making (other references omitted).

207 Ibid.

208 Ibid., p. 313.

209 Spaak (2009/2011), supra note 973, pp. 6-7. For more on the Uppsala School of philosophy, see Oxenstierna (1938).

210 Escorihuela (2003), supra note 967, p. 722. See generally Axel Hagerström, 'Inquiries into the Nature of Law and Moral' (1953). A helpful, although fairly critical account of Hagerström's epistemology and its links to his discussion of law can be found in Jes Bjarup, 'Epistemology and LawAccording to Axel Hagerstrom', in 29 Scandinavian Studies in Law (1985) 13-47.

211 Ibid. The term 'external realism' is borrowed here from analytic philosopher J.R. Searle, 'The Construction of Social Reality,' (1995), p. 150 etc. Jes Bjarup prefers to call Hagerstrom's ontology 'naïve realism', (see Bjarup 1985, supra note 1069, p. 19). Incidently, Bjarup refers to Hagerstrom's realism also as 'direct

even be further specified as psycho-physicalism without excessive concern for verbosity or using too much words (i.e., all of reality is comprehensively reducible to physical objects and psychological states).[212] Scandinavian legal realists also gave their contribution to the legal philosophy. Because they were of the Civil Law tradition, their analysis was not on case-law, but on the reality in the legal aspect of the society including voluntary obedience. Hagerstrom, Anders Vilhelm Lundstedt, Ekelof, Ingemar Hedenius, Karl Olivecrona and Alf Ross belonged to the school. Hagerstrom and Lundstedt have developed their prime thesis "*value nihilsm*" that in science there is no place for normative sentences which do not have any logical meaning and factual content.[213] The legal scholarship employing normative formulae was metaphysical and not scientific and did not reflect reality. Any statements on valid laws should be based on observable facts, which was the facts of regularity of public official behavior and sanctions imposed on law breakers. In his critique of Hans Kelsen's theory of law, put forward in a 1928 review of Kelsen's *Hauptprobleme der Staatsrechtslehre*, Hagerstrom argues that the very idea of the world of the ought is absurd, since this world cannot be thought of as existing alongside the world of time and space.[214] For, he reasons, no knowledge of any reality is possible, except through relating its object to a systematically interconnected whole, and the fact that the two worlds – the world of the ought and the world of time and space – are different in kind means that they cannot be coordinated in a systematically interconnected whole. As he puts it, 'so far as I contemplate the one [world], the other [world] does not exists for me'. The thesis presupposes that the law is obeyed because of the deterrence through imposed sanctions upon law breakers.

Ekelof emphasizes on the importance of moral formation with respect to obedience to the law, although the deterrence of sanctions is admitted as an important factor that causes obedience to the law.[215] Hedeneius holds the validity of a legal rule will have a meaning only if such a meaning is empirical and non-metaphysical and is factually applicable, and therefore the validity should have same meaning as the

idealism', which in that case means that nothing stands in the way of cognition between mind and world (see Bjarup's intriguing analogy between Lenin's and Hagerstrom's respective stances on the theory of knowledge, Jes Bjarup (1985), Ibid., p. 20).

212 Ibid., p. 723 [accompanying text and footnote omitted].

213 Aubert (1983), supra note 956, pp. 10-11.

214 Spaak (2009/2011), supra note 1068, p. 25, referring to Axel Hagerstrom (1953), Kelsen's Theory of Law and the State', in Axel Hagerstrom, Inquiries into the Nature of Law and Morals. Ed. Karl Olivecrona. Trans. C.D. Broad (Uppsala: Kungliga humanistiska vetenskapssamfundet I Uppsala, 1953), pp. 257-298 (p. 267).

215 Aubert (1983), supra note 1072, p. 13.

existing empirical regularity of human behavior.[216] Olivecrona says that legal sanctions will lose their meanings any where if the sovereign cannot functionalize the law provisions in the state-system which is backed up by force. For Ross, a national law system constitutes rules to create and functionalize the state power machinery.[217] But Ross also holds there is a 'legal consciousness' having direct influences upon lawmakers. Ross's legal consciousness corresponds to traditional psychological theory.[218] Many scientists have regarded Ross as a legal theorist whose real intention was to replace traditional legal dogmatics with social-psychological or legal-sociological studies.[219] The science of law being a branch of the doctrine of human behavior ....the legal phenomenon must be found within the field of psycho-physical phenomena constituting the domain of psychology and sociology.[220] In terms of the is/ought division laid out by Karl Llewellyn, Ross clearly delimits legal science to the realm of the 'is' – that is, in his case, the realm of psycho-physical facts – since valuations concerning the shape that the law ought to take are not within the realm of scientific investigation.[221] Any attempt by legal science to confuse the investigation of the factual reality of law and the normative evaluation of the contents of the law derails legal science towards metaphysics again, insofar as that would mean considering that there is any way to discuss values in objective terms.[222] According to Jes Bjarup, Ross has failed to take the consequences of his own position and carry out a regular study of e.g., judicial behavior taking into account all factors motivating judges.[223]

It is clear that Olivecrona in his first edition of *Law as Fact* (1939) had in mind the *social* sciences, especially psychology.[224] Torben Spaak believes that Olivecrona was an ontological, but not a semantic naturalist,

---

216 Ibid, p. 11.

217 Ibid, pp. 11-12.

218 Miller (1985/1986), supra note 1020, p. 400.

219 Dalberg-Larsen (2010), supra note 968, p. 43.

220 Escorihuela (2003), supra note 1071, p. 728, referring to Alf Ross, "Towards a Realistic Jurisprudence" (1946), p. 78.

221 Ibid., p. 723. Lundstedt puts it, as bluntly as always, in the following manner: "The exclusion of allowing value judgments to enter into scientific reasonings as premises or arguments is obvious – if one has decided that science (disregarding abstract mathematics and pure logic) must be empirical, i.e., based on empirical knowledge. Evaluation have nothing to do with such knowledge, as they cannot be any statements of reality, of true facts. Nothing is changed in this respect by the fact that a value judgment in jurisprudence can often be shared by the majority in the community and is sometimes even almost unanimous.' (see Lundstedt 1956, 'Legal Thinking Revised', p. 48).

222 Ibid.

223 Dalberg-Larsen (2010), supra note ,1078, p. 40.

224 Spaak (2009/2011), supra note 1073, p. 10.

and that he probably was not a methodological natularist either. For he clearly believes that everything that exists is composed of natural entities whose properties determine all the properties of that which exists.[225] Olivecrona's adherence to ontological naturalism is clear from his claim that any adequate theory of law must eschew metaphysics and treat the law as a matter of *social facts*. The aim, Olivecrona explains, is to *reduce* our picture of the law to make it correspond with objective reality.[226] The form of legal rules, according to Olivecrona, is imperative, because the lawmakers do not aim to inform us about the existence of certain ideas in their minds, but to impress a certain behavior on us.[227] Statutory provisions are often phrased in the indicative or the subjunctive mood, but they always express an imperative.[228] Olivecrona appears to believe that an utterance functions as an imperative if it is *intended* to be an imperative. But, to determine whether a particular utterance is intended to be an imperative, one needs to consider the whole situation in which the utterance takes place.[229] There is only a *psychological connection*, viz. a connection in a person's mind between the imperative expression and the idea of an action.[230] He says that the word 'ought' and the like are imperative expressions which are used in order to impress a certain behavior on people. *Their sole function is to work on the minds of people*, directing them to do this or that or to refrain from something else – not to communicate knowledge about the state of things. We should note here that the claim that imperatives are psychologically effective is of central importance to Olivecrona's naturalistic theory of law – if they weren't psychologically effective, the theory would be seriously incomplete, since, on Olivecrona's analysis, there are no legal relations the knowledge of which could somehow motivate the citizens to act accordingly.[231] Olivecrona has made a statement on psychological connection in this regard.[232] There is no real judgment behind the sentences. The objective nature of an action is not determined by saying that it should not be undertaken. What lies behind the sentences is something other than a judgment. It is that, in our mind, an imperative expression is coupled to the idea of an action. This is a psychological connection only, though of the utmost importance in social life.

---

225 Ibid., p. 14.

226 Ibid., pp. 15-16, referring to Olivecrona, 'Law as Fact', (Copenhagen: Einar Munksgaard & Oxford: Humphrey Milford, 1939), pp. 25-27.

227 Ibid., p. 32, referring to Olivecrona (1939), Ibid., p. 31.

228 Ibid., referring to Olivecrona, 'Lagens imperative [The Imperative of the Law]', (Lund: Gleerup, 1942), p. 9.

229 Ibid., referring to Olivecrona (1942), Ibid., pp. 16-17.

230 Ibid.

231 Ibid., p. 36.

232 Ibid., pp. 18-19, referring to Olivecrona (1939), supra note 1086, p. 46.

It is interesting to note that John Searle, a leading theorist of performative language, speaks of 'a quasi-magical power of bringing about changes in the world through our utterances'.[233] As J.L. Austin explains, a perfomative utterance, such as 'I promise to lend you $100' or 'I hereby invite you to dinner on Saturday night', has its main verb in the first person present, indicative, active (singular or plural), or is equivalent to such an utterance. It differs from ordinary statement of fact in that he who utters it (i) does not describe or report anything, which means that it cannot be true or false, and (ii) is usually thought to *do* something rather than to (merely) say something.[234] Olivercona's performative imperative seems to parallel Searl's performative language.[235] According to him, if I hand over a watch to my son saying, 'This shall be your property', I am using an imperative form of speech. But I am not commanding him to do anything. The imperative is directed towards his acquiring ownership of the watch.[236] The effect of the utterance is psychological. This is a 'real' effect.[237] With reference to Austin's example, Olivecrona contends that marriage has many consequences. A few performatory words are used that purport to make the parties man and wife. He askes "What happens?" The psychological effect is instantaneous, uniform and far-reaching.[238] The parties are socially classified in a new way, which has consequences of an ethical, religious and legal kind.[239] Performative utterances are not used to report facts; they describe nothing. Their purpose is to establish a new legal relationship; legal consequences are attached to the utterances. They are held to give rise to rights and duties or legal properties.[240] His analysis of the concept of a performative imperative includes a consideration of the nature of the *legal effects* that is supposed to follow from the utterance of such imperatives. Keeping with his belief that there is no such thing as binding force, that there is no legal effect to be found – there is only the psychological fact that people tend to

233 Martin P. Golding, 'Rights, Performatives, and Promises in Karl Olivecrona's Legal Theory', in Ratio Juris Vol. 18 No. 1, March 2005, pp. 16-29 (p. 24), referring to John R. Searle (1991), 'How Performatives Work', in Tennessee Law Review 58, pp. 371-392 (p. 384).

234 Spaak (2009/2011), supra note 1091, p. 39, referring to J.L. Austin, 'How To Do Things With Words', 2nd ed. (J.O. Urmson & Marina Sbisa Eds.), (Cambridge, M.A.: Harvard University Press, 1975), pp. 4-7.

235 Golding (2005), supra note 1092, p. 24, referring to Olivecrona, 'Law as Fact', (London: Stevens & Sons, 1971), p. 134, 218.

236 Ibid., p. 25, referring to Olivecrona 1971, Ibid, p. 134.

237 Ibid.

238 Ibid., referring to Olivecrona 1971, supra note 1095, p. 225.

239 Ibid.

240 Ibid., p. 24. See Olivecrona (1962), 'Legal Language and Reality', in Essays in Jurisprudence in Honor of Roscoe Pound (R.A. Newman, ed.), (Indianapolis, IN:Bobbs-Merril, 1962), pp. 151-191 (p. 174).

believe that there is a legal, and, of course, the (sociological) fact that they tend to *act* accordingly.[241] The consequences of legal performatives then are of a double nature: immediate psychological effects, and the relevance of the acts for action by state organs. The former is a plausible empirical thesis, the latter seems for Olivecrona psychological and plays a crucial role insofar as 'actual effects' are brought about through the medium of a court's feeling bound by the rules.[242]

Olivecrona, who is a psycho-ontological legal realist, explains that in modern states the coercive power of the state is normally kept in the background, and that the citizens do not think of the state as possessing coercive power, but rather as possessing an ideal power to enact binding laws.[243] He adds that if this view is widespread among the citizens, as a result the state will posses *psychological* power, and he points out that these two types of power – coercive and psychological – presuppose one another. Law as fact is what the social reality constitutes the punctual experience of law as the result of the dialectics of belief and compulsion,[244] and therefore the focus is not on the rationalized experience as norm, but on the legal decision by the authorities. A source of law, as well as the judicial process and the doctrines of legal interpretation, [which] must undergo 'a radical change in character of the juridical phenomena themselves, not the juridical rationalizations, are made the starting point of our considerations.[245]

II.1. 6. ANTHROPOLOGICAL LEGAL STUDIES

Law among Trobiand of Melanesia, according to Bronislaw Malinowski, an anthropologist, was not to be found in 'central authority, codes, courts, and constables',[246] but rather in social relations. He holds that the binding forces of Melanesian civil law are to be found in the concatenation of the obligations, in the fact that they are arranged into chains of mutual services, a give and take extending over long periods of time and covering wide aspects of interests and activity.[247] The problem with this approach

241 Spaak (2009/2011), supra note 1093, p. 40.

242 Golding (2005), supra note 1094, p. 26.

243 Spaak (2009/2011), supra note 1100, pp. 55-56, referring to Olivecrona (1971), supra note 1099, pp. 267-268.

244 Escorihuela (2003), supra note 1079, p. 729 [accompanying text omitted].

245 Ibid., referring to Ross (1946), supra note 1079, p. 148.

246 Tamanaha (2008a), supra note 959, p. 391, referring to Bronislaw Malinowski, 'Crime and Custom in Savage Society', (1926), p. 14.

247 Ibid., p. 392, referring to Malinowski (1926), Ibid., p. 76.

was noted by Sally Falk Moore, that the conception of law Malinowski propounded was so broad that it was virtually indistinguishable from the study of the obligatory aspect of all social relationships.[248] Moore says that some writers, following John Griffiths, now take legal pluralism to refer to the whole aggregate of governmental and non-govermental norms of social control, without any distinction drawn as to their source. However, for many purposes this agglomeration has to be disaggregated. For reasons of both analysis and policy, distinction must be made that identifies the provenance of rules and controls.[249] Moore has identified several social phenomena highlighted by legal pluralism, including the way in which the state is interdigitated (internally and externally) with non-governmental, semi-autonomous social fields which generate their own (*non-legal*) obligatory norms to which they can induce or coerce compliance.[250] Under Griffiths's account, the norms of the semi-autonomous social field are *law*. [Griffiths holds those norms are law, but Moore does not]. However, Griffith later changed and asserted: "In the intervening years, further reflection on the concept of law has led me to the conclusion that the word 'law' could better be abandoned altogether for purposes of theory formation in sociology of law". It also follows from the above considerations that the expression 'legal pluralism' can and should be reconceptualized as 'normative pluralism' or 'pluralism in social control" [Griffiths says: normative pluralism, rather than legal pluralism].[251] Nonetheless, the notion of legal pluralism continues to spread. Legal pluralists scholars continue to incorporate Moore's SASF (semi autonomous social field) to identify law, and continue to rely upon Griffiths's analysis.[252]

As to a framework for legal pluralism, six systems of normative ordering are sketched by Tamanaha. *Official or positive legals systems* are linked characteristically to an institutionalized legal apparatus of some kind; they are manifested in legislatures, enforcement agencies, tribunals; they give rise to powers, rights, agreements, criminal sanctions, and remedies. *Customary normative systems* include shared social rules and customes, as well as a social institutions and mechanisms, from reciprocity,

---

248 Ibid., referring to Sally Falk Moore, 'Law as Process: an Athropological Approach', (1978), p. 220.

249 Ibid., p. 394, referring to Moore 1973, 1978, 1998, 1999, 2000.

250 Ibid., p. 95, referring to Sally Falk Moore, 'Certainties Undone: Fifty Turbulant Years of Legal Anthropology 1949-1999' in Sally Falk Moore (ed.), Law and Anthroplogy: A Reader (2005), p. 358 (emphasis added). Moore follows this statement with a footnote that makes an oblique reference to Griffiths, 'The Idea of Sociology of Law and its Relation to Law and to Sociology', in (2005) 8 Current Legal Issues 49, pp. 63-64.

251 Ibid., p. 395, referring to Griffiths (2005), Ibid.

252 Ibid., p. 396.

to dispute resolution tribunals, to councils of traditional leaders. *Religious normative systems* are in some societies an aspect of and inseparable from customary normative systems. *Economic/capitalist normative systems* consists of the range of norms and institutions that constitute and relate to capitalist production and market transactions within social arenas. *Functional normative systems* are organized and arranged in connection with the pursuit of a particular function, purpose or activity that goes beyond purely commercial pursuits. And the last is *community/cultural normative systems*, which are the vaguest category. In general terms, it is an imagined identification by a group of a common way of life, usually tied to a common language and history and contained within geographical boundaries of some kind, but there can be 'communities' of interaction which exist purely on the internet comprised of people from around the world.[253]

The penchant of many legally trained development practitioners and academics to assume that state law and state courts are the solution to the problems faced by these countries is the product of ingrained belief about the state having a monopoly over law. In situations where the state legal system fails to deliver basic services and attempts to reform the system persistently fail, the solution must be found elsewhere. Just as functional alternatives to law may satisfy the requirements of economic development, functional alternatives to law may be available to resolve disputes, maintain order, and coordinate behavior. Customs and customary laws; religious norms and bodies; and community or informal norms and tribunals do a great deal of this work in many settings around the world.[254]

II.2. PRESCRIPTIVE AND/OR NORMATIVE JURISPRUDENCE

The work of legal philosophy and history is generally viewed as auxiliary to law's normativity. Legal philosophy helps legitimate the legal system and clarify its basic concepts, while legal history provides useful data for making normative legal and policy argument. Philosophers and historians are valuable to others in the legal academy because of their relationship to a legal academy dominated by prescriptivism.[255] The theory or philosophy of

253 Ibid., pp. 396-399.

254 Ibid., p. 246. See Customary Justice and the Rule of Law in War-Torn Societies, (Deborah H. Isser ed., forthcoming 2011).

255 Jack M. Balkin & Sanford Levinson, 'Law and the Humanities:An Uneasy Relationship-Essay', in Yale Journal of Law and the Humanities, Vol. 18: 155 (2006), pp. 175-176.

law, according to Finnis, is best done by tracing the human needs to which law – legal systems and the rule of law – is a uniquely appropriate kind of response.[256] These needs constitute the basic reasons for action which are available to make law a set of *reasons for action*. One main human need is (to cut a long story) the need to be treated justly. So law, *positive law*, is needed largely if not wholly as the appropriate response to the need for justice. So *of course* positive law should be just, and should claim to be just, and be such that the claim is true not false. This is a normative need, and any conceptual necessities and historical typicalities that may be established by the formation of concepts and practices in line with this and other normative needs are necessities and typicalities *derivative* from these normative needs or necessities, needs and necessities that not surprisingly are reflected more or less adequately by those established concepts.

Law resists complete invasion by any other disciplines because law's professional orientation produces a curious kind of normative attitude that is quite different from the normativity that appears in many parts of the humanities. By normativity, we mean simply the way that persons within a discipline take normative positions, and the kinds of normative claims that they are expected to make.[257] In law, the form that normativity takes is quite narrow.[258] We might call it prescriptivism – the demand that each piece of scholarship offer some account, however nebulous, of the stakes for how the law should be modified or interpreted or how legal decision-makers should do their job. The demand that legal scholarship be cashed out in policy prescriptions deeply circumscribes the legal imagination and the permissible boundaries of legal scholarship, while

256 Finnis (2014), supra note 916, p. 10.

257 Balkin & Levinson (2006), supra note 1114, pp. 174-175. The idea of "normativity" is presented on the fact that there are many different ways to take a normative position, and many different aesthetics and styles for doing so. For example, one can make normative claims through criticism of the status quo without offering alternatives or through positive proposals for reform, and proposals for reform, in turn, can be directed at improving institutions or conventions, or at individual or group self-awareness or self-improvement. One can criticize (or praise) a person, a practice, a cultural tradition, or an institution. One can work on showing contradiction or inadequacy in reasoning, attempt to demonstrate bad faith, impure motives, self-delusion or hypocrisy, or focus on bad consequences. One can offer normative judgments directly or make them directly through comparative or historical study.Finally, some disciplines and practices insist that they are interested solely in description so that people within them must take normative positions through implication and stealth.

258 Ibid., p. 175. The critique of law's particular normative stance has been made most ably by Pierre Schlag. See PAUL CAMPOS, PIERRE SCHLAG & STEVEN D. SMITH, 'AGAINST THE LAW' (1996); PIERRE SCHLAG, 'LAYING DOWN THE LAW: MYSTICISM, FETISHISM, AND THE AMERICAN LEGAL MIND' (1996).

simultaneously reorienting legal scholarship towards legal practice and policy science.[259] Even though legal scholars, have, over the years, rebelled against the prescriptivism of the legal academy in countless ways, they are continually drawn into the gravitational orbit of law's normativity, which, in turn, reflects law's orientation to legal practice.[260] Constitutional grants of power are seldom absolute. More frequently, they specify the scope of an official's jurisdiction to act authoritatively – that is, they authorize officials to perform some acts but not others. Power-conferring rules typically also prescribe the procedures officials must use in order to act with legal authority.[261]

The success of interdisciplinary studies in law is strongly shaped by the professional orientation of law schools and the prescriptive nature of legal normativity.[262] Law co-opts the insights of social sciences like economics and sociology, or humanistic subjects like history, philosophy or literary criticism and turns them to its own uses. Law uses rhetoric to establish its authority and to legitimize particular acts of legal and political power. The humanities rise and fall in relation to other disciplines to the extent that the humanities help lawyers perform the rhetorical tasks.[263] The humanities play a significant role in the legal academy or the legal profession. The influence of the humanities will be filtered through law's professionalism and prescriptivism, and hemmed in by law's institutional constraints; yet the law will always maintain a genuine ... relationship with the humanities as long as it remains a thoroughly rhetorical enterprise.[264]

The positivists have devoted their best talents to understanding the multiple facets of the actual legal order, and to making the legal process a more effective instrument of human purposes. Iredell Jenkins calls this intention 'the keystone of legal positivism'. The content of the legal order, as defining factual consequences, are dependent on criteria, standards, ends, purposes, and values that have extralegal sources and meaning.[265] The legacy of difficulties arising from a naïve positivism is generally thought to have over-emphasized the role of coercive power. The resulting reaction in

---

259 Ibid.

260 Ibid.

261 Richard H. Fallon Jr., 'Constitutional Constraints', in 97 [No.4] California Law Review (2009), p. 998.

262 Balkin & Levinson (2006), supra note 1119, p. 184.

263 Ibid.

264 Ibid., pp. 186-187.

265 Herbert G. Reid, 'A Philosopher's Perspective on Law: A Study of Morris R. Cohen', (1971), in Americal Journal of Jurisprudence: Vol. 16: Iss. 1, Article 10, p. 243, referring to Iredell Jenkins, "The Matchmaker: Or Toward a Synthesis of Legal Idealism and Positivism", in Journal of Legal Education XII (1959), pp. 1-32, 28, 5-6.

modern jurisprudence against the focus upon coercion reflects a failure to come to grips fully with the underlying methodological issues of descriptive legal theory. Basically, such descriptive theory seeks, or ought to seek, a critically informed understanding of law 'as it is'.[266] We should make at least some efforts to delineate the nature of this kind of understanding. Most importantly, one must seek to appreciate the relevance of our normative deliberations concerning the use of coercion in informing our descriptive undertakings, in particular by helping to structure the analysis of basic legal concepts. Yet much, if not most, descriptive legal theory has ignored this relevance.[267]

It would be the fact that law has the capacity for guidance by providing reasons for action, or that it is related to the state's authority and so on. All these are normative concepts that come from the domain of political philosophy. It is unlikely that our judgments on these matters, *if we seek theoretical illumination* and not a mere report of people's attitudes, are likely to be politically or morally neutral.[268] Finnis elaborates that no one ever can rationally treat as *fact alone* as giving reason for anything, let alone something as demanding and choice-restricting as a law.[269] There must always be some 'evaluative argument' for treating any fact or combination of facts as a 'basis' for identifying a proposition as obligation-imposing or in some other way directive or normative. And, in no legal system responsive to human needs do citizens, judges, or other officials look to the bare social fact of a past legislative act or act of adjudication. Always the reference is to such acts in their intra-systemic context. And that context is, first and foremost, a set of propositions identifying necessary and sufficient conditions of validity both legislative and adjudicative acts and of the legal rules identifiable by reference (directly but in part) to those acts. Contributing both rationale and countless details of content to this

---

266 Nance (1985), supra note 1027, p. 1 [accompanying text omitted].

267 Ibid., referring to David Lyons, 'Founders and Foundations of Legal Positivism' (Book Review), in 82 MICH. L. REV. 722 (1984), p. 727. In a review of H.L.A. Hart's recent work on Bentham, David Lyons observes: "Much of Bentham's works was concerned with the analysis of legal concepts. By this I mean not the identification and interpretation of general principles that are embedded in the law but the explanation in more fundamental terms of the very idea of law and of the more specific ideas such as that of a legal right or obligation. Thus, Bentham was concerned to reveal not just what the law of a particular jurisdiction at a given time requires and allows but also what it is for there to be law, what it is for someone to have a legal right, and so on. A good deal of work within legal philosophy was focused on such abstract questions. But the connection between this seemingly pure theoretical inquiry and the moral concerns or commitments of legal philosophers have not been systematically explored.

268 Priel (2007), supra note 867, p. 152.

269 Finnis (2014), supra note 1115, p. 16.

complex of propositions and intellectual acts (juristic interpretation), will be found 'references' – often silent but detectable by inference – to the desirability of coherence here and now, of stability across time, of fidelity to undertakings, respect for legitimate expectations, avoidance of tyranny, preservation of the community whose laws these are (and of its capacity for self-government), protection of the vulnerable, incentives for investment, maintenance of that condition of communal life we call the Rule of Law, and many other 'evaluative arguments'.

Law is a significant institution saturated with 'oughts', so understanding the question of normativity is an important one.[270] Normative jurisprudence is concerned with explaining what makes legal practice, or particular aspects of it, justified. Most normative jurisprudence is concerned with particular legal doctrines, it is possible to advance normative arguments directed at law in general, such as claims explaining why having law is preferable to some kind of lawless state of nature, why a legal system where legal rules are incrementally developed by judges is superior (or inferior) to a legal system in which many of the legal rules are enacted by legislature and found in a statutory code.[271] Writing from the perspective of normative jurisprudence have challenged the descriptive approach, with argument that any such description of what law is can only be made against a background of an evaluative judgment as to the point or purpose of having law and the goods that having law can secure.[272] In addition to the descriptive theory, [it may be that] law should be practiced quite differently from the way it is in order to optimally achieve law's goal.[273]

Bentham has argued that it is mostly prescriptive claims about law that can be universal.[274] His contrast between 'local' and 'universal' jurisprudence is the distinction between 'the laws of such a nation or nations in particular' and 'the laws of all nations whatsoever'.[275] Bentham recognizes that at the level of description there are endless differences between legal systems. Therefore, the universality of jurisprudence lay for him not at the level of description – here, 'to be, strictly speaking,

270 Priel (2008/2009), supra note 860, p. 35.

271 Ibid., p. 2.

272 Ibid., pp. 4-5. See, e.g., Ronald Dworkin, "Justice in Robes" (2006), pp. 32-34; John Finnis, "On the Incoherence of Legal Positivism", in 75 Notre Dame L. Rev. (2000), p. 1597, ("general description of law will be fruitful only if their basic conceptual structure is .....derived from the understanding of good reasons").

273 Ibid., p. 20.

274 Ibid., p. 1.

275 Ibid., p. 5, referring to Jeremy Bentham, 'An Introduction to the Principles of Morals and Legislation', in JH Burns & HLA Hart, eds., (Clarendon Press, 1996), p. 294.

universal, [jurisprudence] must confine itself to terminology'.[276] Rather, universal jurisprudence was mostly concerned with prescription: It is in the censorial line that there is the greatest room for disquisitions that apply to the circumstances of all nations alike.[277] Bentham's '*An Introduction to the Principles of Morals and Legislation* (1789)' is a presentation of an ethical theory that actions are right insofar as they produce happiness or prevent sufferings, and is an explanation of a political theory that the purpose of civil or criminal laws is to maximize the amount of happiness which may be enjoyed by society. He rejects the notion that the law of reason is a sufficient principle of morality. The law of reason and the law of nature are only theoretical of speculative principles and cannot be practically applied to every moral situation. Bentham defined ethics as the art of producing the greatest possible amount of happiness for oneself and for others; and ethics is both the art of fulfilling one's duty to oneself and the art of fulfilling one's duty to others. According to him, if an act of legislation conforms to the principle of utility, then it tends to increase the total happiness of all individuals. Legal punishments should be proportional to the amount of harm caused by the offenses, but the amount of punishment should not be unjust or arbitrary.[278] For Bentham, what made some laws bad was their lack of utility, their tendency to lead to unhappiness and misery without accomplishing happiness. If a law or an action does not do any good, then it isn't any good. He also promulgated the principle of utility as the standard of right action on the part of governments and individuals. As stated above, actions are approved when they are such as to promote happiness, and disapproved of when they have a tendency to cause unhappiness, and he focused on act-evaluation, not on character evaluation, therefore he shifted from the intrinsic to the instrumental approach, where actions are wrong in virtue of their effect or consequence, thus instrumentally wrong.[279]

Iredell Jenkins says that actually there is both an element of 'morals-in-the-law' important to its outcomes and that outcomes of the law, although sometimes legal may yet be revolting to our sense of justice.[280] Morris Cohen concluded the brief discussion of his legal philosophy as follows: Law, and even the ethical ideal itself, may certainly be viewed as the historic resultant of various social forces. Yet the old problem of natural law, the problem as to what under given conditions the law

---

276 Ibid., referring to Bentham (1996 ed), Ibid., p. 295.

277 Ibid.

278 Driver (2014), supra note 418, § 2.1, referring to Jeremy Bentham (1789) [PML], 'An Introduction to the Principles of Morals and Legislation' (Oxford: Clarendon Press, 1907; Amherst : Prometheus Books, 1988), p. 1 & 310.

279 Ibid., pp. 6-9.

280 Reid (1971), supra note 1124, p. 243, referring to Jenkins (1959), supra note 1124, pp. 28, 5-6.

ought to be, remains. Realism in the law can be combined with genuine idealism in the doctrine of the inherent limitations of legal idealism due to the conditions of human nature, habits, the legal machinery, and the limitations of man's desire for the moral good.[281] Cohen has definitely doubted that it is ....humanly possible to banish the evaluational point of view from an adequate science of law. Such a science must come to ask 'how are we to choose the basic premises of our legal system [and here] we enter the realm of ethics as the science of ultimate human ends'.[282] His whole life and thought may be viewed as including a deep respect for the processes of reason and a continuing concern in the task of establishing ethical norms by the use of reason. He may not have solved the major problems involved in the latter task but he had the insight to face them and the courage to face them honestly. Cohen holds that the *ideal* of legal science will always be, to quote Cairn's formulation, in the direction of a validly constructed postulational system, the postulates of which will be empirical hypotheses. This suggestion explicitly recognizes the importance in their formulation of the role of logic, philosophy, and ethics.[283] In an essay published in 1940, Cohen said: "...since we lack omniscience as to all the possible forms of social adjustment, experimentation, or the process of learning from experience, is indispensable. Law and morality can coincide only in the fundamental assumptions as to the proper procedure to enable us to correct our mistakes. Their common ideal is thus like that of science, to wit, a system that corrects itself by the process of testing principles by their consequences, and conversely, judging actual consequences in the light of principles".[284] After all, Cohen has argued that 'actual practices may be contrary to the policy of the law'. Actual law is never a complete system, as actual, nor the jurist avoid concern for the purpose of the law. Science does not deal only with what actually is. The actual has meaning for science only when judged in the light of some ideal or possible alternatives.[285]

Although Olivecrona is a realist, he admits that legal rules is directive. He holds that legal statements – such as rights statements or statements about duty – fulfill a directive, an informative, or a technical

281 Ibid., p. 245, referring to Cohen, 'Studies in Philosophy and Science', (N.Y.: Ungar, 1949), p. 27.

282 Ibid., p. 251, quoting Cohen, 'Reason and Law', (New York: First Collier Books Edition 1961), pp. 10-15.

283 Ibid., p. 257, referring to Huntington Cairns, 'The Theory of Legal Science', (Chapel Hill: University of North Carolina, 1941), p. 81,143. Cairns, in 1941, suggested initial concentration on the task of constructing only a postulational science of law.

284 Ibid., referring to Cohen (1961), supra note 1141, p. 37.

285 Ibid., p. 254, referring to Cohen, 'Law and the Social Order', (N.Y: Harcourt Brace, 1933), p. 204.

function in legal thinking, and that in regard to its *informative* function, a legal statement may be correct or incorrect, but not true or false. The *correctness* of a legal statement consists in conformity of the statement to an effective system of rules, whereas the *truth* of such statement would consist in correspondence of the statement to brute – as distinguished from institutional – facts.[286] Legal statements are associated with certain consequential ideas on the part of those concerned, and that, if correct, such statements are supported by the coercive power of the state.[287] He does point out that the concept of a right nevertheless fulfills an important function in legal thinking, in that it *guides people's behavior*. He explains that it is essential that the idea of a pattern of conduct should always be awakened in the minds of those concerned and that they should be incited to follow it.[288]

In *Brown v Board of Education*, 347 U.S.(1954), the justices were right, morally speaking, to decide the case as they did and that the country is better as a result. Matters may look different, however, if we imagine the justices to be as prone to moral error as the ordinary lot of humanity.[289] Polanyi has so vigorously shown that even practitioners of the stricter kind of science bring value commitments to their work.[290] In the looser sciences such as sociology some of the best authorities have made plain that not only do personal value judgment necessarily guide the sociologist, but that the most conscientious course with such value judgments is to hold them consciously and state them explicitly.[291] In the 'science of jurisprudence', a looser science still, can one undertake any analysis without a moral purpose, without evaluation of the uses of law, without commitments as to what law should be? Is not analysis clarified, if these purposes, values and commitment are explicitly recorded? The question of purpose is central to the discussion Hart undertakes of the intersecting points of law and morals. Morals influence statutory law; they may, though they need not, guide a

286 Spaak (2009/2011), supra note 1102, p. 62. Spaak means by 'institutional facts' facts that depend on the existence of one or more rules.

287 Ibid., p. 64, referring to Olivecrona (1971), supra note 1094, pp. 259-60.

288 Ibid., pp. 42-3, referring to Olivecrona (1939), supra note 1091, p. 95.

289 Fallon (2009), supra note 1120, p. 1008. See e.g., Jeremy Waldron, 'Moral Truth and Judicial Review', in 43 AM. J. JURIS. 75, 88 (1998) (arguing that we lack any "epistemic apparatus that would enable us to ground any but the most trivial and unhelpful inductions about expertise and institutional competence"); see also Richard A. Posner, 'The Problematics of Moral and Legal Theory,' in 111 HARV. L. REV. (1998), p. 1637.

290 John T. Noonan, Jr., 'The Concept of Law. By H.L.A. Hart. Oxford: Oxford University Press, 1961', in Natural Law Forum, p. 172. See Carl Frederick, 'Book Review of Polanyi, Personal Knowledge'.

291 Ibid. See, e.g., Gunnar Myrdal, 'An American Dilema', (1944), pp. 1043-1046, 1063; Robert S. Lynd, 'Knowledge for What?, (1939), pp. 200-201.

judge making case law; law may be criticized from a moral point of view. Beyond these points of contact, which he says almost any school of 'legal positivism' would admit.[292] Hart notes a further substantial overlapping of law and morals; for a society to be viable, for a legal order to exist, there is what John Noonan considers a limited moral structure built into the law.

Lon L. Fuller broadly and inclusively defines law as the 'enterprise of subjecting human conduct to the governance of rules'.[293] He insists that positivism, by focusing exclusively on the rules which are the product of this process, fails to attend to law as an ongoing *purposive activity*.[294] In particular, Fuller compares his enterprise theory of law with the theorizing of philosophers and sociologists of science, suggesting that the best way to look at law or science is as an activity.[295] He rejects behaviorism (the extreme external point of view) but appears to remain within a basically scientific perspective.[296] He argues: "...a sociologist or philosopher interested primarily in the law of the state, might study the rules, institutions, and problems of this body of parietal law for the insight he might thus obtain into the processes of law generally".[297] It is, then, precisely because the law is a purposeful enterprise that it displays structural constancies which the legal theorist can discover and treat as uniformities in the factually given.[298] Fuller provides us with a connection between the normative concerns of the investigator and the criteria of success of the investigation. Namely, Fuller posits the undeniably legitimate purpose of developing a jurisprudence to 'analyze the fundamental problems that must be solved in creating and administering a system of legal rules'.[299] This purpose is the organizing principle behind Fuller's 'internal morality of law' – the set of normative principles which can be discovered as implicit in, and thereby limiting the effective use of, the different forms of social ordering, such as legislation, adjudication, contract and elections.[300] He points out that the purpose [he has] attributed to the institution of law is a modest and sober one, that of subjecting human conduct to the guidance and control of general

292 Ibid. This is a point well developed by Thomas Broden, 'The Straw Man of Legal Positivism', in 34 Notre Dame Lawyer (1959), p. 350.

293 Nance (1985), supra note 1125, p. 24, referring to L. FULLER, 'THE MORALITY OF LAW' 96 (rev. ed. 1969).

294 Ibid., referring to Fuller (1969), Ibid., Ch. 5, e.g., p. 193.

295 Ibid., n.89, referring to Fuller (1969), Ibid., pp. 118-22.

296 Ibid., p. 24, referring to Fuller (1969), Ibid., pp. 141, 145-51, 162-67.

297 Ibid., p. 25, referring to Fuller (1969), Ibid., p. 125.

298 Ibid., referring to Fuller (1969), Ibid., p. 151.

299 Ibid., referring to Fuller (1969), Ibid., p. 122.

300 Ibid.,referring to Fuller (1969), Ibid., Ch.II. See also FULLER, 'THE PRINCIPLES OF SOCIAL ORDER' (K. Winston ed. 1981).

rules.[301] What Fuller does do is to explore the ways in which the normative principles inherent in the forms of legal ordering constrain the substantive aims attainable through law.[302]

Dworkin notes that David Hume and many other philosophers have insisted that objects or event can be valuable only when and because they serve someone's or something's interests. On this view, nothing is valuable unless someone wants it or unless it helps someone get what he does want.[303] But, as Perry argues that the second sentence here [in Dworkin's note] is a glaring non sequitur. It does not follow, from the Humean view, that nothing is valuable unless someone wants it or unless it helps someone get what he does want. It follows only that nothing is valuable unless it serves someone's or something's interests. That something serves my interests does not entail that I want it (or that it helps me get what I do want). After all, I may not know that something serves my interests, or I may not know what my real interests are. Indeed, that I want something (or that it helps me get what I do want) does not entail that it serves my interests: I may want things that are not good for me – indeed, that are bad for me.[304] Dworkin does of course have such an argument for his stance that legal theory is prescriptive, which rests on at least one prior descriptive claim: that law is a member of a special category of social practices, interpretive practices, that can only bear prescriptive theorizing.[305] Normative concerns cannot be ignored even in building a descriptive theory of law, even though for the purpose of neutrality and objectivity a desire is not to prejudge the normative and empirical connection to be developed. A general theory of law must be normative as well as conceptual.[306] The two dimensions must inform one

301 Ibid., referring to Fuller (1969), Ibid., p. 146.

302 Ibid., n.98. E.g., Fuller (1969), Ibid., Ch. IV.

303 Ari Kohen, 'The Problem of Secular Sacredness: Ronald Dworkin, Michael Perry, and Human Rights Foundationalism' (2006), in Journal of Human Rights 5 (2006), pp. 235-256, (p. 237), referring to Ronald Dworkin, 'Life's Dominion: An Argument about Abortion, Euthanasia, and Individual Freedom', (New York: Vintage Books, 1994), p. 69.

304 Ibid., referring to Dworkin (1994), Ibid.; M. Perry, 'The Gospel According to Dworkin, Constitutional Commentary', (1994) 11 (Winter), p. 178.

305 Adam Tucker, 'The Politics of Legal Positivism: A Reply to David Dyzenhaus', in (2013) 38 Australian Journal of Legal Philosophy, pp. 74-101 (pp. 92-93), referring, inter alia, to Dworkin (2006), supra note 1131, pp. 10-12. For a focused exposition of the notion of an interpretive practice, see also Nicos Stavropoulos, 'Interpretive Theories of Law' (21 September 2008), in Stanford Encyclopedia of Philosophy, Fall 2008.

306 Nance (1985), supra note 1161, pp. 6-7, referring to R. DWORKIN, 'TAKING RIGHTS SERIOUSLY', vii (1978a). The implicit identification made in the text of "practical" and "normative" indicates the use herein of the term "practical" in the broadly normative sense of "with a view to decision and action" rather than the

another; neither can be profitably pursued in isolation. In fact, they are different components of the same general enterprise.[307] Dworkin assumes that the acknowledgement of controversy should not disable judgment of correctness in constitutional law any more that it does in morals.[308] Owen Fiss, among many others, has argued that the courts generally, and the Supreme Court deciding constitutional cases in particular, serve a more important function in elaborating norms than in deciding individual disputes.[309] Alexy argues that principles optimize prescription (*Optimierungsgebote*), within the context of 'value jurisprudence' (*Wertejudikatur*) and the 'tyranny of values' (*Tyrannei der Werte*).[310] Principles, like moral rules, are modeled after obligatory norms of action – not after attractive good. This indicates that principles may have/follow values in themselves. According to Alexy, the balancing of values may be done based on rational argumentation as opposed to mere subjective decision making.[311] Alexy accepts that there is a sense of 'the law' and of cognate or correlated terms such as 'legally valid' and 'legal validity' such that they can be applied with full accuracy to monstrously unjust law.[312]

Finnis displays a highly developed appreciation or the interaction of normative theory and descriptive theory. In reviewing the trend of jurisprudence in this area, Finnis recognizes the progressively greater

---

more narrowly instrumental sense of "workable" or "efficient". This follows FINNIS (1980), supra note 888, p. 12. See generally J. RAZ, 'PRACTICAL REASON AND NORMS', (1975).

307 Ibid. Early modern recognition of the interdependence of the social scientist's normative concerns and his descriptive theory, even (or at least) in the very selection of concepts to be employed, is to be found in the works of Weber. See MAX WEBER ON THE METHODOLOGY OF THE SOCIAL SCIENCES 24, 58, 76-82 (E. Shils & H. Finch ed. 1949); M. WEBER, 'THE METHODOLOGY OF THE SOCIAL SCIENCES', (1949).

308 Fallon (2009), supra note 1148, n.31. See Ronald Dworkin, 'Objectivity and Truth: You'd Better Believe It', in 25 PHIL. & PUB, AFF. (1996), p. 87.

309 Michael Herz, 'Choosing Between Normative and Descriptive Versions of the Judicial Role', in Marquette Law Review Vol. 75, No. 4, 1992, n.171. See Owen M. Fiss, 'The Supreme Court', 1978 Term-Foreword: The Forms of Justice, in 93 HARV. L. REV. 1 (1979); see also Susan Bandes, 'The Idea of a Case', in 42 STAN. L. REV. 227 (1990), pp. 281-292.

310 Martijn W. Hesselink, 'The General Principles of Civil Law: Their Nature, Roles and Legitimacy', in Amsterdam Law School Legal Studies Research Paper No. 2011-35, Centre for the Study of European Contract Law Working Paper No. 2011-14, p. 47, referring to C. Schmitt, 'Die Tyrannie der Werte', 3rd ed., (Berlin: Duncker & Homblot, 1960): 'Wer Wert sagt, will geltend machen und durchsetzen'.

311 Ibid., referring to Alexy (1985, 1994) (Jede Norm ist entweder eine Regel oder ein Prinzip) esp. 143ff, p. 77.

312 Finnis (2014), supra note 1115, p. 4, referring to 58 Am J Juris, p. 105.

incorporation of attention to the practical point of legal institutions into the theoretical constructs of modern jurist, including in particular Austin, Kelsen, Hart and Fuller.[313] Finnis explains this natural impetus by way of a general principle, drawn from Aristotle and Weber, for descriptive analysis of social phenomena: description can best proceed by way of comparison of extant legal practices, conceptions, and institutions with the 'central case' (or 'focal meaning') thereof, i.e., the legal conceptions and institutions hypothetically developed by the exercise of practical reasonableness.[314] His definition of law constitutes what he claims to be such a central case [as a standard for comparison], not as an approximation of the term 'law' in a univocal sense that would exclude from the reference of the term anything that failed to have all the characteristics (and to their full extent) as the central case.[315] Finnis explains that there is thus a movement to and fro between, on the one hand, assessment of human good and of its practical requirements, and on the other hand, explanatory descriptions (using all appropriate historical, experimental and statistical techniques to trace all relevant causal interrelationships) of the human context in which human well-being is variously realized and variously ruined. There is thus a mutual though not quite symmetrical interdependence between the project of describing human affairs by way of theory and the project of evaluating human options with a view, at least remotely, to acting reasonably and

313 Nance (1985), supra note 1165, p. 31. See Finnis (1980), supra note 888, § 1.2. It should be remembered that the term "practical" is used by Finnis, as by Nance, in the sense of "with a view to decision and action," not in the sense of "workable" or "efficient," Id., p. 12.

314 Ibid. See Finnis (1980), Ibid., §§ 1.3 – 1.4. For reasons which are not entirely clear, Finnis restricts the viewpoint from which to hypothetically elaborate his conception to that "in which legal obligation is treated as at least presumptively a moral obligation." Finnis (1980), Ibid., p. 14. This restriction may be unnecessary. See Beyleveld & Brownsword, 'Law as a Moral Judgment vs. the Rules of the Powerful,' in 28 AM. J. JURIS (1983), pp. 115-117.

315 Ibid., referring to Finnis (1980), Ibid., p. 277. The full characterization is as follows: "[T]he term 'law' has been used with a focal meaning so as to refer primarily to rules made in accordance with regulative legal rules, by a determinate and effective authority (itself identified and, standardly, constituted as an institution by legal rules) for a 'complete' community, and buttressed by sanctions in accordance with the rule-guided stipulations of adjudicative institutions, this ensemble of rules and institutions being directed to reasonably resolving any of the community's co-ordination problems (and to ratifying, tolerating, regulating, or overriding co-ordination solutions from any other institutions or sources of norms) for the common good of that community, according to a manner and form itself adapted to that common good by features of specificity, minimization or arbitrariness, and maintenance of a quality of reciprocity between the subjects of the law both amongst themselves and in their relations with the lawful authorities."J. FINNIS (1980), Ibid., pp. 276-277.

well. The evaluations are in no way deduced from the descriptions; but one whose knowledge of the facts of human situation is very limited is unlikely to judge well in discerning the practical implications of the basic values. Equally, the descriptions are not deduced from the evaluations; but without the evaluations one cannot determine what descriptions are really illuminating and significant.[316] Finnis relies on Weber that his 'ideal type', though formed inevitably under the influence of a theorist's perception of importance, does not entail a moral judgment that it is *normatively* ideal.[317] Finnis seems to argue –rather convincingly – that practically relevant, and hence adequate, descriptive theory construction must proceed in conjunction with an increasingly refined elaboration of the ideal manifestation of law, precisely in the sense that the better one's development of such an ideal conception of law, the more informative can be one's description of existing legal systems.[318] And that is all that NLNR [Natural Law & Natural Right] means when it says (as he reports),[319] that The [natural law] tradition explicitly (by speaking of 'unjust *laws*') accords to[320] iniquitous rules of legal validity, whether on the ground and in the sense that these rules are accepted in the courts as guides to judicial decision, or on the ground and in the sense that, in the judgment of the speaker, they satisfy the criteria of validity laid down by constitutional or other legal rules.[321]

Positivists and natural lawyers have struggled for the Janus-faced quality of law.[322] Perhaps, most importantly, it encourages us to consider

---

316 Ibid., p. 32, referring to Finnis (1980), Ibid., p. 17, 19.

317 Ibid., n.127. See Gavison, 'Natural Law, Positivism, and the Limits of Jurisprudence: A Modern Round (Book Review)', in 191 YALE L.J. 1250 (1982), pp. 1264-70.

318 Ibid., pp. 32-33. The point was presaged by Fuller, at least with regard to the various forms of social ordering characteristic of law. See Fuller, 'The Forms and Limits of Adjudication,' in 92 HARV. L. REV. 353 (1978), p. 357. Contrary to at least one of Finnis's critics on this point, he does not claim that one cannot (logically) have any conception of law or legal systems which is not proffered as a normatively (morally) ideal conception. Cf. Gavison (1982), Ibid., pp. 1250, 1264-1270.

319 Finnis (2014), supra note 1171, p. 4, referring to 58 Am J Juris, p. 105.

320 Ibid. As Finnis notes in the Postscript to NLNR p. 467, "this phrase 'accords to' is loose; rather: The tradition accepts that iniquitous rules may satisfy the legal system's criteria of legal validity, and where they do, it does not seek to deny that fact.... (emphasis added). Alexy's 2013 article p. 109 partly quotes and partly paraphrases the remainder on my Postscript comment here; I do not think his paraphrase accurately conveys my point, but need not pursue the matter. He is right to say (p. 110) that the Postscript comment does not make a Radbruchian point."

321 Ibid., referring to Finnis (1980), supra note 1175, p. 365.

322 Nance (1985), supra note 1177, p. 42. Cf. H.L.A. HART, 'LAW, LIBERTY,

the possibility that a developed theory – prescriptive or descriptive in character – may (or may not!) be significantly different if it addresses the paradigmatic category than if it addresses either non-paradigmatic category defined by the satisfaction of one, but not the other, sufficient condition.[323] Dale Nance contends that one may be concerned that in this scheme there is an analytical priority of 'ought' over 'is' which may, if extended, lead to distortion of an 'objective' picture of things. Certainly, the present proposal entails the acceptance of a certain kind of primacy of practical deliberations, particularly those of the official decision-maker, the person facing the legal system's commands, and the social critic. And there are precedents of policy-oriented theorists who allow a particular normative theory to structure, perhaps excessively, their descriptive theory.[324]

David Dyzenhaus's brand of legal prescriptivism attacks legal positivism in three arguments: the argument from authoritarianism, the argument(s) from irrelevance and the arguments from vacuity.[325] His argument that positivism is authoritarianism is developed from the Hobbesian idea that judges are obliged to enforce that as it exists – 'the will of the sovereign as he intended it to be executed'.[326] The argument from authoritarianism presupposes that it is appropriate to appraise legal philosophies in terms of their consequences rather than their inherent soundness.[327] In this respect, Dyzenhaus endorses a position that Julie Dickson calls the beneficial moral consequences thesis: ".. value judgments concerning the beneficial moral consequences of espousing a certain theory of law may legitimately feature in the criteria of success of legal theories".[328] [Dyzenhaus also deploys the argument from authoritarianism as a contribution to the deeper methodological debate.] It is, he claims, itself evidence that the descriptive theorist is mistaken, and should move onto prescriptive ground: It is part of Dworkin's ... accomplishment to have attempted to restore legal philosophy to an examination of its proper, pragmatic roots by reuniting the central questions of legal and political philosophy. .....[T]he costs for contemporary positivists of resisting this attempt is an unwitting collaboration in an authoritarian political project

AND MORALITY', (1963), p. 113.

323 Ibid.

324 Ibid.

325 Tucker (2013), supra note 1164, pp. 91-92.

326 Ibid., p. 78, referring to David Dyzenhaus, 'Why Positivism is Authoritarian', in (1992) 37 American Journal of Jurisprdence 83, 112, 111 and 88.

327 Ibid., p. 79.

328 Ibid., citing Julie Dickson, 'Evaluation and Legal Theory', (Hart Publishing, 2001), p. 9.

of which they should want no part.[329] For Dworkin, then, all conceptual inquiry about law is prescriptive.[330]

In the argument(s) from irrelevance, Dyzenhaus develops two arguments against legal positivism, and both focus on the positivist claim that judges in hard cases exercise a discretion to make new law rather than determine pre-existing legal rights and duties.[331] The first argument from irrelevance takes Hart as its focus. Dyzenhaus sees the value-laden nature of the practice of adjudication as an 'anomaly' for legal positivism and interprets Hart's work on indeterminacy as his response to that anomaly. For Dyzenhaus, the way in which Hart's legal positivism deals with the apparent anomaly ....is to suggest the irrelevance of that practice to its thesis.[332] The second argument from irrelevance focuses on Raz's sense that judges are fully constraint by legal authority only when their judgments about the law are not evaluative.[333] Dyzenhaus finds Raz's claim about discretion peculiar because 'the substance in the ...theory condemns it to practical irrelevance. The measure of 'relevance to practice' upon which Dyzenhaus relies is surprisingly demanding. He unpacks it by constructing a fictional controversy against which the success of legal positivism can be assessed: Suppose that the.....positivist finds that judges in a particular legal order divide between those who adopt a positivistic account of legal authority, in which valid law is the law established in accordance with the Identification Thesis, and those who adopt a Dworkinian account, in which authority accrues only to those statements of the law which are supported by a moral theory which justifies them.[334] At this stage, Dyzenhaus[335] implies that the positivist is 'reduced to reporting that .....there is controversy about the nature of legal authority'. Dyzenhaus says they [the judges] endorse a moral duty to obey the law, whatever its content, direct their decisions accordingly and 'adopt a very conservative view of their role'.

In the argument(s) from vacuity, Dyzenhaus argues that 'positivism is best understood as politically prescriptive' on the grounds that 'any of the marks of positivism as a distinct theory....of law are marks inherited from a political tradition and which can be detached from that tradition only on pain of vacuity.[336] His argument for this position has a complex structure. It

329 Ibid., pp. 81-82, referring to Dyzenhaus (1992), supra note 1185, p. 112.

330 Ibid., p. 92.

331 Ibid., p. 82, referring to David Dyzenhaus, 'Positivism's Stagnant Research Programme', in 20 Oxford Journal of Legal Studies, (2000), p. 703, 704.

332 Ibid., referring to Dyzenhaus (2000), Ibid., p. 708.

333 Ibid., p. 83, referring to Dyzenhaus (2000), Ibid., p. 714.

334 Ibid., p. 84, referring to Dyzenhaus (2000), Ibid., p. 712.

335 Ibid., referring to Dyzenhaus (2000), Ibid., p. 716.

336 Ibid., referring to David Dyzenhaus,'The Genealogy of Legal Positivism', in

consists in a 'genealogical reconstruction of the tradition' which runs from Hobbes to the present day and identifies and culminates in an attack of a shift from positivism's prescriptive origins to the descriptivism of (much) contemporary positivism. This shift, according to Dyzenhaus, can be traced to Austin, who 'does not seem to understand the methodology of legal theory as political'[337] and more significantly, Hart, for whom 'positivism is committed to providing a general theory of law...on value neutral, descriptive ground' whilst remaining 'morally and politically agnostic'.[338] The first argument is aimed at 'inclusive' legal positivism. This argument is Dyzenhaus's version of this concern: All that binds [inclusive positivists to their] tradition is a preamble to their theory that all values have their source in social practices and that social practices give rise to morally repugnant values, so that the presence of morality is a matter of historical and political contingency. That preamble is vacuous because no-one could deny. Here, then, vacuous means undeniable.[339] In the second argument from vacuity, Dyzenhaus turns his attention to exclusive legal positivism. Exclusive legal positivists maintain that moral standards cannot feature in the criteria of legal validity. He objects that this is .. of little assistance to judges in a common law legal order. All the exclusive legal positivist can say to ...judges [in jurisdictions with a bill of rights] is that they have discretion and that they should describe most of what they do in Austinian, quasi-legislative language. Here the kind of vacuity in issue is the virtual irrelevance of theory to practice.[340] Dyzenhaus argues that both kinds of descriptive positivists find themselves retreating to some high ground about the very nature of law, unanswerable to experience and practice because of their political purity.[341]

Dyzenhaus's three arguments linking legal positivism to legislative supremacy are united by the assumption that jurisprudence is properly understood as a prescriptive, rather than purely descriptive, enterprise. The argument from authoritarianism tells us that Dyzenhaus presupposes that jurisprudence is prescriptive. The argument from irrelevance tells us that Dyzenhaus considers prescriptive theory to be aimed at judges and intended to influence the decisions to come to in hard cases. The argument from vacuity tells us that Dyzenhaus supposes that the only kinds of arguments that these prescriptivism can embody are normative political arguments.[342]

---

24 Oxford Journal of Legal Studies, (2004), p. 60.

337 Ibid., p. 86, referring to Dyzenhaus (2004), Ibid., p. 47.

338 Ibid., referring to Dyzenhaus (2004), Ibid., pp. 51-52.

339 Ibid., p. 87, referring to Dyzenhaus (2004), Ibid., p. 55.

340 Ibid., p. 88, referring to Dyzenhaus (2004), Ibid., pp. 60-61.

341 Ibid., referring to Dyzenhaus (2004), Ibid., p. 61.

342 Ibid., pp. 91-92.

Liam Murphy, who shares Dyzenhaus's commitment to prescriptive theory, points out that it is clear that lawyers often argue and judges often decide cases on moral and political grounds. The conceptual question, then, on which legal philosophers disagree, is whether this kind of appeal to political considerations by lawyers and judges is properly understood as part of an argument about what the law (already) is.[343] For Murphy, this agreement is the foundation of an argument in favor of prescriptive theorizing. The disagreement will persist and another way to settle it must be found. Murphy's proposed solution is to move the debate onto political terrain. The reason the disagreement about our equivocal concept matters, he argues, is the extent to which acceptance of one conception of law or another affects political practice. Accordingly, [t]he way to resolve the ....disagreement ....must therefore be to evaluate the practical and political reasons that they offer for their respective positions.[344] Murphy's conclusion is that argument about the nature of law is necessarily prescriptive.[345] Waldron notes in his appeal for more prescriptive positivist theorizing, legal positivists are interested in a cluster of different versions of positivity and can plausibly be understood to be motivated by a variety of values.[346] But he notes that those who resist the general jurisprudence methodology associated with normative positivism may do so.[347] The law, however, is constantly based on notions of morality, and if all laws representing essentially moral choices are to be invalidated under the Due Process Clause, the courts will be very busy indeed.[348] So many laws have (or could be said to have) substantially moral elements.[349] Among the values the Supreme Court of Canada has said are sufficiently 'pressing and substantial' are respect for the inherent dignity of the human person, commitment to social justice and equality, accommodation of a wide variety of beliefs, respect for cultural and group identity, and faith in social and political institutions which enhance the participation of individuals and groups in society.[350]

---

343 Ibid., p. 94, referring to Liam Murphy, 'The Political Question of the Concept of Law', in Jules Coleman (ed.), Hart's Postscript: Essays on the Postscript to the Concept of Law, (Oxford University Press, 2001), p. 372 (emphasis in original).

344 Ibid., referring to Murphy (2001), Ibid.

345 Ibid., p. 95.

346 Ibid., referring to Jeremy Waldron, 'Normative (or Ethical) Positivism' in Jules Coleman (ed.), Hart's Postscipt: Essays on the Postscript to the Concept of Law, (Oxford University Press, 2001), p. 432.

347 Ibid., p. 95, referring to Waldron (2001), Ibid., p. 433.

348 Jamal Green, 'The Rule of Law as a Law of Standards', Justice Stevens's Law of Standard, in 99 the Georgetown Law Journal (2011), pp. 1289-1299 (p. 1294). See 478 U.S. (1986), overruled by Lawrence v. Texas, 539 U.S. 558 (2003).

349 Ibid.

350 Ibid. See Oakes, 1 S.C.R. p. 136.

In Alexander's and Sherwin's words: "Our focus is on rules that are practical (prescriptive) norms and thus can be obeyed or violated, what we call "serious rules .. Serious rules contain a factual predicate or hypothesis and a prescription.... The most important characteristic of a rule, as we use the term, is that it purports to state a prescription applicable to every case that falls within the rule's factual predicate or hypothesis".[351] It may be that Alexander and Sherwin conflate two aspects of Lex's (law giver's) inchoate intent. When Lex legislates, his object is both to determine results and to determine the process by which results are achieved. That is not just to say that Lex is fixing both substantive and procedural law. He is doing more. He is formulating rules in a manner cognizant of adjudication and rule-following behavior. [352] Alexander and Sherwin describe that something as the "gap" between the justification for and instantiation of a rule: In other words, a 'gap' lies between what Lex has reason to prescribe (and his subjects have reason to want him to prescribe) and what his subjects have reason to do, all things considered.[353] The fact that a direction takes the form of a rule would seem to enhance its moral content in a rule-following society because following rules is consistent with the object of Lex's promulgating them.[354] Alexander and Sherwin in their formulation of rules as an elaboration of morality – a conclusion in line with analytical jurisprudence – understand that the data set 'rules' is derived from the substance 'morality' [That may be].[355]

Capturing the same idea as Alexander's and Sherwin's, Frederick Schauer argues that we see rules as essentially frustrating, exercising their influence by getting in the way. They impede access to those facts that would otherwise, under a given theory of justification, be relevant to making the decision, and they interpose facts that would otherwise be irrelevant.[356] Schauer notes that law is a socially constructed concept and, as such, 'it would be open for the people whose collective beliefs and actions construct [the concept of law] to construct [it] in one way rather than another'.[357] Furthermore, the socially constructed concept of law is

---

351 Peter A. Alces, 'The Unruliness of Rules'(2003), Faculty Publication, Paper 129, William & Mary Law School Scholarship Repository, in Michigan Law Review, Vol. 101:2037, May 2003, n.26. See also Schauer (1991), supra note 1043, p. 87.

352 Ibid., n.12.

353 Ibid., p. 2046, referring to Larry Alexander & Emily Sherwin, 'The Rule of Rules: Morality, Rules & The Dilemmas of Law', (Durham: Duke University Press, 2001), pp. viii, 279, p. 54.

354 Ibid., n.27.

355 Ibid., p. 2058.

356 Ibid., n.26. See also Schauer (1991), supra note 1210, p. 87.

357 Tucker (2013), supra note 1206, p. 93, referring to Frederick Schauer, 'The Social Construction of Law: A Reply to Julie Dickson', in 25 Oxford Journal of

not static. Rather, it changes over time and is best understood as emerging through a process of continuous construction and reconstruction.[358] Accordingly, it would be a mistake to assume that the concept of law must always be what it now is.[359] This framework makes space for both descriptive and prescriptive theorizing about the nature of law. Schauer characterizes descriptive jurisprudence as adopting 'a snapshot approach to freezing an image of a continuously moving entity' and contrasts it with prescriptive jurisprudence intended to offer reasons and arguments why a culture should steer and shape its concept of law in this direction rather than that.[360] He acknowledges both the possibility and importance of prescritive jurisprudence.[361] Schauer concludes the responsibility of the moral actor is to afford rules some, albeit not absolute, deference. Rules function, we are reminded, to translate moral principles into a set of directions that can be understood by people who previously disagreed or were uncertain about the meaning of those principles.[362] Morally conscientious citizens, according to Raz, should accept the dictates of legal authorities when they have good reason to believe that the legal authorities can make better decisions than they could make themselves.[363] Those who promulgate authoritative rules 'throw' them in a manner that anticipates the fit between morality and the rule (in light of whatever factors may determine *movement* in that fit). Indeed, the thrower (Lex) may 'put some air under the ball' to permit the receiver (the adjudicator) to adjust as necessary to the ball (the rule) in order to assure a reception, the best fit between the rule and morality. Too limited a conception of the rule-morality fit will obscure the community's reliance on Lex's prescience.[364]

A norm is as an action-guiding or reason-giving precept or principle, deviation of which would provide a ground for reproach within an appropriate domain such as that of morals, law, or etiquette.[365] As to

---

Legal Studies, (2005), p. 493, 496.

358 Ibid., referring to Schauer (2005), Ibid., p. 498.

359 Ibid., referring to Schauer (2005), Ibid. Further, as Raz discusses, (in an argument endorsed by Schauer) the variety is more than merely temporal: 'Different cultures have different concepts of law. There is no one concept of law, and when we refer to the concept of law we just mean our concept'. Joseph Raz, 'The Authority of Law', (Oxford University Press, 2009), p. 32.

360 Ibid., referring to Schauer (2005), Ibid., p. 498.

361 Ibid.

362 Alces (2003), supra note 1215, p. 2041, referring to Alexander & Sherwin (2001), supra note 1214, p. 54.

363 Fallon (2009), supra note 1167, referring to JOSEPH RAZ, 'THE MORALITY OF FREEDOM', (1986), pp. 1018-1020.

364 Alces (2003), supra note 1221, n.12.

365 Fallon (2009), supra note 1222, n.28.

ethical prescriptivity or moral prescription, in any case of collision between legal and moral norms, moral norms claim superior status.[366] Moral norms may of course accommodate legal norms to a considerable extent by requiring officials to obey even morally misguided laws, unless the laws are very seriously unjust.[367] But for an official who takes morality seriously, the question of the force of legal norms will always be a moral question.[368] Del Veiccho says there have been shifts as to another emphasis in the definitions of law, from morals and ethics to force, and back again to ethics. The life of law lies in a struggle against wrong, and can be understood only in correlation with this antagonistic opposite (right v. wrong), which shows the resistence of social reality to the application of law. All values and norms of action are referred to an ethical principle as a basis. Del Veiccho is of the view that the same degree of certainty and naturalness enters morals and law. Whoever denies the existence of natural law should reach, to be consistent, an analogous denial of morality and duty.[369]

One of the elements characterizing the new interpretive approach is the discovery of the importance of choice in the judicial process. Choice means discretion, evaluation and balancing: it means giving consideration to the choice's practical and moral results; and it means employment of not only the argument of abstract logic, but those of economics and politics, ethics, sociology and psychology.[370] As rule prescribes action, normativity of law is prescriptive. In addition to the normativity prescription, there are also prescriptions from other disciplines the issues of which are regulated by the law. In law, there are prescriptions from sociology [in sociology of law], from anthropology [in anthropology of law], and from politics [in politics of law]. Interdisciplinary and multidisciplinary approaches might exist between law and sociology, anthropology or politics. The prevailing laws regulate issues in business such as stock market, commercial papers, insurance, transportation and sales, so prescriptions from principles and practice of stock market, commercial papers, insurance, transportation

366 Ibid., p. 1007. See, e.g., BERNARD WILLIAMS, 'ETHICS AND THE LIMITS OF PHILOSOPHY', (1985), p. 178 (explaining "morality" as a variety of ethical thought by noting that "moral obligation is categorical").

367 Ibid. There is a vast literature on whether, and if so when, there is a moral obligation to obey the law. For an introduction, sse William A. Edmundson, 'State of the Art: The Duty to Obey the Law', in 10 LEGAL THEORY (2004), p. 215.

368 Ibid., pp. 1007-1008.

369 Del Vechhio (1908/1969), supra note 878, p. 155, 163.

370 Oreste Pollicino, 'Legal Reasoning of the Court of Justice in the Context of the Principle of Equality Between Judicial Activism and Self-restraint', in German Law Journal Vol. 05, No. 03,(2004), p. 287. See M. Cappelletti,'The Law-Making Power of the Judges and its Limits', in M.U.L.Rev. (1981), p. 22. The importance of choice in judicial process is accentuated by the willingness of political branches of governments to pass responsibility for difficult decision to the judiciary.

and sales should be taken into account by the law. The prevailing laws also regulate issues in agriculture, mining, property or construction industries, therefore prescriptions from principles and practice of agriculture, mining, property or construction industries should be considered by the laws. The law might or should follow prescriptions from any area any issue of which is provided or regulated by the law. These are other prescriptions in jurisprudence. In this connection, Rod Macdonald has put forward his notion of legal prescriptivism.[371] He calls 'legal prescriptivism' as the notion that law resides in a prescription external to oneself.

As Llewellyn admiringly proclaimed that 'the sociological [school] alone is vital, growing, expanding to meet new needs'.[372] The new thinking, a 'multiform mass of efforts', came out of the sociological school.[373] In analyzing this 'new thinking' the only two tenets Llewellyn identified to which nearly every writer in this movement could agree -- that jurisprudence cannot stand alone; and that the significant aspect of law is law's effect.[374] – appeared in Pound's Jurisprudential agenda from the very beginning. Llewellyn advocated reform of commercial law, arguing that the abstract legal principles that dominated late 19th century and early 20th century commercial codes and court decisions hindered modern business.[375] Llewellyn wanted commercial law to use the insights of economics and modern business practices as guides.[376] Realists demand the integration of social and economic facts into the legal order – the infiltration of psychology, economics, sociology, anthropology and all other natural and social sciences.[377] Llewellyn's chief contribution to jurisprudential literature in recent years consists of an article exploring certain relationships and contacts between the law and the social sciences.[378] As soon as we lawyers become imbued with the conviction that law is an institution, he says, consisting of going practices, relevant specialists, relevant physical equipment, and a manner of organization of the whole, and once we

371 Richard Janda, "Toward Cosmopolitan Law", in (2005) 50 McGill Law Journal / Revue de Droit de McGill, p. 973.

372 Hull (1989), supra note 1007, p. 1312, referring to Karl Llewellyn, 'A Realistic Jurisprudence', Llewellyn Papers, B.I.6.a-c, p. 1.

373 Ibid., referring to Llewellyn, Ibid.

374 Ibid., referring to Llewellyn, Ibid. p. 2.

375 Ibid., p. 1311, referring to Llewellyn, 'The Effect of Legal Institutions Upon Economics', in 15 AM. ECON. REV. (1925), p. 665.

376 Ibid., referring to Llewellyn (1925), Ibid., p. 672.

377 Kennedy (1940), supra note 1011, p. 365.

378 Edgar Bodenheimer, 'A Decade of Jurisprudence in the United States of America: 1946-1956', in Natural Law Forum, (1958), paper 27, p. 50, referring to Llewellyn, 'Law and the Social Sciences, Especially Sociology', in 62 Harv. L. Rev. (1949), p. 1286.

further perceive that this institution serves to produce and maintain 'the groupness of a group' by fighting down and conquering the divergent drives, frictions, and disruptions inherent among human beings, the door are going to be wide open for a fruitful and friendly collaboration between law and the social disciplines related to it.[379] The substance of rule may reflect individualism that might include economics, welfare and a larger intellectual entity. The relationship of rule form and rule substance may be analyzed based on the connection between rules, on the one hand, and economics, welfare and a larger intellectual entity, on the other hand. The connection is structural rather than contextual. It is not a practical or empirically verified connection, but rather a connection in the exact correspondence between the structure of arguments for rules and arguments for economics, welfare and a larger intellectual entity (the Classical theory of laissez-faire). Economic individualism was once much more tightly linked to advocacy of rules that it is today, because they were both parts of a larger intellectual entity. According to that theory, economics could recover general laws about the welfare consequences of particular legal regimes looked at as wholes.[380]

If in descriptive jurisprudence, the focus is much on the description or snapshot of what the law is, whereas the law itself is a normative and/or prescriptive phenomena; in prescriptive jurisprudence, it is the normativity and/or prescriptivity of law which is much focused in the discussion. As Hart has argued, as mentioned in Chapter II.1, that the description of law in descriptive jurisprudence might be the description of normative and/or prescriptive phenomena viewed as law.

As already mentioned, Quine's skeptical holism with the radical relativism eliminates the possibility to maintain a clear distinction between descriptive and normative statements, consequently the normative/ descriptive distinction is unattainable, so the radical distinction between normative theories and descriptive ones is also unattainable. The only thing left is some gradualness between two points. Thus, one argumentative theory is more normative or descriptive than another theory, but not purely normative or descriptive. Theories that tend to the more descriptive end of the descriptive/normative continuity focus on analyzing the actual argumentative discourse and the whole practice that wraps such pieces of discourse. Theories that tend more to the normative end focus on the requirement for sound argument and enable the evaluation and criticism of actual argumentative discourse. Consequently, the descriptive approach

379 Ibid., referring to Llewellyn (1949), Ibid., p. 1289, 1292.

380 Duncan Kennedy, 'Form and Substance in Private Law Adjudication', in 89 Harvard Law Review 1685 (1976), pp. 1745-1746.

to argumentation collapses into the normative one.[381] In line with this, prescriptive jurisprudence and descriptive jurisprudence might merge into naturalized realist jurisprudence in which there is some gradualness between prescriptivity and descriptivity. Descriptive jurisprudence and prescriptive jurisprudence shed the light on the notions of descriptivity and prescriptivity in law, and to ignore either such descriptivity or prescriptivity in viewing the law causes incomplete understanding thereof. A correlation of such descriptivtiy and prescriptivity may appear in or through generativity and transformativity which will be addressed in Chapter IV of this book.

381 Schwed (2001), supra note 1036, p. 8, referring to W.v.O. Quine, 'Pursuit of Truth', (Cambridge, MA.: Harvard University Press, 1990).

CHAPTER III

Rule and Principle of Law as "Competence of Law"

III.1. RULE OF LAW

***

Civil law of ancient Rome was received by the Continental Europe and then retained through codification. The Code of Napoleon did impose the most part of the law, and later on the imposition of codified law was greatly influenced by the French Civil Code of 1804. The precepts of the codification are fundamental, and a legal order is legitimate only when it does not contradict such precepts.[1] For the nominalists, who think of 'the law' as much formalistic concept, there is a set of sorts of timeless rules. Such timeless rules are concepts awaiting discovery by judges for resolving particular situations, and legal obligations are determined based on such formalistic concepts through mechanism as applied within a certain authority frame. Those, who view 'the law' as meaningful rules due to having sufficient factual reference, pay much attention to the law as what we see and experience in life. A superficial examination of legal practices is enough to show what the law and legal obligations are because of, among other things, the fact that law changes and evolves through time, though problems will sometimes appear. Problems will appear in both mechanistic and substantive jurisprudence.[2] For legal positivists, one central aim of jurisprudence is to systematize and clarify legal concepts and legal rules.

A rule of law is an enforceable statement that establishes a standard of conduct. It can be a constitutional provision, a statute, or originate from a rule established by a court in an opinion.[3] Legal rules, according to the positivists, constitute a set of special rules used by the community directly or indirectly to determine which behavior will be punished or coerced by the

1 William Tetley, Q.C., 'Mixed Jurisdictions: Common Law vs Civil Law (Codified and Uncodified)', in 60 La. L .Rev (2000) and La .L. Rev.1999, para IV.1 & 2.

2 Ronald M. Dworkin , 'The Model of Rules', in The University of Chicago Law Review, Vol 35, 1967, p. 16.

3 A. Connelly,'Legal Reasoning : Analyzing Cases and Statues', College's Legal Clinic, University of Kentucky, Lexington, www.law.uky.edu/files/docs/clinic/legal_analysis.pdf, para 1.A.1.

public order.[4] The positivists argue that such cases are to be determined by some official, like a judge, 'exercising his discretion'. Someone has a 'legal obligation' means that his case falls under a valid legal rule that requires him to do or to forbear from doing something. Consequently, there is no legal obligation if there is no valid legal rule applicable to his case.[5] The positivists posit that these special valid legal rules constitute an exhaustive set of 'the law'. Consequently, in the event an appropriate valid legal rule is not found in a certain particular situation, or a seemingly applicable valid rule is vague in a certain particular situation, or for some other reasons, the law is not applicable to such certain particular situation. The law then cannot resolve or determine the case of such particular situation.[6] When there is no such valid legal rule or when such valid legal rules are vague or have furry edges, the judge has her discretion[7].

A rule is a formula for making a decision. Every rule has three separate components: (1) a set of elements, collectively called a test; (2) a result that occurs when all the elements are present (and the test is thus satisfied); and (3) a causal term that determines whether the result is mandatory [shall], prohibitory [shall not] or discretionary [may]. Additionally, many rules have one or more exceptions that, if present, would defeat the result, even if all the elements are present.[8] A rule can be considered as consisting of a conclusion and a number of conditions. Rules are formulated through the interpretation of legal sources, such as statute, social practice and precedent. In the application of a rule to any particular case, the rule must match the description of facts, therefore interpretation and classification deal respectively with the rule and the facts in order to arrive at that match.[9] Legal rules treat elements in different ways. If all elements must be satisfied in order to reach the conclusion called by a rule, the rule treats its elements as 'All Required Elements'. In the event that either element can be satisfied in order to reach the conclusion intended by a rule, the rule treats its elements as 'Alternative Elements'. When the court is required to balance and weigh competing interests from a list of several factors in order to reach the conclusion called by a rule, this way of treating the rule's elements is the 'Factor Test'.[10]

4 Dworkin (1967), supra note 1242, p. 17.

5 Ibid., pp. 17-18.

6 Ibid.

7 Ibid., p. 18.

8 Connelly, supra note 1243, para 1.A.1, referring to Richard K. Neumann, 'Legal Reasoning and Legal Writing', 3rd ed. 1998, Section 2.1, pp. 15-16.

9 Jaap Hage, 'A Theory of Legal Reasoning and a Logic to Match', 15, in Artificial Intelligence and Law 4(3-4), (1996), pp. 199-273.

10 Connelly, supra note 1248, para 1.C.

The legal rules of a community, according to Austin, are the general commands its sovereign has deployed. An obligation means lying under a rule, where such a rule is a general command, and such a command is an expression of desire to make others behave in a particular way, and such a command is backed by the power and will to enforce that expression in case of disobedience. Having a legal obligation means being one among the addressees of some general order of the sovereign, and being in danger of suffering as sanction unless obeying that order.[11] When the sovereign's scheme of orders does not provide for certain contingencies, or when the sovereign's orders are vague or have furry edges, the sovereign (according to Austin) grants those who enforce the law (judges) discretion to make new commands or rules or to adapt old rules, and the sovereign either overturns their creations, or tacitly confirms them by failing to do so.[12]

Hart argues that a legal rule is *normative*, setting a standard of behavior, regulating its subject beyond the threat that may enforce it.[13] A rule is binding not just because of force by some person with physical power who wants it to be so. The person issuing and enforcing a rule must have *authority*, without *authority* such a rule is not a legal rule. Such authority can only come from another rule which is binding on those to whom he speaks. Being bound by a rule must be different from being subject to an injury if one disobeys an order. Being bound by a rule is being obligated, not being obliged. Hart notes rules cannot determine their own application in advance. It is the exercise of judgment which happens when particular facts are subsumed under instances of a general rule (Hart, the Concept of Law, 2nd ed. 1994, p. 130). Rules, precedent or legislation, prove indeterminate, when they are applied at some point to the great mass of ordinary cases. Because of the indeterminacy [or furry edges], rules have been termed an open texture (Hart 1994, *supra*, pp. 127-128).

Schauer describes rules as 'entrenched generalization'. Entrenched makes the properties suppressed by generalization less subject to recall on demand, and entrenched generalizations mould our imagination and apprehension in such a way that methods of thinking that would focus on different properties become comparatively inacceesible. To the extent that generalization becomes entrenched, the inclusions of past generalization facilitate dealing with the future when it is like the past, but the suppressions of past generalizations impede dealing with future when that future departs from our prior expectation.[14] Rules do not channel thought *simpliciter*,

11 Dworkin (1967), supra note 1242, p. 18, referring to J. Austin, 'The Province of Jurisprudence Determined', (1832).

12 Ibid.

13 Ibid., p. 20, referring to Hart (1961), supra note 888, pp. 79-88.

14 Alces (2003), supra note 1223, p. 2041 & n.11, referring to Alexander & Sherwin (2001), supra note 1221, p. 35.

they change the way we think about problems, the way we make choices – they 'mould our imagination'. Insofar as the moral measure of our actions may be determined by reference to the imagination we impose on choice, rules as facts can shift the moral firmament, just as Law and norms are in symbiotic tension.[15] Legal propositions or legal rules are often general, covering [possible] numerous particular cases, so they need interpretation. Elements of a rule are to be scrutinized, including the description of a complete situation and more often also detailed prerequisites, such as concept, agent, time dimension and relationship.[16] Unlike a principle of law [principle of law will be sketched out in Chapter III.2], a rule identifies a particular type of case and indicates the consequences of this type of case. The requirements of a rule constitute a set of characters, and each character may represent a dimension that is made relevant by a legal principle. *All relevant* requirements or characters or *aspects* of the rule must be met to make the rule applicable to that case with the consequences that should appear. Reasons generated by principles for alternatives are (at least in theory) already taken into account in the rule itself. Because of this fashion, there is no need to weigh the outcome of the rule against other possible outcomes.[17] The conceptual structure refers to the rule structure, since rules are concepts. Dickinson (1931) has argued that a rule supplies a structure for the judge's thought to follow.[18] Gottlieb (1968) said that the concept of rule developed ...characterizes rules as devices for the guidance of mental process of inference leading to choices, decisions, actions, attitudes, judgments, conclusions and the like.[19]

Rule is as a means to control action. Rule might restrict executive behavior that tends to place an impermissible low value, such as unreasonable search and seizures or the suspect's testifying against himself, on the rights of the individuals. So, valuation is important, and the valuation might involve debates and different opinions on substantive constitutional guarantees and bureaucratic inherent tendencies. In this situation, formally realizable rules may be deemed much better than standards or principles, because principles impose less restriction than rules and the necessity of delegation of the application function creates an excessive danger of *de*

15 Ibid., n.11, referring to Schauer (1991), supra note 1215, p. 43.

16 Peter Wahlgren, 'Legal Reasoning, A Jurisprudential Model,' Stockholm Institute for Scandinavian Law 1957-2009 ["2009"], p. 206.

17 Hage (1996), supra note 1249, p. 10.

18 Wahlgren (2009), supra note 1256, p. 211, referring to J. Dickinson, 'Legal Rules: Their Function in the Process of Decision', in University of Pennsylvania Law Review, Vol. 79, (1931), p. 849.

19 Ibid., referring to G. Gottlieb, 'The Logic of Choice: An Investigation of the Concept of Rule and Rationality', (London: Georg Allen and Unwin Ltd., 1968), p. 157.

facto nullification.[20] Rules may foster a sense of bureaucratic (or private) autonomy and provide a basis of independent executive power that would be absent under a regime of principles, though the best way to control the bureaucratic subordinate is not always through rules.[21] The restraint of official arbitrariness and certainty have been the two great social virtues of formalized rules at least since Ihering. Official arbitrariness ranging from corruption to political bias has to be avoided through the control by formalized rules. Certainty is valued for its effect on the citizenry, that is to say that publicly promulgated formalized rules may make members of the society know in advance the incidence of official intervention, so they can adjust their activities in advance to take account of them. For the state, this increases the likelihood that private activity will follow a desired pattern. For the citizens, it removes the inhibiting effect on action that occurs when one's gains are subject to sporadic legal catastrophe.[22]

A rule is a basis for reasons, and any rule as the basis for reasons must be a legally valid rule. Legal conclusion must be based on legal reason, and legal reason must in turn be based on legal rule (or principles or goals, etc.). This heavy demand is relaxed somewhat since before reaching a legal conclusion there exist intermediate conclusions which are often classifications that do not need to be based on legal reason. These intermediate conclusions are sometimes dealt with by legal rules. There are sometimes legal rules which deal with classifications. More often, the law borrows from common way of speaking the conditions for the applicability of classifications.[23] Rules are categorized as formalities and as designed directive to deter wrongdoing. This categorization is logically independent of rule formal realizability and generality, meaning that rules designed to deter wrongdoing can be couched in terms of general or particular rules or some combination. In spite of the logical independence, conventional arguments pro and con the use of general rules as designed formalities and as designed directive to deter wrongdoing also appear. The impact of general rule on the parties' willingness to master the language of form is the crucial issue in the argument that rules are as designed formalities. But, the 'chilling' effect of standards/principles on those parties who will come

20 Kennedy (1976), supra note 1239, p. 1706. See Miranda v. Arizona, 384 U.S 436, 455-70 (1966); See also Amsterdam, 'Perspective on the Fourth Amendment', in 58 Mink. L. Rev. (1974), pp. 429-39, On the use of detailed rules by the legislature as a means to curb judicial discretion; Friedman, 'Law, Rules and the Interpretation of Written Document', in 59 NW.U.L.Rev. (1975), p. 752 n.4.

21 Ibid., p. 1707.

22 Ibid., pp. 1688-89, citing Kennedy,'Legal Formality', in 2 J. Leg. Stud. (1973), pp. 365-77.

23 Hage (1996), supra note 1257, p. 15. Cf., A.Valente, 'Legal Knowledge Engineering. A modeling approach' Thesis, (Amsterdam: IOS Press,1995), p. 57.

as close to the forbidden behavior as they can without getting caught is the focus of the argument that rules are as designed to deter wrongdoing.[24]

***

Legal institutions are placed at one pole to prevent certain particular activities that are morally wrong or otherwise flatly undesirable. Most of the law of crimes fits this pattern: laws against murder aim to eliminate murder. Other legal institutions which sometimes are formalistic are placed at the other pole to facilitate private ordering.[25] Those legal institutions facilitating private ordering are supposed to help parties in communicating clearly to the judge on which dispute resolution the parties elect as to any disputes that may arise later between them in their relationship.[26] The idea of formal rule adoption has been familiar for centuries. Montesquieu put it as follows, speaking of the peasants of the Ottoman Empire in the eighteenth century: Ownership of land is uncertain, and the incentive for agricultural development is consequently weakened: there is neither title nor possession that is good against the caprice of the rulers.[27] The adoption of rules sacrifices the precision in the achievement of the objectives lying behind the rules. Adopting rules involves the idea or act of combining things over and placing things under inclusiveness. This combined over – and under inclusiveness, viewed from the 'purpose of the rules', amounts not just to licensing but to requiring official arbitrariness. However, adopting the rule means pursuing less arbitrariness and uncertainty if compared with leaving determinations to the empowered official to apply the principle of 'free will' directly to particular cases.[28] As to formalities, under-inclusion means the rejection to any intention which is against or not in accordance with the prescribed norm. When one did something against the rule, what he did should be rejected by the law. Over-inclusion means treating an intention may include treating its opposite intention. When one intended to enter a contract, the law should also treat him that he actually had the choice to not enter the contract.[29]

---

24 Kennedy (1976), supra note 1262, p. 1695.

25 Ibid., p. 1691, referring to Lon Fuller, 'Consideration and Form', in 41 Colum. L. Rev. (1941), p. 799; Von Mehren, 'Civil LawAnalogues to Consideration: An Exercise in Comparative Analysis', in 72 Harv. L. Rev. (1959), p. 1009.

26 Ibid.

27 Ibid., n.7, quoting C. de Montesquieu, 'Lettres Persanes', (1721), p. 64.

28 Ibid., p. 1689.

29 Ibid., p. 1739, referring to Macauly, 'Private Legislation and the Duty to Read: Business Run by IBM Machine, The Law of Contracts and Credit Cards', in 19 Vand.L.Rev. (1966), p. 1067.

Rules are general, and the generality is vis-à-vis particularity. Generality means that the framer of a legal rule is attempting to kill many birds with one stone. The wide scope of the rule attempts to deal with as many as possible of the different imaginable fact situations in which a substantive issue may arise.[30] A general rule will be over- and under inclusive than a particular rule. Every rule involves a measure of imprecision vis-à-vis purpose. The wider the scope of the rule, the more serious the imprecision becomes.[31] A regime of general rules causes fewer rules altogether. Fewer rules altogether cause fewer cases of first impression and fewer occasions on which a judge is free to choose between conflicting lines of authority. At the same time, formal realizability eliminates the sub rosa lawmaking that is possible under a regime of principles. Formal realizability makes the rule clear, and its application will also be clear. The judge is restricted in his power, and this alone should make the judge more wary of using his power than he would otherwise be.[32] The purpose of [rule]formalities is cautionary and evidentary. Formalities make the parties know what they are doing and make the judge know what they did. Lon L. Fuller began the limitation of the functions of formalities to the cautionary and evidentary to resist openly or defies the modern trend to multiply functions almost indefinitely.[33] Duncan Kennedy uses the cautionary function to include both making the parties think twice about what they are doing and making them think twice about the legal consequences. The evidentiary function includes both providing good evidence of the existence of a transaction and providing good evidence of the legal consequences the parties intended.

***

Hart argues that the basis of a rule's authority is not the physical power of its author. If a rule is accepted as a standard of behavior through practices and is recognized as a reason or justification for the behavior of the community's members and as a reason for criticizing the behavior of those who do not obey it, the rule is deemed as binding.[34] Hart recognizes that

30 Ibid., p. 1689, referring to Ihering, 'Der Geist Des Romsichen Recht' § 4, pp. 54-55.

31 Ibid., p. 1690. This phenomenon is discussed in Surrey, 'Complexity and the Internal Revenue Code: The Problem of the Management of Tax Detail,' in 1969 Law & Contemp. Prob.673, 695-702: See also Amsterdam (1974), supra note 1260, pp. 349,374-377, 388-395.

32 Ibid. On the obligation to formulate rules as a check on discretionary power, see K. Davis, 'Discretionary Justice: A Preliminary Inquiry' (1969), pp. 52-96; Amsterdam (1974), Ibid., pp. 416-428.

33 Ibid.,p. 1691.

34 Dworkin (1967), supra note 1242, pp. 20-21, referring to Hart (1961), supra

rules are of different logical kinds, 'primary' and 'secondary' rules. Primary rules are those that grant rights or impose obligations upon members of the community. Secondary rules are those that stipulate how, and by whom, such primary rules may be formed, recognized, modified or extinguished.[35] Hart (1961) said that they [secondary rules] may all be said to be on a different level from the primary rules, for they are all about such rules; in the sense that while primary rules are concerned with the actions that individuals must or must not do, these secondary rules are concerned with the primary rules themselves. They specify the ways in which the primary rules may be conclusively ascertained, introduced, eliminated, varies, and the fact of their violation conclusively determined. The secondary rules are further divided into: *rules of recognition*, *rules of adjudication* and *rules of change*. Rules of recognition decide criteria for the validity of other kinds of legal rule; rules of adjudication define the procedure to be followed when the primary rules have been set aside; and rules of change define the procedures for the change of primary rules.[36] If a rule is enacted in conformity with some secondary rules which stipulate its enactment, that rule so enacted is 'valid' and shall be binding. So, Hart expressed his fundamental distinction.[37] A rule may be binding because it is accepted or because it is valid. Secondary Rules of recognition are ultimate in a legal system, and there is no more fundamental rules that test the validity of the rules of recognition. The rules of recognition are the only rules whose binding force depends on their acceptance by members of the community, especially its officials. We can apply no mechanical test, but there is no danger of our confusing the rule of recognition of a community with its rules of morality. The rule of recognition is identified by the fact that its province is the operation of the governmental apparatus of legislature, courts, agencies, policemen, and the rest.

Carlos E. Alchourron and Eugenio Bulygin recognize two groups of rules within the secondary system. We have given the name of secondary system or judge system to the set of norms regulating the actions of judges as such. These norms may be divided into two groups: (i) those that determine in what conditions the judges may judge and what types of question they may resolve (norms of competence); and (ii) those that establish obligations and prohibitions for the judges.[38] A. Ross recognizes

---

note 1253, pp. 97-107.

35 Ibid., p. 19, referring to Hart (1961), Ibid., pp. 89-96.

36 Wahlgren (2009), supra note 1259, p. 230, referring to Hart (1961), Ibid., pp. 92-96.

37 Dworkin (1967), supra note 1275, pp. 20-21, referring to Hart (1961), Ibid., pp. 97-107, and passim particularly ch. IV.

38 Wahlgren (2009), supra note 1276, p. 231, referring to C. E. Alchourron & E. Bulygin, 'Normative Systems', Library of Exact Philosophy 5, (Wien: Springler-

three different rules of competence (regulating *personal competence*, *procedural competence*, and *substantial competence*).[39] Tore Stromberg makes a distinction between *rules of conduct* (describing patterns of activities), *rules of qualification* (defining legally relevant qualities), and *rules of competence* (defining legally relevant competences).[40] Alexsander Peczenik separates, among other things, between *constituting norms* and *regulating norms* (A. Peczenick 1987).[41] N.K Sundby and Eckhoff propose a division into *rules* and *guide-lines* (*retningslinjer*).[42] Following Hart's terminology, Wahlgren holds that formal rules are secondary rules. Formal rules and substantive ones have their functions on different levels. Formal rules, in this regard, are similar to methodological rules that govern the process of interpretation. However, little doubt appears as to the similarity between the function of formal rules and that of methodological rules. That is to say, the assumption that formal rules have been developed with a more conscious goal to provide stability to the decision making process and to make possible the accomplishment of rule application of high quality is well grounded.[43] Because the justification in judicial discretion as to the choice of norm pops a rule out of principle, precedent, the text of the Constitution, or some other source of law, and because the chosen rule form disguises the discretionary element involved in applying it to cases, the rule form has the function of keeping up the legitimacy of judicial decision.[44]

***

Unlike Austin, Hart finds the authority of officials and public institutions to create valid legal rules in constitutional standards, 'long customary practice' and 'the relation [of a rule] to judicial decisions'. 'Long customary practice' and ...the relation [of a rule] to judicial decisions, Hart says, generally go

---

Verlag, 1971), p. 151).

39 Ibid., referring to A. Ross, 'Directives and Norms', (London: Routledge & Keagan, Paul, 96 1968).

40 Ibid., referring to Tore Stromberg, 'Rattsordningens byggstenar. Om normtyperna i lag och sedvaneratt', Studentlitteratur, - Extensive Comments on Competence in Skandinavian jurisprudence - Lund, (1988) passim.

41 Ibid., referring to Alexsander Peczenick, 'Rattsnormer', (Stockholm: Norstedts forlag, 1987), pp. 15-32.

42 Ibid., referring to N.K. Sundby, 'Om normer', Universitetsforlaget, Oslo, (1974) – Fiolosofiske problemer XLIII, Scandinavian Studies in Philosophy, Naess, A. ed.- pp. 190-306; T. Eckhoff and N.K. Sundby, 'Rettssystemer' Systemteoretisk innforing i rettsfilosofien, Tanum-Norli, Oslo,(1976), p. 128; N. Jareborg, 'Varderingar', (Stockholm: Norstedts forlag, 1975), pp. 87-97.

43 Ibid., p. 250.

44 Kennedy (1976), supra note 1273, p. 1708.

along with but subordinate to the test of legislation.[45] Ideally, rules take all relevant factors into account so all possible cases can be resolved by rules. This ideal expectation also includes another expectation that any possible case can be resolved by a rule. This indicates that a rule conflict is not expected to happen. When rules conflict, there must be a resolution that leads to one single rule applicable to a case. This means that the application of the other rules should be excluded.[46] When two rules conflict, one supersedes the other by virtue of its greater weight. One of them cannot be a valid rule. This decision must be made by appealing to considerations beyond the rules themselves. The regulation of such rule conflict may be that rules enacted by higher authority supersede rules enacted by lower authority, later enacted rules supersede prior enacted ones, more specific rules supersede more general rules, or something of that sort. A legal system may also prefer the rules supported by the more important principles.[47]

The rules are valid rules, and the validity of which is tested by their *pedigree* or the manner of their adoption, not by using the content of the rules.[48] The grounds of legal propositions should be about what makes legal rules valid, not about what makes legal propositions true. The conditions of norms' validity are sourced-based. Exclusively source-based, the conditions of norms' validity are concerning the norms' pedigree. Laid down by more fundamental source-based norms, or by settled judicial practice, or by some other feature of political history, norms' validity may further depend on certain moral conditions. Interpretivism is the thesis that legal norms' validity is partly dependent upon the best justification of political practice. So, valid norms are those which have the right source and which are consistent with the principles that justify the relevant political practice.[49]

***

Legal rules appear both as rules of substantive nature and as methodological rules. Legal rules are considered due to the doctrine of legal sources (a collection of theories about origin, validity and application of legal rules) or other legally authoritative reasons. Those rules are usually reflected in statutes, in legislative preparatory material (*travaux preparatoires*), in precedents, in work of jurisprudence, or, as at last resource, in regularities

45 Dworkin (1967), supra note 1277, p. 22, referring to Hart (1961), supra note 1277, ch. VII.

46 Hage (1996), supra note 1263, p. 12.

47 Dworkin (1967), supra note 1285, p. 27.

48 Ibid., p. 17.

49 Nicos Stavropoulos, 'Interpretivist Theories of Law', in Stanford Encyclopedia of Philosophy, first published Tuesday, October 14, 2003, p. 5.

that may be perceived as customs.[50] Substantive legal rules prescribe particular outcomes for particular types of cases. The requirements as stated by substantive rules are the basis for justifying particular types of governmental action. Formal logic represents such rules as 'conditional propositions'.[51] Substantive legal rules is therefore *prescriptive* of legal determinations including judicial decisions.

Judge-made laws are laws in Common Law systems, but in Civil Law systems judicial decisions are merely the application of law, not the law itself. The Civil Law systems follow a straightforward understanding of the separation of powers in which the courts have their legitimate function to merely apply the law, and the courts should not usurp the legitimate function of the legislators. Under Civil Law, if the courts make law, the courts wrongfully take the legislative legitimate function. On the contrary, one distinctive feature of Common Law systems is the existence of central areas of law that have no legislative foundation – such as contract, tort, trusts and personal property. Most Common Law jurisdictions still leave these areas on a non-statutory footing. Here the decisions of the courts are the basis of the law.[52]

The substantive content of the Common Law rules was believed to be an embodiment of the idea of freedom. The belief was based on conceptualism. Official intervention to enforce the Common Law rules was believed to be non-discretionary, and this belief was expressed through a complex of doctrines, including *stare decisis*, the non-delegation doctrine, the void for vagueness doctrine, objectivism in contracts, the reasonable person standard in torts, the distinction between questions of law and questions of fact, and the general idea that law tended to develop toward formally realizable general rules. Believing that the Common Law rules were logically derived from the idea of freedom and that there was no discretionary element in their application made the description that the legal order is at least neutral (nonpolitical if not really 'natural') reasonable. The assertion of the 'naturalness' of economic interaction under property and contract rules in 1900 was based on the combination of the beliefs.[53] Which institution should lay down substantive norms is often argued. It is a question as to whether the institutions should be the courts or some other more 'democratically legitimate' institutions such as the legislature, the jury, or private parties pursuing their own objectives through institutions

50 Wahlgren (2009), supra note 1283, p. 202.

51 Vern R. Walker, 'Discovering the Logic of the Logal Reasoning', in WALKER.PRD2, Hofstra University School of Law, Hempstead, New York, USA, 11/6/2007, p. 1693.

52 Grant Lamond, 'Precedent and Analogy in Legal Reasoning', in Stanford Encyclopedia of Philosophy, first published Tuesday, June 20, 2006, p. 15.

53 Kennedy (1976), supra note 1284, p. 1747.

like contract or corporate law. About which institution is the superior or the inferior in the premises is often in conflict. Stereotyped images of what courts, legislators, juries, and private right holders 'ought' to do are appealed by the parties, and a very deep seated idea of the judicial function is that judges apply rules[54].

Precedents have practical authority because they are regarded as partly constituting the law. Because courts are bound to apply the law, and because earlier decisions have practical authority over the content of the law (i.e., over what the law is), later courts are bound to follow the decisions of earlier cases.[55] Precedents should arguably be understood as laying down rules, as the application of underlying principles, and as a decision on the balance of reasons. Precedents operating by laying down rules are akin to statutes. Precedents and statutes lay down rules to apply to later cases whose facts satisfy the requirements for application. In precedents, it is the *ratio decidendi* that represents the rules (the proposition of law) layed down in precedents. It is the *ratio decidendi,* not the *obiter dicta* which is the 'holding' or 'ruling' that is binding upon later cases.[56] A precedent is the decision of a court (or other adjudicative body) which has a special legal significance lying in the court's decision, regarded as having practical, and not merely theoretical, authority over the content of the law. A decision has theoretical authority if the circumstances in which it was made (the identity of the decision-makers, those involved in arguing the case, the availability of evidence or time) provide good reasons for believing the decision to be correct in law. If there are good reasons to believe that an earlier case was correctly decided, and if the facts in a later case are the same as those in the earlier case, then there are good reasons for believing that the same decision would be correct in the later case.[57] Common law rules – those developed by earlier court decisions – are sometimes overruled directly, and sometimes radically altered by further development.[58] If courts had discretion to change established rules, then these rules would of course not be binding upon them, and so would not be law on the positivists' model.

---

54 Ibid., p. 1708.

55 Lamond (2006), supra note 1292, p. 3, 4.

56 Ibid., p. 7, referring to J. Raz,'Law and Value in Adjudication', in The Authority of Law (Oxford: Oxford University Press, 1979); N.D. MacCormick,'Legal Reasoning and Legal Theory', (Oxford: Oxford University Press, 1978, 1994) (especially 82-6, 213-28); L. Alexander, 'Constrained by Precedent', in Southern California Law Review 63 (1989), pp. 1-64; F.Schauer, 'Is the Common Law Law?' in California Law Review 77 (1989), pp. 455-471(pp. 467-471); F. Schauer (1991), supra note 1255, pp. 174-87.

57 Ibid., p. 1, 2.

58 Dworkin (1967), supra note 1287, p. 37,38, citing Wellington & Albert, 'Statutory Interpretation and the Political Process: A Comment on Sinclair v. Atkinson', in 72 Yale L.J. (1963), p. 1547.

The positivist must therefore argue that there are standards, themselves binding upon judges, that determine when a judge may overrule or alter an established rule, and when he may not[59].

In the United States, judge-made law is a part of the law, and statute law is another part. The written opinion of a judge or of a panel of judges is also referred to as a case. A case usually includes a description of given fact, a short history of the legal procedure that brought the case before the court and the court's reasoning in reaching a judicial decision. Judicial decisions are published, or reported, only if they change or clarify a rule of law. Generally, trial level state court decisions are not published. Only some appellate decisions are reported. All cases from the U.S Supreme Court and from state supreme courts are published.[60] Under s3(1) of the European Communities Act 1972, decisions of the ECJ are binding, in matters of Community law, on all courts up to and including the House of Lords. This written law clearly shows a certain trend in European Community law toward the adoption of more substantive legal rules, and practice has really shown the trend.

***

A legislature has the power to change the Common Law or enact a Common Law rule into law by passing legislation. However, the legislature must not exceed its constituional power when enacting legislated rules. A statute may be challenged if it is unconstituional because of having been passed by a legislature which has exceeded its constitutional power. The court may then determine that the statute is unconstitutional and invalid. Any valid statutes must be applied to particular situations by the court through interpretation. Once a statute was interpreted and applied by the court to a particular case, the case becomes precedent.[61] Statutes are formal and written rules of law, passed by federal, state, city or county legislative bodies, with the constitutional power to exercise the legislative function in its jurisdiction. Being written rules of law to proscribe or prohibit future conduct, statutes are written in very general and often vague language. A legislative 'enabling statute' grants the power to certain administrative bodies to enact administrative regulations. There is a hierarchy of statutory law, and the United States Constitution sits at the apex.[62] Statutory rules

59 Ibid., p. 38.

60 Locating The Law, A Handbook for Non-Law Librarians, 5th ed., revised 2011, Southern California Association of Law Libraries (SCALL), Public Access to Legal Information, edited by June Kim, 2011 SCALL, p. 6, 7.

61 Connelly, supra note 1250, para II C & D.

62 Ibid., para II. A.

are subjected to interpretation and reinterpretation, sometimes even when the result is not to carry out what is called the "legislative intent".[63]

The first section of the Sherman Act states that every contract in restraint of trade shall be void. The United States Supreme Court interpreted the provision as a rule, but treated the rule as containing the word 'unreasonable' and as prohibiting only 'unreasonable' restraint of trade. The interpretation by the Supreme Court has demonstrated that a rule and a principle can sometimes play much the same role, but they are different in terms of form alone.[64] The provision may logically function as a rule in the sense that whenever a court finds that the restraint in a contract is 'unreasonable', such a contract is to be deemed invalid; and may also substantially function as a principle in the sense that a variety of other principles and policies must also be taken into account in determining whether or not a particular restraint in particular economic circumstances is 'unreasonable'. The application of rules containing such words depends to some extent upon principles or policies or standards lying behind such rules. Such words make such rules themselves like principles, but do not quite turn such rules into principles, because even the least confining of these terms restricts the kind of other principles and policies on which the rule depends.[65]

Civil law statutes are personal, real and mixed. Personal statutes have persons as their principal object, such as on birth, legitimacy, freedom, the fight of instituting suits, majority as to age, incapacity to contract, to make a will, to plead in person and the like. Personal statutes treat of property only incidentally. A personal statute is universal in its operation, and in force everywhere. Real statutes have property as their principal object and do not provide for persons, except in relation to property; such are those which concern the disposition, which one may make of his property either alive or by testament. A real statute is confined in its operation to the country of its origin. Mixed statutes provide at once for both persons and property. Almost all statues provide for persons in relation to things.[66] Legal rules made by the legislator take into account ethical, religious, moral interests and the interest of justice, of equity, of the public and the highest interests of human kind.[67] It is self-evident that every statute affects these

63 Dworkin (1967), supra note 1298, p. 37, 38, referring to Wellington & Albert (1963), supra note 1298, p. 1547.

64 Ibid., p. 28. See Standard Oil v. United States, 221 U.S. 1, 60 (1911); United States v. American Tobacco Co., 221 U.S. 106, 180 (1911).

65 Ibid., p. 28-29.

66 Legal Definition of Statute, from the 'Lectric Law Library's Lexicon *Statute, http: // www. lectlaw. com/def2/s071, (1995 – 2013 The 'Lectric Law Library) , p. 4.

67 James L. Dennis, 'Interpretation and Application of the Civil Code and the

kinds of interests.[68] Accordingly, the Civil Code is an integrated system of concepts determining conflicts of interests, a structure of command based on value judgment and value ideals.[69] A. Aarnio, R. Alexy and A. Peczenik stated: "The legal order is the sum of legal norms which have been put together (systematized) on a certain basis".[70] The legal order or system is broken down into sub-systems, e.g., civil law, criminal law, etc., and in each sub-system legal rules are commonly systemized in various manners, e.g., around some legal issue or as decompositions of general and special parts. Legal classifications may be made by using certain aspects such as objects or functions as a means, and the notion of rights has long played an important role. A lot of effort has been made to penetrate the content and meaning of legal concepts. Both legal rules and legal concepts are entities which may be studied at different levels.

***

Legal rules in the countries of Romano Germanic family are also held in high esteem and are not considered merely rules that are appropriate to the solution of concrete cases. Legal rules are viewed as rules of conduct, endowed or naturally given with a certain generality, situated above the specific application by the courts or practitioner in any concrete cases. The French *regle de droit* which is situated at the level of a legal principle (*principe juridique*), in Englishmen's viewpoint, appears to be more a moral precept than a truly 'legal rule'.[71] Legal rules are prescriptions for the behavior of men. Rules of law refer only to human behavior; they state how men ought to behave, and say nothing about the actual behavior of men and of the causes thereof.[72] Legal rules in England are precedents which are

---

Evaluation of Judicial Precedent', in 54 Lousiana Law Review - 1993, p. 9, referring to Phillip Heck, 'The Formation of Concepts and the Jurisprudence of Interests', in The Jurisprudence of Interests (M.Magdalena Schoch trans. 1948) ["Heck 1948a"], pp. 130-31.

68 Ibid., pp. 9-10 referring to Heck (1948a), Ibid., p. 131.

69 Ibid., p. 10 referring to Heck (1948a), Ibid., p. 168.

70 Wahlgren (2009), supra note 1290, pp. 210-211, referring to A. Aarnio, R. Alexy and A. Peczenik, 'The Foundation of Legal Reasoning' (1981), p. 423.

71 Tetley (1999/2000), supra note 1241, para V. 12. [part of accompanying text omitted]. A.P. SERENI. 'The Code and the Case Law', in B. Schwarz (ed.). The Code Napoleon and the Common Law World, (New York: New York University Press, 1956), 61 'The civil law regle-juridique may appear at times to an Anglo-American lawyer to be nothing more than an abstract percept or at most a general directive rather than an actual legal provision.

72 Hans Kelsen, 'General Theory of Law and State,' 20th Century Legal Philosophy Series Vol. I, (Anders Wedberg trans.), (New York: Russel & Russel, 1961), p. 37, 38.

at the case level. The English legal rules which, according to French jurists, are situated at the level of particular judicial application are concepts of case-by-case law which give an organizationally unsatisfactory character.[73] Consequently, in Civil law systems every possible situation is governed by a limited number of general principles, so the systems are 'closed' in that sense. In Common law systems, new rules may be created or imported for new facts, therefore the systems are 'open' in that sense.[74]

In Common Law jurisdiction, most rules are found in the jurisprudence, and statutes complete them. In Civil Law tradition, the important principles are stated in the code, while the statutes complete them.[75] Statutory law is of the same paramountcy in Common law and Civil law. However, statutes differ in function in both law traditions. In Civil law jurisdictions, general principles of law are systematically and exhaustively exposed in codes,[76] and the codes provide the core of the law. Particular statutes have their function to complete the codes. In Common law jurisdictions, statutes complete precedents, which then contains the core of the law. Precedents as the core of the law are specific rules applying to specific facts.[77] The function of statutes causes different styles of law drafting in Common law and Civil law traditions. Since the codes should be exhaustive in Civil law jurisdictions, they provide statutory general principles that are not read restrictively and that do not need to be explained. The Civil law codes and statutes are concise or brief (*le style francais*), do not provide definition, do state principles in broad and have general phrases. The principles of law that often appear in rigid doctrine are frozen into the codes and are imposed upon courts.[78] In Common law jurisdictions, statutes cover only the specific part of the law to be reformed and must be precise (*le style anglais*), since the Common Law courts restrict rules to the specific facts they intended to cover.[79] Most Common law rules can be changed from time to time, subject to the doctrine of *stare decisis*.[80]

Judge-made law is the core of Common law, but rules passed by legislature are the core of Civil law. In Civil law tradition, the doctrine's function is to draw from this disorganized mass [cases, books and legal

73 Tetley (1999/2000), supra note 1311, para V.12, referring to R. DAVID/JEC BRIERLY, 'Major Legal Systems in the World Today', third ed. (London: Stevens & Sons, 1985), para 320, p. 358, 359.

74 Ibid., para V. 12, referring to DAVID/BRIERLY (1985), Ibid., para 322, pp. 360-361.

75 Ibid., para III.5.

76 Ibid., para V. 7 [accompanying text omitted].

77 Ibid., para V.7.

78 Ibid., para V.8 [accompanying text omiited].

79 Ibid., para V. 8.

80 Ibid., para V. 11.

dictionaries] the rules and the principles which will clarify and purge the subject of impure elements, and thus provide both the practice and the courts with a guide for the solution of particular cases in the future.[81] That doctrine has a modest function in Common law, where authors are encouraged to distinguish cases and to extract from these specific rules. Common law authors may refuse to draw specific rules with no policy basis and may openly criticize absurd judgments.[82] Specific rules in Common law are extracted from case analyses of similar facts, not identical fact. Common law focuses [more] on fact pattern. Upon such extraction, then through deduction the Common law authors determine the often very narrow scope of each rule, and sometimes propose new rules to cover facts that have not yet presented themselves. Civil law focuses rather on principles. The history of legal principles is traced, the function of legal principles is identified, the domain of legal principle application is determined, and the effects of legal principles in terms of right and obligation are explained. At this stage, general and exceptional effects are deduced. Specifically on principles or apart from statutory analysis required, some induction from the existing case law is involved in determining the area of application of a principle, while some deduction is involved in delimiting exceptions. Common law jurisprudence sets out a new specific rule to a new specific set of facts and provides the principal source of law, while Civil law jurisprudence applies general principles.[83] Wider legal rules in private law matters are allowed more in Civil law than in Common law. Civil law rules are suppletive - the parties are deemed to know the law and hence to be aware of those rules, - while Common law rules are presumptive of the intention of the parties when relevant facts are present.[84]

***

'Rule' is defined in a logically spare manner, as a prescriptive proposition that has a logical structure the most abstract form of which is reflected in the standard conditional proposition, either propositional ('if P then Q') or predicate ('for all x, if x is an F then x is a G').[85] Berkeley contends that internal structure is an appropriate internal mechanism (ideas of something including the law running or working, relating to regularity and predictability). So,

---

81 Ibid., para V.2, referring to DAVID/BRIERLY (1985), supra note 1314, p. 94.

82 Ibid.

83 Ibid., para V.3 & 4.

84 Ibid., para V.12, referring to DAVID/BRIERLY (1985), supra note 1321, para 325, pp. 364-365.

85 S. Brewer, 'Exemplary Reasoning: Semantics, Pragmatics and Rational Force of Legal Argument by Analogy', in 109 HARV. L. REV, 923, (1966), p. 972.

prescriptivity through *structure* is existent in legal propositions, and such prescriptivity is *generative*. A particular rule is often generated from a standard or principle in the application of the standard to a particular case. An ever increasing group of particular rules of this kind are included in the standard, so the standard is general. The generality of the standard means that there are no gaps: it is possible to find out something about how judges will dispose of cases that have not yet arisen. But, formulation of a formally realizable general rule is not attempted within this context. Rather, case law gradually fills in the area with rules so closely bound to particular facts that they have little or no precedential value.[86] Raz also thinks that a rule is *generative*, that is generative of reason. According to Raz (1975), the facts that make a rule applicable to a particular situation constitute an *exclusionary reason* for the rule conclusion. A rule generates exclusionary reasons, reasoning with a rule is somewhat different from reasoning with a principle. They [rule and principle] both are [in combination] a reason for the conclusion of the rule, and a reason not to apply competing goals and principles. So, if these competing goals and principles are not applied, then they do not generate reasons, consequently the reason based on the rule needs not be weighed against other reasons anymore. The rule applies in an all-or-nothing fashion. Raz says that an exclusionary reason is a second order reason not to act for some reasons.[87] Most rules are the product of some kind of decision making, but principles and goals generally are not (Raz 1975, p. 71). Rules are the product of legislation or abstracted from case law. If a rule is applicable to a case, a reason appears for the conclusion of the rule. This reason replaces all other reasons which might be relevant for that case, and the application of the goals and principles which might underlie these reasons would be excluded. The reason generated by the rule is the only available one, and the rule governs the case on its own. The rule applies in an all-or-nothing fashion (Dworkin).[88]

From the above mentioned, it can be concluded that legal rule is normative, setting a standard of behavior, is a reason or justification for

---

86 Kennedy (1976), supra note 1293, p. 1690, referring to Chief Justice Shaw who gave classic expression to this view in Norway Plains v. Boston & Maine R.R.Co. 67 Mass. (I Gray) 263, 267 (1854): It is one of the great merit and advantageous of the common law that, instead of a series of detailed practical rules, established by positive provisions, and adapted to the precise circustamces of particular cases, which would become obsolete and fail, when the practice and course of business, to which they apply, should cease or change, the common law consists of a few broad and comprehensive principles founded on reason, natural justice, and enlightened public policy modified and adapted to the circumstances of all the particular cases which fall within it.

87 Hage (1996), supra note 1286, p. 11, referring to Raz (1975), supra note 1165.

88 Ibid., p. 12, referring to Raz (1975), Ibid.

behavior, is as a means to control action, is a basis for action, is generative of reason, and is prescriptive. Being normative and prescriptive, legal rule is as the *competence* of law as proposed in this book, and the *competence* identifies the manners how legal determinations including judicial decisions can be analyzed and understood. The *competence* underlies its contingent derivatives, which might be manifested in possible and selected legal

determinations including judicial decisions, or, possible and selected alternative dispute resolutions or undisputed legal practices. Legal rules being the *competence* of law is versatile or clever in many different things insofar as it serves as an explanation of the meaning of legal determinations.[89] Legal rule expresses or implies underlying legal regularities or underlying regularities of legal determinations, that is why legal rule (rule of customary law is included) serves as an explanation of legal determinations including judicial decisions. Underlying regularities of legal determinations significantly contribute to the understanding or meaning of law. So, rule of law concerns with the understanding or meaning of law.[90] Rule of law transforms itself into judicial decisions, alternative dispute resolutions, customary or undisputed legal practices through legal reasoning, and such judicial decisions, alternative dispute resolutions, customary or undisputed legal practices further transform themselves into subsequent judicial decisions, alternative dispute resolutions, customary or undisputed legal practices, to be addressed in Chapter IV of this book.

In legal structural perspective, particularly as to the *competence* or deep structure of law, we know that the judicial process under Common law jurisdiction (much through intuition based on professional knowledge) and under Civil law jurisdiction (much through cognitive instrumental mechanism) do have the same meaning, that is, how to produce judicial decisions, but viewed from different angles, or, analyzed from different starting point. Scandinavian realists hold that language (thought) which does not reflect reality is not correct theorizing, then [it might be concluded that] more specifically that language (thought) which does not reflect the reality of human behavior is not correct theorizing. Conversely, the reality of human behavior which is not in accordance with human thought [the law of thought] is [in mathematical expression] not correctly theorized, in the sense that human beings governed by the law of thought tend at least to say 'no' to such behavior, or, human mind does not always agree with or say 'yes' to any fact of human behavior that happens. This shows that human mind has its prescriptive power upon human behavior, at least to

89 Following Chomsky's rationale in generative transformational grammar as described by Richard Nordquist, 'Deep Structure,' About.com.Guide; and Richard Nordquist, 'What is the Difference Between Descriptive and Prescriptive Grammar?,' About.com.Guide.

90 Ibid.

some certain degree. Rule of law [which is conceptual] as the *competence* or deep structure of law is the more stable element of law, as compared to the *performance* or surface structure of law. The stability of rule as a concept is the basis of temporal career of multiplicity (multiple juridical propositions or juridical cases). Rule of law as the *competence* or deep structure of law is the inherent and the very identity and continuity of law.

III.2. PRINCIPLE OF LAW

***

The pseudo-Platonic Greek philosophical dialogue set forth the classical view that there are certain fundamental rules by which human grow and prosper; and that without these present, the human life becomes impotent and full of suffering.[91] In Aristotle's doctrines, man is fundamentally a social animal, thus law should promote man's harmonious living, and the very nature of man causes law to be a certain way.[92] The doctrines indicate there are timeless principles of law. It is not an external ultimate reality which so much dictates what the principles are, rather they are dictated by the psychological nature of human being.[93] Cicero, the Roman great trial attorney and Stoic philosopher, characterized law as the discovery of nature's principles via human reason.[94] The Roman law was itself an attempted exposition of the fundamental legal precepts.[95] *Ius gentium* is one of the fundamental legal precepts, promoting individual autonomy.[96] For the purpose of restoring authority to the maxims stated by the great jurists and creating some order for the mumble jumble of legal materials, not codified, that time, Justinian dedicated a book of his Digest (the 50th) to the gathering of principles (*de regulis juris antiqui*).[97]

91 Miller (1985/1986), supra note 1077, p. 369, referring to Plato, 'Minos,' in CLASSIC OF WESTERN THOUGHT 391 (undated).

92 Ibid., p. 370, referring generally to ARISTOTLE, 'THE POLITICS', (Penguin, 1975), pp. 25-30; C. CONWAY, 'JURISPRIDENCE', (1971), p. 22.

93 Ibid., referring to ARISTOTLE (1975), Ibid., p. 33, 38, 40, 62, 64.

94 Ibid., referring to CONWAY (1971), supra note 1332, p. 22; see also CICERO, 'MURDER TRIALS', (Penguin 1980); B. NICHOLAS, 'AN INTRODUCTION TO ROMAN LAW', (Oxford, 1967), p. 54.

95 Ibid., p. 371, referring to NICHOLAS (1967), Ibid.; see generally JUSTINIAN, 'THE DIGEST OF ROMAN LAW', (C. Kolbert trans. 1979), p. 54.

96 Ibid., pp. 370-371, referring to NICHOLAS (1967), Ibid.

97 Guido Alpa, 'Articles - General Principles of Law', produced by The Berkeley Electronic Press, 1994, http: //digitalcommons. Law.ggu.edu//annlsurvey/voll/iss1/2, para II. p. 4.

In the Renaissance, Hugo Grotius and Francis Bacon attempted to remedy the lack of specificity in the theory of natural law. They each tried to specify the universal legal principles. Grotius introduced the fundamentals, among other things, the allowance of self-defense, the right of personal ownership of property, the right of the people to accept or reject particular laws, the prohibition of battery, the prohibition of larceny, the including in the society's system of justice provisions for reward and punishment, and the use of judges to settle disputes.[98] These fundamentals were criticized as being banal and so of little consequence.[99] Bacon posited that there are a finite number of legal principles, or 'maxims', based on which the judges proceed the judicial decision-making in a particular dispute.[100] His approach showed clearly the notion that the thinking or reasoning process of the lawmakers was as important as, or perhaps more important than the actual recorded legal rules. By his own reading of cases, Bacon noted certain principles recurring, certain harmonies. The recurring principles identified by him were, inter alia, the maxim on causation, which is still in force, that the law favors the proximate and not the remote cause; that ambiguities should be construed against the draftsman of the legal writing; that necessity is the root privilege in criminal law (e.g., that even self-defense derives from necessity); that punishment cannot be increased after the fact; that two parties cannot compromise a third party's right; that ambiguities in legal documents may be cured by the use of extrinsic evidence, etc.

Under the enlightened legal philosophy, Montesquieu, Rousseau and Locke emphasized the super important of individual *liberty* in society. In order to protect individual liberty from being choked off by the centralized power, Montesquieu theorized the necessity of separating the executive, legislative and judicial branches of government.[101] To protect the right of individual man in the society, Rousseau introduced a societal contract theory based on which *governmental* breach was possible.[102] Locke's emphasis on liberty came under natural law philosophy,[103] and the source of the natural

98 Miller (1985/1986), supra note 1331, p. 372, referring to H. GROTIUS, 'DE JURE PRAEDA' (G. Williams trans. 1950), quoted in JURISPRUDENCE, (G. Christie ed. 1973), p. 152.

99 Ibid.

100 Ibid., pp. 372-373, referring to Francis Bacon, 'Maxim of the Law', in JURISPRUDENCE, (G. Christie ed. 1973), p. 884.

101 Ibid., p. 373, referring to B. MONTESQUIEU, 'THE SIPIRIT OF LAW', (1878), pp. 161-163.

102 Ibid., citing J. ROUSSEAU, 'THE SOCIAL CONTRACT', (M. Cranston trans. 1978), p. 58-62.

103 Ibid., referring to J. LOCKE, 'A LETTER CONCERNING TOLERATION,' (Hnhbs-Merril 1979; J. LOCKE, 'TWO TREATIES OF GOVERNMENT', (Cambridge 1960).

law is no longer in divinity – it was just basic to the nature of man.[104] From the Kantian categorical imperative, Karl Larenz derived the principle 'one is a person, a being free to express his own will, only inasmuch as other beings are respected'.[105] From this principle the following principles can be derived: the injustice slavery, the illegality of 'corporal' servitude, the illegality of forced labor inflicted without the necessity of sanctions; and in the positive sense, the legal capacity recognized for all men. The principle Larenz has derived from the Kantian categorical imperative is imminent in paragraph 1.1 of Fundamental German Rights, according to which the dignity of man is intangible. It is indeed from this norm that jurisprudential construction of general rights of individual persons is derived. A derivation of the same principle with respect to the person is the liberty of conscience and worship. The liberty of the will is thus reduced to the freedom to do anything that is not prohibited and anything that does not obstruct the equal liberty on the part of others. As to just rights and the foundation of judicial ethics, Larenz mentions that among the individuality principles of self-determination and contractual autonomy are the principle of equivalence in synallagmatic contracts, and the principles of trust and good faith. He says that among the principles inherent to the community are participation, equality and proportionality, to which he then adds the principles that govern political representation and trial rights (impartiality of the judge and of the trial).

Locre first used legal principles in the sense in his *Espirit du code civil* of 1804. Rudolf von Ihering used them in describing the 'spirit' of Roman rights in introducing legal principles as the points from which the formation and evolution of Roman rights departs (the original principles) and the propulsive force of the mechanism of rights in the system (the unifying criteria).[106] Langdell had searched for fundamental legal principles. He wished to define law and what is basic about law in any society.[107] Other illustrious jurists such as Gustav Radburch and Roscoe Pound, in their works to illustrate the spirit of common law, understand this use of 'principle' as an expression of the spirit of the system.[108] L. De Mauri gathered together two thousand rules in Italy in the first years of the 20th century. The collection of Daguin and Jouanneau was referred by Boulanger during the same time and the years before in France. Recently, a new collection has been made and edited by Roland and Boyer, where principles in the form of a 'brocard' or maxim are considered 'adages of French rights'. James Mans Puigarnau classified rules, maxims and aphorisms, with reference to statements made

104 Ibid., referring to J. Locke, 'Essays on the Law of Nature', in JURISPRUDENCE, (G. Christie ed. 1973), pp. 224-225.

105 Alpa (1994), supra note 1337, p. 5, 6, 7.

106 Ibid., p. 4.

107 Miller (1985/1986), supra note 1338, p. 376.

108 Alpa (1994), supra note 1346, para II, p. 4.

by the Supreme Court of Justice, and put them in order in a catalogue. And, maxims gathered together by Broom before the nineteenth century had been having a notable success in the 1940s in England and in the United States.[109] Legal naturalists hold that timeless legal principles exist, but the positivists, on the contrary, consider there is no timeless legal principle.[110]

***

Guido Alpa concludes that legal principles have originated from legislation, judicial works and legal doctrine.[111] Most sentences in judicial decisions taking legal principles as the ground demonstrate that there are legal principles originated from judicial works. And among the examples of legal principles originating from legal doctrine are *pacta sunt servanda, rebus sic stantibus* and the principles of the employment theory of supposition; of enrichment without cause; of the acquisitive occupation; and of the protection of minors in custody cases connected to the separation of parents. Legal doctrinal writers identified principles of law from judicial practice, politics of rights followed by legislation, and scientific elaboration proposing legal principles to organize diverse and scattered norms in a systematic manner or introducing new legal principles to adapt the system to new necessities, such as consumer protection, protection of savings, and transparency of contract.

The principle of legality in criminal law is explicitly mentioned in the Swedish constitution – RF chapter 2, section 10), under which the famous sentence *nulla poena sine lege, nulla poena sine crimine, nullum crimen sine poena legali* (no punishment without law, no punishment without crime, no crimes without criminal law) is stated, as originally formulated by Paul Johann Anselm von Feuerbach at the beginning of the 19th century.[112] Not only that the principle of legality is that of criminal law, but the principle then also becomes important in all areas of law.[113] The principle of equality

109 Ibid., p. 3.

110 Miller (1985/1986), supra note 1347, p. 368. John Austin gave the most terse statement of this rule. See Austin (1832), supra note 1251 (G. Christie ed. 1973), pp. 471-74.

111 Alpa (1994), supra note 1348, para VII, p. 21.

112 Wahlgren (2009), supra note 1310, p. 254-2555, see, e.g., on the principle of legality in criminal law, N.Jareborg, 'Kriminalisering', in S. Heckscher, A. Snare, H. Takala, J. Vestergaard, eds., Straff och rattfardighet, (Stockholm: Norstedts forlag, 1980), pp. 38-41; M.E. Frankel, 'Criminal Sentence: Law Without Order', (New York: Hill and Wang, 1973), pp. 3-5 and passim.

113 Ibid., see, e.g., RF chapter 8, section 3, H. Stromberg, 'Allman forvaltningsratt', (Malmo: Liber forlag, 1984, 12th ed.), pp. 73-74; Coval & Smith, 'Law and its Presuppositions', (1986), p. 37 "[The doctrine of precedent] follows

before the law (imposing that cases which are similar from the legal point of view should be decided alike) is of fundamental importance for legal reasoning process, and the principle is also fundamental for the legitimacy of legal system.[114] The principle of justice is especially important to uphold in certain kinds of judicial decisions, foremost, in decisions in which the outcome can be described in exact measures and in which irregularities are easily perceived. Justice is of great importance to the persons involved.[115] The principle of individual responsibility is materially found in civil responsibility. The principles of 'respect for the other' are shown in the prohibition of acts of rivalry (Article 833 of [Italian] civil code), the good neighbor rules (Article 872 e ss.), and the prohibition of pollutants (Article 844 e ss.). In the writing on civil responsibility, it is said that he who causes damage is charged with the obligation of indemnification, in a specific form or in an equivalent number. The principle of contractual autonomy is also considered one of the fundamental values. Larenz has observed that in all systems, the principle *pacta sunt servanda* is recorded, even if in each individual case it may be realized differently. Other value-principles are the one concerning the non-retroactivity of the law and the one which concerns the presumption of awareness of the law (*numquam legem ignorare censetur; ignorantia legis non excusat*).[116] In practice, the principles of legality and equality (as well as the doctrine of precedent) imply that sanctions or other rulings determined by judicial decisions must be imposed in accordance with the law.[117]

Von Bogdandy holds that legal doctrines of principles are, in general, parts of discourse internal to law, i.e. operations of the legal system. Such discourse is different from approaches that analyze the material provisions of law from a social science viewpoint which for instance traces the factual constrains or motives affecting the law.[118] What such a discourse claims

---

from the principle of reason that unless we employ predicates and other terms in a consistent manner we have neither consistency in, nor predictability from, our arguments"].

114 Ibid. See also, on the importance of the principle of equality, F. Schmidt, 'Domaren som lagtolkare. In Festskrift tillagnad Nils Herlitz', (Stockholm: Norstedts, 1955), p. 296.

115 Ibid., pp. 254-255.

116 Alpa (1994), supra note 1351, para III, p. 7, 8, 9.

117 Wahlgren (2009), supra note 1355, p. 255, referring to Alchourron & Bulygin (1971), supra note 1280, p. 176.

118 Armin Von Bogdandy, 'Founding Principles of EU Law: A Theoretical and Doctrinal Sketch', in European Law Journal, Vol. 16, No. 2, March 2010, pp. 95-111 (p. 97-98). "Political science uses the sociological term, whereby principles encompass empiric, causal and normative axioms in a broader way," see seminally S.D. Krasner, 'Structural Causes and Regime Consequences', in (1982), 36 International Organization 185, p. 186.

is to deal with argumentative reasons. A principle-oriented scholarship, rather, has its correlations with legal philosophy, and legal philosophy currently often submits arguments on the basis of principles. An identified difference, according to Von Bogdandy, is that the philosophical discourse on principles can proceed deductively, whereas the discourse on principle in the doctrine of law has to be linked to the material provisions of positive legal rules and judicial decisions. The discourse on principles in legal doctrine is hermeneutical and refers to the law in force.

***

In the past, a system under a doctrinal construct was often thought of having idealistic meaning or being crypto-idealistically believed to be inherent in law. Such a system was sometimes dogmatically advanced as the single truth. This doctrinal teaching has been attacked as undemocratic or elitist.[119] In the light of this attack, contemporary endeavors should be directed towards the more humble goal of proposing means to arrange the legal material and develop the law. The idea of single truth is not necessary academically. The academic claim to truth should necessarily be restricted, especially for construction based on principles because of the openness of principle stock, the semantic openness of each principle, and the openness of which principles prevail in particular cases of conflict.[120] The expectations as to what a system can concretely achieve in the operation of law are also reduced in similar manner under the doctrinal constructivism. Consequently, a doctrine of principles as the result of such reduction does not sufficiently have factual references to the practice of law.[121] Since the congress in Hamburg in 1962, researches have shown there are common values underlying western systems and the values are currently expressed by principles. Peter Stein and John Shand illustrate a view of these common values with the use of theoretical models without consulting legislative text or judicial decisions.[122] Stein and Shand believe that they have individualized the common values: the exclusion of violence and the

119 Ibid, p. 100. For seminal study, see H. Kelsen, 'Vom Wesen und Wert der Demokratie', (Scientia Verlag, 2nd reprint of the 2nd edn of 1929, 1981), 23, Ibid,' Der soziologische und der juristische Staatsbegriff,' (Scientia Verlag, 2nd reprint of the 2nd edn of 1928, 1981); M. Everson, 'Is it just me, or is there an Elephant in the Room?' in (2007) 13 European Law Journal 136; J. Murkens, 'The Future of Staatsrecht', in (2007) 70 The Modern Law Review 731.

120 Ibid. On discourses of application, see K.Gunther, 'Der Sinn fur Angemessenheit', (Suhrkamp, 1988), 300.

121 Ibid.

122 Alpa (1994), supra note 1356, para III, p. 5.

value of security; the limits of discretion on the part of the interpreters and of the administration; the responsibility for contractual fulfillment and for illicit deeds; personal liberties; the right to life and privacy; property and protection of reasonable expectations; and the co-operation and limitation of economic initiative for reasons of the public interests.

Legal positivists reject the existence of principles: where the law runs out, courts have discretion. The normative nature of principles are doubted by the realists who argue that principles are not binding in themselves. A principle would be observed because it is held to be binding in itself only in the collective imagination, not really binding in itself. The realists hold that principles are easily under the influence of interpreters to cover, legitimately, their operations.[123] However, 'inclusive positivists', like Coleman and probably Hart, accept the existence of principles to the extent that acknowledged sources of law refer to them.[124] Positivists hold that a judge's decision is either determined by applicable rules or left to the standardless exercise of discretion.[125] The positivists say that principles are not amenable to a test, so principles are not binding law. But since the positivists cannot deny the role of some principles such as those in *Riggs* and *Henningsen*, they must show some other reason why principles cannot count as law. Dworkin strongly argues that if some principles (such as in *Riggs* and *Henningsen*) are not acknowledged to be binding upon judges who require them in order to reach judicial decisions in particular cases; then rules cannot be said to be binding upon judges either, as rules are also required by judges in judicial process for particular decisions. It is true that the authority or weight of a principle cannot be found in an act of Congress, but we make a case for a principle, and for its weight, by appealing to an amalgam of practice and other principles in which the implications of legislative and judicial history figure along with appeals to community practices and understanding. There is no litmus paper for testing the soundness of such a case – it is a matter of judgment, and reasonable men may agree.[126] Kennedy says that standards or principles refer directly to the substantive values or purposes of the community.[127] They involve 'value judgments'. Legal principles have normative nature, and the normative nature of legal principles are nowadays universally recognized. Legal doctrine plays the role as a source and describes legal principles through

123 Ibid., para VII, p. 20.

124 Hesselink (2011), supra note 1171, pp. 15-16, referring to J. Coleman, 'The Practice of principle; In defence of a pragmatist approach to legal theory', (Oxford: OUP, 2001); H.L.A. Hart, 'The Concept of Law,' 2nd ed., (Oxford:Clarendon Press, 1994), 'Postscript'.

125 Dworkin (1967), supra note 1274, p. 34.

126 Ibid., p. 37.

127 Kennedy (1976), supra note 1326, p. 1752.

the works of legal doctrinal writers.[128] Standards or principles or policies are norms other than formally realized rules. Substantive objectives of the legal order, such as good faith, due care, fairness, unconscienability, unjust enrichment and reasonableness, are what principles refer. Kennedy says 'the application of a principle requires the judge both to discover the facts of a particular situation and to assess them in terms of the purposes or social values embodied in the principle'.[129]

Dworkin says that Hart's thesis that most of legal rules are valid because of being created or enacted by some competent institution, a legislature or judges, will not work for the principles cited in *Riggs* and *Henningsen*. The origin of these legal principles is not found in existing legislative products or court's decisions, but in a sense of appropriateness developed in the profession and the public over time. Their continued power depends on this sense of appropriateness being sustained. It is true that a principle of law was cited from an existing precedent or from a statute, but that does not happen in all particular cases. If we could not find such institutional support, we would probably fail to make out our case, and the more support we found, the more weight we could claim for the principle.[130] Therefore Hart's test of pedigree may work for certain part of law only, but does not work for the whole integrity of law.

In hard cases where the existing materials do not yield a distinct answer, principles play an important role in finding the right answer to any question of law. A principle fitting with the relevant legal materials and with the prevailing political morality should be found to answer the question of law in determining the case at hand.[131] Principles play an important role in hard cases like *Riggs* and *Henningsen*, in which principles work energetically to carry most weight. In hard cases, principles play an essential part in arguments supporting judgments about particular rights

128 Alpa (1994), supra note 1362, para VII, p. 21.

129 Kennedy (1976), supra note 1367, p. 1688, referring to A. Hart & A. Sacks, 'The Legal Process', 113 (10th. Ed. 1958), pp. 126-29; Friedman, 'Law, Rules and the Interpretation of Written Document', in 59 NW.U.L.Rev. (1965), pp. 753-54; Dawson, 'Unconscionable Coercion: The German Version', in 89 Harv.L.Rev. 1041 (1976), pp. 1042-1047. The extent to which particular words or categories are regarded as sufficiently "factual" to serve as the basis of formally realizable rules changes through time, is subject to dispute at any particular time, and is a matter of degree. For example, the idea of competition may appear to one writer to be capable of generating precise and predictable answers to particular questions of antitrust law, while another may regard it as no more than a principle, unadministrable except though a further body of per se rules.

130 Dworkin (1967), supra note 1365, p. 41.

131 Hesselink (2011), supra note 1364, pp. 15-16, referring to R. Dworkin (1986), 'Law's Empire'; Dworkin (1978a), supra note 1165.

and obligations. After a judgment is made based on a principle in a hard case, the judgment stands for a particular legal rule (precedent), that is a new legal rule that has never existed before. The court cites principles as its justification for adopting and applying a new rule.[132] In Dworkin's view, principles constitute a ground and support the creation of new rules.[133] Since legal principles are cited by the court in its justification for the adoption and application of new legal rules, the important role of principles have to be considered in the determination of certain particular cases. Principles may be treated the same way as we treat legal rules, and some principles are binding as law, and therefore judges must take them into account in determining legal obligation in judicial decision making. Although a denial to the legal binding character of principles is possible, but in hard cases like *Riggs* and *Henningsen* it is undeniable that the judges reach beyond the rules that they are bound to apply (reach, that is, beyond the 'law') for extra-legal principles they are free to follow if they wish.

Hart argues that the master rule of recognition might stipulate that some custom is considered as law even before the courts recognized it. Dworkin holds that if the master rule says merely that whatever other rules accepted by the community as legally binding are legally binding, then the acceptance is enough to make such custom legally binding.[134] This shows that the validity of such custom as law is that acceptance, and therefore institutional support is not a must for such custom in order to count as law. This also shows that a test by the master rule is not the mere source of validity. The master rule becomes (for these cases) a non-rule of recognition. There is no formulated test of pedigree that relates principles to acts of legislation. Hart's concept of customary law, which is an exception to the positivists' tenet that legal rules are valid after being tested as so by the master rule of recognition, does not hold without abandoning the positivist tenet altogether. So, Hart's version of positivism cannot be adapted through the modification of his rule of recognition to embrace principles. If there is no rule of recognition that can provide a test for identifying principles, why not say that principles are ultimate, and *form* the rule of recognition of our law? Dworkin concludes that treating principles as law means rejecting the positivists' first tenet, that the law of a community is distinguished from other social standards by some test in the form of a master rule. The doctrine of judicial discretion being the positivists' second tenet is trivial or lacking serious efforts in legal elaboration. The third tenet that a legal obligation exits when (and only when) it is imposed by an established rule does not work in hard cases, such as *Riggs* and *Henningsen*. If the tenet is followed, then there is no legal obligation until the court creates a new rule

132 Dworkin (1967), supra note 1370, p. 29.

133 Ibid., pp. 29-30.

134 Ibid., pp. 42-43, 44-45.

(precedent) for the future. The judge may apply that new rule to the parties in the case, but this is *ex post facto* legislation, not the enforcement of an existing obligation.

Dworkin says, "When principles intersect .... one who must resolve the conflict has to take into account the relative weight of each".[135] The policy of protecting automoblie consumers must be weighed in the balancing with the principle of freedom of contract. The weighing cannot be, of course, an exact measurement, and judging that a particular principle or policy is more important than another will often be controversial. Nevertheless, it is an integral part of the concept of a principle that it has this dimension, that it makes sense to ask how important or how weighty it is. Legal rules do not have this dimension.[136] A principle may apply with equal force to cases with very different facts. The application of a principle to non-analogous cases with very different facts shows that principles do not explain the nature of analogical reasoning. Facts of cases are rarely justified solely based on principles, instead a range of considerations are applicable and justify the result.[137] Specific principles replace general principles, and the application of specific principles excludes that of general principles.[138]

***

Dworkin in his theory of jurisprudence closely relates legal principles to his right answer thesis and his idea of law integrity. Law integrity in his complete theory of jurisprudence means the legal system as a seamless web providing answers to all questions of law. Hercules, who is an imaginary judge of superhuman intellectual power and patience and who accepts law as integrity, could derive the rights (and obligations) that individuals have.[139] Dworkin's theory shows clearly the link between principle and coherence. If the general principles of civil law can contribute to making European private law more coherent, and if this increased coherence does not come at too high a price, e.g., in terms of national sovereignty (an important 'if'), then surely their discovery by the European Court of Justice

135 Hage (1996), supra note 1327, p. 5, referring to Dworkin (1978a), supra note 1371, p. 27.

136 Dworkin (1967), supra note 1374, p. 27.

137 Lamond (2006), supra note 1297, p. 23.

138 Hage (1996), supra note 1375, p. 13.

139 Hesselink (2011), supra note 1371, p. 33, referring to Dworkin (1986), supra note 1371, p. 239; and for the latest statement, extending the idea of integrity well beyond the law into a more general theory of value, see R. Dworkin, 'Justice for Hedgehogs', (Cambridge, Massachusetts: Belknap Press, 2011).

must be welcome.[140] Dworkin says that judgment is better understood as the balancing of rules against principles of political morality; these principles do not dictate results, but 'incline a decision one way, though not conclusively'. A principle, according to Dworkin, is 'a standard that is to be observed, because it is a requirement of justice or fairness or some other dimension of morality'. And, he holds that a policy is that kind of standard that sets out a goal to be reached, generally an improvement in some economic, political, or social feature of the community (though some goals are negative, in that they stipulate that some present feature is to be protected from adverse change).[141] We cannot practically assess the moral or economic or political significance of standards in a real administration of justice independently of our assessment of the substantive structure within which they operate. Standards may even be accepted into the predominant conception of how a rule system works, treated as an area of 'inchoacy' or of 'emerging rules'.[142]

Principle justifies a change in a legal rule, and the change is found to be going to, necessarily, though not sufficiently, advance such policy or serve such principles, a judge is permitted to make that change. In *Riggs* the change (a new interpretation of the statute of wills) was justified by the principle that no man should profit from his own wrong; in *Henningsen* certain rules about automobile manufacturer's liability were altered on the basis of the principles and policies Dworkin quoted from the opinion of the court. In changing a legal rule, there must be some principles that count and others that do not, and there must be some principles that count for more than others. It could not depend on the judge's own preference amongst a sea of respectable extra-legal standards, and if it were the case, then no rule could be said to be binding, because a judge on his own preferences as such would freely justify a shift or radical re-interpretation of even the most firmly established rule. A judge could also change existing doctrine by considering some important standards that argue against departure from established doctrine, and these standards are also for the most part of principles and policies that require the courts to pay a qualified deference to the acts of the legislature. They also include the doctrine of precedent, another set of principles and policies reflecting the equities and efficiencies of consistency. The doctrines of legislative supremacy and precedent incline toward the *status quo*, each within its sphere, but they do not command it. Judges are not free, however, to pick and choose amongst the principles and policies that make up these doctrines – if they were, again, no rule could be said to be binding.[143] Practically, principles generate insight through

140 Ibid.

141 Dworkin (1967), supra note 1376, pp. 22- 23.

142 Kennedy (1976), supra note 1369, pp. 1776-1777.

143 Dworkin (1967), supra note 1381, p. 38.

order and supply arguments for creative law application. This practical orientation as stated by the Supreme Court of Canada also constitutes a feature of principle *doctrines*, legal scholarship. The functions of principles are diverse in law application. Principles often increase the number of arguments to be employed to debate the legality of certain acts. Principles increasing the number of arguments strengthen principles' autonomy vis-a-vis legislative political institutions. This happens mostly via a principle-oriented interpretation of a relevant legal rule, be it of primary or secondary law.[144] Von Bogdandy has made a note on the employment of principles.[145] In the employment of principles, those who argue against principles are often held responsible to show that their arguments are not weaker than arguments supported by principles.

Principles generate reasons for conclusion of arguments and help to reach the conclusion; and this reason generation and concluding process constitute a model of reasoning with principles. Two steps are identified in reasoning with principles. First, we apply all relevant and accepted principles with the purpose of gathering all reasons which plead for and against possible conclusions. Then, a 'weighing' process to determine which one of the possible conclusions follows from the collected reasons.[146] In Kennedy's words,[147] standards or policies or principles might represent a substantive compromise between all and nothing. It might mean that principles are not at all adopted when applicable rules are existent; but when applicable rules cannot be identified (in certain particular cases),

144 Bogdandy (2010), supra note 1361, p. 100. Concerning the principle-oriented interpretation of primary law, see Cases C-402/05 and C-415/05 P, para 303; further Case C-50/00 P, Union de Pequenos Agricultores v. Council [2002] ECR 1-6677, para 44; Case C-354/04, Gestoras Pro Amnistia et al v. Council [2007] ECR I-1579, paras 51 et seq.; Case C-355/04, Segi at al v. Council [2007] ECR I-1657, paras 51 etc., concerning the principle-oriented interpretation of secondary law, see Case C-540/03, Parliament v. Council [2006] ECR I-5769, paras 70 et seq.; Case C-305/05, Ordre des barreaux francophones et germanophone [2007] ECR I-5305, para 28.

145 Ibid., pp. 100-101. For an instructive case, see Case C-361/01 P, Kik v. HABM [2003] ECR I-8283, where the ECJ rejects a principle: on this, see F.C. Mayer, 'Europaisches Sprachenverfassungsrecht' in [2005] 44 Der Staat 367, p. 394; this article at the same time demonstrates how legal principles can be generated by legal scholarship.

146 Hage (1996), supra note 1378, p. 13.

147 Kennedy (1976), supra note 1382, pp. 1705-1706, referring to McCloskey, 'Economic Due Process and the Supreme Court: An Exhumation and Reburial', in 1962 SUP. CT. REV. 34, 36-40. On vagueness in contracts as the outcome of compromise, see Macaulay, 'The Use and Non-Use of Contracts in the Manufacturing Industry', in 9 PRACTICAL LAWYER 14-17 (1963). On legislative standards, see Friedman, 'Legal Rules and the Process of Social Change', in 19 STAN. L. REV. (1967), pp. 835-836.

principles are (say totally) adopted in particular cases. Particular cases or substantive demands cause the adoption of principles. Principles could be taken into account in particular cases without overruling precedents. When a precedent as a legal rule was invalidated in any posterior case, such invalidation could be reinterpreted as findings unreasonableness. Experience showed that a principle might lead to the knowledge necessary to formulate a more precise rule. So, principles fit a political strategy for conflict resolution rather than for reasons intrinsic to the social situation in which they will be applied, or to the substantive content of the law in question. Principles or standards thus function as instruments of change.

Fundamental ideas of a legal system are expressed in principles and goals. The interaction of principles and goals for a number of certain cases produces the outcomes which are summarized by legal rules. Principles, goals and rules are used to produce [or generate] legal arguments, but their logical roles are different. These different logical roles are taken into account in the model of legal reasoning. This consideration of the different logical roles constitutes a feature of the legal reasoning.[148] If principles may underlie all kinds of reason such as reason for classification, reason to believe, reasons in the sense of causes and reason for acting, then principles may underlie reasons for arguments in legal reasoning. Principle and goal should be weighed. A goal keeps an eye on only one dimension of a case. In certain cases, the goal to protect parties in good faith intersects with the protection of the right of the owner of stolen things. Someone who in good faith bought a thing, did not know the thing is a stolen thing, and did pay a reasonable price for the thing is protected by the goal to protect parties in good faith. But in such a case, the goal to protect parties in good faith does not protect the right of the owner of that stolen thing. Since goals and principles both have the same narrowness in terms of scope, so in legal reasoning the goal to protect parties in good faith must be weighed against reasons based on the nemo plus-principle.[149] Principles only have their attentions for the aspect of cases that correspond to the conditions being parts of the principles and leave things else out of consideration. Such things out of consideration count for rules, and it is rules which aim to take into account all legally relevant aspects of cases on such things. Reasons based on principles must be weighed, because the views of principles are narrow. A typical legal principle, such as the nemo plus-principle, does not even attempt to avoid narrow-mindedness.[150] Reasons based on principles are of two sets, one set pleads for a certain conclusion, and the other set pleads against that conclusion. Weighing the two sets of argument may

148 Hage (1996), supra note 1386, pp. 3-4.

149 Ibid., p. 8, 9, 10.

150 Ibid., p. 7.

be dealt with in a rational manner if one set can be argued to overweigh the other. There will be no rational solution if such rational weighing is not possible.[151] Alexy characterizes principle as being the optimization of commands which are subject to balancing.[152]

In Hage's illustration, a reason generated by a principle is outweighed by one or more reasons that plead in a different direction.[153] For example, A had stolen an antique clock from B, and then C not knowing that the clock had been stolen by A from B bought and paid the clock at a reasonable price. The fact that B was not the owner of the clock as a reason against C becoming the new owner, may be outweighed by the reason that C acted in good faith and paid a reasonable price for the clock. In other words, the narrow view of a principle is counteracted by one (or more) possible colliding principle (and goal) underlying a reason that pleads in a different direction. By basing the final conclusion on the interaction of all available reasons, the narrow view of principle does not become a major disadvantage. Hage makes a distinction between stating and denoting in connection with the formulation of principles.[154] The distinction can be clarified by another distinction between directions of it popularized by Searle [1983]. Searle's distinction between directions of fit was made by borrowing an example of Anscombe [1957]. For example, Jane made a shopping list to guide what items she would buy at the super market. But after she finished putting all items in the list into a trolley, the supermarket's guard checked all items in the trolley and made his list. Jane's list and the guard's list are the same in terms of the items in the trolley. But the two lists have different functions and have two different directions of fit. Jane's list has a world to word direction, but the guard's list has a word to world direction. And those two directions are directions of fit. Jane's list having the world to word direction of fit is directive, but the guard's list having the word to world direction of fit is descriptive.

Another distinction may also be made, between description and principle. Descriptive sentences have the word to world direction of fit, and consequently descriptive sentences are true or false. But principles have the world to word direction of fit, therefore they do not describe but rather express a connection between types of fact. Although distinct directions of fit do not dictate different logics for reasoning with description and for reasoning with principles, rules or goals; the distinction between those

151 Ibid., p. 13.

152 Bogdandy (2010), supra note 1385, p. 104. For more detail, see R. Alexy, 'Theorie der Grundrechte', (Suhrkamp, 2006), 75 et seq.

153 Hage (1996), supra note 1391, p. 7.

154 Ibid., pp. 6-7, referring to J. Searle, 'Intentionality: An Essay in the philosophy of mind', (Cambridge University Press, 1983); G.E.M. Anscombe, 'Intentions', (Oxford: Blackwell, 1957).

directions of fit provides at least the beginning of explanation of differences in logical behavior between these two categories. The distinction plays an important role in the model of legal reasoning. A standard 'a soldier who flees at the approach of the enemy is coward' is directive, not descriptive of the fact of the world. If that standard is absent, there is no coward soldier, even though many soldiers fled away at the approach of the enemy. The adoption of that standard makes a certain fact (the fact that a soldier fled away at the approach of the enemy) count another fact (the fact that the soldier is coward). So, cowardice will not appear if the standard is absent. This proves that the world to word fit focuses on a different case which is a case under *constitutive* principles.[155] There is the layer of facts which is built on top of the layer of purely physical facts. The psychical world would be the same if standards existed or did not exist. A difference will be existent if standards are adopted. Any difference as appearing due to the adoption of standards lies in the layer of facts which lies on top of the psychical layer. In this connection, Hare writes about 'supervenience' (Hare 1952, p. 80f).[156] Some facts supervene on other facts; and logically, the supervening facts are present if the supervened facts are present. The standard or principle 'any soldier who flees away at the approach of the enemy is coward' makes any fact (that a soldier fled away) a reason of another fact (that the fleeing soldier is coward). So, a principle makes a particular fact a reason of a kind of constitution.

***

General principles could participate in bringing coherence and convergence in the multi-level private law system in Europe.[157] This participation corresponds with the emerging European legal scholarship. Transnational legal scholarship informs general principles to law-makers of state, EU and global levels; and the general principles could play an important role in vertical dialogues between those law-makers. European private law principles and scholarship can find each other in a common European legal space.[158] Sales law in CISG (United Nations Convention on contracts for the international sales of goods 1980), in the consumer sales

155 Ibid., p. 6.

156 Ibid., pp. 6-7, referring to R.M. Hare, 'The Language of Morals', (Oxford University Press: Oxford, 1952), p. 80f.

157 Hesselink (2011), supra note 1380, p. 38, referring to J. Habermas, 'Between Facts and Norms: Contribution to a Discourse Theory of Law and Democracy', (Cambridge: Polity Press, 1996), p. 460.

158 Ibid., compare, with regard to the general principles of EU law, K. Lenaerts & J.A. Gutierrez-Fons, 'The Constitutional Allocation of Powers and General Principles of EU Law', in 47 CMLR (2010), pp. 1629-1669, 1635.

directive (Directive 1999/44/EC on consumer sales and guarantees) and in a number of EU Member States (but not all), is based, at least in part, on similar principles. Rigidity is the character of legislative device. Due to such legislative rigidity, law reform is hampered. Under these circumstances, underlying principles may be helpful in assuring the development of sales and, if possible, its convergence. A multi-level dialogue on a common European private law space could be helpful in removing unnecessary contractions. Ideally, it could even lead to a reflective equilibrium. These all are indicative that general principles of civil law could make an important contribution to coherence and convergence of private law making on national, Europen and global levels.[159]

The general principles of EU law, including equality, proportionality and effectiveness, have their 'constitutional' status in the EU. The general principles are unwritten EU primary law, being on the same level as the founding Treaties. In *Audiolux* the CJEU stated: "The general principles of Community law have constitutional status while the principle proposed by *Audiolux* is characterized by a degree of detail requiring legislation to be drafted and enacted at Community level by a measure of secondary Community law. Therefore, the principle proposed by *Audiolux* cannot be regarded as an independent general principle of Community law".[160] Positivists argue the CJEU decides cases based on Article 19 TUE, the first paragraph of which provides: "The Court of Justice of the European Union ....shall ensure that in the interpretation and application of the Treaties the law is observed". Article 19 TEU (or its predecessor – Article 220 EC) has often been cited to justify the Court in developing general principles of EU law. Thus, the legitimacy of principles is directly derived from the legitimacy of the founding Treaty. Against the positivists, there is an argument that the Court justifies itself by resorting to general principles, and thus provides legitimacy to the principles the Court deems necessary in doing its task. In doing its task, the Court interprets, fills gaps and occasionally corrects rules, following simply from the nature of adjudication.[161] With respect to civil, criminal and administrative law, especially in civil law - for example under the Brussel I regulation on 'civil and commercial matters' - the CJEU has developed a rich case law or substantive law on the (autonomous) interpretation of the 'civil matter' concept, such as shown in Case C-195/02, *Commission of the European Communities v. Kingdom of Spain*, ECR [2004], 1-0785, 40: legal consequences of a civil, criminal and administrative nature.[162]

---

159 Ibid., pp. 33-34.

160 Ibid., p. 23, referring to the CJEU in Audiolux.

161 Ibid., p. 32.

162 Ibid., p. 18.

Legal principles are of general and specific natures. This distinction is similar to the familiar distinction between general and specific private law, and between general and specific contract law. Most of the principles the CJEU have referred so far seem to be general, such as the binding force of contract (*Societe thermale*), discharge by performance (*Hamilton*), good faith and unjustified enrichment (*Messner*). They are principles of general contract law or (even broader) of the general law of obligations. In *Messner* (2009), the CJEU referred to 'the principles of civil law', not the *general* principles of civil law. The ruling in *Messner* (2009), referring to the ruling in the *Amtsgericht* Lahr in Germany, concerned the interpretation of the distance selling directive (Directive 97/7/EC of the European Parliament and of the Council of 20 May 1997) on the protection of consumers in respect of distance contracts (OJ 1997 L 144, p. 19). In *Messner*, principles do the function of gap-filling.[163] In EU law, general principles have three functions: interpretation (*secundum legem*), gap filling (*praeter legem*) and correction (*contra legem*).[164]

The general principles of EU law, Hesselink has noted, have the status of primary law in the EU. Supremacy and, as the case may be, direct effect of EU law should not depend on whether the relevant EU law is written or unwritten.[165] Then, the question is whether or not the general principles of civil law have the primary law status like the general principles of EU law, so whether or not the general principles of civil law have direct effect like the general principles of EU law. But, what seems more relevant to the issue of direct effect is the requirement that legal provisions be sufficiently clear, precise and unconditional. Principles may often be too general to pass this test. Nevertheless, direct effects can only be brought by principles of primary EU law, as seemed to have been suggested in the recent *NCC Construction Danmark* case. Direct horizontal effect on market freedom are accepted by the CJEU in a number of cases, notably Case C-438/05, *International Transport Workers' Federation and Finnish Seamen's Union v. Viking Line AB and OU Viking Line Eesti*, ECR [2007], and Case C-341/05 *Laval un Partneri Ltd v. Svenska Byggnadsarbetareforbundet and Others* [2007] ECR 1-11767. Hartkamp points out an important problem with the

163 Ibid., p. 9, 10, 6, 19.

164 Ibid., p. 19, referring to T. Tridimas, 'The General Principles of EU Law', 2nd ed. (Oxford : OUP, 2006), p. 27ff.; A. Metzger, "Extra legem, intra ius: Allgemeine Rechtsgrundsatze im Europaischen Privatrecht', (Tubingen: Mohr Siebeck, 2009); A.S. Hartkamp, 'The General Principles of EU Law and Private Law', in 75 RabelzZ (2011), p. 256; A-G Trstenjak, 'Opinion in Audilux', delivered on 30 June 2009, Case C-101/08, p. 68.

165 Ibid., p. 20, 21, 22. See A.S. Hartkamp, 'The Effect of the EC Treaty in Private Law: On Direct and Indirect Horizontal Effect of Primary Community Law', in 18 ERPL (2010), p. 548.

direct horizontal effect on market freedom.[166] The problem is that freedom of contract and party autonomy are defeated by the market freedom, whereas private law disputes have traditionally been a matter of balancing the interests of private parties. In this context, the general principles of civil law may provide a solution. They would bring the private law interests, in a way that does not necessarily have to trouble those who fear the constitutionalization of freedom of contract because private autonomy and its limits would enter the equation. In this way all relevant private interests as principles, readily balanced or still to be balanced, could come directly into play. For example, the CJEU has already referred to both the principle of binding force of contract and its traditional counter principle of good faith. The result would be, of course, that the general principles of civil law (or some of them) would gain the constitutional status of primary law. Because accepting the defeat of freedom of contract and party autonomy by the market freedom is a problem if related to the fact of those traditional private law disputes, Hartkamp proposes the exception system be extended to cover direct horizontal effects.

A distinction is usually made as to their origins between principles having sources from the common traditions of the Member States, on the one hand, and principles having sources from that objectives of the EU, on the other. The former could be referred to as bottom-up (inductive) and the latter as top-down (deductive) principles. Bottom-up principles derived inductively from the laws of all Member States do not become legitimate automatically though the fact that top-down principles, derived deductively from the acquis and its objectives, cannot do the job the CJEU wishes the general principles of civil law to do. Merely commonness in the legal systems of all Member States does not constitute a sufficient reason that the bottom up principles are legitimate. A common principle in all Member States may be unjust or may become unjust due to historical changes in law, including private law. But, the absence of the recognition of the common principles in all (the majority of) Member States should not always bar that recognition, since that absence itself might be unjust.[167]

From the above mentioned in this sub-chapter, a conclusion can be drawn that principles of law, general or specific – high level or mid-level, are *normative, prescriptive* (In *Riggs* the change [a new interpretation of the statute of wills] was justified by the principle that no man should profit from his own wrong; in *Henningsen* certain rules about automobile manufacturer's liability were altered on the basis of the principles and

166 Ibid., p. 21, referring to Hartkamp (2010), id.; Hartkamp (2011), supra note 1404.

167 Ibid., pp. 39-40, 41-42.

policies[168]), and *generative,* in the sense that principles of law generate insight and arguments for creative law application, and often increase the number of arguments to be employed to debate the legality of certain acts;[169] principles of law generate reasons for conclusion of arguments and help to reach the conclusion.[170]

III.3. RIGHTS

***

Rights dominate modern understanding of what actions are permissible and which institutions are just. Rights structure the form of government, the content of laws, and the shape of morality as it is currently perceived. To accept a set of rights is to approve a distribution of freedom and authority, and so to endorse a certain view of what may, must, and must not be done.[171] Dworkin and Michael Perry suggest that rights claim all rely on the notion of sacredness. [Dworkin's view is secular, while] Perry's is theological. Perry contends that the sacredness of persons can be equated with the concept of inherent dignity.[172] Perry argues that something is held sacred in virtue of a clear connection to some other holy thing. Sacredness can apply to objects and to people, and it provides the foundation for inviolability.[173] Perry's project is to examine the various secular understanding of the conviction that every human being is sacred – sacred in the strong/objective sense, sacred because of how the world really is, and not because of what we attach value to in the world.[174] For Dworkin, 'something is sacred or inviolable when its deliberate destruction would dishonor what ought to be honored'.[175] Dworkin argues that human life is valuable because of the creative contributions to both nature and humanity. The key component of this argument is the latter notion, the idea that each human being is

168 Dworkin (1967), supra note 1383, p. 38.

169 Bogdandy (2010), supra note 1392, p. 100 [accompanying text omitted].

170 Hage (1996), supra note 1393, p. 13.

171 Leif Wenar, 'Rights', in Stanford Encyclopedia of Philosophy, first published Monday, December 19, 2005; substantive revision Saturday, July 2, 2011, p. 1.

172 Kohen (2006), supra note 1162, p. 246.

173 Ibid., p. 249.

174 Ibid., p. 243, referring to Michael Perry, 'The Idea of Human Rights: Four Inquiries', (Oxford: Oxford University Press, 1998), p. 29.

175 Ibid., p. 238, referring to R. Dworkin, 'Life's Dominion: An Argument about Abortion, Euthanasia, and Individual Freedom', (New York: Vintage Book, 1994), p. 74.

created by her culture and community, as well as her own thoughts. On this point, Dworkin's ideas are very well articulated: The life of a single human organism commands respect and protection, then, no matter in what form or shape, because of the complex creative investment it represents and because of our wonder at the .....processes of nation and community and language through which a human being will come to absorb and continue hundreds of generations of culture and forms of life and value, and, finally, when mental life has begun and flourishes, at the process of internal personal creation and judgment by which a person will make and remake himself, a mysterious, inescapable process in which we each participate, and which is therefore the most poweful and inevitable source of emphaty and communion we have with every other creature who faces the same frightening challenge.[176] Lawrence Becker's 'root idea of a right' is stated: The existence of a right is the existence of a state of affairs in which one person (the right-holder) has a claim on an act or forbearance from another person (the duty-bearer) in the sense that, should the claim be exercised or in force, and the act or forbearance not be done, it would be justifiable, other things being equal, to use coercive measures to extract either the performance required or compensation in lieu of that performance.[177]

[T]he 'rights' conception [of the rule of law] assumes that citizens have moral rights and duties with respect to one another, and political rights against the state as a whole. It insists that these moral and political rights be recognized in positive law, so that they may be enforced upon the demand of individual citizens through courts or other judicial institutions of the familiar type, so far as this is practicable. Rule of law requires, as part of the ideal of law, that the rules in the rule book capture and enforce moral rights.[178] As history makes clear, the most dangerous agents of force, by far, are governments. Ayn Rand observes "A government holds a legal monopoly on the use of physical force". The nature of governmental action is: coercive action, with the threat of physical injury-the threat of property expropriation, imprisonment, or death.[179] Insofar as any force is

---

176 Ibid., p. 245, referring to Ronald Dworkin (1994), Ibid., p. 84.

177 Nance (1985), supra note 1183, n.7, referring to L. BECKER, 'PROPERTY RIGHTS: PHILOSOPHIC FOUNDATIONS', 8 (1977). See also Becker, 'Three Types of Rights', in 13 GA. L. REV. (1979), p. 1197.

178 David Dyzenhaus, 'The Rule of Law as the Rule of Liberal Principle', in Arthur Ripstein ed.'Ronald Dworkin', (New York: Cambridge University Press,2007), pp. 56-81 (p. 56), referring to Ronald M. Dworkin, "Political Judges and the Rule of Law", in A Matter of Principle, (Cambridge, MA: Harvard University Press, 1985), pp. 11-12 (his emphasis).

179 Craig Biddle, 'Ayn Rand's Theory of Rights: The Moral Foundation of a Free Society', in TOS Vol. 6, No.3, Fall 2011, referring to Ayn Rand, 'America's Persecuted Minority: Big Business, in Capitalism: The Unknown Ideal', (New York: Signet, 1967), p. 46.

used against human beings, they cannot live fully as human beings with a human life guided by the judgment of his mind.[180] There are theories of God-given rights, natural rights, and government-granted rights.

***

According to God-given rights theory, an all powerful, infallible, all-good being makes moral law and gives man rights; thus rights exist prior to and apart from any man-made law and cannot be granted or repealed by government.[181] Man is in duty bound to strive to fulfill the designs of his Creator, and humans must exercise their faculties and conduct their lives according to the intention of their Lord and Master. Because humans are under these obligations they are consequently invested with rights, God-given and primordial, antecedent to the State and independent of it. Such are humans' natural rights, granted to them by nature herself, sacred as is their origin, and inviolable. Beside these humans may have other rights given to them by Church or State, or acquired by his own industry and exertion. All these rights, whatever be their source, are the object of the virtue of justice. Justice requires that all persons should be left in the free enjoyment of all their rights.[182] The rights which belong to every human being inasmuch as he is a person are absolute and inalienable. The right to life and limb, the essential freedom which is necessary that a man may attain the end for which he is destined by God, the right to marry and remain single, such rights as these may not be infringed by any human authority whatever. A man himself even has no right to dispose of his own life and limbs; God alone is the Lord of life and death. But a man has the duty and the right to use and develop his faculties of soul and body, and if he chooses he may dispose of his right to use these faculties and whatever advantage they can procure him in favor of another. No person then can become the property of another human being, slavery in that sense is repugnant to the dignity of human nature. But a man may by various titles have the right to the labor of another.[183]

Rights are defined in terms of metaphysical consideration by Grotious and Pufendorf, the naturalists, who define a right as a moral quality or faculty (*qualitas or facultas moralis*). It is established by an act of will by one party that is accepted by the other. The act of will is made

180 Ibid., referring to Rand (1967), Ibid.

181 Ibid.

182 Catholic Encyclopedia: Justice, APA citation, T. Slater, (1910), New York: Robert Appleton Company, Retrieved January 19, 2013 from New Advent: http:/// www.newadvent.org/cathen/08571c,htm ["Catholic Encyclopedia – Justice"].

183 Ibid.

known through a promise, a declaration of will, in which the declarer alienates a part of his liberty, his right to decide over his own actions, to the other party, the promisee. Olivecrona calls this power 'mysterious' presumably because it is not directly observable. A legal right is a mystical power to be enforced by the state.[184] Naturalist John Locke puts it, there is *a law of nature*, and this law *teaches all mankind, who will but consult it, that being all equal and independent, no one ought to harm another in his life, health, liberty, or possessions.*[185] Thomas Jefferson wrote "*Man is endowed by nature with rights", and these rights are a matter of "moral law"; thus they are "inherent", "inalienable", and "unchangeable"*. A free people claim their rights as derived from the laws of nature, and not as the gift of their chief magistrate.[186] Alexander Hamilton wrote: *Good and wise men, in all ages ... have supposed that the deity, from the relations we stand in to himself and to each other, has constituted an eternal and immutable law, which is indispensably obligatory upon all mankind, prior to any human institution whatever. This is what is called the law of nature.... Upon this law depend the natural rights of mankind.*[187] In George Mason's view: *The law of nature are the laws of God, Whose authority can be superseded by no power on earth.*[188] And John Adams held: *Man possesses rights 'antecedent to all earthly government – Rights, that cannot be repealed or restrained by human laws – Rights, derived from the great Legislator of the universe.*[189] In Ishay's words, the most

184 Golding (2005), supra note 1101, pp. 17-18.

185 Biddle (2011), supra note 1421.

186 Ibid., referring to Thomas Jefferson to William Johnson, June 12, 1823, in Writings of Thomas Jefferson, edited by Andrew A. Lipscomb and Albert Ellery, Washingon DC: Thomas Jefferson Memorial Association, 1905, http://press-pubs.uchicago.edu/founders/documents/v_1_ch_15s67.html; Thomas Jefferson, Opinion on French Treaties, 1793, TeachingAmericanHistory.org, http:// teachingamericanhistory.org/library/index.asp?document=623; First Draft of the Declaration of Independence, Papers of Thomas Jefferson, Princeton University, http:// teachingamericanhistory. Org/ library/idex.asp?document623. First Draft of the Declaration of Independence, Paper of Thomas Jefferson, Princeton University, http://www. princeton edu/-tjpapers/ declaration/declaration.html; letter to Major John Cartwright, June 5, 1824, Letters of Thomas Jefferson, University of Virginia Library, http://etext.virgina.edu/etcbin/toccer-new_2?id=JefLett.sgm&images/modeng&data=texts/english/modeng/parsed&tag=public&part=276&division=div1; Thomas Jefferson, 'A Summary View of the Rights of British America,' 1774, in Writings of Thomas Jefferson.

187 Ibid., referring to The Works of Alexander Hamilton: Miscellanies, 1774-1789, Vol. 2, edited by John C. Hamilton, (New York: John F. Trow, 1854), p. 43.

188 Ibid. As quoted in Scott Douglas Gerber, To Secure These Rights: The Declaration of Independence and Constitutional Interpretation, (New York: NYU Press, 1996), p. 106.

189 Ibid., referring to John Adams, Papers of John Adams, vol. 1, (Cambridge,

sense assumes that all men possess equally the sacred rights of 'liberty, property, security, and resistence to opression' [because of their (unstated) connection to 'the Supreme Being in the presence and under the auspices of [whom]' the rights were affirmed by the French National Assembly.[190] A similarly nondescript 'Creator' appears in the American Declarations, though, are the rights themselves, not their ultimate guarantor, because their infringement provided a rallying cry for the revolutions and their protection was at the heart of the radical democratic experiment that the revolutionaries proposed.

All things inferior to human beings fulfill the end of their being by ministering to human wants and necessities. Whatever pertains to the animal, vegetable, or inorganic world may be brought under the ownership and made the property of human beings. The right thus to acquire property which is useful and necessary for an orderly human life, is one of human being's natural rights, and it cannot be taken away by the State. Such rights are antecedent to the State, and in their substance independent of it. The State was instituted to protect and defend such rights, and may indeed make reasonable laws regulating and defining the property rights of its subjects for the common good, but the State cannot take them away or abrogate them altogether. Rights are the appanage of intelligent beings as such, beings who can reflect on themselves, know their own wants, and who can will to supply them by permanently appropriating to themselves objects which are subordinate and which will satisfy those wants. Every human being, therefore, is the subject of rights, even before he has been brought into the world.[191] Not only individuals, but societies of men are the subjects of rights. For men cannot singly and by their own unaided exertions do everything that is necessary for the security and dignity of human existence. For this end man needs the co-operation of his fellows. He has then a natural right to associate himself with others for the attainment of some lawful end, and when such societies have been formed, they are moral persons which have their rights similar to those of natural persons. Such societies then may own property, and although the State may make laws which modify those rights for the common good, is it beyond its power altogether to abrogate them. Men have this power to form themselves into societies.[192]

The largest class of rights which justice requires that we should render to others are rights of ownership. Ownership is the moral faculty of using something subordinate to us for our advantage. A holders of ownership

MA: Harvard University Press, 1977), p. 112 .

190 Kohen (2006), supra note 1416, p. 250, referrring to M. Ishay, 'The Human Rights Reader: Major Political Writings, Essay, Speeches, and Documents from the Bible to the Present', (New York: Routledge, 1997), p. 138, 127.

191 Catholic Encyclopedia - Justice, supra note 1423.

192 Ibid.

rights has the right to exclude others from the enjoyment of what he owns. Were anyone else to make use of it against the reasonable wish of the owner, such use would offend against justice. The right of ownership may be absolute and qualified. Absolute ownership extends to the substance of the property and to all its uses. Qualified ownership may, in the language of divine, be direct or indirect. Direct ownership is of the substance of a thing without its uses, such as the landlord has over a house. Indirect ownership is the faculty of using, but not of disposing of, a thing. When anything definite and determinate is owned by anyone so that he can say – 'This is my property' – he is said by divines to have a right *in re*. If the thing has not yet come into existence though it will come, or it is not separate and determinate, so that he cannot say that it is actually his, but he nevertheless has a strict claim in justice that it should become his, he is said to have a right *ad rem*. Thus a farmer has a right *ad rem* to the harvest of the coming year from his land; when he has harvested his crop he will have a right *in re*.[193] Human nature, its wants and aims, are the source of the fundamental and natural rights of man. By his industry man may occupy and annex to his person material things which are of use to him and which belong to nobody else. Any increases in value of rights belong to the holder of such rights – 'Res fructificat domino'. Rights may be transferred from one to another or modified by a great variety of contracts.[194] Lord Cooke has remarked in *Daly* that some rights are inherent and fundamental to democratic civilized society.[195] Conventions, institutions, bills of rights and the like respond by recognizing rather than creating them. The Common law may not offer a prescriptive list of rights but this does not mean that it is not a rich source of fundamental rights and values, nor that its development has been somehow arrested once the Convention was incorporated into domestic law. As Lord Toulson put it in *Kennedy v The Charity Commission*,[196] it was not the purpose of the Human Rights Act 1998[197] that the common law should become an ossury.

Moral rights, legal rights and customary rights all define domains of rights within the realm of rights of conduct: rights concerning how agents should act. When our reasons within these three different domains conflict, we may have reasons of different kinds of act in different ways. Yet there

193 Ibid.

194 Ibid.

195 Lady Hale, UK Constitutionalism on the March?, a keynote address to the Constitutional and Administrative Law Bar Association on Conference 2014, July 12, 2014, https:// www supremecourt.uk/.../speech-140712.p..., p. 2. R (Daly) v. Secretary of State for the Home Department [2001] UKHL 16, [2001] 2 AC 532, p.[30].

196 Ibid., p. 2.[2014] UKSC 20, [2014] 2 WLR 808, p.[133].

197 Ibid., p. 2.

are also rights entirely beyond the realm of conduct. These are rights to believe, to feel and to want. The realm of rights to believe, to feel and to want are the realms of epistemic, of affective and of conative rights. The realms of epistemic, of affective and of conative rights and the realm of rights to conduct are the four realms of rights.[198]

***

Ayn Rand holds that individuals have a right to life, liberty, property, and the pursuit of happiness. Her conception is rooted in observation of fact. Her theory of rights derives from her more fundamental theory of morality – which derives from her observation of reality, of the nature of values, and of the requirements of life. Morality or ethics, observed Rand, is a code of values to guide man's choices and actions – the choices and actions that determine the purpose and the course of his life.[199] Looking at reality, Rand has noted that a 'value' is 'that which one acts to gain and/or keep'.[200] Values are objects of actions. All living things – and only living things – take actions. *All living things take self-generated, goal-directed actions.* Non-living things take no action and do not generate their actions. Only living organisms have needs, goals, or values; accordingly, only they have a means of acting toward such ends. According to Rand, the concept 'value' presupposes an answer to the question: of value to *whom* and for *what*? [201] It presupposes an entity capable of acting to achieve a goal in the face of an alternative. The objects a living thing acts to gain and keep are its values – values to it. The reason why living things need values is: to *live*. The answer to the question '*for what*' is: for *life*. She has observed that an organism's life is its ultimate value and thus its standard of value – the standard by which all of its other values and actions are to be evaluated. Man does need values in order to live. Moral values – values in the realm of human choice – are facts in relation to the requirements of man's life. Only life makes values possible, and only life makes values necessary. We have to be alive in order to pursue values, and we have to pursue values in order to stay alive. Rand says that metaphysically, life is the only phenomenon that is an end in itself; a value gained and kept by a constant process of action. Epistemologically, the concept of 'value' is genetically dependent upon and derived from the antecedent concept of life. It is only the concept of 'Life' that makes the concept of 'Value' possible.[202] Because human beings are

198 Wenar (2011), supra note 1411, p. 20.

199 Biddle (2011), supra note 1429, referring to Ayn Rand, "The Objectivist Ethics", in The Virtue of Selfishness, p. 13.

200 Ibid., referring to Rand, id., p. 16.

201 Ibid.

202 Ibid., referring to Rand, supra note 1440, p. 18.

individuals – each with his own body, his own mind, his own life – this standard applies to human beings as individuals. Man's life is the standard of moral value – and each individual's own life is his own ultimate value. Each individual is morally an end in himself – not a means to the ends of others.[203] The moral principle here is *egoism*. Egoism (properly understood) is not hedonism or subjectivism; it does not hold 'pleasure' or 'feelings' as the standard of value. Egoism is the recognition of the fact that each individual should act to promote his own life and is the proper beneficiary of his own moral action.[204] Rand sees that although experiencing pleasure and achieving happiness are crucial aspects of human life, they are not and cannot be the standard of moral value. Rand observed, "...happiness can properly be the purpose of ethics, but not the standard. The task of ethics is to define man's proper code of values and thus to give him the means of achieving happiness".

Human beings, Rand sees, survive by volitional means – by choosing to use their mind to identify and pursue the requirements of their lives. Human needs are physical and spiritual. Human beings need food, clothing, shelter, medicine, and other material goods in order to live and prosper. Human beings also need self-confidence, personal goals, romantic love, and other spiritual values in order to thrive. More fundamentally, human beings need knowledge of such needs and knowledge of how to acquire them.[205] According to Rand's observation, first and foremost what human beings must use is reason. Reason is the faculty that identifies and integrates the material provided by human senses,and is human means of understanding the world, human self and human needs. Reason is human means of acquiring knowledge of physical and spiritual needs. It is by means of reason that human beings learn what self-confidence is, why they need it, and how to gain it; the importance of long-range goals, which ones will serve our life and happiness, and which ones will not; the nature of love, and how to build and maintain a wonderful romantic relationship; and so on. On the basis of such observations, Rand identifies reason as our fundamental means of living, our basic life-serving value, and thus our basic moral value.[206] If we want to live and prosper, we must use reason: We must observe reality and think; we must integrate our observations into concepts, generalizations, and principles that correspond to reality; and we must act accordingly. Human beings must act rationally. The moral

---

203 Ibid., referring to Ayn Rand, 'Introducing Objectivism', in The Voice of Reason, (New York: Meridian, 1990), p. 4.

204 Ibid., referring to Leonard Peikoff, 'Objectivism: The Philosophy of Ayn Rand', (New York: Dutton, 1991), pp. 229-230.

205 Ibid.

206 Ibid., referring to Ayn Rand, 'For the New Intellectual', (New York: Signet,1963), p. 134.

principle is: If we are to live and prosper, we must always act on our rational judgment – our basic means of living. A human life is a life guided by the judgment of one's mind. The only thing that can stop a person from acting on his judgment is other people; and the only way they can stop him is by means of physical force.

Rand reasons that because man's life is the standard of moral value, because each person should act to sustain and further his own life, and because physical force used against a person stops him from acting on his basic means of living, we need a moral principle to protect ourselves from people and governments that attempt to use force against us. That principle involves the concept of rights. 'Rights' are a moral concept – the concept that provides a logical transition from the principles guiding an individual's action to the principle guiding his relationship with others – the concept that preserves and protects individual morality in a social context – the link between the moral code of a man and the legal code of a society, between ethics and politics. Individual rights are the means of subordinating society to moral law.[207] The moral law that Rand speaks of here is the principle of egoism – the observation-based moral truth that each individual should act to promote his own life and is the proper beneficiary of his own actions.[208] Individual rights are the means of subordinating society to the truth of egoism. There is only one fundamental right (all others are its consequences or corollaries): a man's right to his own life. The right to life means the right to engage in self-sustaining and self-generated action – which means: the freedom to take all the actions required by the nature of a rational being for the support, the furtherance, the fulfillment and the enjoyment of his own life. Such is the meaning of the right to life, liberty and the pursuit of happiness.

***

Blackstone identified three primary rights: the right of personal security, personal liberty and private property, with auxiliary rights including importantly access to justice. Dicey argued that rights stemmed from remedies,[209] which certainly puts access to the courts at the forefront of rights protection.[210] Linguistic usage makes a distinction between a right

207 Ibid., referring to Ayn Rand, "Man's Rights", in The Virtue of Selfishness, p. 108.

208 Ibid., referring to Rand, Ibid., p. 110.

209 Lady Hale (2014), supra note 1437, p. 2. See Dicey, 'An Introduction to the Study of the Law and the Constitution', (Macmillan, 1965).

210 Ibid. 'Of the Absolute Rights of Individuals', Blackstone's Commentaries

concerning one's own behavior and a right to somebody else's behavior. In colloquial language we make still another distinction. We say not only that one has a right to a certain behavior; we say also that one has a right to a certain thing. Property is the typical example of a right to a certain thing. That I own a certain thing means that I have a right to this thing. Hence a distinction is made between *jus in rem*, that is a right to a thing, and *jus in personam*, that is a right to demand that somebody else *shall* behave in a certain way, the right to somebody else's behavior, for instance, the creditor has a right to demand that the debtor shall pay a certain sum of money.[211] Deontological and consequentialist approaches are two leading philosophical approaches to explaining which fundamental rights of conduct there are, and why these rights should be respected. Another approach to the justification of rights might be called 'contractual'.[212] Under the deontological approach, all natural rights theories fix upon features that humans have by their nature, and which make respect for certain rights appropriate. Status theories belonging to the tradition of natural rights theories hold that human beings have attributes that make it fitting to ascribe certain rights to them, and make respect for these rights appropriate. This is a justification which starts with its base on the natural status of rightholder and then arrives immediately at the right. Under consequentialist approach, instrumental theories hold that respect for particular rights is a means for bringing about some optimal distribution of interests. This is a justification that begins with the desired consequence (like maximum utility) and works backward to see which rights-ascription will produce those consequences. Instrumental theories describe rights as instruments for achieving an optimal distribution of interest. According to the contractual approach, agents agree to the basic terms of their relations. Such agents having been properly situated and motivated under such agreement choose principles, for example, within Scanlon's contractualism that no one could reasonably reject, or in Rawls's original position. The fundamental principles within these contractual theories are defined by rights due to the close connection between rights and what the theories' agents have strong reason to want.[213] Rawls states that the role of the right of personal property is to allow a sufficient material basis for a sense of personal independence and self-respect, both of which are essential for the development and exercise of the two moral powers.[214] Scanlon states his opinion on basic rights.[215] Reasonable individuals have reason to insist on

on the Laws of England (1765-1769).

211 Kelsen (1961), supra note 1312, p. 75.

212 Wenar (2011), supra note 1438, p. 21.

213 Ibid., pp. 21-26.

214 Ibid., referring to John Rawls, 'A Theory of Justice', (Cambridge, MA: Harvard Univesity Press, 1993), p. 293.

215 Ibid., referring to T. Sanclon, 'Rights, Goals, and Fairness', (2003), in

basic rights, which give them important forms of protection and control over their own lives.

Ihering has based his theory of duty in the maintenance of one's rights, firstly, on the connection between rights and personality; and secondly, on the solidarity of law and rights. In the beginning, there is egoism. Human beings begin their lives as pure egoists, that is as individual persons. Individual persons live together, and this forms a legally organized society that generates an ethical personality. Being ethical is a certain life-renewal which takes possession of the legal system as a completed construction. Therefore, the world of law is always conceived with ethical support.[216] Each individual person has her own end or conscious purpose. In a society, each individual person's end is associated with the other society-members' individual ends to form social ends attributed to the law.[217] In his theory, Ihering distinguishes the objects resting on egoistic self-assertion (physical, economic, and legal objects) of the individual from those based on social self-assertion, which correspond to ethical objects of individual self-assertion. This distinction is adopted by Ihering as the plan of a doctrine of evolution, to show how "one object is connected with another, the higher to the lower; and not simply connected, but the one derived from the other as a consequence of itself by the force of necessity. From the egoistic self-assertion to the social-self assertion, individual egoism serves itself, transforms into social ends, and produces the material for the legal structure. This is the organization of social power controlled by the State for these objects, for security of the social conditions of life. The ethical spirit, which is characterized by the identity of individual ends with objects of the community, makes its entrance then into this legal structure for the purpose of setting up therein its dominion. That which is conformable to law, and what is ethical, therefore, are not contrary to what conforms to purpose.[218] The relation of rights to personality is admirably stated. In truth, our rights involve a parcel of our social worth, our honor. Whoever violates our rights, attacks our worth, our honor. If rights had not been accepted as isolated interests, as appears in the fourth volume of the 'Geist', Ihering would not have hit upon personality, and it would not have been possible for him to take the position that the assertion of a right is moral self-assertion.[219] Furthermore, Ihering's theory has developed to focus on the thought of the independence of legal rules on social purposes.

Waldron 1984, pp. 137-52, p. 4.

216 Merkel, supra note 953, p. 449.

217 Ibid.

218 Ibid., p. 445.

219 Ibid., p. 443-444.

For Joseph W. Bingham the concept of rights is a 'mental tool', like our concepts of rules and principles. While nothing in reality corresponds to them, these mental tools enable us to classify and manipulate the 'concrete' materials in the field of law. These mental tools, as ideas in the mind, have causal effects. Bingham no where denies the reality of these ideas or the reality of the idea of a right.[220] Many of the notable successful rights challenges in recent years have been based on the common law, including the rejection of the admission of evidence obtained by torture in *A (No.2)*[221] (in which Lord Bingham observed that the English common law had regarded torture and its fruits with abhorrence for over 500 years) and the requirements of open justice highlighted in *the Guardian News and Media* case.[222] The recognition of the importance of these rights is accompanied by a principle of statutory construction – the principle of legality – which requires Parliament expressly to legislate to limit fundamental rights – and thus openly to confront the political controversy entailed.[223]

Raz says that when someone claims her right, she gives someone else an exclusionary reason: a second-order reason not to act on some first-order reason.[224] Dworkin's trumping metaphor characterizes the normative force of rights in the stronger terms of conclusive reasons.[225] Each right trumps competing considerations in most circumstances, but there are certain circumstances in which another right with higher priority – or a pressing non-right consideration – determines what may or should be done. From this perspective, the conclusive reasons implied by rights assertions really are conclusive, but only within certain circumstances. Every right is absolute, within a specifically delimited space. The theoretical position at the end of this line of thought is called "specificationism".[226] The specificationist holds that each right is defined by an elaborate set of qualifications that specify when it does and when it does not apply: a set of qualifications that define the right's 'space'.[227] Windscheid's will-power

220 Golding (2005), supra note 1424, p. 22. See Joseph W. Bingham (1912), 'What is the Law?', in Michigan Law Review 11:1-109.

221 Lady Hale (2014), supra note 1449, p. 3. A v. Secretary of State for the Home Department (No. 2) [2005] UKHL 71, [2006] 2 AC 221.

222 Ibid. R (Guardian News and Media Ltd.) v. City of Westminster Magisters Court (2012) EWCA Civ 420, [2013] QB 618.

223 Ibid. R v. Secretary of State for the Home Department (ex parteSimms) [2000] a AC 115, 131.

224 Wenar (2011), supra note 1452, p. 16, citing Raz (1975), supra note 1329, pp. 35-48.

225 Ibid., referring to R. Dworkin, 'Rights as Trumps,' in Waldron 1984, pp. 153-167.

226 Ibid., p. 17, referring to R. Shafer-Landau, 'Specifying Absolute Rights', in Arizona Law Review, 37 (1995), pp. 209-224.

227 Ibid., p. 16.

(*Willensmacht*) theory, in essence, is typical of a whole group of writers. A right is a power exerted by the will of one person over that of another. But no longer is it the result of an individual's power over his own actions which he has transferred to another. In connection with what Ihering has contended, Ihering was concerned with the substantive content of the law and the reason for the creation of legal rights. Rights are bestowed in order to protect interests worthy of protection. A right is a legally protected interest, the legal security in enjoying certain advantages.[228] Government-granted rights theorists say that any laws created by governments dictate the rights and non-rights of the people who live under those governments. Stephen Holmes and Cass Sunstein elaborate: "[R]ights are powers granted by the political community: thus, an interest qualifies as a right when an effective legal system treats it as such by using collective resources to defend it".[229]

Olivecrona says that Hagerstrom has given a psychological and historical explanation of rights language. We cannot identify a right with a factual situation; a right (in private law) is believed to be created by operative facts but we cannot find such facts.[230] He in fact maintains, the idea of a right 'does not signify anything at all; it does not even refer to something existing, in imagination only, as the centaurs'.[231] It is a 'hollow word', Olivecrona does point out that the concept of a right nevertheless fulfills an important function in legal thinking, in that it *guides people's behavior*. He explains that it is essential that the idea of a pattern of conduct should always be awakened in the minds of those concerned and that they should be incited to follow it. This may easily be done by means of such notions as that of a right.[232] The term 'right' can fulfill this function by expressing an *imperative*, according to which the right-holder shall be allowed to act in such and such a manner and to maintain control over that to which he has a right, whereas others may not act in the same manner or interfere with the object of the right.[233] The term 'right' fulfills a *directive* function. Olivecrona's explanation is largely psychological. His book 'Law as Fact' contains an intensive attack on metaphysical and naturalist accounts

228 Golding (2005), supra note 1460, p. 18, referring to Olivecrona (1971), supra note 1148, p. 148.

229 Biddle (2011), supra note 1439, referring to Stephen Holmes & Cass Sunstein, 'The Costs of Rights: Why Liberty Depends on Taxes', (New York: W.W. Norton & Company, 2000), p. 17.

230 Golding (2005), supra note 1468, p. 21, referring to Karl Olivecrona, 'Legal Language and Reality' (1962), in Essays in Jurisprudence in Honor of Roscoe Pound. Ed R.A. Newman, 151-91, (Indianapolis, IN: Bobbs-Merrill), pp. 160-169.

231 Ibid., p. 19, referring to Olivecrona (1971), supra note 1468, p. 183.

232 Spaak (2009/2011), supra note 1145, p. 42-3, referring to Olivecrona (1939), supra note 1147, p. 95.

233 Ibid., p. 43, referring to Olivecrona (1939), Ibid., p. 96; Olivecrona (1962), supra note 1470, p. 182.

of such central legal terms as 'rights' and 'duty'.[234] His primary problem is to explain what a right and duty really are, and how rights and duties can be created by operative facts such as verbal declaration. He wants to use scientifically concrete concepts only, meaning 'concepts corresponding to reality'.[235] Finally, Olivecrona points out that the term 'right' sometimes fulfills a technical functions, in the sense that it ties two sets of rules in a way that facilitates our efforts to render the content of those rules.[236] He describes the function as follows: "the expression 'right of property' serves as a connecting link between two sets of rules: on the one hand the rules about the acquisition of property, on the other hand penal rules and rules about damages, etc., which refer to the situation where one person is the owner of an object and another person does something with regard to the object".

***

Paralleling what have been mentioned above, there are two main theories of the function of rights: the will theory and the interest theory. Will theorists maintain that a right makes the rightholder 'a small scale sovereign'.[237] More specifically, a will theorist asserts that the function of a right is to give its holder control over another's duty. In Wesley Hohfeld's terms, will theorists assert that every right includes a Hohfeldian power over a claim. In colloquial terms, will theorists believe that all rights confer control over others' duties to act in particular ways.[238] Influential will theorists include Kant, Savigny, Hart, Kelsen, Wellman and Steiner. Interest theorists maintain that the function of a right is to further the right-holder's interests. An owner has a right not because owners have choices, but because the ownership makes owners better off. The contest between will-based and interest-based theories of the function of rights has been waged for hundreds of years. Important interest theorists include Bentham, Ihering, Austin, Lyons, MacCormick, Raz and Kramer.[239] Other recent analyses of

234 Golding (2005), supra note 1471, p. 16, citing Karl Olivecrona (1971), supra note 1471.

235 Ibid., referring to Olivecrona (1962), supra note 1473.

236 Spaak (2009/2011), supra note 1473, pp. 44-45, referring to Olivecrona (1962), Ibid., pp. 189-90.

237 Wenar (2011), supra note 1464, pp. 10-11, referring to H.L.A. Hart, 'Essays on Bentham: Studies in Jurisprudence and Political Theory', (Oxford: Clarendon Press, 1982).

238 Ibid., referring to Wesley Hohfeld, 'Fundamental Legal Conception,' W. Cook (ed.), (New Haven: Yale University Press, 1919).

239 Ibid.

what rights do for rightholders attempt to combine the strengths of both of the leading theories. Sreenivasan put forward a hybrid analysis of the claim-right that grafts the interest theory onto the will theory: here the function of the claim-rights is to endow the right-holder with the amount of control over another's duty that advances her interests.[240] Cruft suggests an inclusive analysis where all rights are 'of value' in securing the right-holder's autonomy or interests.[241] Wenar abandons the idea that all rights have any single function at all, describing instead several distinct functions that rights perform.[242]

The seemingly interminable debate between these two major theories has encouraged the development of alternative positions on the function of rights. 'Demand' theories fill out the idea that, as Feinberg puts it : A right is something a man can stand on, something that can be demanded or insisted upon without embarrassment or shame.[243] For Darwall, to have a claim-right includes a second-personal authority to resist, complain, demonstrate, and perhaps use coercive measures of other kinds, including, perhaps, to gain compensation if the right is violated.[244] On Skorupski's account rights specify what the right-holder may demand of others, where 'demand' implies the permissibility of compelling performance or exacting compensation for non-performance.[245] Though there are disputes over the function of rights and the history of rights language, most agree that rights have special normative force. As Mill wrote about the trumping power of the right to free expression: If all mankind minus one were of one opinion, mankind would be no more justified in silencing that one person than he, if he had the power, would be in silencing mankind.[246] The reasons that rights provide are particularly powerful or weighty reasons, which override

---

240 Ibid., p. 13, referring to G. Sreenivasan, 'A Hybrid Theory of Claim-Rights', in Oxford Journal of Legal Studies 25 (2005), pp. 257-74; G. Sreenivasan, 'Duties and Their Disrection', in Ethics, 120(3) (2010), pp. 465-494.

241 Ibid., referring to R. Cruft, "Rights: Beyond Interest Theory and Will Theory?" in Law and Philosophy, 23 (2004), pp. 347-97.

242 Ibid., referring to L. Wenar, 'The Nature of Rights', in M. Kramer, C. Grant, B. Colburn, and A. Hatzistavrou (eds.), The Legacy of H.L.A. Hart, (Oxford: Oxford University Press, 2005), pp. 251-73.

243 Ibid., p. 12, referring to J. Feinberg, 'Social Philosophy', (Englewood Cliffs, NJ: Prentice-Hall, 1973), p. 58-59.

244 Ibid., referring to S. Darwall, 'The Second-Person Standpoint', (Cambridge, MA: Harvard University Press, 2006), p. 18.

245 Ibid., referring to J. Skorupski, 'The Domain of Reasons', (Oxford: Oxford University Press, 2010), XII.6, XIV.2-3.

246 Ibid., p. 16, referring to J. Mill, On Liberty; page reference in the text is to the reprint in J. Mill, On Liberty and Other Essays (1859), S. Collini (ed.), (Cambridge; Cambridge University Press, 1989) , p. 20.

reasons of other sorts. Rights as "trump" is stated in Dworkin's metaphor.[247] Rights give reasons to treat their holders in certain ways or permit their holders to act in certain ways, even if some social aim would be served by doing otherwise.

***

As to categories of rights, there are a right to life, a right to choose; a right to vote, to work, to strike; a right to one phone call, to dissolve parliament, to operate a forklift, to asylum, to equal treatment before the law, to feel proud of what one has done; a right to exist, to sentence an offender to death, to launch a nuclear first strike, to castle kingside, to a distinct genetic identity; a right to believe one's eyes, to pronounce the couple husband and wife, to be left alone, to go to hell in one's own way. Making sense of persistent rights-assertions in great variety, we class rights together by common attributes. Rights-assertions can be categorized, for example, according to: -*Who is alleged to have the right*: children's rights, animal rights, workers' rights, state's rights, the rights of people; - *What actions or states or objects* the asserted right pertains to: Rights of free expression, to pass judgment; rights of privacy, to remain silent; property rights, bodily rights; - *Why* the rightholder (allegedly) has the right: Moral rights are grounded in moral reasons, legal rights derive from the laws of the society, customary rights exist by local convention; and – *How the asserted right can be affected* by the rightholder's actions: The inalienable right to life, the forfeitable right to liberty, and the waivable right that a promise be kept. Many of these categories have sub-categories, for instance, natural rights are the sub-class of moral rights that humans have because of their nature; the rights of political speech are a sub-class of the rights of free expression.[248]

Hohfeld discovered the four basic components of rights, known as "the Hohfeldian incidents". The four basic 'elements' are the privilege, the claim, the power and the immunity.[249] Privilege-rights mark out what their bearer has no duty not to do. Your right to paint your bedroom red is a privilege, but you have no duty not to paint it red. Every claim-right correlates to a duty in (at least) one duty-bearer. What is distinctive about the claim-right is that a duty-bearer's duty is 'directed at' or 'owed to' the right-holder, for example, the employee's claim-right to wages payment from the employer. A claim-right can also require duty-bearers to refrain from performing some actions, such the child's claim-right correlates to

247 Ibid., referring to Dworkin (1984), supra note 1465.

248 Ibid., pp. 2-3.

249 Ibid., pp. 3-4, referring to Hohfeld (1919), supra note 1478.

a duty in every other person not to abuse her. Hart called privileges and claims 'primary rules': rules requiring that people perform or refrain from performing particular actions.[250] Powers and immunities, according to Hart, are 'secondary rules' - rules that specify how agents can introduce, change, and alter primary rules.[251] A promisor exercises a power-right to create in the promisee a claim that the promisor will perform a certain action. The promisor's exercise of her power-right to promise creates in the promisee a claim that the promisor do what she promised to do. This Hohfeldian power is the incident that enables agents to alter primary rules. Witnesses in court have an immunity-right not to be ordered to incriminate themselves, and civil servants have a right not to be dismissed after a new government comes to power. These immunities correspond to an absence of a power in some other party to alter the rightholder's normative situation in some way.

Each of the 'atomic' incidents – the privilege, claim, power, and immunity – can be a right when it occurs in isolation. But these atomic incidents also bond together in characteristic ways to form complex rights, for example, the property right that has its molecular structure, comprising the 'first-order' rights and the 'second-order' rights. The first-order rights are your legal rights directly over your property, and the second-order rights are your legal rights concerning the alteration of the first-order rights. The privilege on the first level entitles you to use your property. The claim correlates to a duty in every other person not to use your property. On the second level, you have several powers with respect to your claim (you may waive the claim, annul the claim, or transfer the claim), and your immunity prevents others from altering your first-order claim over your property (your immunity prevents others from waiving, annulling, or transferring your claim over your property).[252]

The distinction between active and passive rights (Lyons) maps neatly onto the Hohfeldian incidents. The privilege and the power are 'active' rights that concern their holders' own actions; and the claim and the immunity are 'passive' rights that regulate the actions of others.[253] A distinction between negative and positive rights is popular among some normative theorists, especially those with a bent toward libertarianism. The holder of a negative right is entitled to non-interference, while the holder of a positive right is entitled to provision of some good and service. A right against assault is a classic example of a negative right, while a right

250 Ibid., referring to Hart (1961), supra note 1285.

251 Ibid., pp. 4-5.

252 Ibid., p. 7.

253 Ibid., p. 8, referring to D. Lyons, 'The Correlativity of Rights and Duties', in Nous, 4 (1970), pp. 45-57.

to welfare assistance is a prototypical positive right (Narveson).[254] Since both negative and positive rights are passive rights, some rights are neither negative nor positive. Privileges and powers cannot be negative rights; and privilege, powers, and immunities cannot be positive rights.

Rights often appear to conflict. For example, when the public's right to protest conflicts with the government's right to keep order in public property, on a certain day we will judge in favor of the public's right, in given different circumstances we will judge in favor the government's right.[255] When rights appear to conflict like this, the usefulness of the image of rights as trumps begins to dim. Both of these rights are trump cards, yet it does not appear that one right always trumps the other. A specificationist will attempt to dispel any appearance of conflict of rights. For example, a specificationist will say that what is colloquially referred to as 'the public's rights to protest' is actually, on closer examination, the public's rights to protest, unless the protest would cause serious risk to life or property, or would lead to the spread of a deadly disease, or.... Similarly, the government's rights should really be specified more fully as the rights: ...to control what happens on public property, but not to the extent of stopping peaceful protest, unless the protest would lead to the spread of deadly disease, but not... On the specificationist view, rights never conflict, they fit together like pieces in a jigsaw puzzle, so that in each circumstance there is only one right which determines what is permitted, forbidden or required. Rights are always, to use Steiner's phrase, 'compossible' (Steiner 1994).[256] Rights sometimes support each other. Henry Shue argues that both rights of security and rights of subsistence are 'basic rights' because they are indispensable for the full enjoyment of all other rights – while other rights are non-basic because they are not indispensable for the enjoyment of these two.[257] Nickel develops a typology of supporting relations between rights.[258] One right strongly supports another when it is logically or practically inconsistent to endorse the implementation of second right without endorsing the simultaneous implementation of the first. Nickel argues that the strength of

254 Ibid., referring to J. Narveson, 'The Libertarian Idea, Peterborough', (Ontario: Broadview, 2001).

255 Ibid., referring to W. Sinnott-Armstrong, 'Moral Dilemmas and Rights,' in H.E. Mason (ed.), Moral Dilemmas and Moral Theory, (New York: Oxford University Press, 1996), pp. 48-65; F. Kamm, 'Intricate Ethics', (Oxford: Oxford University Press, 2007), pp. 262-301.

256 Ibid., referring to H. Steiner, 'An Essay on Rights', (Oxford: Blackwell, 1994).

257 Ibid., p. 19, referring to Henry Shue, 'Basic Rights: Subsistence, Affluence, and U.S. Foreign Policy', (Princeton: Princeton University Press, 1996).

258 Ibid., referring to J. Nickel, 'Rethinking Indivisibility: Towards a Theory of Supporting Relation between Human Rights', in Human Rights Quaterly 30 (2008), pp. 984-1001.

supporting relations between rights varies with quality of implementation. Poorly implemented rights provide little support to other rights, while ones that are more effectively implemented tend to provide greater support to other rights.

In Germany, rights in the Basic Law are circumscribed by duties and are often limited by objectives and values specified in the constitutional text, the Constitutional Court receives considerable guidance in determining the legitimacy of a state purpose.[259] In Canada, in *Oakes*, 1 S.C.R the reason for the government's rights violation must 'relate to concerns which are pressing and substantial in a free and democratic society'. The particular language of the Canadian formulation derives from the language of section 1 of the Charter of Rights and Freedom, which subjects rights guaranteed therein to 'such reasonable limits prescribed by law as can be demonstrably justified in a free and democratic society'.[260] Rights are what the rule of law protects, and, such protection is provided under the rule of law which is prescriptive and generative. In this perspective, rights and the protections thereof are central to the prescription of law in order to generate legal determinations including judicial decisions, alternative dispute resolutions, customary practice, and undisputed law practice in real life.

III.4. LEGAL PRESCRIPTIVITY

III.4.1. ETHICAL PRESCRIPTION

III.4.1.1. MORAL-IN-THE-LAW

As already mentioned in Chapter II.2, Bentham defined ethics as the art of producing the greatest possible amount of happiness for oneself and for others; and ethics is both the art of fulfilling one's duty to oneself and the art of fulfilling one's duty to others. According to him, if an act of legislation conforms to the principle of utility, then it tends to increase the total happiness of all individuals. Bentham promulgated the principle of utility as the standard of right action on the part of governments and individuals.

259 Green (2011), supra note 1207, n. 35. See DONALD P. KOMMERS, 'THE CONSTITUTIONAL JURISPRUDENCE OF THE FEDERAL REPUBLIC OF GERMANY', 46 (2d ed. 1997).

260 Ibid., pp. 1293-1294, referring to Canadian Charter of Rights and Freedom, Part I of the Constitution Act, 1982, being Schedule B to the Canada Act, 1982, c. 11, § 1 (U.K.).

Actions are approved when they are such as to promote happiness, and disapproved of when they have a tendency to cause unhappiness.[261] Morris Cohen is of the opinion that the limitation of man's desire for the moral good is one of some causes of the inherent limitation of legal idealism which can be combined with legal realism.[262] An adequate science of law must come to ask: "how are we to choose the basic premises of our legal system [and here] we enter the realm of ethics as the science of ultimate human ends".[263] Cohen holds that the *ideal* of legal science will always be, to quote Cairn's formulation, in the direction of a validly constructed postulational system, the postulates of which will be empirical hypotheses. This suggestion explicitly recognizes the importance in their formulation of the role of logic, philosophy, and ethics.[264] According to Cohen in an essay published in 1940, since we lack omniscience as to all the possible forms of social adjustment, experimentation or the process of learning from experience is indispensable. Law and morality can coincide only in the fundamental assumptions as to the proper procedure to enable us to correct our mistakes. Their common ideal is thus like that of science, to wit, a system that corrects itself by the process of testing principles by their consequences, and conversely, judging actual consequences in the light of principles.[265]

It has already been mentioned also in Chapter II.2 that, in *Brown v Board of Education*, 347 U.S.(1954), the justices were right, morally speaking, to decide the case as they did and that the country is better as a result. Matters may look different, however, if we imagine the justices to be as prone to moral error as the ordinary lot of humanity.[266] Fuller suggests no serious discontinuity between the 'legislative' considerations of (non-legal) moral duty and those of legal duty.[267] This can be easily associated with

261 Driver (2014), supra note 1137, § 2.1, quoting Jeremy Bentham (1789) [PML], 'An Introduction to the Principles of Morals and Legislation', (Oxford: Clarendon 1907), p. 1 & 310.

262 Hebert G. Reid, 'A Philosopher's Perspective on Law: A Study of Morris Cohen', in the American Journal of Jurisprudence, Vol.16: Iss. 1, Article 10, 1971, p. 245, referring to Cohen (1949), supra note 1140, p. 27.

263 Ibid., p. 251, referring to Cohen (1961), supra note 1143, pp. 10-15.

264 Ibid., p. 257, referring to Cairns (1941), supra note 1142, p. 81, 143. Cairns (1941) suggested initial concentration on the task of constructing only a postulational science of law.

265 Ibid., referring to Cohen (1961), supra note 1503, p. 37.

266 Fallon (2009), supra note 1227, p. 1008. See, e.g., Waldron (1998), supra note 1148 (arguing that we lack any "epistemic apparatus that would enable us to ground any but the most trivial and unhelpful inductions about expertise and institutional competence"); see also Posner (1998), supra note 1148, p. 1637.

267 Nance (1985), supra note 1417, p. 30. In fairness to Fuller, it should be pointed out that another part of his theory illustrates his concern about moralistic

a view that any act constituting a breach of a moral duty is appropriately proscribed or put publicly out of the protection by law, aside from certain, seemingly incidental matters ('casuistry') concerning the fair administration of the proscription. Radbruch insists on the moral neccessity in the law.[268] Whether similarly or by entailment, the moral necessity that rulers rule according to law is a neccessity qualified by the moral neccessity to take steps to preserve the community and its members against threats which the community has not forfeited its right to be defended from, including steps contrary to the law and even the constitution.

The most commonly endorsed method of moral inquiry among contemporary moral philosophers is John Rawl's 'reflective equilibrium'.[269] First, we identify a set of moral intuitions of particular cases, then we set aside among such moral intuitions those which are clearly the products of distorting influences. After that, we seek to unite the remaining intuitions under a set of more general principles. We seek principles that both imply and explain our particular judgments. But the match between principles and intuitions will inevitably be very imperfect in the first instance. A candidate principle which has some implications that conflict with other intuitions may be modified or left away. If the principle has considerable explanatory power with respect to a wide range of intuitions and cannot be modified without significant sacrifice of this power, we may instead decide to reject the recalcitrant or disobedient intuitions. In this way we make reciprocal adjustments between intuitions and principles until

---

authoritarianism and provides something of a barrier thereto. Indeed, the main thrust of the gambling example is to illustrate the difference between "the morality of aspiration" (based upon the effort to live fully and well) and "the morality of duty" (based upon the effort to limit one's actions in the minimal ways necessary for communal life). For Fuller, the former bears a close affinity to the substantive aims of law, the latter to the "internal morality of law." Fuller (1969), supra note 1163, Chs. 1-11. If Fuller's only point is that the moral considerations concerning the substantive aims of law are properly much more like those of the morality of duty than those of the morality of aspiration, then perhaps the present criticism is misdirected. Moreover, since Fuller deplores much of the moral escalation by which moral aspirations become moral duties (footnote omitted), it is clear that his general inclination is to keep the category of moral duties relatively small and thereby restrict the category of candidates for the duties of citizens under substantive law. See also Fuller (1969), Ibid, pp. 132-33, Ch IV; Fuller (1981), supra note 1159, p. 67.

268 Finnis (2014), supra note 1180, n. 50, quoting Gustav Radbruch, 'Statutory Lawlessness and Supra-Statutory Law', in Oxford Journal of Legal Studies 26 (2006), p. 1,7 - translated by Bonnie Litschewsky Paulson and Stanley L. Paulson, the original is Radbruch,'Gesetzliches Unrecht und ubergezetzliches Recht', (1946) 1 Suddeutsche Juristen-Zeitung 105.

269 Rawls (1971), supra note 449, pp. 19-21& 48-51;Bishop & Trout (2005), supra note 165.

our beliefs at various levels of generality are all brought into a state of harmony, or reflective equilibrium.

Dworkin holds that judgment of correctness in constitutional law is made in morals. By building in 'justified coercion' to the concept of law, most legal theorists[270] think Dworkin has limited his theory to a subset of legal systems in which legal coercion is morally justified, thus making it a case of 'particular jurisprudence'.[271] Polanyi has so vigorously shown that even practitioners of the stricter kind of science bring value commitments to their work.[272] In sociology, personal value judgment necessarily guides the sociologist, and the most conscientious course with such value judgments is to hold them consciously and state them explicitly.[273] In the 'science of jurisprudence', one can undertake any analysis without a moral purpose, without evaluation of the uses of law, without commitments as to what law should be? However, morals influence statutory law; they may, though they need not, guide a judge making case law; law may be criticized from a moral point of view. Hart notes a further substantial overlapping of law and morals; for a society to be viable, for a legal order to exist, there is what Noonan considers a limited moral structure built into the law.[274] Finnis straightforwardly argues that a moral obligation, at least if falling within the rubric of justice, is *ipso facto* an obligation which may properly be backed by coercive sanctions, such sanctions being 'of very secondary importance'.[275] Alexander and Sherwin in their formulation of rules as an elaboration of morality – a conclusion in line with analytical jurisprudence – understand that the data set 'rules' is derived from the substance 'morality' [That may be].[276] The central case of a legal system, they say, is one whose valid norms are at least presumptive moral requirements, and that it is therefore impossible for the theorist to describe the central case of law without engaging in some moral theorizing to determine what would have to be true of a legal system that actually generated moral obligations.[277] Schauer concludes that rules function to

---

270 Langlinais & Leiter (2012), supra note 964, p. 19, referring to Hart (1994), supra note 1364, pp. 240-242; Brian Leiter, 'Naturalizing Jurisprudence', (Oxford: Oxford University Press, 2007), p. 159.

271 Fallon (2009), supra note 1506, n.31. See Dworkin (1996), supra note 1167, p. 87.

272 Noonan (1961), supra note 1151, p. 172 [accompanying text omitted].

273 Ibid. See e.g., Myrdal (1944), supra note 1150, p. 1043-1046, 1063; Lynd (1939), supra note 1150, pp. 200-201.

274 Ibid., p. 172. A point well developed by Broden (1959), supra note 1151.

275 Nance (1985), supra note 1507, p. 36.

276 Alces (2003), supra note 1255, p. 2058.

277 Langlinais & Leiter (2012), supra note 1510, p. 15, referring to John Finnis, "Law and What I Truly Should Decide", in The American Journal of Jurisprudence

translate moral principles into a set of directions that can be understood by people who previously disagreed or were uncertain about the meaning of those principles.[278] According to Raz, morally conscientious citizens should accept the dictates of legal authorities when they have good reason to believe that the legal authorities can make better decisions than they could make themselves.[279] Del Vecchio says there have been shifts as to emphasis in the definitions of law, from morals and ethics to force, and back again to ethics.[280] The life of law lies in a struggle against wrong, and can be understood only in correlation with this antagonistic opposite (right v. wrong), which shows the resistence of social reality to the application of law. All values and norms of action are referred to an ethical principle as a basis (Del Vecchio, p. 155, 163). Law, according to Del Vecchio, is the part of Ethics which establishes the bases of coexistence between several individuals. Without law one could not even concieve of a society. *Ubi societas, ibi jus*. Since *Ubi homo, ibi societas*, we can conclude, *Ubi homo, ibi jus*.

Hazard holds that 'morals' refer to 'the notion of right and wrong that guide each of us individually and subjectively in our daily existence'.[281] The interpretation of laws must be based upon how well laws 'conform our conduct to the demand of morality'.[282] As also already said in Chapter II.2, the law is constantly based on notions of morality, and if all laws representing essentially moral choices are to be invalidated under the Due Process Clause, the courts will be very busy indeed.[283] Fallon is of the contention that a norm is as an action-guiding or reason-giving precept or principle, deviation of which would provide a ground for reproach

48 (2011), pp. 107-129.

278 Alces (2003), supra note 1516, p. 2041, referring to Alexander & Sherwin (2001), supra note 1254, p. 54.

279 Fallon (2009), supra note 1511, p. 1028, referring to Raz (1986), supra note 1222, pp. 1018-1020.

280 Ben W. Palmer and John W. Giles, 'PHILOSOPHY OF LAW. GIORGIO DEL VECCHIO', translated by Thomas Owen Martin from the Eighth Edition, forward by Brendan F. Brown, - THE ART OF ADVOCACY. LLOYD PAUL STRYKER, in Cath. U.L.Rev. (1954), p. 147..

281 Geoffrey C. Hazard Jr., 'Law, Morals, and Ethics', in (1995) Faculty Scholarship Series, Paper 2372, Yale Law School Legal Scholarship Repository, p. 451.

282 W. Bradley Wendel, 'Legal Ethics Is About the Law, Not Morality or Justice: A Reply to Critics', Wendel.A3Edit, 1 February 1993, 7, in Major Reference Books-Wiley Online Library, International Encyclopedia of Ethics, 2013, referring to Heidi M. Hurd, 'Interpreting Authorities', In Law and Interpretation (Andrei Marmor ed. 1995), p. 405, 425.

283 Green (2011), supra note 1499, p. 1294. See 478 U.S. (1986), overruled by Lawrence v Texas, 539 U.S. 558 (2003).

within an appropriate domain such as that of morals, law, or etiquette.[284] In any case of collision between legal and moral norms, moral norms claim superior status.[285] Moral norms may accommodate legal norms to a considerable extent by requiring officials to obey even morally misguided laws, unless the laws are very seriously unjust.[286] For an official who takes morality seriously, the question of the force of legal norms will always be a moral question.[287] Beyleveld and Brownsword define natural law to include the following definition of the nature of a law: 'Rule X is a law (is legally valid) if, only if, there is a moral right to *enforce* X'.[288] Those who promulgate authoritative rules 'throw' them in a manner that anticipates the fit between morality and the rule (in light of whatever factors may determine *movement* in that fit). Indeed, the thrower (Lex) may 'put some air under the ball' to permit the receiver (the adjudicator) to adjust as necessary to the ball (the rule) in order to assure a reception, the best fit between the rule and morality.[289] Some members of society, according to Priel, are substantive natural lawyers in the sense that they believe that putative legal systems that are grossly immoral are not legal systems, or that grossly immoral laws are not laws.[290] The importance of moral in the law is forwarded by Iredell Jenkins.[291] There is actually an element of 'morals-in-the-law' important to its outcomes and the outcomes of the law, although sometimes legal may yet be revolting to our sense of justice.

---

284 Fallon (2009), supra note 1519, n.28.

285 Ibid., p. 1007. See, e.g., Williams (1985), supra note 1225, p. 178, (explaining "morality" as a variety of ethical thought by noting that "moral obligation is categorical").

286 Ibid. There is a vast literature on whether, and if so when, there is a moral obligation to obey the law. For an introduction, see Edmundson (2004), supra note 1226, p. 215.

287 Ibid., pp. 1007-1008.

288 Nance (1985), supra note 1515, n.158, referring to Beyleveld & Brownword (1983), supra note 1175, p. 82 (emphasis supplied).

289 Alces (2003), supra note 1528, n.12.

290 Priel (2007), supra note 1127, p. 149. See, e.g., Fuller (1969), supra note 1512; Radbruch (2006), supra note 1508, p. 1; Robert Alexy, 'The Argument from Injustice: A Reply to Legal Positivism', trans. Bonnie Litschewski Paulson & Stanley L. Paulson (Oxford : Oxford University Press, 2002).

291 Reid (1971), supra note 1502, p. 243, referring to Jenkins (1959), supra note 1139, pp. 28, 5-6.

III.4.1.2. JUSTICE

***

Justice means giving each person what he or she deserves or, in more traditional terms, giving each person his or her due. Justice and fairness are closely related terms that are often today used interchangeably. There have, however, also been more distinct understandings of the two terms. While justice usually has been used with reference to a standard of rightness, fairness has often been used with regard to an ability to judge without reference to one's feelings or interests; fairness has also been used to refer to the ability to make judgments that are concrete and specific to a particular case.[292] The most fundamental principle of justice – as widely accepted since Aristotle - is the principle that 'equals should be treated equally and unequals unequally'. Contemporarily, this principle is sometimes expressed: Individuals should be treated the same, unless they differ in ways that are relevant to the situation in which they are involved.[293] Justice teaches us to give to another what belongs to him. Man's natural rights are the object of the virtue of justice. Justice requires that all persons should be left in the free enjoyment of all their rights.[294] In the *Republic* of Plato, almost every issue individual person or society would regard as ethical comes in under the notion of justice (*dikaosoune*). However, in modern times, justice covers only part of individual morality. Individual justice most naturally refers to moral issues having to do with goods or property. It is unjust for someone to steal from people or not to give them what he owes them, and it is unjust if someone called upon to distribute something good (or bad or both) among members of a group uses an arbitrary or unjustified basis for making the distribution.[295] According to Plato, the just individual is someone in whom reason governs passion and ambition through such a vision. Individual justice precisely consists in such a state of the soul.[296] Aristotle's account of justice as a virtue anchors individual justice in situational factors that are largely external to the just individual. Situations and communities are just, according to

292 Velasquez et al (1990), supra note 371, p. 1.

293 Ibid., p. 2.

294 Catholic Encyclopedia-Justice, supra note 1434.

295 Mark LeBar and Michael Slote, 'Justice as A Virtue,' in Stanford Encyclopedia of Philosophy, first published Friday, March 8, 2002; substantive revision Wednesday, September 8, 2010, (2016), p. 1.

296 Ibid., p. 2.

Aristotle, when individuals receive benefits according to their merits, or virtue; those most virtuous should receive more of whatever goods society is in a position to distribute (exemptions from various burdens or evils counting as goods). This is what we would today call a desert-based conception of social justice.[297] What Plato and Aristotle both say about the virtue of justice clearly reflects the commitment to rationalism.[298] Under the influence of Plato and Aristotle, much subsequent thinking about justice (especially in the Middle Ages) emphasized the role of reason both in perceiving what is just and in allowing us to act justly rather than to give in to contrary impulses or desires.

The philosopher Immanuel Kant and others have pointed out, human beings are all equal in this respect: they all have the same dignity, and in virtue of this dignity they deserve to be treated as equals. Whenever individuals are treated unequally on the basis of characteristics that are arbitrary and irrelevant, their fundamental human dignity is violated.[299] The foundation of justice can be traced to the notions of social stability, interdependence, and equal dignity. As Rawls has pointed out, the stability of a society depends upon the extent to which the members of that society feel that they are being treated justly. The members of a community, Rawls holds, depend on each other, and they will retain their social unity only to the extent that their institutions are just.[300] According to Velasquez, Andre, Shanks and Meyer, any moral decision treats all persons equally. If not, we must determine if the difference in treatment is justified.[301] But justice is not the only principle to consider in making ethical decisions. Sometimes principles of justice may need to be overridden in favor of other kinds of moral claims such as rights or society's welfare.

Distributive justice, feminist justice, retributive or corrective justice, compensatory justice and restorative justice are in the discourse in doctrinal writing. Distributive justice refers to the extent to which society's institutions ensure that benefits and burdens are distributed among society's members in ways that are fair and just. Another important kind of justice is retributive or corrective justice, which refers to the extent to which punishments are fair and just, taking into account relevant criteria such as the seriousness of the crime and the intent of the criminal, and discount irrelevant criteria such as race. Compensatory justice refers to the extent to which people are fairly compensated for their

297 Ibid.

298 Ibid.

299 Velasquez et. al (1990), supra note 1532, p. 3.

300 Ibid.

301 Ibid., pp. 3-4.

injuries by those who have injured them; just compensation is proportional to the loss inflicted on a person.[302]

A claim in justice, or a right in the strict sense, is a moral and lawful faculty of doing, possessing, or exacting something. The owner of a house has the right to exclude others from the enjoyment of its uses, it belongs with all the advantages which it can confer to him alone. If anyone else made use of the house against the reasonable wish of the owner, then he who made use of the house in such a manner would offend against justice. The right of ownership may be absolute or qualified. Such ownership is the principal object of the virtue of justice as it regulates the relation of man with man. Justice between man and man is called individual, particular, or commutative justice, because it is chiefly concerned with contracts and exchange. Individual justice is distinguished from social, for not only individuals have claims in justice against other individuals but a subject has claims against the society to which he belongs, as society has claims against him. Justice requires that all should have what belongs to them, and so the just man will render to the society, or State, of which he is a member, what is due to it. The justice which prescribes this is called legal justice. On the other hand, the individual subject has claims against the State. It is the function of the State to protect its subjects in their rights and to govern the whole body for the common good.[303] If the power of State violates the natural rights of individual persons, the power commits injustice, just like in the event individuals do the same.[304] There is a controversy among authorities as to whether commutative, legal and distributive justice are so many species of one common genus, or whether commutative justice is in reality the only species of justice in the strict sense. For justice is something which is due to another; neither more nor less is satisfied.[305]

To the extent Christian writers allied themselves with Plato and Aristotle, they emphasized on agapic love. Such love seems to be a matter of motivationally active feeling rather than of being rational. In particular, the 'moral sentimentalists' Hutcheson and Hume treated morality as grounded in something other than reason, and the influence of Christian ideas and ideals of agapic love on Hutcheson (at least) is well documented. According to Hutcheson, the individual virtue of justice (ultimately) consists in being motivated by universal benevolence through a moral sense (or sensitivity), not through reason, and he explicitly denies that benevolence can ever conflict with true justice.[306] Hume saw (or believed he saw) that individual

---

302 Ibid., p. 3.

303 Catholic Encyclopedia- Justice, supra note 1534.

304 Ibid.

305 Ibid.

306 LeBar & Slote (2010/2016), supra note 1535, p. 3.

justice at least sometimes conflicts with what benevolence would motivate us to do.[307] He holds that being virtuous depends on feelings and feelingful motives like benevolence and symphaty rather than on reason, and that the virtue of justice is not natural, but rather should be considered 'artificial', because it depends for its existence on human conventions and artifices and because the primary motive to justice is a sense of justice (of duty).

***

The theories of distributive justice include Strict Egalitarianism, Rawls' theory of justice, Luck Egalitarianism, desert-based principle, welfare-based principle (i.e., utilitarianism), libertarian principle, and feminist principle. The 'Luck Egalitarianism' literature comprises varying attempts to design distributive principles that are appropriately sensitive to considerations of responsibility and luck in economic life. Desert-based principle similarly emphasize the moral role of responsibility and luck but are distinct because they approach these factors through claims about what people deserve due to their work. Advocates of welfare-based principles (of which utilitarianism is the most famous) do not believe the primary distributive concern would be material goods and services. Material goods and services are valuable only in so far as they increase welfare. Hence, they argue, distributive principles should be designed and assessed according to how they affect welfare, either its maximization or distribution. Advocates of libertarian principles, by contrast to each of the principles so far mentioned, generally criticize any distributive ideal that requires the pursuit of economic 'pattern', such as maximization equality of welfare or of material goods. They argue that the pursuit of such patterns conflicts with the more important moral demands of liberty or self-ownership. Feminist principles hold that existing distributive principles tend to ignore the particular circumstances of women, and that women often have primary responsibility for child-rearing and on average, spend less of their lifetimes than men in the market economy.[308]

Distributive principles vary in numerous dimensions. They vary in what is considered relevant to distributive justice (income, wealth, opportunities, jobs, welfare, utility, etc.); in the nature of the recipients of the distribution (individual persons, groups of persons, reference classes, etc.); and on what basis the distribution should be made (equality, maximization, according to individual characteristics, according to free

307 Id., p. 4.

308 Julian Lamont and Chisti Favor, 'Distributive Justice', in Stanford Encyclopedia of Philosophy, first published Sunday, September 22, 1996; substantive revision Wednesday, January 2, 2013, pp. 1-2.

transactions, etc.).[309] Principles of distributive justice are therefore best thought of as providing moral guidance for the political process and structures that affect the distribution of economic benefit and burdens in societies. The first relatively simple principle of distributive justice examined is Strict Egalitarianism, according to which every person should have the same level of material goods and services. The principle is most commonly justified on the grounds that people are morally equal and that equality in material goods and services is the best way to give effect to this moral ideal. There are a number of direct moral criticisms made of strict equality principles: that they unduly restrict freedom, that they do not give best effect to the moral equality of persons, that they conflict with what people deserve, etc.[310] But the most common criticism is a welfare-based one related to the Pareto efficiency requirement:[311] that everyone can be materially better off if incomes are not strictly equal.

Governments continuously make and change laws and policies affecting the distribution of economic benefits and burdens in their societies. Almost all changes, whether they regard tax, industry, education, health, etc. have distributive effects. As a result, every society has a different distribution at any point in time. At every time now, each society is faced with a choice about whether to stay with current laws, policies, etc. or to modify them. The practical contribution of distributive justice theory is to provide moral guidance for these constant choices. Distributive justice theory is a practical enterprise. It is important to acknowledge that there has never been, and never will be, a purely libertarian society or Rawlsian society, or any society whose distribution conforms to one of the proposed principles, so rather than guiding ideal societies. Distributive principles provide moral guidance for the choices that each society faces now and every year.[312]

The distribution of material goods and services is not the only economic distribution which is important to people. The distribution of opportunity is also important. Equality of opportunity is often contrasted favorably with 'equality of income' or strict egalitarianism, by those who believe that we can show equal concern, respect, or treatment of people without them having the same material goods and services, so long as they have equal economic opportunities.[313] Rawl claims that 'natural lottery' is immoral, because if society is structured so that people's prospect for

---

309 Ibid., p. 2.

310 Ibid., pp. 1- 2.

311 Ibid., p. 5,7, referring to Joseph Carens, 'Equality, Moral Incentives and the Market', (Chicago: Chicago University Press, 1981).

312 Ibid., pp. 3-4.

313 Ibid., p. 11.

gaining more economic goods are not largely determined by factors for which they are responsible but rather largely by luck, then the society is open to the charge of being unfair.[314]

The desert-based principles differ primarily according to what they identify as the basis for deserving. While Aristotle proposed virtue, or moral character, to be the best desert-basis for economic distribution, contemporary desert theorists have proposed desert-bases that are more practically implemented in complex modern societies. Most contemporary desert theorists have pursued John Locke's lead in this respect. Locke argues people deserve to have those items produced by their labor and industry, the products (or the value thereof) being a fitting reward for their effort (Miller 1989). Locke's underlying idea was to guarantee to individuals the fruits of their own labor and abstinence.[315] According to the contemporary desert theorist, people freely apply their abilities and talents, in varying degrees, to socially productive work.[316] Distributive systems are just insofar as they contribute incomes according to the different levels earned or deserved by the individuals in the society for their productive labors, efforts, or contributions. The main moral objection to desert-based principles is that they make economic benefits depend on factors over which people have little control. The problem is most pronounced in the case of productivity-based principles – a person productivity seems clearly to be influenced by many factors over which the person has little control.[317]

Rawls makes clear his belief in the inadequacy of benevolence or sympathetic human sentiment in formulating an adequate conception of social justice.[318] Rawls's positive view of justice is concerned primarily with the justice of institutions or (what he calls) the 'basic structure' of society; justice as an individual virtue is derivative from justice as a social virtue defined via certain principles of justice.[319] He also contends that the idea of what people distributively deserve or merit is derivative from social justice rather (as with Aristotle and/or much common-sense thinking) providing the basis for thinking about social justice.[320] A conception of social justice is to be regarded as providing in the first instance a standard whereby the

---

314 Ibid., p. 11, referring to Rawls (1971), supra note 1509.

315 Ibid., p. 18, referring to David Miller, 'Market, State, and Community', (Oxford: Clarendon Press, 1989).

316 Ibid., referring to Joel Feiberg, 'Justice and Personal Desert,' Doing and Deserving, (Princeton, NJ: Princeton University Press, 1970), pp. 55-94.

317 Ibid., p. 19.

318 LeBar & Slote (2010/2016), supra note 1546, p. 7 [footnote omitted].

319 Rawls (1971), supra note 1554, p. 13, 110.

320 Ibid., p. 3, 133.

distributive aspects of the basic structure of society are to be assessed.[321] Rawls proposes the following two principles of Justice: (1) Each person has an equal claim to a fully adequate scheme of equal basic rights and liberties, where the equal political liberties, and only those liberties, are to be guaranteed their fair value; and (2) Social and economic inequalities are to satisfy two conditions: (a) They are to be attached to positions and offices open to all under conditions of fair equality of opportunity; and (b) they are to be to the greatest benefit of the least advantaged members of society.[322] The principle 2b is known as the Difference Principle. If it is possible to raise the absolute position of the least advantaged further by having some inequalities of income and wealth, the Difference Principle prescribes inequality up to that point where the absolute position of the least advantaged can no longer be raised.[323] No society can be a scheme of cooperation which men enter voluntarily in a literal sense; each person finds himself placed at birth in some particular position in some particular society, and the nature of this position materially affects his life prospect. Yet a society satisfying the principles of justice as fairness comes as close as a society can to being a voluntarily scheme, for it meets the principles which free and equal persons would assent to under circumstances that are fair.[324] Rawls' theory is one of the theories of distributive justice. Rawls has introduced the notion of 'original position' from which the principles of justice are derived. The original position is the appropriate initial status quo, and thus the fundamental agreements reached in it are fair. This explains the propriety of the name 'justice as fairness' - it conveys the idea that the principles of justice are agreed to in an initial situation that is fair.[325] The original position as above stated requires the parties to make a collective agreement, and therefore the restrictions on valid undertakings as well as the publicity and finality conditions are an essential part of the agreement for the two principles.[326] The principles of justice are chosen behind a veil of ignorance, says Rawls.[327] This ensures that no one is advantaged or disadvantaged in the choice of principles by the outcome of natural chance or the contingency of social circumstances. Since all are similarly situated and no one is able to design principles to favor his particular condition, the principles of justice are the result of a fair agreement or bargain.

---

321 Ibid., p. 9.

322 Ibid., pp. 60-61.

323 Lamont & Favor (2013), supra note 1548, p. 8.

324 Rawls (1971), supra note 1559, p. 13.

325 Ibid., p. 12.

326 Ibid., p. 183.

327 Ibid., p. 12.

The Difference Principle that constitutes Rawls' alternative distributive principle permits diverging from strict equality so long as the inequalities in question would make the least advantaged in society materially better off than they would be under strict equality.[328] Rawls deliberately invokes Kantian rationalism (or anti-sentimentalism) in explaining the intellectual or theoretical motivation behind his construction, and the two principles of justice that would be agreed upon under the contractual conditions represent a kind of egalitarian political liberalism.[329] Roughly, those principles stress (equality of) basic liberties and opportunities for self-advancement over considerations of social welfare, and the distribution of goods in society (according to the Difference Principle) is then supposed to work to the advantage of all (especially the worst-off members of society). Rawls argues that a utilitarian principle of justice dictating simply the maximization of overall social well-being would not be accepted in his original position and is accordingly less plausible than the conception of justice embodied in his own two principles and the construction that leads to them.

When explaining how individuals (within a just society) develop a sense and/or the virtue of justice, Rawls invokes the work of Jean Piaget who saw moral development as akin to the other sorts of development he so famously studies.[330] Piaget treats moral development, therefore, as principally involving increasing cognitive sophistication. Piaget sees that sophistication as a matter of taking more and more general or universal views of moral issues, and the Kantian and rationalist idea that morality rests on and can be justified in terms of considerations of universality or universalizability seems to underlie or to be much presupposed in Piaget's contention about moral development. Rawls gives distinct arguments for believing that it is rational to *retain and act upon* a sense of justice, and stresses the need for a sufficient general appreciation and rational understanding of social relations as the grounding basis of a sense of duty or of justice.[331] Lawrence Kohlberg claims that the highest stage of such development (as taken by Rawls from Piaget) involves a concern for justice and human rights based on universal principles, and Kohlberg relegated sheer concern for relationships and for individual human well-being to lower stages of the process.[332] He saw the ordering of the different stages in Piagetian fashion as basically reflecting differences in rational understanding: those whose moral thinking involved the invoking of universal principles of justice and rights were said to show a more advanced

328 Lamont & Favor (2013), supra note 1563, p. 1, 2.
329 LeBar & Slote (2010/2016), supra note 1558, p. 7.
330 Ibid., p. 8.
331 Ibid.
332 Ibid.

cognitive development than those whose moral thought appeals primarily to the importance of relationships and of human well-being or suffering.

Later luck egalitarians claim that those with unequal natural endowments should receive compensation.[333] Luck egalitarians continue to refine such aspects of their theories as (a) what they believe is the relevant conception of equality of opportunity, (b) how much of a role luck should play in the distribution of economic benefits and (c) what is the best conception of 'luck'.[334] Advocates of Luck Egalitarian principles argue that the Difference Principle does not fully capture the moral roles they believe luck and responsibility_should play in principles of distributive justice.[335]

Dworkin in his theory *Resource Egalitarianism* presented his key insight in terms of a distinction between 'ambitions' and 'endowments'.[336] Dworkin uses the term 'ambitions' to cover the realm of our choices and what results from our choices, such as the choice to work hard, or to spend money on expensive luxuries. His term 'endowments' refers to the result of brute luck, or those things over which we have no control, such as one's genetic inheritance, or unforeseeable bad luck. Dworkin agrees with Rawls that natural inequalities are not distributed according to people's choices, nor are they justified by reference to some other morally relevant fact about people, so people should not end up worse off as a result of bad luck in the natural lottery. In terms of sensitivity to 'ambitions', Dworkin argues that provided people have an 'equal' starting point (in Dworkin's case, resources) they should live with the consequences of their choices. People who choose to work hard to earn more income should not be required to subsidize those choosing more leisure and hence less income. Like later

333 Lamont & Favor (2013), supra note 1568, p. 13, referring to Richard Arneson, 'Liberalism, Distributive Subjectivism, and Equal Opportinuty for Welfare', in Philosophy and Public Affairs, 19 (1990), pp. 158-194; Marc Fleurbaey, 'Egalitarian Opportunity', in Law and Philosophy:An International Journal for Jurisprudence and Legal Philosophy, 20 (2001), pp. 499-530; A. Swift, 'The Value of Philosophy in Nonideal Circumstances', (2008), in Social Theory and Practice: An International and Interdisciplinary Journal of Social Philosophy, 34 (2010), p. 363-387; G. Sher, 'Real-World Luck Egalitarianism', in Social Philosophy and Policy, 27 (1) (2010), pp. 218-232.

334 Ibid., quoting Arneson (1990), Ibid.; Fleurbaey (2001), id.; Swift (2008), Ibid.; Sher (2010), Ibid.

335 Ibid., p. 9, 10.

336 Ibid., pp. 12-13. See Ronald Dworkin, 'What is Equality Part 1: Equality of Resources', in Philosophy and Public Affairs, 10 (1981) ["1981a"], pp. 185-246; Dworkin, 'What is Equality Part 2: Equality of Welfare', in Philosophy and Public Affairs, 10 (1981) ["1981b"], pp. 283-345; Dworkin, 'Sovereign Virtue', (Cambridge, MA: Harvard University Press, 2000).

luck egalitarians, Dworkin's recommendation[337] is that those with unequal natural endowments should receive compensation.[338]

Robert Nozick has advanced this version of libertarianism. He proposes a 3-part 'Entitlement Theory': If the world were wholly just, the following definition would exhaustively cover the subject of justice in holdings: (a) A person who acquires a holding in accordance with the principle of justice is entitled to that holding; (b) A person who acquires a holding in accordance with the principle of justice in transfer, from someone else entitled to the holding, is entitled to the holding; (c) No one is entitled to a holding except by (repeated) applications of (a) and (b).[339] The complete principle of distributive justice would say simply that a distribution is just if everyone is entitled to the holdings they possess under the distribution. The statement of the Entitlement Theory includes reference to the principles of justice in acquisition and transfer. The principle of justice is designed to specify fair contracts while ruling out stealing, fraud, etc. According to Finnis, Nozick's principle of justice in holdings is that holdings are just which are justly acquired from an unowned state or justly received from someone else who held them justly.[340] Moreover, the only justification for taking such just holdings from someone to give to another arises under a principle of 'rectification' for a (sufficiently serious) wrong done to the recipient by the person being taken from, with appropriate accounting for wrongs done between predecessors.

Finnis cites Nozick's arguments in favor of an 'entitlement' theory of justice in holding and the argument against redistributive taxation that is derived therefrom.[341] Nozick explicitly indicates a role, albeit a subsidiary one, for the principle of distributive justice in dealing with special problem of rectification – namely, situations in which the principle of rectification unaided by such distributive principles yields a non-unique prescription.[342] Nozick's arguments emphasize the 'moral side-constraints' which limit the legitimate actions of everyone, including the state.[343] Most importantly, Nozick frequently reminds the reader that justice in terms of what may

337 Ibid., p. 13, referring to Arneson (1990), supra note 1574; Fleurbaey (2001), supra note 1579; Swift (2008), supra note 1579; Sher (2010), supra note 1574.

338 Ibid., referring to Arneson (1990), Ibid.; Fleurbaey (2001), Ibid.; Swift (2008), Ibid.; Sher (2010), Ibid.

339 Ibid., p. 20, referring to R. NOZICK, 'ANARCHY, STATE AND UTOPIA (1974), p. 151.

340 Nance (1985), supra note 1528, p. 34, referring to Finnis (1980), supra note 1172, pp. 186-188.

341 Ibid. See Nozick (1974), supra note 1579, Ch. 7.

342 Ibid., n.138. See Nozick (1974) Ibid., p. 153n.

343 Ibid., referring to Nozick (1974), Ibid., Part I, esp. Ch.3.

be required of someone under threat of coercion is distinct from justice in terms of what one ought voluntarily to do.

The Difference Principle uses the market as a means of helping the least advantaged, utilitarian principles use it as means of achieving the distributive pattern maximizing utility, and desert-based principles rely on it to distribute goods according to desert, etc. In contrast, advocates of libertarian distributive principles rarely see the market as a means to some desired pattern, since the principle(s) they advocate do not ostensibly propose a 'pattern' at all, but instead describe the sorts of acquisitions or exchanges which are just in their own right. The market will be just, not as a means to some pattern, but insofar as the exchanges permitted in the market satisfy the conditions of just acquisition and exchange described by the principles.[344] Libertarians argue that the Difference Principle involves unacceptable infringements on liberty, property rights, or self-ownership.[345]

***

Welfare-based principles are motivated by the idea that what is of primary moral importance is the level of welfare of people. The concerns of other theories – material equality, the level of primary goods of the least advantaged, resources, desert-claims, or liberty – are as derivative concerns. They are only valuable in so far as they affect welfare, so that all distributive questions should be settled entirely by how the distribution affects welfare. Philosophers tend to restrict themselves to a small subset of the available welfare functions, and most philosophical activity has concentrated on a variant known as utilitarianism. Historically, utilitarians have used the term 'utility' rather than 'welfare' and utility has been defined variously as pleasure, happiness, or preference-satisfaction. Bentham argued that the experience of pleasure was the only thing with intrinsic value, and all other things had instrumental value insofar as they contribute to the experience of pleasure or the avoidance of pain. His student John Stuart Mill broadened this theory of intrinsic value to include happiness, or fulfillment. Modern philosophers since Kenneth Arrow, though, tend to argue that intrinsic value consists in preference-satisfaction, i.e., in 'individuals' having what they want.[346] Under utilitarian theories, in their classical form, a racial preference – that the members of some minority racial groups have less material benefits – counts like any other in determining the best distribution. If racial preferences are widespread and are not outweighed

344 Lamont & Favor (2013), supra note 1573, p. 20.

345 Ibid., p. 9, 10.

346 Ibid., p. 14.

by the minority's contrary preferences, utilitarianism will recommend an inegalitarian distribution based on race if there is no some other utility-maximizing alternative on offer.[347] As already mentioned above, Rawls articulated that utilitarianism fails to take seriously the distinctness of persons.[348] The complaint against utilitarianism is that it takes this principle, commonly described as prudent for individuals, and uses it on an entity, society, unlike individuals in important ways. However, in the case of society as a whole, there is no single experiential entity – some people suffer or are sacrificed so that others may gain. It is often argued against utilitarianism that it is immoral to make some people suffer so that there is a net gain for other people.

Feminist conception of distributive justice varies; theorists who name themselves feminists defend positions across the political spectrum. John Stuart Mill gives one of the clearest early feminist critiques of the political and distributive structures of the emerging liberal democracies. Mill argued that the principles associated with the developing liberalism of his time required equal political status of women. The principles include a rejection of the aristocracy of birth, equal opportunity in education and in the marketplace, equal rights to hold property, a rejection of the man as the legal head of the household, and equal rights to political participation.[349] Susan Moller Okin[350] argues that the consequence of the institution of the nuclear family is a position of systematic material and political inequality for women. Okin and others demonstrate that women have substantial disadvantages on competing in the market because of childrearing responsibilities which are not equal shared with men. As a consequence, any theory relying on market mechanism, including most liberal theories, will yield systems which result in women systematically having less income and wealth than men. Feminists who follow Mill believe that a proper recognition of the position of women in society requires that women be given equal and the same rights as men have, and that these primarily protect their liberty and their status as equal persons under the law. Government regulation should not prevent women from competing on equal terms with men in educational, professional, marketplace and political institutions.

***

347 Ibid., p. 15.

348 Ibid., referring to Rawls (1971), supra note 1564.

349 Ibid., p. 24, referring to John Stuart Mill, 'The Subjection of Women', (1869).

350 Ibid., p. 25, referring to Susan Moller Okin, 'Justice, Gender and the Family', (New York: Basic Books, 1991).

The absolute or strictest version of retributivism sees its moral rules as clear and absolute mandates applying to each person in all situations, in order to avoid all failures of desert. Such moral rules would include not only the imperatives captured by criminal law itself but also the moral duty to punish all those (and only those) who deserve punishment. This is often described as a *deontological (agent-relative)* understanding, since its commands apply to each individual actor and action, rather than seeking to maximize 'the good' overall.[351] Retributive literature has a lot of references to the principle of desert-based punishment as a moral duty and to the corresponding claim that the retributive principle does not merely authorize punishment but affirmatively calls for its imposition on those who deserve it.[352] The view dates back at least as far as Kant and Hegel, and it continues to appear in contemporary writing as well.[353] In theory, the duty-to-punish view creates a clear affirmative goal for the application of the retributive principle: punish everybody who deserves it, to the full extent of their desert.[354] Another version of retributivism is the threshold model to also avoid serious failures of desert. This version shares the absolute model's position that imposing desert-based punishment is a moral duty, but it considers the duty less categorical or universal than the absolutist approach. Under this view, sometimes called *threshold deontology*, moral

351 Michael T. Cahill, 'Retributive Justice in the Real World', in Washington University Law Review, Vol. 85:815(2007), p. 826, referring to Michael Moore, 'Placing Blame: A General Theory of the Criminal Law' (1997), p. 156 ("The deontological' or 'agent-relative' retributivist regards the act of punishing the guilty as categorically demanded on each occasion, considered separately").

352 Ibid., also referring to Mitchell N. Berman, 'Punishment and Justification', in 118 Ethics (forthcoming Jan. 2008), p. 28.

353 Ibid., pp. 826-827, referring to Immanuel Kant, 'The Metaphysics of Morals', 105 (Mary Gregor ed. & trans.), (Cambridge Univ. Press, 1996/1797), (describing retributive punishment as a "categorical imperative" that "must always be inflicted upon [a criminal] only because he has committed a crime); G.W.F. Hegel, 'Elements of the Philosophy of Right', 127, (Allen W. Wood ed., H.B. Nisbet trans.), (Cambridge Univ. Press, 1991/1821), ("Both the nature of crime and the criminal's own will require that the infringement for which he is responsible should be cancelled"); Igor Primoratz, 'Justifying Legal Punishment', 74 (1997) ("A full-fledged retributive theory sees in the offense committed not only the ground of the right to punish, but the source of the duty to punish as well, Hegel is a true retributivist: his doctrine ... is primarily an attempt to establish the second of the two claims); Stephen P. Garvey, 'Is It Wrong to Commute Death Row? Retribution, Atonement, and Mercy', in 82 N.C. L. Rev. 1319 (2004), p. 1324, ("Retributive justice obliges the state to punish an offender because and to the extent, but only to the extent, he deserves to be punished.... [T]he state cannot shrink its obligation to do justice"); Moore (1997), supra note 1591 (citing Michael Moore's references to duty to punish).

354 Ibid., p. 828.

duties are generally binding but may be violated if adherence would lead to some particularly bad result.[355] Cahill says that this model allows that in some (presumably rare) cases, other considerations could trump that duty and permit a violation of the desert principle.[356] Thus, where the absolutist model would categorically forbid intentional infliction of injury or death on an innocent person under any circumstances, the threshold model might allow torturing or even killing if doing so would, for example, save an entire city from destruction. Second, according to Cahill, this model would appear to scale the magnitude of that duty according to the magnitude of the moral wrongdoing involved in an offense.

Typically, retributive concerns will outweigh other (i.e., consequentialist) considerations, but as the relevant bad consequences of following the desert principle become serious enough, they may trump retribution. Michael Moore's discussion of this dynamic looks primarily at the situation where consideration of consequence trumps retribution.[357] Quoting Igor Primoratz, Cahill says that by the same logic, it may also be true that in some cases the retributive concerns favor punishment but are small enough that significant consequential costs will trump them, militating decisively against punishment. Such variations in the level of obligation to punish would presumably track the moral gravity of the offense in question: we may forgo punishment for less serious crimes, but must punish more serious ones.[358] Consequentialist Retributivism is to maximize deserts, with the consideration that the nature of the moral call for desert-based punishment does not demand punishment of each individual offender but rather sets the goal of maximizing the *total* amount of desert-

355 Ibid., p. 830, referring to Moore (1997), supra note 1593, p. 1568 n.13 (A 'threshold' deontologist refuses to violate a categorical norm of morality until not doing so produces sufficient bad consequences as to pass some threshold – then, he will override such categorical norms");

356 Ibid., p. 833, referring to Moore (1997), Ibid., p. 719; and saying "The relative moral gravity of different offenses might turn on various factors, but two prominent factors would surely be the level of culpability required (so that intentional wrongdoing would be more serious than reckless wrongdoing) and the extent of the harm caused or risked (so that causing death would be more serious than causing injury). Other factors or subfactors, such as whether harm is actually caused or "merely" risked, might be more controversial in terms of their bearing on the seriousness of the offense).

357 Ibid., p. 830, referring to Moore (1997), supra note 1596, p. 719 ("It just is not true that one should allow a nuclear war rather than killing or torturing an innocent person. It is not even true that one should allow the destruction of a sizeable city by a terrorist nuclear device rather than kill or torture an innocent person").

358 Ibid., p. 831, referring to Primoratz, (1997), supra note 1593, p. 149.

based punishment,[359] even if this means sacrificing deserved punishment in some cases for the sake of pursuing it in others. Because this approach interprets desert-based punishment as a 'good' to maximize, rather than an *ex ante* and inviolate command, it has been described as *consequentalist* (as opposed to deontologist) retributivism.[360] Significantly, according to Polinsky and Shavell, the Consequentialist Retributivism perspective does not merely seek to find room for retribution as one component of a standard consequentialist scheme, as some defenses of desert-based punishment do, for those accounts defend the practice as *instrumentally* valuable insofar as it generates other good consequences (such as making people happy or preventing crime).[361] Cahill concludes that the most sensible means for incorporating retributive goals into a general theory of criminal justice is to adopt the approach of 'consequantialist retributivism'.[362] Under consequantialist retributivism, the underlying justification for punishment

---

359 Ibid., saying "Obviously, maximizing deserved punishment is distinct from maximizing punishment altogether. Any retributivist system would seek to avoid undeserved punishment at least as strenuously as it would seek to impose deserved punishment, if not more so" and "It is unclear whether retributivism is neutral as between "false positives" (undeserving people who are punished) and "false negatives" (deserving people who fail to be punished), or whether retributivism should be seen as valuing the avoidance of punishing the innocent more highly than the imposition of punishment on the guilty; and referring to Louis Kaplow & Steven Shavell, 'Fairness versus Welfare,' (2002), p. 342 n.103 (expressing uncertainty as to retributivism's view of how to balance positive value of deserved punishment against negative value of punishing the innocent); Richard A. Bierschbach & Alex Stein, 'Mediating Rules in Criminal Law', in 93 VA. L. Rev. (2007), p. 1208 (defending claim that retributivism is "agnostic" between these two kinds of error and "expresses no strong preferences for whether [evidentiary] rules skew more toward the side of false positives of more toward false negatives"); Russel L. Christopher, 'Deterring Retributivism: The Injustice of "Just" Punishment', in 96 NW. U.L. Rev. 843 (2002), pp. 912-913, (discussing the debate within retributivism as to whether punishing the innocent is worse than failing to punish the guilty).

360 Ibid., p. 833, referring to Moore (1997), supra note 1597, pp. 156-59.

361 Ibid., referring to Mitchell Polinsky & Steven Shavell, 'The Fairness of Sanction: Some Implications for Optimal Enforcement Stratetgy', in 2 AM, L. & Econ. Rev. (2000), p. 223, (incorporating "taste" or preference for retribution into economic analysis of punishment); and Paul H. Robinson, & John M. Darley, 'The Utility of Desert', in 91 NW. U.L.Rev. (1997), p. 453, (defending desert-based punishment as the best way to achieve deterrence); Jean Hampton, 'Correcting Harms Versus Righting Wrongs: The Goal of Retribution', in 39 UCLA L. Rev. 1659 (1992), p. 1659 n.2 (citing Hampton's own previous work offering a "moral education" theory of punishment, and asserting continuing adherence to the position that "moral education and deterrence should be goals of any well-designed system of punishment").

362 Ibid., p. 870.

rests on a more general balancing of its consequences, and retributive goals count as only one factor in that balancing. Retributive justice, then, may enter the real world, but in doing so, it must allow other considerations to share space on the ideal plane where criminal law's motivating principles reside.

***

Paradigmatic cases of compensatory justice involve someone being injured (the victim), a person committing the injury (the victimizer), and quantifiable damage that can be restored by the vistimizer through the paying of compensation or the return of stolen goods.[363] There is a rift in the moral fabric when someone injures someone else. The agent of harm needs to do something to repair the rift and make things right. There have been several suggestions put forward as to what actions would result in 'making things right'; restoration of equality; restoration of the *status quo ante*; making the victim whole; and material reparation plus apology.[364] Foreshadowed by Aristotle's characterization that the law's role is to govern rectificatory justice as treating two participants as equal, Bernard Boxhill argues that compensatory ('reparatory') justice not only repairs the physical damage caused by the injury, but also underlines that fact that the victim is worthy of respect.[365] The *stated* theoretical goal of contemporary tort law is 'restoration of the *status quo ante*'. Expounded upon by Justice Brewer in 1893, compensation's goal is to provide the 'full and perfect equivalent' of what was lost, and so to restore completely the *status quo ante*.[366] Jeffrie Murphy and Jules Coleman describe 'corrective or rectificatory justice' as evening out unjust gains and losses.[367] Loren Lomasky presents another version of the goal of compensatory justice – that it should make the 'injured party' whole. He relates this 'making whole' to being 'at least as well

363 Rene A. Hill, 'Compensatory Justice: Over Time and Between Groups', in The Journal of Political Philosophy: Volume 10, Number 4, 2002, (Oxford, UK and Malden, MA: Blackwell Publishers, 2002), pp. 392-415 (p. 392).

364 Ibid., pp. 393-398.

365 Ibid., pp. 393-394, referring to Aristotle's Nichomachean Ethics, Book V, chapter four; Bernard Boxhill, 'Morality of Reparation', in Barry R. Gross (ed.), Reverse Discrimination, (Buffalo, N.Y.: Prometheus Books, 1977), pp. 270-278.

366 Ibid., pp. 394, referring to Robert Goodin, 'Compensation and redistribution,' in John Chapman (ed.), Nomos XXXIII: Compensatory Justice, (New York: New York University Press, 1991), pp. 143-77 (p. 145).

367 Ibid., p. 396, referring to Jeffrie Murphy & Jules Coleman, 'Philosophy and private law', in Jeffrie Murphy and Jules Coleman, The Philosophy of Law: An Introduction to Jurisprudence, (Totowa, N.J.: Rowman and Allanheld, 1984).

off as before the transgression occurred'.[368] Whatever compensatory plan has been invoked, Boxhill maintains that justice has not been reinstated, even if material reparations have been paid, if the victimizer has not acknowledged that he/she was wrong or mistaken.[369] Rene Hill holds that equal consideration means other people are openly acknowledged as being equals, and this means victims are owed the affirmation of equality which an admission of error brings.[370]

To summarize the suggestions above mentioned, Hill has adopted as a working definition Lomasky's two-tiered explanation of the goal of compensation: (1) to render the situation as it was before the injury, or restoration of the *status quo ante*, or if that is not possible, (2) to make the "injured party whole" by rendering her 'at least as well off as before the transgression occurred'.[371] This allows for repair that will not take one back to the original situation but removes the impediments to project pursuit caused by the injury.[372] The victim may now be in a different place with different resources at her disposal, but she should be able to move forward once again. The central goal of compensation is to restore the victim to some baseline point, and an apology may or may not be thought central to that process. Apology may be imposed upon the wrongdoer if it is thought necessary by the victim.

***

Restorative justice is a new way of looking at criminal justice that focuses on repairing the harm done to people and relationships rather than on punishing offenders. This new focus on healing and the related empowerment of those effected by a crime seems to have great potential for enhancing social cohesion in our increasingly disconnected societies. Restorative justice and its emerging practices constitute a promising new area of study for social sciences. The foundational postulate of restorative justice is that crime harms people and relationships and that justice requires the healing of the harm as much as possible.[373] Restorative justice

368 Ibid., referring to Loren Lomasky, 'Compensation and the bounds of rights', in John Chapman (ed.), Nomos XXXIII: Compensatory Justice, (New York: New York University Press, 1991), pp. 13-44 (p. 16, 27).

369 Ibid., p. 397, referring to Boxhill (1977), supra note 1605, pp. 274-275.

370 Ibid.

371 Ibid., p. 398, referring to Lomasksy (1991), supra note 1608, p. 16, 27.

372 Ibid., pp. 398-399.

373 T. Wachtel and P. McCold, 'In Pursuit of Paradigm: A Theory of Restorative Justice', in Paper presented at the XIII World Congress of Criminology, 10-15

is a collaborative process involving those most directly affected by a crime, called the 'primary stakeholders', in determining how best to repair the harm caused by the offense.

Structurally, a theory of restorative justice proposed by T. Watchel and P. McCold explains the how, what and who of restorative justice theory. [374] Everyone with an authority role in society faces choices in deciding how to maintain social discipline. Until now, Western societies have relied on punishment, usually perceived as the only effective way to discipline those who misbehave or commit crimes. The punitive approach, with high control and low support, is also called 'retributive', having a tendency to stigmatize people. The permissive approach, with low control and high support, is also called 'rehabilitative' and tends to protect people from experiencing the consequences of their wrongdoing.[375] The theory of restorative justice proposes how to relate the harm caused by the offense to the specific needs of each stakeholder created by that offense, and to the restorative responses required to meet those needs. This causal structure distinguishes the interests of the primary stakeholders from those indirectly affected. The primary stakeholders are the victim and his community of care and the offender and his community of care. The harm done, needs created and the restorative responses of primary stakeholders are specific to the particular offense and require active participation to achieve the greatest healing. The secondary stakeholders who are not emotionally connected to the specific victims and offenders include those who live nearby or those who belong to educational, religious, social or business organizations and the whole society represented by government officials is to support and facilitate the process in which the primary stakeholders determine for themselves the outcome of the case. When criminal justice practices involve only one group of primary stakeholders, as in the case of governmental financial compensation for victim, the process can only be called 'partly restorative'. When a process such as victim-offender mediation includes two principal stakeholders but excludes the communities of care, the process is 'mostly restorative'. Only when all three sets of primary stakeholders are actively involved, such as in conference or circles, is a process 'fully restorative'.[376] Restorative justice, Wachtel and McCold hold, is ideally achieved through a cooperative process involving all the primary stakeholders in determining how best to repair the harm done by the offense.[377] A criminal justice system

August 2003, Rio de Janeiro.

374 Ibid., referring to T. Wachtel & P. McCold (2000), Stakeholder Role – McCold (1996, 2000) and the Restorative Practices Typology - McCold & Wachtel (2002)'.

375 Ibid.

376 Ibid.

377 Ibid.

that merely invokes punishment to offenders and sidelines victims does not address the motional or relational needs of those who have been affected by crime. In a world where people feel increasingly alienated, restorative justice restores and builds positive feelings and relationships. A restorative criminal justice system aims not just to reduce crime, but to reduce the impact of crime as well.

***

Corrective justice is about correcting the outcomes of actions performed in violation of our duties. Corrective justice is about correcting wrongs. Jules Coleman in 1982 argued that corrective justice consisted in and required, first and foremost, the rectification, annulment or neutralization of those wrongful losses and wrongful gains caused by wrongful actions. The 'Annulment Conception' of Corrective Justice was built out of the conjunction of the well-known principle of unjust enrichment with its mirror principle, more precisely, the principle of unjust loss. The 'Annulment Conception' provided us with part of what we want out of a conception of corrective justice, more precisely, with what Coleman calls a 'ground for recovery and grounds for liability', that is to say, arguments to, respectively, sustain, both, the claims of those that ask for compensation from specific others and the duties of those that were asked specifically by others to provide compensation.[378] In 1992 Coleman's *Risk and Wrongs* (Cambridge 1992) showed partial change in his original view, arguing that the 'Annulment Conception' was to some extent lacking because it failed to properly correlate the wrongful loss of the victim with the wrongful gain of the tortfeasor and thereby, it failed to properly explain a very essential aspect of both, corrective justice and tort law, more precisely its agent-relative nature, that is, the ability of corrective justice and tort law to source reasons that only apply to some people – the tortfeastor and the victim of the harm – but not to others.[379] A plausible conception of corrective justice, according to Coleman, had to consist in, and provide, not only a ground of recovery' and a 'ground for liability' but also in a 'mode of rectification', that is to say, an indication of the particular way in which

378 Carlos Rosenkrantz, 'A Compensatory Conception of Corrective Justice Revisited,' in Dirrito & questioni pubbliche, Vol. 12 (2012, pp. 109-135, citing Jules Coleman, 'Corrective Justice and Wrongful Gain', in 11J. Legal Stud, (1982), 421; Jules Coleman, 'Risks and Wrongs', (Cambridge 1992) ["Coleman 1992a"], p. 309.

379 Ibid., referring to Jules Coleman, 'The Mixed Conception of Corrective Justice', in 77 Iowa L. Rev. (1991-1992), p. 427.

compensation has to be effectuated.[380] The 'Annulment Conception' did say that the rectification, annulment and repairment of the wrongful loss could not add itself a new wrongful gain or a wrongful loss. It is always wrong to create a corrective injustice in order to rectify a wrongful loss if it is possible to correct a loss without doing so – but 'this constraint (of) the set of possible modes of rectification' was radically insufficient since it did not explain why, and if at all, the victim has to be compensated by and only by the tortfeastor.

Coleman emphasizes that there is a deeper reason for duties in corrective justice to direct us to annul gains and losses, deeper than the mere fact that they are gains and losses, and this was that their annulment is itself required by the norms that regulate the relationship that links the person that endured the loss to the person that, while procuring a gain, caused the loss.[381] Coleman assertively claims that only wrongful losses fall within the ambit of corrective justice. It is wrongful losses that must be annulled; and the threat of creating new ones that restricts the institutions we might develop for rectifying existing one. Compensation in corrective justice is a way of respecting the claims associated with rights ownership in the case of liability rule rights; it is a way of repairing wrongs in the case of property rule rights.

***

Morris Cohen contended that the fact that ethical views as to what is fair and just are, and always have been, streaming into the law through all the human agencies that are connected with it, judges and jurists as well as legislature and public opinion. Indeed, the body of the law could not long maintain itself if it did not conform in large measure to the prevailing sense of justice.[382] Rational argument, however, depends upon recognizing the logical distinction between judgments of what is and of what ought to be, Cohen argued. He insists on the elementary understanding that from the simple fact that a specific law or state of affairs exists, we cannot derive a logical conclusion as to whether it ought or ought not to continue to exist unless, of course, we have incorported a premise favoring or disfavoring change. Clear logical analysis must be an integral part of the search for

380 Ibid., referring to Jules Coleman, 'Epilogue to Risks and Wrongs', (1992) ["Coleman 1992b"] Spanish translation at http; // papers.ssrn.com/sol3/papers.cfm= abstract_id=1621881, 18 ; Coleman (1992a), supra note 1618, p. 308, 306.

381 Ibid., referring to Coleman (1992a), Ibid., p. 306/312, 306, 341.

382 Reid (1971), supra note 1531, p. 244, referring to Cohen, 'Reason and Nature', first edition, (N.Y. : Harcourt Brace, 1931), p. 426.

justice in modern jurispridence.[383] Cohen regarded the principles of justice as part of social ethics and not to be identified with personal morals or ethics. In his view the courts could not, realistically, ignore the problem of justice in American constitutional law because the bill of rights incorporated particular popular principles of justice. The problem of justice was a recurrent one. The prevalent legal theory in the United States made a blatant identification between the is and the ought (the law was both the will of the people and the expression of immutable justice, as it ought to be in each case).[384] Cohen advocated responding to unsatisfactory judicial results with rational efforts at improvement of the judicial process rather than attempts to drop the ethical question in law. [385]

The rationalistic attention to a system of rules was rooted in a genuine substructure, primarily the need of certainty in human transactions and security against unforeseen changes. But over-attention to fixity and formality in law leads to uncertainty that is supposed to be prevented, and, in addition, unworkability. And so in the history of law, says Cohen, we find waves calling for flexibility, attention to actual experience and justice.[386] In particular situation purely formal considerations alone are not enough to determine whether a law is just in content. Concretely, equality before law, which is a formal principle of legal justice, may be had (in the sense that officials give no favors to a particular party) but the question of the justness of the law's material content remains. Questions of justice are not legitimately dispensed with by confusion of the formal and the material elements in law. Cohen holds that distinguishing the formal and the material elements of justice in law is one aspect of avoiding the complete identification of law with justice or their complete divorce. In Cohen's words: "Principles of justice are assumed in almost all branches of the law, but they are applied to the concrete material of social life, and the conclusion is based ... not merely upon ethics, but also on the factual judgments and the juristic technique that operates within them".[387] Cohen quoted Spinoza: "He who tries to fix and determine everything by law will inflame rather than correct the vices of the world". These limits of the legal machinery (always humanly operated) make for part of the truth of this statement. Concentrating on justice exclusive of a concern for consequences is iniquitous and imprudent.

---

383 Ibid., pp. 244-245, referring to Cohen (1961), supra note 1505, pp. 172-173, 183.

384 Ibid., pp. 248, referring to Cohen (1931), supra note 1622, pp. 404-410.

385 Ibid., pp. 247-248.

386 Ibid., p. 248, 250-251.

387 Ibid., referring to Cohen (1933), supra note 1144, p. 256; Cohen (1931), supra note 1124, pp. 420-425. Cohen quoted Spinoza from The Tractatus Theol. Polit., Ch.20.

III.4.2 PRESCRIPTIONS FROM OTHER DISCIPLINES

This sub-chapter is presented in light of the notion of prescriptivity and the interdisciplinary and multidisciplinary approaches as already sketched out in Chapter I.2.4. The relationship between philosophy and history in jurisprudence has been dominated by prescriptivism.[388] Herbert Reid has noted that the positivists have devoted their best talents to understanding the multiple facets of the actual legal order, and to making the legal process a more effective instrument of human purposes.[389] In expressing his contention on prescriptivity of law, Iredell Jenkins argues as to *the keystone of legal positivism,* "The content of the legal order, as defining factual consequences, are dependent on criteria, standards, ends, purposes, and values that have extralegal sources and meaning".[390] Referring to Cappelletti, Oreste Pollicino says that one of the elements characterizing the new interpretive approach is the discovery of the importance of choice in the judicial process.[391] Choice means discretion, evaluation and balancing: it means giving consideration to the choice's practical and moral results; and it means employment of not only the argument of abstract logic, but those of economic and politics, ethics, sociology and psychology.

Kennedy contends that the substance of rule may reflect individualism that might include economics, welfare and a larger intellectual entity. The relationship of rule form and rule substance may be analyzed based on the connection between rules, on the one hand, and economics, welfare and a larger intellectual entity, on the other hand. The connection is structural rather than contextual. It is not a practical or empirically verified connection, but rather a connection in the exact correspondence between the structure of arguments for rules and arguments for economics, welfare and a larger intellectual entity (the Classical theory of laissez-faire). Economic individualism was once much more tightly linked to advocacy of rules that it is today, because they were both parts of a larger intellectual entity. According to that theory, economics could recover general laws about the welfare consequences of particular legal regimes looked at as wholes.[392] New principles of law are being developed to meet the new situations that arise. Every new invention and every new business practice introduces a

---

388 Balkin & Levinson (2006), supra note 1123, pp. 175-176.

389 Reid (1971), supra note 1622, p. 243.

390 Ibid., referring to Iredell Jenkins (1959), supra note 1531, pp. 1-32, 28, 5-6.

391 Pollicino (2004), supra note 1229, p. 287. See Cappelletti (1981), supra note 1229. The importance of choice in judicial process is accentuated by the willingness of political branches of governments to pass responsibility for difficult decision to the judiciary.

392 Kennedy (1976), supra note 1387, pp. 1745-1746.

number of situation for which there may be no existing rule of law. For example, how could there have been a law governing the liability of a food canner to the consumer before canning was invented? How could there have been a law relating to stocks and bonds before those instruments came into existence? How could there have been a law with respect to the liability of radio and television broadcasters before such methods of communication were developed?[393]

As already stated before, law resists complete invasion by any other discipline because law normativity is quite different from the normativity that appears in many parts of the humanities.[394] In law, the form that normativity takes is quite narrow.[395] As rule prescribes action, normativity of law is prescriptive. In addition to the normativity prescription as such, there are also prescriptions from other disciplines the issues of which are regulated by the law. Drawing on the work of Talcott Parsons, Roberto Unger remarks that many things besides law may fit into the category of normative order, for example, a society's religion and art.[396] To the extent that law can be differentiated from these other aspects or normative order, it is distinguished by its primary emphasis on externally observable behavior and on the use of secular sanctions to penalize or redress deviant conduct.

Law takes prescription from stockholding practice. Concerning the duty to maximize shareholder value in the context of selling a company, *Revlon, Inc. v. MacAndrews & Forbes Holdings, Inc.*, 506 A. 2d 173 (Del. 1986) holds that if: (i) the directors initiate an active bidding process to sell the company; (ii) the directors abandon the company's long-term strategy and seek an alternative transaction involving the breakup of the company; or (iii)

the directors engage in a plan or transaction that results in a 'change in control' of the company, then they must run a fair process aimed at maximizing stockholder value by getting the best price, and they must ensure full disclosure to stockholders called upon to approve the sale of a company. In that case on page 182 the Court also held that once it became certain that the corporation was for sale, ...[t]he duty of the board

---

393 Ronald A. Anderson, Ivan Fox and David P. Twomey, Business Law, UCC Comprehensive Volume, twelfth edition, (Cincinnati; West Chicago, ILL; Dallas; Pelham Manor, N.Y; Palo Alto, California: South Western Publishing, Co, 1984), p. 27.

394 Balkin & Levinson (2006), supra note 1628, pp. 174-175 [footnote omitted].

395 Ibid., p. 175. The critique of law's particular normative stance has been made most ably by Pierre Schlag. See Campos et. al (1996), supra note 1117; Schlag (1996), supra note 1117.

396 Nance (1985), supra note 1580, n.102.

had thus changed from the preservation of Revlon as a corporate entity to the maximization of the company's value at a sale for the stockholders' benefit.. This holding was then followed in *Paramount Communications, Inc. v. Time, Inc.*, 571 A.2d 1140, 1150-51 (Del. 1989)."[397] In a different case, *Burbank v. Lockheed Air Terminal, Inc.*, 411 US 624 (1973), prescription from air traffic management and environment has been followed by the law. As to that case, the federal government has adopted laws regulating aviation and noise (the federal Aviation Act of 1958 and the Noise Control Act of 1972) and such legislation preempted the field and excluded state action. Local regulations would place an unreasonable burden on interstate commerce because it would be very difficult to plan flight schedules if each airport had its own landing time. Moreover the bunching of flights to avoid local curfews would produce even greater noise and would increase the danger of collision by increasing traffic density. From the nature of the activity, a single, national control, excluding all local regulation was essential. Local state regulation was therefore prohibited.[398] In *Arizona v. Arizona Mines Supply Co.*, 107 Ariz 199, 484 P2d 619(1971), the judicial decision followed prescription from environment consideration. In the decision of the case, the evidence could not be admitted on the question of guilt. If the air was polluted, the defendant was guilty even though it did not have any intent to pollute the air and even though it had sought to prevent it. This is so, because society makes the mere doing of the act a crime for the reason that society is harmed when the air is polluted regardless of why it was polluted. After the question of guilt was decided, the evidence could be considered, however, in determining what sentence to impose and whether to put the defendant on probation.[399]

On January 13, 2011 the Swiss Supreme Court, following prescription from financial industry in its decision in Case n° 6B_223/2010, concluded that retrocession should be characterized as a *consideration for services* and might thus be kept by the bank. The Court's decision clarified the scope of the Swiss 2006 landmark case law in Case n° 4C.432/2005 as determined on March 22, 2006, on the issue of retrocession in Swiss financial industry.[400]

So, for law, as already mentioned before, there are prescriptions from

397 Irwin H. Warren and Bradley R. Aronstam, 'Delaware's Business Judgment Rule and Varying Standards of Judicial Review for Assessing Director Conduct in M&A Transactions', Weil, Gotshal & Manges LLP – New York, NY, the Canadian Institute – November 2007, p. 21. See Revlon, Inc. v. MacAndrews & Forbes Holdings, Inc., 506 A. 2d 173 (Del. 1986); and Paramount Communications, Inc. v. Time, Inc., 571 A.2d 1140, 1150-51 (Del. 1989).

398 Anderson, et al (1984), supra note 1633, p. 74.

399 Ibid., p. 76.

400 Ibid.

sociology as in sociology of law, from anthropology as in anthropology of law, and from politics as in politics of law. Cross-disciplinary or interdisciplinary [or multidisciplinary] approaches might happen to law and sociology, anthropology or politics. The prevailing laws regulate issues in business such as stock market, commercial papers, insurance, transportation and sales, so prescription from principles and practices of stock market, commercial papers, insurance, transportation and sales are then followed by the law. The prevailing laws also regulate issues in agriculture, mining or construction industries, therefore prescriptions from principles and practices of agriculture, mining or construction industries are followed by the laws. The law might or should or do follow prescriptions from any areas, such as environment or medical, any issue of which is provided or regulated by the law. These are all prescriptions from other facets of life for jurisprudence. Rod Macdonald has called 'legal prescriptivism' as the notion that law resides in a prescription external to oneself.[401] Balkin and Levinson have stated their opnion on the success of interdisciplinary studies in law.[402] Strongly, it is shaped by the professional orientation of law schools and the prescriptive nature of legal normativity, and the law co-opts the insights of social sciences like economics and sociology, or humanistic subjects like history, philosophy or literary criticism and turns them to its own uses.

It has probably always been true that, as McHugh has recently obseved, judges, even of the highest courts, lack the power to issue legal prescriptions commanding the kind of literal obedience which is due to statutes.[403] The correctness of this observation is borne out by the long-established maxim that judicial pronouncements as to the law must be read as subject to the underlying facts (*secumdum subjectam materiam*).[404] Facts of/in other facets or dimensions of life or other branches of science are taken into account in law. Prescriptions from sociology, economics, politics, environmental science, medical science, etc are undeniably taken into account by the law when the law regulates issues of fact of/in those facets of life. This indicates that prescriptivity fills the gap between normativity and descriptivity as sketched out in Chapter I.2.6.

401 Janda (2005), supra note 1230, p. 973.

402 Balkin & Levinson (2006), supra note 1634, p. 184.

403 HK Lucke, 'Ratio Decidendi: Adjudicative Rationale and Source of Law', in Bond Law Review, Vol. 1 [1989], Iss. 1, Art. 2, p. 38.

404 Ibid., pp. 38-39.

III.5. LEGAL SANCTION

***

Sanctio in Roman law meant that a rule of conduct was prescribed with the authority of the emperor. All the measures taken for disobeying the law, having punitive, preventive or remedial character are sanctions.[405] Many societies (at various times and places) do the following: (a) recognize that deviations from certain standards of conduct threaten the community (the system of public order as a whole); (b) invoke collective methods of dealing with such non-conformers; (c) inflict measures of incapacitation upon the non-confomers, and to this end rely eventually upon deprivation of status and privilege either permanently or pending transformation of the individual into conforming personality.[406] Sanctions prescribed by the legal order are socially immanent (as distinguished from transcendental) sanctions; besides, they are socially organized (as distinguished from mere approval or disapproval).[407] Sanctions are provided by the legal order to bring about certain human behavior which the legislator considers to be desirable. The sanction is made a consequence of the behavior which is considered detrimental to society and which, according to the intentions of the legal order, has to be avoided.[408] 'Sanctions' in the specific sense of the word appear – within national legal orders – in two different forms: as punishments (in the narrower sense of the word) and as civil executions.[409]

A sanction is 'as a detriment imposed for doing what is forbidden'.[410] Sanctions can be authorized and administered either to promote wise policies or to enforce constitutional norms.[411] Sanction is used as appropriate for remedial or preventive measures. The importance of the nature of a sanction lies mostly in the involvement of culpability and the personal character of the sanction. Punitive sanctions are only applied as a consequences of a culpable and illicit form of conduct (an intentional act or negligence) and it must have a personal character, which means that other persons, who were not involved in the infringement, can not be held

405 Elena Mihaela Fodor, 'General Principles of Administrative Sanctions in the Romanian, Law', in Fiat Justitia, nr.1/2007, p. 1.

406 George H. Dession, 'Sanctions, Law and Public Order', in HeinOnline, 1 Vanderbilt Law Review 14 (1947-1948), p. 10.

407 Kelsen (1967), supra note 897, p. 33.

408 Kelsen (1961), supra note 1451, pp. 50-51.

409 Kelsen (1967), supra note 1647, pp. 108, 109.

410 Fallon (2009), supra note 1224, n.104, quoting Robert Cooster, 'Prices and Sanctions', in 84 COLUM. L. REV. 1523 (1984), p. 1523.

411 Ibid., p. 999.

responsible for the purposes of the sanction. Remedial sanctions are also applied against culpable illicit conduct, but in many situations they can also be applied against non-culpable illicit conduct, as long as prejudice has occurred. Remedial sanctions can be imposed against another person – a successor or another person designated or allowed by the law.[412] The technique of public order is the 'know-how' of use of sanctions, as noted by Dession.[413] In the 'know-how', sanctions are negative in themselves to preserve desired aspects of a culture or, as the case may be, to promote desired culture change.

It is a basic hypothesis that the negative sanctions have a positive social role, there are recurring types of situations in which a net value gain (measured in terms of the shaping and distribution of the values of the culture) can most economically be achieved by a discriminating application of value-depriving sanctions. In all contemporary societies recourse to negative sanctions is the ultimate response of power and authority to deviation deemed dangerously destructive of the values sought by power and authority to be maximized or at least maintaned.[414] Under penal law, sanctions are grouped into main sanctions, complementary sanctions and accessory sanctions.[415] Under administrative law, the contraventional sanctions are grouped into main sanctions and complementary sanctions. In both branches of the law the main sanctions have a punitive character while the complementary and accessory sanctions have a predominantly preventive or remedial character and may be added to the main sanctions.[416]

In the standard model of public enforcement of law, sanctions are evaluated in terms of their deterrent benefits and their costs, but there is no sense in which sanctions are considered to be fair or unfair.[417] People tend to believe that a sanction should not be out of proportion to the gravity of the act committed. To take beliefs concerning the fairness of sanctions into account, theoretical writers assume that individuals obtain what we refer to as *fairness-related utility* or *disutility* from the imposition of sanctions on others. Individuals might feel better off as a result of punishment of

---

412 Fodor (2007), supra note 1645, pp. 1-2.

413 Dession (1947/1948), supra note 1646, p. 8.

414 Ibid., p. 13.

415 Fodor (2007), supra note 1652, p. 2.

416 Ibid.

417 A. Mitchell Polinsky and Steven Shavell, 'The Fairness of Sanctions: Some Implications for Optimal Enforcement Policy', in American Law and Economics Review V2 N2 (2000), pp. 223-237 (pp. 223-224). For example, the issue of fairness is not discussed in two recent surveys of the economic literature on public enforcement – Mookherjee (1997) and Polinsky and Shavell (2000) – and is only briefly mentioned in a third – Garoupa (1997, p. 284).

violators, perhaps due to *retributive satisfaction*, or individuals might feel worse off, because of emphaty for violators. Fairness of sanctions must derive from what individuals want, as opposed to philosophical principles that might or might not be connected to individuals' preferences. The *fairness ideal* is [when] the sanction measures fairness-related utility or minimizes fairness-related disutility.[418] The *conventional deterrence ideal* is [when] the sanction maximizes social-welfare and [when] fairness is ignored. The *full deterrence ideal* is [when] the sanction maximizes social-welfare and [when] fairness-related utlity is recognized in defining the full harm, and [when] fairness is otherwise ignored.[419] The optimal sanction reflects both fairness and deterrence considerations, it is between the fairness ideal and the full deterrence ideal, and it may be greater or less than the conventional deterrence ideal.[420]

Polinsky and Shavell have noted that Wittman (1974) analyzes optimal sanctions solely from the perspective of achieving retributive fairness, ignoring deterrence; he does not consider the optimal probability of catching injures.[421] Ehrlich (1982) discusses optimal enforcement under alternative concepts of justice; in the part of his analysis, in which he considers retribution, he assumes that there is a social cost from failing to sanction injurers (those who escape liability), but he does not allow for the possibility that the sanctions that are imposed on injurers (on those who are caught) might be unfair. Miceli (1991) derives the optimal sanction and the optimal accuracy of the prosecutorial process (as opposed to the optimal probability of detection) when deterrence and the fairness of sanctions are taken into account. Waldfogel (1993) studies empirically whether actual sanctions are better explained by considerations of deterrence or fairness (in the sense that sanctions are proportional to the harm caused), and suggests that deterrence concerns better explain sanctioning practice. Diamond (1997) investigates the optimal sanction with respect to both deterrence and fairness when the probability of detection is fixed; he does not consider the optimal probability of detection because his analysis is in the context of private lawsuits for damages. Lando (1997) examines how fairness concerns affect the optimal due care standard under the negligence rule in tort law; he, too, does not study the likelihood of sanctions. In Lando's analysis, the fairness-related utility or disutility experienced by the injurer and the victim are taken into account, but not, as here, that of other parties as well.

---

418 Ibid., p. 224.

419 Ibid., pp. 224-225. The full deterrence ideal does not take into account the effect of sanctions on social welfare that is unrelated to deterrence – that is, the effect of sanctions on fairness-related utility when the number of individuals who commit the harmful act is held constant.

420 Ibid., p. 225.

421 Ibid., n.7.

The existence of sanction changes moral calculus. More particularly, the way sanctions change moral calculus reveals something about the function of the interrelation between morality and rules. Alexander and Sherwin state that [i]f we assume that at some point, a threat of punishment assumes moral significance, either because punishment will cause grave harm to the actor or because it will cause indirect harm to others, then sanctions can tip the balance of reason in favor of compliance with rules.[422] In the case of a rule-sensitive-moral judge, Alexander and Sherwin hold that [p]unishment can have a corrective function with respect to moral costs that follow from the example of an unpunished violations of rules; punishment can make morally right a violation that otherwise would be wrong because it would undermine the value of the rule.

***

Kenneth Mann seems to assume that civil sanctions function as an alternative to more vigorous criminal prosecutions. It lessens the need to use the criminal law to sanction wrongs and permits a more flexible response to the wrongful conduct. While the reach of the criminal law has expanded consistently, the availability of punitive civil sanctions has avoided some of the inflation of criminal law that would otherwise have occurred.[423] In some situations the applicable 'civil' sanctions (denaturalization, deportation, or indefinite commitment of individuals, decrees of divestiture, divorcement or dissolution addressed to industrial or commercial organizations) are far more depriving than any applicable 'criminal' sanctions. A more functional classification of sanctions involving deprivation might distinguish between those utilizating deprivation as an instrument, and those to which deprivation was incidental.[424]

---

422 Alces (2003), supra note 1255, p. 2051-2052, referring to Alexander & Sherwin in a collection of these essays: L. Alexander, 'Are Procedural Rights Derivative Substantive Rights?, in 17 LAW & PHIL (1998), p. 19; L. Alexander, 'The Banality of Legal Reasoning', in 73 NOTRE DAME L. REV. (1998), p. 517; L. Alexander, 'With Me, It's All er Nuthin': Formalism in Law and Morality, in 66 U. CHI. L. REV. (1999), p. 530; Emily Sherwin, 'A Defense of Analogical Reasoning in Law', in 66 U. CHI. L. REV. (1999), p. 1179 ["Alexander & Sherwin 1998/ 1999"], p. 77.

423 Franklin E. Zimring, 'The Multiple Middlegrounds Between Civil and Criminal Law', in 101 The Yale Law Journal 1901(1992), p. 1904, citing Kenenth Mann, 'Punitive Civil Sanctions: The Middleground Between Criminal and Civil Law', in 101 YALE L.J. (1992), p. 1863.

424 Dession (1947-1948), supra note 1653, p. 15.

Tort law does *not* purport to provide remedies proportional to the injurer's wrong; normally, compensation is the remedy, whatever the nature of the tort or wrong is.[425] To be sure, the compensatory remedy is scaled to the severity of the harm caused, and, in that sense, is proportional.[426] But the tort remedy usualy does not vary with the culpability of the injurer.[427] Most of tort law is governed by a negligence standard. There are relatively few categories of intentional torts and even fewer categories of recklessness and strict liability. To be sure, a number of distinct torts address distinct forms of conduct and social harm other than the physical harm that negligence law protects.[428] The main functions of tort law are: (1) plaintiff obtains damages as compensation (or redress) and (sometimes) in exess of compensation; (2) defendant pays damages as compensation (or redress) and (sometimes) in exess of compensation; (3) deterrence of future torts (by the threat of future tort liability); (4) loss-spreading; and reinforcement of social norms (Arguably, the failure to impose liability also reinforces [different] social norms).[429] The normative principles – most often offered by way of justification, but hardly exhaustive - underlying tort law are: (1) corrective justice or vindications of rights (this principle adopts an *ex post* perspective) ; (2) distributive justice; (3) deterrence in order to promote efficiency; and (4) deterrence in order to prevent wrongs or rights-violations.[430]

For a civil sanction to constitute punishment, the legislature must create the penalty and the court must implement the sanction for the purpose of punishing.[431] Proving that a sanction is punitive [under

---

425 Kenneth W. Simons, 'The Crime/Tort Distinction: Legal Doctrine and Normative Perspectives', in Widener Law Journal, Vol. 17 (2008), p. 721. See John C.P. Goldberg & Benjamin C. Zipursky, 'Tort Law and Moral Luck', in 92 CORNELL L.REV. 1123 (2007), pp. 1142-1143.

426 Ibid. Even this type of proportionality is undermined: by the difficulty of impossibility of providing genuine compensation for certain types of harms, such as pain and suffering or loss of enjoyment of life, and by the problem that wrongful death and survival statutes do not compensate for the loss of enjoyment of life when the tort victim suffers an early death. Moreover, for certain types of intentional wrongs, such as civil rights violations, and perhaps invasions of privacy and other emotional harms, tort remedies might more aptly be characterized as reflecting respect for the victim or some types of redress for the rights-violation than as compensatory.

427 Ibid.

428 Ibid., p. 722.

429 Ibid., pp. 725-726.

430 Ibid., pp. 727-728.

431 Patrick S. Nolan, 'Double Jeopardy's Multipunishment Protection and Regulation of Civil Sanctions after United States v. Ursery', in 80 Marquette Law Review (1997), p. 1107. See 303 U.S. 391 (1938).

multipunishment analysis] is difficult as courts will presumably look to a non-remedial regulatory purpose for the sanction and show deference to the legislature.[432] Courts use a variety of indicators to decide whether the legislature intended a civil sanction to punish. In deciphering the legislature's intent, legislative history, statutory language, and procedural structures provide the most important indications for determining the nature of the sanctions.[433] In particular, legislation that contains separate criminal and civil sanctions accompanied by separate procedures suggests the legislature enacted the separate civil sanction to be a non-punitive remedial measure.[434] The *Kennedy-Ward* intent test offers a seven-factor method [*see* footnote] of determining the punitive nature of a sanction and provides a narrow focus for judical subjectivity.[435] The deferential language of the test acknowledges the legislature's power to simultaneously punish and regulate.[436] Consequently, legislatures have much leeway in crafting both punitive and remedial mechanism.[437] Legislative intent is rarely recorded, especially on a state level, so the reasons for a statutory enactment can be impossible to discover.[438] When legislative history for a statute can be found, it usually shows conflicting legislative motivations among various legislators.[439] [In case damages are more severe than criminal sanctions], it is more accurate to speak of 'extracompensatory' rather than 'punitive' damages insofar as this category of damages might be justified for reasons other than *punishing* the defendant.[440] In legal terms, tort law grants

432 Ibid. See Fleming v. Nestor, 363 U.S. 603, 617-621 (1960).

433 Ibid. See Mitchell, 303 U.S. p. 399.

434 Ibid. See United States v. One Assortment of 89 Firearms, 465 U.S. 354, 363 (1984); Mitchell, 303 U.S., p. 399.

435 Ibid., p. 1108. See Kennedy, 372 U.S. pp. 168-69. The Court highlighted seven factors for determining if a civil proceeding requires procedural due process safeguards afforded criminal defendants: "Whether the sanction involves an affirmative dissability or restraint, whether it has historically been regarded as a punishment, whether it comes into play only on a finding of scienter, whether its operation will promote the traditional aims of punishment – retribution or deterrence, whether the behavior to which it applies is already a crime, whether an alternative purpose to which it may rationally be connected is assignable for it, and whether it appears excessive in relation to the alternative purpose assigned are all relevant to the inquiry [into whether a proceeding is penal or remedial], and may often point in differing directions.

436 Ibid. See Kennedy, 372 U.S., pp. 168-169.

437 Ibid. See Kennedy, 372 U.S., pp. 168-69; see also Fleming v Nestor, 363 U.S. 603, 617-621 (1960) (holding that a statute will always carry the presumption of constitutionality).

438 Ibid. See J. Morris Clark, 'Civil and Criminal Penalties and Forfeitures: A Framework for Constitutional Analysis', in 60 MINN. L. REV. 379 (1976), p. 443.

439 Ibid. See United States v. O'Brien, 391 U.S. 367, 384 (1968).

440 Simons (2008), supra note 1670, p. 726. For example, "punitive" damages

a remedy of restoration or damage compensation if an injurer violates a property right that is protected by law against violation by anyone: namely, if the injurer acts illegally. The legal remedy is triggered by an illegal act for which the tortfeasor is responsible under the *culpa* doctrine. This legal manner of reasoning again reflects the autonomist concept of civil law, entailing that where damage was caused against the categorial intent of *neminem laedere*, this leads to the imposition of a sanction.[441]

In France, traditionally the structure of civil liability rested on three bases; fault, risk and guarantee. The three, depending on the circumstances, could operate in an autonomous manner, but which most often were found in combination.[442] The study of the development of French civil liability since its origin shows a continuing slippage which indicates a clear withdrawal from 'fault' in favor of 'guarantee'. By linking civil liability solely to the goal of indemnifying the victim it is to be noted that, certainly in the second half of the 19th century, civil liability expanded in scope and gained strength[443] but it appeared particularly as a true right of indemnity conferred on the person who suffered loss.[444] The development of the system of civil liability in France, and the new place that 'fault'[445] occupies, undoubtedly helps explain the process of reinforcing the rights of victims and if the compensation of victims is the corollary of civil liability, the goal is undeniably being better

---

might be awarded in order to require the injurer to pay societal damages for harms to people other than the victim. See Catherine M. Sharkey, 'Punitive Damages as Societal Damages', in 113 YALE L.J. 347 (2003), pp. 349-352. Or they might be awarded in order to provide optimal deterrence in cases where the probability of detention of the tort is unusually low, as many economically oriented scholars have advocated. See A. Mitchell Polinsky & Steven Shavell, 'Punitive Damages: An Economic Analysis,' in 111 HARV.L.REV. 869 (1998), pp. 890-891.

441 Claus Ott and Hans-Bernd Schafer, 'The Dichotomy Between Property Rules and Liability Rules: Experiences from German Law', in Erasmus Law Review, Volume 01 Issue 04, 2008, p. 44.

442 Yves-Louis Sage, 'Reinforcing the Rights of the Victim in the French Law on Civil Liability', in (1998) 28 VUWLR, p. 543, referring to P Guiho et G Peyrard, 'Doi Civil. Les Obligations,' (Tome I, "Les Sources," Edit L'Hermes, 1991), p. 418.

443 Ibid. Fault plays a secondary role. For both courts and academics, the tortfeaser's behavior was no longer the only issue. Finding its origin in the theory of risks and its consecration by the case law, the current concern is to provide the victim, with adequate indemnification. On this subject, see notably F Terre, 'Propos sur la responsibilite civile,' Archives de Philo Dr 1977, T 22, p. 37.

444 Ibid.

445 Ibid., p. 569, referring to A Tunc, 'Introduction au volume XI, Torts', [Encyclopedie Internationale de Driot Compare, 1975. "To limit the civil liability domain to somebody's fault is a myth....but it does not mean that fault must be banned from the law of civil liability", in G. Vinney. RIDC 1976, p. 581.

and better attained.[446] The French system represents simply different efforts to redefine the place of fault in civil liability.[447] It may be said that law has had to adapt the transformation of society and the new demands for compensation for loss, and that could not happen other than at the cost of revision of the basis of liability.[448]

In Germany, tort law focuses on property rights, which include private property and the rights to life, health, and bodily intergrity, as well as on the other comparable entitlements,[449] including the protection of an individual's name.[450] Ott and Schafer say that these entitlements are protected by property rules (injunctions, *actio negatoria*) and also by liability rules granting damage compensation. Tort law contains a general rule of damage compensation in case of wilful infliction of damage in violation of *bonos mores*.[451] The German Civil Code of 1900 restricted damage compensation to payments for pain and suffering in cases of bodily harm and deprivation of personal freedom. Subsequently, German courts adhered strictly to the rules of the Civil Code. It was only after World War II that they embarked on a new approach to overcome the restriction of the Civil Code regarding the protection of privacy. A property right of privacy was established and integrated into tort law by the Federal Court of Justice (*Bundesgerichtshof*) and was continously developed, beginning with judgement in 1956 and 1958.[452] This development can be explained as a reaction to ongoing social change, including the decline of traditional barriers based on social norms protecting privacy, as a response to new technologies of information and communication permitting deep intrusions into privacy, and last but not least a reaction to the increasing relevance of the mass media.[453] Protection of the right to privacy by liability rules was indeed the predominant approach of German courts and legal doctrine until very recently. Infringement of these rights, as noted by Ott and Schafer, were regarded as torts, resulting in claims for damage compensation.

---

446 Ibid.

447 Ibid., referring to A Tunc, 'Quatorze ans après: Le systeme d'indemnisation neo-zelandais', in RIDC, 1-1989, p. 140; T. G. Ison, 'Accident Compensation: A Commentary on the New Zealand Scheme' (London: Croom Helm, 1980): "Changes to the Accident Compensation System: An International Perspective" in (1993) 23 VUWLR, 25.

448 Ibid.

449 Ott & Schafer (2008), supra note 1681, p. 50. See § 823 Abs. 1 BGB.

450 Ibid. See § 12 BGB.

451 Ibid.

452 Ibid., p. 51.

453 Ibid., p. 52-53.

***

In Common law systems, the payment of damages constitutes true fulfillment of the contractual promise. Whereas, in Civil law systems, contract liability is an effect arising from breach or sanction.[454] Thus, for a civil lawyer, the amount of damages as contractually agreed upon is always intended to be higher than the loss.[455] In the field of penalty clauses in contract law, Common law courts may declare unenforceable a penalty sum as agreed upon under contract by virtue of the principle of just compensation,[456] and Civil law courts may only reduce a grossly excessive contractual agreed sum for penalty. Such agreed sums exceeding the actual loss of the promise are unlikely to be enforced by Anglo-American judges,[457] and those deemed extremely high by Continental European judges are also moderated.[458]

The most illustrative case on the American common law of penalties is *Banta v. Stamford Motor Co.,* (1914) opinion which firstly delineated the test to determine whether a provision for the payment of a contractually agreed [stipulated] sum in the event of a breach of contract will be regarded as one for liquidated damages.[459] This test was formed by three conditions:

---

454 Ignacio Marin Garcia, 'Enforcement of Penalty Clauses in Civil and Common Law: A Puzzle to be Solved by the Contracting Parties', in European Journal of Legal Studies, Volume 5, Issue 1 (Spring/Summer 2012), pp. 98-123. Judge Holmes noted that 'the duty to keep a contract at common law means a prediction that you must pay damages if you do not keep it, - nothing else' - Holmes (1897), supra note 903, p. 457, 477. See also Fernando Pantaleon Prieto, 'Las nuevas bases de la responsabilidad contractual' in (1992) 46 Anuario de Derecho Civil 1719, 1737-1740.

455 Ibid. See Ugo Mattei, 'The Comparative Law and Economics of Penalty Clauses in Contracts', in 43 Am. J. Comp. Law, 427 (1995), p. 428.

456 Ibid. In these jurisdictions, contract law does not aim to force the promisor to perform, but to compensate adequately the aggrieved promise, E. Allan Farnsworth, 'Contracts,' (4th edn, Aspen 2004) 811. Regarding the principle of just compensation, the holdings of two cases, one American and the other English, are very illustrative of the fact that in common law systems freedom of contract encompasses such a wide autonomy for the parties to enter a contract, but a much more restrictive one to arrange remedies against its breach. First, in Jaquith v Hudson, 5 Mich. 123 (Mich. 1858), the Supreme Court of Michigan stated that 'courts will not permit the parties by express stipulation, or any form of language, however clear the intent, to set it aside.' Second, in Addis v Gramophone Co. [1909] AC 488 (HL), the House of Lords insisted that 'damages for breach of contract [are] in the nature of compensation, not punishment.'

457 Ibid. Nevetheless, English law and American state laws present substantially different regimes governing liquidation of damages, with respect to the analysis of its validity and the legal consequences for a penalty clause.

458 Ibid.

459 Ibid., p. 84. See Banta v. Stamford Motor Co., 92 A 665 (Conn. 1914), the

(1) the damages to be anticipated as resulting from the breach must be uncertain in amount or difficult to prove; (2) there must have been an intent on the part of the parties to liquidate them in advance; and (3) the amount stipulated must be a reasonable one, that is to say, not greatly disproportionate to the presumable loss or injury.[460] The subsequent case law further elaborated this test in such a way that the second condition, the intent of the parties, did not survive over time;[461] and the third condition has been relaxed in the sense that the reasonableness of the amount agreed/ stipulated may also be ascertained in the light of both the anticipated or actual loss, instead of only the anticipated loss at the time of contracting (in *Banta*, the so-called presumable loss).[462] In addition, the difficulty of proof of loss at the moment of contracting as the other relevant factor for the assessment of the reasonability of the amount stipulated still continues,[463] although the case of proof alone should not be purported to deem the agreed sum as a penalty.[464]

Supreme Court of Errors of Connecticut upheld as a valid liquidation of damages the agreed sum of $ 15 a day for delay in the delivery of a luxury yacht priced at $ 5,500.

460 Ibid. See Banta v. Stamford Motor Co, Ibid., pp. 667-668.

461 Ibid. Restatement (Second) of Contracts § 356v cmt c (1981): 'Neither the parties' actual intention as to its validity nor their characterization of the term as one for liquidated damages or a penalty is significant in determining whether the term is valid.' See also Wassenar v. Panos, 331 N.W.2d 357 (Wis. 1983), ruling the Supreme Court of Wisconsin that the 'subjective intent of the parties has little bearing on whether the clause is objectively reasonable'; Farnsworth (n 1) 817, explaining that the inquiry goes to whether the effect of upholding the stipulation improperly compels performance; Joseph M. Perillo, 'Corbin on Contracts,' (11th edn, vol. 11, Lexis Nexis 2005) 427, stating that, even in those jurisdictions which formally keep intention as an independent factor, intention is derived from an objective test, so this prong of the test is redundant.

462 Ibid. The clash between the classical requirement that the sum must be a genuine pre-estimate of the harm (reasonableness ex ante) and the alternative that the sum must be reasonable at the time of breach when compared with the actual harm (reasonableness ex post) remains unsolved. In this vein, the Restatements have never opted for one of them, and then Uniform Commercial Code either. Restatement (First) of Contracts § 339(1) (1932), without referring to any of the two criteria; Restatement (Second) of Contracts § 356 cmt b (1981), explicitly admitting both criteria, albeit acknowledging that each one leads to different results; UCC § 2-718(1) (1977).

463 Ibid. Restatement (Second) of Contracts § 356 cmt b (1981): 'If the difficulty of proof of loss is great, considerable latitude is allowed in the approximation of anticipated or actual harm. If, on the other hand, the difficulty of proof of loss is slight, less latitude is allowed in that approximation.

464 Ibid. Dan B. Dobbs, 'Law of Remedies,' vol. 3 (2nd edn. West 1993), claiming that this is the right interpretation of Restatement (Second) of Contracts § 356(1); William D. Hawkland, 'Uniform Commercial Code Series,' § 2-718:03,

The French Civil Code, as enacted in 1804, established the literal enforcement of conventional penalties in Article 1152: .. [T]orsque la convention porte que celui qui manquera de l'executer paiera une certain somme a titre de dommages-interest, il ne peut etre alloue a l'autre partie une somme plus forte ni moindre...[465] The Napoleonic Code was the model for the neighboring nations (Belgium, Italy, Portugal and Spain) and their laws copied this regulation. Nonetheless, the liberal principle of literal enforcement of penalties [as originated from Roman law] was progressively abandoned,[466] and most European legislation converged on allowing the judge to moderate those contract penalties which are grossly excessive. Thus, the judicial review of penalty clauses on the grounds of equity is the solution widely accepted by Continental European laws, since Germanic

vol. 2 (Clark Boardman Callaghan 1994), with respect to the UCC § 2-718(1) (1977), advocating that, in contrast with other common law jurisdiction, the difficulty of proof of loss at the moment of contracting has never been a requirement for the validity of the agreed damages clause in American contract law.

465 Ibid., p. 85. 'Where an agreement provides that the party who fails to perform it will pay a certain sum as damages, the other party may not be awarded a greater or lesser sum,' French Civil Code http://www.legifrance.gouv.fr accessed 10 March 2012.

466 Ibid. The Italian Civil Code enacted in 1942 (Article 1384); the Portugese Civil Code enacted in 1966 (Article 812); and in Belgium, without any statutory reform, after the Belgian Cour de cassation Judgment, 24 November 24, the case law considers that extravagant contract penalties are against the public order and, for this reason, void. In 1975, the French Civil Code was reformed too. Law No. 75-597 of 9 July 1975, JO 10 July 1975 7076, added a second paragraph to Article 1152: 'Neanmoins, le juge peut moderer ou augmenter la peine qui avait ete convenue, si elle est manifestement excessive ou derisoire. Toute stipulation contraire sera repute non ecrite ('Nevertheless, the judge may moderate or increase the agreed penalty, where it is obviously excessive or ridiculously low. Any stipulation to the contrary shall be deemed unwritten,' French Civil Code http://www.legifrance.gouv.fr accessed 10 March 2012). This article let the judge to increase or decrease a penalty found to be disproportionate. Moreover, Law No. 75-597 reformed Article 1231, governing the reduction of the penalty in case of partial performance, stating that Article 1152 was also applicable: "Lorsque l'engagement a ete execute en partie, la peine convenue peut etre diminuee par le juge a proportion de l'interet que l'execution partielle a procure au creancier, sans prejudice de l'application de l'article 1152. Toute stipulation contraire sera reputee non eerite' ('Where an undertaking has been performed in part, the agreed penalty may be lessened by the judge in proportion to the interest which the part performance has procured for the creditor, without prejudice to the application of Article 1152. Any stipulation to the contrary shall be deemed not written,'French Civil Code http://www.legifrance.gouv.fr accessed 10 March 2012). Therefore, the same penalty might be reviewed by a French judge on the grounds of partial performance and on the grounds of equity.

legal systems do also opt for it (Austria, Germany and Switzerland).[467] With some differences concerning the grounds of the judicial review, European civil law systems share the same concept of penalty clause: a provision seeking to deter breach by requiring the payment of extra-compensatory damages.[468]

***

In the United States, civil consequences of criminal conviction exist in disparate state and federal statutes and regulations,[469] but generally there are two categories of civil consequences of a criminal conviction. The first is sanctions that flow from the fact of conviction.[470] Within those consequences, some are automatically applied and some are applied on a discretionary basis, which unsurprisingly leads to wide variation.[471] The second penalties that follow are often discretionary, from the underlying conduct.[472]

467 Ibid., p. 86. German Civil Code (BGB § 343), although the German Commercial Code (HGB § 348) excludes contracts between professionals in the scope of their activity. Both Austrian law (§ 1336.2 Austrian Civil Code, ABGB) and Swiss law (Article 163-3 Code des obligations) admit the judicial review of disproportionate penalties too, but without a different regime for commercial contracts.

468 Ibid., pp. 86-87.

469 Colleen F. Shanahan, 'Significant Entangelments: A Framework for the Civil Consequences of Criminal Convictions,' in 49 American Criminal Law Review 2012, p. 1394. See, e.g., Am. Bar Ass'n Criminal Justice Section, Collateral Consequences Project AM. BAR. ASS'N, http://isrweb.isr.temple.edu/projects/accproject/ (last visited Mar. 5, 2012) (listing 38,012 consequences).

470 Ibid. See AM. BAR. ASS'N, ABA STANDARDS FOR CRIMINAL JUSTICE: COLLATERAL SANCTIONS AND DISCRETIONARY DISQUALIFICATION OF CONVICTED PERSONS 12 (3d ed. 2004), http://www.fedcure.org/information?USSC-Symposium-0708/dir_16Love_collateralsanctions.pdf. For example, certain convictions can lead to disqualification from voting and jury service, disqualification from federal benefits ranging from student loans to public housing, and deportation.

471 Ibid. Court Security Improvement Act of 2007, Pub. L. No. 110-177, 121 Stat. 2534 (codified as amended in scattered sections of 26 and 28 U.S.C).

472 Ibid., pp. 1394-1395. For example, those who engage in "drug-related criminal activity" (as determined by a housing agency's administrative process, not by the fact of conviction) are excluded from federally funded housing benefits. Thus, the fact of conviction does not automatically impose the consequence, and a conviction is not the only basis for imposition of the consequence. See Lease Requirements, 24 C.F.R. § 966.4 (1)(f)(12)(i)(B) (2001); see also Jenny Roberts, 'Ignorance Is Effectively Bliss: Collateral Consequences, Silence, and

One category of civil consequences of criminal convictions is additional imprisonment imposed on the defendant by civil statute in addition to the incarceration imposed by a criminal sentence. This situation arises in different context including civil commitment, the use of the plea to impose a different criminal sentence than that charged, and revocation of parole. Civil commitment – whether for mental health reasons or under a state's sexual violent predator – is a civil consequence of a criminal conviction that leads to additional detention.[473] There are other civil consequences of criminal convictions that are deprivation of liberty, but do not involve additional incarceration. The classic example of this type of consequence is sex offender registries. A sex offender registry is plainly civil – stemming from a civil statute and involving civil law – but also necessarily flows from a criminal conviction.[474] A final category of civil consequences of criminal convictions [that is useful to help understand the significant entanglement framework] is financial loss. Certainly, a number of civil consequences of criminal convictions can fall in this category, but two are useful for explanatory purposes. The first is loss of licensing or access to a job, and the second is forfeiture of assets as a civil penalty subsequent to conviction.[475]

Criminal law, in theory at least, contains a proportionality principle, requiring that the punishment 'fit' the crime. Punishment should be proportional to the culpability of the actor and the seriousness of the harm or wrong he has committed or threatened.[476] Criminal law contains a much broader spectrum of fault or culpability than does tort law. The spectrum is wider along two dimensions: the state of mind or *mens rea* element and the conduct or social harm element. Thus, the requisite culpable state of mind in criminal law ranges from strict liability to negligence to recklessness to knowledge to purpose, with punishment varying according to *mens rea*. (The multiple degrees and categories of homicide are the best example of this range). And the conduct or social harm element also ranges enormously.[477] The main functions of criminal law are (1) the state inflicts stigma on defendant; (2) the state inflicts suffering on defendant; (3) deterrence of future crimes (by the threat of criminal sanctions); (4) the state incapacitates the defendant (sometimes); and (5) reinforcement of

---

Misinformation in the Guilty-Plea Process', in 95 IOWA L. REV. 119 (2009), p. 136 n.65 (providing examples of cases where nolo contendere pleas still incur collateral consequences).

473 Ibid., p. 1419. See, e.g., Marco T. Torres, 'Direct and Collateral Consequences after Padilla v. Kentucky,' 22 S.C.Law.16 (2011) (discussing civil commitment in the context of South Carolina's Sexually Violent Predator Act).

474 Ibid., p. 1423.

475 Ibid., p. 1425.

476 Simons (2008), supra note 1680, pp. 720-721.

477 Ibid., p. 722.

social norms. The normative principles – suggestive, but nonexhaustive - underlying criminal law are retributive justice, expressive or communicative justice, deterrence in order to promote efficiency and deterrence in order to prevent serious wrongs or rights-violations.[478] One common formulation of retributive justice is that the state should punish defendant according to what he justly deserves. Expressive or communicative justice focuses on whether the state should communicate, through public condemnation, that defendant has committed a serious wrong.[479] The purpose of criminal law is to put convicted criminals behind bars, or to label those convicted of a crime as criminals.[480]

The continental schools can be roughly divided into two categories – the absolutists and the relativists.[481] For the absolutists, punishments are not a means to an immediate practical goal, but rather, they flow as logical consequences from a well-defined view of society and the nature of 'justice'.[482] The relativists, on the other hand, regard the law solely as a means to prevent certain undesired social activities.[483] The classicists accepted the basic outlines of the theory of just retribution but complemented it by explaining that deterrence or 'general prevention'[484] lies behind the theory

478 Ibid., pp. 729-730.

479 Ibid.

480 Ibid., p. 727.

481 Michael Brush, 'Comments – The Swedish Penal Code of 1965', in 67 Duke Law Journal (1968), p. 68. The classification proposed here is admittedly oversimplied. One must bear in mind, of course, that elements of both categories must enter into any comprehensive theory of criminal law. Nevertheless, the categorization is useful analytically, despite its limitation.

482 Ibid. The absolute theories tend to emphasize a process of societal intergration and idealistic balance in which the injury to society brought by a crime can only be compensated by the suffering and punishment of the individual criminal. Exacting "just retribution" is thought to restore balance to the community. Originally, this theory rested upon a religuous foundation, but with Immanuel Kant its basis descended to secular authorities. Although Kant's thinking had little direct effect upon Brottsbalken [Criminal Section], its impact upon the criminal law of Western Germany is pronounced. See generally Simson, 'Straffrattens Utveckling i Tyskland och Forslaget till Ny Strafflag', in 48 SvJT 594 (1968).

483 Ibid. The primary relative theory is advanced by the advocates of individual prevention. The most unique theoretical contribution made by this approach is the idea that punishment should improve the criminal by reforming him.

484 Ibid., p. 69. The current Swedish debate over the goals and values of the criminal law process centers around two terms: "allmanpreventiva" functions and "individualpreventiva" functions. These two terms most closely correspond respectively to the English categories of "deterrence" and "rehabilititation". In order to emphasize the shade of difference between the Swedish and English categories, a literal English translation of the terms, namely "general preventive" and "individual preventive", is utilized. Two other terms figure prominently today

of balance and that just retribution is necessary to maintain obedience to the laws.[485] Johna Hagstromer's version of the relativist school stressed individual prevention, and he recommended that the object of criminal law should be to neutralize the potential for crime commission by taking away the desire or by terminating the opportunity.[486] The desire could be removed through fines and imprisonment, depending upon the intensity of the will to criminality. The opportunity could be removed through imposing the death penalty or life imprisonment. According to David Nehrman Ehrenstrahle

---

in American criminal law debates ' "retribution" and "prevention". The Swedish equivalent of the term "retribution" is "vedergallning," but it no longer occupies any pace whatsoever in Swedish discussion. The term "prevention" as used in the United States refers primarily to the prevention of crime by an individual offender through having him remain in prison or executing him. Sweden has no death penalty, except in time of war, and the detention of a person in prison to prevent his further criminality does not enter into general debates, exept to the extent they concern the sanction of internment. See these: (1) Internment was originally created in 1927 with two alternative types of sentence – one intended for dangerous recidivists with mental problems, and the other for dangerous recidivists without serious mental difficulties. See 1927 SFS 107-10. It was discovered, however, that the latter category did not in fact exist. Thus, Brottsbalken established one category of internment for all recidivists and dangerous and difficult criminals. Conversation with Professor Hans Thornstedt, Faculty of Law, University of Stockholm, May 13, 1966. See also I BECKMAN, HOLMBERG, HULT & STRAHL, 'BROTTSBALKEN JAMTE FORKLARINGAR', 14 (1955); BRINCK, NYQUIST & OHLSON, 'STRAFFRATT GRUNDLAGGANDE LAROBOK I, ALLMAN STRAFFRATT ENLIGT BROTTSBALKEN', 355 (1965); 1955 NORDISK KRIMINALISTIK ARSBOK 31; (2) Conversation with Professor Hans Thornstedt on May 13, 1966; see BROTTSBALKEN, ch. 26, §§ 6-7 (1965); (3) Qwist, Om Tidsobestamda Straff 17 (1966) (student paper); (4) The problems that can arise from internment provisions are aptly illustrated by the classic case in the field, In re Maddox, 351 Mich. 358, 88 N.W. 2d. 470 (1958). This case involved a civil commitment under the Michigan sexual psychopath law. The offender was committed to the state penitentiary without a trial on the basis that his past behavior (several arrests and some minor convictions) indicated that he was a dangerous sexual psychopath. His commitment was for an indefinite term, and psychiatrists for the state declared that his mental problem required the "treatment" of being placed in a prison in precisely the same position as all other prisoners. The Michigan court ordered state officials to commit the offender to a genuine mental institution for treatment, or to release him within one month. This function might be considered to be included within the "individual preventive" function.

485 Ibid. The notion produced a problem for those who recommend such measures as conditional sentencing where the punishment was not at all certain. A certain survival of the theory of regularity is found in the modern view that certainty of discovery is more important than imposing a sanction. See STRAHL, 'DEN SVENSKA KRIMINALPOLITIKEN,' (1961), p. 93.

486 Ibid., pp. 60-70.

(1756), the purpose of punishment is purely practical.[487] As regards the punished, after a convicted has served the sentence either he cannot or dare not harm others or break the law in any other way, and as regards the rest of the society, the executed punishment is a warning.[488] Nils Fredrik Biberg (1776-1827) has advocated the view that a person is punishable only if he breaks the law knowingly and willingly.[489] He contended that temporarily mental derangement might exempt from punishment.

A penalty is punishment imposed on a wrongdoer, usually in the form of imprisonment or fine; especially, a sum of money exacted as punishment for either a wrong to the state or a civil wrong (as distinguished from compensation for the injured party's loss). Though usually, for crimes, penalties are also sometimes imposed for civil wrong.[490] The use – and misuse – of the methods of criminal law, since through centuries have been relied upon as the ultimate sanctions for the achievement and preservation of public order. Criminal sanctions are concieved as a distinctively motivated sub-class of negative sanctions or collectively enforced deprivations of value; and crime as a distinctively experienced sub-class of deviational or value depriving behavior.[491] In a period of world crisis, with advances in technology forcing an accelerated social change, the public order problem may be posed in terms of a maximum preservation of basic values in the process of such change. There is the premise that the prime function of the administration of criminal sanctions, as of other institutional arrangements in any given society, is to maximize the values of the culture.[492] Law and criminology have, indeed, come to speak of social protection (through deterrence and rehabilitation, when possible, and otherwise through incapacitation) rather than exclusively in the older symbols of vengeance, retribution and expiation. This involves recognition that deprivation should bear a rationally demonstrable relation to a desired end.[493] The modern sociological school of criminal law was led by Franz

487 Christer Svennerlind, 'Philosophical Motives For the Swedish Criminal Code of 1965,' in Philosophical Communication, Web Series, No. 52, 2009, p. 2. David Nehrman Ehrenstrahle (1695-1769), a professor of Swedish and Roman law at the University of Lund from 1721, had written excellent commentaries on the Swedish legal system of his time.

488 Ibid.

489 Ibid., p. 3. He was a Swedish legal philosopher. His lectures were published in Biberg 1830. Cf. Ovarsell, 1993, p. 85.

490 Shanahan (2012), supra note 1715, p. 1403, referring to BLACK'S LAW DICTIONARY 1247 (9th ed. 2009).

491 Dession (1947-1948), supra note 1664, p. 8.

492 Ibid., p. 10, 12.

493 Ibid., p. 14.

von Listst (1851-1919).[494] [In Sweden] An important methodological contribution of the sociological school was the introduction of dualistic system of sanctions. Under this system, penalties are tied both to specific crimes to serve the general preventive function and to the particular situation of the offender to serve the individual preventive function.[495] Social defense theorists emphasize the individual preventive function of the criminal law and endorse imprisonment or fines only where the science of criminology has not advanced far enough to provide other alternatives. The basic recommendations of this school include: (1) protect society rather than punish offenders; (2) neutralize offenders by non-punitive measures such as treatment; (3) effect individual prevention rather than general prevention; (4) humanize the law to maintain the dignity of the offender.[496]

According to the provision in Chapter I, Section 3 of the Swedish Penal Code the sanctions for a crime are either *punishments* or *other sanctions for a crime*. The concept of criminal sanction (sanction for a crime) is consequently broader than the concept of punishment. Punishments are only fines and imprisonment. In addition to these punishments, there are also conditional sentence, probation and committal for special care as sanctions for a crime. In addtition to these sanctions for a crime the law also states some special consequences of a crime: Apart from a sanction, a crime may, in accordance with what is provided, result in forfeiture of property, corporate fines or some other special consequences defined by law and may also entail liability for the payment of damages.[497]

A diversification in the sanctions available through the criminal law has paralleled the diversification of civil sanctions. [In the United States] The Federal Criminal Code of 1984 greatly expanded the range of criminal fines,[498] and both federal and state criminal sanctions now include options like restitutions, the payment of some enforcement costs, and reparative remedies such as community service.[499] This diversification of the criminal sanction is directly relevant to the expansion of civil sanctions in two ways. First, the development of criminal sanctions in new directions suggests that the desire to avoid procedural protections associated with

494 Brush (1968), supra note 1721, p. 70.

495 Ibid.

496 Ibid., p. 71. See generally ANCEL, 'SOCIAL DEFENSE' (Routledge & Paul trans., 1965).

497 Per Ole Traskman (2003), 'Harmonisation des Sanctions Penales – Constant: Sweden', in M. Delmas-Marty edition, in DC3595CH14-RAPPORTS-NATIONAUX, pp. 185-186. [the author is an LL.D. Professor of Criminal Law, University of Lund].

498 Zimring (1992), supra note 1663, p. 1904.

499 Ibid.

criminal prosecution is not the sole force behind the trend toward more diversified sanction systems. The same forces are evidently at work within the criminal justice systems.[500] Second, the increased variety of criminal sanctions alters the opportunity costs associated with the restriction of civil sanctions. If only civil sanctions could provide very large money fine, the comparative advantage of large fines would become part of the argument for supporting the civil sanctioning system. Once the criminal law catches up with administrative systems in the size and variety of available money sanctions, the case for a civil system must rest on considerations other than the types of sanctions available.[501]

As to crime victims, the Council of Europe's recommendations on the position of the victim within the framework of criminal law and criminal procedure and on the assistance to victims and the prevention of victimization refer also to the new concern for the crime victim and frame victim policies designed also to recognize the crime victim in the system of criminal sanctions. Among the policies derived from the victim's perspectives - it is restitution (or compensation) and victim-offender-conciliation which in one way or another have been incorporated into penalty systems. However, restitution or compensation orders are mostly attached to probation or suspended prison sentences or serve as conditions to be fulfilled in exchange for non-prosecution.[502] It is interesting to see why restitution suddenly received so much attention in the 1980s and how these grounds may fit into penal policies developed since then. Different answers can be found here. It's first of all the perspective of the victim which has to be taken into consideration. It has been claimed that victims of crime are marginalized in the criminal processes, which emphasizes solely the offender. Indeed, concentrating the criminal procedure and criminal penalties on the offender [being] matched with the legal theory as prevention, either pursued through individual or general deterrence or through rehabilitation or incapacitation represented the main goal of criminal law and its implementation. When rehabilitative efforts as well as deterrence failed to demonstrate at least significant effects, the vacuum left behind could be easily filled with a new rationale for responding to the offender: restitution and compensation for the victim.[503] In particular, from the victims' policy perspective, compensation and restitution are open to various crime policies. These devices can be used to make the system more punitive and to demonstrate the offenders' accountability. It seems that

---

500 Ibid.

501 Ibid.

502 Hans-Jorg Albrecht, 'Sanction Policies and Alternative Measures to Incarceration: European Experiences with Intermediate and Alternative Criminal Penalties', in Resource Material Series No. 80. UNAFEI, Tokyo (1987), p. 37.

503 Ibid.

recently the punitive aspects of compensation and restitution are receiving more recognition. From a practical point of view, however, it must be noted that compensation and restitution constitute a main response or a sole penalty range far behind imprisonment, probation and day-fines.[504]

Germany has adopted a two-track system of criminal sanctions: one track for criminal punishment (which requires a finding of guilt and the determination of a fine or a prison sentence) and another providing for so-called measures for rehabilitation and protection of public security.[505] The second track measures do not depend on personal responsibility. Instead, they are the consequence of a finding of danger[ousness] (based on assessment of risks presented to the court by forensic psychologists or psychiatrists) and a corresponding need for treatment of preventive detention.[506] This two-track approach is based on the belief that proportional punishment limited by the principle of personal guilt may not be sufficient to respond effectively (in terms of public protection) to habitual offenders or offenders suffering from mental deseases or addictions to alcohol or drugs who are likely to recidivate. German criminal law (as well as the criminal law of other continental European countries, such as Denmark, Austria, and Switzerland) therefore provides for a line of criminal sanctions that pursues prevention of serious recidivism alone. In Germany, preventive detention (*Sicherungsverwahrung*) may be imposed in place of a prison sentence of two years or more if – besides some formal conditions referring to prior convictions – the status of a habitual felon and danger[ousness] are established.[507] When considering developments in the second track (measures of rehabilitation and security), we find a long-term decline in the number of offenders sentenced to incapacitating preventive detention. This trend was reversed in the mid-1990s, when dangerous-sexual-offender legislation widened the applicability of preventive detention. This development was stopped by a series of decisions of the European Court of Human Rights and ultimately by a landmark decision of the German Federal Constitutional Court declaring all second track provisions related to preventive detention (*Sicherungsverwahrung*) to be unconstitutional (due to violation of the principle of proportionality) and fixing a time limit of 2013 for the Federal Parliament to enact legislation in line with the Basic

504 Ibid.

505 Hans-Jorg Albrecht, 'Sentencing in Germany: Explaining Long-Term Stability in the Structure of Criminal Sanctions and Sentencing', in Law and Contemporary Problems, Vol. 76:211, (2013), p. 213, referring to Hans-Jorg Albrecht, 'Security Gaps: Responding to Dangerous Sex Offenders in the Federal Republic of Germany', in 16 FE. SENT'G REP. 200 (2004), p. 2004.

506 Ibid.

507 Ibid.

Law (*Grundgesetz*, German Constitution).[508] Hassemer has interpreted the role of the second track as relieving the system of criminal penalties and sentencing from pressure to consider danger[ousness] and security when imposing criminal punishment. A system of punishment determined and restricted by personal guilt will be in all societies – focusing on risk and the management of risk – confronted with an enormous pressure to accept risk and the prevention of risk as a salient goal.[509] Criminal courts thus have responded to the amendment of 1998 as Hassemer has suggested.[510]

The German system of criminal sanctions is simple and provides for only two penal sanctions: day fines and imprisonment. Day fines come with a minimum of five-day finess and a maximum of 360-day fines; prison sentence in general may range from one month to fifteen years.[511] Criminal punishment after the reform was imposed in the same way and with the same result as was done before. The course of criminal punishment evidently does not reflect security concerns. This is in line with decisions of the Federal Court of Justice (*Bundesgerichtshof*) holding that incapacitation may not be invoked as grounds in sentencing since the second track of criminal sanctions provides for exclusive rules regarding security and protection of the public.[512] The second track of sanctions, a major issue of law reform aiming at protection of the public in the 1990s and in the new millennium does not affect the structure and stability of criminal punishment, but serves evidently as a safety valve that exposes few offenders (a negligible number in terms of structure and structural impact) assessed to be dangerous in rather complex and complicated proceedings to indeterminate confinement.[513]

In the Netherlands, the principal penalties are set out in article 9 of Dutch Criminal Code in order of severity (according to the opinion of the Dutch legislator) as follows: imprisonment; detention; service penalty; a fine.[514] The system of Dutch criminal law incorporates general

---

508 Ibid., p. 221.

509 Ibid., referring to Winfried Hassemer, 'Sicherheit durch Strafrecht', in 7 HRRS-STRAFRECHT (2006), p. 131.

510 Ibid., p. 226, referring to Hassemer (2006), Ibid., p. 133.

511 Ibid., p. 215.

512 Ibid., p. 226.

513 Ibid., p. 229.

514 Tijs Kooijmans, 'Harmonisation Des Sanction Penales – Constant : The Netherland,' Scientific Bureau of the Supreme Court of the Netherlands and the Law School of the Erasmus University, Rotterdam, in a report edited by M. Delmas-Marty, 2003: 200. Capital punishment for ordinary crimes was abolished in 1870. For military crimes and war crimes capital punishment was abolished in 1983 but in practice it has not been used since 1950. See P.J.P. TAK, 'the Dutch Criminal Justice System', Essay on Dutch Criminal Policy, in Wolf Legal Production,

minimum penalties: general provisions in which the minimum penalties for (in principle all) offences are described. Dutch criminal law doesn't incorporate special minimum penalties.[515] The law incorporates special maximum penalties: each criminal provision incorporates the maximum (custodial and pecuniary) penalty prescribed for specific offences. The limits of the maximum penalties are prescribed in general provisions. The system of special maximum penalties is supplemented by general and special aggravating and mitigating circumstances.[516] The Dutch Criminal Code acknowledges three additional penalties: deprivation of specific rights; forfeiture; publication of judgment.[517] The Dutch system of criminal sanctions not only incorporates (principal and additional) penalties, but also measures.[518] Unlike the penalties, the measures do not primarily react to an offence but to an unwanted situation that has been constituted or revealed by the offence. For that reason, the primary aim of measures is not to punish an offender but to finish the unwanted situation. For example, the aim of the measure of withdrawal [of goods from market] is to finish the unwanted situation that a dangerous object is in circulation.[519] Unlike the penalties, the measures do not primarily react to an offence and their primary aim is not to punish (retribute).[520]

Nijmegen, 2002, p. 59. According to article 114 of the Dutch Constitution, capital punishment cannot be imposed.

515 Ibid. pp. 200-201. The law of the European part of the Kingdom of the Netherlands doesn't acknowledge special minimum penalties. The Criminal Code of the Dutch Antils incorporates a few provisions (articles 438a and 438b) with special minimum penalties for second offenders, and so does some other legislation of the Dutch Antils. In October 2002, two members of the second Chamber (Lower House) introduced a legislative proposal introducing minimum penalties for grave offences such as murder and rape. However, there seems to be much opposition to this proposal. Therefore, it is not sure whether this proposal will ever become a law.

516 Ibid. pp. 203.

517 Ibid., p. 201. The term additional is misleading insofar that in cases in which the law allows the imposition of an additional penalty, this penalty may be imposed either separately or in conjunction with principal penalties and in conjunction with other additional penalties. See article 9 paragraph 5 of Criminal Code. Specific additional penalty in (article 7 of) the Economic Offences Act is the whole or partial close down of the company of the convicted person. A specific additional penalty in (article 179, 179a and 180 of) the Road Traffic Act 1994 is the disqualification from driving.

518 Ibid., p. 202. See for an extensive overview T. Kooijmans, 'Op maat geregeld?' (Deventer: Kluwer, 2002).

519 Ibid. For that reason, it seems plausible that this measure could be imposed in order to withdraw objects that have been used in terrorist actions.

520 Ibid.

***

Administrative penalties are a mechanism for enforcing compliance with regulatory legislation. They are monetary penalties assessed and imposed by a regulator without recourse to a court or independent administrative tribunal.[521] An administrative penalty is payable when the regulator, not a court, determines that a breach of the regulatory legislation has occurred.[522] A recent survey of the use of administrative penalties in Canada observed that it is only relatively recently that they have become a favorite tool among regulators, but they have been increasingly used to engender compliance and cooperation from the 'regulated community', to secure environmental or consumer protection.[523] In most cases, administrative penalties are imposed on individuals and businesses that have been licensed to undertake regulated activities. Administrative penalties are used in these cases to enforce the terms of the license.[524] Some critics have argued that administrative penalties are, despite their characterization by regulators and legislators, essentially [for] criminal or quasi-criminal offences. If this is the case, extra-judicial assessment of 'guilt' would likely conflict with section 11 of the *Charter of Rights and Freedom*.[525] The constitutionality of administrative penalties was addressed in 2004 by the Supreme Court of Canada in *Martineau v. MNR*, 2004 SCC 81,[2004] 3 S.C.R. 737, where the Court upheld provisions in the Customs Act allowing customs officials to declare property illegally imported into Canada forfeit without obtaining a court order. Although the provision in question was not an administrative penalty in the strict sense, it is analogous

521 Law Reform Commission of Saskatchewan, Administrative Penalties, Final Report, University of Saskatchewan, Saskatoon, SK S7N 5A6, March 2012, p. 2. Thus, the Australian Law Reform Commission (ALRC) defined administrative penalties as "sanctions imposed by the regulator, or by the regulator's enforcement of legislation, without intervention by a court or tribunal": ALRC, Principled Regulation: Federal Civil and Administrative Penalties in Australia (Final Report) (March 2003), p. 78.

522 Ibid. Because administrative penalties are not characterized as offences, they are not quasi-criminal in nature. Assessment of a penalty is not an offence, nor is a conviction registered.

523 Ibid., referring to Amanda Tait, 'The Use of Administrative Monetary Penalties in Consumers Protection' (Ottawa: Public Interest Advocacy Centre (PIAC), 2007, p. 5.

524 Ibid.

525 Ibid., p. 4, referring to Peter Hogg, who has written extensively on the Charter, made the contention in strong terms in an Opinion Letter dated October 17, 2005, written on behalf of the Retail Council of Canada and presented at hearings on Bill C-19, An Act to amend the Competition Act.

in allowing a regulatory sanction to be imposed without recourse to the courts. The *Martineau* decision establishes the proposition that administrative penalties are not objectionable in principle; but the decision is unlikely to end questions about administrative penalties. Although the adequacy of safeguards was not directly in issue in *Martineau*, the Court assumed that the administrative regime met the minimum standards of natural justice, and that its purpose was truly regulatory rather than punitive.[526]

During the past ten years [in the United States], the assessment of dollar fines for violations of federal regulations has become the most popular sanction utilized by administrative agencies to enforce their regulatory schemes.[527] The use of these fines,[528] termed civil money penalties,[529] has

526 Ibid., pp. 4-5.

527 Russel L. Hewit and Wiliam P. Wallace, Jr., 'Administrative Civil Money Penalties and the Right to Jury Trial-Notes & Comments', in Washington and Lee Law Review Vo. XXXIII -1976, p. 719. The amount of civil money penalties collected by federal agencies nearly doubled from 5.8 million dollars in 1967 to 10.5 million dollars in 1971. Additionally, it was estimated that the 1971 figure would probably triple within a few years. Goldschmid, 'An Evaluation of the Present and Potential Use of Civil Money Penalties as a Sanction by Federal Administrative Agencies', in 2 RECOMMENDATIONS & REPORTS OF THE ADMINISTRATIVE CONFERENCE OF THE UNITED STATES, 896, 903, 905 (1973).

528 Ibid. The money penalty is but one of many sanctions available to administrative agencies for enforcing their regulations. For a discussion of other enforcement techniques see Gellhorn, 'Administrative Prescription and Imposition of Penalties', in 1970 WASH. U. L. Q., p. 265; McKay, 'Sanctions in Motion: The Administrative Process', in 49 IOWA L.REV. (1964), p. 441; Murphy, 'Money Penalties – An Administrative Sword of Damocles', in 2 SANTA CLARA LAWYER, (1962), p. 113.

529 Ibid. A money penalty may be either criminal or civil. To determine whether a sanction is civil or criminal, courts generally consider the purpose of the sanction – if it is primarily remedial it is considered civil, if it is primarily punitive it is considered criminal. See Kennedy v. Mendoza-Martinez, 372 U.S. 144 (1963); United States ex rel Marens v. Hess, 317 U.S. 537 (1943). However, in an administrative proceeding money penalties re considered civil because an agency may not impose criminal sanctions. I K. DAVIS, 'ADMINISTRATIVE LAW TREATISE', § 2.13 (1958); L. JAFFE, 'JUDICIAL CONTROL OF ADMINISTRTIVE ACTION', 109-15 (1965); 1 T. VOM BAUR, 'FEDERAL ADMINISTRATIVE LAW', § 81 (Supp. 1947). To avoid an improper delegation of the judicial authority to decide criminal actions, Congress merely labels money penalties assessed by administrative agencies as "civil", and the court generally accept this congressional characterization. See Halvering v. Mitchell, 303 U.S. 391 (1938); Hepner v. United States, 213 U.S. 103 (1909); Atlas Roofing Co. v OSHRC, 518 F.2d 990 (5th Cir. 1975); Goldschmid (1973), supra note 1779, at part C, 913-16; Comment, The Imposition of Administrative Penalties and the Right to Trial by Jury – An Unheralded Expansion of Criminal Law? 65 J. CRIM. L & C. 345, 351-53 (1974).

increased primarily because they are administratively advantegeous. According to Goldschimd as quoted by Hewit and Wallace, the penalties affect only the wrongdoer; they are flexible, thereby enhancing an agency's ability to achieve its statutory goals; and they are less severe than other administrative sanctions, such as license revocation.[530]

Administrative sanction, according to Articicle 5:2 of Dutch General Administrative Law Act [text as per October 1, 2009], is an obligation imposed or an entitlement withheld by an administrative authority on account of a violation. In addition to administrative sanction, the Act also defines reparation sanction and punitive sanction. Reparation sanction is an administrative sanction intended to fully or partially undo or terminate a violation, to prevent repetition of a violation or to eliminate or limit the consequences of a violation; and punitive sanction is an administrative sanction intended to inflict harm on the violator. Under Article 5:40, punitive sanction is administrative fine which is in form of an unconditional obligation to pay a sum of money. A reparation sanction may be imposed as soon as there is a clear threat of a violation (Article 5:7). A reparation sanction is in form of an adiministrative enforcement order, which requires full or partial reparation of the violation, and empower the administrative authority to carry out the order itself if it is not carried out or not carried out in time (Article 5:12). Any order subject to a financial penalty means a reparation sanction which requires full or partial reparation of the violation and requires payment of a sum of money in the event the order is not carried out or not carried out in time (Article 5: 31d). An administrative authority should not impose an administrative fine if criminal proceedings have been brought against the violator for the same act and the hearing has started or a punishment order has been

---

Several commentators have critized the courts' ready acceptance of administrative money penalties as "civil" merely because Congress has so designated the penalties. The commentators assert that the courts have failed fully to analyze the nature of the penalties and that, therefore, a defendant is deprived of constitutional rights guaranteed to one accused of a crime. See Charney, 'The Need for Constitutional Protections for Defendants in Civil Penalty Cases', in 59 CORNELL L. REV. (1974), p. 478; McKay (1964), Ibid., pp. 443-45; One commentator, however, favors the use of civil money penalties by administrative agencies. He emphasizes that an important function of the money penalties is to punish individuals for, and deter other individuals from, violating administrative regulations. He concludes that money penalties designated as civil by Congress will be accepted by the courts of the penalties; "(1) are rationally related to a regulatory (or revenue collecting) scheme; (2) do not deal with offenses which are mala in se .....; [and] (3) may be expected to have a prophylactic or remedial effect." Goldschimd (1973), Ibid., p. 914 (footnote omitted).

530 Ibid., pp. 719-720, referring to Goldschimd (1973), Ibid., pp. 910-911.

issued (Article 5:44). An administrative fine imposed on account of an act which is also a criminal offence is cancelled in the event the court of appeal, applying article 12i of the Code of Criminal Procedure, orders that the offender must be prosecuted for the offence (Article 5:47).

Administrative sanction in Romanian law can be divided into *contraventional sanctions*, considered to be the most important category, and *other administrative sanctions*. Government Ordinance No. 2/2001 regulates the legal regime for contraventions. Initially, a new sanction was added to the main sanctions established by Law No. 32/1968: obliging the offender to carry out community service. To the framework dispositions in Government Ordinance No. 2/2001,[531] the Ordinance added dispositions concerning the procedure for applying and executing the sanctions of contraventional imprisonment and obliging the offender to carry out community service. According to the Ordinance, contraventions that are sanctioned by obliging the offender to carry out community service can only be laid down in specific laws and must always have a fine as an alternative sanctions. The definition of contravention, according to Law No. 32/1968, was that a contravention had been an illicit form of conduct with a lesser degree of social danger compared to a penal offence. Government Ordinance No. 2/2001 excludes from the definition of contravention the proviso that it has a lesser degree of social danger compared to a penal offence. According to Fodor, legal literature still agrees, however, that the reduced degree of social danger is a characteristic of the contravention as well as of any conduct that results in an administrative offence.[532] Features of contraventional sanctions that mirror their penal origin are the division of sanctions into main sanctions – having a punitive character – and complementary sanctions – having a predominantly preventive or reparatory character.[533] Complementary sanctions have also been established, such as the confiscation of goods, closing down production or preventing a certain activity, suspending the activity, suspending or withdrawing a licence for developing an activity, blocking a bank account, halting certain works and restoring land to its original conditions. These complementary sanctions are mostly of a preventing or reparatory nature.[534] Administrative sanctions may have a punitive character, such as a fine. Other measures are of a predominantly preventive nature. Administrative sanctions with a remedial character are considered to be, for example, surcharges or prohibiting certain works and restoring land to its original condition.[535]

531 Fodor (2007), supra note 1655, p. 3.

532 Ibid., p. 4.

533 Ibid.

534 Ibid., p. 3.

535 Ibid., p. 6.

Legal sanctions are remedial or punitive. They are remedial in the sense that they are designed to compensate or recoup losses. Being punitive, sanctions are designed to penalize actions breaking the law and do have the character of punishment. Sanctions do also have the character of deterrence to discourage, stop or prevent from acting by fear, danger, difficulty, or other considerations which disheartens or countervails the motive for the act. Legal sanctions under administrative law, such as money penalties and license suspension or revocation, are to be imposed upon any violations of regulatory legislation. Legal sanctions safeguard the normativity and prescriptivity of legal rule. Legal sanctions the theories of which follow, *inter alia*, the theories of justice as sketched out in Chapter III.4.1.2 are prescribed by rule of law that generates legal determinations including judicial decisions, alternative dispute resolutions, and customary or undisputed law practice in society.

CHAPTER IV

Transformational-Generative Legal Reasoning

IV.1. FACT-FINDINGS

IV.1.1. FACT

Facts of a particular case determine which legal rule is applicable. Facts make legal rules applicable. Which facts are the facts of a certain case will be clear if such a case is described. Thayer distinguishes between 'primary facts' and 'secondary or ultimate facts'.[1] Fact-finding is the establishment of facts of a case. A fact is either a state of thing, that is, in existence, or a motion, that is, an event (1 Benth.Jud.Ev.48). Fact (*factum, fait*) stands in lawbooks for an act, or as designating what exists, in contradistinction to what should exist (*de facto* as contrasted to *de jure*), or indicating things, events, actions, conditions, as happening, existing, really taking place (Thayer, Evid. 190) (Black's Law Dictionay, p. 706). Thayer asserted: "The question of whether a thing be a fact or not, is the question of whether it is, whether it exists, whether it be true".[2] He argues that 'the right inference or conclusion [from these primary facts], in point of fact, is itself [a] matter of fact'.[3] The interpretation of writing, when conducted on the basis of the ascertained facts, involved questions of fact, not law.[4] According to Thayer, questions of fact mean questions of 'ultimate fact', the facts 'in issue to be decided by the jury'.[5] Justice Frankfurter, in *Baumgartner v United States,* also distinguished ultimate facts from primary or evidentiary fact, in an attempt to break out from the constraints imposed by Rule 52(a) upon the review of findings of fact by reviewing courts[6]. In *Goodman v. Lukens Steel Co,*[7] the process of fact identification is sometimes described as

1 George C. Christie, 'Articles – Judicial Review of Findings of Fact, 1992, in NORTHWESTERN UNIVERSITY LAW REVIEW, Vol. 87, No. 1, n.112, referring to James B.Thayer, 'A Preliminary Treatise on Evidence at the Common Law', (1898), p. 194.

2 Ibid., p. 38, referring to Thayer (1898), Ibid., p. 191.

3 Ibid., n.23, referring to Thayer (1898), Ibid., p. 194.

4 Ibid., n.112, referring to Thayer (1898), Ibid., pp. 203-204.

5 Ibid., referring to Thayer (1898), Ibid., p. 197.

6 Ibid., p. 54. See Justice Frankfurter in Baumgartner v. United States.

7 Ibid., p. 38. See e.g., Goodman v. Lukens Steel Co., 483 U.S. 656, 665 (1987).

the process of establishing 'historical fact'.[8] Christie thinks that Thayer's analysis is not sufficient. It is untenable to consider that 'reasoning' is the ultimate facts only. In addition, the notion of 'inference' which includes the ultimate facts only does not capture the evaluation and characterizing the mass of evidence as presented to it. Roy Stone proposes fact categories: *alpha* facts and *aleph* facts.[9] *Alpha* facts were the facts determined by direct observation; *aleph* facts were the facts determined by reflection after all the evidence is in.

As it stands, Montrose's distinction between 'words which refer to classes of facts and words which refer to particular facts' is in need of some further clarification. We employ words of the first type continually when we refer to particular facts. The purpose of descriptive statements of the facts in judgments is to acquaint the reader with the relevant events, to put him in the position in which he would be if he had personally witnessed the events which led to the dispute. If the reader is already familiar with a thing, the best way of evoking it for him is to use its name. No 'level of generality' problem can arise, for names are entirely specific: they simply 'point to' some temporally and spatially unique thing. We are concerned with the judicially established version of the facts which may or may not differ from the true facts. Moreover, the statement of the facts which we find in judgments is already heavily selective: much that cannot be of any legal relevance has already been ignored. The judge will usually only establish and relate what is conceivably of some legal relevance.[10] The description of fact under a legal rule usually comprises several relevant pre-requisites, indicating that how to find one disqualifying fact which excludes the whole situation or eliminates a large number of possibilities is probably the most effective way in initial identification steps.[11] Jaap Hage identifies elementary fact which constitutes a reason in legal reasoning. Take an imaginary example that 'John took away Mary's car and Mary did not allow him to take away her car'. These facts constitute an elementary compound fact, being the reason, that is a *constitutive* reason, to legally classify John as a thief.[12]

In the debate on the distinction of jurisdictional and constitutional fact, Monaghan noted that the difficulty experienced by the Court in *Bose Corp. v. Consumers Union of United States, Inc.,* (466 U.S. 485 (1984)) in trying to apply (and extend) the doctrine of constitutional fact 'had its origin in the 'vexing' distinction between 'questions of law' and 'questions of fact.

8 Ibid., n.123.

9 Ibid., p. 38, referring to Roy Stone-deMontpensier, 'The Compleat Wrangler' in 50 MIN.L.REV. 1001 (1966), pp. 1009-1010 & n.27.

10 Lucke (1989), supra note 1643, p. 43.

11 Wahlgren (2009), supra note 1357, p. 214.

12 Hage (1996), supra note 1410, p. 5.

Some commentators, such as Louis Jaffe, have rejected this distinction as 'fundamentally incoherent', but Monaghan believes, "...[t]he incoherence argument seems vastly overdrawn". Law and fact are not opposites but rather concepts that have a 'nodal quality; they are points of rest and relative stability on a continuum of experience.[13] 'Factual findings' should not be construed to mean simply 'facts', as opposed to 'opinion' or 'conclusions' (*Beech Aircraft Corp.. v. Rainey*, 488 U.S. 153, 161-70 (1988). A factual finding unless it is a simple report of something observed, is an opinion as to what more basic facts imply (*Beech Aircraft*, 488 U.S. p. 168).[14] As to 'facts', Christie has drawn a certain conclusion.[15] All our conclusions are the product of some mental process, and this does not prevent some of our conclusion from being more open to challenge than others.

IV.1.2. ESTABLISHED FACT

Facts to be determined by a fact-finder in a legal case are relevant facts to some appropriate standard of proof. Highly specific evidence may prove particularized facts. The public prosecutor in criminal cases must specifically prove the allegation that all elements of the accused crime were factually committed by the defendant 'beyond a reasonable doubt'. The plaintiff in any civil case must prove it was 'more probable than not' that the defendant violated the law in the manner as argued, and this standard is known as proving the case to a 'preponderance of the evidence'. In the event that a sort of presumption in certain typical civil cases must be solved, another standard known as 'substantially more probable than not' or 'clear and convincing' applies. For example, in *Geneva Pharm., Inc. v. Glaxosmithkline* PLC, 349 F. 3d 1373, 1377 (Fed. Cir. 2003),[16] an accused patent infringer who asserts invalidity of the patent as a defense must prove invalidity by clear and convincing evidence to overcome a presumption that the patent is valid.

Trial information from the evidence received by jury is carefully controlled

13 Christie (1992), supra note 1784, p. 27, referring to Henry Monaghan, 'Constitutional Fact Review', in 85 COLUM. L. REV. (1985), p. 233. Monaghan notes that Jaffe (1965), supra note 1781, pp. 546-545, was among those who argued that this distinction is "fundamentally incoherent.

14 Ibid., n.119. See Beech Aircraft Corp. v. Rainey, 488 U.S. 153, 161-70 (1988), citing, inter alia, McCormick, 'on Evidence', 27 (Edward E. Clearly et al. eds., 3d ed. 1984), and Richard O. Lempert & Stephen A. Saltzburg, 'A Modern Approach to Evidence,' 449 (2d ed. 1982).

15 Ibid.

16 Shawn Kolitch, 'Constitutional Fact Finding and the Appropriateness of Empirical Data in Constitutional Law', in Lewis & Clark Law Review, Vol. 10:3,(2006), p. 674.

by the evidence law. This control follows the notion that jurors may overvalue or otherwise misuse various items of admittedly relevant information, so the exclusion of some relevant evidence is required by the law of evidence due to a distrust of the reasoning capacities of ordinary people. According to FRE of USA 403, a judge may exclude relevant evidence ...if its probative value is substantially outweighed by the danger of unfair prejudice, confusion of the issues, or misleading the jury..." Similarly, in order to prevent jurors from giving too much weight to information from someone who is not appearing in court, hearsay evidence is excluded. These perhaps show that the most important feature of evidence law is to exclude what figures prominently in everyday reasoning.[17] Holmes describes the process of fact identification as "*hearing evidence.. concerning what the conduct was*".[18]

Wilson holds that facts are the empirical data to be identified and classified by judges. Buchanan and Headrick say that facts are the facts that suggest some possible applicable rules. The facts being encountered in trial fact-finding have first and foremost to be related to the *legal system*.[19] Wilson argues that in this process the judge performs the mental operations of 'identification' and 'classification': identification of the empirical data – be it a present object or evidence of parts action – and its classification under a relevant legal figure.[20] The process of reasoning involved in the judge's interpretation of facts as legally relevant is made up of two heterogeneous, irreducible elements: his knowledge of the normative – legal system, whose rules, principles, categories and definitions provide the scheme of interpretation, and the evidence of the facts in the case at hand. Buchanan and Headrick say that [t]here is the process of fact recognition and characterization. The facts suggest some possibly applicable rules: these rules and the cases using them suggest the relevance and importance of certain facts. The rules that are being explored will influence the decision about which facts are relevant.[21] Working with these interrelation is one aspect of recognizing relevant facts in legal problem solving.[22] The identification process interacts with the search for legal descriptions and with the recollection (by law professionals) of prerequisites used in legal

17 Barbara Spellman & Frederick Schauer, 'Legal Reasoning', University of Virginia School of Law, February 2012, in Public Law and Legal Theory Working Paper Series 2012-09, pp. 27-28.

18 Christie (1992), supra note 1788, p. 38, referring to Oliver W. Holmes, 'Law in Science and Science in Law,' in 12 HARV. L. REV. (1899), p. 104.

19 Wahlgren (2009), supra note 1786, pp. 207-208, referring to A. Wilson, 'The Nature of Legal Reasoning,' 278, 279 (1982); B.G. Buchanan & T.E. Headrick, 'Some Speculation About Artificial Intelligence and Legal Reasoning,' 53 (1970).

20 Ibid., referring to Wilson (1982), Ibid., pp. 278, 279.

21 Ibid., referring to Buchanan & Headrick (1970), supra note 1794.

22 Ibid., p. 208.

description, and the interaction swings to and fro or back and forth between actual situation and legal description.

Various sub-processes, at least three, occur in legal identification. First, superfluous information including irrelevant or unnecessary facts often appears, so the relevant facts should be recognized and the irrelevant ones should be left out. This fact selection is what Bing and Harvold refer to as 'extracting the legal problem out of the totality'.[23] Secondly, there is also the possibility that relevant facts are few or not sufficient or incomplete, so one or more facts should be established. Referring to such a situation, Alchourron and Bulygin put forward a term 'gap of knowledge'. Third, it is also possible that the elements of description is disputed, and mutually exclusive or inconsistent facts are submitted, such as by opposing parties, in trials. It may also happen that the concepts used in the description of situation is vague, as Hart similarly refers to as 'problem of the penumbra' and Alchourron and Bulygin refer to as 'gap of recognition'.

Kelsen tries to avoid every epistemological break in judicial process by totally absorbing the *questio facti* into the *questio juri*. In empirical science there is empirical verification of natural facts, but in judicial process there is the fact of judicial ascertainment [by the judge who is the competent authortity] of empirical fact. A *legal fact* is the ascertainment itself, not a natural fact ascertained by a judge in judicial process. Thus the judicial decision has specific truth-criteria, distinct from the criteria of natural or empirical facts, but parallel with the criteria of empirical facts. The distinction resides in the normative appointment of the judge who is authorized to establish the facts to be determined in judicial process.[24] However, descriptive doctrinal writers, such as Alchourron & Bulygin, say that judicial decisions are descriptive of empirical facts (not from the control of empirical truth) and of legal rules. They argue that the absorbing of factual truth into legal truth is not acceptable, since 'empirical truth is only one and only upon it the judicial decision must be based'. The pronouncement of a judge must be measured by what has factually happened. The facts are what they are, not what judges say they are. Judge's task has many peculiarities that are not absorbed in mere description. Many determining factors contribute to fact determination in judicial process. Such determining factors have a normative character. Viola holds that the choice among different descriptions of the same fact

23 Ibid., referring to J. Bing & T. Harvold, 'Legal Decisions and Information Systems', Universitetsforlaget', Oslo (1997), p. 18; Alchourron & Bulygin (1971), supra note 1357, p. 18, 33; H.L.A. Hart, 'Positivism and the Separation of Law and Morals', in Harvard Law Review, Vol. 71 (1958), p. 607.

24 Francesco Viola, 'Judicial Truth', in Persona y Derecho, 32, 1995, p. 252, referring to Hans Kelsen, 'Reine Rechtslehre' (Wien: Auflage, Deuticke, 1960), p. 244.

has its contribution to judicial fact determination, in addition to the law of evidence. P.G. Stein says that the judge is judge of evidence too. A judge must establish [trial fact] if there are sufficient element for the evidence of a fact.[25] However, the fact identification is connected to the interpretation of legal rules. Such interpretation is often as the presupposition of the judicial fact determination as far as the judge must ascertain only all certain facts to which a legal rule has to be applied. In addition, as Wroblewski says, it is possible to design a typology of fact in accordance with the way in which the corresponding legal rules define them.

The assertions relating to what happened, 'usually responding to inquiries about who, when and where' inquiries, according to Jaffe as quoted by Monaghan, can be made by those who do not view the applicable law. Law thought may not necessarily get involved in fact identification.[26] It is in Christie's words that a more useful method of analysis would focus on the manner to answer the question of fact, such as by direct observation and by 'accepting or rejecting the testimony of witnesses who are reporting their own observations'.[27] Allen and Pardo say there is no essential epistemological difference between fact and law. Making any propositional claims about what the law is, regardless of what 'law' is in mind, is making claims of facts.[28] Lawson argues that [a] proposition by definition is the sort of statement that can be either true or false. Whatever one's metaphysical theory of law may be, any positive propositions derived from that theory are, from an epistemological standpoint, claim of fact. Any established proposition of fact or law in any context needs evidentiary support. This must entail three steps: applying rules of admissibility of evidence, employing analytic methods for measuring and combining the significance or weight of that evidence, and requiring the combined evidence's weight to exceed some standard before declaring the proposition proved. The concern here is the application of proof standards. The need for standards of proof and the effect of standards of proof on interpretive outcomes are not determined by or are free from the admissibility and significance rules

25 Ibid., p. 256, referring to P.G.Stein, 'Judgments in the European Legal Tradition', in La sentenza in Europa. Metodo, tecnica e stile, (Cedam: Padova, 1988), p. 29; J. Wroblewski, 'Meaning and Truth in Judicial Decision', second edition by A. Aarnio (Helsinki: A-Tieto Oy, 1986), p. 108.

26 Christie (1992), supra note 1793, pp. 28-29, referring to Monaghan (1985), supra note 1788, pp. 235-239.

27 Ibid., p. 39.

28 Kevin M. Clermont, 'Jurisdictional Fact', in Cornell Law Review Vol. 91, Cornell Law Library, Scholarship@Cornell Law: A Digital Repository, Cornell Law Faculty Publication, 7-24, 2006, pp. 1001-1002, referring to Ronald J. Alen & Michael S. Pardo,'Essay, The Myth of the Law-Fact Distinction', in 97 Nw. U. L. Rev. (2003), p. 1770.

of one's theory of interpretation.[29] Clermont's conclusion is that accepting a proposition is, at least implicitly, invoking a standard of proof, therefore the necessity of such standard of proof is just as real for law as for fact.[30] The trial judge, according to S.S. Diamond & M.R. Rose and J.R.P. Ogloff & V.G. Rose, may give two types of instruction to jurors. First, immediate instructions during trial is that jurors should forget information they have heard or should use some information for one purpose but not for an (obvious) other purpose.[31] For example, a witness might blurt out that he knew the defendant because they had been in prison for robbery at the same time. If the defense lawyer objects and makes a motion to strike, and the judge sustains, she will immediately instruct the jury to disregard that evidence. Then, before deliberating, the jurors are instructed about both the content of the law to the case at hand and about general procedures they should use to decide the case. The instruction about general procedure to be used to determine the trial fact includes the mandate that the jurors determine the fact in accordance with the instructed law, and not based on what they think is the right result. As to the extraction of relevant facts, Bing says that [t]he initial extraction of relevant facts or circumstances is tentative.[32] The lawyer has available, as a latent resource, the full bag of details comprising the problem as part of the world, with all its parties, witnesses and documents. At any time, the lawyer may refer back to this wealth of details, sift through them once more for extracting new facts to replace or supplement those made available in the first selection.

Spellman and Schauer say that the question of fact in any legal disputes is the initial question, since the first thing the 'trier of fact', be it jury or judge, must do is 'fact-finding', and the question of what consequences (the question of law) flow from what happened.[33] Schauer holds that judges tend to be comparatively free to consider all relevant trial information in countries where jury trial is absent.[34] In the United States, judges sitting

29 Ibid., referring to Gary Lawson, 'Proving the Law', in 86 Nw. U. L. Rev. (1992), pp. 861-77 (p. 863, 865).

30 Ibid., p. 1002.

31 Spellman & Schauer (2012), supra note 1792, p. 28, referring to S.S. Diamond & M.R. Rose,'Real Juries', in Annual Review of Law and Social Sciences,1 (2005), pp. 255-284; J.R.P.Ogloff & V.G. Rose,'The comprehension of judicial instructions' in N.Brewer& K.D. Williams(Eds.),Psychology and Law:An empirical perspective, (New York: Guilford, 2005).

32 Wahlgren (2009), supra note 1794, p. 213, referring to Jon Bing, 'Legal Decision and Computerized System', in P. Spiegel ed., From Data Protection to Knowledge Machines: The Study of Law and Informatics, in Computer/Law Series 5 (Deventer: Kluwer Law and Taxation Publishers, 1990), pp. 223-250 (p. 228).

33 Spellman & Schauer (2012), supra note 1806, p. 8.

34 Ibid., p. 31, referring to F. Schauer, 'On the supposed jury-dependence of evidence law', in University of Pennsylvania Law Review 155 (2006), pp. 165-202.

without juries often tell lawyers that many rules of the evidence law will be disregarded or interpreted loosely to allow more evidence to be taken into account. In the event some subject matter may be related to the legal system (if only through several succeeding steps), then there is a possibility to initiate alternative fact eliciting sequences, and the established facts contained in the elaborated chain of evidence may be eventually linked to explicit prerequisites in the legal system.[35] The facts of the case are the facts with which the Supreme Court will deal in case brought from Court of Appeal by writ of review, and are the facts that were proven or admitted, not deductions or conclusions as to duty of parties or negligence (*Llorens v. McCann*, 187 La. 642, 175 So. 442, 444 – Black's Law Dictionary, 4th edition, by the Publisher's Editorial Staff, 1957, p. 709).

***

Lord Simonds took into account the 'evaluation' of facts by distinguishing between the 'perception and evaluation of facts'.[36] The evaluation of facts captures the point that some factual matters can only be resolved by a process of reflection. Distinguishing the perception of facts from the evaluation of facts was considered as the equivalent of distingushing specific facts from inference from those facts. Goodhart equates the evaluation and inference of facts, though at some places in his paper he seems to suggest they are different. Lord Simonds and Goodhart regarded 'the appellate courts of England as free to substitute their evaluations for those of the trial courts as they would be to substitute their inferences for those of the trial courts'. Christie contends differently that inference conjures up logical process and potentially right answers, but evaluation conjures up the exercise of judgment.

With regard to the elements in background knowledge, Benjamin Cardozo of legal realism argues that in this mental background every problem finds its setting. We may try to see things as objectively as we please. None the less, we can never see them with any eyes except our own. And on general level relating to this issue, Wittgenstein posits that the mental picture is the picture which is described when someone describes what he imagines.[37] What appear ahead of us are different opinions about the nature of law as well as appropriate classification of legal elements.

35 Wahlgren (2009), supra note 1807, p. 221.

36 Christie (1992), supra note 1801, p. 42.

37 Wahlgren (2009), supra note 1810, pp. 209-210, referring to Ludwig Wittgenstein, 'Philosophical Investigation', (Oxford: Basil Blackwell, 1953), p. 115.

At a more general level, legal positivists and legal realists may represent two basic models of legal identification.[38] Wahlgren has noted, uncertainty appears commonly because of legal professionals' failure to recognize the elements communicated to them, because the reports they receive are imprecise or incomplete from legal viewpoint, e.g., due to the witnesses' poor memory or missing written information on some details. Other causes of uncertainty are the fact that people make mistakes about what they have seen, or the fact that some information about past events is no longer available, or the fact that conflicting reports of past events are submitted by, for example, opposing parties having different opinions about how to describe a situation, or simply because people consciously tell lies.[39]

Various methods are employed to reduce uncertainty. There are methods employed through rules with the purpose of finding a balance between trustworthiness and the necessity to determine each issue being submitted. Other methods appear to focus on indications on various degrees of *evidential strength* (*degrees of certainty, degrees of possibility*). Among the former methods are a rule of the old Swedish procedural code and a similar rule in France. Under the Swedish procedural act (RB 17:29) wording of 1918, unanimous statements made by two witnesses should be treated as undisputable evidence. According to the similar rule in France, if the witnesses were female, three unanimous statements were necessary to establish sufficient evidence.[40] Lindell says the possibilities to establish substantive truth values about the past events using formal rules of evidence have turned out to be restricted.[41] Consequently, there is awareness that many judicial systems are abandoning detailed regulations in favor of a more or less free process, accepting less restricted principles such as 'the best evidence rule'. Among the latter methods focusing on the degrees of *evidential strength* is the Swedish legislation providing a rich selection of more or less well defined levels of confirmation.[42] Certain statutes provide that legal consequence may occur if a certain condition can be assumed. Other statutes provide that rules may apply with a growing degree of evidential strength depending upon whether something is reasonable, may be presumed, may be suspected, for good reasons may be suspected, for good reasons is beyond any reasonable doubt, is obvious, and so forth.

38 Ibid., referring to Benjamin N. Cardozo, 'The Nature of the Judicial Process', (New Heaven: Yale University Press, 1921), p. 13.

39 Ibid., p. 217.

40 Ibid.,p. 218, referring to P.O. Ekelof, 'Rattegang: Fjarde haftet', (Stockholm: Norstedts forlag, 1977, 4th revised ed.), (Institutet for rattsvetenskaplig forskning XXXVIII), note 24a (1977).

41 Ibid., referring to B. Lindell, 'Sakfragor och rattsfragor', (Uppsala: Iustus forlag, 1987, Skrifter fran jurisdika fakulteten I Uppsala 11), pp. 62-95.

42 Ibid., p. 220.

With regard to clarifying uncertainty, three manners are identified by Wahlgren, namely by undertaking a contextual investigation, by what is called the *definitional approach*, and by shifting into law-search. Relating to the undertaking of contextual investigation, Ekelof points out that the method employed for the coherence analysis of evidence is found in various case reports.[43] When conflicting facts appear, a contextual investigation has been suggested to be the most effective way to resolve uncertainty. According to Lindell, in cases where fact-assertions conflict, the best way to resolve uncertainty is to investigate which of the two conflicting stories that accounts for the largest number of elements in the disputed chain of events.[44] MacCormick suggests that the only type of test which we have available to us for verifying contested assertions about the past is this test of 'coherence'; taking all that has been presented to us in the way of real or testimonial evidence we work out a story that hangs together, which makes sense as a coherent whole.

IV.1.3. JUDICIAL TRUTH

Judicial truth means the truth *within* the judicial decision, not the truth *of* the judicial decisions. Since the judicial decision concerns both facts and norms, the truth-question must be divided into the *questio facti* (factual truth) and into the *questio juris* (legal truth). Factual truth and legal truth which both cannot be solved in the same way cause the judicial decision as their final result to have no epistemological unity. Epistemological break cannot be avoided.[45] L.Ferrajoli in *Diritto e ragione,Teoria del garantismo penale*, Laterza ; Bari 1989, at 39 says the problem of judicial truth does not concern the conclusions, i.e., specifically the decision. It is the ascertainment of facts in particular cases is what the problem of judicial truth usually concerns. This viewpoint importantly requires the distinction, if any, between judicial truth and the truth stated in empirical science.[46] In contrast to Kelsen's conception which frees judge from the control of empirical truth, descriptive writers of legal doctrine argue that judicial truth is descriptive of empirical fact.[47] There is only one truth, which is descriptive truth, and this truth concerns all judgment, including legal judgment or

---

43 Ibid., pp. 220-221, referring to P.O. Ekelof, 'Om vardering av strukturala bevis', in H.T. Klami ed. Rattoch Sanning: Ett bevisteoretiskt symposium I Uppsala 26-27 maj 1989 (1990).

44 Ibid., referring to Lindell (1987), supra note 1816, pp. 255-256; N. Mac Cormick, 'Legal Reasoning and Legal Theory', in Clarendon Law Series, (Oxford: Oxford University Press, 1978), p. 90.

45 Viola (1995), supra note 1799, pp. 249-250.

46 Ibid., p. 251, referring to Wroblewski (1986), supra note 1800, p. 180.

47 Ibid., p. 255.

judicial decision. Along these line, however, the epistemological break is unavoidable.

Viola indentifies three large spheres, namely *descriptive truth*, *hermeneutic truth* and *practical truth*, into which the truth-games are growing in many shapes. With regard to descriptive truth game, the intention of the player is directed to knowing how the things are. A describing statement and described things are the elements to be related. The quality of being true in such a describing statement depends on its certain relation to fact or the actual 'state of affairs'. The descriptive statement refers to its *referents.* But, the confusion, as the old neopositivist did, between the meaning and referent of a term and the meaning and referent of a statement should be avoided. The referents of several terms may be established directly by means of non-linguistic procedures, and such reference precedes and determines meaning. On the contrary, the referent of a statement is determined by its meaning, and only upon understanding of the meaning may the question arise about the truth of such statement. Different manners of asserting things are identified, depending upon the distinction of disciplinary fields of investigation. Descriptive truth statements tend to be organized according to some fundamental viewpoints under which reality is going to be scrutinized. So, it is clear that the search for descriptive truth presupposes another activity, i.e., understanding. Understanding as well may be considered not only as an element of the game of descriptive truth, but also a truth game itself. [48] Judicial truth is empirical truth of science itself; and the truth of judicial decision, as far as it concerns the questions of fact, resides in the conformity to natural facts.[49]

Practical-truth game is Viola's thesis, which is ruled by a distinct intention. Practical truth which includes descriptive truth and hermeneutic truth presupposes a specific intention. The elements of relationship in practical truth game are actions: the factual actions to be judged and the "ought" as the measure or the ideal model.[50] Descriptive and hermeneutic truths are now subjected to particular conditions of practice which are determined by its specific finality. This finality does not reside in saying how the things are, or in saying what they mean, or in saying how they ought to be. The problem is of the relationship between how the things are or the 'is' and how they ought to be or the 'ought'. So, all the conditions of a truth-game are present in the practical truth game: a relation between two things, an examination of correspondence or conformity and the possibility of objective control based on non-hypothetical criteria.

---

48 Ibid., pp. 260-261.

49 Ibid., p. 255, referring to Alchourron & Buligyn, 'Limits of Legal Logic and Legal Reasoning', in A.A. Martino (ed.), Pre-proceedings of the III International Conference on Logica Informatica Dirotto, (Firenze, 1989).

50 Ibid., pp. 262-264.

The fact in a particular case to be determined exists only in one empirical way of existence, therefore the way of ascertaining judicial truth has to be one only, i.e., scientific verification. However, because judges are assigned to identify and interpret the rule to be applied, the judicial process also considers aspects in which empirical truth is put aside.[51] Natural scientists look for the cause of event, while judges look for the reason of action. Facts to be scrutinized by natural scientists are natural or empirical facts, but facts to be scrutinized by judges in judicial process are *institutional facts*.[52] Viola is of the opinion that to know an institutional fact one needs to value it. Consequently, inside the game of practical truth the descriptive and hermeneutic exploration interweave in an inseparable way.

Practical truth game questions an event and its happening. The event is no longer accounted on its necessity, since the event is not considered as a natural fact that happened as it did and then it is not disputed but only verified. In the game of practical truth a particular action is questioned. If such particular action is different (from the measure), then to value the reasons that justifies its happening is required.[53] Consequently, empirical events, Viola contends, should not be explained in causality only in judicial process, but should also be examined on the reason of action.[54] The identification of action requires interpretation and reason-balancing. So, judges should test the soundness of the reason of action. In its turn this activity of interpretation as well is sustained by reasons. The judge must justify the ascertainment of the fact-situation and his judgment on it. Unlike scientific investigation that cannot be limited in any manner, a judicial investigation has to reach a definitive result, since its final term is not a theoretical truth, but a practical one. In addition, a judicial decision determining an action is an act of application that fits into the general framework of judicial practice and preserves its identity, rectifying what has occurred. A judicial decision includes truth-declaration and truth-establishment, rectifying what has actually happened. This is the full sense of practical truth.

IV.2. RULE IDENTIFICATION

***

Legal reasoning in which rule identification is a part starts with confronted

51 Ibid., pp. 251- 252.

52 Ibid., p. 263, referring to N. MacCormick & O. Weinberger, 'An Institutional Theory of Law', (Dordrecht: Reidel, 1986).

53 Ibid., pp. 262-263.

54 Ibid., pp. 263-264.

legal issues. Legal professionals here depend upon how familiar they are with the situations at hand. There are cases in which law professionals immediately recognize the descriptions of cases and make decisions instantly without additional effort. There are also cases in which law professionals do not recognize any piece of information, the whole situation as well as its elements is a total mystery.[55] In legal reasoning, an attempt is made to establish a general description of the case which includes a search for relevant facts. At the same time, rule identification is conducted, searching for a legal proposition in order to establish a legal rule applicable to the facts.[56] Dennis has quoted Heck as to judicial process.[57] In judicial process the appropriate legal precept is to be identified and selected, and then the judge is to apply the precept to the facts of a certain case in order to reach the correct solution. In each case, the judge must understand the nature of a legal concept before selecting an applicable legal rule.

The doctrine of law source is the most noticeable explicit guide for rule identification. Raz says: "It is common ground to all legal positivists that the law has social sources, i.e., that the content and existence of the law can be determined by reference to social facts and without relying on moral considerations". As to the source of law, there is a hierarchy among different kinds of legal rules, and this hierarchical order sometimes provides rather firm indications on how rule identification ought to be conducted. According to the order, any elements of a lower level may have to be extracted only if higher level elements fail to give sufficient information (Compared to Hart, 1961).[58] The sucessful result of rule identification has something to do with the effective management of several sub-processes. Rule identification is to consider the close relationship between the form and substance of rule. It is the text of legal rule which constitutes the fundamental communication medium in this regard. Rule identification is practically almost always dependent upon the effective retrieval of legal documents. A good sense of the language, an ability to transform the encountered fact description into relevant legal language, and elaborated and rich background knowledge are much useful in this process. The relevant point of law must be found, and all relevant items of legal knowledge must be established.[59] In reading a

55 Wahlgren (2009), supra note 1812, pp. 203-204.

56 Ibid., p. 205.

57 Dennis (1993), supra note 1307, p. 9, referring to Heck (1948a), supra note 1309, p. 134; Phillip Heck, 'The Jurisprudence of Interests: An Outline', in The Jurisprudence of Interests, translated by M. Magdalena Schoch, 1948 ["1948b"], p. 35.

58 Wahlgren (2009), supra note 1830, pp. 222-223, referring to J Raz, 'The Authority of Law: Essays on Law and Morality', (Oxford: Clarendon Press, 1979), p. 53; Cf/. Hart (1961), supra note 1490, pp. 92-93.

59 Ibid., p. 222.

related statute, the focus is usually on one specific section that provides for the relevant materials.[60] Wahlgren says that law professionals' immediate recollection of relevant legal categories have significant influence upon legal identification, particularly in the initial stages.[61] In addition, the factual situation and existing legal description of similar things, such as available concepts, previous cases, and rules of substantive nature, also influence fact identification and rule identification.

Hart contends the identification of primary rules of obligations is conducted based on a secondary rule of recognition. The provisions of 'authoritative criteria for identifying primary rules of obligation' are to be followed. The criteria may be in the form, including reference to an authoritative text; to legislative enactment; to customary practice; to general declarations of specific persons, or to past judicial decisions in particular cases.[62] As to the secondary system or secondary rule of recognition, Alchourron and Bulygin have termed it the 'judge system' regulating judges' actions.[63] Monaghan's distinction among *law declaration, fact identification*, and *law application* is to resolve the allocation of power among the various participants in judicial process.[64] We can place the process of rule identification under the function of law application within that distinction. Law application involves relating the legal rule to the fact established during the fact-finding process based on evidence, or in other words the rule to be identified must be some certain rule relating to the facts of the case. Since legal propositions are not formulated in great detail, the function of relating rules to facts is not merely mechanical, but the function is a complex psychological process, frequently involving judgment. Many of the claims about a distinctively legal reasoning, according to Spellman and Schauer, pertain to the resolution of uncertain questions about the law rather than about the fact.[65] Determining the requirements of a rule may also mean that rule identification is as attempt to identify the requirements or elements of a rule, matching the facts as (already or still being) established.

***

60 Ibid., p. 226.

61 Ibid., p. 212.

62 Ibid., p. 231, referring to Hart (1994), supra note 1510.

63 Ibid., referring to Alchourron & Bulygin (1971), supra note 1798, p. 151.

64 Christie (1992), supra note 1811, p. 28, referring to Monaghan (1985), supra note 1801, pp. 235-239.

65 Spellman & Schauer (2012), supra note 1808, p. 9.

In Common law tradition, rule identification is conducted through a process which is a usually internal and fairly intuitive or automatized chain of cognition. In the process, standards of proof for law and burdens of proof for law are in play. Often, it is obvious which party is pushing an issue of law and so bears the burden of persuasion. Yet, burdens on law can shift under the influence of canons of interpretation.[66] Cases in which legal professionals can use intuition based on their structured professional knowledge are for instance the cases in situations where the nature of the upcoming issues can be easily determined in advance and in which the law is stable and clear. Benjamin Cardozo says: "Of the cases that come before the court in which I sit, a majority, I think, could not, with semblance of reason, be decided in any way but one. The law and its application alike are plain. Such cases are predestined, so to speak, to affirmance without opinion".[67] The concept of legal rules is criticized by legal realists who often underline the importance of cases and examples. Legal identification, including fact identification and rule identification, is understood on the importance of cases and examples. Dyer and Flower have made the following summary: " [A]lthough numerous legal crib notes exist which attempt to explicitly formulate the rules of contracts, most lawyers look down on learning law in this way. Instead law schools claim to teach by a Socratic method of reasoning and debate which is extremely example-based. Law students examine famous and prototypic cases. In our experience, when a lawyer is given a situation to analyze, he or she immediately recalls one or more prototypic cases which involve similar issues."[68]

In hard cases, the language of an applicable rule is unclear, or applicable rules are more than one so it is not clear which one should apply, or the language of a plainly applicable rule is clear but causes the outcome which, according to the interpreter, applier, decider, or enforcer of the rules, is wrong.[69] These also cause difficulties in rule identification process. A hypothetical rule prohibiting vehicles in a public park (Hart, 1958; Schauer 2008a) is an example of hard case.[70] If the rule expressly prohibited cars, it was clear that all cars were prohibited. Following this, when the fact shows that somebody parked a car in a public park, the

66 Clermont (2006), supra note 1803, p. 888, 868, 895, 877.

67 Wahlgren (2009), supra note 1833, p. 204.

68 Ibid., p. 212, referring to M.G.Dyer & M. Flowers,'Toward Automating Legal Expertise', in Walter, C. (eds), Computing Power and Legal Reasoning, (St. Paul: West Publishing Company, 1985), p. 7.

69 Spellman & Schauer (2012), supra note 1840, p. 10.

70 Ibid., p. 11, referring to Hart (1958), supra note 1798, pp. 593-629; F.Schauer,'A critical guide to vehicles in the park', in New York University Law Review, 83 (2008), pp. 1109-1134 ["Schauer 2008a"].

rule is easily identified to be made applicable. Fact first, rule follows. But the rule prohibits vehicles, not cars, so when bicycles, baby carriages, wheelchairs, and skateboards (none of which are either clearly vehicles or clearly not vehicles) are parked there, will the hypothetical rule be definitely identified as the applicable rule? People can and sometimes do reason in such a deductive or syllogistic way when they are given clear rules and presented with clear instances of application.[71] In such situation, the judge would then have discretion to decide the issue as she thought best, or would try to determine the purpose behind the rule, or perhaps would try to imagine what the original maker of the rule would have thought should be done in such a case.

Consistent with the Legal Realist view about rules, Joseph Hutcheson, a Texas-based federal judge, claims that it is a mistake to suppose that the judge would first look to the text of the rule, the purpose behind the rule, the evidence of legislative intent, and the like in order to decide the case winding up in court. Rather, the judge would initially, and based largely on the particular facts of the case rather than the law, come up with an initial 'hunch' about how the case ought to be decided. Then, and only then, would the judge seek to find a rule to support that result.[72] Subsequent Realist reinforced this theme, albeit rarely with systematic empirical approach.[73] Spellman and Schauer conclude that the realists, like Hutcheson and Frank, do not follow the notion of rule identification. They thinks that legal rules are not to be identified as applicable rules, but legal rules are used as the justification of what judges have decided.

In Common law countries, multiple and inconsistent rules may apply to the same event, allowing for more decisions that seem to be based on motivated reasoning. Moreover, when there are multiple potentially applicable rules, judges, even judges with no preferred outcome, will be influenced by, among other things, their background and training in determining which rule are retrieved or ignored.[74] In addition, if judges seek coherence and consistency, they may well select

71 Ibid., referring to J. St. B.T. Evans, J.L. Barston and P. Pollard,'On the conflict between logic and belief in syllogistic reasoning', in Memory and Cognition, 11(1983), pp. 295-306; L.J. Rips, 'Two kinds of reasoning', in Psychological Science, 12 (2001), pp. 129-134.

72 Ibid., p. 12, referring to Joseph Hutcheson Jr., (1929), 'The judgment intuitive: The function of the "hunch" in judicial decision', in Cornell Law Journal, 14, pp. 274-288.

73 Ibid. See, e.g. Frank (1930), supra note 1040.

74 Ibid., p. 14, referring to B.A. Spellman, 'Judges, expertise, and analogy,' in D, Klein & G. Mitchell (Eds.), The psychology of judicial decision making (pp. 149-163), (New York: Oxford, 2010).

legal rules and sources that are consistent with the others they have retrieved, and ignore those that would make coherence more difficult.[75] Cases and examples are important in rule identification in legal reasoning. Prototypic cases involving similar issues play an important role in assessment of legal rule to apply.[76] Peter O'Niel concludes that the reasoning and problem solving behavior demonstrated by our expert involves the construction of rich semantic models developed on the basis of prototypical stories and expectations from previous case experiences across multiple contexts. These previous case experiences are used for gathering information to develop theories about the case, gauge what typically fits within expectations, notice anomalies, and generate mentally simulated predictions about how the new case may be concluded.[77] Mental models are summarized in the form of 'stories' and 'legal theories' by our expert and reflects particular characterizations and instantiations of the components models outlined. Legal experiences in the form of prototypical stories and expectations from previous cases is similar to the notion forwarded by Dyer and Flowers that the access to 'a legal memory organized around abstract conceptual issues' is crucial in legal identification.

***

The law is viewed as a network of component structures that exist on different levels of abstraction, namely document level, text level, concept level, rule level and rule system level. Rule identification in the process of legal reasoning must also consider the nature of the material that is to be retrieved. Analyses of relations between different kinds of legal knowledge [materials] have to be made, using the network. As to document level, rule identification in practice, says Bing, is

75 Ibid., referring to K.J. Holyoak & D. Simon, 'Bidirectional reasoning in decision making by constraint satisfaction', in Journal of Experimental Psychology: General, 128 (1999), pp. 3-31; D. Simon, L.B. Pham, Q.A. Le and K.J. Holyoak, 'The emergence of coherence over the course of decision making', in Journal of Experimental Psychology: Learning, Memory, and Cognition, 27 (2001), pp. 1250-1260.

76 Wahlgren (2009), supra note 1842, p. 212, referring to Dyer & Flowers (1985), supra note 1843, p. 57.

77 Ibid., referring to D.P. O'Niel 'A Process Specification of Expert Lawyer Reasoning', in Paper - Proceeding the First International Conference on Artificial Intelligence and Law, ACM Press, New York (1987), p. 57; Dyer & Flowers (1985), Ibid., p. 53.

closely related to document retrieval.[78] Various kinds of document must be investigated before a legal issue can be identified. Several different categorizations of legal documents have been suggested. Legal concepts [of right] are primarily technical tools for representation. Rule identification is achieved by using a vehicle of inference in which there can be found systematic connection between facts (f) and consequences (c).[79] Legal concepts may be however less technical, in the sense that they should not necessarily be made immediately relevant to rule application. Frandberg distinguishes between legal concepts with the systematization function (*systematiserande R-begrepp*) and legal concepts which constitute rule elements (*regelkonstituenter*).[80] The view that legal concepts may be less technical is the view on legal concepts with the main function to provide a convenient general label in order to facilitate communication about a number of related legal concepts. Here, it is not so important to observe concept structures as a crucial part in legal thought process, but it is important to observe conceptual structures as the fundamental corpus of legal knowledge, and that various kinds of legal concepts are basic building blocks in all fields of the law. The Continental (dogmatic) jurisprudence has its major objectives to clarify the meanings of legal concepts and their relationships with each other. Consequently, legal concept structures are vital for the understanding of how relevant legal materials may be retrieved.

In Civil law tradition, rule identification must employ a deep analysis beyond the text level. The process of searching for a rule to be indentified involves immediate access to a rich spectrum of legal concepts. Each instantiated legal concept might have a decisive influence on the succeeding sequences of the search process. This follows from the basic function of legal concept, which is to tie elements to each other in a legally relevant way.[81] The objective of rule identification is to find a *complete legal rule* that matches the current case, not only an isolated legal description. The relationship between elements of such a legal rule

78 Ibid., pp. 224-225, referring to Jon Bing, 'Handbook of Legal Information Retrieval', (Amsterdam: North-Holland Publishing Company, 1984), pp. 74-84.

79 Ibid., p. 229, referring to A. Ross, 'Tu – Tu,' in Borum, O.A. Illum, Knud, eds., Festskrift till Henry Ussing, (Kobenhavn: Juristforbundet/Nyt Nordisk Forlag, Arnold Busck, 1951), pp. 468-484 (English version: Harvard Law Review, Vol. 70 (1956/57), pp. 812-25, also reprinted in Sc.St.L. Vol. 1 (1957).

80 Ibid., pp. 227-228. Cf. A. Frandberg, 'Till fragan om de juridiska begreppens systematic: En studie i jurisdik begreppsbildning', in Tidsskrift for rettsvitenskap (1985), pp. 79-116 (p. 84).

81 Ibid., p. 227, referring to L. Lindahl, 'Definitioner, begreppsanalys och mellanbegrepp i juridiken', in Rationalitet och emperi i rattsvetenskapen, Stockholms universitet, Stockholm, (1985), pp. 37-49 (Juridiska fakulteten i Stockholm, skriftrerien nr. 6), p. 43 – original text in Swedish.

must be identified. A description of antecedent or consequence must be established. The corresponding antecedent or consequence have to be found in order to get something out of the description of such a legal rule. A vague definition of such a legal rule may, for instance, have to be combined with an illustration of a prerequisite in a case-report or in an amended regulation.[82]

The doctrine of law sources is basically a theory of substantive law and may be viewed as a collection of methodological rules or 'managing rules' (Compare with Hart,1961, on rules of recognition; and Stromholm, 5th ed. 1996).[83] And as a collection of methodological rules, the doctrine is essential for the guidance for rule identification in many ways. In Civil law traditions, the most important thing in rule identification is almost always to investigate legislated or statutory laws which are prevailing. In such investigation, first the legislative preparatory materials should be looked upon, and then case law reports may supply examples of how a legal rule is to be applied in practice. In the event there is no sufficient legal information from such official materials and previous case reports, then an appeal to equity/justice or customs or the works of jurisprudence may be made.

In judicial process, the appropriate legal precept is to be identified and selected, and then the judge is to apply the precept to the facts of a certain case in order to reach the correct solution.[84] More difficult cases give more complex choices of legal rules, interpretations and ways of rule application. More than one legal rules, different interpretations of the same legal concept and various ways applicable to the facts are identified. In each case, the judge must understand the nature of a legal concept before selecting an applicable legal rule. Every legal concept functions to delimit contradictory or competing interests and to guide judicial decision on the settlement of the contest between more than one interests. It is necessary that such judicial decision must be based on the legislator's evaluation of each relevant interest, which in turn must rest on his value judgments emanating from his notion of a desirable social order.

---

82 Ibid., pp. 228-229, referring to Peczenik (1987), supra note 1281; Sundby (1974), supra note 1282, p. 387; T. Eckhoff, 'Rettskildelaere', (Oslo: Johan Grundt Tanum Forlag, 1971) (reale hensyn), pp. 44-51.

83 Ibid., p. 223. Cf. Hart (1961), supra note 1833, at 92-93; S. Stromholm, 'Ratt, rattskallor och rattstillampning: En Larobok I allman rattslara, Norstedts juridik, Stockholm, (5th ed.1996), (Institutet for rattsvetenskaplig forskning CIX) , pp. 317-321.

84 Dennis (1993), supra note 1832, pp. 8-9, citing Heck (1948a), supra note 1832, p. 134.

IV.3. LEGAL INTERPRETATION

IV.3.1. DOCTRINAL VIEWS

***

Interpretation means a mental process by human beings, affecting reality by something which declares to be true the situation as object of interpretation.[85] According to V. Knapp, in general, interpretation is to give meaning to the characters, i.e., appearing of meaning of the signs. Interpretation is an essential part of the legal regulation procedure. The main role of interpretation can be seen in correct practical application of law but it is impossible to apply a legal rule correctly without affecting its meaning.[86] Interpretation is required in adjudication. Adjudication is a hermeneutical process whereby norm application is interconnected with a description of the circumstances and a concretization of generally valid norms: interpretive issues are finally decided by the meaning equivalence between the description of facts in the case at hand and the descriptive requirements of applicable norms.[87] In Aristotelian theory of reasoning, accepted legal interpretation relates to the rationality of reasoning (*logos* argument), rather than *ethos* (rhetorical) argument based on the character of speaker or *pathos* argument based on emotion.[88] Interpretation is at the intersection of the debate about different methods of interpretation (or forms of legal reasoning) and broader questions on the proper role of courts in a democratic society; and this is a function of hermeneutics, institutional constraints and normative preferences, determining judicial outcomes in light of an existent body of rules. [89] The concrete interpretation to be given to legal rules is therefore a product of legal reasoning and of the institutional

85 Bohumila Salachova and Bohumil Vitek, 'Interpretation of European Law, Selected Issues', in Acta Universitatis Agriculturae et Silviculturae Mendelianae Brunensis, Volume LXI, Number 2, (2013), p. 2717, referring to D. Houbova, 'Interpretace prάva', in J. Harnavel, et.al. Teorie prάva, Plzeñ: Aleš Čeněk, 2008, p. 361.

86 Ibid. Cf. V. Knapp, 'Teorie prάva' (Praha: C.H. Beck, 1995), p. 168.

87 Elina Paunio, 'Beyond Predictability – Reflection on Legal Certainty and the Discourse Theory of Law in the EU Legal Order', in German Law Journal, Vol. 10 No. 11, (2009), p. 1473. See Habermas (1996), supra note 1397, p. 218.

88 Ibid., p. 1483, 1487.

89 Miguel Poiares Maduro, 'Interpreting European Law: Judicial Adjudication in a Context of Constitutional Pluralism', in Vol. 1 EJLS No. 2 (2007), pp. 2-3.

constraints and normative preferences that determine the role of courts in a given political community. *Ethos* and *pathos* may be effective means of persuasion, but from a theoretical viewpoint they are both incomplete. This is because neither type of argument shows that the argument itself is correct. Essentially, *logos* concerns providing factually accurate and logically meaningful reasons in support of the outcome. This is particularly important in the context of legal reasoning. Factual argumentation means that conclusions follow from accurate assumption and factual information: in order to convince the linguistically as well as culturally pluralistic legal community, the rightness of a particular interpretation requires all three types or arguments.

Acquiring meaning or interpretation is the process in which man learns about himself only through his acts, through the exteriorization of his life and through the effects it produces on others. It is in a durable acquisition where the objectifications of life tend to deposit and sediment themselves, as at this point it is said in the objective Hegelian spirit that *life graps life*. And the only really significant difference between psychological interpretation and exegetical interpretation stems from the fact of this objectification of life. Life contains the power to surpass itself through meaning.[90] The text to be interpreted was reality itself and its *interconnection* (*Zusammenhang*). Understanding a text from the past is preceded by a historical interconnection. The coherence of history first, and the coherence of text later.[91] Perfectly perceiving that *life grasps life* can only be done by the mediation of units of meaning which arise above the historical flux. Text must be unfolded, no longer towards its author, but towards its immanent sense and towards the world it opens up and discloses. Paul Ricouer argues that the reader may seek, not something hidden behind the text, but something disclosed in front of it; not the internal constitution of the text, but that which points towards a possible world.[92] To understand a text at this level is to move from its sense to its reference, from that which it says to that which it says it about. In Ricouer's theory, with the mediation of structural analysis .. it seems possible to situate explanation and interpretation along a unique *hermeneutical arc* and to integrate the opposite attitudes of explanation and understanding within an overall conception of reading as the recovery of meaning.

Interpretation paves the way for reflection. Philosophical reflection leads to a deeper understanding of human existence, and hermeneutics is

---

90 Thompson (1981), supra note 295, p. 52.

91 Ibid., p. 48, 53.

92 Ibid., p. 5, referring to Paul Ricouer, 'What is a text? Explanation and understanding'.

the route to such reflection.[93] If hermeneutics is the route to philosophical reflection, then reflection cannot escape from the conflict of interpretation. Ricouer holds there is no general hermeneutics, no universal canon of exegesis, but only disparate and opposed theories concerning the rules of interpretation.[94] A suggestion by Ricouer is that, on the first approximation, the notion of meaning may be analyzed into two basic dimensions, comprising both an objective aspect or that which the sentence means [as having an ideal sense and a real reference, - following Frege], and a subjective aspect or that which the speaker means.[95] Only interpreting the signs of desire enables reflection to regain the archaic heritage which it has lost.[96] Desire and need, action and motive, pleasure and pain are among the issues being focused by the philosophy of will, which according to Ricouer,[97] is to reflect upon the affective and volitional dimensions of human existence.

The theory of interpretation elaborated by Ricouer is closely connected to the concept of the text. As to the characteristics of written discourse, there are forms of distanciation. One form implies that the objective meaning of a text is something other than the subjective intentions of its author. In another form, the emancipation of written discourse from the interlocutors and circumstances of the dialogical situation engenders two possible attitudes towards the text, namely, suspending any judgment concerning the referential dimension of the text, treating the latter as a wholly worldless and self-enclosed entity, or, abandoning this *ephocé* and seek to unfold the non-ostensive references of the text.[98] Ricouer makes the transition from semantics to hermeneutic proper with the formulation of a concept of the text.[99] The text is a work of discourse, which is a structured totality that cannot be reduced to the sentences whereof it is composed. Speaking and writing are alternative and equally legitimate modes of the realization of discourse. The realization of discourse in writing nevertheless involves a series of characteristics which effectively distance the text from the conditions of spoken discourse.

***

93 Ibid., p. 6.

94 Ibid., referring to Paul Ricouer, 'Freud and Philosophy: An Essay on Interpretation', translated by Denis Savage, (New Heaven: Yale University Press, 1970), pp. 26-27.

95 Ibid., p. 11.

96 Ibid., p. 8.

97 Ibid., p. 6.

98 Ibid., pp. 14-15.

99 Ibid., p. 13.

Originalism, intentionalism and purposivism are interpretive doctrines.[100] According to intentionalism, the constitutional text should be interpreted based on the subjective intent of the framers. Originalism teaches that the constitution is to be understood according to the reasonable reading of the constitutional text at the time of its adoption. The purpose of legal texts is central to the interpretive doctrine of purposivism according to which the Constitution is to be interpreted based on its purpose. The main problem of interpretation [is n]ot what the meaning of words in the rule is, but whether the words authorized the inference made in reliance on them, Hart says. Vagueness or indeterminacy of legal propositions appear within jurisprudential literature, as often referred to as *open texture*. It is on the concept or rule level the problems of vagueness most frequently appear. In Peczenik's words, ambiguity of law causes problems on the rule level and such problems are then referred to as instances of *rule collision* [101] In the application of law by a legal organ, the cognitive interpretation of the law to be applied is combined with an act of will by which the law-applying organ chooses between the possibilities shown by cognitive interpretation.[102] One cannot obtain by interpretation the only correct statutes from the Constitution, and one cannot either obtain by interpretation the only correct judicial decisions from the statute.[103] The first steps of classical methodology of legal interpretation were laid down by F.C. von Savigny in the 19th century. By legal interpretation Savigny means the ideas included in statutes.[104] There are several methodological rules of interpretation, causing the existence of several methods of interpretation. Methods or canons of interpretation have been submitted from alternative standpoints and listed on priority basis. When the law is ambiguous, one or some methodological rules of interpretation may be employed based on the priority. The term "*canons of interpretation*" is derived from a categorization outlined by Savigny, who submitted four basic canones (guide-lines) of legal interpretation; (i) textual factors, (ii) logical, systematical factors, (iii) historical factors, and (iv) functional, teleological factors.[105] Savigny's construction in which

100 Aharon Barak, 'Comparative Law, Originalism and the Role of a Judge in a Democracy: A Reply to Justice Scalia – in the Fulbright Convention, January 29, 2006, (www fullbright.org.il/...for.../Barrak_50th_symposium_ speech.doc, B.1 & 2).

101 Wahlgren (2009), supra note 1851, pp. 234-235, refering to Hart (1961), supra note 1858, pp. 123-126.

102 Kelsen (1967), supra note 1649, p. 354.

103 Ibid., p. 353.

104 Salachova & Vitek (2013), supra note 1860, p. 2717. To specification of Savigny's conception of law interpretation viz., e.g. P. Hollander, 'Filosofi práva', (Plzeň: Aleš Čeněk publisher, 2006), pp. 220-224.

105 Wahlgren (2009), supra note 1876, p. 236, referring to Savigny (1840), supra note 931, pp. 206-330.

interpretation is on the ideas in statutes should apply the grammatical, logical, historical and systematical methods.[106] According to Savigny, these methods do not stand independently and the interpreter is not allowed to use them arbitrarily, but if the interpretation should be successful they *shall* operate in the interconnection. To the list of methods Savigny did not include the teleological method but he considered purposes to be the auxiliary means of finding the meaning (reason) of statutes and of internal value of interpretation result, especially in connection with analysis of vague and unclear terms.

In terms of sequence of interpretive methods, Salachova and Vitek argue that the grammatical method stands first. In case of situation when the legal provision, after using the grammatical method, is clear and unambiguous, this interpretation *shall* not be excluded by other means of interpretation attained through different methods. Other methods are suitable if the legal provision is unclear and ambiguous and the grammatical interpretation fails. In a situation when the meaning is ambiguous, it is necessary to use the teleological interpretive method. And when the interpreted text remains ambiguous, the systematic interpretation is then used, by focusing on the relationships between the text and other provisions. Internal compliance of provisions can be guaranteed by the systematic interpretation (case 101/63 *Wagner*).[107] Close adherence to interpretation based on verbal [grammatical] formulas cannot be expected, says Johnstone, because the application of statutes to cases involves so many conditions existing and so many power and judgment conflicts to be resolved and compromised, although the rules and principles of statutory interpretation have been phrased too exactly and have been expected to operate too precisely.[108] In addition, language is inherently ambiguous in nature, causing great restrictions to the amount of precision possible. All these make the law of statutory construction unable to operate with mathematical precision.

***

As noticed by doctrinal writers, grammatical interpretation decreased in its use in the court's practice, and another type of written law interpretation

---

106 Salachova & Vitek (2013), supra note 1879, p. 2717.

107 Ibid., p. 2718.

108 Quintin Johnstone, 'An Evaluation of the Rules of Statutory Interpretation', in Kansas Law Review, Vol 3 (1954), Yale Law School Legal Scholarship Repository, Faculty Scholarship Series, p. 22.

grew by the end of the 19th century.[109] 'Some of the code provisions had become obsolete', they were no longer used, 'and the industrial revolution, as well as economic, political and other societal changes had occurred'.[110] Conceptualism in France and Europe was reacted by a non-mechanical conception of judicial process, such as by Francois Geny in his theory of 'free scientific research', which provides that judges are bound by the text of the written law only when, and to the extent that, the text is clear.[111] Otherwise, considerations of social, economic and moral factors involved in the particular case or considerations within the context of the basic principles and values reflected in the legal system as a whole, have to be made by judges. This is to be done in order to 'arrive at a rule that best promotes justice and social utility for the given situation'.[112] The new interpretive approach was called the 'revolt against formalism',[113] and it is characterized by two innovative elements, which both display elements of judicial creativity: the method of systematic interpretation and the relevance of the choice element for the judges. According to the former, interpretation should not only be guided by textual and historical arguments; elements of the system and of purpose will have to come at play. These elements can be found by consulting tradition, case-law and literature, and by rethinking the cohesion of the different chapters of the legal system.[114] The second element characterizing the new interpretive approach is the discovery of the importance of choice in the judicial process: evaluation and balancing: giving consideration to the choice's practical and

---

109 Claire M. Germain, 'Approach to Statutory Interpretation and Legislative History in France', in Duke Journal of Comparative & International Law, Vol. 13:195, Special Issue 2003, p. 198, referring to H. Mazeaud, J. Mazaud and Francois Chabas, 'Lecons de Droit Civil', t.1. (12th ed. 2000), p. 172.

110 Ibid., referring to Francois Geny, 1 'Method d'Interpretation et Sources du Droit Prive Francais', (2nd ed. 1919).

111 Dennis (1993), supra note 1859, p. 6, referring to Jaro Mayda, 'Geny's Methode After 60 Years: A Critical Introduction', in Francois Geny, Methode d"Interpretation et Sources en Droit Prive Positif v, x, (Louisiana State Law Institute trans., 2nd ed.,1954).

112 Ibid., pp. 6-7, referring to Arthur T. von Mehren & James R. Gordley, 'The Civil Law System', 2nd edition, 1997, pp. 1127-1142 (p. 1138).

113 Pollicino (2004), supra note 1631, p. 286. This expression tended to accentuate the element of pure and mechanical logic in judicial decision making, while neglecting or concealing the voluntaristic discretionary elements of choice. In France, where the rejection against formalism started, the spokesman of the new generation of lawyers was Geny. He embodied the reaction of legal theory against the excessive legalism of the post-codification era.

114 Ibid., p. 287, referring to T. Koopmans, 'The Theory of Interpretation and The Court of Justice', in Liber Amicorum in Honor of Lord Slynn of Hadley (D. O'Keeffe & A. Bavasso eds., 2000), Vol. 1, Jud. Rev. in Eur. Union L., Kluwer L. Int'l 48 (2000).

moral results; employment of not only the argument of abstract logic, but those of economics and politics, ethics, sociology and psychology.[115] Another method is the social purpose method, advocated by Louis Josserand.[116] A judge using this method is to identify 'the social purpose or objective of the legislation' in judicial process for concrete cases.

A non-mechanical approach to judicial process was also developed by the Jurisprudence of Interests school of thought in Germany. Phillip Heck has summarized: "*What the legislator intends is the protection of interests*". At the same time, however, the legislator realizes that he is unable to capture the variety of life situations and to regulate them so completely that logical subsumption furnishes the correct delimitation in each individual case. The judge should be more than a legal automaton functioning according to the laws of logical mechanics. The judge should stand by the legislator's side as an intelligent helpmate, who does not merely consider the words and the commands of the laws but who enters into the intentions of the legislator and applies the value judgments embodied in the law to situations not expressly regulated by the law, with the aid of his own evaluation of interests.[117] In Switzerland, Max Rumelin has noted, Article 1 of the Swiss Civil Code of 1907 provides that judges should decide cases not clearly covered by the text of the code on the basis of customary law or, where no such rule exists, in accordance with the rules that the judge would have established as a legislator.[118]

When the code refers the judge to his own judgment in the formulation of concepts in frequent cases, he is required to resort to the method of rule-making,[119] either by express delegation (judicial decision),[120] or by the use of indeterminate words which demand appraisal of value, such as 'fault'.[121] ['Fault' is also delineated into relative degrees of severity

---

115 Ibid. See Cappelletti (1981), supra note 1631, p. 22. The importance of choice in judicial process is accentuated by the willingness of political branches of governments to pass responsibility for difficult decision to the judiciary.

116 Germain (2003), supra note 1884, p. 199, citing E. Steiner, 'French Legal Method', (2002), p. 64.

117 Dennis (1993), supra note 1886, p. 7, referring to Heck (1948a), supra note 1859, pp. 101, 103-04.

118 Ibid., referring to Max Rumelin, 'Development in Legal Theory and Teaching During My Lifetime', in The Jurisprudence of Interests 2, 23 [M. Magdalena Schoch trans., 1948]; Germain (2003), supra note 11891, p. 199, citing Rene David, 1 'Le Droit Francais.' 145 [1960].

119 Ibid., p. 12, referring to Heck (1948b), supra note 1832, p. 41.

120 Ibid. See e.g., La. Civ.Code arts. 372, 1589, 1852, 1960, 1986, 1999, 2033, 2324.1.

121 Ibid. See e.g., La. Civ.Code arts 112, 577, 599, 614, 628, 799, 973, 1250, 1260, 1261, 1268, 1270, 1386, 1506, 1569, 1701, 1772, 1800, 1804, 1812, 1813, 1814,

in Louisiana Civ. Code art. 3506(13)], 'good faith',[122] or 'public order' or 'public policy'.[123] The judge is also required to resort to the method of rule-making through appraisal of interests, when concepts or rules of statute law are contradictory or totally lacking, causing a 'gap' in the statute law.[124] In Heck's thesis, in the event there are gaps in the code, judges who must make judicial decisions should resort to either analogy or rule-making to give form to a concept or rule so as to adjust the conflict of interests.[125]

James Dennis holds that in essence, a non-mechanical judicial process treats the Civil Code, the courts and the public with more honesty and respect than a methodology based on the fiction that the legal order is a 'complete,' 'gapless' system of legal concepts that was intended to be an inexhaustible source of new material and that for each concrete factual situation a decision must be deducible from existing abstract legal rules by means of juridical logic.[126] Quoting Geny, Dennis believes if judges were confined to a function of subsuming facts under concepts deduced or construed from abstract legal rules, the jurisprudence would be less in touch with reality and more legalistic because judges and lawyers are more apt to disagree and split hairs about abstract concepts than the real human interests in conflict in particular situations.[127] Dennis is of the opinion that the legislative history of modern statutes reflects a struggle for the protection of interests rather than conceptual accuracy and consistency.[128] When the particular constellation of interests has already been evaluated by the legislator, and a rule based on such evaluation has been legislated, judges are bound by the delimitation of such interests as already legislated, and the method of logical subsumption is to be applied.[129] In this matter,

---

1873, 2004, 2057, 2298, 2312, 2315, 2315.2, 2323, 2324(B), 2374, 2433, 2489, 2536, 2552, 2597, 2695, 2699, 2721, 2723, 2759, 2760, 2902, 3003, 3018, 3022, 3167, 3217(9), 3237(11).

122 Ibid. See e.g., La. Civ.Code arts. 96, 468, 486, 487, 488, 496, 518, 522, 523, 524, 528, 529, 670, 742, 1759, 1770, 1950, 1963, 1975, 1983, 1996, 2021, 2028, 2035, 2311, 2480, 2529, 2811, 2814, 2822, 2830, 2831, 3033, 3050, 3158(B), 3475, 3480, 3481, 3482, 3486, 3490, 3491, 3536.

123 Ibid. See e.g., La. Civ.Code arts. 7, 1851, 1968, 2012, 2030, 2329, 3520, 3538, 3540.

124 Ibid., p. 13, citing Heck (1948b), supra note 1894, p. 41.

125 Ibid., p. 11, citing Heck (1948a), supra note 1908, p. 155 ; see La. Civ. Code art. 4.

126 Ibid., p. 7.

127 Ibid., p. 8, referring to Francois Geny (1954), 'Methode d'Interpretation et Sources en Droit Prive Positif', # 220 n. 606, (Louisiana State Law Institute trans., 2nd ed. 1954), or, [Francois Geny, '1 Methode d'Interpretation et Sources du Droit Prive Francais', (second ed. 1919)].

128 Ibid., p. 6, referring to Heck (1948b), supra note 1899, pp. 34-35.

129 Ibid., p. 10, referring to Heinrich Stoll, 'The Role of Concepts and

there are scholars viewing that what happens is the logical subsumption of clear facts to the rule, but other scholars argue that what happens is an analysis of interests, being made 'intuitively' based on judges' structured professional knowledge without logical instrumental process.[130] Logical subsumption should be employed only if its result is in harmony with that objective.[131] The Civil law system has always used the method of analogy, where according to Heck[132] 'analogy' also includes the inverse, *argumentum e contrario*.[133] If the facts of a particular case are not foreseen by the code provision, what the judge must do is first to determine the conflict of interests underlying the dispute. Then the judge must examine if same [similar] conflict of interests underlies other factual circumstances that have already been clearly provided by legislation. In the event the answer is in the affirmative the judge must decide such similar conflict of interests in the same way, by transferring the value decision or the balance of interests contained in the code provision to the facts of the dispute before him.

In 1935, statutory interpretation by using legislative history was attacked by Henri Capitan, arguing that 'parliamentary discussions lead to the expression of personal views, rather than a general sense of the spirit of the law'. In France in 1970s, a legislative reform happened. It was 'a new period of legislative reform' where 'the exegetic method and use of legislative histories enjoyed a resurgence of interest'.[134] Under French law, there is no certain strict canons of interpretation to be followed, and there is no provisions on interpretation under French Code. Judges and scholars are given by the drafters of Code Napoleon a flexible room to interpret the principles to particular cases, since 'the drafters intended only to set general principles'.[135] According to Portalis, one of the four drafters of the Civil Code, the function of statute is to establish through a broad view the general maxims of the law; to establish principles rich in consequences and not to descend into the detail of questions, which could arise on every question. It is up to the judge and the jurist imbued with the general spirit

Construction in the Theory of the Jurisprudence of Interests', in The Jurisprudence of Interests, (M. Magdalena Schoch trans., 1948), p. 262.

130 Ibid., p. 40, referring to Heck (1948a), supra note 1900, p. 185.

131 Ibid., p. 10, referring to Heck (1948a), Ibid., p. 185.

132 Ibid., p. 12, citing Heck (1948b), supra note 1903, p. 41.

133 Ibid., p. 11, citing Heck (1948b), Ibid., p. 41; Heck (1948a), supra note 1906, pp. 180-181. See also Geny (1954), supra note 1902, ## 107, 165, 166.

134 Germain (2003), supra note 1891, p. 199, referring to Henri Capitant, 'L'Interpretation des Lois d'Apres les Travaux Preparatoires', D.H, 1935, Chr. 77.

135 Ibid., pp. 195-196, referring to Rene David, 'French Law', (1959), in 166 Michael Kindred trans., (Lousiana State University Press, 1972); H. Mazeaud, J. Mazaud, & Francois Chabas, 'Lecons de Droit Civil', t.1 (12th ed. 2000), p. 81; Alfred Rieg (1978), 'Rapport Francais sur le droit civil', in 29 Travaux de L'association Henri Capitant (1978), pp. 70-71.

of the law, to direct their application.[136] Mazeaud, Mazaud, and Chabas[137] stated that the meaning of statutes is not always clear, interpretation is needed on the meaning and scope of the text. Rene David distinguishes 'among grammatical, logical, historical (including legislative history) and teleological interpretations.[138] Alfred Rieg sees the difference between looking at the intention of the legislature, which is particularly appropriate for recent laws, and looking at the social purpose of the law, particularly for old laws.[139] And Jean Carbonnier says there are three main methods of statutory interpretation as the exegetic method, the method of social purpose, and the free scientific research method.

French scholars contend that exegetic and teleological interpretations are major methods of interpretation to be followed. The exegetic interpretation 'making use of legislative history', and the teleological interpretation restricting to the social objective of the statute 'have several different variations'.[140] In the nineteenth century, the exegetical school of thought propounded that revealing the solution in concrete cases needed a careful and sufficient study of the text.[141] Logical methods of interpretation were used, such as analogous interpretation, *e contrario* interpretation and inductive interpretation. Interpretation by analogy is used 'to resolve difficulties encountered in the practice of applying the code', by using the rule of a similar case, in the event the written law is silent. An *e contrario* interpretation gives a conclusion regarding any analyzed situations which are contrary to a given legal proposition. This means that in the event the legal proposition prohibits a thing, then anything contrary to the thing is not prohibited.[142] Interpretation by induction starts 'from the principle set by the legislator, and expands it to other situations'.[143] Mazeaud, Mazaud and Chabas said that when the law was already clear, there was no need

136 Ibid., referring to John Bell, 'French Legal Culture', 72 (2001), quoting original French text in Discours Preliminaire in Naissance du Code Civil 41 (F. Ewald ed. 1989).

137 Ibid., p. 196, referring to Mazeaud et al, (2000), supra note 1910, p. 82, 107.

138 Ibid., p. 201, referring to David (1959, 1972), supra note .1910, pp. 140-46.

139 Ibid., referring to Rieg (1978), supra note 1910, pp. 82-83; Jean Carbonnier, 'Droit Civil', 177 (12th ed. 1979), p. 179.

140 Ibid., p. 197.

141 Ibid., p. 198, citing Andrew West, et. al., 'The French Legal System, An Introduction', (1992) (2nd ed. 1998).

142 Wahlgren (2009), supra note 1880, p. 243, referring to Stig Stromholm (1996), supra note 1858, p. 411.

143 Germain (2003), supra note 1909, p. 198, referring to Mazeaud et, al. (2000), supra note 1912, p. 172; A. Weill, 'Droit Civil', 185-186b (4th ed. 1979).

for interpretation in the application.[144] In the event the law was obscure, a judge would examine the *travaux preparatoires* to discover the legislature's intent and 'the meaning of obscure provisions' as meant in the legislature's clear thought. In the event the legal system does not provide sufficient reasoning for interpretation, the investigation may be extended beyond the available legal propositions and may include previously described legal *solutions* by employing analogy.

***

One central characteristic of interpretation is that interpretation is a Janus-faced concept, encompassing both a backward-looking conserving component, and a forward-looking creative one. In legal interpretation, judges seek to conserve the currently existing content of the law as well as to supplement, modify, or bring out something new in the law, in the course of reasoning from the content of the law to judicial decisions. The right balance between the conserving and creative elements of legal interpretation and the constrains upon judges as they undertake the balancing are the concerns of jurists and legal theorists in their writing on interpretation.[145] The pragmatic judge will go beyond the 'orthodox legal materials' to consider, inter alia, rules' purposes, social policies, and possible consequences.[146] Richard Posner continues: "A systemic value that requires particular emphasis is the importance of preserving language as an effective medium of communication. If judges did not generally interpret.. statutes in accordance with the ordinary meaning of the sentences appearing in those texts, certainty of legal obligation would be seriously

144 Ibid., referring to Mazeaud et.al. (2000), Ibid., p. 172.

145 Julie Dickson, 'Interpretation and Coherence in Legal Reasoning', in Stanford Encyclopedia of Philosophy, first published Tuesday, May 29, 2001, substantive revision Wednesday, Feb.10, 2010, §2, p. 5. See O. Fiss,'Objectivity and Interpretation', in Stanford Law Review, 34(1982), pp. 739-763; Dworkin (1986), supra note 1379; A. Marmor, 'Interpretation and Legal Theory', (Oxford: Clarendon Press, 1992); A. Marmor, 'Interpretation and Legal Theory', revised 2nd edition, (Oxford: Hart Publishing, 2005); T.A..O. Endicott, 'Putting Interpretation In Its Place', in Law and Philosophy, 13 (1994), pp. 451-79; J. Raz, 'Why Interpret?', in Ratio Juris, 9(1996), pp. 349-63 ["Raz 1996a"]; J. Raz, 'Intention in Interpretation' in RP.George (ed.),TheAutonomy of Law, (Oxford: Clarendon Press, 1996) ["Raz 1996b"].

146 Ofer Raban, 'Real and Imagined Threats to the Rule of Law: On Brian Tamanaha's Law As A Means To An End', (2007), in Virginia Journal of Social Policy and the Law,Vol.15, 2008, p. 478, referring to Richard Posner,'Law, Pragmatism, and Democracy', (2003), p. 67.

undermined. For judges in the run-of-the-mill ....cases to subordinate this consideration to a weighing of case-specific consequences would therefore be unpragmatic".[147] When the consequences are not catastrophic or absurd, it is usually sensible to go with the plain meaning of a statute or contract in order to protect expectations and preserve ordinary language as an effective medium of legal communication.[148] Indeed, although judges should strive to achieve the best results, only in the extreme case would a judge be justified in disregarding the legislative judgment [as to what these best results are].[149] The judges have a natural inclination to see what they are doing as interpreting the legal materials, such as contracts, statutes, constitutions, treaties or precedents. The judges' inclinations are related to the best feature of a concern for the rule of law: the determination not to subject the parties and the community to the arbitrary will of an official.[150]

Joseph Raz views, when we interpret the law, we should primarily establish the existence and meaning of any purportedly authoritative directives of legal institutions and the decisions of those institutions are the originals to be interpreted in the case of law.[151] He insists that proper legal interpretation requires one to understand the legislation as meaning what the legislator said.[152] John Gardner, elaborating Raz's thesis, thinks that the possibilities are endless, .. So long as one can work out more or less how the relevant others will read what one says or does, one can also adapt what one says or does to anticipate their readings. If one can work out that the relevant others are perverse types who will always read 'cat' to mean 'dog', one can make the dog-regulating laws one means to make by passing a Cat Regulation Act. By this feedback route, one has the power intentionally to determine what law one makes even though the norm of interpreting that law ....gives one's text a quirky meaning (i.e., is not textualist).[153] So 'perverse positivists' need not be textualist; but textualism is the only practical alternative for reasonable one.[154] Legal reasoning is at all interpretative.[155] Raz is doubtful of a certain

---

147 Ibid. See Posner (2003), Ibid., p. 62.

148 Ibid. See Posner (2003), Ibid., p. 82.

149 Ibid. See Posner (2003), Ibid., p. 71.

150 Timothy A.O. Endicott, 'Legal Interpretation', in A. Marmor (ed.), Routledge Companion to Philosophy of Law, (Routledge, 2012), in Legal Research Paper Series – Paper No. 39/2011, June 2011.

151 Dickson (2010), supra note 1920, p. 7.

152 Raban (2007/2008), supra note 1921, n.66, referring to Joseph Raz, 'Intention in Interpretation', in the AUTOMONY OF LAW 249, 271 (Robert P. George ed., 1999).

153 Ibid., referring to John Gardner, 'Legal Positivism, 5 ½ Myths', in 46 Am. J. Juris. 199 (2001), p. 219.

154 Ibid.

155 Dickson (2010), supra note 1926, p. 14, referring to J. Raz, 'Ethics in the

kind of account of interpretation in the form of a theory which purports either to operate as a recipe for concocting good interpretation, or to provide us with a general account of how to evaluate interpretation as good or bad, right or wrong.[156] Finnis 1987 holds that pervasive incommensurabilities exist in the criteria by reference to which we are supposed to adjudge one interpretation to be better than other, so interpretation in legal reasoning may not lead judges to one right answer.[157] Interpretive pluralism, according to Raz (2009), is a basic feature of the concept of interpretation, and several different and incompatible interpretations of the same object are probable, all of which can be good.[158]

Timothy Endicott sees people's conviction are significantly different. The considerations supporting a conclusion about justice do not become stronger as the conclusion shows a better fit with what people do or believe, or, the considerations do not get weaker as the conclusion demonstrates a worse fit with what people do or believe. Then, the problem can be answered by Dworkin's suggestion that the 'leeways' are drawn less tightly around the interpretive data for justice than for law. There is no general reason to try to fit judgments of justice to any body of data, so interpretation may be required in seeking justice. Concerning reasonableness, it is the courts or other decision-makers which should identify the reasons, 'without constraint from the law'.[159] Tim Endicott relies on three general propositions and two specific ones concerning interpretation.[160] The general propositions are: (1) interpretation is of an object (that is, a good interpretation depends on true propositions that refer to the object); (2) interpretation is creative (that is, an interpretation does not simply state what everyone knows if they are familiar with the object, but ascribes to it a meaning that someone else might dispute); and (3) interpretation is rational (there can be reasons for arriving at an interpretation). And the two specific propositions are: (1) a legal interpretation gives a rule for the application of the law (it is applicable, not generalizing); and (2) a legal interpretation is articulate or propositional (i.e., it can be expressed in propositions).

***

Public Domain' (Oxford: Clarendon Press, 1994), ch.o.

156 Ibid., p. 9, referring to J. Raz, 'Between Authority and Interpretation', (Oxford: Oxford University Press, 2009).

157 Ibid., p. 12, referring to John Finnis, 'On Reason and Authority in Law's Empire', in Law and Philosophy, 6 (1987), pp. 357-380.

158 Ibid., referring to Raz (2009), supra note 1931.

159 Endicott (2011), supra note 1925.

160 Ibid.

As to the debate between formalism and anti-formalism at the root of American jurisprudence, Judge Posner has written that [this] jurisprudential disagreement is not less important by virtue of being unavowed by most judges. It is the disagreement between the severely positivistic view that the content of law is exhausted in clear, explicit, and definite enactments by or under express delegation from legislatures, and the natural lawyer's or legal pragmatist's view that the practice of interpretation and the general terms of the Constitution (such as 'equal protection of the laws') authorize judges to enrich positive law with the moral values and practical concerns of civilized society. Neither approach is entirely satisfactory. The first buys political neutrality and a type of objectivity at the price of substantive injustice, while the second buys justice in the individual case at the price of considerable uncertainty and, not infrequently, judicial willfulness. It is no wonder that our legal system oscillates between the approaches.[161] Justice Antonin Scalia and his allies are formalists, attacking legislative intent. They hold that legislative intent does not exist and that the law on the books is the only law. The ordinary meaning of statutory language is to govern statutory interpretation.[162] Under Justice Scalia's new formalism, legislative history is out, and the canons of statutory interpretation are back in.[163]

161 Phillip P. Frickey, 'Revisiting the Revival of Theory in Statutory Interpretation: A Lecture in Honor of Irving Younger', in 84 Minn. L. Rev. 199 (1999), p. 220. See United States v. Marshall, 908 F.2d 1312, 1334-35 (7th Cir. 1990) (enbanc) (Posner, J., dissenting) (emphasis added), aff'd sub nom. Chapman v. United States, 500 U.S. 453 (1991).

162 Ibid., p. 204, referring to Phillip P. Frickey, 'From the Big Sleep to the Big Heat: The Revival of Theory in Statutory Interpretation, in 77 MINN. L. REV. (1992), pp. 254-256.

163 Ibid., p. 206. Respect for the canons had been in decline since Karl Llewellyn's famous essay suggested that for every canon there was a counter-canon. See Karl N. Llewellyn, 'Remarks on the Appellate Decision and the Rules or Canons About How Statutes Are to Be Construed', in 3 VAND. L. REV. (1950), p. 395. About the time that Scalia lent support to canonical methodology, several scholars were suggesting various theories under which the canons play a legitimate role in statutory interpretation. See William N. Eskridge, Jr., 'Public Values in Statutory Interpretation', in 137 U. PA. L. REV. 1007 (1989), p. 1011, (observing that canons may represent "public values" drawn from the Constitution, statutes, and common law); Geoffrey P. Miller, 'Pragmatics and the Maxims of Interpretation', in 1990 WIS. L. REV. pp. 1179, 1183, 1191-225 (discussing how textual canon may be consistent with philosophical linguistics); David. L. Shapiro, 'Continuity and Change in Statutory Interpretation,' in 67 N.Y.U. L. REV. 921 (1992), pp. 927-941 (arguing that canons promote legal stability); Cass R. Sunstein, 'Interpreting Statutes in the Regulatory State', in 103 HARV. L. REV. 405 (1989), pp. 462-503, (arguing that canons should provide principles for interpreting statutes in post-New Deal regulatory circumstances). For a list of the canons used by the current Supreme Court, see William N. Eskridge, Jr., & Phillip P. Frickey, 'The Supreme

Formalism follows its basic premise that predictability, certainty and the constraint of judicial discretion make law 'law'. And formalism separates courts from legislatures and administrative bodies. The desire for legal predictability and certainty might be achieved through Justice Scalia's *judicial* pronouncement of a method for statutory interpretation – text plus canons. Formalism is a top-down rule of law methodology, where canons can trump ordinary textual meaning.[164]

Anti-formalists also attacked the old conventional wisdom that defended legislative intent. Bill Eskridge in his 1987 article says that statutory law, like constitutional law and common law, are dynamic rather than static, and the meaning of statutes has evolved over time in many circumstances.[165] In 1990, Eskridge and Frickey focused on a pragmatic approach to defining and, in limited circumstances, redefining statutory meaning.[166] They put forward their descriptive arguments that courts in statutory interpretation had commonly considered 'textual meaning, legislative intent, and functional purposes', all measured against the factual litigation context - and normatively as well - that 'this kind of critical pragmatism was appropriate' since its purpose was 'to construct practical answers to concrete problems in light of the relevant textual, institutional, and contextual perspectives'.

***

On the current methods of statutory interpretation in France, Claire Germain summarizes that: (1) When a text is clear, it should be applied and not interpreted, unless an absurd result would follow[167]; (2) When a text is ambiguous or obscure, courts look for the will of the legislature; for that, a judge first examines the text itself with care and considers commentaries written about the text; and this is not limited to the provision to be applied but includes the chapter or the entire law; and often a provision is obscure

Court 1993 Term – Foreword: Law as Equilibrium', in 108 HARV. L. REV. 26 (1994), pp. 97-108.

164 Ibid., p. 207.

165 Ibid., p. 204, referring to William N. Eskridge, Jr., 'Dynamic Statutory Interpretation', in 135 U. PA. L. REV. (1987), p. 1487.

166 Ibid., referring to Wililam N. Eskridge, Jr & Frickey, 'Statutory Interpretation as Practical Reasoning', in 42 STAN. L. REV. 321 (1900), pp. 345-362, 362-384.

167 Germain (2003), supra note 1918, p. 201, referring to Mazeaud et. al. (2000), supra note 1918, p. 182; Rieg (1978), supra note 1914, pp. 74-78.

only if separated from its context[168]; (3) If this study is insufficient, courts often go to the *travaux preparatoires* to discover the legislature's thinking; and the Cour de cassation agrees with this process, but also states that the *travaux preparatoires* never bind the court, and Rene David calls the process the historical method of interpretation[169]; (4) When a text does not directly provide the solution for a dispute, judges need at least to start from a text to situate the rule that they will design; and French judicial decisions almost always invoke a text, and it is exceptional for a court not to refer to a legal text; and sometimes courts invoke general principles of law[170]; and (5) If the legislative history is confused, or the law is too old, the judge will look at other considerations and use what the scholarly writers call the teleological interpretation method.[171] So, what the courts employ are the exegetic method and legislative history method, in case the text is recent; the teleological approach is employed in the event the written law is already old and there is no legislature's thinking expressed.

Allison Connelly identifies three methods of statutory interpretation.[172] If the statutory text is so clear and unambiguous, the plain meaning rule method applies. If a statute appears to be unambiguous on its face, its meaning must be determined from the [statute] itself without resort to any 'outside evidence' (Black's Law Dictionary 1188, 8th ed. 2004). If the language of statute is ambiguous and its meaning is not clear, other evidence to establish legislative intent can be used (Extrinsic Evidence – Legislative Intent & History). Canons are rules or guides used to interpret a statute when the legislative intent of the statute cannot be determined. Textual Canons are used to infer the meaning of a statute from its textual structure. *Expressio unius est exclusio alterius* (to express on thing – as in a statute – is to exclude other things not mentioned), *ejusdem generis* (of the same class or genus and applicable to all catch words after a list), and *in pari material* (statutes having a common purpose or common subject matter should be construed together) are examples of Textual Canons. Substantive Canons can also be used and are principles that are derived from the legal effect of a rule, for example: when the same rules should be used to construe and interpret statutes; the more specific statute supersedes the general one, and later statutes supersedes earlier ones; and courts should broadly construe remedial statutes.

In rule-based reasoning, the statute is broken into separate elements,

168 Ibid., p. 202, referring to Mazeaud et. al. (2000), p. 182.

169 Ibid., referring to David (1959, 1972), supra note 1913, p. 143.

170 Ibid., referring to David (1959, 1972), Ibid., p. 186.

171 Ibid., referring to David (1959, 1972), Ibid., p. 147; Rieg (1978), supra note 1942, p. 84.

172 Connelly, supra note 1301, para III.D.5.a & b.I, II & III.

says Connelly.[173] Once the statute has been broken into the separate elements, the statutory text must be interpreted and understood by first reviewing the statute to determine whether there is a definition section, and then noting any words of authority such as *shall* for mandatory, *shall not* for prohibitory, *may* for discretionary and *is* for declaratory. The facts of the case are to be matched with each element of the statute to see if the element is proven.

Wilson Huhn has identified there are five types of legal arguments: text argument, legislative history and drafter's intent argument, precedent argument, tradition argument and policy argument.[174] Text argument is forwarded when the legal rules are written laws, and this argument focuses on the text of constitutions, statutes and codes as opposed to judicial opinions or the Common law. Legislative History and Drafter's Intent Argument should be based on what the legislator meant when the legal text was enacted. In the precedent argument, a legal rule is what the courts in their precedents have said it means. According to the tradition argument, the rules have a meaning that is the traditional way members of community have acted in the past. And, policy argument follows the notion that the rule should conform to the underlying values and interests that the rule is designed to serve.

IV.3.2. TEXTUALIST METHOD

When the words of the statute seem to have a clear meaning all by themselves, but the meaning is not in accordance with the legislative intent, which of these is to be privileged in statutory interpretation? When more than one meaning are identified, which of these is to be privileged? In terms of more practical concerns, the meaning which is more practical, or more consistent with the broader legal landscape, or simply more in accord with common sense is considered. If the interpretation consistent with clear legislative intent produces a dysfunctional or absurd outcome, must that interpretation be privileged as against these more practical concerns? Justice Scalia's vivid and relevant theory on statutory interpretation has much been followed by practice in state courts.[175] In a dissenting opinion in 1991, Justice Scalia wrote: "I thought we had adopted a regular method for interpreting the meaning of language in a statute: first, find the ordinary meaning of the language in its textual context; and second, using established canons of construction, and ask

173 Ibid., para III.D.1,2,3 & 4.

174 Ibid., para II. 1, 2, 3, 4, 5, referring to Wilson Huhn, '5 Types of Legal Argument,' 12 (2002).

175 Frickey (1999), supra note 1936, pp. 202-203.

whether there is any clear indication that some permissible meaning other than the ordinary one applies".[176]

In *Caminetti v. United States*[177] it has been held that the old 'plain meaning rule' is a familiar notion to lawyers. When a statute has a plain meaning or is unambiguous, in accordance with the "plain meaning rule" the court must stick with that meaning. But in interpreting an ambiguous statute the court is free to consult the legislative history, statutory purposes and other potential sources of meaning.

Close view of statutory texts is today carried on in legal practice. In examining and defining the critical words of statutory texts, today's practitioners use the language and context of statutory provisions as reference. But, contemporary lawyers should also endeavor, as far as the text permits, to give effect to the purpose and policy which are clear in statutory language. So, the texts are to be viewed in its entirety, and its objects may be held as far as possibly. Michael Kirby agrees with James Raymond that more convincing meaning of the statutory language will be exposed if the exposition moves beyond purely linguistic explanation. When the interpreter discloses 'deep-lying' considerations or responses to a linguistic problem, she or he will truly explain why the conclusion stated was reached.[178] The judicial task is fundamentally textual, with the text as the anchor for the task of any lawyer or citizen in interpreting and applying legislation. Straying too far from the text is not permitted.[179] Obedience to the text, Kirby says, has a constitutional foundation, based on the respect to the democratic character of parliamentary law-maker, speaking to the courts in the words that the law-maker has formally adopted.[180]

As shown in the ECJ case law, where the wording of an EU law provision is clear and precise, the ECJ will never ignore the clear and precise wording of an EU law provision,[181] in order to be in accordance with

176 Ibid., p. 206. See Chisom v. Roemer, 501 U.S. 380, 404 (1991) (Scalia, J., dissenting).

177 Ibid., p. 210, 211. See Caminetti v. United States, 242 U.S. 470, 485 (1917).

178 Michael Kirby, 'Statutory Interpretation: The Meaning of Meaning', School of Accounting and Law Symposium on Statutory Interpretation, Chapter House, St. Paul's Cathedral, RMIT University, Melbourne, August 13, 2009, p. 30, 31, 32.

179 Ibid., p. 25. See Trust Co. v. Commissioner of State Revenue (2003) 77 ALJR 1019, p. 1029 [66[-[68].

180 Ibid.

181 Koen Lenaerts and Jose A. Gutiérrez-Fons, 'To Say What the Law of the EU Is: Methods of Interpretation and the European Court of Justice', in EUI Working Paper AEL 2013/9, European University Institute – Academy of European Law, p. 7. See e.g., Case C-220/03 BCE v. Germany [2005] ECR I-10595, para 31; Case C-263/06 Carboni e dericati [2008] ECR I-1077, para 48; and C-48/07 Les Vergers

the principle of legal certainty and to the principle of inter-institutional balance enshrined in Article 13(2) TEU.[182] In accordance with the maxim *interpretatio cessat in claris*, only an obscure text may be interpreted in a way that departs from the usual meaning of the words contained therein.[183] As noted by AG Jääskinen, 'the literal interpretation and the clear meaning may not be synonymous as the literal meaning of a provision may be ambiguous'.

IV.3.3. TELEOLOGICAL METHOD

In law, the teleological or purposive interpretation seeks to find the meaning of the normative act by highlighting the finalities of the interpreted normative act.[184] In this hermeneutic approach, the trichotomy practiced by Origen in analyzing a text is essential: a first and literal level has a guiding character, based on the relationship between thought and words, thus giving us the direct meaning of the text; the second level is the soul, of an evocative order for the receiver; and the third, of a spiritual order, is the one which bears the essential meaning of the text, this being the level at which the method or the teleological interpretation criterion operates.[185] The major difficulty of the teleological interpretation rests in the accurate deceleration of the distinction between the spirit of law and the will (intention) of the legislator. This represents the concordance point when *telos* is demonstrated, the original purpose of instituting a law order in the Fundamental Law, as detectable in the Constitution, can be found.[186] According to I. Huma, [the] purpose is a representative criterion of valuable judgments, which the teleological approach uses, while the historical approach is causal-analytical, and it identifies direct motivations; it operates in the world of facts as facts, not of the ideal which transcends them, by using ascertained

---

du Vieux Tauves [2008] ECR I-10627, para 44.

182 Ibid. See e.g., Case C-582/08 Commission v. United Kingdom [2010] ECR I-07195.

183 Ibid. See Opinion of AG Jääskinen in Case C-582/08 Commission v. United Kingdom [2010] ECR I-07195, para 27 (referring to Opinion of Advocate General Mayras in Case 67/79 Fellinger [1980] ECR 535, p. 550.

184 Lucian-Sorin Stănescu, 'The Teleological Interpretation and the Discovery of the Constitution's Efficiency Meanings', in Fiat Iustitia No. 1/2014, p. 230, referring to I. Craiovan, 'Tratat de teoria generală a dreptului', Universul Juristic, Bucharest, 2007, p. 427.

185 Ibid., referring to Gh. Mihai, 'Argumentare si interpretare in drept', Ed. Lumina Lex, Bucharest, 2001, p. 199.

186 Ibid., referring to Eremia, 'Interpretarea juridica', (Bucharest: All, 1998), p. 73.

or mostly ascertained judgments.[187] D.C. Danisor shows that the purpose of law identifies itself with the reason of law (*ratio legis*) which is also called 'the spirit of the law', and it is formulated in a preamble or in an express disposition of the text itself [although this procedure is kind of rare].[188] This attracts attention in a justified manner that in order to better interpret a text it is essential to clearly notice this law reason, to admit, for instance, which are the interests that the law tends to protect, which are the abuses which it wants to stop, which is the political or social result that it tends to realize, etc.

Following Rawls' thesis on legitimacy as a constant that determines the ongoing evaluation of the performance of a political regime, implying the continuation of the trial of reassurance and affirmation of consent at the original social contract (joining consent),[189] Lucian-Sorin Stănescu concludes that the teleological role of interpretation appears as a bridge between the vision of the Founding Fathers and the current meaning of constitutional text, and its use becomes mandatory in order to ensure the continuity of its goals.[190] By abstracting one of Ihering's theories, Craiovan holds that the purpose or *telos* [as a future state, anticipated and desired, and as a product of the voluntary human action and the ideal, and as a representation of an always desired but never fully reached model, interacting in law, not being isolated by the philosophical layers and the social and political contex],[191] is [in] the creator of the whole law; and the law is the frame in which the state organizes, by constraint, the insurance of life conditions of the society. By consequence, the existence and insurance of the society represent the final purpose of law.[192] Rudolf Stammler's opnion relates law with fairness.[193] The law is justified as far as its purposes are fair: in this conception, the content of a norm is fair when in its determined conditions it corresponds to the social ideal, whereas the social ideal is the conception of a perfectly free human will community, [...] in which each individual assimilates the objective and general purposes of the others.

Courts are bound by the constraints of legal reasoning as defined by

---

187 Ibid., referring to I. Huma, 'Probleme controversate privind tehnica istorica in interpretarea dreptului', in EIRP Proceedings, Vol. 1, (2006), "Danubius" University, Galati, p. 14.

188 Ibid., pp. 230-231, referring to D.C. Danisor, I. Dogaru & Gh. Danisor, 'Teoria generală a dreptului', (Bucharest: C.H. Beck, 2006), p. 396.

189 Ibid., p. 237, referring to F. Peter, 'Political Legitimacy', in Stanford Encyclopedia of Philosophy [Summer 2010 Edition], Edward N. Zalta (ed.), http://plato.stanford.edu/archives/sum2010/entries/legitimacy/

190 Ibid.

191 Ibid., p. 166.

192 Ibid., p. 231, referring to Craiovan (2007), supra note 1959, p. 167.

193 Ibid., referring to Craiovan (2007), Ibid., p. 167.

the limits imposed by the text, by the logical rules of practical reasoning,[194] and by the systemic requirements of coherence and consistency.[195] In this respect, teleological reasoning reinforces the Court's accountability as it increases transparency as to its normative choices.[196] *Telos* signifies a higher constraint, that is pure reference to wording or intent. It binds courts to a consistent normative reading of those provisions. Teleological interpretation can also be seen as more faithful to the democratic outcomes since it prevents textual manipulation of the legal rules. In fact, an interpretation that pays attention to the goals of the rule, and not simply its wording, prevents opportunistic behaviors and minimizes the risk of an interpretive manipulation of the legislation. Brian Tamanaha argues that judges formerly were explicit oriented toward strictly following the law, but they were never completely blind to ends.[197] With the rise of instrumentalism [Posner's included], judges are encouraged to strive to achieve purposes or ends, while paying attention to the legal rules. Both orientations consider rules and ends. The former approach makes it clear, however, that the rules control, unless the outcome is absolutely absurd or impossibly outrageous (a high threshold rarely met). The latter approach makes consideration of ends a routine matter, and thus always a threat to affect the application of the legal rules.

The favorable method of interpretation utilized by the ECJ is the teleological method, which seeks to interpret a rule by taking into account the purpose, aim and objective it pursues. AG Fennelly noted '[t[he characteristic element in the [ECJ]'s interpretive method is [...] the so-called teleological approach'.[198] Teleological method of interpretation is perfectly consistent with the dynamic and evolving nature of the European Community, which over the years has changed its objectives and its plans from a purely economic approach to a broader system of values which affects social and environmental issues; and the protection of human rights.[199]

A principal corollary, developed early on, to the teleological method, is the doctrine of 'effectiveness' or '*effect utile*'.[200] The Court of Justice of

194 Maduro (2007), supra note 1864, p. 10, referring to Robert Alexy, 'A theory of legal argumentation', (Oxford: Clarendon, 1989).

195 Ibid., referring to Dworkin (1986), supra note 1920; McCormick (1978), supra note 1296.

196 Ibid.

197 Raban (2007/2008), supra note 1927, ch. iv, referring to Brian Tamanaha, 'Law As A Means To An End: Threat to the Rule of Law', 2006, p. 233.

198 Lenaerts & Gutiérrez-Fons (2013), supra note 1956, p. 24, referring to Fennelly (1996), infra note 1975, p. 664.

199 Pollicino (2004), supra note 1888, p. 289.

200 Nial Fennelly, 'Legal Interpretation at the European Court of Justice', in Fordham International Law Journal, Volume 20, Issue 3, Article 4, (1996), p. 674.

the European Community seeks above all, effectiveness, consistency and uniformity in its case law and in the application of Community law.[201] On the basis of teleological arguments, being the decisive interpretation in European law, a breakthrough was achieved on certain decisions as well as on certain fundamental shifts in understanding of the importance of European law.[202] The interpretive principle of effectiveness (*effect utile*)[203] is reflective when interpreting European law by using the teleological method of interpretation, which means not only taking into account the objectives (to which the teleological method leads) but also the effort to reach the goal as effectively as possible (case C 292/89 *Antonissen*).

Due to the pluralism of languages and legal traditions [in EU], bringing with them conceptual problems of translation, teleological interpretation is also the more appropriate form of guarantying a uniform application of EU law at the national level. Teleological interpretation not only enables the ECJ to engage in gap filling, but may also be relied upon with a view to reducing the scope of application of EU law (so-called 'teleological reduction'). Bengoetxea has observed[204] that teleological interpretation first aims to secure the *effect utile* (effectiveness) of the EU law provision in question (the so-called 'functional interpretation').[205]It is only after examining the normative context in which the EU law provision in question is placed that the interpretation that best preserves the effectiveness of that provision may be chosen. So, teleological interpretation goes hand in hand with systematic interpretation. When an EU law provision is ambiguous or incomplete, it must be interpreted in light of the objectives it pursues (the so-called 'teleological interpretation *stricto sensu*').[206]

See, e.g., Bauhuis v. Netherlands, Case 46/76, [1977] E.C.R. 5.

201 Ibid.

202 Salachova & Vitek (2013), supra note 1881, p. 2719.

203 Ibid., referring to D. Sehnalek, 'Princip effet utille v unijnim pravu', in V. Tyc, et.al., Vybrane otazky pusobeni prava Evropske unie ve sfere ceskeho pravniho radu, (Brno: Masarykova univerzita, 2011), p. 65.

204 Lenaerts & Gutiérrez-Fons (2013), supra note 1973, p. 25, referring to J. Bengoetxea, 'The Legal Reasoning of the European Court of Justice', (Oxford: Clarendon, 1993).

205 Ibid. Regarding the effectiveness of Article 101 and 102 TFEU, see e.g., Case C-439/08 VEBIC [2010] ECR I-12471, para 64. Regarding the preliminary reference procedure enshrined in Article 267 TFEU, see e.g., Joined Cases C-188/10 and C-189/10 Melki and Abdeli [2010] ECR I-5667, para 45. Regarding the primacy of directly effective provisions of EU law, see Case C-409/06 Winner Wetten [2010] ECR I-8015, para 56.

206 Ibid. For example, in Case C-101/01 Lindqvist [2003] ECR I-12971, the ECJ ruled that '[i]n the light of the purpose of the directive [i.e. the protection of the right to respect for private life], the expression data concerning health used in Article 8(1) thereof must be given a wide interpretation so as to include information

IV.3.4. CONTEXTUALIST / SYSTEMATIC METHOD

In ECJ case law, accepted interpretive criteria include linguistic, systemic and contextual as well as teleological arguments.[207] In more recent years [after the *van Gend en Loos* case], the idea of 'context' has been added [to the teleological method of interpretation],[208] and the prevailing wording, varying minimally from case to case, has been that it is necessary when interpreting a provision of Community law to consider not only its wording, but also the context in which it occurs and the objects of the rules of which it is a part.[209] Teleological interpretation in EU law does not refer exclusively to a purpose driven interpretation of the relevant legal rules. It refers to a particular systemic understanding of the EU legal order that permeates the interpretation of all its rules. In other words, the ECJ interprets a rule in light of the broader context provided by the EU legal order and its 'constitutional *telos*'. There is a clear association between the systemic (context) and teleological elements of interpretation. It is not simply the *telos* of the rules to be interpreted that matters but also the *telos* of the legal context in which those rules exist.[210] Various forms of contextual interpretation may be combined and interconnected, so efficient interpretation implies interpreting activities through sifting or carefully examining large volumes of text encompassing not only a lot of legal matter of a substantial nature, but also considerations of legal propositions of intentional and methodological nature originating from different kinds of legal sources. When explicit methodological support is available, it is possible to employ *methodological interpretation*.[211] Methodological interpretation is used when legal propositions of a substantive nature are interconnected with methodological rules. One example of such a rule of a very distinct nature appears in the Swedish legislation concerning vehicles, where the third section in the statute on road traffic (SFS 1972:603) stipulates that if a certain vehicle or type of

---

concerning all aspects, both physical and mental, of the health of an individual,' Ibid., para 50.

207 Paunio (2009), supra note 1862, p. 1484. See in more detail Bengoetxea (1993), supra note 1979, pp. 218-270.

208 Fennelly (1996), supra note 1975, p. 664. Possibly because of the inclusion of the expression in the Vienna Convention.

209 Ibid. See Merck v. Hauptzollant Hamburg-Jonas, Case 292/82, [1983] E.C.R. I-3781, 3792, 12; see e.g., Bosphorus v. Minister for Transport, Case-85/95, [1996] E.C.R. I-3953, I-3982 11, [1996] 3 C.M.L.R. 257, 293; Peter Leifer and Others, Case C-85/94, [1995] E.C.R. I-3231, 22. By now this has become "the constant case law" of the Court. E.J.M. de Jaeek, Case C-340/9430, slip op. pp. 1-5, 17 (Eur. Ct.J.Jan. 1997).

210 Maduro (2007), supra note 1969, p. 5.

211 Wahlgren (2009), supra note 1917, p. 241.

vehicle cannot be classified in accordance with the lists of vehicles in the statute, the issue of classification should be submitted to the Road Traffic Security Administration.

As to statutory interpretation, the High Court of Australia has adopted some other necessary principles, and amongst those principles are: 1/ Where the applicable law is expressed in legislation the correct starting point for analysis is the text of the legislation and not judicial statements of the Common law or even judicial elaborations of the statute;[212] 2/ The overall objective of statutory construction is to give effect to the purpose of parliament as expressed in the text of the statutory provisions[213] and 3/ In deriving meaning from the text, so as to fulfill the purpose of parliament, it is a mistake to consider statutory words in isolation. The proper approach demands the derivation of the meaning of words from the legislative context in which those words appear. Specifically, it requires the interpreter to examine at the very least the sentence; often the paragraph; and preferably the immediately surrounding provisions (if not a wider review of the entire statutory context) to identify the meaning of the words in the context in which they are used.[214]

Among several approaches, *contextual interpretation* is the most obvious and uncontroversial approach to clarify legal propositions by means of finding explicit indicators on how to reduce difficulties concerning vagueness and ambiguity of law in handling a certain issue within the legal system.[215] And when indicators from the legal system cannot be utilized for some reasons, *supplementary interpretation* through the application of various kinds of technical approaches may complementary be employed to transform legal propositions.[216]

---

212 Visy Paper Pty Ltd v. Australian Competition & Consumer Commission (2003) 216 CLR 1 at 10 [24], fn35).

213 Kirby (2009), supra note 1953, p. 4. See Project Blue Sky Inc v. AMA (1998) 194 CLR 355, p. 381 [69]; M. D. Kirby, 'Toward A Grand Theory of Interpretation: The Case of Statutes and Contracts', (2003), in 24 Statute Law Review 95, p. 99.

214 Ibid., pp. 4-5. See Collector of Customs v. Agfa Gevaert Ltd. (1996) 186 CLR 389, p. 397 applying R v. Brown [1996] 1 AC 543, p. 561 per Lord Hoffmann; Minister for Immigration & Multicultural Affairs v. Khawar (2002) 210 CLR 1, p. 36 [109]; SGH Ltd v. Commissioner of Taxation (2002) 210 CLR 51, p. 91 [88].

215 Wahlgren (2009), supra note 1986, p. 235, referring to Jan Hellner, 'Rattsteori: En introduktion', (Stockholm: Juristforlaget, 1988), p. 65; for a somewhat different perspective, K.T. Jackson, 'Definition in Legal Reasoning', in Jurimetrics Journal, Vol. 25, (1985), pp. 379-384, on applying various types of legal definitions to facts.

216 Ibid., referring to Hellner (1998), Ibid., p. 69.

IV.3.5. COMPARATIVE LAW METHOD

In so far as the ECJ combines a teleological interpretation of EU law with a construction of that law grounded in a comparative law method, the objectives pursued by the EU are aligned with those set out in national constitutions, thereby creating a 'common constitutional space' which, needless to say, does not threaten national sovereignty.[217] One of the values of constitutional pluralism [in EU] and of a proper comparative law methodology is the learning and experimentalism it promotes among different legal orders. It creates a framework for attributing between different legal solutions which compete in answering to what might be a common problem.[218] As a consequence, a comparative law methodology that would amount to a simple arithmetic exercise will also ignore the value of constitutional pluralism. The methodology of comparative law to be employed by the Court has to balance the respect of national legal traditions with the need to accommodate them to the specific needs of the EU legal order. In other words, it is not simply a question of determining what legal solution is common to the national legal orders, but also, or mostly, a question of determining what legal solution fits better with the EU legal order (in light of its broader set of rules and principles and of its context of application). The comparative law methodology to be employed by the Court must be shaped by a requirement of consistency within the EU legal system.[219]

The comparative analysis by MacCormick indicates that various legal systems have generated different kinds of methodological rules concerning rule conflicts, and that .. no system has yet succeeded in establishing any clearly articulated picture of the law at this level.[220] First, if the conflicting rules vary in status due to formal reasons, the principle of *lex superior legi inferior derogate* may be employed.[221] Secondly, if one of the conflicting rules is older than the other, the principle of *lex posterior legi priori derogate* may be used.[222] Thirdly, if one of the conflicting rules can be seen as a more specialized regulation of a certain issue, the principle

217 Lenaerts & Gutiérrez-Fons (2013), supra note 1979, p. 28.

218 Maduro (2007), supra note 1985, p. 7.

219 Ibid.

220 Wahlgren (2009), supra note 1990, pp. 244-245, referring to N. D. MacCormick, 'Interpreting Statutes: A Comparative Study', in Robert S. Summer ed. (Aldershot: Dartmouth Publishing Company Ltd, 1991), pp. 527-530.

221 Ibid., referring to J.W.F. Saundberg, fr. Eddan t. Ekelof: Repetitorium om rattskallor i Norden, Studentlitteratur/Akademisk forlag/Institutet for offentlig och internationell ratt, (1978), p. 200.

222 Ibid., referring to Stromholm (1996), supra note 1917, p. 506.

of *lex specialis legi generali derogat* may come into use.[223]

IV.3.6. PRECEDENTIAL ARGUMENT

As Huhn has identified that precedent argument is a type of legal arguments. In the precedent argument, a legal rule is what the courts in their precedents have said it means. It is the *ratio decidendi* that constitutes the legal rule in precedent argument under the *stare decisis* doctrine in Common law jurisdiction.[224] In Common law jurisdictions, statutes are to be objectively constructed according to certain rules standing by themselves,[225] such as that an enactment must be read as a whole, and that special provisions will control general provisions, so as to meet the subjects' reasonable understandings and expectations[226] [as compared with Civil law tradition, where the first step in interpreting an ambiguous law, according to Mazeaud, is to discover the intention of the legislator by examining the legislation as a whole, including the '*travaux preparatoires*', as well as the provisions more immediately surrounding the obscure text].[227] If Civil law codes and statutes are the primary source of law under Montesquieu's theory, Common law statutes have to be read against a case law background. If Civil law judges are influenced by Rousseau's theory that the State is the source of all rights under the social contract, English judges favor Hobbes's theory that the individual agreed to forfeit to the State only certain rights.

As to the precedent argument, Grant Lamond's conclusion is that the *ratio decidendi* of the earlier case at a formal level is a rule, with the argument that later courts have the power to modify the rule in the earlier case when the fact of the later case and that of the earlier case show some

---

223 Ibid., referring to Stromholm (1996), Ibid., p. 414; See also, for a more comprehensive analysis of how to make choices between several possible rules, A. Frandberg, 'Om analog anvandning av rattsnormer: En analys av analogibegreppet inom ramen for en allman juridisk metodologi', (New York: Hill and Wang, 1973), passim.

224 Connelly, supra note 1947, para II. 1, 2, 3, 4, 5, referring to Huhn (2002), supra note 1949, p. 12.

225 Tetley (1999/2000), supra note 1313, para V.9, referring to Sir Courtney, ILBERT, 'Legislature Methods and Forms', (Oxford: Clarendon Press, 1901), pp. 250-251.

226 Ibid. However, Sir Courtney (1901), Ibid., p. 250, sets some presumptions that the legislature did not intend to alter the rules or principles of the common law beyond what is expressly declared, or to oust or limit the jurisdiction of the superior courts.

227 Ibid., referring to H. Mazeuad, 'Lecons de Droit Civil', in Francois Chabas, ed., 11 Ed., (Paris: Montchrestien, 1996), t.1, vol.1, para 110, p. 172.

difference.[228] However, the ruling in the later case must not be inconsistent with the result in the precedent case. The only formal constraints on the later court are that: (1) in formulating the *ratio decidendi* of the later case, the factors in the *ratio decidendi* of the earlier case must be retained, and (2) the ruling in the later case must be such that it would still support the result reached in the precedent case. If the legislators have the power to either annul or to amend legal rules, precedents in Common law jurisdictions are considered the rules up and until they are overruled.

IV.3.7. DWORKINIAN INTERPRETIVISM

Ronald Dworkin's general theory of interpretation is designed to assist in guiding judges to the one right answer in a case before them. For Dworkin, the aim of legal interpretation is to 'constructively interpret' the social practice of law, by imposing purpose upon it such as, to make of it the best possible example of the form or genre to which it is taken to belong.[229] There is no limit to judicial interpretation through language in the Common law, and within this context Dworkin distinguishes 'enactment force' from 'gravitational force'. Enactment force is about 'the limits on the political decisions ascribed to an authority and set by language'; and gravitational force is a kind of authority that 'escapes .... Language'. It is explained by the principle of fairness, the fundamental ground of precedent system, on likeness as to principle. The gravitational force of earlier decisions is limited 'to the extension of the arguments of principle necessary to justify those decisions'.[230] Dworkin claims that his theory is not recipe-like in the sense of providing judges with a detailed step program for correct judicial decision-making. Interpretivism as developed by Dworkin views that legal rights and duties are determined by the scheme of principle that provides the best justification of certain political practices of a community: a scheme identifiable through an interpretation of the practices that is sensitive both to the facts of the practice and to the values or principles that the practices serve.[231] Dworkin's two components, which are: the practice exists and serves some interests or purposes or enforces principle, and, the requirements of the practice are what are sensitive to its point and therefore the strict rules must be understood or applied or modified or qualified or limited by that point, must both be satisfied, having important consequences in respect

228 Lamond (2006), supra note 1377, pp. 9-10.

229 Dickson (2010), supra note 1930, pp. 9-10, referring to Dworkin (1986), supra note 1970, p. 52.

230 Dyzenhaus (2007), supra note 1419, p. 65, referring to Dworkin (1978a), supra note 1371, p. 13.

231 Stavropoulos (2003), supra note 1289, p. 1.

of the practice's character.[232] The interpretive data are identified as 'the practices and paradigms of that concept', our collective behavior in using that concept 'the shared practices of calling institutions, people and actions just and unjust'.[233]

The interpreter formulates a hypothesis, i.e. to postulate a value that could justify the practice's requirement. In conforming to the practice's requirement, participants behave in certain way to serve the value. The interpreter in his hypothesis attributes a rationale or point is attributed to the relevant practice. An equally complex hypothesis is then constructed by the interpreter to explain and justify all the facts of a large number of specific practices, many of which might have different directions. In order to achieve equilibrium among all the relevant practice, the interpretivist may then introduce a superhuman character, the ideal interpreter, which Dworkin calls 'Hercules'. The introduction of the superhuman character merely helps illustrate that any candidate of legal interpretation is open to the challenge that it does not cohere with a certain part of the law, where both the interpreter and challenger agree what that part requires.[234] Dworkin says 'For every route Hercules took from that general conception to a particular verdict, another lawyer or judge who began in the same conception would find a different route and end in a different place, as several of the judges in our sample cases did. He would end differently because he would take leave of Hercules, following his own lights, at some branching point sooner or later in the argument. So, Dworkin's distinction between fit and justification is merely a device for organizing complex interpretations and so for facilitating the representation of alternative interpretations involved in notional and actual disputes.

Interpretivism claims that values justify precise kind of authority and precise way of decision-making, which determine our duties, including any specific cases in which the values may dictate that the facts about authoritative decision-making alone determines our duties. Interpreting the practices consists in assigning to the practices the content that best fits and justifies them. Dworkin's distinction between fit and justification, as tests of interpretive success, is explicitly a mere heuristic devise.[235] In Dworkin's 'constructive' theory of interpretation, a good interpretation must meet two requirements of the dimension of fit and justification. An interpretation should fit its object, and the object must be justified. A good interpretation

232 Ibid., p. 6.

233 Endicott (2011), supra note 1934, § 3, on Deciding what is just, citing R.Dworkin, 'Justice for Hedgehogs', (Cambridge, Mass. ; Harvard University Press, 2011), p. 157, 162.

234 Stavropoulos (2003), supra note 2006, pp. 8-9, 12.

235 Ibid., pp. 10-11, referring to R. Dworkin (1982), 'Natural Law Revisited', in U. Florida Law Review, 34: 165; Dworkin, (1986), supra note 2004, pp. 229-263.

is the one which fits the justified object. To find an interpretation that succeeds on the dimensions of fit and justification, the interpreter needs to start with two questions: (1) what is it that the interpretation must fit?; and (2) what would make that material look good? The first thing an interpreter should do is the 'pre-interpretive' stage where the interpreter identifies that an interpretation fits the 'interpretive data'.[236] What follows the 'pre-interpretive' stage is the 'interpretive' stage, being the second stage, where the interpreter decides what virtues would make the interpretive data look good. Then the 'post-interpretive' stage follows the second stage, and in the 'post-interpretive' stage 'the interpreter decides what conclusion would best meet the two requirements of fit and justification'. Any inconsistency with the interpretive data (a 'defect of fit')[237] will not defeat an interpretation that shows better overall fit and justification than an alternative interpretation; but such an inconsistency will have to be noticed in the post-interpretive conclusion.[238]

Dworkin has noticed that 'Hard Cases' should be considered under written constitution, statues and the Common law. The legislature's constitutional responsibilities are to be considered by any judge in statutory interpretation. The language of the statute is to be interpreted, and the individual rights affected by plausible interpretation should be considered. It will be deemed in accordance with the policy of the statute if the judge combines such interpretation with such consideration. The judge should connect alternative interpretations to the legislature's constitutional responsibilities, and the statutory interpretation that best ties the language the legislature used to its constitutional responsibilities should be considered. The interpretation that best puts to practice the judge's sense of the legislature's constitutional responsibilities must be selected by the judge.[239] Dworkin says: "...a judge deciding a hard case must seek to show that her or his interpretation of the law is best on two dimensions – fit and soundness".[240] The soundest among interpretations that fit or are consistent with relevant institutional history should be the interpretation the judge must show. The history is in its best moral light in her or his interpretation. 'The set of principles that shows all the law of a particular jurisdiction in its best light' is what Dworkin terms a theory of law.[241]

---

236 Endicott (2011), supra note 2008, on Deciding what is just, citing Dworkin (2011), supra note 2008, p. 176.

237 Ibid., on Deciding what is just, citing Dworkin (1986), supra note 2010, p. 257.

238 Ibid., on Deciding what is just.

239 Dyzenhaus (2007), supra note 2005, p. 64, referring to Dworkin (1978a), supra note 2005, pp. 108, 109-110.

240 Ibid., p. 65, referring to Dworkin (1986), supra note 2012.

241 Dennis (1993), supra note 1892, p. 65.

IV.3.8. HABERMAS' THESIS ON INTERPRETATION

Habermas stresses the importance of a particular paradigm of law in guiding the process of interpretation. A paradigm of law is based on a particular understanding of the legal system: it is an implicit social theory of a legal system.[242] More specifically, it makes the rationality of the interpretive process explicit by reference to a specific purpose.[243] Additionally, building a bridge between predictability and acceptability respectively is connected to the distinction between justification discourses and application discourses. Justification discourses refer to the lawmaking process, whereas application discourses are relevant in adjudication.[244] The fact that a norm is valid before application means that it has been impartially justified; a valid decision in a particular case requires that it has also been impartially applied.[245] The validity of the general norms does not therefore guarantee validity in an individual case. Understood this way, application discourses in legal adjudication concern a norm's appropriate reference to a situation, not its formal validity.[246]

According to Habermas, predictability means that when engaging in a communication process nearly all lawyers are convinced that the proposed interpretation is acceptable. The criterion is therefore whether clear argument on an interpretation may be reached among authorized experts but not whether everyone would reach the same interpretation in all possible situations.[247] [Legal decision and, more specifically, legal argumentation aiming at justifying those decisions are directed towards an audience.[248] This perspective might be characterized by means of

242 Paunio (2009), supra note 1982, p. 1472, referring to Habermas (1996), supra note 1862, pp. 194-195.

243 Ibid., referring to Dworkin (1986), supra note 2015, p. 52.

244 Ibid., pp. 1472-1473, referring to Klaus Günther, 'A Normative Conception of Coherence for a Discursive Theory of Legal Justification', in 2 Ratio Juris, (1989), p. 155, 157. See also Jürgen Habermas, 'Justification and Application', 1993, p. 35.

245 Ibid., p. 1473. [See, inter alia, Alexsander Peczenik, 'On Law and Reason', (1989), p. 142, on the conceptual difference between valid norms and their validity as acts performed].

246 Ibid. See Habermas (1996), supra note 2017, p. 217. Habermas seems to suggest that in modern legal systems courts need to engage in both discourses of justification and application, since the political process does not alone justify norms sufficiently from a communicative perspective.

247 Ibid., p. 1480.

248 Ibid., p. 1481. See Chaim Perelman & Lucie Olbrechts-Tyteca, 'The New Rhetoric: A Treatise on Argumentation', (1971); Chaim Perelman, 'Justice et Raison', (1963), whose notion of an ideal audience and its role from the viewpoint of acceptability of argumentation is connected with Habermas's views.

the following regulative principle related to legal adjudication:] legal interpretation should aim to secure the support of the majority in a rationally reasoning legal community.[249] The interrelationship between argumentation and audience is based on Chaim Perelman's theory of argumentation where the relationship between rational and reasonable is analyzed. Rational argumentation is aimed at a universal audience to which all rational persons belong (an essentially ideal audience).[250] Legal interpretation (adjudication) is also dialectical: it proceeds as a dialogue between the court and its audience.[251] In legal interpretation, however, a close connection exists between convincing and acceptable adjudication: they are both related to the outcome in a particular case.[252] For a particular legal decision (judgment) to be acceptable from the viewpoint of argumentation (or as to reasonableness), it must correspond to the values of the audience.[253]

Although it is impossible to make legal interpretation predictable in the strict sense [in EU law], some degree of predictability may be created by making determinacy a question of agreement among language users, or in this case the EU legal community.[254] In this respect, ECJ legal reasoning may be regarded as the primary means for facilitating communication – if it succeeds – leads, if not necessarily to consensus then at least to rational agreement as to the legal paradigm to be followed in interpreting EU law. In this sense, principles expressing values of the legal community may function as a basis for a dialogue between the ECJ and national courts. Consequently, such value-discussions, says Allan Risas as quoted by

249 Ibid. See Aulis Aarnio, 'The Rational as Reasonable', (1987), pp. 226-227.

250 Ibid. This universal audience in fact corresponds to Habermas's "ideal speech situation" where the possibility of manipulation and persuasion has been eliminated and therefore all participants are in the same position. See Jürgen Habermas, 'The Theory of Communicative Action', in Vol. 1: Reason and the Rationalization of Society, (1984), p. 86.

251 Ibid. See for a critical account of dialectics of legal interpretation, see Allan Rosas, 'The European Court of Justice in Context: Forms and Patterns of Judicial Dialogue', in 1 European Journal of Legal Studies, (2007), p. 125. He essentially argues that dialectical legal interpretation is characterized by conflict, power and normativity.

252 Ibid., p. 1483, referring to Mirjami Paso, 'Viimeisella Toumiolla Soumen Korkeimman Oikeuden ja Euroopan Yhteisöjen Toumioistuimen Retorikka', 2009, p. 353.

253 Ibid. See Aarnio (1987), supra note 2024, pp. 185-195. The requirement of rationality consists of L-rationality and D-rationality.

254 Ibid., p. 1489. See Jan Engberg, 'Statutory Text as Instances of Language(s): Consequences and Limitations on Interpretation', in 29 Brooklyn Journal of International Law (2004), p. 1155. See also F. Schauer (2008a), supra note 1845, p. 1109, 1123; Rosas (2007), supra note 2026, p. 14.

Paunio, may also act as a foundation for creating an agreement within the EU legal community on suitable legal interpretations in accordance with the dominant legal paradigm.

IV.4. CONSTRAINT AND PRESCRIPTIVITY ON LEGAL REASONING

***

Human mind which is discursive is sensitive to regularity. Regularity is seen due to similarity [and difference]. The normativity of law may appear because of the constraints of regularity in terms of similarity. The normativity of law as caused by the constraints of regularity prescribes the formulation, formation and application of law. Constraint, according to Braman, is defined as something that limits the freedom to act spontaneously; or some physical, moral or 'other' force that compels somebody to do something or limits their freedom of action.[255] Fallon has noted that a constraint does not need to be absolute in order to count as constraint.[256] Attempting to unpack the idea of legal constraint, we start by distinguishing non-compliance with law from reasonable disagreements about law. Next, we address the difficulty of 'observational equivalence", whereby actions consistent with law may be taken for nonlegal reasons, and whereby actions inconsistent with law may occur even though law acted as a constraint. Finally, we explore several relationships that affect law's capacity to constrain: between law's role in constraining government action and its role in constraining (and thus enabling) government, between law and law enforcement, and between law and judicial review.[257] Legal compliance, Bradley and Morrison say, can mean different things in different contexts. In some circumstances, complying with the law could mean adhering to a view that is ultimately deemed to be the correct one.

As much as other officials, judges and justices are normatively constrained by validly enacted law, including statute that regulate their

255 Eileen Braman, 'Constraint in Legal Decision Making', prepared for the Workshop on Exploring the Judicial Mind, University of Virginia, March 30-31, 2007, p. 2. [accompanying text omitted].

256 Fallon (2009), supra note 1524, p. 1009.

257 Curtis A. Bradley and Trevor W. Morrison, 'Presidential Power, Historical Practice, and Legal Constraint', Essay, in Columbia Law Review, Vol. 113:1097, (2013), p. 1114, 1116.

jurisdiction.[258] Fallon says that statutory constraints on judges and justices have enormous importance. It is nearly impossible to imagine a justice who would not feel constrained to enforce any law enacted by Congress, despite her personal disapproval of it, unless she had a good legal reason to hold it unconstitutional. A recent example comes from statutes specifying penalties for criminal offenses that some judges have regarded as draconian.[259] The constraining effect of law could stem from either internal or external considerations. Obviously, if an actor has internalized the normative force of a legal rule, the rule is having an effect. This is what is sometimes referred to as the 'Hartian' perspective.[260] But even if an actor has not internalized the rule, there is legal effect, if sanctions for non-compliance are affected

---

258 Fallon (2009), supra note 2031, p. 1014. Because Article III of the Constitution does not require Congress to create any lower federal courts at all, U.S. CONST. art. III § 1, lower federal courts possess jurisdiction only insofar as jurisdiction is conferred by statute. See RICHARD H. FALLON Jr. ET AL., 'HART & WECHSLER'S THE FEDERAL COURTS AND THE FEDERAL SYSTEM,' 244-67 (5th ed. 2003), pp. 330-337. Although Article III expressly confers both original and appellate jurisdiction on the Supreme Court, the appellate jurisdiction is subject to "such Exceptions.....as the Congress shall make". U.S. CONST. art. III, § 2, cl. 2. With Congress having regulated the Court's appellate jurisdiction since the 1789 Judiciary Act, the Court's current appellate jurisdiction is almost entirely governed by statute. See 28 U.S.C §§ 1251-59 (2006). Although it is almost universally agreed that some possible statutory limitations on the Court's jurisdiction would violate the Constitution, see FALLON ET AL, Ibid., pp. 334-35, 337, the bounds on congressional power have seldom been tested and remain much debated. See. Ibid., p. 337-342.

259 Ibid. A number of judges have criticized statutes that establish mandatory minimum sentences – including life sentences without the possibility for parole – for drug offenses. See, e.g., John Caher, 'Judge Gives 'Small-Time' Dealer 'Unjust' Mandatory Life', in LEGAL INTELLIGENCER, Jan. 20, 2006, p. 4. When Northern District of New York Judge David N. Hurd was forced under 21 U.S.C. § 846 to impose a life sentence on a "relatively small-time drug dealer," he remarked: "The increment of harm in this case bears no rational relationship to the increment of punishment that I must impose. This is what occurs when Congress sets [a] mandatory minimum sentence which distorts the entire judicial process." Ibid. (quoting Judge Hurd). In United States v Booker, 543 U.S. 220, 226-27 (2005), the Court held that any factual predicate for the imposition of a sentence comes within the province of the constitutional right to trial by jury, but it did not question that Congress may prescribe mandatory penalties for crimes as statutory defined, which the Court had earlier held constitutional in McMillan v. Pennsylvania, 477 U.S. 79 (1986), and Harris v. United States, 536 U.S. 545 (2002).

260 Bradley & Morrison (2013), supra note 2032, p. 1122. See Richard H. Pildes, 'Law and the President', in 125 Harv. L. Rev. (2012), p. 1404 n.9 (describing Hartian perspective as "the classic account of law as a practice that is experienced as normatively binding" (citing H.L.A. Hart, 'The Concept of Law', 2d ed. 1994).

by the norm's legal status.[261] Thus, law can act as a constraint even if the law is not internalized by the actor. That is, law can [externally] constrain even what Oliver Wendell Holmes referred to as a 'bad man', as long as the existence or strength of the relevant sanctions is tied at least in part to the fact that the norm in question is a legal norm.[262] As to sanction, the core idea is a familiar one, often associated with Holme's 'bad man'. One who obeys the law only because he concludes that the cost of non-compliance exceeds the benefits is still subject to legal constraint if the cost of non-compliance is affected by the legal status of the norm. This is true even though the law is likely to impose less of a constraint on such 'bad man' than on those who have internalized legal norms, and even though it is likely to be difficult in practice to disentangle internal and external constraints.[263] In many contexts, Bradley and Morrison argue, internal and external constraints probably do not operate independently.[264] In particular, it seems plausible that practices followed out of fear of external sanctions can become internalized as a result of habit or what has been called the 'normative power of the actual' – that is, the tendency of people to give normative significance to that with which they are familiar.

External constraints do not function by inspiring officials [including judges and justices] with a sense of legal or moral obligation. Instead, external constraints inhere in the unwanted consequences that failure to comply with the law, or at least with expectations that are traceable to the Constitution, would frequently engender.[265] In some cases, officials may be

---

261 Ibid., pp. 1122-1123. But see Fallon (2009), supra note 2033, p. 981 (describing perspective under which "it is only refracted through individual minds and consciences that legal norms can be motivationally efficacious").

262 Ibid., p. 1123. See Pildes (2012), supra note 2035, p. 1392-1393 ("[T]he premise .....is that public officials obey the law not for normative reasons but only when the benefits of legal compliance in specific contexts outweigh the costs"); see also Holmes (1897), supra note 1695, p. 457, 459 ("If you want to know the law and nothing else, you must look at it as a bad man, who cares only for the material consequences which such knowledge enables him to predict, not as a good one, who finds .....reasons for conduct.....in the vaguer sanctions of consceince").

263 Ibid., p. 1137. See Holmes (1897). Ibid., p. 459; see also Fallon (2009), supra note 2033, p. 981 [accompanying text omitted]; Pildes (2012), Ibid., pp. 1392-1393 [accompanying text omitted]; see also Holmes (1897), Ibid., p. 457, 459 [accompanying text omitted].

264 Ibid., p. 1140. The phrase apparently originated with Georg Jellinek, 'Allgemeine Staatslehre' [General Theory of the State] (1921), p. 338; see also Morris Cohen, 'The Basis of Contract', in 46 Harv. L. Rev. 553 (1933), p. 582, (stating ceremonies "have what Jellinek has called the normative power of the actual, that is, they control what we do by creating a standard of respectability or a pattern to which we feel bound to conform").

265 Fallon (2009), supra note 2033, p. 983. External constraints are the sole

externally constrained because they know that failure to comply with legal requirements for the valid exercise of their power would result in their acts being treated as legal nullities. Political scientists concern themselves more frequently with constraints, especially as perceived by officials whom they assume to be rational maximizers of their personal, typically ideological, preferences.[266] The political question doctrine obliges the Supreme Court to treat other branches' determinations of some constitutional questions as controlling.[267] In other words, determinations by the political branches in political question cases constrain the courts from reaching any other conclusions.[268]

Courts reason in normative terms (by appeal to a certain normative conception of their legal order) and they are bound by the constraints of legal reasoning as defined by the limits imposed by the text, by the logical rules of practical reasoning,[269] and by the systemic requirements of coherence and consistency.[270] In the context of ambiguous or conflicting

---

focus of those who deploy rational choice or economic analysis. See, e.g., John O. McGinnis, 'Constitutional Review by the Executive in Foreign Affairs and War Powers: A Consequence of Rational Choice in the Separation of Powers', in LAW & CONTEMP. PROBS., Autumn, 293 (1993), pp. 295-305. For pioneering explorations of how strategic or game theoretical assumptions regarding human motivation might be incorporated into a basically Hartian framework, see JULES L. COLEMAN, 'THE PRACTICE OF PRINCIPLE,' 92-95 (2001); Gerald J. Postema, 'Coordination and Convention at the Foundation of Law', in 11 J. LEGAL STUD. 165 (1982), pp. 182-197. For an interesting discussion suggesting that positive political scientists should have a place for the internal point of view in their theories, see John Ferejohn, 'Positive Theory and the Internal View of Law', in 10 U. PA. J. CONST. L. 273 (2008), p. 280.

266 Ibid., p. 977. Indeed, Ferejohn (2008), Ibid., p. 273, 280, treats as a necessary element of a "positive theory" that it includes a description of "the institutional, physical, and fiscal constraints" of relevant actors, along with "the preferences of the agents, the sets of actions each can take....and a description of the outcomes that arise as a function of the actions taken by the agents," For some examples of political science scholarship viewing judges as rational maximizers operating subject to constraints, see LEE EPSTEIN & JACK KNIGHT, 'THE CHOICES JUSTICES MAKE', (1998), pp. 9-10; McNollast, 'Politics and the Courts: A Positive Theory of Judicial Doctrine and the Rule of Law', in 68 S. CAL. L. REV. (1995), p. 1631.

267 Ibid., p. 1011. See Nixon v. United States, 506 U.S. 224 (1993).

268 Ibid. But cf. Louis Henkin, 'Is There a "Political Question" Doctrine?', in 85 YALE L.J. 597 (1976), p. 622-623, (arguing that the so-called political question doctrine is "an unnecessary, deceptive packaging of several [independent] established doctrines" and has no further, legally valid scope).

269 Maduro (2007), supra note 1993, p. 10, referring to Alexy (1989), supra note 1986.

270 Ibid., referring to Dworkin (1986), supra note 2018; Neil McCormick

provisions, *telos* signifies a higher constraint, that is pure reference to wording or intent, preventing opportunistic behaviors and minimizing the risk of an interpretive manipulation of the legislation.[271] Even if the President is advised that there is a minimally plausible argument in favor of the action in question, the law might still constrain him not to act if the argument is perceived as being too weak. The *relative percieved strength* of a legal arguments might have a constraining effect.[272] Braman argues that constraint is not *undiscoverable* - and legal models of decision making are not unfalsifiable (cf. Segal and Spaeth 1993, 33-34). What we need are fair, theoretically based, tests of constraint.[273] When legal types talk about constraint they are usually referring to professional norms and/or obligations that require judicial actors to use legal presumptions, rules and authority in reaching decisions.[274] Attempts to justify legal authority without reference to meaningful external constraint are fundamentally flawed, as argued by Braman who characterizes constraint as a "democratic good" particularly important for legitimizing the distributive choices of unelected judges. As such, scholars in all disciplines, but particularly political science, should be deeply concerned with finding constraint in legal decision making.

A norm does not need to be perfectly enforced in order to constrain. Of course, as the legal realists have emphasized, one cannot get an accurate picture of the law by looking only at the law on the books rather than the law in action.[275] The point here, however, is simply that the lack of *perfect*

(1978), supra note 1970.

271 Ibid.

272 Bradley & Morrison (2013), supra note 2035, p. 1117. Whether this scenario involves "law" acting as a constraint will depend to some extent on one's definition of law. Under a Dworkinian conception of law, pursuant to which there is a single best reading of the legal materials, a mere plausibility constraint might not be a legal one. See, e.g., Dworkin (1986), supra note 2045, p. 231 (suggesting there will be best legal interpretation in terms of fit with prior legal materials and principles). Even under that conception, however, one could reasonably describe the plausibility constraint as "law-related".

273 Braman (2007), supra note 2030, p. 5. See Howard Gillman (2001), 'What's Law Got to Do with It? Judicial Behavioralists Test The "Legal Mode" of Judicial Decision-Making', in Law and Social Inquiry 36, pp. 465-504 (p. 486). ("[I]f some contemporary positivists are willing to make empirical claims about the determinate influence of rules, then it is not unreasonable for scholars such as Spaeth and Segal to ask them to formulate those claims in ways that allow for hypothesis testing"). This is what Braman attempts to do in her essay.

274 Ibid., p. 2, 4. [accompanying text omitted].

275 Bradley & Morrison (2013), supra note 2047, pp. 1126-1127. See e.g., Llewellyn (1931), supra note 1062, p. 1222 (noting "some rules [are] mere paper").

enforcement of a legal rule does not mean the rule does not exist, or that it does not constrain.[276] Enforcement doesn't need to be formal.[277] Even when the likely enforcement mechanisms are entirely informal, we think they should count for purposes of evaluating whether law operates as a constraint. Outside the area of constitutional law, it is generally accepted that law can act as a constraint even when it takes the form of customary norms, and even when it is subject primarily to informal enforcement.

***

As Madison explained in *The Federalist 51*, it surely would be a mistake to assume that the Constitution is enforced – or that officials are constrained – by normative constraints alone. Rather, the Constitution creates institutions – including the electorate – that are empowered to establish non-normative or "external" constraints of official actions.[278] The overall structure of constitutional constraints is that the Constitution embodies the assumption, whether right or wrong, that presidential and legislative action is more dangerous than presidential and legislative inaction and, accordingly, that presidential and congressional action should be subject to an especially dense network of constitutional constraints.[279] Because the Constitution helps constitute the institutional and cultural framework in which judges and presidents experience both power and constraint, there is no independent baseline of non-constraint from which to measure the constitutional constraints on judges or presidents.[280] By constituting the offices of president and Supreme Court justice, for example, the Constitution helps establish widely accepted understanding of what presidents and justices can (and cannot) lawfully do. These understanding then function as constraints.[281] Insofar as officials regard the Constitution from an internal point of

276 Ibid., p. 1127.

277 Ibid. See e.g., Avner Greif, 'Institutions and the Path to the Modern Economy: Lessons from Medieval Trade' (2006); Avner Greif, Paul Milgrom & Barry R. Weingast, 'Coordination, Commitment, and Enforcement: The Case of the Merchant Guild', in 102 J. Pol.Econ. (1994), p. 745.

278 Fallon (2009), supra note 2040, p. 983. See THE FEDERALIST No.51 (James Madison) (Clinton Rossiter ed., 1961), p. 322.

279 Ibid., p. 985.

280 Ibid.,p. 988. See STEPHEN HOLMES, 'PASSIONS AND CONSTRAINT',(1995), p. 163 (observing that "constitutional rules are enabling, not disabling).

281 Ibid., p. 987.

view, they will be constrained by constitutional norms or be subject to normative constraints.[282]

There is a type as called 'direct normative constraint' on adjudication. Insofar as judges and justices take an internal point of view on legal norms, they are subject to normative constraints defined by the Constitution and by surrounding rules of recognition and adjudication (many of which are only tacit). Although the justices are the Constitution's ultimate interpreters for some purposes, they have a duty to follow the law in discharging their function.[283]

[While] some rules of recognition tell justices how to identify valid law, others, applicable to other officials, characteristically direct those other officials to accept judicial interpretations as binding – even when those other officials think the judges made mistakes.[284] Common law theories call for judges to accord authority to prior judges' and justices' interpretations of constitutional language.[285] Normative constitutional constraints take the form of constitutionally inspired *experiences* of obligation, for it is only as refracted through individual minds and consciences that legal norms can be motivationally efficacious.[286] In speaking of normative constraints, Fallon assumes that at least some officials are sometimes motivated to act out of a sense of constitutional obligation, even when their rational self-interest

282 Ibid., p. 980. See generally THE OXFORD COMPANION TO PHILOSOPHY 626 (Ted Honderich ed., 1995) (charaterizing a norm as an action-guiding or reason-giving precept or principle, deviation from which would provide a ground for reproach within an appropriate domain such as that of morals, law, or etiquette).

283 Ibid, p. 1003, referring to HART (1994), supra note 1510, pp. 145-46.

284 Ibid, p. 1015. See, e.g., Hutto v Davis, 454 U.S. 370, 375 (1992) (per curiam) ("[U]nless we wish anarchy to prevail within the federal judical system, a precedent of this Court must be followed by the lower federal courts no matter how misguided the judges of those courts may think it to be."); Cooper v Aaron, 358 U.S. 1, 18-19 (1958) (explaining that "[n]o state legislator or executive or judicial officer can war against the Constitution without violating his undertaking to support it," and that all officials are thereby bound by the Supreme Court's constitutional interpretations); see also Larry Alexander & Frederick Schauer, 'On Extrajudicial Constitutional Interpretation', in 110 HARV. L. REV. (1997), p. 1362 (offering an unqualified defense of Cooper" and its assertion of judicial primacy").

285 Ibid., p. 1012. See generally David A. Strauss, 'Common Law Constitutional Interpretation', in 63 U.CHI. L. REV. 877 (1996), p. 883 (defending an approach to constitutional interpretation under which "[m]ostly the courts decide cases by looking to what the precedents say").

286 Ibid., p. 981. See, e.g., Frederick Schauer, 'Has Precedent Ever Really Mattered in the Supreme Court', in 24 GA. ST. U. L. REV. 381 (2007), pp. 391-396 (examining the role of the "felt obligation" to follow precedent in the Supreme Court).

or political values would otherwise lead them to act differently,[287] however, it seems natural to assume that a central function of the Constitution is to constrain officials.[288]

Indirect normative constraints exist insofar as officials are duty-bound to treat other officials' interpretations or dictates as legally authoritative. It will be helpful to distinguish two subcategories of indirect constraints. First, insofar as the Constitution imposes an obligation on officials to accept someone else's constitutional interpretations as binding, it subjects them to *mediated* constraints. Significantly, it is more the norm than the exception for officials to understand themselves as constrained to accept judicial, and especially Supreme Court, interpretations of the Constitution, even if they believe that the court erred.[289]

Justice Stevens wrote in *McDonald*,[290] the 'conceptual core' of the Due Process Clause .. safeguards, most basically, 'the ability independently to define one's identity', the individual's right to make certain unusually important decisions that will affect his own, or his family's destiny, and the right to be respected as a human being ...[291] Significantly, that core not only defines substantive individual rights under the Fourteenth Amendment, but is a fundamental constraint on the government's objectives when it acts

287 Ibid.

288 Ibid., p. 975 and n.1. Cf. HOLMES (1995), supra note 2055, p. 241.

289 Ibid., p. 996. For a prominent defense of the idea that officials are bound by judicial interpretations of the Constitution even when they disagree with those interpretations, see Alexander & Schauer (1997), supra note 2059, p. 1359; see also Larry Alexander & Frederick Schauer, 'Defending Judicial Supremacy: A Reply', in 17 CONST. COMMENT. (2000), p. 455 (responding to criticism of the idea that other officials must adhere to the Supreme Court's constitutional rulings). For diverse opposing views, see, for example, Edwin Meese III, 'The Law of the Constitution', in 61 TUL. L. REV. (1987), p. 979; Sanford Levinson, 'Could Meese Be Right This Time?' in 61 TUL. L. REV. (1987), p. 1071; Michael Stokes Paulsen, 'The Most Dangerous Branch: Executive Power to Say What the Law Is', in 83 GEO. L. J. 217 (1994), pp. 343-45; Mark v. Tushnet, 'The Hardest Question in Constitutional Law', in 81 MINN. L. REV. 1 (1996), pp. 25-28.

290 Green (2011), supra note 1523, p. 1296. See McDonald v. City of Chicago, 130 S. Ct. 3090-91 (2010) (calling substantive due process "consonant with the venerable 'notion that governmental authority has implied limits which preserve private autonomy', a notion which predates the founding and which finds reinforcement in the Constitution's Ninth Amendment" (footnote omitted); City of Cleburne v Cleburne Living Ctr., 473 U.S. 432, 452 (1985) (Stevens, J., concurring) ("[T]he word 'rational' – for me at least – includes elements of legitimacy and neutrality that must always characterize the performance of the sovereign's duty to govern impartially").

291 Ibid., p. 1295. See McDonald v. City of Chicago, Ibid., p. 3020, 3101 (2010) (Stevens, J., dissenting) (citations omitted).

in a way that implicates those rights: the requirement of legality is what prevents substantive due process from being an oxymoron. In *Brown v. Plata*, 131 S.Ct. at 1928-29 (citing *Hutto v. Finney*, 437 U.S. 678, 687, n.9, 98 S.Ct. 2565, 57 L.Ed. 522 (1978)), it was held, "Courts may not allow constituional violations to continue simply because a remedy would involve intrusion into the realm of prison administration".

***

Decision rules have their constraining force. It has to do with the level of discretion in the aplication of specific decision rules that are supposed to govern decision makers' analyses.[292] Perhaps the most commonly discussed issue in this vein is whether and to what extent decision makers are constrained by the application of precedent.[293] Braman and Nelson (forthcoming) have detailed a critique of extant operationalizations of the constraining influence or precedent.[294] Conventional wisdom holds that "black-letter rules" confine decision makers to a greater extent than more flexible 'legal standards.'[295] If conventional wisdom is right decision makers in the rule condition should be less influenced by their attitudes and there should be less variance across decision makers within that condition.[296]

Two relatively non controversial tasks of judges are as 'law interpreter' and as 'decision maker on rights and duties of disputing parties'. As 'interpreters of law', judges are not free to decide cases according to their personal views because they are constrained by appropriate sources of legal reasoning and canon of interpretation. Technical training in the

292 Braman (2007), supra note 2048, p. 25.

293 Ibid., referring to Cass R. Sunstein, 'On Analogy in Legal Reasoning', in Harvard Law Review, 106(3) (1993), pp. 741-789; Emily Sherwin, 'A Defense of Analogical Reasoning in Law', in University of Chicago Law Review. 66(4) (1999), pp. 1179-1197; Daniel Simon, 'A Third View of the Black Box: Cognitive Coherence in Legal Decision Making,' in University of Chicago Review 71 (2004), p. 511.

294 Ibid., n.5.

295 Ibid., p. 26. See, e.g., Schauer (1991), supra note 1215; Pierre Schlag, 'Rules and Standards', in University of California Law Review 33 (1985), p. 379; Kathleen M. Sullivan, 'The Supreme Court 1991 Term: The Justice of Rules and Standards', in Harvard Law Review 106 (1992), pp. 22-123. Braman has been trying to operationalize this for some time and have yet to come up with a psychological theory to express this expectation that seems almost intuitive to legally trained individuals (it might be the kind of decision domain where there is no psychological theory that neatly corresponds with conventional legal wisdom – but Braman is open to suggestions which is why Braman specifically mentions it here).

296 Ibid.

tools of legal analysis enable judges to separate reason from personal biases in their deliberations; and it is the predominance of reason that endows judge-made law with legitimacy in our constitutional democracy.[297] Both judges' own accounts[298] and psychological theories stressing the importance of socialization and social roles in influenzing human behavior[299] attest to the plausibility of claims that judges seek to comply with distinctively legal obligation. Judges and justices are deeply socialized, beginning with their training as law students, to believe that there are legal norms independent of personal preference and that judges have an obligation to do what the law requires.[300] For those who have internalized norms, those norms as

297 Ibid., p. 11. This notion of expertise as a source of judicial authority is uniquely reflected in our constitutional structure. Federal judges are insulated from politics. They serve for life during "good behavior." The democratic justification for this protection is not to allow judges to pursue their policy preferences unchecked – although notable judicial scholars have argued such behavior is the result of this particular institution – but rather, to allow judges to apply their expertise without having to worry about pleasing particular constituencies or government officials. Such concerns, it is assumed, interfere with judges' expert interpretation of what the law requires in particular cases. As Alexander Bickel put it "judges have or should have the leisure, the training, and the insulation to follow the ways of the scholar in pursuing the ends of government" (1986, 25-6).

298 Fallon (2009), supra note 2053, p. 992. See, e.g., Texas v. Johnson, 491 U.S. 397, 420-21 (1989) (Kennedy, J., concurring) (explaining that the Court's decision, which held that a conviction for flag burning violated the First Amendment, "exacts its personal toll," but that "sometimes we must make decisions we do not like", because "they are right, right in the sense that the law and the Constitution, as we see them, compel the result"); Griswold v Connecticut, 381 U.S. 479, 527 (1965) (Stewart, J., dissenting) (explaining that while the ban on contraceptives was "an uncommonly silly law", the Court was "not asked...to say whether we think this law is unwise, or even asinine", but whether "it violates the United States Constitution"); Confirmation Hearing on the Nomination Before the S. Comm. on the Judiciary, 109th Cong. 56 (2006) (statement of Samuel A. Alito, Jr.) ("The judge's only obligation – and it's a solemn obligation – is to the rule of law. And what that means is that in every single case, the judge has to do what the law requires."): CARDOZO (1921), supra note 1813, p. 114 (describing the constraints on judicial creativity "established by the traditions of the centuries, by the example of other judges, ...by the collective judgment of the profession, and by the duty of adherence to the pervading spirit of the law"); Henry J. Friendly, 'Judicial Control of Discretionary Administrative Action', in 23 J. LEGAL EDUC. 63 (1970), p. 64 (citing Lord Halsbury and Chief Justice Marshall for a view of law-bound discretion that "sounds remarkably like what judges do, or think they do").

299 Ibid. For a survey of such theories, see B.J. Biddle, 'Recent Development in Role Theory' , in 12 ANN. REV. SOC. (1986), p. 67.

300 Ibid. See, e.g., Mark Tushnet, 'Constitutional Interpretation, Character, and Experience,' in 72 B.U. L. REV. 747 (1992), p. 751 (emphasizing "limits on what properly socialized judges do"); Adrian Vermeule, 'Instrumentalisms', in 120 HARV. L. REV. 2113 (2007), p. 2132, reviewing Tamanaha (2006), supra note 1972

decision rules frequently determine behavior.[301] A very interesting question having to do with legal decision rules involves the 'order of operation' legal decision makers are supposed to follow when considering arguments and authority. Akin to mathematics, there is a logical sequence decision makers are supposed to follow when reasoning through cases where certain types of grounds are availabe for a decision.[302] Understanding the mix of conscious and unconscious goals in the mind of legal decision makers and how norms and context operate to facilitate and frustrate these goals is the key to understanding how constrains operate in legal decision making.[303]

'Attitudinalists' literatue assumes that Supreme Court justices are single-minded maximizers of their political preferences who face few, if any, constraints in voting to advance their ideologies.[304] Any debates between 'attitudanlists' like Segal and Spaeth and 'post-positivist' legal scholars like Dworkin and Ackerman are debates about the *degree* and *mechanism* of extralegal influence in judges' decision making. Their conclusions are similar: the law does not (and perhaps cannot) constrian legal decision-makers in all cases.[305] Post-positivist legal theorists spend a great deal of

---

('[T]he internalized sense of legal rule-following by officials and the public....is part of what we call 'the rule of law').

301 Ibid. See, e.g., Christine Horne, 'The Internal Enforcement of Norms', in 19 U. CHI. L. REV.(1995), p. 943; Richard A. Posner, 'Social Norms and the Law: An Economic Approach', in AM. ECON. REV., May 1997, p. 365, (explaining that judges follow "norms governing judicial behavior," because failing to do so means 'not playing the judicial' game, and the "judicial selection procedures select for persons who want to play the judical game"); Symposium, The Legal Construction of Norms, 86 Va. L.REV. (2000), p. 1577.

302 Braman (2007), supra note 2067, p. 23.

303 Ibid., pp. 6-7.

304 Fallon (2009), supra note 2073, p. 978. See JEFFREY A. SEGAL & HAROLD J. SPAETH, 'THE SUPREME COURT AND THE ATTITUDINAL MODEL'(1993), p. 360 (asserting that the influence of non-attitudinal factors appears to be "overwhelmingly insubstantial"). Although the attitudinal model has attracted increasing criticism, many of the most telling political scientific critiques – which identify constraints to which judges and justices must respond "strategically" (rather than always voting in straightforward accord with their ideologies) – share the attitudinalists' assumption that legal decision-makers experience no normative constraints arising from legal obligations to obey the Constitution. See e.g., Lee Esptein et al, 'The Supreme Court as a Strategic National Policymaker', in 50 EMORY L. J. 583 (2001), p. 592 (proposing a "strategic approach" that "starts off with" the attitudinalist premise that justices are "single-minded seekers of legal policy"" but assumes that they must behave strategically in order to advance their policy goals effectively).

305 Braman (2007), supra note 2077, p. 8. Of course Dworkin (1993) and Ackerman (1991) go on to argue for the legitimacy of judicial decision making in the absence of constraint as long as judges rely on "fundamental" or "judicial"

time in debates among legal academics trying to justify departures from doctrine in favor of 'fundamental' or 'judicial' values, there is a lack of meaningful constraints. The absence of meaningful constraint or objective criteria by which judges can make distributive choices calls the legitimacy of such choices into question and enlists state authority in the enforcement of what are essentially personal preferences about litigants or competing legal (or policy) arguments. Any expectation of objectivity or equality before the law becomes illusory in the absence of external constraints.[306] A final aspect of argumentation where we could benefit from psychological approaches to decision making is, of course, related to the ultimate goal of legal argument: persuasion. A final point related to persuasion and legal decision making is that several studies have evidence suggesting individual differences in how decision makers respond to constraining authority related to attitudinal/ideoligical traits of the decision makers.[307] Until now, as noted by Braman, legal scholars and political scientists all assume law has constrained or (failed to constrain) uniformity across different types of decision makers.

Understanding how stylized norms of appropriate behavior succeed and fail to shape legal decision making will go along way in advancing our understanding of cognitive processes more generally.[308] Moreover, knowing how norms and context operate in the mind of decision makers will only improve our understanding of where the requirements of democratic theory tax the boundaries of human capacity[309] and where traditional

---

values. Segal and Spaeth (1993, 2002) do not attempt to legitimate judicial decisions in the absence of constraint. Indeed part of the power of their empirical investigation is their implicit (and explicit) critique of traditional conception of judicial authority. This is not to say that political scientists are not interested in such issues. Gillman (2001) argues for a conception of legitimacy that involves whether or not judges act "sincerely" in their attempt to apply legal principles to particular cases. While Braman is sympathetic to Gillman's argument that a lack of volition in the application of values and/or ideology takes some of the "blame" off judges engaged in the exercise of unconstrained decision making (see discussion of "bottom-up" vs, "top-down" mechanism of extralegal influence Braman 2004), the subjective state of mind of decision makers can not resolve the ultimate issue of democratic legitimacy.

306 Ibid., p. 13.

307 Ibid., p. 21, referring to Braman (2006) findings suggesting differences in response to controlling precedent); Kirk A. Randazzo, Richard W. Waterman and Jeffrey A. Fine, 'Checking the Federal Courts: the Impact of Congressional Statutes on Judicial Behavior', in Journal of Politics 68(4) (2006), pp. 1006-1017 (finding differences in response to legislative authority).

308 Ibid., pp. 9-10.

309 Ibid., p. 10, referring to Jerome Frank, 'Are Judges Human? Part One: The Effect on Legal Thinking of the Assumption that Judges Behave Like Human

conceptions of legal enterprise as a legitimizing factor may yet have force in justifying court outcomes.[310] A sort of normative constraint involves the specific application of stylized rules of decision making in legal reasoning [Issues related to Decision Rules].[311] An issue related to argumentation has been raised by Stone-Sweet who argues that we should reconceptualize our thinking about constraint to encompass the range of plausible arguments adversaries could raise in litigation rather than the more narrow attention extant research has paid to relevant choice sets created by selected arguments.[312] On this view, argumentative choices themselves represent an important part of the constraining influence of law.

The ability of decision makers to apply required *presumptions* in their legal analyses is potentially involved in constraint important source. The ability to comply with rules about where reasoning should "start from" has important consequences for the administration of justice in our judicial system. Presumptions are not just important in criminal matters – they are also used in more mundane, but important of legal reasoning.[313] The start might affect the outcome in legal reasoning. Legal reasoning is kind of work with a purpose, and here the purpose is to make the case come out the way the judge's sense of justice tells him it ought to, in spite of what seems at first like the *resistence* or *opposition* of 'the law'.[314] Resistence or opposition is the characteristic of the law when the judge anticipates it as a constraint on how-he-wants-to-come-out. But if his initial sense had been that the law was 'on his side' it would be a resistence or opposition from the point of view of the disputing parties. The image changes according to how the law initially presents itself in relation to how-the judge-wants-to-come-out. But in each case the judge is suggesting that one of the ways in which we experience law (not the only way, as we'll see) is as a medium in which one pursues a project [determination], rather than as something that tells us what we have to do. When we approach it this way, law constrains

---

Beings', in University of Pennsylvania Law Review 80(1931), pp. 17-53 ["1931a"]; Jerome Frank, 'Are Judges Human? Part Two: As Through a Class Darkly', in University of Pennsylvania Law Review 80(1931), pp. 233-267 ["1931b"].

310 Ibid.

311 Ibid., p. 22 [footnote omitted].

312 Ibid., p. 20, referring to Alec Stone-Sweet, 'Path Dependence, Precedent and Judicial Power,' in On Law Politics and Judicialization, ed. Ian Saphiro and Alec Stone-Sweet (New York: Oxford University Press, 2002), talking about this sort of constraint in more formal/economic terms – but it's hard imaging the psychological literature could not significantly contribute to our understanding of constraint in this respect.

313 Ibid., p. 24.

314 Duncan Kennedy, 'Freedom and Constraint in Adjudication: A Critical Phenomenology, Critical Legal Studies, Critical Phenomenology of Judging', in 36 Journal of Legal Education (1986), p. 526.

as a physical medium constraints – you can't do absolutely anything you want with a pile of bricks [judicial-making is metaphorized as a project of making a building out of bricks], and what you can do depends on how many you have, as well as on your other circumstances. In this sense, that you are building something out of a given set of bricks, and such a set constrains you, controls you, deprives you of freedom. On the other hand, the constraint a medium imposes is relative to your chosen project – to your choice of what you want to make.[315] The medium doesn't tell you what to do with it – that you *must* make the bricks into a doghouse rather than a garden wall. In the same sense, the judge is free to work in the legal medium to justify the one disputing party's actions against its opponent. How the judge's argument will look in the end depend in a fundamental way on the legal materials – rules, cases, policies, social stereotypes, historical image – but this dependence is a far cry from the inevitable determination of the outcome in advance *by the legal materials themselves.*

As to adjudication constriant, we should understand both freedom and constraint as aspects of the experience of work – chosen project constrained by material properties of the medium – rather than thinking in the back of our mind of a transcendentally free subject who 'could do anything', constrasted with a robot programmed by the law. One might accept the notion that legal argument is manipulation of the legal materials understood as a medium and still believe that the medium constrains very tightly.[316] The second way in which the judges experiences the law as a constraint in his hypothetical is that it is one of the determinants of what we might call the 'legitimacy costs' of deciding for one of the disputing party. The very notion of legitimating power is that the judge can reduce the percieved distance between what the law requires and what he decrees just by decreeing it. In order to improve his reputation, he has to write an opinion that will convince the good faith observer struggling to understand what the law is that in fact the judge's result was not out of the ordinary at all. In other words, the judge can build up his legitimating power through instances of persuading people through legal argument.[317]

In thinking about the sources of constraint in legal decision making, two broad categories come to mind: (1) constraint imposed by legal authority and/or application of appropriate rules of decision making (normative constraint), and (2) constraint that results from the institutional context in which judges make decisions ('contextual

315 Ibid.

316 Ibid., p. 527.

317 Ibid., p. 529.

constraint').[318] Normative constraints are not always efficacious, any more in law than in morals. A constraint – including the paradigmatic threat of criminal punishment – can remain a constriant even if it fails to determine conduct in every instance.[319] Direct normative constraints are reflected in an official's unmediated, personal interpretation of the written Constitution or other sources of legal authority. They manifest themselves through what some scholars have termed a 'Protestant' approach to constitutional law, in which each person decides for herself what the Constitution and other legal norms mean without acknowledging anyone else's interpretations as epistemically authoritative.[320] As already mentioned, Supreme Court justices, too, are subject to mediated normative constraints, including prior Court precedents. There are additional mediated normative constraints which are the political question doctrine, deferential standards of review, long unchallenged executive practice and constitutional theories.[321] The mediated constraint that the justices most commonly acknowledge involves the doctrine of *stare decisis*.[322] Absent good reason not to do so, the justices consider themselves bound by previous Supreme Court decisions.[323] Courts always say that *stare decisis* is a principle of policy, not an inexorable constitutional command.[324]

Pragmatic constraints take into account the goals and purposes of the agent, recognizing that 'the purpose will guide selection' of relevant similarities. *Semantic* constraint represent estimates of the degree to which people regard source and target items as being alike.[325] Justice

---

318 Braman (2007), supra note 2080, pp. 16-17.

319 Fallon (2009), supra note 2079, p. 994.

320 Ibid., p. 996. See generally SANFORD LEVINSON, 'CONSTITUTIONAL FAITH'(1998), pp. 9-53; Thomas C. Grey,'The Constitution as Scripture', in 37 STAN. L. REV. 1, 17 (1984), pp. 3, 5-9.

321 Ibid., p. 1008, 1011, 1012.

322 Ibid., p. 1009. See, e.g., Dickerson v. United States, 530 U.S. 428, 443 (2000) (describing how "the principles of stare decisis weigh heavily against overrruling [the rule established in Miranda v. Arizona, 396 U.S. 868 (1969) now, "even if the Court would not agree with Miranda's reasoning or holding in the first instance).

323 Ibid. See, e.g., Dickerson v. United States, Ibid. (explaining that stare decisis "carries such persuasive force that we have always required a departure from precedent to be supported by some 'special justification'" (quoting United States v. IBM Corp., 517 U.S. 843, 856 (1996)).

324 Ibid. See, e.g., Seminole Tribe of Fla v. Florida, 517 U.S. 44, 63 (1996) ("[W]e always have treated stare decisis as a 'principle of policy,' (quoting Helvering v. Hallock, 309 U.S. 106, 119 (1940), and not as an 'inexorable command.' (quoting Payne v. Tennessee, 501 U.S. 808, 828 (1991)").

325 Paul Bartha, 'Analogy and Analogical Reasoning', in Stanford Encyclopedia of Philosophy, first published Tuesday, June 25, 2013, § 3.5.1, referring to K.

Stevens wrote that contexts are taken into account in order to further the underlying purposes of a given constitutional or statutory text.[326] This indicates that context is determinant. Sources of contextual constraints have to do with issues related to group decision making and issues related to accountability. On issues related to group decision making, one very interesting aspect about group decision making in American legal system is that whether you take a 'strategic' or 'sincere' psychological approach to judicial policy motivations – the presence of others in the decision process acts as a constraint on the ability of judges to reach outcomes they most prefer.[327] Judicial accountability (by constraining the power of courts in individual decisions and subjecting them to a normative, and not political, scrutiny with regard to the normative preferences they attribute to their legal order), and, the coherence and integrity of the legal order (by fitting individual decisions into a coherent whole) are secured only by the methods of interpretation used by courts as well as their institutional and value choices.[328] This reflects (or which ought to reflect) a certain systemic understanding of the normative preference and institutional constraints of the legal order in which those courts operate.

Constraints upon judicial interpretation, according to Owen Fiss, is supplied by 'disciplining rules' in the form of standard which are constitutive of the profession of judging.[329] The constraints upon judicial interpretation supplement the rules of language which already constrain all language users in their attempt to understand texts. Furthermore, what constrains judges in judicial interpretation are both the need to be faithful to the original legal text which they are interpreting and supplementary norms of interpretation which are constitutive of the judicial role.

In the broadest sense, the role of courts is a function of the hermeneutics, institutional constraints and normative preferences that determine judicial outcomes in light of an existent body of rules. The concrete interpretation to be given to legal rules is therefore a product of legal reasoning and of the institutional constraints and normative preferences that determine the role of courts in a given political community.[330] The methods of interpretation used by courts as well as

---

Holyoak & P. Thagard, 'Analogical Mapping by Constraint Satisfaction', in Cognitive Science, 13(1989), pp. 295-355; K. Holyoak & P. Thagard, ' Mental Leap: Analogy in Creative Thought', (Cambridge, MA: MIT Press, 1995).

326 Green (2011), supra note 2065, p. 1291 [footnote and accompanying text omitted].

327 Braman (2007), supra note 2093, p. 27.

328 Maduro (2007), supra note 2044, p. 3.

329 Dickson (2010), supra note 2004, pp. 8-9, referring to Owen Fiss, 'Objectivity and Interpretation', in Stanford Law Review, 34 (1982), pp. 739-763.

330 Maduro (2007), supra note 2103, p. 2-3.

their institutional and value choices reflect (or ought to reflect) a certain systemic understanding of the normative preference and institutional constraints of the legal order in which those courts operate. This might occur by constraining the power of courts in individual decisions and subjecting them to a normative, and not political, scrutiny with regard to the normative preferences they attribute to their legal order. Understood in this way, a theory of judicial adjudication or a judicial philosophy (which ought not to be confused with a judicial ideology or, even less so, with a political ideology) serves not only to objectivise and constrain the subjective preferences of judges but to also define and legitimize the proper role of courts in a given political community.[331] Institutional constraints may raise from the constitutional context, in particular with regard to the relations among courts. In this context, the role played by the Court (ECJ in European law) is also a function of institutional constraints and the interpretation of legal rules is only properly understood in light of the interplay between courts and other actors.[332] Through a series of very clever pre vs. post judgment experimental manipulations Tetlock (1983, 1985) and Tetlock, Skitka and Boettger (1989) have shown that accountability concerns do not only influence how decision makers justify their choices, *but how they think* about the decisions for which they may be held accountable.[333] Judges have multiple audiences including litigants, attorneys, legal academics, other judges, members of ideological group (Baum 2006).[334] A judge's desire to 'court', appease, or satisfy any one of these audiences can act as a real constraint on their decisional behavior. Moreover, where judges have a prior record of deciding cases in a certain way, memorialized in written opinions accounting for prior decisions,

---

331 Ibid., p. 3.

332 Ibid., p. 4, referring to M.P. Maduro, 'Contrapunctual law: Europe's Constitutional Pluralism in Action', in N. Walker, Sovereignty in Transition, manuscript by Neil Walker, not yet published, forthcoming in the proceedings of the conference: Rethinking Constitutionalism in an Era of Globalization and Privatization," organized by the Floersheimer Center for Constitutional Democracy at Benjamin N. Cardozo School of Law, New York School of Law, University of Paris I (Panthéon-Sorbonne), the International Journal of Constitutional Law (I-CON), and the U.S. Association of Constitutional Law.

333 Braman (2007), supra note 2102, p. 29, referring to Phillip E. Tetlock, 'Accountability and the Complexity of Thought', in Journal of Personality and Social Psychology 45(1983), pp. 74-83; Philip E. Tetlock, 'Accountability: A Social Check on the fundamental Attribution Error', in Social Psychology Quarterly 48 (1985), pp. 227-236; Phillip E. Tetlock, L. Skitka and R. Boetrger, 'Social and Cognitive Strategies for Coping with Accountability Conformity, Complexity and Bolstering', in Journal of Personality and Social Psychology. 57 (1989), pp. 632-640.

334 Ibid., p. 30, referring to Lawrence Baum, 'Judges and Their Audiences'(Princeton NJ: Princeton University Press, 2006).

consistency motives (Abelson *et al* 1968)[335] are likely to kick in and act as a futher constraint on decisional behavior.

Judges and justices are constrained by the prospect that some decisions they might imaginably render would be treated as nullities or otherwise prove inefficacious.[336] While some rules of recognition tell justices how to identify valid law, others, applicable to other officials, characteristically direct those other officials to accept judicial interpretations as binding – even when those other officials think the judges made mistakes.[337]

***

Legal constraint and legal prescriptivity are mutually related, in the sense that legal prescriptivity may appear through or in legal constraint, and legal constraint turns itself to be legal prescriptivity. As above mentioned in Chapter III.4, law follows prescriptivity from moral and disciplines other than law. Moral issues and issues of other disciplinary studies as adopted by law become the issues of law, and this is admitted by prescriptive jurisprudence which together with descriptive jurisprudence constitute law in complete view. A huge amount [if not majority] of judicial decisions have also been prescribed by dimensions of life other than legal dimension.

Legal constraint causes prescription to be followed in legal

335 Ibid., referring to Robert P. Abelson, 'Psychological Implications,' in R. Abelson, E. Aronson, W. McGuire, T. Newcob, M. Rosenberg and P Tennenbaum (Eds.) Theories of Cognitive Consistency; A Sourcebook, (Chicago: Rand McNally, 1968).

336 Fallon (2009), supra note 2094, p. 1015. See, e.g., Kenneth Einar Himma, 'Making Sense of Constitutional Disagreement: Legal Positivism, the Bill of Rights, and the Conventional Rule of Recognition in the United States', in 4 J.L.SOC'Y 149, 154 (2003), p. 154; McNollgast, 'Politics and the Courts: A Positive Theory of Judicial Doctrine and the Rule of Law', in 68 S. CAL. L. REV. (1995), pp. 1641-1647.

337 Ibid. See, e.g., Hutto v. Davis, 454 U.S. 370, 375 (1992) (per curiam) ("[U]nless we wish anarchy to prevail within the federal judical system, a precedent of this Court must be followed by the lower federal courts no matter how misguided the judges of those courts may think it to be".); Cooper v. Aaron, 358 U.S. 1, 18-19 (1958) (explaining that "[n]o state legislator or executive or judicial officer can war against the Constitution without violating his undertaking to support it", and that all officials are thereby bound by the Supreme Court's constitutional interpretations); see also Alexander & Schauer (1997), supra note 2064, p. 1362 (offering an unqualified defense of Cooper" and its assertion of judicial primacy").

reasoning for judicial decision making. Legal constraint limits judges in adjudication in order to choose the best alternative of reasoning so as to shun arbitrary decision. In pursuing the best reasoning, adjudication is to follow prescriptivity that directs toward what is just, reasonable and acceptable by the community.

IV.5. STARE DECISIS

***

An important consequence of precedents' practical authority is this: since courts are bound to apply the law, and since earlier decisions have practical authority over the content of the law (i.e., over what is the law), later courts are bound to follow the decisions of earlier cases. This is commonly known as the *doctrine* of precedent, or *stare decisis* (i.e., standing by things decided).[338] *Stare decisis* carries such persuasive force that we have always required a departure from precedent to be supported by some 'special justification'.[339] The principles of *stare decisis* weigh heavily against overruling [the rule established in *Miranda v. Arizona*, 396 U.S. 868 (1969) now, even if the Court would not agree with *Miranda*'s reasoning or holding in the first instance].[340] Judicial decisions are based on the verdicts and reasoning that have governed relevantly similar cases, according to the doctrine of *stare decisis*.[341] The Common Law, then, might have limited its doctrine of *stare decisis* by holding that later courts were not bound by earlier decisions that were wrongly decided. Instead it developed a different practice –that of 'overrulling', whereby some courts were given a limited power to deprive earlier decisions of their binding status on the basis that they are wrongly decided.[342]

There are three ways in which precedents should be understood: (1)

338 Lamond (2006), supra note 2003, p. 4.

339 Fallon (2009), supra note 2111, n.155. See United States v. IBM Corp., 517 U.S. 843, 856 (1996).

340 Ibid., n.154. See Dickerson v. United States, 530 U.S. 428, 443 (2000).

341 Bartha (2013), supra note 2100, § 4.4, referring to E. Levi, 'An Introduction to Legal Reasoning', (Chicago: University of Chicago Press, 1949); K. Llewelyn, 'The Brumble Bush: On Our Law and its Study', (New York: Oceana, 1960) ["Llewelyn 1960a"]; R. Cross and J.W. Harris, 'Precedent in English Law', fourth ed., (Oxford: Clarendon Press, 1991); Sunstein (1993), supra note 2068.

342 Lamond (2006), supra note 2113, p. 4.

as laying down rules, (2) as the application of underlying principles, and (3) as a decision on the balance of reasons. As to (1), the rule laid down in the earlier case is represented by the *ratio decidendi*.[343] As to (2), it is argued, whether the earlier decision must be followed in the later case turns on applying the *best justification* for the earlier decision, but not the best justification for that decision, taken in isolation. Rather, what is binding in law is the set of principles which best fit and justify the totality of the results in past decisions.[344] As to (3), if a precedent is not laying down a rule, nor binding in terms of its underlying justification, how should it be regarded? One alternative is to think of the precedent as representing a decision on the balance of reasons in the individual case before the court that later courts are required to treat as correctly decided (see Lamond 2005).[345] The precedent court took a range of facts into account in reaching its decision. Those facts ground reasons for reaching some particular legal conclusion.

Determining the *ratio* is not a mechanical exercise: it involves understanding what was decided in a case – by reference to what was said in the judgment of earlier cases, and the general understanding of that area of the law. The *precedent court's* own justification for its decision plays an important role in determining the level of abstraction of the factors in the *ratio*, and for providing arguments for a narrower or wider reading of those factors.[346] A stated *ratio decidendi* may be too narrow and in need of being broadened, or it may be too braod in some respects and too narrow in others, so that it later becomes authority for a proposition quite different from the one originally stated (Bayesian model is required). When a narrow rationale is stated in a judgment, a broadening of the rule in later cases may well be appropriate. The analogical extension of *rationes decidendi* to appropriate weaker cases is a legitimate part of the Common law process [Lord Atkin in *Donoghue*].

Applying lessons of the past to solve problems of the present and future is a basic part of human practical reason.[347] In day to day life

---

343 Ibid., p. 7.

344 Ibid., p. 12. See e.g., M. Moore, 'Precedent, Induction, and Ethical Generalization', in Goldstein 1987, p. 201, 210; cf. Dworkin, 'Hard Cases', (1975), reprinted in 'Taking Rights Seriously', (London: Duckworth, 1978 rev.Ed,), pp. 110-113.

345 Ibid., p. 13, referring to G. Lamond, 'Do Precedents Create Rules?', in Legal Theory 15 (2005), pp. 1-26.

346 Ibid.

347 Mary Garvey Algero, 'The Sources of Law and the Value of Precedent: A Comparative and Empirical Study of a Civil Law State in a Common Law Nation', in Louisiana Law Review, Vol. 65, (2005), p. 782. See Interpreting Precedents: A Comparative Study 1 (D. Neil MacCormick & Robert S. Summers eds., 1997), p. 1. See also William Thomas Tete, 'The Code, Custom and the Courts: Notes Toward

we often consider precedent, or what we have done in the past, to help us make decisions and create rules, whether we do so consciously or unconsciously. We strive to bring some consistency to our actions in dealing with our coworkers, students, children and friends so that we will be fair in our dealings with others and will be recognized as such.[348] These same motivations are at work in judicial system around the world, whether the systems are grounded in the Civil law tradition, the Common law tradition, or some other tradition; a reliance on precedent creates certainty and stability for those parties operating in a jurisdiction, and precedent is valued in legal jurisdictions worldwide.[349] The practice of following precedent can be justified by two main practical considerations. First, and above all, the practice is *conservative*: it provides a relatively stable basis for replicable decisions. People need to be able to predict the actions of the courts and formulate plans accordingly. *Stare decisis* serves as a check against arbitrary judicial decisions. Second, the practice is still reasonably progressive: it allows for the gradual evolution of the law. Careful judges distinguish bad decisions; new values and a new consensus can emerge in a series of decisions over time.[350]

The principle of fairness requires 'that like cases be treated alike', where likeness with respect to principle is to be followed.[351] The doctrine of Common-law follows the basic pattern: .. a process ... in which a proposition descriptive of the first case is made into a rule of law and then applied to a .... similar situation.[352] 'Recognition of a similarity between cases, announcement of a rule fashioned from the material facts of the first case and application of the rule to the second case' are to be done in the process

---

a Louisiana Theory of Precedent', in 48 Tul. L. Rev. 1, (1973), p. 6, ("If someone else has already considered a similar problem, it is only logical to look to the prior reasoning").

348 Ibid. See Frederick Schauer, 'Precedent', in 39 Stan. L. Rev. 571(1987), pp. 57-73.

349 Ibid. See Interpreting Precedents: A Comparative Study 1 (D. Neil MacCormick & Robert S. Summers eds., 1997), p. 2; see also Interpreting Statutes: A Comparative Study 1 (D. Neil MacCormick & Robert S. Summers eds., 1991), p. 487 (concluding that, together with any applicable statutes, "precedents are the most frequently used materials in judicial opinions," regardless of whether precedents are considered to have the force of law or not).

350 Bartha (2013), supra note 2116, § 4.4, referring to Levi (1949), supra note 2116; Llewelyn (1960a), supra note 2116; Cross & Harris (1991), supra note 2116; Sunstein (1993), supra note 2116.

351 Dyzenhaus (2007), supra note 2014, p. 65, referring to Dworkin (1978a), supra note 2014, p. 113.

352 Dennis (1993), supra note 2116, p. 4, referring to Edward H. Levi, 'An Introduction to Legal Reasoning 1'(1951).

of judicial reasoning.[353] The Common-law system allows the court in adjudicating a case ...to exercise a great deal of flexibility in deciding which previous case to be chosen as a precedent.. based on sufficient similarity and 'in formulating a rule based upon the material facts of the precedent case'.[354] With reference to Hart, Dennis says that the use of precedent in Common Law must admit the following: No single correct method can be found for determining the rule for which a case stands, and therefore, more than one acceptable formulation of the rule to be extracted from a precedent are accepted, and any rule extracted from a case is subject to two types of creative judicial activity: narrowing of the rule by admitting some exception not considered before and widening of the rule by discarding a restriction in the rule as formulated from the earlier case, on the ground that it has not been required previously by any rule of statute or precedent.[355]

On the rule-making view of precedent, lower courts have the power to narrow the rules laid down by the higher courts, just so long as the narrower rule would still support the result reached in the earlier case.[356] An integral part of legal reasoning using precedents is the practice of *distinguishing*. Distinguishing involves a precedent not being followed even though the facts of the later case will fall within the scope of the *ratio* of the earlier case. As the later case falls within the scope of the earlier *ratio* (i.e., within the scope of the rule), one might expect that the decision in the later case must be the same (unless the court has the power to overrule the earlier case and decides to do so). In legal reasoning using precedents, however, the later court is free not to follow the earlier case by pointing to some difference in the facts between the two cases, even though those facts do not feature in the *ratio* of the earlier case.[357] The difficulty in the scope of distinguishing arises from the fact that distinguishing is not restricted to the application of the justification provided by the earlier decision. Any good argument can provide the basis for distinguishing, for example by showing that the novel facts in the later case provide considerations which *outweight* the original justification: it is not that the original justification is inapplicable to the novel facts, it is simply that those facts raise additional considerations that are more compelling. So later courts go beyond what was done in the earlier decision in determining whether to distinguish the later case.[358]

One of the ways purporting to deal with the problem of distinguishing

---

353 Ibid., referring to Levi (1951), Ibid.

354 Ibid.

355 Ibid., p. 5, referring to Hart (1961), supra note 1876.

356 Lamond (2006), supra note 2117, p. 10.

357 Ibid., p. 8.

358 Ibid., p. 12.

on the rule mode is to argue that the 'rule' for which the decision is binding is not the precedent court's ruling, but something narrower - the 'material facts' that were 'necessary' for the result of the case (See Goodhart 1930, 1959; and see also Burton 1995, 25-58, 60-5 on 'case –specific facts' and Eisenberg 1988, 51-4 on 'minimalist' and 'result-centered' technique). The effect of such an approach is to narrow what is regarded as binding in the case to those facts which were crucial to the actual outcome, rather than the stated ruling applied to those facts.[359] The effect of distinguishing, then, is that the later court is free not to follow a precedent that, *prima facie*, applies to it, by making a ruling which is narrower than that made in the precedent case. The only formal constraints on the later court are that: (1) in formulating the *ratio* of the later case, the factors in the *ratio* of the earlier case must be retained, and (2) the ruling in the later case must be such that it would still support the *result* reached in the precedent case. In short, as already mentioned, the ruling in the second case must not be inconsistent with the result in the precedent case, but the court is otherwise free to make a ruling narrower than that in the precedent. A later court must *either* follow or distinguish a binding precedent – a disjunctive obligation.[360]

Courts exist to resolve disputes.[361] Their decisions rest on the law rather than on personal preferences or public pressure, on 'judgment'

---

359 Ibid., p. 11. See Arthur L. Goodhart, 'Determining the Ratio Decidendi of a Case', in Yale Law Review, 40 (1930) ["1930a"], pp. 61-83; Arthur .L.Goodhart, 'Ratio Decidendi of a Case', in Modern Law Review 22 (1959), pp. 117-124; see also S. Burton, 'An Introduction to Law and Legal Reasoning', 2d ed., (Boston: Little Brown,1995), pp. 25-58, 60-5, on 'case –specific facts'; M. Eisenberg, 'The Nature of Common Law', (Cambridge, Mass.: Harvard University Press, 1988), pp. 51-54 on 'minimalist' and 'result-centered' technique.

360 Ibid., p. 9.

361 Herz (1992), supra note 1168, p. 726. For a standard exposition of this position, see generally the lectures by former Senator Sam Ervin in SAM J. ERWVIN, JR & RAMSEY CLARK, ROLE OF THE SUPREME COURT: POLICY MAKER OR ADJUDICATOR (1970). A more recent scholarly statement of essentially the same idea is MARTIN H. REDISH, THE FEDERAL COURTS IN THE POLITICAL ORDER 3-28 (1991). Professor Redish sees the core constraint on judicial authority as being "the Representational principle": "The Representational principle posits that, within constitutionally established boundaries, the representative branches of government may make policy decisions, free from judicial power to ignore or overrule them simply on grounds of social, political, or moral disagreement. This principle flows from the fundamental values underlying democratic systems in general and the American system in particular: the right of the populace to have basic policy choices made by representatives whom it has chosen and whom it may replace if, on balance, their policy choices do not coincide with the wishes of a majority of the electorate. Ibid., p. 4.

rather than on 'will'.[362] Justices Marshall and Blackmun were united against the rest of the Court in *Payne v. Tennessee*,[363] invoking precedent and *stare decisis* and warning of the danger of judges mistaking their personal predilections for the law.[364] In *James B. Beam Distilling Co. v. Georgia*,[365] Justices Marshall and Blackmun were joined by Justice Scalia, of all people, in insisting, against the other six members of the Court, that judges find law rather than make it, that they thus lack the power to change the law, and that Article 111 forbids prospective decisions because that is not how the Common law operated in the eighteenth century.[366] Justice Blackmun argued that judges are not policymakers; their primary task is to resolve disputes by 'apply[ing] rules reflecting the policy choices made by, or on behalf of, those elected to legislative and executive positions'.[367]

There are innumerable instances in which the exact scope of a precedent is gradually defined by subsequent cases. Most commonly this occurs when the language of an earlier opinion is narrowed and circumscribed by subsequent cases. Goodhart (1930) discusses the example of *Rex v. Fenton*, 1 Lew. C.C. 179 (1830) which contained the following language: "If death ensues as the consequence of a wrongful act, an act which the party who commits it can neither justify nor excuse, it is not accidental death, but manslaughter". Fifty-three years later, *Regina v. Franklin*, 15 Cox C.C. 163 (1883), held that 'a civil wrong ...is immaterial to this charge of manslaughter'. *Regina* thus narrowed the scope of *Rex* by restricting the wrongful acts that can give rise to manslaughter to criminal, as opposed to merely civil wrongs.[368] [Analogy should not only be between a case and a case, but should be in series between the case at hand and a number of precedents]. In *Daley v. Lees* [1926] I K.B. 46, Lord Hewart, C.J., says: "One has to approach the matter on the pure question of law whether *Parker v. Talbot* applies and governs this case.... I am compelled to take a

---

362 Ibid., pp. 726-727, referring to THE FEDERAL LIST No. 78, p. 399 (Alexander Hamilton) (Max Beloff ed.,1987); see Osborn v. Bank of the United States,22U.S. (9 Wheat) 738, 866 (1924) (Marshall,C.J.) ("Courts are the mere instruments of the law, and can will nothing).

363 Ibid., p. 728. See 111 S. Ct. 2597 (1991).

364 Ibid. See III S. Ct. 2597 (1991), pp. 2619-2625 (Marshall, J., joined by Blackmun, J., dissenting). Justice Stevens also file a dissent, which Justice Blackmun joined. Ibid., p. 2625.

365 Ibid. See 111 S. Ct. 2439 (1991).

366 Ibid. See 111 S. Ct. (1991), Ibid., pp. 2449-2450 (Blackmun, J., joined by Marshall, J., and Scalia, JJ, concurring in the judgment).

367 Ibid., p. 731. See Gregory v. Ashcroft,111 S.Ct.(1991),pp. 2415-2418 (Blackmun,J., dissenting).

368 L. Karl Branting, 'A Computional Model of Ratio Decidendi', in Artificial Intelligence and Law, March 1993, Vol.2, Issue 1, pp. 1-31(p. 12), referring to Goodhart (1930a), supra note 2134.

course and expound a view which, if the matter were open, I should not take or expound". In *Williams v. Guest, Keen and Nettlefolds* [1926] I K.B. 504, Lord Justice Atkin said: "I agree that the appeal should be dismissed, and I do so solely because I consider that this Court is bound by the decision in *Steel v. Cammell, Laird and Co.*, which it is impossible to distinguish from the facts of this particular case".[369] In *United States v. Halper*, 490 U.S. (1989), Justice Steven argued that the express statement of *Halper's* holding was much narrower, prohibiting only successive sanctions where "the second sanction may not fairly be characterized as remedial, but only as a deterrence or retribution".[370] Justice Stevens also found that the Court had clarified the narrowness of *Halper's* breadth in *Ursery*.[371] According to Justice Stevens' concurrence,[372] the *Hudson* decision departed from the decisions in *Halper* and *Department of Revenue of Montana v. Kurt Ranch* , 511 U.S. (1994) chiefly by adopting the multi-factor test in *United States v. Ward*, 448 U.S. (1980) and thus 'recalibrating' the method of determining when a civil sanction is punitive. Assessing the potential impact stemming from adoption of the multi-factor test, Justice Stevens concluded that while it would be difficult to predict the effect, the factors seem very close to the reasoning in *Halper*, and the effect may be negligible.

Under the principle of *stare decisis*, the Court will allow its legal errors to stand unless *policy* considerations - the 'special justification' of impracticality or unworkability - require abandoning them. *Stare decisis* is thus exactly the opposite of the usual conception of judicial decisionmaking, under which courts are bound to follow the law, even if it is inconvenient or silly. Instead, courts *ignore* the law, unless doing so is inconvenient or silly. The legal mandate is soft, the policy considerations hard.[373] Prospective overruling and *stare decisis* share a more abstract link. A prospective

369 Arthur L. Goodhart, 'Case Law in England and America', in CORNELL LAW REVIEW, Volume XV, Number 2, February 1930 ["1930b"], pp. 177-178.

370 Lisa Melenyzer, 'Double Jeopardy Protection from Civil Sanctions after Hudson v. Uniteed States', in 89 J. Crim. L & Criminology 1007 (1998-1999), p. 1033. See Hudson v. United States, 118 S.Ct. (1997) p. 498 n.3 (Stevens, J., concurring in judgment) (quoting United States v. Halper, 490 U.S. 435, 448-449 (1989), abrogated by 118 S. Ct. 488 (1997). Justice Stevens quotes the express statement of the Halper holding:" We ... hold that under the Double Jeopardy Clause a defendant who already has been punished in a criminal prosecution may not be subjected to an additional civil sanction to the extent that the second sanction may not fairly be characterized as remedial, but only as a deterrent or retribution." Ibid. (Stvenes, J., concurring in judgment).

371 Ibid. See Hudson, 118 S.Ct. (1997), p. 498 (Stevens, J., concurring in judgment).

372 Ibid., p. 1034 (Stevens, J., concurring in judgment).

373 Herz (1992), supra note 2136, n.144, referring to Maurice Kelman, 'The Forked Path of Dissent', in S. Cr. REV. 227 (1985), pp. 231-232.

decision assumes a system of precedent; unlike a retroactive decision, it is meaningful precisely and only because future courts will adhere to it. The forward-looking aspects of precedent are identified.[374] Joint opinion of O'Connor, Kennedy, and Souter, JJ., in *Planned Parenthood v. Casey, 112 S. Ct. 2791, 2815* (1992), described *stare decisis* as involving a 'promise of constancy' by which 'the Court implicitly undertakes to remain steadfast'.[375]

The precise operation of *stare decisis* varies from one legal system to another. It is common for courts lower in a judicial hierrarchy to be strictly bound by the decisions of higher courts, so that Federal Court judges in the United States are bound by decisions of the Federal Court of Appeal for their circuit, and the English Court of Appeal is bound by decisions of the House of Lords. The lower court is 'strictly' bound because it has no power to overrule the higher court's decision. Equally, most appeal courts are bound by their own earlier decisions, though they are generally entitled in certain circumstances to overrule those decisions. There is enormous variation in the circumstances that are necessary for a court to overrrule one of its decisions: at a minimum it must regard the earlier decision as wrongly decided, but generally more is required than this, e.g., that the decision is 'clearly' or 'plainly' wrong. Finally, Lamond argues that courts are generally not bound by the decisions of lower courts: the House of Lords for example is not bound to follow decisions of the Court of Appeal and is free to overrrule such decisions if it takes a different view of how the case should have been decided.[376] Court hierarchy and court powers in terms of hierarchy are taken into account in this argument, so higher courts are not bound by lower courts' decisions.

IV.6. JURISPRUDENCE CONSTANTE

Modern legal systems, whether generally labeled 'common law systems' or 'civil law systems' employ different doctrines to determine the value placed on precedent. Typically, Common law legal systems have been associated with the doctrine of *stare decisis*, under which courts are bound by precedent, and Civil law systems have been associated with doctrines such as the French doctrine of *jurisprudence constante*, which, in simple terms, recognizes that a line of prior, consistent decisions may be persuasive

374 Ibid., n.182. On the forward-looking aspects of precedent, see Schauer (1987), supra note 2123, p. 571.

375 Ibid., n.185.

376 Lamond (2006), supra note 2131, p. 5.

evidence of the proper interpretation of the law.[377] Mary Algero contends that legal systems worldwide influence each other daily as individuals and entities do business and otherwise interact across jurisdictional lines, and courts across the world are called upon to interpret each other's laws and procedures.[378] In Civil law jurisdictions, the availability of reported judicial decisions has allowed precedent to become more widely known, perhaps filling the role that "custom" palyed in sixteenth century France,[379] thereby increasing the consideration of precedent in traditional Civil law and mixed jurisdictions.[380] Meynial demonstrated that 'the importance of case law, the care with judicial decisions, the influence of case commentaries on legal practice and later on judicial decisions and other scholars' writings had been observed and scrutinized. The code was affected by case law.[381] Ledru-Rollin who was a lawyer at the Cour de Cassation and the editor in chief of the Journal du Pallais has written that case law has arisen from the law, little by little, impresses itself within equity, reflects the morals (or customs, *moeurs*), the ideas, and new discoveries, and from submissive slave, proclaims itself queen in turn.

The [foregoing] general propositions may be superseded, however, by the doctrine of *jurisprudence constante*. When a series of decisions forms a constant stream of uniform and homogeneous rulings having the same reasoning, the doctrine grants the cases considerable persuasive authority

377 Algero (2005), supra note 2122, p. 783. See Catherine Valcke, 'Quebec Civil Law and Canadian Federalism', in 21 Yale J. Int'l L., 83 (1996), p. 83 & n.106, in which the author denounces any similarity between the doctrines of stare decisis and jurisprudence constante, explaining that in a civil law system the repetition of a particular interpretation of a code article may simply reinforce the rationality of the earlier decisions, but it in no way creates or changes the law or lessens the burden on judges to interpret the code. She explains that stare decisis is necessary in a common law system to maintain consistency when judges are filling in gaps in the law, thus exercising a lawmaking function. This gap-filling is not necessary in a civil law system in which the source of law is a code that is "gapless" and judges' primary duty is to apply that law logically, rather than try to create consistency of interpretation. Ibid., pp. 79-80, 83, 85 & n.106. But see Dennis (1993), supra note 2127, p. 7-8, in which Judge Dennis opines that the Louisiana Civil Code, as well as the French Civil Code, were not intended to be a "gapless system of legal rules." See also Francesco G. Mazzotta, 'Precedents in Italian Law', in 9 Mich. St. U.-DCL J. Int'l L. (2000), p. 141 (discussing the Italian doctrine of giurisprudenza constante).

378 Ibid., p. 780.

379 Ibid., p. 781, referring to I Marcel Planiol, 'Treatise on the Civil Law'(Louisiana State Law Institute trans., 12th ed. 1959), pp. 8-9.

380 Ibid.

381 Germain (2003), supra note 1942, p. 197 citing E. Meynial, 'Les recueils d'arrets et les arretistes', in Le Code Civil, 1804-1904, 1 Le Livre du Centenaire 173 (1903); Mazeaud et. al., (2000), supra note 1943, p. 186.

and justifies, without requiring, the court in abstaining from new inquiry because of its faith in the precedents.[382] The doctrine of *jurisprudence constante*, according to Geny, is warranted on the ground that the long continuous use and influence of precedent indicates that it is in harmony with the code, that deviation from the precedent series more so than from a single precedent would impair the social values protected by precedent, and that the practice suggested by the decisions may have originated usages containing the germ of future custom.[383] Some French scholars have argued that customs must necessarily arise from judges who rule on disputes and enforce general, unwritten rules accepted in the society. Others have argued that customs come from the people through general usage over time that is enforced through some type of social sanction.[384] According to Marcel Planiol, customary law is law which has not been sanctioned by legislation. It consists of traditional rules established little by little in the course of time, and which are often difficult to ascertain.

Article 455 of the French Code of Civil Procedure requires courts to explain the reasoning behind their decisions and making a judicial decision based solely on a precedent is illegal.[385] In France, the law of

---

382 Dennis (1993), supra note 2127, p. 15, citing Geny #149 and Harriet S. Daggett et. al., 'A Reappraisal Appraised: A Brief for the Civil Law of Louisiana', in 12 Tul. L. Rev. 12 (1937), pp. 15-26.

383 Ibid., citing Francois Geny, 'Methode d'Interpretation et Sources en Droit Prive Positif, § 149 nn.104-05 (Louisiana State Law Institute trans., second ed. 1954).

384 Algero (2005), supra note 2152, p. 794-795. See Planiol (1959), supra note 2154, p. 9 & n.6. Professor Planiol has described custom as the rules that governed particular areas in France that were at some point in the 1500s written down (in some ways similar to the Restatement of United States law, which is drafted by the American Law Institute). He distinguishes written law, which is enacted by legislatures, from customary law, which he says must necessarily arise from judges who are ruling on disputes. Ibid.; Marcel Planiol was a professor of civil law studies in France who wrote one of the preeminent treatises on the French Civil Code in the late 1800s and early 1900s. Professor Planiol's treatise was translated by the Louisiana State Law Institute in 1959 and since that time it has served as a valuable resource concerning the meaning of the Louisiana Civil Code.

385 Ibid., p. 788, referring to Michel Troper & Christophe Grzegorczyk, 'Precedent in France', in Interpreting Precedents: A Comparative Study (D. Neil MacCormick & Robert S. Summers eds., 1997), pp. 115, 117-19 (citing N.C.P, art. 455). The article provides: "The judgment must state succinctly the respective claims of the parties and their arguments (moyens); it must be reasoned (motive)." N.C.P.C. art. 455 (George A. Bermann & Vivian Grosswald Curran trans., Juris Publishing, Inc. 1998). See also C. Civ. Art. 5 (George A. Bermann & Vivian Grosswald Curran trans., Juris Publishing, Inc. 1998) (providing: "Judges are forbidden to decide by way of a general and rule-making (reglementaire) decision the cases submitted to them").

civil wrong (torts, delicts) is based upon five relatively short articles of the Code Civil (§§ 1382-1386). Formally, the law is found in those five articles, and a court decision is legally flawed or cracked in value if it does not cite at least one of them as the basis for its ruling. But there is a vast body of cases interpreting and applying those articles, and these cases are regularly cited before the courts to assist them in reaching their decisions, even though judgments themselves do not mention earlier cases. In substance, then, if not in form, this area is partly constituted by judge-made law.[386]

Despite the lack of bindingness of 'precedents', the decisions of higher courts in the French judicial systems certainly have force for the lower courts whose decisions will be appealable to those higher courts. These lower courts must conduct their own analysis of the cases that are presented to them in light of the applicable enacted law, but they decide cases knowing that the higher court may reverse them should they decide in such a way that is inconsistent with the higher court's earlier decisions.[387] Thus, the decisions of the higher courts can provide an 'authoritative argument' to the lower courts on how to interpret the enacted law, though 'the lower court has no legal obligation to follow that argument'.[388] This method of allowing precedent to play an important role, though not allowing it to bind courts, has been described as creating a '*de facto* obligation' to follow precedents, which arises from the hierarchy within the court system.[389] French courts are only bound to follow the official sources of law – the Constitution, European law, statutes and codes – even though precedents are frequently cited to explain how to interpret and apply these sources.[390] Thus, these cases interpreting statutes have, in many ways, become a *de facto* source of law to lower courts because they represent the accepted interpretation of the statutes.[391] As to this,

386 Lamond (2006), supra note 2151, p. 16.

387 Algero (2005), supra note 2159, p. 789, referring to Troper & Grzegorczyk (1997), supra note 2160, p. 117-119; see also Yvon Loussouarn, 'The Relative Importance of Legislation, Custom, Doctrine, and Precedent in French Law', in 18 La. L. Rev. 235 (1958), p. 258.

388 Ibid., referring to Troper & Grzegorczyk (1997), Ibid., p. 111. See also Nina Nichols Pugh, 'The Structure and Role of Courts of Appeal in Civil Law Systems', in 35 La. L. Rev.(1975), p. 1170; Loussouarn (1958), Ibid., p. 258.

389 Ibid., referring to Troper & Grzegorczyk (1997), Ibid., pp. 118-119.

390 Ibid., referring to Troper & Grzegorczyk (1997), Ibid., pp. 112-113, 117. See also Germain (2003), supra note 2156, p. 195; Loussouarn (1958), supra note 2163, pp. 250-254 (discussing the role of custom as a source of law in France).

391 Ibid., p. 779, 789, referring to Troper & Grzegorczyk (1997), Ibid., pp. 118-119. Professors Troper and Grzegorczyk explained: "A precedent is binding to the extent that a decision by a lower court contrary to a precedent by a superior court can be reversed by that superior court. But, as already mentioned, French courts

Algero argues, traditionally, in Civil law systems respect is paid to prior judicial decisions under such doctrines as the doctrine of *jurisprudence constante*, though they are not considered to be law.

The doctrine of *jurisprudence constante* plays a significant role in EU law for the sake of uniformity. In the United Kingdom, the *jurisprudence constante* of the European Union courts is recognized. The phrase 'clear and constant jurisprudence' seems to have made its first appearance in *R (Alconbury Development Ltd) v. Secretary of State for the Environment, Transport and the Regions,* where Lord Slynn, having acknowledged that section 2 of HRA did not require that national courts consider themselves bound by Strasbourg decisions, said at para 26: "In the absence of some circumstances it seems to me that the court should follow any clear and constant jurisprudence of the European Court of Human Rights".[392] In *R (Ullah) v. Special Adjudicator* [2004] UKHL 26; [2004] 2 AC 323, 350, Lord Bingham of Cornhill said in para 20: "In determining the present question, the House is required by section 2(1) of the Human Right Act 1998 to take into account any relevant Strasbourg case law. While such case law is not strictly binding, it has been held that courts should, in the absence of some special circumstances, follow any clear and constant jurisprudence of the Strasbourg court: R (Alconbury Development Ltd) v. Secretary of State for the Environment, Transport and the Regions [2003] 2 AC 295, para 26".[393] In *Secretary of State for the Home Department v AF and others* [2009] UKHL 28 the late and much lamented Lord Rodger might be supposed to have been slightly less than wildly enthusiastic about the effect of the decision in Strasbourg in *A v. UK* [Application no. 3455/05] on the decision that the House of Lords felt forced to reach in *AF* when he said: "Even though we are dealing with rights under a United Kingdom statute, in reality, we have no choice: Argentoratum locutum iudicium finitum – Strasbourg has spoken, the case is closed".[394] Now the Supreme Court has paved the way by its decision in *Horncastle*, but without suggesting that the result in *AF* would be any different, Lord Kerr proposes that the final words of that wonderful judgment might now be amended to read *Argentoratum*

---

have no obligation to follow a precedent as such, but only to the extent that it is considered by the superior court as the "correct" application of a rule. What the precedent stands for is the rule".

392 Ibid.

393 Lord Kerr, 'Clifford Chance Lecture, 25 January 2012, The UK Supreme Court, The modest underworker of Strasbourg?; Judgments – In re P and others (AP) (Appellants) (Northern Ireland)', Parliament home page > Parliament business > Publications and Records > Lords Publications > Judgment Index > Judgment.

394 Ibid.

locutum, nuhnc est nobis loquendum - Strasbourg has spoken, now it is our time to speak.[395]

In some Civil law systems, the doctrine of *jurisprudence constante* or *'giurisprudenza constante'* calls on these courts to recognize the persuasive value of a long line of precedents.[396] A consideration of the value of precedent in France, Italy, Spain and Louisiana reveals this practice.[397] The Italian system considers precedents in much the same way as the French system. Italian courts are only bound to follow the official sources of law – codes, constitution and statutes – even though precedents are frequently cited to explain how to interpret and apply the statutes.[398] In fact, according to Francesco Mazzota, 'precedents are now by far *the most important* justificatory material used in judicial opinions', and they far surpass any reliance on academic or professional writings.[399] Like in French law, the decisions of higher courts in Italian law have great influence on and are persuasive to lower courts, though the decisions lacks bindingness.[400] These lower courts can adopt a different position on a legal issue; however, they are expected to adequately explain the reasons for disregarding the decision of the higher court if they choose not to follow the precedential decisions. The lower courts have a right, not an obligation, to apply the previous ruling. Thus, the decisions of the higher courts are instructive to the lower courts on how to interpret the enacted law. Moreover, in addition to a consideration of the level of the court that rendered a prior decision, the persuasive value of prior decisions is significantly increased when a line of cases, as opposed to only one case, supports a particular interpretation

---

395 Ibid.

396 Algero (2005), supra note 2162, p. 787. See Johnson v. St. Paul Mercury Ins. Co., 236 So. 2d. 216, 218 (La. 1970). See also Mazzotta (2000), supra note 2152, p. 141 (discussing the Italian doctrine of giurisprudenza constante); Valcke (1996), supra note 2152, n.106 (explaining that under the doctrine of jurisprudence constante in a civil law system, the repetition of a particular interpretation of a code article may simply reinforce the rationality of the earlier decisions, but it does not create or change the law); Dennis (1993), supra note 2180, p. 15.

397 Ibid., p. 788.

398 Ibid., p. 789-790, referring to Mazzota (2000), supra note 2171, p. 153.

399 Ibid., p. 790, referring to Mazzotta (2000), Ibid., p. 153.

400 Ibid., referring to Michele Taruffo and Massimo La Torre, 'Precedent in Italy', in Interpreting Precedents: A Comparative Study (D. Neil MacCormick & Robert S. Summers eds., 1997), pp. 154-55. See also Mazzotta (2000), Ibid., p. 141, 137 (explaining that it is unusual for a lower court to render a decision that is inconsistent with a decision of the Corte di Cassazione and noting that decisions of the Corte di Cassazione are most persuasive, followed by decisions of the appellate courts); Pugh (1975), supra note 2163, p. 1186. But see Ibid., p. 134 (noting that the Italian Constitution does not subordinate lower courts to higher courts) (citing Cost. art. 107(3)).

of the law, in which the interpretation is considered *'giurisprudenza constante'* or *'consolidata'*, and courts are 'bound' by the interpretation 'except for very good countervailing reasons'.[401]

In Spain, a fundamental principle of law is that the judge is bound by (statutory) law and not by 'precedent',[402] This statement is based in large part on the fact that *jurisprudence* or precedent is not listed in the *Codigo Civil* (the Civil Code of Spain) as one of the sources of law, which are legislation, custom and general principles of law.[403] However, article 1(6) of the *Codigo Civil* recognizes that *'jurisprudence* of the court shall serve as a complement to the legal order with the doctrine that, in a constant manner, may be established by the Supreme Court, in its interpretation of legislation, customs and the general principles of law'.[404] When the Spanish higher court decides two cases in the same line, it will be said to have created a *jurisprudence* (formerly *doctrina legal*) which if not followed by the lower courts becomes reversible error (Quizlet). Spanish procedural law allows an appeal to the *Tribunal Supremo* when two intermediate appellate courts have reached inconsistent decisions in similar cases.[405] In this circumstance, Alergo views, the decision of the Tribunal Supremo establishes the *jurisprudence* on the issue, and other courts face reversal if they decide differently. This system provides yet another recognition of the value of precedent in the Spanish legal system.

With regard to the decisions of intermediate appellate courts and trial courts and with regard to the Louisiana Supreme Court considering its own prior decisions, the doctrine of *jurisprudence constante* still applies, that is, a consistent line of judicial decisions on a particular issue is entitled to great weight and is considered persuasive as to what the law is.[406] Further, just one decision by a court to which a lower court's decision is appealable is often given great weight and persuasive value. Other Civil law jurisdictions seem to be gravitating in a similar direction, though many have not expressly

---

401 Ibid., pp. 790-791, citing Taruffo & La Torre (1997), Ibid., pp. 155, 160-1.

402 Ibid., p. 791, referring to Alfonso Ruiz Miguel & Francisco J. Laporta, 'Precedent in Spain', in Interpreting Precedents: A Comparative Study (D. Neil MacCormick & Robert S. Summers eds., 1997), pp. 259, 269 (quoting Constitutional Court ruling 49/1985).

403 Ibid. Article 1(1) of the Codigo Civil (the Civil Code of Spain) provides in part: "The sources of the Spanish legal order are legislation, custom and the general principles of law". C.C. art. 1(1) (trans. Julio Romanach, Jr., Lawrence Publishing Co., 1994).

404 Ibid. Art. 1(6).

405 Ibid., p. 792, referring to Miguel & Laporta (1997), supra note 2177, p. 274.

406 Ibid., pp. 780-781. See section III.D on Judicial Decisions and section IV on Surveys of Louisiana Judges of her article above.

recognized that judicial decisions can have any binding force.[407] As to the interpretation of sources of law and the use of precedent, Algero has observed that Louisiana is among several jurisdictions that have employed a principle referred to herein as *systemic respect for jurisprudence*, which is somewhat of a hybrid of *stare decisis* and *jurisprudence constante*.[408] This term refers to a respect for prior decisions that is influenced by the legal system's court hierarchy, the accepted sources of law in the jurisdiction, a desire to maintain consistency and constancy of law, and the need to allow some flexibility to allow the law to develop.

In Louisiana, this doctrine has been described as follows: [W]hen, by repeated decisions in a long line of cases, a rule of law has been accepted and applied by the courts, these adjudications assume the dignity of jurisprudence constante; and the rule of law upon which they are based is entitled to great weight in subsequent decisions.[409] Nevertheless, although many Civil law jurisdictions have recognized some form of the restrained doctrine of *jurisprudence constante*, the prevalence and availability of reported decisions and the hierarchical nature of modern court systems have led to the recognition that even a single decision by a highly ranked court may carry great weight or even serve as a *de facto* binding authority.[410] Custom is the other source of law in Louisiana. The Louisiana Civil Code provides, "Custom results from practice repeated for a long time and generally accepted as having acquired the force of law. Custom may not abrogate legislation".[411] Commenting on the meaning of custom in Louisiana, William Thomas Tete has explained that custom is established by a practice or usage by the people in general, and a common belief that this practice is necessary as required by law.[412] After consideration of the

407 Ibid., p. 781. See section II.B for discussions of precedent in France, Italy and Spain. See also Interpreting Precedents: A Comparative Study 1 (D. Neil MacCormick & Robert S. Summers eds., 1997).

408 Ibid.

409 Ibid., p. 787. See Johnson v. St. Paul Mercury Ins. Co., 236 So. 2d. 216, 218 (La. 1970). See also Mazzotta (2000), supra note 2175, p. 141 (discussing the Italian doctrine of giurisprudenza constante); Valcke (1996), supra note 2171, n.106 (explaining that under the doctrine of jurisprudence constante in a civil law system, the repetition of a particular interpretation of a code article may simply reinforce the rationality of the earlier decisions, but it does not create or change the law); Dennis (1993), supra note 2157, p. 15.

410 Ibid., pp. 787-788, referring to Troper & Grzegorczyk (1997), supra note 2166, pp. 103, 119, 122-23, 130-31; Pugh (1975), supra note 2175, p. 1202 (recognizing pressure upon lower courts in civilian jurisdictions to follow decisions of higher courts) [other references omitted].

411 Ibid., p. 794. See La. Civ. Code, art. 3.

412 Ibid., p. 795, referring to Tete (1973), supra note 2122, p. 12 (citing Loussouarn (1958), supra note 2165, p. 248).

Spanish law in Louisiana at the time the early drafts of the Code were being made, that the meaning of custom, Tete holds, includes customs that arise from the judiciary's repeated enforcement of a rule.

German's legal system treats a line of cases as customary law, and the use of customary law looks at consistent line of judge decided cases (Quizlet). The jurisprudence of the German Federal Constitutional Court (FCC) directly binds all German courts and agencies pursuant to Sec. 31 para. 3 of the Federal Constitutional Court Act.[413] In the case *Schuth*, as mentioned by Martin Reufels and Karl Molle, the German Federal Labor Court (FLC) referred to the leading decision of the FCC of June 4, 1985.[414] The FLC emphasized that due to the right of self-determination of the church not only the public labor laws but also the ecclesiastical labor law applies to employer-employee-relationship. Thus, the application of public labor laws must not question the constitutionally protected characteristics of the ecclesiastic employment. Therefore, the catholic church is entitled to base its employer-employee-relationships on the overall concept of a Christian community. Furthermore, the church can demand from its employees to accept and to obey the catholic doctrine and deontology even in their private conduct of life. This includes the outstanding importance of marriage which constitutes not only a contract but an indissoluble sacrament. This concept of marital fidelity does not contradict the basic principles of the legal system, in particular the prohibition of arbitrariness, the concept of morality, and the *ordre public*. The German Federal Labour Court Judgment[415] of July 3, 1981, (2 AZR 235/02) *Neue Zeitschrift fur Arbeit*, 2004, 21(8) was the determination on a case in which remedial measures by the employer could not be expected reasonably. This was certainly probable when the employer tried to solve the issue internally in vain,[416] and the employer had the onus of presentation and the burden of proof regarding these facts, and this is suggested by the *constant jurisprudence* of FLC regarding the onus of presentation and the burden of proof regarding the reason for dismissal and proof of employee's possible arguments.

---

413 Martin Reufels and Karl Molle, 'Labour Law within the Recent Jurisprudence of the European Court of Human Rights', in Jurisprudencija / Jurisprudence, 2012, 19(4), pp. 1567-1583 (p. 1568).

414 Ibid., p. 1571.

415 Ibid. See German Federal Labour Court's Judgment of July 3, 1981, (2 AZR 235/02). Neue Zeitschrift fur Arbeit, 2004, 21(8), p. 430.

416 Ibid. See Federal Labour Court, September 6, 2007, Judgment (2 AZR 264/06). Neue Zeitschrift fur Arbeit, 2008, 25(11), pp. 636-641; Federal Labour Court, June 17, 2003, Judgment (2 AZR 123/02). Neue Zeitschrift fur Arbeit, 2004, 21(10), pp. 564-567(p. 566); Federal Labour Court, August 6, 1987, Judgment (2 AZR 226/87). Neue Juristische Wochenschrift, 1988, 41(7), pp. 438-439.

In Germanny, the sources of administrative law are statutory law sources: Constitution, acts of Parliament, delegated legislation/regulations, by-laws; and unwritten administrative law – case law.[417] In relation to the unwritten administrative law and case law, it is stated that judge-made law is as reaction to the need to concretize the written law. The written law needs to be concretized to be applied in individual cases, and the development of *constant jurisprudence* is required for the concretization and application. *Constant jurisprudence* is not a real source of administrative law, but the interpretation of administrative law by the courts.[418]

In Case 7 Ob 302/05w, the Austrian Supreme Court (*Oberster Gerichtshof*) confirmed that according to its *constant jurisprudence* the conformity of the goods to the purposes for which goods of the same description would ordinarily be used – Art. 35(2)(a) CISG – is to be assessed according to the standards in the country of the seller. It is up to the buyer to take into account the provisions and standards of its country and, if needed, to include them into a specific agreement according to Art. 35(1) or (2)(b). If the buyer had failed to specify particular requirements [in contract] as to the quality of the product, no liability of the seller would have been assumed.[419]

In the European Union, the Court of Justice of the European Union (CJEU) ruled in Case C-400/10 PPU J McB v LE, 5 October,[2010] ECR I-nyr at para 53 that where Charter rights paralleled ECHR rights, the Court of Justice should follow any *clear and constant jurisprudence* of the European Court of Human Rights, noting that: "It is clear that the said Article 7 [of the EU Charter] contains rights corresponding to those guaranteed by Article 8(1) of the ECHR. Article 7 of the Charter must therefore be given the same meaning and the same scope as Article 8(1) of the ECHR, as interpreted by the case-law of the European Court of Human Rights (see, by analogy, Case C-450/06 Varec [2008] ECR I-581, paragraph48)".[420] Mirjami Paso as quoted by Paunio says that the ECJ typically uses references to its own case

417 Stelkens, U., 'Administrative Law and State Liability', University of Speyer, in Lehrstuhl fur Offentliches Recht, insbesondere deutsches und europaisches Verwaltungsrecht, in DHV - Deutsche Hochschule fur Verwaltungswissenschaften Speyer, § 3 Sources of Administrative Law.

418 Ibid.

419 Austrian Supreme Court (Oberster Gerichtshof), 25 January 2006 [7 Ob 302/05w], translation by Jan Henning Berg, edited by Institute fur auslandisches und internationales Privat- unde Wirtschaftsrecht de Universitat Heidelberg, Daniel Nagel, editor, Queen Mary Case Translation Programme, CISC CASE PRESENTATION.

420 Aidan O'Neil QC, 'How the CJEU uses the Charter of Fundamental Rights', in eutopialaw, EU Law: Comment and Analysis, posted on April 3, 2012 by eutopialaw.

law as arguments for justifying its decisions.[421] The ECJ uses its own case law to support the outcomes in particular cases, but does not necessarily explain why these cases are relevant and what makes them similar to the case in question. Arguably, analogical reasoning based on previous case law plays a key role in ECJ reasoning. This approach ties individual cases to a longer line of cases and therefore may be argued to enhance consistency.

IV.7. INTUITION IN JUDICIAL DECISION MAKING

***

Aristotle's practical reason and habitual upbringing have been translated and interpreted by philosophers and psychologists among other things to include intuition as evidence in philosophy and as a vehicle of awareness in moral philosophy in order to see the moral reality.[422] In relation thereto, Aristotle's phrase has been 'In the end, the decision regarding what to do rests with perception'.[423] In line with this, Aquinas holds that human separate faculty of practical reason exists; and the faculty lets human beings know the good by intuition. Any opinion which had been held long enough and deeply enough, John Stuart Mill contended, was sanctified by reliance on intuitions. It was the great intellectual buttress of social, moral, political, and intellectual conservatism.[424] Justice is grasped intuitively through long and deep habit for practical reason.[425] Kant also sees human's separate faculty of practical reason by which moral truth is grasped.[426] In moral philosophy or ethics, keeping promise is self-evident responsibilty

421 Paunio (2009), supra note 2017, p. 1486. See Paso (2009), supra note 2045, p. 364. The ECJ also often refers to relevant legal sources, principles, and legislation, without opening these arguments by explaining why they are relevant and what their content is.

422 McNaughton (2016), supra note 429.

423 Skelton (2012), supra note 420, § 5 (Moral Epistemology). See RG (The Right and Good) 42; OJ 127; AT (Aristotle, sixth ed., London: Routledge, 1995) 1 109b23, 1126b$.

424 McMahan (2013), supra note 428, referring to Alan Ryan, 'The Passionate Hero, Then and Now', in New York Review of Books (December 8, 2011), pp. 59-63(p. 62).

425 Paul H. Robinson, Robert Kurzban and Owen D. Jones, 'The Origins of Shared Intuitions of Justice', in Vanderbilt Law Review, Volume 60, Number 6, November 2007, p. 1652, referring to James Q. Wilson, 'The Moral Sense', (1997), p. 40.

426 Siegel (2009), supra note 378, p. 38.

or duty we immediately apprehend with no need to prove, and the sense of duty is among the things which are intrisincally valuable.[427] The process of immediate apprehension of an actual fact, being, or relation between fact and being and its results is referred to as intution. Kant distinguishes between empirical intuition and pure intuition.[428] The knowledge of objects through sensation was empirical intuition, whereas our perception of space and time as the forms a priori of sensibility is pure intuition.

Some philosophers hold that an intuition is a *sui generis* occurent propositional attitude, variously characterized as one in which a proposition *occurently* seems true,[429] in which 'a proposition is *presented to* the subject as true',[430] or 'which *pushes* the subject to believe a proposition'.[431] Bealer claims that when you have an intuition that A, it seems to you that A. Here 'seems' is understood, not in its use as a cautionary or 'hedging' term, but in its use as a term for a genuine kind of conscious episode.[432] Philosophers endorsing such view hold that perceptual (and other) experiences have propositional contents and seek to provide an account of the distinctive features of intuition, perception and other seemings or experiences.[433] Philosophical inquiry relies on *a priori* intuitions, but scientific thought experiments rely upon physical intuition. Physical intuitions do not present themselves as necessary, while *a priori* intuitions do.[434] It has thus been assumed that 'intuitions always take propositions as their objects'.

---

427 Skelton (2012), supra note 2198, referring to Kant's Ethical Theory (Oxford: Oxford University Press, 1954), p. 42; cf. Robert Audi, 'The Good in the Right: A Theory of Intuition and Intrinsic Value', (Princeton: Princeton University Press, 2004).

428 Catholic Encyclopedia, Intuition, APA citation, George Sauvage (1910), New York: Robert Appleton Company, Retrieved January 15, 2013, from New Advent :http://www.newadvent.org/cathen/ 08082b.htm) ["Catholic Encyclopedia-Intuition"].

429 Joel Pust, 'Intuition', in Stanford Encyclopedia of Philosophy, first published Tuesday, December 4, 2012, § 1.3, referring to G. Bealer, 'Intuition and the Autonomy of Philosophy', in DePaul and Ramsey 1998; G. Bealer, 'Modal Epistemology and the Rationalist Renaissance', in Concievability and Possibility, T. Gendler and J. Hawthrone (eds) (New York: Oxford Univesity Press, 2002); J. Pust, 'Intuition as Evidence', (New York: Garland/Routledge, 2000); M. Huemer, 'Skepticism and the Veil of Perception', (Lanham, MD: Rowman and Littlefield, 2001); M. Huemer, 'Moral Intuition', (New York: Palgrave Macmillan, 2005).

430 Ibid., referring to E. Chudnoff (2011a), 'What Intuitions are Like', in Philosophy and Phenomenological Research, 83, pp. 625-654.

431 Ibid., referring to O. Koksvik, 'Intuition', Ph. D. Thesis, Australian National University (2011) [preprint available from the author].

432 Ibid., referring to Bealer (1998), supra note 2204, p. 207.

433 Ibid..

434 Ibid. See e.g., Bealer (1998), supra note 2207, p. 165.

Intuitions are naturally suggested to be considered as the primary data in philosophical inquiry, even though such suggestion is not free from attack.[435] According to the epistemological rationalist, some propositions are believed because of being justified by rational intuition, not by sense of experience, introspection, or memory.[436] Being justified not by experience is the position of rationalist. One traditional argument for rationalism might include principles of classical logic, basic arithmetic, analytic propositions, color or shape exclusion principles, and transitivity claims, to appeal to various propositions. Treating intuitions as evidence in philosophy is best thought of as viewing that, with respect to many core questions of philosophy, justification for believing that things are true consists (at least substantially) in our having suitable intuitions[437].

William James is the first who argues that 'cognition takes place in two different modes: .. intuition and rational thinking. Intuition works effortless and is fast, whereas rational thinking is analytical, requires efforts, and is slow. Cognitive scientists consider intuition as 'quick first assessment of a given situation' which is provisional and is to be further checked.[438] H.A. Prichard argues that moral intuition grasps the good and duty.[439] He holds that goodness seems to be a simple monadic property. The things that can have this property are states of affairs, people and actions. An act can be thought of as good, but whenever we do so, we are really thinking of its motives; a good act is one from a good motive. Prichard claims that the ground for our duty to ensure certain outcomes lies not in their value but in their nature, and this is just a form of intuitionism in its conception of our duties.

In general, William Ross says, there are those who argue that intuition is self-supporting insofar as the general claim that intuitions provide *prima facie* justification for belief in their content is itself intuitive. This may be because of the fact that intuitions seem to be the only source of justification for claims about justification, reason, evidence and other epistemic concepts.[440] Intuition may be deemed as distinctive from other commonly reputed sources of evidence, in connection with

---

435 Ibid., § 2.

436 Ibid., § 3, referring to L. Bonjour, 'In Defense of Pure Reason', (Cambridge; Cambridge University Press, 1998); Bealer (1998), supra note 2209.

437 Ibid.

438 Maria Popova, The Science of "intuition", (Brain Pickings, New York, 2012). Massimo Pigliiucci explores in a chapter of 'Answer for Aristotle: How Science and Philosophy Can Lead Us to A More Meaningful Life' (public library).

439 Jonathan Dancy, 'Harold Arthur Prichard', in Stanford Encyclopedia of Philosophy, first published Monday, January 26, 2009, substantive revision Friday, Jan. 31, 2014, §§ 3, 4.

440 Pust (2012), supra note 2204, § 4.

whether we are *prima facie* justified in accepting the contents of our intuitions. The distinctive feature of intuition, according to Ross, is that only intuition is clearly capable of epistemic self-support because it is the only source which produces non-doxastic states with *epistemically normative content*.[441]. Epistemic circularity is that intuitions is treated as an independent defense of the appeal to intuitions. Epistemic circularity in the epistemology of intuition appears unavoidable.

Recently, a number of philosophers have argued that the epistemic credentials of intuitions can be defended by appealing to similarities between perceptual justification and intuitive justification' or 'to a general doctrine regarding non-inferential justification. Perceptual dogmatism, intuitive dogmatism and general dogmatism do justify intuition. According to general dogmatism, intuitions, as characterized by the various versions of the *sui generis* state, are 'a source of justification'. It seems extremely plausible that 'if perceptual dogmatism is true, then so is intuitive dogmatism'.[442] Ross concludes, appeals to dogmatism of any sort are ultimately justified only if intuitions do provide *prima facie* justification and so cannot serve as an independent defense of the appeal to intuitions.

Intuition signifies *hunch*, clear meaning, and completely independent of further analysis. A common folk usage of the word *intuition* is to mean 'natural knowing', a knowing that is independent of the usual logic of evidence. Instead, other qualities inherent in or accompanying these insights confirm their validity to the knower. Intuition in this way is synonymous with *truth*; however, from the point of view of another person it may be at best subjective truth. In contrast to what have already been mentioned, intuitions in the sense of an understanding of the whole may rest on logical or rational processes, therefore intuition in this sense implies that a pattern, logical sequence, or understanding appears to the mind as a whole, that the whole is seen in a single instant. These different meanings of intutions all shares the idea that the events or processes referred to occur in the absence of conscious mental will. The process of intuition can then be seen as a bridging function that brings information content which is originally outside of consciousness into awareness in the absence of directed mental activity. Intuition as a bridging function brings the power of the unconscious into conscious thought. Through intuition, the unconscious with its vast memory banks, its associative accessing system, its speed, and its ability to process multiple items in parallel,

---

441 Ibid.

442 Ibid., referring Huemer (2005), supra note 2230; M. Huemer, 'Compassionate Phenomenal Conservatism', in Philosophy and Phenomenological Research, 74 (2007). pp. 30-55; Chudnoff (2011a), supra note 2205; Koksvik (2011), supra note 2232.

greatly enriches the ability of conscious mental activity to manipulate logic and construct empiric tests.[443]

M. Huemer in his Principle of Phenomenal Conservatism (PPC) holds briefly, that 'it is reasonable to assume that things are the way they appear'. Appearance has propositional content, but is not a belief. For Huemer, 'appearance' is a broad category that includes mental states involved in perception, memory, introspection, and intellection. An initial, *intellectual* appearance is an 'intuition.' An intuition of an event, says Heumer, is a state of its seeming, not dependant upon inference from other beliefs, and as a result from thinking about the event, as opposed to perceiving, remembering, or introspecting.[444] Intuition is at bottom about 'the brain's ability to pick up on certain recurring patterns', on habitual basis, so more practice (in certain area of activity) gives more and faster ability to the brain to 'generate heuristic solutions to the problem we happen to face' (in that area). Charles Siegel says that intuitionists claim that 'our reason knows directly that certain things are good', in the same way that 'our reason knows directly that the axioms of geometry are true'.[445] Intuitionists use the word 'intuition' to mean 'direct, certain, rational knowledge, such as the knowledge we have of the axioms of geometry'.

***

There is an 'inbuilt conservatism' (Singer 2005:347) in any method of moral justification that gives an important role to moral intuitions.[446] G.E. Moore claims that humans have a direct intuitive knowledge of the human good that is independent of our observation of human nature.[447] Things which are intrinsically good are things that should exist for their own sake. Human's intuitive awareness grasps 'goodness'.[448] Intuitively the intuitions seems right. Empirical investigation can tell us many things about the

443 Lois D. Isenman, 'Toward An Understanding of Intuition and Its Importance in Scientific Endeavor', in Perspective in Biology and Medicine, 40, 3 Spring 1997, University of Chicago.

444 McNaughton (2016), supra note 2197, referring to M. Huemer, 'Ethical Intuitionism', (Palgrave Macmillan, 2006), p. 99, 102.

445 Siegel (2009), supra note 2201, p. 36.

446 McMahan (2013), supra note 2199, referring to Ryan (2011), supra note 2199, p. 1022:62.

447 Siegel (2009), supra note 2220, p. 38.

448 Chaffee (2008), supra note 427, citing H.A. Prichard, 'Does Moral Philosophy Rest on a Mistake?' in 21 Mind 21 (1912), pp. 21-22, referring to Moore, 'Principia Ethica', # 10 (1903).

world, but it does not seem that it can tell whether certain acts are right or wrong, good or bad. This is not to say that our moral views are not revisable in the light of empirical findings. So, our moral intuition tells us whether the consequences of our actions are good or not, and empirical situations are taken into account.[449] Prichard has made a claim on right or wrong and intuition.[450] Moral philosophy is simply an attempt to prove and rationalize preexisting intuitions about what constitutes right and wrong.

Some moral truths are known intuitively; that is, non-inferentially, but not through sense-experience.[451] Huemer's claim that we can extend the range of Principle of Phenomenal Conservatism to cover intellectual intuition. In this context, the discourse covers the phenomenal sense and the doxastic sense. The phenomenal sense is where things can *seem* or *look* a certain way, in virtue of their perceptual appearance. The doxastic sense is the one in which there is nothing phenomenal about experience, such as certain mathematical results. Certain mathematical results *seem* to be correct in our mind without presenting anything phenomenal. There is no way that true correct mathematical judgments *look*.[452] McNaughton's remark on Huemer's view demonstrates classes of intuition.[453] There is a class of intuitions in which there are general evaluative remarks to which one might appeal in argument, such as 'it is unjust to punish an innocent person'; and there is another class of intuitions in which there is initial moral response to particular moral scenario.

We are directly aware of moral truths. Intuition is a form of that awareness, and is just a part of our awareness of moral facts. Intuitions are just the vehicles of our awareness, which we 'see through' to the moral reality.[454] Intuitions, according to Huemer, are what we are inclined to believe, *prior to reasoning*. They are the starting points from which we reason to our final beliefs. In moral judgment, once the process of reflective equilibrium is under way, some adjustments will have to be made. What we think of our initial judgments through intuition may vary when we later reflect on them. So, intuition is often independent of belief, and intuition provides the sort of constraint needed for adjudicating between competing moral ethics.[455] Intuitive apprehension of the moral principles and laws is the basis of intuitional ethical theories (Shaftesbury, Hutcheson Reid, Dugald Stewart).

---

449 Stratton-Lake (2014), supra note 400, § 2.1.

450 Chaffee (2008), supra note 2223.

451 McNaughton (2016), supra note 2219.

452 Ibid.

453 Ibid.

454 Ibid., referring to Hummer (2006), supra note 2219, pp. 121-122.

455 Ibid.

In situations in which deliberation and reflection are not possible, morality must ensure that people are equipped with dispositions to believe and act in certain ways. According to philosophers conceding that intuitions may reliably guide actions, intuitions do not have any proper role in reasoning about moral problems.[456] Jonathan Haidt concludes that 'moral judgments' derive from 'quick automatic evaluations (intuitions)'.[457] Hauser's conclusion is that ...much of our knowledge of morality is ... intuitive, based on unconscious and inaccessible principles.[458] If such judgments were the product of a set of principles of morality learned from others, it would be a straightforward matter to derive the 'wrongness' of acts from these principles, just as mathematical inferences can be made from a set of axioms and subsequently explained by reference to them.[459] According to Jeff McMahan, a moral intuition is a moral judgment, typically about a particular problem, a particular act, or a particular agent.[460] It is also possible that moral intuition is about a moral rule or principle. Moral intuition arises on its own, not the result of inferential reasoning. Moral intuition does not necessarily cause the way of sense perception to come out instantaneously. Long considerations may get involved in complex particular cases in order to distinguish and assimilate its various relevant feature – in much the same way that one might have to examine the many details of a highly complex work of art in order to judge or appreciate it.

The basic moral and axiological propositions are non-inferential knowable because they are self-evident or knowable on the basis of an understanding alone.[461] A responsibility is self-evident just as a mathematic axiom, or the validilty of a form of inference, is evident.[462] We apprehend the algorithm in the particular cases after repeated exposure to particular instances of its application, by a process of intuitive induction.[463] What comes first in time is the apprehension of the self-evident *prima facie* rightness of an individual act of a particular type. From this we come by reflection to apprehend the self-evident general principle of *prima facie* duty.[464] When moral intuition grasps the *prima facie* duties themselves,

---

456 McMahan (2013), supra note 2221.

457 Robinson et al. (2007), supra note 2200, p. 1886, referring to Jonathan Haidt, 'The Emotional Dog and Its Rational Tail' (2001), pp. 814, 819-820 (discussing the automaticity of such judgment).

458 Ibid., referring to MARCH D. HAUSER, 'MORAL MINDS: HOW NATURE DESIGNED OUR UNIVERSAL SENSE OF RIGHT AND WRONG', (2006), p. 125.

459 Ibid.

460 McMahan (2013), supra note 2231.

461 Skelton (2012), supra note 2202. See RG 20N1, 29; FE 320.

462 Ibid. See RG 29: also 12,13; KT (Kant's Ethical Theory) 42.

463 Ibid. See FE 170.

464 Ibid. See RG 33; also FE 170.

it is a grasping of a moral general truth. Moral intuition is a grasping of a truth. Our abilities to have correct moral intuition depend on our moral upbringing, the moral habits we have formed, through which we formed virtues and vices.[465] Actions can be judged to be right and that it is our moral intuition that tells us whether or not an action is right.[466] March Hauser says: "In such small scale societies, fairness was most likely an effective proxy for judging punishable acts". He suggested how evolution could have led to the human capacity for morality,[467] and concludes,'much of our knowledge of morality is intuitive, based on unconscious and inaccessible principles'.[468] As already mentioned, according to Rawls' 'reflective equilibrium', we begin with a set of moral intuitions about particular cases, filter out those that are the obvious products of distorting influences, and then seek to unify the remaining intuitions under a set of more general principles.[469] Dennis Krebs argues that deference gives rise to moral behavior involving adherence to and respect for the rules and laws of authority.[470] Robinson and Darley contend that judgments about justice are more the product of intuition than reasoning.[471] This has been shown by [s]ocial science evidence. Included in these intuitions are especially intutions about violations as might be classified as the core of criminal wrongdoing.

***

The subtractive aspect of Bergsonian perception is: only that which is relevant to our practical concerns is perceived. This means that in itself a thing possesses, as pure 'image', an infinite number of aspects that are neglected in any one concrete act of perception. Thus in the report drawn by a judge of a case – the judge's perception of the case, in other words

465 Jan Garrett, 'A Simple and Usable (Although Incomplete) Ethical Theory Based on the Ethics of W.D. Ross', Last Revision: August 10, 2004, in Ted Lockhart's academic web page on W.D. Ross, http://www.wku.edu/~jan.garrett/ethics/rossethc.htm,, p. 8,9.

466 Stratton-Lake (2014), supra note 2224, § 2.1.

467 Robinson et.al. (2007), supra note 2232, p. 1646.

468 Ibid., p. 1686, referring to HAUSER (2006), supra note 2233, p. 125.

469 McMahan (2013), supra note 2235, referring to Rawls (1972), supra note 749.

470 Robinson et.al. (2007), supra note 2242, p. 1650, referring to Dennis L.Krebs, 'The Evolution of Moral Behaviors', in Handbook of Evolutionary Psychology: Ideas, Issues, and Applications, (Charles Crawford & Dennis L. Krebs eds. 1998), p. 337, 342.

471 Paul H. Robinson and John M. Darley, 'Intuitions of Justice: Implications for Criminal Law and Justice Policy', in 81 S. Cal. L. Rev. 1 (2007), p. 3.

– only those aspects of the case relevant to the principle guiding the judge's interpretation will be perceived.[472] In Henri Bergson's terms the legal archive is seen as virtual in the 'pure past of the law'. Bergson distinguishes inattentive perception from attentive perception. In his notion of inattentive perception, a thing is a mere trigger for the inrush of practical useful abstract recollection. Following this, Lefebvre counts for the everyday workings of the court as 'inattentive judgment'.

A legal reasoning process starts when we are faced with legal issues, and initially the information available does not frequently make us able to arrive at legal decisions. How we are familiar with the situations based on past experience plays an important role. Efforts have to be made. As already mentioned, when we have experiences of similar past cases, we will immediately recognize the legal description and be able to make instant decisions without additional or bigger efforts. When we do not recognize any piece of information at all, the whole situation will be something we do not know.[473] Structured [past] professional knowledge helps much in recognizing the situations and in arriving at decisions in the area of law.

Fairness is among those to be achieved in legal decision making. Robert Trives says: "[A] sense of fairness has evolved in human beings as the standard against which to measure the behavior of other people, so as to guard against cheating in reciprocal relationships".[474] An indication as demonstrated by a wide variety of empirical studies is that there are broadly shared intuitions by people that serious wrongdoing should be punished. People also share intuitions about relative blameworthiness of different transgressions.[475] Shared intuitions about what constitutes serious wrongdoing, about serious wrongdoing should be punished and about the relative blameworthiness of offenders happen across demographics and cultures.[476] In this connection, Graeme Newman holds that considerable agreement as to the amount of punishment which is appropriate to each offense is clearly in existence,[477] and that 'general agreement in ranks [of

---

472 John Protevi, 'Alexandre Lefebvre, The Image of law: Deleuze, Bergson, Spinoza, (Stanford University Press, 2008), Chap 3, Cont Philos Rev.', in Book Review, Springer Science+Business Media B.B. 2009, Published online: May 26, 2009.

473 Wahlgren (2009), supra note 1995, pp. 203-204.

474 Robinson et.al. (2007), supra note 2245, p. 1650, referring to Krebs (1998), supra note 2245, p. 337, 342; Robert Trivers, 'Social Evolution' (1985).

475 Paul H. Robinson and Robert Kurzban, 'Concordance & Conflict in Intuitions of Justice', in 91 MINN. L.REV. 1829 (2007), pp. 1854-1855.

476 Robinson et.al. (2007), supra note 2249, p. 1639.

477 Ibid., p. 1637, referring to GRAEME NEWMAN, 'COMPARATIVE DEVIANCE: PERCEPTION AND LAW IN SIX CULTURES" (1976), p. 140.

offence seriousness]' occurs across all countries.[478] People from different cultures might share the intuition about wrongdoing and a view on each offence's relative seriousness, and the amount of punishment to be imposed varies.[479]

In what is arguably the most famous passage in the Common Law, Justice Holmes states: "The life of the law has not been in logic: it has been experience. The felt necessities of the time, the prevalent moral and political theories, intuitions of public policy, avowed or unconscious, even the prejudices which judges share with their fellow-men, have had a good deal more to do than the syllogism in determining the rules by which men should be governed".[480] An aspect of legal reasoning is that immediate recognition of the facts of cases based on past experience leading to immediate legal description occurs in certain cases in which the nature of the upcoming issues can be easily determined in advance and in which the law is stable and clear. This gives little possibility of mistakes concerning the identification of relevant facts. As already mentioned, this aspect of legal reasoning is often neglected in works of analytical jurisprudence, but is reflected in the writing of Benjamin Cardozo[481] that the law and its application alike are plain, and court cases are predestined to affirmance without opinion. Joseph Hutcheson claimed that a judge would first come up with an initial 'hunch' about how a case ought to be decided, upon having grasped the facts of the case, then she would seek to find a rule to support that result, or seek to interpret a fuzzy rule in such a way as to justify that result.[482] The Realist perspective, as exemplified by Hutcheson's reference to a 'hunch', sees even judicial reasoning as having heavy doses of thick, intuitive, and perhaps heuristic quick decision making.[483] Several legal scholars have suggested that judges, just like ordinary people, often come quickly to an intuitive decision but then sometimes override that decision with deliberation. They state, 'the intuitive system appears to have a powerful effect on judges' decision making',[484] and then suggest various

478 Ibid., referring to Newman (1976), Ibid., pp. 141-143, 135-48.

479 Ibid., n.14.

480 Trevino (1994), supra note 961.

481 Wahlgren (2009), supra note 2248, p. 204, referring to Cardozo (1921), supra note 2073, p. 164.

482 Spellman & Schauer (2012), supra note 1844, p. 12, referring to J. Hutcheson, Jr., 'The judgment intuitive: The function of the "hunch" in judicial decision', in Cornell Law Journal, 14 (1929), pp. 274-288.

483 Ibid., referring to K.E. Stanovich, 'Who was rational? Studies of individual differences in reasoning', (Mahwah, NJ: Erlbaum, 1999).

484 Ibid., p. 13, referring to C. Guthrie, J.J. Rachlinski, & A.J. Wistrich, 'Blinking on the bench: How judges decide cases', in Cornell Law Review, 93 (2007), pp. 1-43 (p. 43).

ways in which the legal system should increase the likelihood that judges will use the more logical, systematic and deliberate legal reasoning in deciding cases.[485]

***

If law is a science, law must study natural phenomena, since every branch of science studies natural phenomena. And judicial behavior is a natural phenomenon, so, according to Cassius Keyser, law is to study it.[486] Sciences including the science of law allow prediction. In this connection, Keyser says: "An attempt to predict based on legal science or a branch thereof employs the assumption or postulate that a given pattern of judicial behaviors will repeat itself when the corresponding stimuli and conditioning circumstances repeat themselves".[487] In 1941 Huntington Cairns said that all social sciences study human behavior,[488] and so if jurisprudence is scientific it will study behavior too.[489] Social sciences evidence suggests that judgments about justice are more the product of intuition than reasoning. Judgments about justice are quickly arrived at, and are frequently held with strong feelings of certainty; and the reasons for the judgments are generally not consciously accessible to us.

Following Noam Chomsky's theoretical structure in language learning, Paul Robinson, Robert Kurzban and Owen Jones argue that 'people have a specific ability to acquire intuitions of justice'. The intuitions result from an acquisition mechanism similar to the one as already elaborated by Chomsky and are acquired over the course of development both as a child and as an adult.[490] Robinson, Kurzban and Jones specifically suggest that shared intuitions of justice reflect shared evolved psychological

---

485 Ibid., pp. 12-13, referring to Hutcheson (1929), supra note 2257; Stanovich (1999), supra note 2258; Guthrie et al., (2007) Ibid., p. 43.

486 Robert G. Scofield, 'Goodhart's Concession: Defending Ratio Decidendi From Logical Positivism and Legal Realism in the First Half of the Twentieth Century', in (2005) 16 The King's College Law Journal, p. 315, referrin g to Cassius J. Keyser, 'On the Study of Legal Science', in 38 Yale Law Journal 413 (1929), p. 415.

487 Ibid., referring to Keyser (1929), Ibid., p. 418.

488 Robinson et.al. (2007), supra note 2251, p. 1685.

489 Scofield (2005), supra note 2261, p. 315, referring to Cairns (1941), supra note 1504.

490 Robinson et.al. (2007), supra note 2263, p. 1642, referring to NOAM CHOMSKY, 'KNOWLEDGE OF LANGUAGE: ITS NATURE, ORIGIN, AND USE' (1986), p. 3.

adaptations in human mind. In order to bridge from the general notion of evolved psychological adaptations to that of shared intuitions of justice, a brief foundation for the idea that preferences – and indeed loosely "moral" sentiment – can evolve is needed. There is ample reason, at both theoretical and empirical levels, to believe that human minds share a wide variety of preferences that range from the hedonic to the moral.[491] Complex functional human psychological and behavioral traits are the results of adaptations through natural selection. These include traits relating to the particular challenges of group living, which include aggression, competition, cooperation, deception, and moral sentiments enabling the evaluation of good and bad behaviors.[492] The intuitions leading to judgments, and laws surrounding incest, has been shown through experimentation not to derive from logical rationale.[493]

Shared intuitions of justice also reflect common evolutionary history. This has been suggested by evolved behavioral predisposition through which the influence of, among other things, environment and evolutionary process exists on human problem-solving. Robinson, Kurzban and Jones argue that human sociality has laid the foundation for an evolved predisposition to acquire shared intuitions of justice. Evolution has in particular contributed to intuitions that physical harm, the taking of property and cheating in exchanges are matters for particular attention and condemnation.[494] Shared intuitions of justice contribute to the ability

491 Ibid., p. 1644.

492 Ibid., p. 1645, referring to FRANS B.M. DE WALL, 'GOOD NATURED: THE ORIGINS OF RIGHT AND WRONG IN HUMANS AND OTHER ANIMALS' (1996); THE HANDBOOK OF EVOLUTIONARY PSYCHOLOGY (David Buss ed. 2005); INVESTIGATING THE BIOLOGICAL FOUNDATIONS OF HUMAN MORALITY (James P. Hurd ed. 1996); ROBERT WRIGHT, 'THE MORAL ANIMAL: THE NEW SCIENCE OF EVOLUTIONARY PSYCHOLOGY' (1994); Dennis Krebs, 'The Evolution of Morality', in THE HANDBOOK OF EVOLUTIONARY PSYCHOLOGY, p. 747, 768.

493 Ibid., referring to EDVARD WESTERMARCK, 'THE HISTORY OF HUMAN MARRIAGE' (5th ed. 1971) (1891), pp. 218-239 (arguing that natural selection eliminated injurious inbreeding tendencies); Irene Bevc & Irwin Silverman, 'Early Proximity and Intimacy Between Siblings and Incestuous Behavior: A Test of the Westermarck Theory', in 14 ETHOLOGY & SOCIOBIOLOGY (1993), p. 171; Debra Lieberman et.al, 'Does Morality Have a Biological Basis?: An Empirical Test of the Factors Governing Moral Sentiments Relating to Incest', in 270 PROC: BIOLOGICAL SCIENCE SCI (2003), p. 819; also Haidt (2001), supra note 2232, p. 814; Jonathan Haidt & Matthew Hersh, 'Sexual Morality: The Cultures and Emotions of Liberals and Conservatives', in 31 J. APPLIED SOC. PSYCHOL.(2001), p. 191. This insistence applies even to cases in which, for example, the consummated sex act is between adult siblings, fully consensual, one time, and incapable of leading to pregnancy, pp. 197, 213-14.

494 Ibid., p. 1646, referring to HAUSER (2006), supra note 2243, pp. 108-

of an individual or group to punish, and an advantage to understanding victimhood and to the concurrent condoning of punishment of wrongdoers evolved.[495] When the intuitions of justice are already in existence, publicly rejecting the principles of the system in which the intuitions exist is disadvantageous.[496] Intuitions of justice cause strong pressure that favors any variant in humans which acquires the intuitions, thus stabilizes them and makes them essentially universal in the species.[497] Decision makers are often focused on reaching specific desired conclusions, the motivation to reach an antecedently desired conclusion will affect their information search and recall, as well as other components of the decision making process.[498] Spellman and Schauer say that we believe that intuitions arise from knowledge, and, thus, an experienced judge's intuition about a case will reflect her knowledge of other similar cases.[499] She may arrive at the opinion consistent with her values not because she consciously decided which way to rule, but because her previous knowledge and belief gave her a justifiable intuition.

109.

495 Ibid., pp. 1651-1652, referring to WILSON (1997), supra note 2220, quoting John Stuart Mill's belief that our sense of justice involves a "desire to punish wrongdoers, even when we are not the victims").

496 Ibid., p. 1653. Indeed, formal game theoretical analyses have shown that punishment can lead individuals to behave in accordance with an arbitrarily wide array of norms. Robert Byod & Peter J. Richerson, 'Punishment Allows the Evolution of Cooperation (or Anything Else) in Sizable Group', in 13 ETHOLOGY & SOCIOBILOGY (1992), p. 171.

497 Ibid., [accompanying text omitted].

498 Spellman & Schauer (2012), supra note 2257, p. 5, referring to Z. Kunda, 'Motivated inference: Self-serving generation and evaluation of casual theories', in Journal of Personality and Social Psychology, 53 (1987), pp. 636-647; Z. Kunda, 'The case for motivated reasoning', in Psychological Bulletin, 108, pp. 480-498; D.C. Molden and E.T. Higgins, 'Motivated thinking', in K.J. Holyoak & R. G. Morrison (Eds.), The Cambridge handbook of thinking and reasoning, (New York: Cambridge, 2005), pp. 295-317.

499 Ibid., p. 39 – Endnote No. 2, referring to Spellman (2010), supra note 1849; see D. Kahneman & G. Klein, 'Conditions for intuitive expertise: A failure to disagree', in American Psychologist, 64 (2009), pp. 515-526.

IV.8. DEDUCTIVE REASONING IN JUDICIAL DECISION MAKING

***

Defined broadly, deduction is reasoning in which a conclusion is compelled by known facts. The specific form of deductive reasoning as found lurking below the surface of most judicial opinions and briefs is the 'syllogism' – a label logicians attach to any argument in which a conclusion is inferred from two premises.[500] Deductive reasoning, as Aristotle taught long ago, is based on the act of proving a conclusion by means of two other propositions.[501] Traditionally, the syllosism's three parts are called the major premise, the minor premise and the conclusion. The major premise states a broad and generally applicable truth: 'All men are mortal'. The minor premise states a specific and usually more narrowly applicable fact: 'Socrates is a man'. The conclusion then draws upon these premises and offers a new insight that is known to be true based on the premises: 'Socrates is a mortal'.[502] Legal syllogism was recognized by the 18th century reformer Cesare Beccaria.[503] Beccaria expressly advocated that, in the area of criminal law, judges should follow syllogistic reasoning: In every criminal case, a judge should come to a perfect syllogism: the major premise should be the general law; the minor premise, the act which does or does not conform to the law; and the conclusion, acquittal or condemnation.

---

500 Ruggero J. Aldisert, 'Stephen Clowney and Jeremy D. Peterson, in LOGIC FOR LAW STUDENTS: HOW TO THINK LIKE A LAWYER', in University of Pittsburgh Law Review Vol. 69:1 (2007), p. 3; Timothy R. Zinnecker, 'Syllogism, Enthymemes, and Fallacies: Mastering Secured Transactions Through Deductive Reasoning', in 56 Wayne L. Rev. 1581 (2010), p. 1586. See also LEWIS H. LARUE, 'GUIDE TO THE STUDY OF LAW: AN INTRODUCTION', (2d ed., 2001), p. 172 ("In the kingdom of law, the syllogism reigns supreme"); IRVING M. COPI & CARL COHEN, 'INTRODUCTION TO LOGIC', (8th ed. 1990), p. 191 ("I consider the invention of the form of syllogism one of the most beautiful, and also one of the most important, made by the human mind", [quoting German philosopher and mathematician Gottfried Leibniz]); John Dewey, 'Logical Method and Law', in 10 CORNELL L. Q. 17 (1924), p. 21, (stating that the form of logic "which has had greatest historic currency and exercised greatest influence on legal decisions, is that of the syllogism"). But see Robert F. Hanley, 'Brush Up Your Aristotle', in 3 J. ASS'N LEGAL WRITING DIRECTORS 145 (2006), p. 147 ("Syllogism are for professors. They have a tone of condescension").

501 Aldisert et al (2007), Ibid., p. 2.

502 Ibid., p. 4.

503 Huhn (2002), supra note 1999, p. 814.

During the 19th century, law was equated with science, and legal reasoning was thought to be a species of deductive logic. Consistent with this notion, judicial opinions have traditionally been summarized in the form of syllogism, that is, as arguments of deductive logic. Historically, law was considered as a science and was thought to have the same underlying structures. Both law and science consist of sets of rules; both are concerned with predicting events; both legal reasoning and scientific reasoning use a framework of deductive logic to reason from general principles to particular results; and both legal principles and scientific principles evolve over time. Over the last century, however, legal scholars have rejected the identification of law with science. The principal difference between law and science is that while science is based on and must be reconciled with objective observations of nature, law arises from value judgments.[504]

Deduction has a fundamental role. The process of arriving at a concrete outcome in any legal context is an essentially deductive enterprise. The following set of successive arguments, Sinclair says, shows the usefulness of deduction in clarifying and directing inquiry[505]: All rules of X sort should be adopted. Y is a rule of X sort. Y should be the rule adopted. To justify the major premise, on the issue of why X-type rules should be adopted: All rules serving Z1 – Zn policies should be adopted over other rules. All rules of X sort serve Z1 – Zn policies. Therefore, all rules of X sort should be adopted. Similar reasoning dictates the decision on whether policies Z1 – Zn predominate over another set of concerns, and so on. At each step of the progression a deductive approach helps isolate the issues and provide the answer. This progression illustrates the guiding role of deduction. In formulating issues and selecting propositions to pursue, deduction structures legal thought by laying out the relationship between the various concepts involved in a question.

Analysis of legal reasoning leads to the conclusion that on the various levels at which arguments occurs, deduction constitutes the very structure of legal reasoning. In fact, deductive organization characterizes legal argument and gives it its ultimate cogency.[506] Legal reasoning is a process of inference – the process of passing from certain premises which are assumed to be true, to other premises distinct from the first but deemed to follow from them, to reach a logical conclusion.[507] In deductive legal reasoning, the conclusion must follow from the premises as a matter of

504 Ibid., p. 818.

505 Kent Sinclair Jr, 'Legal Reasoning: In Search of an Adequate Theory of Argument', in 59 CAL. L. REV. 821 (1971), p. 834.

506 Ibid., p. 833.

507 Peter N. Swisher, 'Teaching Legal Reasoning in Law School', in 74 Lib. J. 534 (1981), p. 536, referring to T. GREENWOOD, 'THE DICTIONARY OF PHILOSOPHY', (1942), pp. 264-265.

logical necessity; if one accepts the premises, then one must also accept the conclusion, since it is logically compelling or *conclusive*. Reasoning is conclusive where the conclusion follows from the premises; it is *inconclusive* where the premises support, but do not compel, the conclusion.[508] Several authors have described the application of a rule as a case of deduction [e.g. MacCormick 1978, and Alexy 1978]. An example of this type of legal reasoning is: 'Rule: Thieves are punished. Fact: John is a thief. Conclusion: John is punishable'.[509] Huhn views that although legal reasoning may be logical in form, in substance it is evaluative.[510] Although syllogistic reasoning plays a central role in briefing judicial opinions, logic alone cannot describe hard cases. When we attempt to reduce a judicial opinion to an argument of deductive logic, the aspect of legal reasoning that are not deductive are exposed.

***

Common law starts with experience, and experience determines the rule to be applied. Civil law starts with general formal rule, and experienced is to be classified as instance of general rule, in which experience is the operative fact of the rule. Because of the different starting point, the processes follow different directions. In Civil law countries or in the EU, deduction from general rule or legal principle is done, however by the time a substantive particular rule is created, such a substantive particular rule is considered in legal reasoning. In deductive reasoning, case briefs are not mere syllogism, they are chains of syllogism ('polysyllogism'), in which the conclusions of syllogisms earlier in the chain supply the premises of syllogisms that are later in the chain.[511] Sinclair argues that the justification for a deductive conclusion is not questioned once the premises on which it is based have been established.[512] In practical deductive reasoning, content, and not effect, is the issue, the conceptual structure of our minds and language, and not our psychological responses.

It has been assumed that legal rules and decisions are deduced directly from legislation, previous cases, and secondary authorities. All legal questions may be decided by an appeal to rules which are definite and unchanging and whose application is thoroughly predictable. Fuller

508 Ibid., referring to TWINNING AND MIERS, 'HOW TO DO THINGS WITH RULES' (1976), pp. 139-140.

509 Hage (1996), supra note 1787, p. 4.

510 Huhn (2002), supra note 2279, p. 862.

511 Ibid., p. 819.

512 Sinclair (1971), supra note 2280, p. 855.

assumes 'a gapless system of pre-existing law, from which a solution for every new case could be obtained by deduction'.[513] Various authoritative legal pronouncements form the premises of an argument the conclusion of which constitutes a valid decision.[514] Wasserstrom is of the opinion that in such a system the applicable law would operate as the major premise of a syllogism, while a proposition describing the particular facts of the case would serve as the minor premise. The judge would apply formal logic and announce the conclusion deducible from the premise.[515] MacCormick cautions that deductive reasoning is only of limited usefulness, in that it presupposes certain premises whose soundness cannot be demonstrated by deduction alone.[516] Some of these premises are established by resolving certain problems that inevitably emerge when statutory or case-law rules are applied to specific fact situations. The resolution of this problem of classification necessarily involves 'making a choice between two rival norms as acceptable propositions of law'.[517] As mentioned in Clarendon Law Series[518]: It is sometimes possible to justify legal decisions by deductive arguments whose premises are valid rules of law and propositions of 'proven' fact. Given certain presuppositions about the nature of legal systems and the obligations of legal officials such justifications are conclusive. But we can run out of rules without running out of the need for legal decisions – because rules are unclear, or because the proper classification of relevant facts is disputable, or even because there is dispute whether there is or is not any legal ground at all for some claim or decision at law. The really interesting question about legal argumentation is: how can it proceed when in this sense we do 'run out of rules.

The United States Supreme Court in *Marbury v Madison*, 5 U.S. (1 Cranch) 137, 173-76 (1803) held: "The Judicial Department's province and duty is to say what the law is. The Supreme Court is the Judicial

---

513 Ibid., p. 831, referring to Fuller, 'Introduction to THE JURISPRIDENCE OF INTERESTS xix', (M. Schoch ed., 1948).

514 Ibid., pp. 831-832.

515 Ibid., citing R. WASSERSTROM, 'THE JUDICIAL DECISION' (1961), p. 15.

516 Stephen Kloepfer, 'Book Review: Legal Reasoning and Legal Theory, by Neil MacCormick', in Osgoode Hall Law Journal 18.4 (1980), pp. 674-682 (p. 675). MacCormick argues that two of the fundamental assumptions of positivistic legal theory are (1) that it is possible for a judge to identify all rules that have the status of law, and (2) that "every judge has in virtue of his office a duty to apply each and every one of those rules which are 'rules of law' whenever it is relevant and applicable to any case brought before him". Clarendon Law Series (Oxford: Clarendon Press, 1978), p. 54.

517 Zinnecker (2010), supra note 2275, p. 675.

518 Ibid., referring to Clarendon Law Series, (Oxford: Clarendon Press, 1978), p. 100.

Department. Therefore, the province and duty of the Supreme Court is to say what the law is". In *Griswold v. Connecticut*, 381, 483-86 U.S. 479 (1965), the Court's holding was: "A law is unconstitutional if it impacts the zone of privacy created by the Bill of Rights. The law banning contraceptives impacts the zone of privacy created by the Bill of Rights. Therefore, the law banning contraceptives is unconstitutional".[519] Justice Blackmun's opinion in *Roe v. Wade*, 410 U.S. 113, 153 (1973) was: "This right of privacy, whether it be founded in the Fourteenth Amendment's concept of personal liberty and restrictions upon state action, as we feel it is, or, as the District Court determined, in the Ninth Amendment's reservation of rights to the people, is broad enough to encompass a woman's decision whether or not to terminate her pregnancy". Implicit within Justice Blackmun's statement is the following syllogism - Major Premise: The right of privacy is guaranteed by the Fourteenth or Ninth Amendment. Minor Premise: A woman's decision to terminate her pregnancy is protected by the right of privacy. Conclusion : Therefore, a woman's decision whether to terminate her pregnancy is protected by the Fourteenth and Ninth Amendment. The ideas are floating around in Judge Blackmun's sentence, but it requires some work on the reader's part to parse them into two premises and a conclusion.[520] Deductive reasoning is *generative*, in the sense that it generates the court's holding (conclusion) through inference from general rules (major premises) and factual situations (minor premises).

The principle behind syllogism is that what's true of the universal is true of the specific. In deductive reasoning, we reason from the general to the particular. Accordingly, if we are unsure about the nature of the general, we can't draw proper conclusions about the particular. We can only draw a conclusion about the particular after we demonstrate that it is part of the universal class.[521] A clear, well-constructed syllogism ensures each conclusion is well-supported with evidence and gives a judge recognizable guideposts to follow his desired footpath through the law.[522] Sometimes a legal writer doesn't mention all parts of syllogism, leaving the readers to read between lines. Logicians are certainly aware that an argument can be founded on a syllogism although not all parts of the syllogism are expressed. They even have a name for such an argument: an enthymeme.

---

519 Aldisert et al, (2007), supra note 2276, pp. 4-5.

520 Ibid., p. 7.

521 Ibid., pp. 9-10.

522 Ibid., p. 5. The foremost advocate of clear rules and formalism in American jurisprudence may be Justice Antonin Scalia. See Wilson Huhn, 'The Stages of Legal Reasoning: Formalism, Analogy, and Realism', in 48 VILL. L. REV. 305 (2003), p. 310. Justice Scalia argues that a formalist approach to legal reasoning ensures predictability and fairness. Antonin Scalia, 'The Rule of Law as a Law of Rules', in 56 U. CHI. L. REV. 1175 (1989), pp. 1182-1183.

Often, enthymemes are used for efficiency's sake. If a premise or conclusion is obvious, then the writer can save her precious words to make less obvious points.[523]

IV.9. SUBSUMPTION OF FACT TO RULE / COGNITIVE INSTRUMENTAL MECHANISM

***

The notion of many provisions, approximately 20,000 paragraphs, in the Prussian Code of 1794 to assumingly cover all cases seems to be hopeless for Savigny. He contends that what should be done is 'to learn the method of finding rules, not the rules themselves'[524], and to find 'leading principles'. With the leading principles, a 'completeness of a different kind' could be achieved in reality.[525] According to Kant, to create rules which connect recognition and action by applying general sentences to concrete situations is impossible, since doing so will always need additional rules stating whether such general sentences fit concrete cases or not – and this leads to infinite recursion. At this point, only some technical or pragmatic rules are possible.[526] In order to make subsumption possible, all pragmatic jurisprudence therefore, according to Savigny, can be understood just in a technical pragmatic way, at least as long as the model of application moulds jurisprudence, not understood as regard to recognition of rules.

In Kant's critique of judgment, the distinction between determinant and reflective judgment is identified. Kant contrasts judgment to reason's legislation. Reason's legislation is the faculty which is legislative over an objective order. Judgment by contrast is self-legislating, properly, it is a heuristic faculty with regard to law. The task of 'finding' the law is indicated, more precisely, as the specific activity of the reflective faculty

523 Ibid., p. 8.

524 Joachim Ruckert, 'Friedrich Carl von Savigny, the Legal Method, and the Modernity of Law', in JURIDICA INTERNATIONAL XI/2006, pp. 55-67, § 3.6, referring to F.C. von Savigny, 'Vom Beruf unserer Zeit fur Gesetzgebung und Rechtswissenschaft', Heidelberg 1814, various reprints, critical edition in F.C. von Savigny, Politik und Neuere Legislationen, Materialien zum "Geist de Gesetzgebung,' H. Akamatsu, J. Rukert (eds.) (Frankfurt am Main, 2005), p. 211 (=1827, fol. 94v).

525 Ibid., referring to Von Savigny (1814), Ibid.

526 Ibid., § 3.7, referring to I. Kant, 'Kritik der Urteilskraft', 3rd ed. 1799 (original work: Berlin 1790): Savigny (1814), supra note 2300.

of judgment.[527] Kant describes the faculty of judgment's peculiar relation to law as a 'searching for laws'. In other words, the reflective faculty of judgment has its necessary starting point in experience; judgment's activity is not dependent on principles or cases offered by any other mental power. For reflective judgment, only experience can provide any specific case *a posteriori*; but for determinant judgment, *a priori* rules should be applied through subsumption.[528] Judgment must be supported by legal reasoning or legal justification. From logical perspective, the acceptability of legal justification is based on a necessary condition that any argument underlying justification be reconstructable as a logically valid argument. Another condition is that any arguments brought forward as justification are acceptable if they are in accordance with legal standards. However, only if logical validity applies, judicial decisions will follow from legal rules and facts. Logical validity as a standard of soundness of legal reasoning is, in the view of some authors, related to the requirement that any legal decisions should be based on general rules.[529]

The notion of 'dogmatic law' is drawn from Deleuze's *Difference and Repetition*, which develop a concept of the 'dogmatic image of thought'. The singular becomes the particular when subsumed under a general law (on repetition). The transcendental judgment reinstates the dogmatic image through Kant's emphasis on conditions of possible experience (on Kant). The image of law is drawn from most of Western philosophical tradition in which thought is dogmatic when it dwells in the realm of opinion which sees recognition as the essence of thought. Thought is what happens when things are recognized as instances of pre-existing categories. Thus the dogmatic image of law is where cases are recognized as instances of pre-existing rules, or is where legal judgment is subsumptive.

Aarnio, Alexy, MacCormick and Peczenik draw a distinction between *formal, material* and *procedural* aspects of justification. Formal and material aspects are distinguished in the reconstruction of legal decision justification.[530] The formal aspect is deployed in the internal

527 Angelica Nuzzo, 'Reflective Judgment, Determinative Judgment, and the Problem of Particularity', in Washington University Jurisprudence Review, Volume 6 / Issue 1, 2013, p. 10, referring to IMMANUEL KANT, ' CRITIQUE OF JUDGMENT' ("KANT, JUDGMENT"), pp. 18-20, (Werner S. Pluhar tarns., 1987 (1970), pp. 179-181).

528 Ibid., referring to KANT (1987,1970), Ibid., p. 16.

529 Eveline Feteris and Harm Kloosterhuis, 'The Analysis and Evaluation of Legal Argumentation: Approaches from Legal Theory and Argumentation Theory', in Studies in Logic, Grammar and Rethoric 16 (29) 2009, p. 312.

530 Ibid., pp. 315-316, 317, referring to Aarnio (1987), supra note 2028; R. Alexy, 'On balancing and subsumption. A Structural comparison,' Ratio juris 16 (4)(2003), p. 433-449; MacCormick, 'Legal deduction, legal predicates and expert

justification in which any argument should be reconstructed as a logically valid argument, comprising legal rule and fact as premises, and judicial decision as conclusion. However, since the central of external justification is the material aspects, a question then arises: Can facts and legal rules in the internal justification be considered acceptable in the external justification? In connection with the question, the reconstruction of easy cases and hard cases is distinguished in trying to answer the question. In easy cases, MacCormick says that a *deductive argument* can be used to defend the decisions. Following Wroblewski, Aarnio uses syllogistic logic for analyzing legal arguments. Aarnio calls such *deductive justification* an *internal justification*. In hard cases, applicable norms are not clear yet, and this may cause missing premises for syllogistic deduction. If there are missing premises, a further justification by means of a chain of arguments, MacCormick calls a *secondary order justification*, is required. Within this context, subordinate arguments in argument chain are required for successful justification. Alexy calls the whole chain of arguments the *internal justification*, which is concerned with the formal reconstruction of premises for complete justification. It is Alexy's contention that legal decision must follow logically from at least one universal norm together with other premises. From MacCormick's and Alexy's views, it can be deduced that missing premises should be made explicit, in order to make syllogistic deduction possible. But Alexy does not specify how hidden assumption must be made explicit. Aarnio holds that all implicit elements of incomplete syllogism must be made explicit, in order to defend and reconstruct the elements of the internal justification in the external justification. This connection between internal [formal] justification and external [substantive] justification is tried by creating premises from legal principles through interpretation of legal principles.

Legal reasoning in a broader perspective starts with fact-findings, and at the same time applicable rule is identified. The objective of the process is to enable subsumption of facts under the applicable rule, which is the general description of the facts in the legal-system. Legal subsumption must not be, however, performed haphazardly. In subsumption, methodological rules determine and explain the presupposition for rule application as well as determine how rule applications ought to be completed. In this context it is therefore proper to acknowledge a special rule application process.[531] This is a process-based method, but there is another method which is a content-based method.

***

systems', in International Journal for the Semiotics of Law V (14) (1992), pp. 181-202; A. Peczenik, 'The Basis of Legal Justification', Lund, 1983; Peczenik (1989), supra note 2020.

531 Wahlgren (2009), supra note 2256, p. 205.

Rule-based analysis can originate from a case or a statute. In the analysis, an applicable rule should be broken down into separate elements, and the facts should be subsumed to each element in order to see whether or not the element is satisfied. If a precedent uses, or a statute requires a balancing test to overcome controversial issue, then satisfying the element needs weighing and balancing different interests or factor to achieve a fair outcome.[532] Rule-based reasoning is the reasoning in which rule application means the satisfaction of rule's conditions.[533]

A rule does not take into account all relevant aspects. Due to this, it may be the case that a rule is not applied although such a rule is applicable. Scope limitation, rule exception and goal exception are considered.[534] Satisfaction of rule's requirements is necessary, but not sufficient for rule applicability. A rule is applicable to a case, if and only if its conditions are satisfied, and its application is not excluded. If the application of a rule would be against the purpose of the rule, this is the reason why not to apply the rule. Fuller gave an example of a prohibition to sleep in the railway station, the purpose of which was to prevent tramps from spending their night in the station (Fuller 1958). To apply the rule to a traveler who fell asleep a few minutes while awaiting a retarded late train would be against the purpose of the rule.[535]

In Hage's illustration, the constitution of reason [from facts] is identified elementarily in cases where a principle or rule has some requirements to be totally satisfied. John took away Ellen's car, with the intention to appropriate the car. In that case, the facts that (1) John took away the car, (2) The car belonged to Ellen, and (3) John intended to appropriate the car, *together* become a constitutive reason why John is a thief. Neither one of these facts by itself is a constitutive reason. It is also possible that there are a factual reason for a particular conclusion and another factual reason against that particular conclusion in one particular case. If the rule applicable to the case is formulated with a negative conclusion to be proven, any facts denying the satisfaction of requirements are first to be identified. Then any facts proving the satisfaction are allowed to attack the denying facts.[536] In the subsumption method,[537] a rule identifies a particular type of case and indicates the consequences of this type of case. Each type has a set

532 Connely, supra note 1999, para III.A & B.

533 Hage (1996), supra note 2284, p. 4.

534 Ibid., p. 13, 18.

535 Ibid., p. 19, referring in part to L.L. Fuller, 'Positivism and Fidelity to law: A Reply to Professor Hart', in Harvard Law Review 71 (1958), pp. 630-672.

536 Ibid., p. 16.

537 Ibid., p. 10.

of characteristics as stated in the rule's requirements. Each characteristic, which is a requirement/element of the rule, may represent an aspect of the case, and such an aspect is made relevant by a legal principle. The rule has the pretension to take all relevant aspects of the case into account and to indicate the outcome based on said all relevant aspects. Because of this pretension, there is no need to weigh the outcome against other possible outcomes, since the reasons for such possible alternative outcomes have been (at least in theory) taken into account in the rule, and they need not to be taken into account again.

In subsuming fact to rule, Michael Hoppman sees asymmetrical situations with one accusation at a time.[538] When there are several requirements of an applicable rule to be satisfied, the defense argument proving that one requirement is not satisfied cancels the accusation entirely. On the other side, the accuser must prove the satisfaction of all the requirements. In all norm-based accusation, Hoppman argues, there is an "asymmetrical burden of proof" in criminal law, under which the prosecutor must prove all points (satisfaction of all requirements of rule) in several conjunctive claims, but the defense must merely invalidate one of these points to gain acquittal. Reasonable doubt about any of these points (and there are others) secures acquittal.

***

Rule-based reasoning through subsumption are syllogistic. Alexy has tried to prove that principle-based reasoning is also syllogistic. This syllogistic method constitutes mental construction in terms of formal-technicality of what has factually happened in the first place, but the mental construction is carried in court through formal technicality in court hearing. The starting point of principle-based reasoning is the notion of reason. A reason is elementary, and such elementary reason forms a compound reason which is significant for the presence of some other fact, which is the conclusion. The first fact that John took away Mary's car and the second fact that Mary did not allow John to take away her car form a compound reason why John is a thief. The first fact is a *constitutive* reason that makes John a thief; and the second fact is an *epistemic* reason constituting evidence that John is a thief. The first and the second facts form the compound reason which is the

538 Christian Kock, 'Michael Hoppmann, Argumentative Verteidiguing: Grundlegung zu einer modernen Statuslehre. Neue. 5, (Berlin: Weidler, 2008). 223 pp.', Department of Media, Cognition, and Communication, University of Copenhagen.

basis for an argument for the conclusion that John is a thief.[539] Reasons are amenable to 'weighing'. Since more than one reasons, reason for and reason against, a particular conclusion is possible, doctrinal writers such as Raz and Peczenik argue that weighing reasons should be done.

On reason, Hare holds that 'universalisable' is another important feature of reason.[540] If a fact of type-T is significant for a conclusion of type-C, then all facts of type-T are significant for conclusions of type-C. This presupposes that facts of type-T are significant since they belong to type-T and the conclusions of which belong to type C. So, if the fact that John is a thief is the reason why he is punishable, then in general any fact that who(m)soever is a thief is the reason why he is punishable. The latter formulation can be considered as the expression of a *principle*: Thieves are punishable. The fact that John committed a crime based on the principle 'Thieves ought to be punished' is made the reason why John ought to be punished. This reason contributes to the conclusion that John ought to be punished. If there are reasons why John ought not to be punished or if these reasons are outweighed by the reason that John committed a crime, this weighing of reasons leads to the conclusion that John ought to be punished. This makes use of the structure proposed by Toulmin.[541] There are two steps to the conclusion that John ought to be punished.[542] First, the fact that John has committed a crime leads us to an intermediate conclusion that this fact becomes the reason why John ought to be punished. Then, the intermediate reason (possibly in combination with other reasons) leads us further to the conclusion that John ought to be punished. Both steps are *constitutive* and *ontological*, the principle of which makes the fact the reason for (or – if there are also other reasons – contributes to) the conclusion that John ought to be punished. This argumentation is the mental (verbal) reproduction of the constitution.

***

According to Alexy, the form of legal rule application is subsumption: applying legal rules to facts.[543] In his theory Alexy tries to demonstrate

539 Hage (1996), supra note 2308, p. 5, referring to Raz (1975), supra note 1464; Raz (1979), supra note 1833; Peczenik (1989), supra note 2305.

540 Ibid., with reference to R.M.Hare, 'Freedom and Reason', (Oxford: Oxford University Press, 1963, e.a).

541 Ibid., p. 8, with reference to S.E. Toulmin, 'The Uses of Argument', (London, New York: Cambridge University Press, 1958).

542 Ibid.

543 Harm Kloosterhuis, 'Toward a Typology of Argumentation based on Legal

that to construct weighing and balancing as a rational form of reasoning is possible. He uses a decision of the German Federal Constitutional Court (BVerfG) on the inability of someone to attend court hearings (BVerfGE vol. 51, p. 324). The colliding principles to be weighed and balanced in the case were the basic right to life and to inviolability of physical body and the principle of criminal justice system functioning, in a situation where 'there was a clear and specific danger that the defendant would forfeit his life or suffer serious bodily harm in case the trial was held'. The Court did not solve the problem by declaring that one of the principles was invalid or by introducing an exception. Instead, the Court determined a *conditional priority* for one of the colliding principles over the other. The Court held that the former principle should have priority over the latter. The basic right was deemed to have greater weight and therefore was prioritized over the functioning of criminal justice system (BVerfGE vol. 51, 234, p. 346). Conceptualizing the rational way of principle balancing, Alexy introduces the Law of Balancing: 'The greater the degree of non-satisfaction of, or detriment to, one right or principle, the greater must be the importance of satisfying the other'. (Alexy, 2003, p. 436). Alexy's analysis of weighing and balancing demonstrates that the judicial decision has been considered to have followed logically from a general norm together with further statements/ premises.

Determining judicial decision systematically and logically which can be done by legally-trained minds only is the traditional view of legal reasoning.[544] The traditional view is more logical, systematic and deliberative.[545] It is more process-based rather than content-based. In this more process-based argumentation, the emphasis is on following, applying and interpreting formal, written and authoritative rules, as well as within a framework of such rules.[546] In the traditional view, decision makers can be trained to just follow an authority with which they might disagree, and indeed much of the training in law school is devoted to inculcating just the kind of distinction between obedience to legal authority and taking into account that which otherwise seems morally and decisionally relevant.[547] Using the formal law to produce outcomes

---

Principles', Hacia una tipologia de argumentacion basada en principios legale, in COGENCY Vol. 3, No. 2, Summer 2011, pp. 67-80 (p. 69, 70, 71), citing Alexy (2003), supra note 2305, p. 435; R. Alexy, 'The Structure of Legal Principles', in Ratio juris 13(3) (2000), pp. 294-304 (p. 297); Alexy (2003), Ibid., p. 436.

544 Spellman & Schauer (2012), supra note 2273, p. 2.

545 Ibid., p. 12, referring to K.E. Stanovich, 'Who is rational? Studies of individual differences in reasoning', (Mahwah, NJ: Erlbaum, 1999).

546 Ibid., p. 10.

547 Ibid., p. 6, 35, citing F. Schauer,'Thinking like a lawyer: A new introduction to legal reasoning', (Cambridge, MA: Harvard, 2009).

in the first place is, Spellman and Schauer say, what the traditional view of legal reasoning maintains.

IV.10. PURSUIT OF CERTAINTY AND FAIRNESS

IV.10.1. ANALOGY IN LEGAL REASONING

***

Arguments from precedent and analogy are characteristic of legal reasoning. Legal reasoning differs in a number of ways from the sort of reasoning employed by individuals in their everyday life.[548] The most promising available defense of analogical reasoning may be found in its application to case law. This involves analogical reasoning based on pragmatic justification. Judicial decisions, as viewed by Levi, Llewelyn, Cross & Harris, and Sunstein, are based on the verdicts and reasoning that have governed relevantly similar cases, according to the doctrine of *stare decisis,* which, as already mentioned, is *conservative,* which provides a relatively stable basis for replicable decisions, which serves as a check against arbitrary judicial decisions, which is still reasonably progressive, and which allows for the gradual evolution of the law.[549]An analogical argument in legal reasoning is an argument that a case should be treated in a certain way because that is the way a similar case has been treated. Arguments by analogy complement arguments from precedent in two ways: (i) they are used when the facts of a case do not fall within the *ratio decidendi* of any precedent, in order to assimilate the result to that in the analogical case; and (ii) they are used when the facts of a case do fall within the *ratio decidendi* of a precedent, as a basis for distinguishing the case at hand from precedent. The force of an argument from analogy is different from that from the precedent. An indistinguishable precedent must be followed unless the court has the power to overrule the earlier decision and does so. By contrast, arguments from analogy vary in their strengths: from very 'close' analogies (which strongly support a result) to more 'remote' analogies (which weakly support a result). Analogies do not bind: they must be considered along

548 Lamond (2006), supra note 2161, p. 2.

549 Bartha (2013), supra note 2116, § 4.4, referring to Levi (1949), supra note 2125; Llewelyn (1960a), supra note 2125; Cross & Harris (1991), supra note 2125; Sunstein (1993), supra note 2125.

with other reasons in order to reach a result.[550] Spellman sees a connection between pre-existing knowledge, question-framing and analogy.[551] There is possibility that judges choose relevant analogies (or precedents), as better or worse, applicable or inapplicable, not because of any particular desired outcomes but rather because of their own preexisting knowledge and the way they frame their questions.

Application of precedents without the medium of rules proceeds by way of analogical reasoning: inferences are based upon perceived factual similarities which are thought to justify the same legal treatment. An argument can be mounted to the effect that precedents are not truly binding even when applied in this seemingly compelling way: if the strongest possible case for application is the case involving the closest possible factual similarity, and if growing dissimilarity weakens the case for application, then a precedent would never be completely binding, for some difference between the precedential facts and the facts of later cases can always be detected. Factual dissimilarities may either weaken or *strengthen* the case for the application of a precedent.[552]

The reason-based approach to analogical reasoning focuses on the justifications for the analogical case (for two very different accounts, see Raz 1979, pp. 201-6 and Brewer 1996). It considers the extent to which the rationale for the decision in the earlier case is applicable to the case at hand. The reason-based approach helps to explain why individual cases, and individual doctrines, can ground analogies. It also explains what is accurate in the principles-based approach, since some of the considerations underlying analogical cases will be principles. But there are more legal considerations than principles, and these too play a role in analogical reasoning.[553] Institutional decision-makers often regard earlier decisions as being relevant even when the decision at hand is different from the original ones, by citing them as analogies. They will argue that since an earlier decision was made on same matter, it would be inconsistent now to decide the present case differently.[554] It is widely agreed that the existence of an analogy depends ultimately upon the *justification* for the

550 Lamond (2006), supra note 2323, pp. 20-21.

551 Spellman & Schauer (2012), supra note 2319, p. 26, referring to Spellman (2010), supra note 2274; Spellman & Holyoak (1992), supra note 588; B.A. Spellman and K.J. Holyoak (1996), 'Pragmatic in analogical mapping', in Cognitive Psychology, 31, pp. 307-346.

552 Lucke (1989), supra note 1785, p. 46.

553 Lamond (2006), supra note 2325, p. 24. For two very different accounts see Raz (1979), supra note 2314, pp. 201-206; S. Brewer, 'Exemplary Reasoning: Semantics, Pragmatics, and the Rationale Force of Legal Argument by Analogy', in Harvard Law Review 109 (1996), pp. 923-1028.

554 Ibid., p. 3.

analogical decision. The facts in a case may fall outside the *ratio decidendi* of an existing precedent, and thus the court is not bound by the precedent. On the other hand the *justification* for the earlier decision may apply to the later case, and thus provide an argument from analogy. Analogies, like precedents, Lamond says, arise within a doctrinal context.[555] An analogy may either be to another case or to another legal doctrine, and the analogy rests on there being some common characterization of the facts in both cases or the two doctrines which are relevant to the issue.

***

Since what to be viewed through analogy in legal reasoning are the facts of the case, analogy is closely related to *ratio decidenci* that incorporates the facts of the case. It is the facts established by the judge, which determine *ratio decidendi.* Dias has illustrated this with reference to one of the most famous precedents, *Donoghue v. Stevenson,* A.C. 562 (1932) : "what is important in law is the statement of facts rather than even their truth. The House of Lords remitted the case to the Scottish court for trial on the ruling laid down by the House, but this did not take place because of the death of one of the parties. So the truth as to whether or not there was a snail in the bottle was never established and is irrelevant to the ruling".[556] Even the most clearly stated *ratio,* Dias argues, will not necessarily be given an operation in accordance with its literal meaning. A judge is able to declare the precedent in which the *ratio* was stated inapplicable by pointing to a *significant factual difference* between the precedent and the case before him, and then to distinguish the precedent 'on the facts'.[557] It is the factual facts of the precedcent which are incorporated in the *ratio decidendi* [Lucke]. One should never quote general language from an opinion, divorced from the factual context in which the language was delivered [Gilmore]. The long-established maxim is that judicial pronouncements as to the law must be read as subject to the underlying facts (*secundum subjectam materiam*).[558] Although the *ratio* is to be understood as incorporating the actual facts of the precedent, there is no way implying that judges should not also seek to articulate a generalized version. In *Donoghue v. Stevenson,* Lord Atkin provided a carefully worded rationale intended to embrace no more than truly like cases[559] – a rationale which has a good chance of being

555 Ibid., p. 21.

556 Lucke (1989), supra note 2327, p. 42. See [1932] AC 562.

557 Ibid., p. 40, referring to Dias, 'Jurisprudence'(5th edn 1985), pp. 145-146.

558 Ibid., p. 38.

559 Ibid., p. 51. See [1932] AC 599: "A manufacturer of products, which he

respected and applied by other judges. When a narrow rationale is stated in a judgment, a broadening of the rule in later cases may well be appropriate. The analogical extension of *rationes decidendi* to appropriate weaker cases is a legitimate part of the common law process.

Goodhart's debate switched from the realm of deductive logic to that of analogical logic.[560] Where the facts in the later case are the 'same' as those in the earlier case, the application of precedent is binding.[561] Later courts whose case-facts fall within the scope of the *ratio* must *consider* the precedent, but do so in order to consider whether the differences in facts between the later and the precedent cases justify deciding the cases differently.[562] It is often argued that reasoning by analogy and distinguishing precedents are mirror image of each other: given the facts of two cases, the question is whether there is a good reason for treating them differently (e.g., Eisenberg 1988, 87). In case of distinguishing, a precedent must be followed unless there are good reasons for treating it differently.[563] Lamond argues if there are good reasons to believe that an earlier case was correctly decided, and if the facts in a later case are the same as those in the earlier case, then there are good reasons for believing that the same decision would be correct in the later case.[564]

There is an influential view on analogy, and such a view regards it as grounded in the *principles* that underlie existing cases.[565] The principles must map the decided cases precisely, or must depart from only a small proportion of them. If the principle(s) identified in this process apply to the instant case, then that provides a good reason in favor of the result supported by the principle. A more common view, however, is that a principle that makes best sense of a series of cases or doctrines are morally imperfect. Where principles are used as arguments for a result, earlier cases tend to be cited as illustrations of the application of the principle, rather than as analogies to the facts of the case at hand. If another case is cited as providing an analogy, the emphasis will be on how 'close' the

---

sells in such a form as to show that he intends them to reach the ultimate consumer in the form of which they left him with no reasonable possibility of intermediate examination, and with the knowledge that the absence of reasonable care in the preparation or putting up of the products will result in an injury to the consumer's life or property, owes a duty to the consumer to take that reasonable care."

560 Ibid., p. 49. See Mirehouse v. Rennell (1832) 8 Bing 490, 515.

561 Lamond (2006), supra note 2328, p. 5.

562 Ibid., p. 14.

563 Ibid., p. 22.

564 Ibid., p. 3.

565 Ibid., p. 22, 23. See e.g., MacCormick (1978, 1994), supra note 2045, pp. 152-94; Eisenberg (1988), supra note 2134, pp. 83-96; Sunstein (1993), supra note 2324.

analogy is, i.e., on how specific the common characterization of the facts of the two cases is, and how that characterization relates to the rationale for the earlier decision. The more specific an analogy, the stronger; the more abstract the characterization, the weaker the argument as an analogy. The reason for this is that the more specific the analogy, the less room there is for distinguishing the two cases, whereas the more abstract the analogy the more grounds on which the two cases may be regarded as significantly different.

***

When you reason by analogy, you draw parallels between your factual situation and cases that have already been decided. Cases are made by their facts, so you have to compare and contrast the facts and circumstances of your case with the decided case. If the key facts are similar, you can draw the analogy. If the key facts are different, then you may have to apply a different rule. The role of the court is to resolve disputes by interpreting rules and law and applying them to the facts of a dispute in order to reach a conclusion of law. A conclusion of law is the determination of whether or in what manner a specific rule of law applies to a specific set of facts. You must compare the important facts in the opinion with the new set of facts in the present controversy to identify similarities and differences. If there are similarities between the facts and the rule of law in the opinion and the present controversy, you can make a prediction regarding the outcome of the controversy.[566]

As said in Chapter I.3.2, on learning by analogy and constraint transfer, Winston, Binford, Katz & Lowry have detailed: 1/ a natural language interface translates English sentences describing a precedent and a problem into links in a semantic net; 2/ a matcher determines a correspondence between the parts of the precedent and the problem; 3/ an analogizer determines if the questioned link in the problem is supported by the given links in the problem, and to do this, the analogizer transfers the CAUSE links supplied by the precedent onto the problem; and 4/ a rule generator constructs an if-then rule to capture that portion of the causal structure in the precedent that is ferreted out by the problem. The *then* part of the if-then rule comes from the questioned link in the problem. The *if* parts come from links identified by the transferred CUASE structure. In more complicated situations, no single precedent can supply enough causal structure. Consequently, several precedents must be strung together. A new precedent is sought whenever there is a path in the transferred CAUSE

566 Connelly, supra note 2307, para III.C.

structure that does not lead to an already established link in the problem.[567] Winston, Binford, Katz & Lowry propose a synthesis of two sets of ideas: ideas about learning from precedents and exercises developed at MIT and ideas about physical description developed at Stanford.[568] Their purposes are to explain how physical identification can be done using functional definition, and to show how to learn physical models using functional definitions and specific acts of identification.[569] [a number of precedents strung together is practiced in legal reasoning]. Most cases turn on a dispute about the facts – who did what, when, and to whom. In these cases the job of the court is to decide on the evidence before it whose version of the facts to endorse. The parties in such cases agree about the law that applies to their dispute, they simply disagree about what actually happened. In other cases there can be a dispute over the applicable law.

In many cases before the courts, judges take horizontal and vertical relations into account, similar to Hesse's material analogy, in mapping the similarities [and difference] between precedents and cases at hand. Applying Hesse's material analogy in legal reasoning means applying the similarity-matching of features of identified precedent(s) and those of the case at hand, and the similarity-matching of relations between features of the precedent(s) on the one hand and relations between features of the case at hand on the other hand. The aim of this mapping is to see the insight of the case at hand for problem solving. Extending the field analogy yet a step further, Kennedy says, we can use it to incorporate the 'broadening' and 'narrowing' of holdings into our analysis.[570] Narrowing the holding by restating it as a rule that depends for its application on many potentially idiosyncratic details of the particular case, is a shortening of the line that extends through the fact-situation in the field. It means that there will be fewer hypothetical fact-situations 'covered' by the holding, and the case will therefore have less structuring effect on the field around it. Broadening is the opposite maneuver.

Analogical reasoning helps to make the outcome of cases more predictable by giving weight to existing legal decisions and doctrines. But it only does so against a certain background, one where despite decision-makers not sharing a uniform normative outlook there is a large measure of agreement on the existence and importance of certain values. A certain level of agreement is required for decision-makers to see a case as analogous, since that rests on what they judge to be the proper justification for the earlier decision. The use of analogies in law, then, serves to compensate for

567 Winston et al., (1983), supra note 652, pp. 433-434.
568 Lamond (2006), supra note 2336, p. 5.
569 Winston et. al, (1983), supra note 2342, p. 433.
570 Kennedy (1986), supra note 2089, p. 533.

some of the indeterminacy which flows from fragmented materials and the pluralism of decision-makers. That a close analogy exists usually provides a good reason for deciding the case the same way, since it renders the law more applicable than it would otherwise be, and enables lawyers to predict more accurately how a situation will be treated by the law. Of course, this is only a relative value: analogies can be defeated by other considerations if there is a good basis for distinguishing, or if its merits are too weak.[571]

Concerning the justification for analogical reasoning, in law, analogies carry a weight additional to the merit of the case. There are a number of possible indirect benefits that accrue from the practice of analogical reasoning, such as exposing judges to a wider variety of fact situations than the particular set before them, making them consider the views of other judges in previous cases and exerting a conservative pressure on individual decision-makers.[572] Consistency may provide a rationale for a limited exercise of analogy. Where an earlier case has settled some indeterminacy in the application of the law, and where the rationale for the earlier decision is equally applicable to the later facts, then it would be inconsistent to decide the later case differently.[573] In addition to consistency, analogical reasoning also supports legal coherence. MacCormick's theory of precedent, his subsequent model of *ratio decidendi* and an established doctrine of precedent form part of a coherent system of 'complex interplay between considerations of principle, consequentalist arguments and disputable points of interpretation of established valid rule. The complex interplay is called 'second-order justification', which requires consistency with pre-established and binding *ratio decidendi*, coherence with established law [judicial decisions should be coherent with established general principles], and considerations of consequentialist arguments in which the preferable ruling, as compared to any other alternatives, should be in light of its goal and consequences.[574] In practice, the outcome of a case may be uncertain not simply because the correct result is rationally indeterminate, but because the decision-makers are fallible. Given this, a precedent supported by analogy as practiced in law has a number of advantages due the fact that it may make institutional decisions replicable (see Eisenberg 1988, 10-12, 23-24, whose coinage it is; and Schauer 1987, 597-8). Replicability means that decisions are more predictable than if they were made *de novo* each time.[575] This, in turn, allows individuals to make

571 Lamond (2009), supra note 2343, p. 26.

572 Ibid., p. 25. See Sherwin (1999), supra note 2068.

573 Ibid.

574 Dickson (2010), supra note 2104, p. 19, referring to N. MacCormick, 'Coherence in Legal Justification', in A. Peczenik et al (eds.), Theory of Legal Science, (Dordrecht: D. Reidel Publishing, 1984).

575 Lamond (2006), supra note 2346, p. 19.

plans that are consistent with the law and to avoid falling foul of it, and hence allows them to be guided by the law.[576]

As already mentioned in Chapter I.3.2, analogies are widely recognized as playing an important *heuristic* role, as aids to discovery. They have been employed, in a wide variety of settings and with considerable success, to generate insight and to formulate possible solutions to problems. Since the strongest justification for analogical reasoning lies in the value of replicability, consistency and preditability, analogical reasoning pursues certainty.[577] Since judges match, vertically and horizontally, the similarities between the facts of the case at hand and those of the precedent, it is not unreasonable to say that judges employ a sort of analogy similar to Hesse's material analogy. This may mean: generating the *ratio decidendi* (*legal insight*) of the case at hand by similarity-matching between the facts of the case at hand and those of the precedent based on the already known *ratio decidendi* (*legal insight*) of the precedent. Analogy is therefore generative. What analogy *generates* is the *ratio decidendi* (*legal insight*) of the case at hand, from the *ratio decidendi* of precedent. The generated *ratio decidendi* of the case at hand is similar to the *ratio decidendi* of the precedent. Again, since analogy generates insight (see Chapter 1.3.2, especially, on Hesse's material analogy), analogy is *generative*. Because the core of analogy in legal reasoning is similarity, and as already mentioned that similarity, according to Hahn, Chater and Richardson (2003), is *transformational* (see Chapter 1.3.1), analogy in legal reasoning is *transformational*. And Kemp, Bernstein and Tenenbaum (2005) have also revealed that similarity is *generative* (*see* Chapter I.3.2). In conlcusion, analogy in legal reasoning the core of which is similarity is *generative-transformational* or *transformational-generative*.

IV.10.2. CONSISTENCY AND COHERENCE IN LEGAL REASONING

***

The argument from consistency is related to arguments in favor of 'formal' justice, i.e. that two cases which are the same (in relevant respects) should be treated in the same way. The claim of consistency is also sometimes put in terms of 'equality' ; to treat the later case differently to the first would

576 Ibid.

577 Bartha (2013), supra note 2324, p. 2.

be to fail to treat the parties equally. If a legal system is morally legitimate and has authority over those subject to it, then it is inconsistent for one person to be treated less or more favorably by the law than another person whose situation is legally indistinguishable. Other things being equal, legal decisions should be consistent across time and/or decision-makers. So concerns of consistency provide some justification for treating earlier decisions as sources of law, rather than approaching each question anew when arises again.[578] Equality does not demand the repetition of mistakes. Taken in isolation from other considerations (such as expectations and predictability), equality does not support the bindingness of incorrect decisions. An argument for following earlier wrong decisions is not followed in efforts to pursue certainty through *stare decisis*.[579]

The aspects of consistency play an important role in any particular instance of evaluation. The desire for consistency is well recognized in the legal domain and it is also something that often appears in discussions concerning legal reasoning. In rule application, evaluation may have to examine a composed decision or a set of rules on an aggregated level. Predictability, equality, etc are of direct relevance to evaluation as well. In the process of evaluation consistency means that legal decisions (bills) must be in line with previous decisions (statutes), not contradicting them. In practice, this means that if there is a statute or a legal precedent concerning similar matters, it must be possible to relate the intended decision to the previous proposition.[580] Habermas argues that the socially integrative function of legal systems requires that adjudication must simultaneously satisfy the conditions of consistent decision-making and rational acceptability.[581] It follows that, legal certainty requires that decisions are consistent with the framework of the existing legal system.[582]

It is generally accepted that consistency is a precondition of normative coherence.[583] In relation to normative coherence and second-

578 Lamond (2006), supra note 2350, pp. 16-17.

579 Ibid., pp. 17-18.

580 Wahlgren (2009), supra note 2306, pp. 262-263. See e.g., The Statute of the International Court of Justice, Article 38; Carlos E. Alchourron & Eugenio Bulygin, 'Normative System', (Wien: Springer-Verlag, 1971) (Library of Exact Philosophy 5), p. 172; Peczenik (1983), supra note 2305, p. 91; N. MacCormick & R. Summers, 'Interpreting Statutes: A Comparative Study', S. Robert eds., (Aldershot: Dartmouth Publishing Company Limited, 1991) passim.

581 Paunio (2009), supra note 2196, p. 1472, referring to Habermas (1996), supra note 2021, pp. 194-237.

582 Ibid., referring to Habermas (1996), Ibid., pp. 198-199.

583 Russel Hinchy, 'Judicial Method and Advocates' Immunity in the High Court of Australia and the House of Lords', in Murdoch University Electronis Law Journal, 12 1(2006), pp. 187-208 (p. 191), referring to A. Schiavello 'On "Coherence"

order justification, an appreciation of the distinction between consistency and coherence is important. According to Guest, the requirement of coherence in the law is more than just consistency or, what Dworkin prefers to call it, 'bare consistency'. Bare consistency just amounts to the absence of logical contradiction between two statements of law. Coherence must, rather, be consistency 'in principle', that is, it must 'express a single and comprehensive vision of justice'.[584] Legal theorists and legal philosophers were to develop coherence theories because of the predominant force of coherence theories in modern philosophy, and the significant role played in law and adjudication by the concepts of legal and factual knowledge, legal and factual justification, legal and factual truth, and ethical truth and justification. The development of implicit and explicit coherence theories by legal scholars is expected since precedent and analogical reasoning have been explained in manners that resemble, and in ways that can be characterized as, holistic and coherence theories.[585] Normative coherence is the consistency not of logic but of principle. Value and normative judgments are normatively coherent if they employ distinctions and similarities that are principled and reasonable as opposed to those which are arbitrary and unreasonable. Judgments of normative coherence employ a substantive rather than a formal conception of reason.[586]

The version of coherentism in the fields of ethics and law would be what Hage calls 'constructive coherentism', a version that differs fundamentally from epistemic coherentism.[587] Constructive coherentism is 'merely' a particular form of constructivism, namely the view that the best argument about a position consists in showing that this position is an element of a coherent set of positions.[588] M. Moore has given a central role to coherence in his theories of facts, morality,[589] law, and legal reasoning.[590]

---

and "Law": An Analysis of Different Models', in 14 Ratio Juris (2001), p. 236.

584 Ibid., referring to R. Dworkin (1986), supra note 2047, pp. 39-40; S. Guest, 'Ronald Dworkin', (1992), pp. 39-40.

585 Kress (1984), supra note 700, p. 370. The importance of precedent and the related requirement of treating like cases alike suggest that coherence theories are especially appropriate in theories of adjudication.

586 Jack M. Balkin, 'Understanding Legal Understanding: The Legal Subject and the Problem of Legal Coherence', [originally published] in 103 Yale L. J. 105 (1993), p. 10.

587 Hage (2003), supra note 747, p. 2.

588 Ibid., p. 10.

589 Kress (1984), supra note 2360, pp. 370-371, referring to M. Moore, 'Moral Reality', in 1982 WIS. L. REV. 1061 (1982), p. 1106-1110.

590 Ibid., p. 371, referring to M. Moore, 'Law, Language and Ethics', (tent. Ed. 1981) (unplublished casebook on file with the California Law Review); M. Moore, 'A Natural Law Theory of Interpretation', (Feb. 25, 1984) (originally presented at the University of Southern California Interpretation Symposium, forth-coming

The importance of 'coherence' in law is often considered as the context of the strongest justification for analogical reasoning which lies in the value of replicability.[591] The law is essentially a social phenomenon, which exists, directly or indirectly, through being accepted by the relevant members of a community. A typical example of this view is the Hartian concept of law. According to this view, the law consists of a set of rules which derive their status as legal rules from being indentified as such at the hand of, in the last instance, a rule that is accepted by the officials of a legal system. Knowledge of the content of law is, on this view, knowledge of a part of social reality, and this kind of knowledge would be covered by an epistemic theory such as epistemic foundationalism or epistemic coherence.[592] Amongst those legal theorists taking an interest in the role of coherence in legal reasoning, there is general agreement both that the coherence in question must amount to more than logical consistency amongst propositions[593] and that it is not clear from many coherence accounts exactly what this something more amounts to.[594] Legal coherence is the normative coherence of legal justification. The law (or a part of the law) is coherent if principles or policies that could justify it form a coherent set. MacCormick argues that the basic idea is of the legal system as a consistent and coherent body of norms whose observance secures certain valued goals which can intelligibly be pursued all together.[595] According to coherence in terms of unity of principle in a legal system, the coherence of a set of legal norms consists in their being related either in virtue of being the realization of some common value or values, or in virtue of fulfilling some common principle or principles.[596] The need for

---

in volume 58 of the Southern California Law Review). See generally Moore, 'The Semantics of Judging', in 54 S. CAL. L. REV. (1981), p. 151.

591 Lamond (2006), supra note 2353, p. 25, referring to MacCormick (1978), supra note 2340, pp. 153, 187-188; Sunstein (1993), supra note 2340, pp. 778-779; see also Raz (1979), supra note 2328, pp. 204-206 on 'partial reform.'

592 Hage (2003), supra note 2362, p. 9, referring to Hart (1994), supra note 1510.

593 Dickson (2010), supra note 2349, p. 16, referring to Kress (1984), supra note 2360; N.MacCormick, 'Coherence in Legal Justification', in A. Peczenik et al (eds.), Theory of Legal Science, (Dordrecht: D. Reidel Publishing, 1984); Marmor (1992), supra note 1920; Marmor (2005), supra note 1920; R. Alexy & A. Peczenik, 'The Concept of Coherence and Its Significant for Discursive Rationality', in Ratio Juris, 3 (1990), pp. 130-147.

594 Ibid., referring to Kress (1984), Ibid.; Peczenik (1989), supra note 2314; Marmor (1992), Ibid.

595 Balkin (1993), supra note 2361, p. 11 & n.19, referring to MacCormick (1978), supra note 2366, p. 106.

596 Dickson (2010), supra note 2368, p. 16, referring to MacCormick (1984), supra note 2368.

coherence explains and justifies judicial role.[597] MacCormick espouses a view of the role which coherence can play in adjudication and gives an indication of how we might think of the links between interpretation and coherence in legal reasoning.[598] According to MacCormick, in deciding a case according to law, courts should first of all interpret the existing law in order to establish a coherent view of some branch of the law, and they should do this by showing how that branch of law is justified according to some coherent set of principles or values which underlie it. The court should then use this view of the law in order to justify its decision in a new case which comes before it.

With regard to the law, Dworkin has proposed the standard on constructive interpretation, according to which, propositions of law are true if they figure in or follow from the principles of justice, fairness, and procedural due process that provide the best constructive interpretation of the community's legal practice. As we will see 'best constructive interpretation' has strong links with coherentism.[599] Dworkin advocates coherence in the relationship between a proposition entailed in a judicial decision and precepts of law that are exterior to the decision itself.[600] According to Dworkin, principles, not policies, are primarily relevant to determining the coherence of the legal system, despite the fact that policies play some role in proper interpretation of statutes.[601] Dworkin says that when a judge confronts a legal question he should first determine the settled law in the jurisdiction.[602] Settled law consists of the complete institutional

597 Balkin (1993), supra note 2370, n.26.

598 Dickson (2010), supra note 2371, p. 18, referring to MacCormick (1984), supra note 2371.

599 Hage (2003), supra note 2367, p. 8, referring to R. Dworkin, 'Law's Empire', (London: Fontana, 1986), p. 225.

600 Simon (2004), supra note 2068, n.20.

601 Balkin (1993), supra note 2372, n.23, referring to R. Dworkin, 'Taking Rights Seriously' (7th prtg. 1980), pp. 107-110.

602 Kress (1984), supra note 2364, p. 378. The account that follows is largely taken from Dworkin's inaugural lecture as Professor of Jurisprudence at Oxford, "Hard Cases". DWORKIN (1978a), supra note 2126, In his reply to critics, Dworkin amends the theory, giving a tentative account of the tradeoff between the dimension of fit (explanation of the settled law) and the dimension of moral appeal (justification of the settled law). Roughly put, the best theory of settled law is the most morally appealing theory of all those theories that exceed a set threshold of fit. Ibid., pp. 340-342. In yet more recent writings, Dworkin suggests that the threshold of fit is not an absolute minimum, but only a rule of thumb. A theory that is sufficiently better on moral grounds than any theory that meets the threshold of fit may be the best theory of settled law even if it does not quite reach the threshold. See e.g., Dworkin, "Natural" Law Revisited, in 34 U. FLA. L. REV. (1982), pp. 171-172.

history of the jurisdiction including constitution(s), enactment and repeal of statutes, judicial pronouncements and perhaps administrative rulings. To simplify somewhat, settled law is the explicit, clear, black letter law.[603] Some aspects of the settled law may be disregarded as mistakes.[604] Those parts of institutional history that are no longer persuasive to courts, legislatures, and the legal profession are particularly vulnerable to being labeled mistakes. So too are those parts that are unjust.[605] Adjusting the settled law by deleting mistakes is a subtle process that Dworkin has described as seeking a 'reflective equilibrium' between the institutional facts and a coherent theoretical structure that could justify those facts.[606] The picture that Dworkin sketches of legal justification (in hard cases) is not completely the same as, but nevertheless quite similar to, the picture of narrow reflective equilibrium.[607] The basic idea is that a set of legal materials, cases and legislation, is used to induce legal principles. These principles are both brought in harmony (coherence) with the legal materials and a normative theory about law and its relation to politics and ethics. The resulting principles are then used to formulate 'new' rules (which may very well be the old ones) and to solve cases with them. Just like narrow reflective equilibrium, Dworkin's constructive interpretation

---

The greater emphasis that Dworkin's writings since "Hard Cases" place on substantive moral considerations and consequent lesser role played by the notion of fit suggests that the new theory may not be a strict coherence theory. (Whether the new theory is a pure coherence theory will depend upon whether moral theory, and the full theory that combines or adjudicates between moral appeal and fit, are pure coherence theory). [A sentenece is omitted].

Additionally, this interpretation of "Hard Cases" may be inaccurate if Dworkin intends his theory of legal truth to parallel those aspects of Quine's theory of evidence that reject the analytic/synthetic distinction in favor of a "continuum" of propositions from those at the center of our field of beliefs to those at the periphery. See Quine (1980a), supra note 700, pp. 42-46; But see DWORKIN (1980), Ibid., pp. 164-165 (denying that Quine's theory is an accurate picture of the technique of reflective equilibrium that is analogous to common law adjudication and distinguishing the natural and constructive models of theorizing) [Two sentences are omitted].

603 Ibid. Dworkin's theory is more complex because it attempts to explain and justify not only currently operative law but, in addition, the enactment and repeal of a statute and a judicial decision and its later overriling. See e.g., DWORKIN, (1978a), Ibid., p. 342, 360; Dworkin (1982), Ibid., p. 165, 166, passim.

604 Ibid., referring to DWORKIN (rev. ed. 1978a), Ibid., p. 118-123.

605 Ibid., referring to DWORKIN (rev. ed. 1978a), Ibid., p. 122-123.

606 Ibid., referring to DWORKIN (rev.ed. 1978a), Ibid., pp. 155, 159-68. The term "reflective equilibrium" derives from Rawls, who employed the concept in connection with moral theory and the theory of justice.

607 Hage (2003), supra note 2374, pp. 9-10, referring to Dworkin (1986), supra note 2374.

keeps factual information outside the process of mutual adaptation. Moreover, just like narrow equilibrium may be broadened to make it include other kinds of positions, Dworkin's constructive interpretation may be broadened to make it include other positions. Arguably, if they are both sufficiently broadened, they become both versions of constructive coherentism and they do not even differ from each other anymore.

Dworkin has argued that judges do and should determine the right answer in hard cases by deciding whether the proposition advocated by the plaintiff or by the defendant provides a better fit or coheres better with the best theory of settled law.[608] For Dworkin, in adjudicating cases, judges should seek to constructively interpret the law, i.e. to impose purpose on it in order to make of it the best possible example of the form or genre to which it is taken to belong (chs. 2 & 3). In *Law's Empire,* Dworkin argues that such a justification can best be provided when the law is viewed as the organized and coherent voice of what he refers to as a 'community of principle' i.e. a community whose members accept that their fates are linked by virtue of the fact that their rights and responsibilities are governed by common principles. So for Dworkin, we must interpret law as coherent, in the sense of speaking with one voice, because by doing so, we understand law as the voice of a community of principle.[609] In line with Dworkin's theory of law as integrity as a coherence account, there is something about the nature of law which makes it particularly ripe for explanation via coherence accounts:[610] coherence, in the sense of interpreting the law as speaking with one voice as integrity requires, is a value which is supposed to have special relevance in the legal realm, in terms of the role which it should play in guiding judges seeking to interpret the law correctly.[611] Alexy and Peczenik recognize that weighing and balancing the criteria of coherence will be a complex matter, but appear to assume that it will always be possible to establish which is the most coherent of rival sets of propositions.[612] Barbara Levenbook notes, Dworkin's account of integrity in adjudication requires judges to attempt to view the legal system as a whole as exhibiting coherence and speaking with one voice

608 Kress (1984), supra note 2377, p. 370, referring to Dworkin (rev. ed. 1978a), supra note 2377, p. 283; see also Ibid., p. 44, 340-42, 360. See generally Ibid., p. 81-130; Dworkin (1982), supra note 2377; Dworkin, 'No Right Answer?', in 53 N.Y.U. L. REV. I (1978) ["1978b"], pp. 28-29.

609 Dickson (2010), supra note 2373, p. 21, referring to Dworkin (1986), supra note 2382.

610 Ibid., p. 14, 15. See Kress (1984), supra note 2383; S. Hurley, 'Natural Reasons', (Oxford: Oxford University Press, 1989).

611 Ibid.

612 Ibid., p. 16, referring to Alexy & Peczenik (1990), supra note 2368.

in interpreting the law.[613] Levenbook argues that law is only locally coherent.[614]

There must be a common base to which coherence account in law are addressed. Raz's suggestion in this regard is that coherence accounts in law take court decisions and legislative and regulatory acts as their base. He distinguishes between coherence accounts of law and coherence accounts of adjudication. In the case of a coherence account of law, the whole of what the law *is* is determined by applying a coherence test to the court decisions and legislative and regulatory acts of a given jurisdiction. A coherence account of adjudication, however, accepts that the vagaries of politics and the influence of political considerations on legislative and judicial decisions make it unlikely that the settled law of a jurisdiction will exhibit coherence to any great extent.[615] Raz argues if courts choose the (according to law) morally best outcome to a case over an outcome which coheres better with the settled law, then some problematic consequences may ensue, such as that they may introduce conflicting rules reflecting conflicting social and economic purposes into the law, and hence create a considerable degree of dissonance with regard to existing legal doctrines in a given area of law. This may provide one reason why sometimes courts should give greater weight to considerations of coherence with pre-existing law in deciding cases which come before them, rather than striking out in a (albeit otherwise morality preferable) direction which coheres less well with settled law.[616] Raz also champions local over global coherence in adjudication, and his argument concerning the limitation of the reforming role of courts, and the way in which this sometimes militates in favor of coherence playing a role in judicial decision making, is intended to support local coherence only.[617] Peczenik (1994) claims that while the goal of the kind of doctrinal interpretation undertaken by legal scholars (which he refers to as 'legal dogmatics') is to establish the unity of an entire legal system, the judicial interpretation undertaken by judges is of a far more local variety, as it is concerned merely with the norms applicable to the case

---

613 Ibid., p. 20, referring to B.B. Levenbook, 'The Role of Coherence in Legal Reasoning', in Law and Philosophy, 3 (1984), pp. 355-374.

614 Balkin (1993), supra note 2376, n.24, referring to Levenbook (1984), Ibid., p. 355, 371.

615 Dickson (2010), supranote 2384, p. 17, referring to J. Raz, 'The Relevance of Coherence', in J. Raz, Ethics in the Public Domain, (Oxford: Clarendon Press, 1994) ["Raz 1994a"].

616 Ibid., p. 20, referring to Raz (1979), supra note 2366; Raz (1994a), Ibid.

617 Ibid., p. 22, referring to Levenbook (1984), supra note 2389; Raz (1994a), Ibid.; A. Peczenik, 'Law, Morality, Coherence and Truth,' in Ratio Juris, 7 (1994), pp. 146-76.

in question, and because a coherent interpretation of those norms may decrease their coherence with other legal norms.

If we hold that legal reasoning in the sense that it is reasoning from the content of law to the outcome which judges should adopt in a case before them, is wholly[618] or mainly[619] interpretive, then we can reformulate the questions concerning how much emphasis is to be placed upon coherence in adjudication in terms of the extent to which, in interpreting the law, we should interpret it in such a way as to realize the value of coherence in judicial decisions. Such questions are, for example: Is coherence the sole desideratum which should guide judges in interpreting the law, or is it merely one feature of a successful such interpretation, and, moreover, is it a necessary feature, or one which, although desirable, may be overridden by competing values, which judges should also try to realize in interpreting the law? Levenbook contends that any plausible account of adjudication must make room for the kind of 'area-specific coherence' which she believes is necessary in the case of law.[620] Levenbook (1984) holds that it is a necessary condition for a judicial decision to be legally justified that it coheres with some part of the established law. She contracts her understanding of this requirement with that adopted by MacCormick (1978). According to Levenbook, while MacCormick also holds that minimal coherence with some part of the established law is a necessary condition of a judicial decision being justified, he nevertheless contends that, so long as this minimal standard is met, further considerations of coherence which are also relevant to the decision can be defeated on consequentialist grounds.[621] Against granting a too modest role to considerations of coherence in legal reasoning, Levenbook argues that a judge who, within the limits allowed to him by the law, adopts a decision which is better on moral grounds over one which displays greater congruence (suitableness) with the trend or spirit of the existing law has made a mistake, and has adopted a legally unjustified decision.Granting a strong role to considerations of coherence is to place considerable emphasis on the backward-looking aspect of adjudication, as such an approach may require judges to place greater value on adhering what has gone before, rather than on doing what would otherwise, on moral grounds, be the right thing.

***

618 Ibid., p. 8, referring to Dworkin (1986), supra note 2382.

619 Ibid., referring to J. Raz, 'On The Nature of Law', Archive fur Rechts und Sozialphilosophie, 82 (1996) ["1996c"], pp. 1-25.

620 Ibid., p. 22, referring to Levenbook (1984), supra note 2389; Raz (1994a), supra note 2390; Peczenik (1994), supra note 2392.

621 Ibid., p. 19, referring to Levenbook (1984), Ibid.; MacCormick (1978), supra note 2340.

The strongest justification for analogical reasoning lies in the value of replicability. This is often put in terms of the importance of 'coherence' in the law.[622] Arguments in favor of coherence normally emphasize its instrumental value. This is tied up with the replicability of legal decision-making. There are two important characteristics of legal decision-making. The first is the *fragmentary* nature of legal materials. The second is the *plurality* of decision-making bodies. Legal materials – precedents, statutes, conventions, principles – are fragmentary in two senses: (a) they are the work of many different hands at different times and with different outlooks and (b) different areas of law owe more to some hands and times than others. As a result legal doctrine tends to exhibit only a thin global coherence, whereas it may possess a thick local coherence. The pluralism of decision-makers is also two-fold: (a) there are many individuals making decisions using the same body of materials, and (b) these individuals do not share a uniform evaluative outlook. Given the fragmentary nature of legal material and the plurality of decision-makers there is considerable scope for disagreement when decision-makers are faced with novel questions.[623]

In fact, the claim that coherence and the dominant conception of precedent lead to the linear ordering problem is true because precedent serves as a principle of conservation in coherence theories of law.[624] Coherence theories are as simply one particularly favored way of spelling out what has been called the dominant conception of precedent.[625] The notion of coherence in this book is specific, in legal reasoning or in adjudication. This book takes the notion of coherence of justification in which a legal rule [as a concept or a rule category] is as a coherent set. A legal rule or a rule category on a particular issue [as a coherent set] has many justified members, and such justified members are the *rationes decidendi* in cases on the same particular issue. For example, a legal rule or a rule category [as a coherent set] on the issue of the starting point to determine the deprivation of liberty has its justified members including the *rationes decidendi* in *Engel* (1976), *Guzzardi (19870), HL (2004), Storck (2005), Kedzior (2012), Stanev (2012)* and *Mihailovs (2013),* since those *rationes* are on the same particular issue, namely the starting point to determine any deprivation of liberty. In other words, the *rationes decidendi* in *Engel* (1976), *Guzzardi (19870), HL (2004), Storck (2005), Kedzior (2012), Stanev (2012)* and *Mihailovs (2013)* belong to [or, are justified members of] a coherent set, which is a rule category on the starting point for determining any deprivation of liberty.

---

622 Lamond (2006), supra note 2366, p. 25, referring to MacCormick (1978), Ibid., p. 153, 187-8; Sunstein (1993), supra note 2366, pp. 778-779: see also Raz 1979, supra note 2391, pp. 204-206 on 'partial reform.'

623 Ibid.

624 Kress (1984), supra note 2383, p. 401 [accompanying text omitted].

625 Ibid., p. 401-402.

Coherence transforms *ratio decidendi* to *ratio decidendi* within a certain rule category as a coherent set on same particular issue, through similarity, and based on consistency. Since coherence is taken into account through similarity, and similarity is generative-transformational (see Chapter I.3.1), coherence is therefore generative-transformational.

IV.10.3. ANALOGY AND COHERENCE IN CASES

In the doctrine of *stare decisis,* it is clear that precedents must be followed by later cases. In Civil law tradition, the doctrine of *jurisprudence constante* is [to some certain extent] followed, although formally each case is determined *de novo*. Under the EU law, the ECJ case law is strongly taken into account. *Rationes decidendi* of the ECJ's decisions are determinantly considered in judicial decision making in Member States' courts, ECHR and EFTA Court. These all employ analogical logic and take coherence into account in adjudication in which analogy and coherence are *generative-transformational* or *transformational generative* in nature, as already addressed in Chapter I.3. Examples of the employment of analogy and the consideration of coherence through *transformational-generative* legal reasoning in cases are mentioned rightly below.

The United States Supreme Court's holding in *Roth v. United States,* 354 U.S. 476 (1957) was that ".. implicit in the history of the First Amendment is the rejection of obscenity as utterly without redeeming social importance", and that "obscenity is not within the area of constitutionally protected speech or press..." The Court's holding in *Memoirs,* 383 U.S. 413 (1966) adopted a three-part test for obscenity. The *Memoirs* test provided that the following 'three elements must coalesce' for material to be found obscene. [I]t must be established that (a) the dominant theme of the material taken as a whole appeals to a prurient interest in sex; (b) the material is patently offensive because it affronts contemporary community standards relating to the description or representation of sexual matters; and (c) the material is utterly without redeeming social value.[626] *Roth* and *Memoirs* were followed by subsequent cases. *Books, Inc. V. United States,* 358 F.2d 935, 937 (1st Cir. 1966) has stated that obscenity determinations must be ...[g]uided by the controlling opinions of the justices in the majority in the three cases decided March 21, 1966 in the Supreme Court of the United States [of which *Memoirs* was one] ...as well as [by] earlier cases such as *Roth*...(citation omitted), rev'd, 388 U.S. 449 (1967). *Huffman v. United*

626 Mark Alan Thurmon, 'When the Court Divides: Reconsidering the Precedential Value of Supreme Court Plurality Decisions', in Duke Law Journal Vol. 42:419 (1992), p. 430, 423. See Roth v. United States, 354 U.S. 476 (1957) and Ibid., p. 484, 485; Memoirs, 383 U.S. 413 (1966) and Ibid., p. 418.

States, 470 F.2d 386, 393 (D.C. Cir. 1971) referred to the obscenity test as 'The *Roth-Memoirs* Obscenity Standard'. In *Southeastern Promotion, Ltd. v. Oklahoma City*, 459 F.2d 282, 283 (10th Cir. 1972), the *per curiam* decision has noted that the obscenity standard is to be found in *Roth* and *Memoirs*. In *United States v. Groner*, 479 F.2d 577 (5th Cir. 1973) (en banc), the majority of judges endorsed the *Memoirs* plurality as consistent with the *Roth* principles.[627] The obscenity standards that had been found in *Roth* and *Memoirs* were followed by the *rationes decidendi* in *Books Inc, Huffman, Southeastern Promotion, Ltd* and *Groner*. The legal reasoning in each of the following cases: *Books Inc, Huffman, Southeastern Promotion, Ltd* and *Groner,* had generated [been *generative* of] the *rationes* in each of those cases themselves by employing analogy with *Roth* and *Memoirs* and by taking 'coherence' into account on the issue of obscenity. Analogy and coherence had played significant role in the legal reasoning, and the legal reasoning was transformational-generative since analogy and coherence are transformational-generative (See Chapter I.3). Consequently, the *rationes* of *Roth* and *Memoirs* and those of *Books Inc, Huffman, Southeastern Promotion, Ltd* and *Groner* are similar and are justified members of a category of rule [as a coherent set] on obscenity.

In *Stone, 911 A.2d,* the court's holding was: "[T]he right of a stockholder to prosecute a derivative suit is limited to situations where either the stockholder has demanded the directors to pursue a corporate claim and the directors are incapable of making an impartial decision regarding whether to institute such litigation".[628] In *Tooley v. Donaldson, Lufkin & Jenrette, Inc.*, 845 A.2d 1031, 1036 (Del. 2004), with reference to [*White v. Panic*, 783 A.2d 543, 550 (Del. 2001) and] *Stone, 911 A.2d at 366-67,* the court held at 1033: "In most situations, the board of directors has sole authority to initiate or to refrain initiating legal actions asserting rights held by the corporation. This authority is subject to the limited exception, defined in Chancery Rule 23.1, permitting stockholders to initiate a derivative suit to enforce unasserted rights of the corporation without the board's approval where they can show either that the board wrongfully refused the plaintiff's pre-suit demand to initiate the suit or, if no demand was made, that such demand would be a futile gesture and is therefore excused".[629] The court's holding in *Tooley* was that a derivative action is one brought by stockholders on behalf of a corporation to remedy harm done to the corporation itself, as opposed to stockholders individually, and that

627 Ibid., p. 449, n.146.

628 Warren & Aronstam (2007), supra note 1637, pp. 7-8, see Tooley v. Donaldson, Lufkin & Jenrette, Inc., 845 A.2d 1031, 1036 (Del. 2004); Hawes v City of Oakland, 104 U.S. 450, 462 (1881); White v Panic, 783 A.2d 543, 550 (Del. 2001).

629 Ibid.

the business judgment rule also has a procedural component in addition to the substantive protection of the decisions of independent, disinterested, well-motivated and well-informed directors.[630] By employing analogical logic between *Stone* and *Tooley* and taking 'coherence' into accout, the *Tooley* court has generated [through *generative* legal reasoning] the standard on [t]he right of a stockholder to prosecute a derivative suit. The standard of the issue in *Tooley* is similar [showing *transformation* since similarity is as transformation] to the standard of the same issue in *Stone*. Transformational-generative legal reasoning [employing analogy and taking coherence into account] took place in *Tooley* adjudication.

As to fair dealing and fair price, in *Weinberger v. UOP, Inc.*, 457 A.2d 711 (Del. 1983) the court held that fair dealing 'embraces questions of when the transaction was timed, how it was initiated, structured, negotiated, disclosed to the directors, and how the approvals of the directors and the stockholders were obtained'; and fair price relates to the economic and financial considerations of the [challenged transaction], including all relevant factors: assets, market value, earnings, future prospects and any other elements that affect the intrinsic or inherent value of a company's stock.[631] In 2006, *Gesoff v. IIC Indus Inc.*, 902 A.2d 1130, 1144 (Del. Ch. 2006) quoted *Weinberger* [at 701, 708] that: "According to the now familiar words of [the *Weinberger*] opinion, entire fairness has two aspects: fair dealing and fair price. This test, however, is not a 'bifurcated one between fair dealing and price. All aspects of the issue must be examined as a whole since the question is one of entire fairness".[632] This example also shows that analogy and coherence plays significant role in legal reasoning, that is transformational-generative legal reasoning.

The following cases are some other examples of transformational-generative legal reasoning in judicial decision-making. In *Durkin* (Appellant) *v. DSG Retail Limited and another* (Respondent) (Scotland), Hilary Term [2014] UKSC 21, [633] the United Kingdom Supreme Court gave its judgment on March 26, 2014. The principal issue was whether Mr. Durkin was entitled to rescind (cancel) the credit agreement on rescission of the sale agreement (as per Lord Hodge, para 1). It was early in 2004, Mr. Durkin raised an action in Aberdeen sheriff court against both DSG and HFC. He sought a declarator that he had validly rescinded both the sales contract and the credit agreement and claimed damages (as per Lord

630 Ibid.

631 Ibid., p. 16. See Weinberger v. UOP, Inc., 457 A.2d 701, 708 (Del. 1983).

632 Ibid., p. 15, see Gesoff v. IIC Indus Inc., 902 A.2d 1130, 1144 (Del. Ch. 2006).

633 Durkin (Appellant) v. DSG Retail Limited and another (Respondents) (Scotland), on 26 March 2014, Hilary Term [2014] UKSC 21, On appeal from: [2010] CSIH 49.

Hodge, para 8). Sheriff Tierney followed the opinion in *United Dominions Trust Ltd v. Taylor* 1980 SLT (Sh Ct) 28 and held that section 75 of the 1974 Act had the effect that Mr Durkin had been entitled to rescind and has rescinded both the sales contract and the credit agreement. The sheriff awarded Mr Durkin (i) £8,000 for injury to his credit, (ii) £6,880 for the extra interest with which he had to pay and (iii) £101,794 for the loss of a capital gain arising from his inability to purchase the Spanish property in 2003 (as per Lord Hodge, para 9). Aberdeen sheriff court's holding was that *United Dominions Trust Ltd* and the case of Mr. Durkin's before him were alike therefore should be treated alike. Analogical reasoning was employed therein, and was generating Aberdeen sheriff court's holding that Mr. Durkin was entitled to rescind the credit agreement on rescission of the sale agreement. HFC cross-appealed to the Inner House of the Court of Session against the sheriff's findings (i) that section 75 of the 1974 Act enabled Mr Durkin to rescind the credit agreement, (ii) that HFC was in breach of its duty of care, and (iii) that HFC's breach of duty had caused the second and third heads of loss. HFC did not dispute the award of £8,000 if it had been in breach of its duty but submitted that there was no evidence to entitle the sheriff to make the awards which he did under the second and third heads of loss (as per Lord Hodge, para 10). The Inner House of the Court Session, in [2010] CSIH 49, amended the sheriff's findings of fact to exclude Mr Durkin's claims for loss of interest and the loss arising from his inability to purchase the property in Spain (as per Lord Hodge, para 11). The Supreme Court viewed that the credit agreement was conditional upon the survival of the supply agreement. The debtor on rejecting the goods and thereby rescinding the supply agreement for breach of contract might also rescind the credit agreement by invoking this condition (as per Lord Hodge, para 26). Then, it was determined by the Supreme Court that the appeal was allowed, and that Mr. Durkin was entitled to rescind and validly rescinded the credit agreement by giving notice to HFC in about February 1999. Damages resulting from HFC's breach of its duty of care are confined to injury to Mr Durkin's credit in the sum of £8,000. The parties were given an opportunity to agree the date from which interest should run and the rate or rates of interest to be applied (as per Lord Hodge, para 40).[634] The Court's legal reasoning by employing analogy between *United Dominions Trust Ltd* and the case of Mr. Durkin before Aberdeen sheriff court [on the one hand] and the case at hand (*Durkin* as Appellant *v. DSG Retail Limited and another as* Respondent (Scotland) [on the other hand], was *generative*, in the sense of generating the Court's holding in the case at hand. The legal reasoning was also transformational, since the *rationes decidendi* or standards on that particular issue in the three cases are similar [similarity as *transformation*] as they have been produced through the principle 'like cases should be treated alike'. The *rationes* in the three cases are justified

634 Ibid.

members of a rule category [following the notion of coherence in this book] on that particular issue.[635]

The United Kingdom Supreme Court on February 1 and 2, 2012 heard the case of *Assange (Appellant) v. The Swedish Prosecution Authority (Respondent),* Easter Term [2012] UKSC 22. In the Court's decision, Lord Phillips described in brief the fact of the case. Mr Assange was accused of having committed offenses against two women in Stockholm in August 2010. The Swedish Prosecution Authority issued a European Arrest Warrant ("EAW") signed by Marianne Ny, a prosecutor, requesting the arrest and surrender of Mr Assange. He had been, at the time, in England, as he still was when the EAW was issued. Mr Assange failed to challenge the validity of the EAW before the District Court Judge and subsequently on appeal to the Divisional Court on a number of grounds.[636] This appeal to the Supreme Court of the United Kingdom related to the validity of EAW. Section 2(2) in Part 1 of the Extradition Act 2003 ('the 2003 Act') requires an EAW to be issued by a 'judicial authority'. Mr Assange contended that the Prosecutor did not fall within the meaning of that phrase and that, accordingly, the EAW was invalid (para 1). In discussing '*the critical question*' on the meaning of 'judicial authority', Lord Phillips viewed that the significant safeguard against the improper or inappropriate issue of an EAW laid in the antecedent process which formed the basis of the EAW, rather than the function of the issuing authority.[637] In the case at hand, reference was made to *Piaggio (Germany)* - 14 February 2007, Court of Cassation Sez 6 (Italy), where a challenge was made to the issue of EAW by a public prosecutor. In *Piaggio (Germany),* the appellant challenged the issue by the Hamburg Public Prosecutor's Office of an EAW on the ground that it should have been issued and signed by a judge. The Italian Court of Cassation has rejected this contention for the reasons, inter alia, that the provision [of article 1(3) of Law no 69/2005] allegedly requiring signature of a judge does not refer to the EAW, but to the precautionary measure based on which the EAW is issued, and that the guarantee provided by said article 1(3) is directly connected with the substantial custodian guarantee concerned with the basic conditions underlying the EAW, which must be subject to jurisdiction. The guarantee does not relate to the act of requesting the Member State to grant extradition.[638] The fact of warrant issuance by a judiciary authority is not the true guarantee (para 62). Lord Phillips declared: "However the Court of Cassation has given an

---

635 Ibid.

636 Assange (Appellant) v. The Swedish Prosecution Authority (Respondent), on 30 May 2012, Easter Term [2014] UKSC 22, On appeal from: [2011] EWCH Admin 2849.

637 Ibid.

638 Ibid.

interpretation of this provision in line with the Framework Decision (my emphasis)" (para 63). Furthermore, Lord Phillips reasoned that the phrase 'judicial authority' is used in the Framework Decision to describe different authorities performing different functions at different stages of the overall process. The contexts permit the issuing judicial authority to have different characteristics from the executing judicial authority and, indeed, for the phrase judicial authority to bear different meaning at the state of execution of the EAW dependent upon the function being performed (para 75). Lord Phillips' conclusion was that the 'issuing judicial authority' bears the wide meaning embracing the Prosecutor in the present case. All that weighs the other ways is the narrower meaning that the English phrase naturally bears. For this reason Lord Phillips concluded that the Prosecutor in this case fell within the meaning of 'issuing judicial authority' in the Framework Decision'(para 76). Mr Assange's challenge to the validity of the EAW failed (para 80). Lord Phillips dismissed the appeal and the dismissal was agreed by Lord Walker, Lord Brown, Lord Kerr and Lord Dyson, therefore the majority Members of the House of Lords dismissed the appeal.[639] The *ratio* of *Assange* and that of *Piaggio (Germany)* are similar and are justified members of a coherent set which is the legal rule on the issuer of EAW, because the *rationes* were generated through analogy and coherence in tranformational-generative legal reasoning.

The UK Supreme Court, in P (by his litigation friend the Official Solicitor) (Appellant) v. Cheshire West and Chester Council and another (Respondent), and, P and Q (by their litigation friend, the Official Solicitor (Appellant) v. Surrey County Council (Respondent) – Hilary Term [2014] UKSC 19, had strung together the rationes decidendi in several like cases, Engel (1976), Guzzardi (1987), HL (2004), Storck (2005), Kedzior (2012), Stanev (2012) and Mihailovs (2013), for similarity-matching [in analogical reasoning] with the two cases at hand, on the issue of the starting point to determine the deprivation of liberty.[640] When doing so, by considering the concrete situation of the persons concerned as the starting point in determining deprivation of liberty, the Court's legal reasoning in the cases at hand has generated the rationes thereof that the appellants' liberty has been deprived. The rationes of Engel (1976), Guzzardi (1987), HL (2004), Storck (2005), Kedzior (2012), Stanev (2012), Mihailovs (2013) and those of the cases at hand are similar and are justified members of the rule category

639 Ibid.

640 P (by his litigation friend the Official Solicitor) (Appellant) v Cheshire West and Chester Council and another (Respondent), and, P and Q (by their litigation friend, the Official Solicitor (Appellant v Surrey County Council (Respondent) – The Supreme Court of the United Kingdom's Judgment of 19 March 2014, Hilary Term [2014] UKSC 19 on appeal from: [2011] EWCA Civ 1257;[2011] EWCA Civ 190.

or the legal rule [as a coherent set] on [the starting point of] deprivation of liberty, since the rationes have been generated through analogy and coherence in transformational-generative legal reasoning.

On 9 June 1998 the Court of Palermo in Italy declared Mr. Domenico Rancadore guilty 'of the crime under the Criminal Code [of Italy]'. He was sentenced to nine years in prison, with a year on probation after his release, because it had been shown that he belonged to an extremely dangerous armed mafia type organization (page 3). Then, the appeal court, in its judgment dated 21 July 1999, upheld conviction on the basis of participatory conduct in Cosa Nostra 'by far the most dangerous of the mafia organizations' (page 4). The sentence was reduced by the appeal court to seven years in jail (including two years for the aggravating circumstances in paras 4 and 6 of the Criminal Code) (page 4), due to information lack about his particular prominent and effective position within the organization.[641] An application was filed with the Westminster Magistrates' Court on 17 March 2014 by the judicial authority in Italy for the extradition of Mr. Domenico Rancadore. The case was *The Court of Appeal, Palermo, Italy v. Domenico Rancadore*, before Judge Howard Riddle, Senior District Judge (Chief Magistrate), in The Westminster Magistrates' Court. The Westminster Magistrates' Court in its judgment followed the *ratio decidendi* in *Hayle Abdi Badre v. Court of Folrence* [2014] EWHC 614 and declared that Rancadore should be extradited.[642] The Westminster Magistrates' Court employed analogical reasoning and held that the two cases were analogous. What happened between *Rancadore* and *Badre* was transformational-generative process [in legal reasoning in *Rancadore*] by employing analogy and taking coherence into account.

The joint majority in *D'Orta-Ekenaike v. Victoria Legal Aid and Another* (2005) 214 ALR 92 addressed whether it should reconsider the High Court of Australia's previous decision concerning advocates' immunity in *Giannarelli v. Wraith* (1988) 165 CLR 543. In *Giannarelli* the High Court of Australia considered the immunity at Common law and also the impact of the *Legal Profession Practice Act 1958 (Vic)* on the issue. The joint majority in *D'Orta-Ekenaike* said that the issue was whether the Court should reconsider the decision in *Giannarelli* that 'at common law an advocate cannot be sued by his or her client for negligence in the conduct of a case in court, or in work out of court which leads to a decision affecting the conduct of a case in court'. The joint majority in *D'Orta-Ekenaike* took the 'rule' from *Giannarelli* [from the judgment of Mason

---

641 Judgment of the Westminster Magistrates' Court in the case: the Court of Appeal, Palermo, Italy v. Domenico Rancadore, Judiciary of England and Wales, p. 8, 3, 4.

642 Ibid.

CJ in *Giannarelli*].[643] Analogical reasoning through similarity-matching between *D'Orta-Ekenaike* and *Giannarelli* was generative, in the sense of generating the *ratio* of *D'Orta-Ekenaike* on the issue of the advocate immunity at common law and the impact of *Legal Profession Practice Act 1958 (Vic)*. The *rationes* of the two cases are similar and are justified members of the rule category [as a coherent set] on that particular issue, because coherence has been taken into account in the legal reasoning of *D'Orta-Ekenaike*.

In a case before the German Federal Court of Justice (*Bundesgerichtshof*), the plaintiff, a professor of law faculty, claimed the defendant (an advertising company) that he had suffered an unauthorized attack on his personality right in the defendant's advertisement for ginseng tonic, and that the advertisement had caused the impression that the plaintiff published an opinion on a controversial topic not in his major for money and unprofessionally lent his name to advertizing a doubtful product. In reliance on BGHZ 26, 346 (*Herrenreiter*), the plaintiff claimed DM 10,000 as satisfaction for the harm done to him. The *Bundesregerichtshof* in its decision in the case at hand, BGHZ 35, 365, NJW 1961, 2059, on September 1961 observed the provisions of §§ 253 and §§ 823 I BGB and cited the judgment in BGHZ 26, 349 (*Herrenreiter*). Following the judgment in BGHZ 26, 349 (*Herrenreiter*), the Supreme Court held that satisfaction might be awarded to the plaintiff who had been affected by the blameworthy infringement of his personality right. The satisfaction was the compensation for immaterial damages.[644] Similarity-matching was employed in legal reasoning by the *Bundesgerichtshof* between the case at hand and BGHZ 26, 349 (*Herrenreiter*). The *ratio* of the case at hand and that of BGHZ 26, 349 (*Herrenreiter*) are similar and are, in terms of adjudicative coherence, justified members of the rule category as provided under §§ 253 and §§ 823 I BGB, particularly on the question of compensation for immaterial damages relating to the infringement of personality right.

The Munich Local Court [*Amtsgericht*] in Germany heard *Somm* Case No. 8340 Ds 485 Js 173158/95. In its decision on July 15, 1998 the court addressed the issue on 'representation of pornographic writings' as provided under §§184 para. 3 no. 2,11 para. 3 of Penal Code. Regarding the meaning of the term 'representation', the court cited, inter alia, the judgment of the German Supreme Court in BGHSt 13, 375, 376, in which

643 Hinchy (2006), supra note 2358, p. 194.

644 P. Schlechtriem, B. Markesinis and S. Lorenz, 'Decisions of the Federal Court of Justice (Bundesgerichtshof)', Bundesgerichtshof (Sixth Civil Division), 19 September 1961 BGHZ 35, 362 = NJW 1961,' 2059 (W. Rotelmann NJW 1962, 736 and H. Hubmann = VersR 1962, 350, 562), first published in the German Law Archive courtesy of: Translated German Cases and Materials, translated by F.H. Lawson and B.S. Markesinis, HTLM edition by Lawrence Schafe.

representation had meant 'physical signs which embodied an idea and were perceptible by the senses, whereby the physical embodiment had to last for a certain period'. By citing the judgment of the Federal Court of Justice in NJW 1976, 1984, the court held that providing access should require that another person was given the possibility of gaining knowledge of the pornographic content of writings by sensual perception. The court, also citing the judgment of Higher Regional Court of Stuttgart, NStZ 1992, 38, held that the characteristic features of the term 'representation' had been present in the case at hand since the pornographic data content stored on the newsserver of CompuServe USA for its customers in Germany as ascertained in the statement of facts were physical signs which embodied ideas and the embodiment lasted for a certain period of time. Representation through physical transfer was not required; electronic transfer was considered to fall within the term 'representation'. Providing access to content was given when electronically stored information might be accessed and displayed on the monitor being used by the person receiving it.[645] Having observed §§184 para. 3 no. 2,11 para. 3 of Penal Code, the court employed analogical reasoning between the case at hand (*Somm* Case) and the previous similar cases (BGHSt 13, 375, 376; NJW 1976, 1984; and NStZ 1992, 38) and therefrom generated the holding in the case at hand on that particular issue with regard to the 'representation' of pornographic writings. The *rationes* in *Somm* Case; BGHSt 13, 375, 376; NJW 1976, 1984 and NStZ 1992, 38 are similar and are justified members of the rule category [as a coherent set] as provided under §§184 para. 3 no. 2,11 para. 3 of Penal Code on that particular issue. Transformational-generative legal reasoning [employing analogy and taking coherence into account] has occured in the adjudication of *Somm* Case.

The Swedish Supreme Court in its decision of November 26, 2004 in Case T 2593-01 *Andersson v. Sweden* followed the substantive legal rules on State Liability for breach of EEA law as already laid down in the EFTA Court's decision in Case E-9/97 *Sveinbjornsdottir v. Iceland* [1998], the ECJ's decision in Case C-140/97 *Rechberger and Others v. Austria* [1999], the Icelandic Supreme Court's decision in Case 236/1999 *Iceland v. Sveinbjornsdottir* [December 16, 1999], the Norwegian Supreme Court's decision in *Finanger (No.2)* and the Liechtenstein Supreme Court's decision of March 7, 2010 in Case CO.2004.2 *Liechtenstein v. Dr. Tschannet (No.2).*[646] In terms of analogical reasoning and on coherence

645 "CompuServe Case" (Somm Case), Local Court [Amtsgericht] Munic, File No. 8340 Ds 465 Js 173158/95, Judgment dated July 15, 1998, translation and commentary by Christopher Kuner, http ;// www. kuner.com/data/reg/somm. html.

646 Halvard H. Fredriksen, 'The Troubled Relationship between the Supreme Court of Norway and the EFTA Court–Recent Developments', [Univ.of Bergen], in

account [transformational-generative legal reasoning], the *rationes* of those cases are similar and justified members of the rule category [as a coherent set] on State Liability for breach of EEA law. Evolution of substantive law has happened through generativity and transformation.

The Netherlands Supreme Court in its decision on June 2013, in *H. Lundbeck A/S v. Alfred E. Tiefenbacher, Centrafarm BV*, ECLI: NL: HR:2013:BZ4115, vacated the decision of the appellate court and referred it back to the Court of Appeal. The Supreme Court's decision resolved, inter alia, the issue of [pharmaceutical] substance protection, in which a patentee can also get protection for a substance (compound) made by a (novel and) inventive process, even if the composition and the possible characteristics of such substance are already known (par.4.3).[647] The decision followed Lundbeck's arguments that the substance which had been provided in the manner and with which the state of the art had been consequently enriched was (novel and) inventive (par. 4.2).[648] Under the doctrine set out in Case T-595/90 by Technical Boards of Appeal, novel substances which can be fully envisaged but not yet made can still be considered to be non-obvious and therefore patented if the claimed method for preparing such substance is the first to achieve this in an inventive manner. Following the doctrine in the judgment in Case T-595/90 and subsequent decisions of the Technical Boards of Appeal, and citing the judgments in *BHG 10 September 2009, Xa ZR 130/07* and UKHL 12[2009]- 25 February 2009 - *Generics (UK) Limited and others v H. Lundbeck A/S.),* which had determined the same issue, the Supreme Court in the case at hand (*H. Lundbeck A/S v. Alfred E. Tiefenbacher, Centrafarm BV*) held Lundbeck's patent for 'escitaliopram' to be valid. The Supreme Court has recognized 'compound protection'.[649] Between *H. Lundbeck A/S v. Alfred E. Tiefenbacher, Centrafarm BV* on the one hand and T-595/90, *BHG 10 September 2009, Xa ZR 130/07* and UKHL 12[2009]-25 February 2009 - *Generics (UK) Limited and others v. H. Lundbeck A/S* as strung together on the other hand, the Dutch Supreme Court employed analogical reasoning for legal consistency. The *rationes* of those cases fall within the same legal rule on 'substance protection', or, the *rationes* of the cases are justified members of the rule category on 'substance protection', showing coherence consideration [as also in *Lundbeck* adjudication].

Bergen Open Researh Archive (BORA) (2014), p. 23.

647 Alexander Tsoutsanis, 'Finding Vredo (pat.pending): The Dutch Supreme Court Decision of 'Escitalopram' in Lundbeck v. Tiefenbacher et al.', in Journal of Intellectual Property Law & Practice 2014, Berichten Industriele Eigendom 2014/2, pp. 41-45, February 12, 2014, p. 41.

648 Ibid., p. 43.

649 Ibid., in the abstract.

The Dutch Supreme Court in its decision in Case *RuneScape Theft* – LJN : BQ9251, Supreme, J. 10/00101, on January 31, 2012 held that the virtual nature of the objects itself does not preclude the state to be regarded as 'goods' in the sense of Article Sr. 310. The Court's holding in *RuneScape Theft* resolved similar issues as in HR 23 May 1921, NJ 1921, p. 564 that electric power should be regarded as 'goods' in the sense of Article Sr. 310, as in HR 11 May 1982, NJ. 1982/583 in which bank money could be regarded as 'goods' belonging to other parties.[650] The Dutch Supreme Court might be understood to have taken into account the similarity-matching between those cases in deciding the meaning of 'goods' under Article Sr. 310. Coherence is obviously considered in the adjudication of *RuneScape Theft*.

Regarding AdWords, in *Wintersteiger* [2010] the Austrian court followed its precedents in keyword cases - *Wein & Co*, OGH 17 Ob 1/07g, 20 March 2007 and *Berg Spechte NI*, OGH 17 Ob 3/10f, 21 June 2010 - and applied a surprisingly restrictive standard in respect to trade mark infringements through keyword advertising, apparently assuming that the average Austrian internet-users were fairly unskilled, naïve and fully unaware of the fact that the last line of an ad indicated the website/URL to which the ad was linked.[651] In *Wintersteiger* [2010], the Austrian court employed analogical reasoning between the case at hand (*Wintersteiger* [2010]) and the two previous similar cases: *Wein & Co*, OGH 17 Ob 1/07g [2007] and *Berg Spechte NI*, OGH 17 Ob 3/10f [2010], particularly on the standard in respect to trade mark infringements through keyword advertising. The court's holdings in the three cases are similar and justified members of the rule category on that issue, proving that coherence has been taken into account in *Wintersteiger* adjudication.

The EFTA Court in its decision in Case E-18/11 *Irish Bank Corporation Ltd v. Kaupping nf* (advisory opinion of September 28, 2012) [the case at hand] acknowledged that according to the wording of Article 34 of the Surveillance and Court Agreement (SCA) Act there is no obligation on national courts of last instance to make any reference to the EFTA Court (para. 57). But the Court added: "At the same time, courts against whose decisions there is no judicial remedy under national law will take due account of the fact that they are bound to fulfill their duty of loyalty

---

650 R. Reynolds, 'Full Text of Ruling of the Dutch Supreme Court', RuneScape-Dutch Supreme Court's Decision, LIN:BQ9251, by IVPN Administration, February 1, 2010, under sub-heading III: Satisfy the other condition for criminal liability under Article 310 of the Penal Code – item 333.

651 Maximilian Schubert (Rechtsreferent) and Birgit Clark (Rechtsanwaltin), 'Wintersteiger', – Austrian Supreme Court refers jurisdiction question in AdWord cases to the ECJ, in Journal of Intellectual Property Law & Practice, 2011, Vol. 6, No. 5, pp. 289-290.

under Article 3 EEA". The Court notes in this context that EFTA citizens and economic operators benefit from the obligation of courts of the EU Member States against whose decisions there is no judicial remedy under national law to make a reference to the ECJ (Case C-452/01 Ospelt and Schlossle Weissenberg [1993] ECR I-9743). This had shown that the EFTA Court cited [and followed] the ECJ's decision in *Ospelt.*[652] In the case at hand, the EFTA Court also cited [and followed] its decision in Case E-14/11 *DB Schenker v. EFTA Surveillance Authority*, judgment of December 21, 2012. In the opinion of the EFTA Court in *DB Schenker*, the fact that Regulation No. 1049/2001 secures public access to, inter alia, Commission documents means that the EFTA Surveillance Authority is required to ensure at least the same degree of openness for 'reason of reciprocity' (paragraph 121). A conclusion could be drawn that the EFTA Court's decision in the case at hand (*Irish Bank)* seemed to suggest that concrete legal implications could be deduced from 'reason of reciprocity' also with regard to a possible obligation of the national courts of the EFTA States to turn to the EFTA Court.[653] In Norway, as to the issue of referral to the EFTA Court, the Supreme Court in *Personskadeforbundet (*Rt. 2012 p. 1793) and in *STX and Others v. The Norwegian State* – March 5, 2013, judgment of March 5, 2013, cited [and followed] the EFTA Court's decision in *DB Schenker*, the EFTA Court's decision in *Irish Bank* and the ECJ's decision in *Ospelt.*[654]Analogy and coherence consideration occured in legal reasoning in *Personskadeforbundet* and *STX,* therefore the *rationes decidendi* of those five cases are similar and are justified members of the rule category [as a coherent set] on referral to the EFTA Court under EU law.

The Norwegian Supreme Court in *Personskadeforbundet* also cited [and followed] the EFTA Court in *Nguyen*, the ECJ in *Ferreira* January [2001] and the ECJ in *Bernaldez* [1996], on the issue of state liability in insurance industry according to the Motor Vehicle Insurance Directives.[655] Following the ECJ's interpretation of the directives in *Ferreira*, the EFTA Court in *Nguyen*, upon a referral from Oslo City Court, made it clear that to except redress for non-economic injury ('pain and suffering') from the compulsory insurance system under national law was not compatible with the directives. The EFTA Court in *Nguyen* held further that the said breach of EEA law was sufficiently serious to entail state liability.[656] In its decision in *Personskadeforbundet*, the Norwegian Supreme Court held that the wording of the directives was not sufficiently precise to hold the government liable from the point of entry into force of the EEA Agreement, however

652 Fredriksen (2014), supra note 2421, p. 5.

653 Ibid., p. 16.

654 Ibid.

655 Ibid., p. 9, 10, 11.

656 Ibid.

the Supreme Court also held that the ECJ in *Bernaldez* had clarified the interpretation of the directives to such an extent that the maintenance thereafter of the rule excepting redress for non-economic injury from the compulsory insurance coverage constituted a sufficient serious breach of EEA law to entail state liability.[657] Analogical reasoning between the case at hand (*Personskadeforbundet*) [on the one hand] and *Nguyen* and *Bernaldez* as strung together [on the other hand] was employed by the Norwegian Supreme Court. This analogy involved the decisions of ECJ, EFTA Court and the Norwegian Supreme Court, concerning the interpretation or application of the Motor Vehicle Insurance Directives. The analogy generated the Supreme Court's holding in the case at hand on that particular issue of interpretation. The Supreme Court's holding is similar to the holdings in *Nguyen* and *Bernaldez*; showing coherence consideration in legal reasoning in the three cases, where those holdings are similar and justified members of the same rule category on how the Directives should be interpreted or applied. It has been seen there that generativity and transformativity push the evolution of law.

The EFTA Court in Case E-9/97 *Sveinbjornsdottir v. Iceland* [1998] EFTA [Court Report 95] held that the EEA States should be held liable for breach of EEA law. This principle was the followed by the ECJ and the highest courts of the EFTA States. The ECJ in Case C-140/97 *Rechberger and Others v. Austria* [1999] ECR I-3499 and the Supreme Court of Iceland in its judgment of December 16, 1999 in Case 236/1999 *Iceland v. Sveinbjornsdottir* followed this principle.[658] The Supreme Court of Liechtenstein in its decision of March 7, 2010 in Case CO.2004.2 *Liechtenstein v. Dr.Tschannet (No.2)* also cited the EFTA Court in *Sveinbjornsdottir,* the ECJ in *Rechberger* and the Icelandic Supreme Court in *Sveinbjornsdottir.*[659]Analogical reasoning and coherence consideration occured in and between *Sveinbjornsdottir v. Iceland* [EFTA,1998], *Rechberger and Others v. Austria* [1999], *Iceland v. Sveinbjornsdottir* [Iceland Supreme Court,1999] and *Liechtenstein v. Dr. Tschannet (No.2).* The court-holdings in the four cases are similar and are justified members of the same legal rule on liability of EEA Member States for breach of EEA law.

Van Gend en Loos v. Nederlandse Administrative de Belastingen (1963)-Case 26/62 (1963) ECR 1, (1963) CMLR 105 was the first and famous case before the ECJ, dealing with the principle of direct effect of EC Treaty to protect individual rights. In that case, a Dutch company objected to the Dutch customs law on the ground that the law is incompatible with

657 Ibid.

658 Ibid., p. 23.

659 Ibid.

Article 12 [of EU] Treaty, prohibiting increases in import duties. The ECJ held that Article 12 had to be interpreted as producing direct effect and creating individual rights, and the national courts of the Member States had to protect the rights and establish the principle of 'direct effect'. Article 12 of EC Treaty on customs duties on imports from Member States to other Member States should be enforced before domestic courts.[660] The ECJ ruled that the protection of EU law applied to individuals as well as member states, created the principle of direct effect.[661] Two years after *Van Gend,* the second famous case before the ECJ was *Costa v. ENEL* (1964)-Case 6/64 (1964) ECR 585 CMLR 425-in 1964 in which an Italian, Flaminio Costa, refused to pay a $3.00 electric bill on the ground that Italy's nationalization of electric companies violated Article 37 of the EEC Treaty.[662] Costa was claiming before his local court that the Italian law was incompatible with the EC Treaty. The local court referred the question to the ECJ for a preliminary ruling. Upon such reference, the ECJ held that the unlimited duration of the Community, the autonomy of Community power, both internally and externally, and especially the limitation of competence or transfer of powers from the states to the European Community should be emphasized.[663] In consideration that the Member States had effectively transferred their sovereign rights under Community law, the Court ruled that Community law takes precedence over national law and cannot be overridden by domestic legal provisions, however framed.[664] In the event that EU law is contradictory to national laws, EU law is the higher authority, thus establishing the supremacy of the ECJ.[665] In *Costa* the ECJ expanded on its constitutional theory of the Community, declaring that the Member States had created a sovereign Community by limiting their own sovereign rights.[666] The principle of supremacy of EU law as laid down in *Van Gend* and *Costa* was followed by the ECJ's later decisions, in *Internationale Handelsgessellschaft v. Einfuhr* – Case 11/70 (1970) ECR 1125; (1970) CMLR 255 and *Simmenthal SPA*_(1978) – Case 106/77 (1978) ECR 629; (1978) 3 CMLR 263.[667] In Italy, in *Simmenthal*

660 Elena Papageorgiou, 'The European Court of Justice and the Supremacy of EC Law', Law Office of Community Law, the Law Office of the Republic of Cyprus, pp. 8-9, referring to Wayne Ives, 'European Union Law', in Civitas 01/2006, last update: Lucy Hatton, 07/2011, www.civitas.org.uk/eufacts, (CIVITAS Institute for the Study of Civil Society 2006).

661 Ibid., referring to Ives (2006), Ibid.

662 Ben Aston, 'How does Community Law Affect National Soverignty?' : Politics of Governance: The European Union, 25.02.04, at benaston.com, p. 4.

663 Papageorgiou, supra note 2435, pp. 9-10.

664 Aston (2004), supra note 2437, p. 4.

665 Ives (2006), supra note 2435.

666 Papageorgiou, supra note 2438, pp. 9-10.

667 Ibid., p. 11.

the Italian first instant court concerned requested the ECJ to determine if the Italian court should wait for its repeal from the Constitutional Court prior to determining the case. Upon having been referred, the ECJ held that the national court was under a duty to give full effect to Community law even where there was a conflicting provision of national law and without awaiting a higher court to rule on the matter. *Simmenthal* is an interesting case, since it spells out the practical implications for the Community legal order concerning the principles of EU law supremacy and direct effect.[668] Analogical reasoning and coherence consideration occured there in *Simmenthal*. The substantive rules on the principle of EU law supremacy as laid down in *Van Gend, Costa, Internationale Handelsgessellschaft* and *Simmenthal* are similar in terms of law, and they are justified members of the rule category on that principle. The principles of EU law supremacy and direct effects laid down by the ECJ's decision in *Van Gend* had first been generated through deduction from EC Treaty, and the ECJ's decision being the particular legal rule applicable to *Van Gend* then generated another transformed similar particular ruling in *Costa*. The ruling in *Costa* furthermore caused the generative transformational process in *Internationale Handelsgessellschaft* so as to produce another similar / transformed particular ruling there. Furthermore, the ruling in *Internationale Handelsgessellschaft* constituting the particular rule applicable to that case generated another similar / transformed particular ruling being the legal rule applicable or enforceable in *Simmenthal*.

In Case C-106/89, *Marleasing SA v. La Commercial de Alimentacion SA* (1990) ECR 1-4135 (1992)1 CMLR 305, at 4146, the ECJ interpreted the terms of an unimplemented directive as it applied between private individuals, by observing: "In applying national law, whether the provisions in question were adopted before or after the directive, a national court called upon to interpret it is required to do so, as far as possible, in light of the wording and purpose of the directive in order to achieve the result pursued by the latter". In addition, in conformity with Article 10 TEU, national courts are required to fully effectivate EU law and to interpret all national legislation in the light of all relevant EU law, regardless of whether the particular provision is of direct effect [*Van Colson* (1984)]. Then, the Court held in *Francovich* (1991): "The full effectiveness of Community rules would be impaired and the protection of the rights which they grant would be weakened if individuals were unable to obtain compensation when their rights are infringed by a breach of Community law for which a Member State can be held responsible". So, the state may be held responsible in respect of breaches of EU law, and liable in damages for the non-implementation of a directive. These are all based on the *principle of direment ct effect* which principally protects individuals and often gives them rights which they can

668 Ibid., p. 12.

rely upon as against Member States. The doctrine sets up a mechanism for the citizens of Europe to plead before national courts the provisions of EU legislation.[669] The ECJ's holdings in *Marleasing SA* and *Francovich* followed its holdings in *Marshall v. Southmpton and South - West Area Health Authority* (1986)[Case 152/84 (1986) ECR 723, (1988)1 CMLR 688] and *Van Duyn v. Home Office* (1974) [Case 41/741 (1974) ECR 1337, (1975)1 CMLR]. The dimension of fit has been clear in and between *Marleasing SA, Francovich, Marshall,* and *Van Duyn*. The ECJ pursues legal certainty through consistency and coherence in judicial decision-making.

The Chamber of European Court of Human Rights in Strasbourg in the merits of *Vassis and Others v. France*, ECHR 190 (2013) pointed out that it had previously accepted, in its decisions in *Rigopoulos and Others v. Spain* (application no. 37388/97, January 12, 1999) and in *Medvedyev and Others v. France* (application no. 3394/03, March 29, 2010), that the detention of crew members for several days, to allow time for the vessel to be escorted to the territory of the respondent State, was not incompatible with that requirement of promptness, in view of the existence of 'wholly exceptional circumstances' justifying such a delay. The Chamber also cited its decision in *Moulin v France* (application no. 37104/06), 23 November 2010 in which it was held that there was no longer any need to address the question whether a French public prosecutor could act as a 'judge', within the meaning of Article 5 § 3. The Chamber observed that the intervention of a public prosecutor at the beginning and in the course of police custody did not itself raise any difficulty, provided the person in custody was subsequently presented to a 'judge or other office authorized by law to exercise judicial power' within a time-frame that met the requirements of Article 5 § 3. The Chamber held unanimously that the placement of Mr. Vassis, Mr. Bardoulis, Mr. Kamara, Mr. Taylor and Mr. Thomas (applicants) into police custody for 18 days was deprivation of liberty. Despite being in the police custody for 18 days, the applicants had had to wait a further 48 hours, after arrival in Brest [from the high seas], to be brought before a judicial authority, even though the circumstances of the case did not justify such a delay. The placement, according to the Chamber, constituted a violation of Article 5 § 3 (right of liberty and security) of the European Convention on Human Rights.[670] Material analogical reasoning vertically and horizontally had been employed by the ECHR between *Vassis* [2013] on the one hand and *Rigopoulos* [1999] and *Medvedyev* [2010] as strung together on the other hand. The analogical reasoning was *generative* of the *ratio* in *Vassis*

---

669 Ibid., pp. 23-24.

670 Press Release issued by the registrar of the European Court of Human Rights, ECHR 190 (2013) 27.06.2013, Drugs traffickers detained on the high seas for 18 days without judicial supervision should have been brought before a judicial authority immediately they arrived in France, Strasbourg, 2013.

[2013]. The *rationes* in the three cases are similar in terms of law and they show the dimension of fit. Generativity and transformativity are shown to exist in the evolution of law from *Rigopoulos* [1999] to *Medvedyev* [2010] to *Vassis* [2013].

From the cases as mentioned above, it is true that Common law and Civil law traditions have the same goal in the sense of pursuing legal certainty and fairness through maximizing consistency and coherence in law. It is also true that both traditions tend to be closer in that regard. Generativity and transaformativity push that trend. Legal transformational-generative process happens domestically, transnationally, between EU Law and EU Member States' national laws, and within EU Law.

IV.10.4. LEGAL CERTAINTY AND FAIRNESS

***

The struggle between legal certainty and equity is as old as the law itself. Only the labels have changed: while formerly discussion proceeded in terms of *ius strictum* and *ius aequum*, the expressions currently preferred, especially in Germany, are 'legal certainty' and 'justice (in individual cases)'; equity is the need for deciding current, concrete disputes adequately, by giving due weight to the special and perhaps unique circumstances of each case.[671] Legal certainty is the public interest in clear, equal, and foreseeable rules of law.[672] At the beginning of the 20th century, the idea of certainty of law was in its heyday. Legal theory continued to reflect the constancy of economic development and international peace which existed until 1914 – at least so far as Western Europe and America are concerned. The promotion of legal certainty has been with a view to eliminating the legal risk of business and of other transactions by making them clearly predictable. Even after World War I, the tendency towards legal certainty continued to be dominant in many instances. To a large extent, this was probably due to two reasons. First, many people were inclined to ignore, as much as possible, the basic transformation of their environments, and to return to the old standards (e.g., the gold standards) as soon as practicable. Secondly, lawyers often consciously tend to oppose revolutionary change

671 Paul H. Neuhaus, 'Legal Certainty Versus Equity in the Conflict of Law', in 28 Law and Contemporary Problems, (Fall 1963), pp. 795-807, Duke Law Scholarship Repository Journal LCP, Vol. 28, No.4 (1963), p. 795.

672 Ibid.

and to defend traditional values.[673] Clear and determinate legal rules are essential for freedom. Friedrich Hayek explained the thesis as follows: "The law tells [the individual] what facts he may count on[,] and thereby extends the range within which he can predict the consequences of his actions".[674] The law is 'data on which the individual can base his own plans' which means that 'in most instances the individual needs never be coerced unless he has placed himself in a position where he knows he will be coerced'.[675] Hayek says that the ability of the individual to avoid the coercive power of the state – that is to say, his freedom – is therefore dependent upon certain attribute of the law – principally among those is 'its ...certainty'.

The political and economic development of the leading countries may have been decisive. A certain stabilization after the changes and disturbances brought by World War II and its immediate aftermaths; the integration of Europe and, generally, of the free world; and finally, increasing contacts with underdeveloped countries – are the factors that may contribute today or in the near future to strengthening the quest for legal certainty.[676] "Capitalistic enterprise cannot do without legal security", wrote Weber, "because such security was essential for the investment of capital".[677] "Bourgeois interests" need a legal system that 'function[s] in a calculable way', and calculability means, in turn, an unambiguous and clear legal system.[678] Some writers have since summed up the thesis that markets cannot function without a clear and precise definition of who owns what (property rights), who may do what to whom (civil and criminal law), and who must pay whom to protect their interests (contract law).[679]

Dworkin states that in an advanced legal system, one which is thick with constitutional rules and practices, and dense with precedents and statutes, the antecedent probability of such 'ties' is much lower and the

673 Ibid., p. 797.

674 Ofer Raban, 'The Fallacy of Legal Certainty: Why Vague Legal Standards May Be Better For Capitalism and Liberalism', in Public Interest Law Journal Vol. 19, 175 (2010), p. 178, citing Friedrich A. Hayek, 'The Constitution of Liberty' (1960), pp. 156-157.

675 Ibid., referring to Hayek (1960), Ibid., p. 21, 167.

676 Neuhaus (1963), supra note 2446, p. 802.

677 Raban (2010), supra note 2449, p. 177, referring to Max Weber, 'Economy and Society', in Guenther Roth & Claus Wittich eds., (Univ. of California Press, 1978), p. 883.

678 Ibid., referring to Weber (1978), Ibid, p. 847.

679 Ibid., p. 178, referring to Daniel W. Bromley & Jeffry A. Cochrane, 'A Bargaining Framework for the Global Commons 6 (United States Agency for International Development', Working Paper No. 21, 1995), available at http://ageconsearch.umn.edu/bitstream/11899/1/wp21.pdf.

predictability of the outcome therefore much higher.[680] A different sort of theory from Dworkin's, leading to the same conclusion that law becomes more certain, has been advanced by Landes and Posner.[681] A system with a larger and newer capital stock corresponds to a legal system that contains a great deal of law. Such a system results in greater certainty.[682] Landes and Posner argue that two phenomena affect the capital stock of precedents-depreciation and new investment-work in opposition to one another to maintain an 'equilibrium' of certainty in the law. First, precedent depreciates over time; its informational value declines because of changing circumstances. In particular, the value of precedent as a source of legal doctrine is reduced by changes in social and economic conditions, in legislation, in judicial personnel, and in other parameters of legal actions.[683] Second, opposing the force of precedential depreciation is constant new instrument. Landes and Posner describe a 'production function' of legal precedents, which senses the level of uncertainty and counteracts it to restore certainty. When in a given case the controlling precedent is depreciated and the outcome is therefore somewhat uncertain, parties will differ in their predictions of the outcome and accordingly will be more likely to litigate their dispute to a conclusion, thus creating a precedent or one of a string of precedents that will settle this issue and restore certainty by rising the stock of legal capital back to the desired level.[684] In order for

680 Anthony D'Amato, 'Legal Uncertainty', in 71 California Law Review 1-55 (1983), pp. 1-55 (p. 4), referring to R. Dworkin, 'Taking Rights Seriously' (1997), p. 286. "Ties," in Dworkin's analysis, can occur only when superhuman (Herculean) judges are unable to choose one of two possible results as the "right" one.

681 Raban (2010), supra note 2452, p. 6, referring to William Landes & Richard Posner, 'Legal Precedent: A Theoretical and Empirical Analysis', in 19 J.L. & Econ. (1976), p. 249 (accompanying text omitted).

682 D'Amato (1983), supra note 2455, p. 6.

683 Ibid. Landes and Posner offer this following example of depreciation of precedent: "To illustrate, a decision involving a collision between two horse-drawn wagons is bound to lose some of its precedential value when wagons are replaced by cars and trucks, and a decision turning on the difference between "trespass" and "trespass on the case" may lose all of its precedential value when the common-law forms of action are abolished by statute. In general, passage of time reduces the flow of services of a precedent, and this reduction represents the depreciation or absolescence of legal capital." (Landes & Posner (1976), Ibid., p. 263 – footnote omitted).

684 Ibid. As Landes & Posner state: "Suppose that the stock of legal capital, and hence the flow of information on the likely outcomes of potential legal disputes, were temporarily below the desired (long-run equilibrium) level. This might be due to new legislation or other unanticipated changes in economic or social conditions that rendered part of the existing capital stock obsolete. With the resulting increase in uncertainty, more disputes would arise, parties to a dispute would find it more difficult to forecast the outcome of litigation, and litigation would increase. The

the new investment mechanism to sustain the desired level of certainty, Landes and Posner suggest, bias is simply that the more uncertain the law, the more likely are the disputants to litigate rather than to settle because their estimates of the probable outcome diverge.[685] The fruit of litigation - the decision of the case - in turn makes the law certain for everyone else.

***

The dichotomy between predictability and acceptability is connected to the classic division between valid norms and their validity as action.[686] It concerns the distinction between what is valid in itself and what can gain validity as an act performed. Formal predictability suggests that law is immobile, independent, and pre-established as well as pre-settled. Substantive acceptability, however, concerns the more flexible aspect of law and adjudication; it refers to law's reflexibility, fluidity, and context-sensitivity. These two distinct and sometimes apposing values come together in the notion of legal certainty.[687] Legal certainty requires a balance between stability and flexibility. Following the hermeneutical footsteps of legal theorists such as Aarnio and Peczenik, a distinction can be made between formal and substantive legal certainty; between predictability and acceptability of legal decision-making.[688] Formal legal certainty implies that laws and, in particular, adjudication must be predictable: laws must satisfy requirements of clarity, stability, and intelligibility so that those concerned can with relative accuracy calculate the legal consequences of their actions as well as the outcome of legal proceedings. Substantive legal certainty, then, is related to the rational acceptability of legal decision-making. In this sense, laws and adjudication are predictable and must

result would be a temporary increase in the production of precedents (investment) until the discrepancy between actual and desired capital was eliminated (Landes & Posner (1976), Ibid., pp. 269-270 – footnote ommited).

685 Ibid. The now more experienced Judge Posner still adheres to his early position. In his remarks to a luncheon at the Court of Appeal on May 12, 1982, Judge Posner stated that simply increasing the number of precedents also increases the number of particular conflicts that are "solved" by some of the precedents, thereby increasing predictability.

686 Paunio (2009), supra note 2356, p. 1469.

687 Ibid., citing Georg Henrik von Wright,'Norms and Actions:A Logical Inquiry', (1963).

688 Ibid., referring to Aarnio (1987), supra note 2305, p. 3; Peczenik (1989), supra note 2369, p. 31; Alexander Peczenik, 'Vad är Rätt? Om Demokrati, Rattssäkerhet, Etik Och Jurisdik Argumentation', 1995, p. 43.

be accepted by the legal community in question.[689] A rule consciously striving to ascertain their actual understanding – rather than one that blindly follows the literal language of their agreement – would appear to prove *more*, not less, predictability.[690] Those who believe that clear and unambiguous rules produce more certainty and predictability need not think that *any* clear rule does so. The claim pertains only to *well-crafted* rules, not to ill-concieved ones; and the external evidence rule or the rule of explicit verbal consent may be ill-concieved. The proper comparison is therefore between well-crafted and strictly-followed clear and unambiguous rules, and well-crafted vague standards. It is here that bright-line rules are bound to perform better predictability-wise.[691] It is generally believed that legal rules provide the virtues of certainty and predictability, while legal standards afford flexibility, accommodate equitable solutions, and allow for a more informed development of the law.[692] Raz holds that since the law should strive to balance certainty and reliability against flexibility, it is on the whole wise legal policy to use rules as much as possible for regulating human behavior because they are more certain than [standards].[693] Kaplow says that [s]tandards ...increase the cost and difficulty of prediction [while] rules are defined [by] the ease with which private parties can predict how the law will apply to their conduct.[694] According to Posner,[695][t]he rule of law implies (as the name suggests) a preference for rules over standards. Although a legislature, by issuing a standard, announces in advance of the regulated conduct that anyone who engages in that conduct now risks a sanction, in practice this announcement does not amount to much ... [because it] does not tell people what is permitted and what is not permitted, though it gives them something of an idea. Scalia puts forward: [A]nother obvious advantage of establishing as soon as possible [clear and definite rules]: predictability. Even in simpler times uncertainty has been regarded as incompatible with the Rule of Law. Rudimentary justice requires that those subject to the law must have the means of knowing what it prescribes.[696] Schauer contends that since following a rule may produce a suboptimal decision in some particular case, the question of the comparative value of

689 Ibid.

690 Raban (2010), supra note 2456, p. 178.

691 Ibid., p. 186.

692 Ibid., p. 175 [accompanying text omitted].

693 Ibid., referring to Joseph Raz, 'Legal Principles and the Limits of Law', in 81 Yale L.J. 823 (1972), p. 841.

694 Ibid., referring to Louis Kaplow, 'The General Characteristics of Rules', in 5 Encyclopedia of Law and Economics 512-13, (Boudewijn Bouckaert & Gerrit De Gees eds. 2000).

695 Ibid., pp. 175-176, referring to Eric A. Posner, 'Standards, Rules and Social Norms', in 21 Harv. J. L. & Pub. Pol'y 101 (1997), p. 113.

696 Ibid., p. 176, referring to Scalia (1989), supra note 2297, p. 1175, 1179.

rule-based reliance is the question of the extent to which a decision-making environment is willing to tolerate suboptimal results in order that those affected by the decision in that environment will be able to plan.[697] Sunstein is of the opinion: "A system committed to the rule of law is... not committed to the unrealistic goal of making every decision according to judgments fully specified in advance. Nonetheless, ...[f[requently a lawmaker adopts rules because rules narrow or even eliminate the ....uncertainty faced by people attempting to follow ....the law. This step has enormous virtues in terms of promoting predictability and planning".[698]

However, differently, Fuller holds that many of our social, moral, and economic decisions involve polycentric situations which have multiple elements with mutual influence over each other.[699] Such polycentric situations are best governed by vague standards and not by clear rules. Life can be complicated. And so it is unsurprising that our normative standards are replete with such concepts – and that, consequently, so are our laws, which are often mere formalizations of these non-legal (or pre-legal) standards. Thus vague and indeterminate legal standards often produce more certainty and predictability than any alternative bright-line rule because they replicate, one-for-one, the social, moral, economic, or political norms that already prevail, and which, given the nature of the phenomena they describe, cannot be reduced to clear and unambiguous language.

***

Sure enough, insurance companies (and other sophisticated repeat players) may and do take the law and its interpretive methodology into account when contemplating their actions. But even willingness and ability to consult the law and its interpretive methodology in advance, and to act

697 Ibid., referring to Schauer (1991), supra note 2070. In earlier paragraph Schauer notes that "the argument from reliance [i.e., predictability] ....presupposes a commonality of understanding between the relying addressees [i.e., those subjected to the law] and the enforcers [i.e., judges] on whose actions reliance is placed". Ibid., p. 138. That is absolutely correct, and is one reason why the best rules can reduce predictability when compared with vague standards. But instead of drawing this conclusion, Schauer moves to commit the fallacy by identifying rules with predictability insofar as "addressees and enforcers" share "a common language". Ibid., p. 139.

698 Ibid. See 83 Cal. L. Rev. 953 (1995), pp. 1021-1022.

699 Ibid., p. 189. Fuller borrowed the notion of "polycentric situations" from Michael Polany. See Michael Polanyi, 'The Logic of Liberty: Reflections and Rejoinders', (1951), p. 171.

accordingly, would be futile in many cases if the governing methodology is textualism. Literal interpretation may defy parties' expectations for myriad reasons, including but not limited to the use of ill-conceived contractual terms, reliance on industry non-contractual understandings, or failure to realize what a contractual provision may mean in certain unforeseen circumstances. Textualist analysis – or, for that matter, clear and unambiguous rules – can facilitate predictability only when people can configure them their prediction. But oftentimes people cannot. There is little reason to think that courts engaged in textualist interpretation can better promote predictability. This is especially true, given that non-textualist interpretation (which often, of course, ends up following the text) consciously takes into account people's expectations, while textualism does not.[700]

In a democratic and pluralist society, the standards for judgment cannot be purely personal or irrational; the judge must be guided by generally recognized standards capable of rational cognition. The practical need for uniformity and predictability of decisions and the dignity of the individuals, which is incompatible with arbitrary judicial fiat, create an abiding need for objective standards of law.[701] The past has made us suspicious of a purely logical-deductive and stationary approach to terminology and systematic analysis. The development and the adaptable application of the law must remain possible in a changing world, and each value judgment must proceed from an exact analysis of the facts. But dispite the myriad of actual fact situations and possible points of approach to the decision of concrete cases, the lawyer should always strive to express the solution of individual cases in clear terms, and seek to fit them into a larger framework. In Ernst Rabel's words, there should be 'system construction from below'.

Habermas argues that the socially integrative function of legal systems requires that adjudication must simultaneously satisfy the conditions of consistent decision-making and rational acceptability, a view closely connected to Aarnio's thesis.[702] It follows that, on the one hand, legal certainty requires that decisions are consistent with the framework of the exsisting legal system. The claim to legitimacy demands decisions that are not only consistent in relation to the surrounding legal system, but that should also be rationally justified so that all participants can accept them as rational decisions. The rationality problem which Habermas discusses

700 Ibid.

701 Neuhaus (1963), supra note 2451, pp. 802-803, referring to Ernst Rabel, 'Die Fachgebiete des Kaiser Wilhelm-Instituts für ausländisches und internationales Privatrecht 1900-1093', in 3 25 Jahre Kaiser Wilhelm-Gessellschaft 77 (1937), p. 109.

702 Paunio (2009), supra note 2461, p. 1472, referring to Habermas (1996), supra note 2357, pp. 194-237.

is the following: how can continually evolving and developing law be applied in a way that guarantees both certainty and rightness?[703] Or, more specifically: how can the appropriateness of selective decisions be justified so that all participants perceive them as acceptable?[704] The answer to these questions is related to the idea of a paradigm of law that guides adjudication.[705] A paradigm of law is based on a particular understanding of the legal system: it is an implicit social theory of a legal system.[706] More specifically, it makes the rationality of the interpretive process explicit by reference to a specific purpose.[707] Additionally, according to Klaus Gunther, building a bridge between predictability and acceptability respectively is connected to the distinction between justification discourses and application discourses.[708] Justification discourses refer to the lawmaking process, whereas application discourses are relevant in adjudication.

Habermas says that the certainty of law can be secured on a different level.[709] He introduces the concept of *procedure-dependent certainty* of law in order to resolve the paradoxical relationship between certainty and acceptability. In essence, procedural rights guarantee legal persons the possibility of a fair procedure. Instead of guaranteeing certainty of outcomes in individual cases, procedural legal certainty assures a discursive clarification of the pertinent facts and legal questions.[710] In this respect, Habermas contends, what is important is not the predictability of the outcome itself, but rather, the certainty that legal persons have the opportunity to affirm their legal situation in a court procedure according to a predetermined set of procedural rules.[711] Importantly, because it is impossible to create laws that are precise at the outset, legal certainty is guaranteed on the one hand by procedural means (creating procedural predictability) and on the other hand by means of argumentation (rational acceptability).[712] His theory of law is based on the idea that balancing predictability and substantive legal certainty is

---

703 Ibid., referring to Habermas (1996), Ibid., pp. 198-199.

704 Ibid., referring to Habermas (1996), Ibid., pp. 202.

705 Ibid.

706 Ibid., referring to Habermas (1996), supra note 2479, pp. 194-195.

707 Ibid., referring to Dworkin (1986), supra note 2382, p. 52.

708 Ibid., pp. 1472-1473, referring to Klaus Günther, 'A Normative Conception of Coherence for a Discursive Theory of Legal Justification', in 2 RATIO JURIS (1989), p. 155, 157. See also Jürgen Habermas, 'Justification and Application'(1993), p. 35.

709 Ibid., p. 1474.

710 Ibid., referring to Habermas (1996), supra note 2481, p. 220.

711 Ibid., referring to Habermas (1996), Ibid., p. 388.

712 Ibid., p. 1475.

possible through procedural guarantees.[713] Habermas proposes a reflexive form of communicative action to resolve the problem of how the legal community can agree on a specific legal paradigm, so that the problem of indeterminacy in legal decision-making can be resolved. For Habermas, the paradigmatic preunderstanding of law can limit the indeterminacy of legal decision-making and guarantee a sufficient degree of legal certainty in so far as the paradigm is shared by all citizens and expresses the self-understanding of the entire legal community.[714]

Predictability should not be understood as meaning that every person identically interprets legal texts without communicating with others. Rather, it means that when engaging in a communication process nearly all lawyers are convinced that the proposed interpretation is acceptable. The criterion is therefore whether clear argument on an interpretation may be reached among authorized experts but not whether everyone would reach the same interpretation in all possible situations.[715] A shift occurs from emphasizing formally predictable outcomes to substantive legal certainty that essentially requires rationally acceptable legal decision-making and, consequently, substantively acceptable legal reasoning.[716] Essentially, to realize the aim of (rationally) acceptable legal decision-making and as a result, substantive legal certainty, the interpretive choices made by a court must be acceptable not only normatively but also rationally so that they conform to the values of that particular community.[717] Habermas puts an emphasis on the role of procedural guarantees.[718] In essence, the emphasis may be understood as a way of balancing between predictability and context-sensitive legal interpretation, the fact that both laws and contexts of interpretation change means that something is needed to guarantee at least some level of stability. In this sense what remains stable and predictable is the procedure itself.

***

713 Ibid., p. 1478.

714 Ibid., p. 1476. See Habermas (1996), supra note 2486, pp. 222-223. Habermas tries to develop Dworkin's One Single Right Answer thesis beyond the monological, judge-centered view that seems to be at the center of Dworkin's theory. Indeed, Dworkin does not address the issue of different legal paradigms that are simultaneously present in a given community. See also, Dworkin (1986), supra note 2482, p. 225.

715 Ibid., p. 1480.

716 Ibid., p. 1479.

717 Ibid., p. 1482. See also Dworkin (1986), supra note 2489, p. 255.

718 Ibid., p. 1490. See Habermas (1996), supra note 2489, p. 386.

Habermas's theory seems to be a useful point of reference because of the importance he places on procedural guarantees and communication [between relevant legal actors] in balancing certainty and acceptability in adjudication. These also appear to form the basic ingredients of legal certainty in EU law. Tentatively, and on a purely theoretical level, the formula for legal certainty could be the following: predictable procedure plus rationally acceptable and transparent legal reasoning in accordance with the underlying values of the legal community in question equals legal certainty.[719] Concerning adjudication in the context of EU, focusing on the European Court of Justice (ECJ), legal certainty encompasses both its formal and substantive elements and is generally considered as one of the most important principles in national legal systems: emphasis is nonetheless placed on predictability.[720] The principle of legal reasoning is also used as an interpretive tool in its reasoning by the ECJ. Legal reasoning is also used as an underlying, perhaps even an ideal, principle expressing the fundamental rationality of the EU legal order, more specifically on the more general aspects of ECJ legal reasoning. It is presumed that the ECJ can, by way of argumentation, assure more legal certainty.[721] The teleological approach to interpreting EU law which the ECJ has adopted is often said to collide with the principle of legal certainty.[722] Interpreting EU legislation by reference to systemic and, in particular, teleological considerations is said to run contrary to ideas associated with the principle of legal certainty, especially that of predictability. On this view, teleological interpretation disregarding the wording of a rule makes adjudication within the context of EU law particularly unpredictable.[723] This shows that systemic teleological interpretation may cause uncertainty.

Drawing from Habermas's discourse theory of law, the principle of legal certainty may be conceptualized within the context of EU law from the viewpoint of ECJ legal reasoning.[724] In ECJ case law, considerations of legal certainty (i.e., predictability) are sometimes weighed against other

719 Ibid., p. 1492.

720 Ibid., p. 1470. It should be noted that the concept of legal certainty is generally used in Civil Law systems. In Common Law, the closest equivalent would be the principle of rule of law. See e.g., Peczenik (1989), supra note 2463, p. 31.

721 Ibid.

722 Ibid., referring to Isabel Schubel-Pfister, 'Enjeux et perspectives du multilinguisme dans l'Union europeenne: après l'élargissement, la "babelisation', in 488 488 REVUE DU MARCHE COMMUN ET DE L'UNION EUROPEENNE, 2005, p. 332; Hjalte Rasmussen, 'Towards a Normative Theory of Interpretation of Community Law', (1993), p. 33.

723 Ibid.

724 Ibid. The choice of a systemic theory as the basis for Paunio's analysis is explained by the fact that the principle of legal certainty has been of particular interest to theorists with a background in Civil law systems.

principles such as that of effectiveness and uniformity in particular.[725] In EU, guaranteeing legal certainty through procedural means (creating procedural predictability) and argumentation (rational acceptability) may be argued that legal certainty consists in a combination of procedural safeguards and argumentation. In this respect, the ECJ's role is to support its decisions by reasons that convince the legal community of the suitability of the decisions. In this respect, the role of the EU legal community[726] is of particular importance in determining the acceptability of ECJ case.[727] The adversarial procedure to which Habermas implicitly refers in describing legal certainty in procedural terms does not as such exist in the EU. The preliminary ruling procedure is a case in point. Under this procedure, after a national court has referred a question to the ECJ, all parties to the proceedings before that court, the Member States as well as the Commission and other European institutions (under certain conditions) are allowed to take part in the proceedings before the ECJ. In this respect, the procedure in reality transforms the referred question from a simple legal dispute between two parties in a national setting to a larger EU-related legal question bearing not only on the actual case to be decided by the referring court but also on other similar cases. In a certain sense, the procedure at the ECJ resembles lawmaking instead of traditional adjudication. In this procedure, different legal paradigms compete based on different standards for balancing between values, principles and policies.[728] Predictable procedure in the EU is not enough to guarantee legal certainty in the substantive sense. In addition to procedural guarantees, substantive legal certainty requires transparent and open argumentation.[729] Indeed, ECJ legal reasoning may be described as essentially *meta-teleological*: decisions are based on a small number of recurring general and abstract purposes. These include effectiveness of Community law, uniformity of application, legal certainty and legal protection.[730] Paunio notes that substantive legal

---

725 Ibid., pp. 1475-1476. See, inter alia, Case 238/84, Criminal proceedings against Hans Röser, 1986 E.C.R. 795; Case 173/88, Skatteministeriet v. Henriksen, 1989 E.C.R. 2763; Case C-64/95, Konservenfabrik Lubella Friedrich Büker GmbH & Co. KG v. Hauptzollamt Cottbus, 1996 E.C.R. I-5105; Case C-161/06, Skomo-Lux s.r.o. v. Celni feditelstvi Olomouc, 2007 E.C.R, I-10841.

726 Ibid., p. 1476. Here the concept of a legal community is understood in the strict sense: that is, as primarily encompassing the juristic community operating in the EU legal system, both on national and EU levels.

727 Ibid. See e.g., Thomas Wilhelmsson, 'Yleiset opit ja pienet kertomukset ennakoitavuuden ja yhdenvertaisuuden nökökulmasta', in 102 LAKIMIES 199, 220 (220) on predictability of argumentation.

728 Ibid., p. 1479.

729 Ibid., p. 1478.

730 Ibid., p. 1483, 1490, referring to Mitchel Lasser, 'Judicial Deliberations: A Comparative Analysis of Judicial Transparency and Legitimacy' (2004), p. 211-

certainty depends on whether the legal community in question accepts the arguments advanced to support and justify a specific outcome in a case at the ECJ.

***

While clear and determinate legal rules are superior, by *definition*, insofar as the predictability of application is concerned, vague legal standards are often better in allowing people to predict the consequences of their actions.[731] Hayek, for all his early insistence on unambiguous rules fixed and announced beforehand, had come to realize the truth of legal certainty later in life.[732] In 1973, at age seventy-four, he returned from his experience of thirty odd years in the common law world to the civil law atmosphere and seemingly recognized that judicial decision might in fact be more predicatable if the judge was also bound by generally held views of what was just, even when they were not supported by the letter of the law.[733] Hayek's insight should receive the wider recognition it deserves. It has long been recognized that vague legal standards and a non-textualist judiciary would often produce better regulative results (of this there is no better proof than the practices of our legislature and courts). And yet, these practices are too often seen, even if advantageous, as setbacks to certainty and predictability. Missing is the realization that these standards, and these judicial practices, may be superior precisely because they enhance the certainty with which the people can predict the consequences of their actions. The extensive use of vague legal standards, Raban argues, no doubt harbors dangers.[734] Vague standards can easily mask arbitrariness, inconsistency, and injustice, and can also (of course) generate uncertainty. Their proper use requires good faith, professionalism, and intelligence, and therefore depends on a high caliber legal profession.

Certainty is connected with stability and flexibility. In balancing between stability and flexibility of law, consistency is to be maintained, since law is as norm which provides for fact pursuant to pattern of regularity. The claim of consistency is sometimes put in terms of 'equality' [or 'justice'], whereas justice might be viewed as 'fairness'. Therefore, consistency to be

---

229.

731 Raban (2010), supra note 2465, p. 190.

732 Ibid., referring to Friedrich A. Hayek, 'The Road to Serfdom', (1944), p. 72.

733 Ibid., referring to Friedrich A. Hayek, 'Law, Legislation, and Liberty', (1973), p. 117.

734 Ibid., pp. 190-191.

maintained by legal reasoning through coherence has to do with the pursuit of fairness, in addition to the pursuit of legal certainty.

IV.11. CONCLUDING REMARK

***

Legal reasoning is a kind of work with a purpose, and the purpose is to make the case come out, in which, among other things, the law initially presents itself in relation to how-the judge-wants-to-come-out.[735] Rationalists assume that legal decisions are the product of rational decision-making process, emanating naturally from prescribed forms of logical inference, namely deduction, induction and analogies. However, Critical Legal Study questions the veracity of Rationalist-account and portrays the decision-making process as fundamentally inconsistent with these logical forms of inferences.[736] The distinction between the Rationalist and Critical positions can be understood by comparing their conceptualization of the term 'reasoning'.[737] Reasoning stands for the articulation of the rationale for a decision. The term 'reasoning' can also be used to denote the actual processes of inference, that is, the mental processes by which people advance from one state of belief to the next. While the Rationalist view implicitly equates the two senses of the term, the Critical view drives a wedge between them, asserting that legal decisions are driven by factors that are incompatible with or unrelated to the espoused premises, analogies, and facts.

Legal reasoning includes fact-findings, rule identification and rule application or interpretation. Interpretation or law application is constrained by legal normativity and prescriptivity. Interpretation through various methods, such as textual, contextual/systematic, teleological and precedential methods, might be subjected to methods/canons of interpretation. The methods of interpretation reflect (or ought to reflect) a certain systemic understanding of the normative preference and institutional constraints of the legal order in which courts operate.[738] It might be textual and/or contextual interpretation and the methods/canons of interpretation, which form legal normativity or legal internal constraint. Constraints upon judicial interpretation is supplied by 'disciplining rules' in

735 Kennedy (1986), supra note 2345, p. 526.
736 Simon (2004), supra note 2375, pp. 511-512.
737 Ibid., p. 514 [accompanying text omitted].
738 Maduro (2007), supra note 2105, p. 3.

the form of standard which are constitutive of the profession of judging.[739] What constrains judges in judicial interpretation is the need to be faithful to the original legal text which they are interpreting and supplementary norms of interpretation which are constitutive of the judicial role. Such an approach is capable of securing the coherence and integrity of legal order (by fitting individual decisions into a coherent whole) and judicial accountability (by constraining the power of courts in individual decisions and subjecting them to a normative scrutiny with regard to the normative preferences they attribute to their legal order).

In addition to normative preference or legal normativity or internal legal constraint, other constraints on law or legal reasoning from moral, justice, law's goal and other aspects of life (or other disciplines) also exist. Moral norms may accommodate legal norms to a considerable extent by requiring officials to obey even morally misguided laws, unless the laws are very seriously unjust.[740] But for an official who takes morality seriously, the question of the force of legal norms will always be a moral question.[741] Some members of society are substantive natural lawyers in the sense that they believe that putative legal systems that are grossly immoral are not legal systems, or that grossly immoral laws are not laws.[742] Iredell Jenkins says that there is actually an element of 'morals-in-the-law' important to its outcomes and the outcomes of the law,[743] although sometimes legal may yet be revolting to our sense of justice.[744] Morris Cohen concluded that it is humanly possible to banish the evaluational point of view from an adequate science of law. Such a science must come to ask: ' .. how are we to choose the basic premises of our legal system [and here] we enter the realm of ethics as the science of ultimate human ends.'[745]

Ethics or moral philosophy is where the notion of justice is addressed. Justice is a central part of ethics and should be given due consideration in our moral lives. Any moral decision treats all persons equally. If not, we must determine if the difference in treatment is justified. But justice is not the only principle to consider in making ethical decisions. Sometimes principles of justice may need to be overridden in favor of other kinds of moral claims such as rights or society's welfare. Nevertheless, justice is an expression of our mutual recognition of each other's basic dignity, and an acknowledgment that if we are to live together in an interdependent

739 Dickson (2010), supra note 2390, p. 8, 9 [footnote omitted].

740 Fallon (2009), supra note 2114, p. 1007 [accompanying text omitted].

741 Ibid., pp. 1007-1008.

742 Priel (2007), supra note 1530, p. 149 [footnote omitted].

743 Reid (1971), supra note 1629, p. 245.

744 Ibid., p. 243.

745 Ibid., p. 251.

community we must treat each other as equals.[746] Aristotle's account of justice as a virtue anchors individual justice in situational factors that are largely external to the just individual. Situations and communities are just, according to Aristotle, when individuals receive benefits according to their merits, or virtue; those most virtuous should receive more of whatever goods society is in a position to distribute (exemptions from various burdens or evils counting as goods). This is what we would today call a desert-based conception of social justice. A just individual is one who has rational insight into her own merits in various situations and who habitually (and without having to make heroic efforts to control contrary impulses) takes no more than what she merits, no more than her fair share of good things.[747]

As mentioned in Chapter III.4 on Legal Prescriptivity, law follows prescriptivity from moral and disciplines other than law. Moral issues and issues of other disciplinary studies, such as economics, sociology and medical science, as adopted by law become the issues of law, and this is admitted by prescriptive jurisprudence which together with descriptive jurisprudence constitute law in complete view.

***

Common law starts with experience, and experience determines the rule to be applied. The practice under the principle of *stare decisis* is *conservative*: it provides a relatively stable basis for replicable decisions. People need to be able to predict the actions of the courts and formulate plans accordingly. *Stare decisis* serves as a check against arbitrary judicial decisions. The practice is still reasonably progressive: it allows for the gradual evolution of the law. Careful judges distinguish bad decisions; new values and a new consensus can emerge in a series of decisions over time.[748] The French doctrine of *jurisprudence constante* recognizes that a line of prior consistent decisions may be persuasive evidence of the proper interpretation of the law.[749] Legal systems worldwide influence each other daily as individuals and entities do business and otherwise interact across jurisdictional lines, and courts across the world are called upon to interpret each other's laws and procedures.[750] Under EU law, the ECJ typically uses

746 Velasquez et al.(1990), supra note 1539, pp. 3-4.
747 LeBar & Slote (2010/2016), supra note 1569, p. 2.
748 Bartha (2013), supra note 2352, § 4.4.
749 Algero (2005), supra note 2171, p. 783 [footnote omitted].
750 Ibid., p. 780.

references to its own case law as arguments for justifying its decisions.[751] The ECJ uses its own case law to support the outcome in particular cases. Arguably, analogical reasoning based on previous case law plays a key role in ECJ reasoning. This approach ties individual cases to a longer line of cases and therefore may be argued to enhance consistency.

Analogical reasoning is of pragmatic justification.[752] Arguments by analogy complement arguments from precedent, in which they are used when the facts of a case do fall within the *ratio decidendi* of a precedent, as a basis for distinguishing the case at hand from precedent.[753] Analogy is closely related to *ratio decidendi* that incorporates the facts of the case.[754] Analogical reasoning helps to make the outcome of cases more predictable by giving weight to existing legal decisions and doctrines. The strongest justification for analogical reasoning lies in the value of replicability.[755] This is often put in terms of the importance of 'coherence' in the law.[756] Analogical reasoning supports legal certainty and coherence.[757] Analogy is widely recognized as playing an important heuristic role, as aids to discovery. Analogy has been employed, in a wide variety of settings and with considerable success, to *generate* insight and to formulate possible solutions to problems.[758] Analogy generates the *ratio decidendi* of the case at hand, through similarity mapping between precedent(s) and the case at hand. While generating *ratio decidendi* through similarity mapping, analogy at the same time transforms the *ratio decidendi* of precedent to the *ratio decidendi* of the case at hand, where both of them belong to the same rule category, therefore analogical reasoning is generative-transformational.

Civil law upholds that the general formal rule is to be deduced in order to generate particular rule. Civil law starts with general formal rule, and experienced is to be qualified as instance of general rule, in which experience is the operative fact of the rule. In Civil law countries, more clearly in the EU, as well as in Common law countries, deduction from general rule or legal principle is done to create *category exemplar(s)* or *prototype(s)*, but by the time a substantive particular rule is created, such a substantive particular rule is considered *a category exemplar* or *a prototype* in legal reasoning. This shows that deductive reasoning is also generative.

---

751 Paunio (2009), supra note 2477, p. 1486 [footnote omitted].
752 Lamond (2006), supra note 2397, p. 2.
753 Ibid., pp. 20-21.
754 Lucke (1989), supra note 2331, p. 42. See [1932] AC 562.
755 Lamond (2006), supra note 2527, p. 25.
756 Ibid., pp. 25-26.
757 Dikson (2010), supra note 2514, p. 22.
758 Bartha (2013), supra note 2523, p. 2.

Consistency may provide a rationale for a limited exercise of analogy.[759] In the process of evaluation for predictability and equality, consistency means that legal decisions must be in line with previous decisions, not contradicting them.[760] The claim of consistency is also sometimes put in terms of 'equality': to treat the later case differently to the first would be to fail to treat the parties equally.[761] Consistency is the necessary condition of coherence. The development of coherent theories is expected since precedent and analogical reasoning have been explained in manners that resemble holistic and coherence theories.[762] Arguments in favor of coherence normally emphasize its instrumental value. This is tied up with the replicability of legal decision-making.[763] The importance of 'coherence' in the law is often of analogical reasoning for replicability and certainty.[764] The struggle between legal certainty and equity is as old as the law itself. Only the labels have changed: while formerly discussion proceeded in terms of *ius strictum* and *ius aequum*, the expressions currently preferred, especially in Germany, are 'legal certainty' and 'justice (in individual cases)'. Equity is the need for deciding current, concrete disputes adequately, by giving due weight to the special and perhaps unique circumstances of each case.[765] There is general agreement that coherence must amount to more than logical consistency amongst propositions.[766] Legal coherence is normative coherence of legal justification. The basic idea is that legal system is as a consistent and coherent body of norms whose observance secures certain value goals which can intelligibly be pursued all together.[767] However, law is locally coherent.[768] Any plausible account of adjudication must make room for the kind of 'area-specific coherence' which is necessary in the case of law.[769] Even though principles are primarily relevant to determining the coherence of the legal system as a whole, [770] courts, in deciding a case according to law, should first of all interpret the existing law in order to establish a coherent view of some branch of the law or of a legal rule on certain particular issue.[771]

---

759 Lamond (2006), supra note 2530, p. 25.
760 Wahlgren (2009), supra note 2355, p. 262.
761 Lamond (2006), supra note 2534, p. 16.
762 Kress (1984), supra note 2399, p. 370.
763 Lamond (2006), supra note 2536, p. 25.
764 Ibid.
765 Neuhaus (1963), supra note 2476, p. 795.
766 Dickson (2010), supra note 2532, p. 16.
767 Balkin (1993), supra note 2389, p. 11 & n.19 [footnote omitted].
768 Ibid., n.24.
769 Dickson (2010), supra note 2541, p. 22.
770 Balkin (1993), supra note 2542, n.23.
771 Ibid., n.26.

Coherence theories constitute simply one particularly favored way of spelling out what has been called the dominant conception of precedent.[772] The notion of coherence in this book is coherence of justification in which a legal rule [as a concept or a rule category] is as a coherent set. A legal rule or a rule category on a particular issue [as a coherent set] generates many justified members through legal reasoning, and such justified members are the *rationes decidendi* in cases on the same particular issue. Coherence also transforms *ratio decidendi* into another *ratio decidendi* belonging to the same legal rule as a coherent set. Coherent effect is taken into account through similarity-mapping between a precedent or a bunch of precedents and the case at hand. Deduction from a general rule to a court decision every time judicial decision making is conducted may also be considered as within this coherence theoretical framework, but analogical logic in substantive law adjudication follows a more concrete, predictable and consistent process of judicial decision making and therefore guarantees more certainty and more fairness. Legal certainty has to do with procedural predictability and rational acceptability.[773] Substantive legal certainty essentially requires rationally acceptable legal decision-making and, consequently, substantively acceptable legal reasoning.[774]

To conclude this chapter, it is proven or revealed that legal reasoning in which analogy is employed and coherence is taken into account is generative-transformational. It is undeniable that analogy is generative-transformational, since analogical reasoning is done through similarity-matching where similarity is generative-transformational (see Chapters I.3.1 and I.3.2). Coherence has also been revealed generative-transformational (see Chapter I.3.4). Generative-transformational coherence happens by being supported by consistency for the sake of replicability, predictability, stability and certainty; and the claim of consistency is also sometimes put in terms of 'equality' [or 'justice'], and justice might be viewed as 'fairness'. (see, inter alia, Rawls). So, consistency and coherence brigde legal certainty and justice as fairness. The bridging forms continuum which makes legal certainty and fairness go along together [in the sense that they are not always contracdictory one against the other] at least to some certain extent or in certain particular circumstances. Legal reasoning through analogical logic and coherence, being generative-transformational or transformational-generative, enhances the pursuit of legal certainty and fairness.

772 Kress (1984), supra note 2537, pp. 401-402.

773 Paunio (2009), supra note 2526, pp. 1475-1476.

774 Ibid., p. 1479.

CHAPTER V

Legal Determination

V.1. JUDICIAL DECISION

V.1.1. OVERVIEW ON JUDICIAL DECISION

Goodhart pointed out that although nearly all the books on jurisprudence, from the time of Austin onward, had stated that it was necessary to distinguish between the general principle of a case, which constitutes the *ratio decidendi*, and the concrete decision, few attempts have been made to state any rules by which these general principles can be determined.[1] The concrete decision is binding between the parties to it, but it is the abstract *ratio decidendi* which alone has the force of law as regards the world at large.[2] A distinction must be drawn between the legal principle for which the reasoning in a decision stands and the binding force of the order made in the case. When the High Court of Australia overrules a previous legal decision of the Court, the *ratio decidendi* of that decision will no longer be binding as a legal precedent. However, this will not affect the validity and effect of the actual orders and judgment that have been made in the case whose legal principle has been overruled. The reasons for this were outlined in *Ruddock v. Taylor* (2005) 79 ALJR 1534, per Kirby J at [169]-[172][3]: "Before a party – or the community – is excused from compliance with the orders of this Court it is necessary for the Court to examine the question and itself set aside, or vary, any orders earlier made, if that course is justified. No person may decide for themselves to ignore orders of this Court or treat them as invalid so long as such orders remain in force".

Olivecrona proceeds to argue that the actual role of the courts is that of being a lawgiver for particular cases. The legal rules, whether laid down through acts of legislation or evolved in some other way, cannot supply exact patterns of behavior for every contingency.[4] There is always a margin

1 Goodhart (1959), supra note 2134, p. 118.

2 Lucke (1989), supra note 2529, p. 38, referring to Paton, 'Jurisprudence', (1946), p. 159; Salmond, 'Jurisprudence', (7th edn 1924), p. 201.

3 Michael Kirby, 'International Academy of Comparative Law Conference', July 17, 2006, in Precedent-Report on Australia , pp. 3-4.

4 Torben Spaak, 'Karl Olivecrona on Judicial Law-Making' 2, in Ratio Juris, 2009, Vol. 22, Issue 4: pp.483-498 ["2009a"], quoting Olivecrona (1971), supra note 1146, p.211.

for deciding which of two or more alternatives are to be deemed lawful. There are *operative facts* to be classified by the court under names such as contract, promise, payment, marriage, etc. This is a step in the application of the law. It requires something more than ascertaining some facts; these facts *have also to be evaluated*, with the result that the court either declares them to constitute a contract, a promise, a payment, a marriage, etc., or rejects the proposed classification. Likewise, evaluations are made with regard to the *law*. Texts and pronouncements are evaluated when they are classified as laws and precedents.[5] In connection with judicial decisions where legal classification occurs, Sunstein holds that judges might agree on the outcomes of individual cases without having agreed upon which general theory best accounts for those outcomes. Judges might agree on a general principle, but not on what that principle requires in particular cases. Judges might agree on a 'mid-level' principle without having agreed about both the general theory underlying it and particular cases falling under it.[6] Olivecrona's stance that courts necessarily create law is both similar to and different from Kelsen. Kelsen, as is well known, holds that every act of judicial decision-making is both an act of law application and an act of judicial law-making.[7] Kelsen views judicial decisions in the context of sharp distinction between reason and volition, between cognition and decision, and between science and politics. A judicial decision is an individual norm, being the final goal of legal judgment. Any judicial decision is the act of will, not of cognition.[8] Kelsen (1960) said: "The judgment that an act of human behavior, performed in time and space, is 'legal' (or 'illegal') is the result of a specific, namely normative, interpretation".[9]

Every judgment of normative conformity is an interpretation of norms, and more than one possible meanings might appear in the interpretation of a norm. S.L. Paulson is of the opinion that any judicial decision is not merely the act of cognition, but it is also the act of will in which judges' will determines which one of those meanings to pick up. Judges cannot identify a norm without determining its content. In concrete cases, judges choose a certain meaning of the content, and the general

5 Ibid., p. 3, referring to Olivecrona (1971), Ibid., p. 214 (Emphasis added).

6 Dickson (2010), supra note 2544, p. 11, referring to C. Sunstein, 'Legal Reasoning and Political Conflict', (New York & Oxford: Oxford University Press, 1996), p. 36.

7 Spaak (2009a), supra note 2553, n.13, citing Kelsen (1960), supra note 1799, p. 347.

8 Viola (1995), supra note 1820, p. 252, referring to Kelsen (1960), Ibid., p. 244-245.

9 Wahlgren (2009), supra note 2535, p. 214, referring to John Dickinson, 'Legal Rules: Their Function in the Process of Decision', in University of Pennsylvania Law Review, Vol. 79 (1931), pp. 833-868 (p. 849).

frame of a norm does not construct the meaning as chosen, but the chosen meaning tends to construct the general frame. Therefore, the judgment of normative conformity is in the field of choice and, consequently, not of truth.[10] The truth is not in question in judicial decisions and therefore judicial decisions are not in the field of truth. The issue is directly of the concern of the right application of a normative criterion and its use as a guide for a particular action for the sake of justification based on legal reasoning. The target of this legal reasoning is the acceptability of judicial decisions for the legal system considered, not the truth. Rightness and truth seem to be separated strongly. Even though Kelsen and Paulson [and some other writers] hold that judicial decisions are not in the field of truth, Viola argues that in this matter judges believe they play the truth-game through grasping a truth and making true affirmations. This is the meaning of the *jus dicere*.[11] Reasons of a judicial decision, Aarnio says, are not entirely of 'legal' dimension, but the 'legal' dimension is only a part of them. Objective criteria of judgment, according to Tapani Klami, can be found in the general rules of logic and argumentation, common sense, the framework of culture and consensus concerning experience and values, the recourse to probability, and so on. Judges are not given a delegation of arbitrary power in using reasons, but they are to consider those objective criteria.[12] Viola argues that judges should not decide according to his/her personal opinion but should apply pre-existent normative criteria.[13] The *Sollen* of an action is its measure or its ideal model. Differently, the attitudinal model postulates the Supreme Court justices consistently vote to decide cases in ways that directly reflect their ideological values.[14] Joseph Francis is a Realist, with the thesis that a judge first decides what conclusion he wishes to come to, and then later develops arguments to justify the conclusion. Such operative facts constituting the legal category will depend upon the judge's behavioral patterns in which there are things, such as, the legal

10 Viola (1995), supra note 2557, p. 254, referring to Kelsen (1960), supra note 2557; S.L. Paulson, 'Kelsen on Legal Interpretation', in "Legal Studies", 10, 2, (1990), pp. 136-152.

11 Ibid., p. 259.

12 Ibid., p. 253, referring to Aarnio (1987), supra note 2463; H. Tapani Klami-J. Sorvettula-M. Hatakka, 'Evidence and Legal Reasoning: On the Intertwinement of the Probable and the Reasonable', in "Law and Philosophy" 10 (1991), pp. 73-107.

13 Ibid., p. 262.

14 Fallon (2009), supra note 2515, p. 1003. See SEGAL & SPAETH (1993), supra note 2079, p. 228; JEFFREY A. SEGAL & HAROLD SPAETH, 'THE SUPREME COURT AND THE ATTITUDINAL MODEL REVISITED'; HAROLD J. SPAETH & JEFFREY A. SEGAL, 'MAJORITY RULE OR MINORITY WILL: ADHERENCE TO PRECEDENT ON THE U.S. SUPREME COURT' (1999). According to SEGAL & SPAETH 1993), Ibid., p. 364, the impact of "internal and external non-attitudinal factors ....appears to be minimal.

consequences the judge wants to happen, the judge's sense of justice, and his sense of contemporary values.[15] As Segal and Spaeth pithily summarize their causal theory, '[William] Rehnquist vote[d] the way he [did] because he [was] extremely conservative; [Thurgood] Marshall voted the way he did because he [was] extremely liberal'.[16]

Any judicial decision outlines the facts, talks about evidence and refers to the legal rule. The legal rule may be statutory or precedent on which the judicial decision is grounded. It is the legal reasoning or the *ratio decidendi* which constitutes the consideration behind judicial decision.[17] Judicial decisions are justified by legal process. Judicial decisions, says Viola, are to be shown as being grounded on the rational and consistent application of legal rules.[18] It is the truth to which a judicial decision belongs. The tradition of legal process is where the pursue for the truth in judicial decision is rooted, and the movement towards the truth sustains the conviction that a court's judgment sees the issues as a clear-cut either/or, black and white affair. Declaring a winner and a loser is an important feature of European courts' judgments. R.W.M. Dias puts an emphasis on the prescription of relevant rules.[19] Any judicial decision in dispute is to determine which party's actual behavior is in conformity with the prescription in the relevant legal rule and which party's actual behavior is not.

Compared with Common law judgments, Civil law judgments are more formalistic and shorter, comprising the *motifs* (reasons) and the *dispositif* (order). In Common law judgments, the facts are extensively exposed and compared with the facts of previous cases, and the specific rule of law which is relevant to the facts of the present case is then decided or created. Judges in Civil law tradition first identify the relevant legal principles and then verify if the facts support their application, and only the

15 Scofield (2005), supra note 2264, referring to Joseph F. Francis, "Three Cases on Possession – Some Further Observation", in 14 St. Louis Law Review (1928), p. 22, 23.

16 Fallon (2009), supra note 2563, p. 1003, citing SEGAL & SPAETH (1993), supranote 2563, p. 65.

17 The Australasian Legal Information Institute (AustLII) – Free, comprehensive and independent access to Australasian Law, A joint facility of UTS and UNSW Faculties of Law, last update 28 August 2018. .

18 Viola (1995), supra note 2559, p. 250, citing P.G. Stein,'Judgments in the European Legal Tradition'in La sentenza in Europa, Metodo, tecnica e stile: Padova 1988, pp. 27-41 (p. 27).

19 Ibid., pp. 249-250, referring to R.W.M. Dias, 'Autopoiesis and the Judicial Process', in Rechtstheorie 11 (1980), pp. 257-283 (p. 258), and citing Montesquieu.

facts relevant to the advanced principle thus need be stated.[20] William Tetley holds that Civil law relies rather on the courts to choose or even create the appropriate remedy in setting the rights and obligations in judging lawsuits, and there is no clearly defined system of remedies. In Common law the courts having jurisdiction in their decisions set the rights and obligations *au fur et a mesure* that they are called to rule on them. Specific rights can be found only through precedents.[21] Judgments in Commom law system have paradigmatically five aspects, which are a recitation of the facts of the case, an identification of the legal issue (dispute) to be resolved, the reasoning over the appropriate resolution of such issue (dispute), the ruling resolving the issue, and the result or outcome of the case, following the ruling.[22] Judicial decisions in Civil law system should follow the principles of law as expressly or implicitly contained in the Code through judicial process which takes the legal methodology serving the achievement of practical goals. Civilian legal methodology is, therefore, 'important not only for judges but for all legal scholars who wish to assist judges in their functions'.[23] Legal decisions such as judicial decisions and transaction lawyers' decisions give rise to more foreseeable effects. Legal decisions as existing due to legal reasoning process may be more explicit and visible, in the sense that legal decisions have direct effects [due to formal reasons]. Challenge to legal decisions is required in order to motivate the transformation of such legal decisions. In addition to the *judex factie* and *judex juris*, legal decisions should also take into account the consequences thereof.[24] Gottlieb says that every decision necessarily leads to some reasonably foreseeable consequences for the parties and for those closely associated with them.

20 Tetley (1999/2000), supra note 2000, para. V.6.

21 Ibid., § V.14.

22 Lamond (2006), supra note 2538, p. 5, 6. For more detailed discussion, see D.N. MacCormick, 'Why Cases Have Rationes and What These Are', in Goldstein 1987 ["MacCormick 1978a"], p. 170ff.

23 Dennis (1993), supra note 2157, p. 5, referring to Heck (1948b), supra note 1907.

24 Wahlgren (2009), supra note 2558, p. 203, 246. Cf. Gottlieb (1968), supra note 1259, p. 74.

V.1.2. RATIO DECIDENDI

***

Ratio decidendi has been touched in Chapter IV.10.1 on 'Analogy in Legal Reasoning' and Chapter V.1.1. on 'Overview on Judicial Decision'. *Ratio decidendi* or the *ratio* is to be understood, and it is the understanding (*verstehen*) that captures the *ratio*, since determining the *ratio* is not a mechanical exercise, but it involves understanding what was decided in a case. The understanding is the one of the judgment and of the focused area of law.[25] Therefore, the *ratio* of the case at hand is the understanding of it. The *ratio* of a case represents the 'holding' or 'ruling', – it is the aspect of the case which is binding on later courts. The rule laid down in the earlier case is represented by the *ratio*.[26] The precedent court's own justification for its decision plays an important role in determining the level of abstraction of the factors in the *ratio*, and for providing arguments for a narrower or wider reading of those factors. The *ratio* of the precedent sets the outer limit of what is binding on later courts.[27]

Classically, the *ratio decidendi* of a case is 'the principle of law propounded by the judge as the basis of his decision', or in other words, the classical theory holds that the *ratio* is the rule or principle that the court deciding a case considers necessary for the result reached in the case.[28] The *ratio* is the underlying principle of judicial decision [Salmond, Jurisprudence, 7th edn., 1924, at 201].[29] The *ratio* was the principle of law which the judge considered necessary to the decision [Paton, Jurisprudence (1946), at 159]. Following the definitions by Paton and Salmond, the *ratio* of the case at hand is the generality expression of the case itself, without taking the facts of the case at hand into account in understanding the *ratio*.[30] In precedents, it is the *ratio decidendi* that represents the rules (the proposition of law) laid down in precedents. It is the *ratio decidendi* which is the 'holding' or 'ruling' that is binding upon later cases.[31] A technique

25 Lamond (2006), supra note 2571, p. 13.

26 Ibid., p. 7.

27 Ibid., p. 13.

28 Lucke (1989), supra note 2551, p. 38, referring to 'Ratio Decidendi and the House of Lords', (1957), 20 MLR 124.

29 Ibid., referring to Paton (1946), supra note 2551, p. 159; Salmond (1924), supra note 2551, p. 201.

30 Ibid., p. 39. See [1901] AC 495, 506.

31 Lamond (2006), supra note 2574, p. 7, referring to Raz (1979), supra note

of finding the governing doctrine of a case was provided by Eugene Wambaugh, a prominent Englsih legal scholar during the late nineteenth and early twentieth centuries: "In order to make the test, let him first frame carefully the supposed proposition of law. Let him then insert in the proposition a word reversing its meaning. Let him then inquire whether, if the court had concieved the new proposition to be good, and had had it in mind, the decision could have been the same. If the answer be affirmative, then, however excellent the original proposition may be, the case is not a precedent for that proposition, but if the answer be negative the case is a precedent for the original proposition and possibly for other propositions also".[32] In short, when a case turns on only one point the proposition or doctrine of the case, the reason of the decision, the *ratio decidendi*, must be a general rule without which the case must have been decided otherwise. Wambaugh's method, based on principles of judicial restraint, remains useful for determining which portions of a decision warrant precedential respect. He provides four principles to guide the search for a *ratio decidendi*: (i) the Court's duty to decide the very Case: Hypothetical Cases – the first key to the discovery of the doctrine of a case is found in the principle that the court making the decision is under a duty to decide the very case presented and has no authority to decide any other; (ii) the Court's duty to follow a general Rule ....[T]he second key to the discovery of propositions of law, is the principle that the court must pass upon each case precisely as it would pass upon a similar case, that is to say, in accordance with a general rule; (iii) [t]he very Words of the Court not the Doctrine of the Case – accordingly, the third key to the discovery of the doctrine of reported case is the principle, or rather the caution, that the doctrine of the case is not the language of the judges. In so far as the words of the judges go beyond the precise doctrine necessary to the decision, laying down a different rule or a broader rule, they are mere *dicta*; (iv) Doctrine in the Mind of the Court: Necessity for Deliberation: ...this fourth principle is, that a case is not a precedent for any proposition that was neither consciously nor unconsciously in the mind of the court. It is a duty of the court to deliberate.. What makes decisions of value as precedents is the fact that they are based upon reasoning and not upon chance. If it can be shown that there was no deliberation, it follows that the case is of no authority for any proposition whatever.

1833; MacCormick (1978), supra note 1970, (especially 82-6, 213-28), Alexander (1989), supra note 1296; Schauer (1989), supra note 1296, pp. 467-471; F. Schauer, 'Playing by the Rules: A Philosophical Examination of Rule-Based Decision-Making in Law and in Life, (Oxford: Oxford University Press, 1991), pp. 174-187.

32 Thurmon (1992), supra note 2401, pp. 423-424, referring to Eugene Wambaugh, 'The Study of Cases', (Boston: Little, Brown & Co., 1984, second ed.), § 11-12 [footnote and accompanying text omitted].

The 'classical theory' regards the *ratio decidendi* as the principle of law propounded by the judge as the basis of his decision, and Montrose accepts that the 'classical theory' be correct.[33] Cross and Harris articulated the classical theory: 'The ratio decidendi of a case is any rule of law expressly or impliedly treated by the judge as a necessary step in reaching his conclusion, having regard to the line of reasoning adopted by him, or a necessary part of his direction to the jury'.[34] However, in *Quinn v. Leatham* [1901] AC 495, 506, Lord Halsbury gave an affirmation that the *ratio* should be understood with consideration of the facts of the case.[35] *Quinn v. Leatham* [1901] AC 495, 506 affirmed the maxim as follows: "Every judgment must be read as applicable to the particular facts proved or assumed to be proved, since the generality of the expressions which may be found there are not intended to be expositions of the whole law but governed and qualified by the particular facts of the case in which such expressions are to be found".[36] *The ratio decidendi* of a precedent consists of a single, unique proposition of law 'without which the case must have been decided otherwise'. Rupert Cross illustrated the untenability of this view with the example of *Donoghue v. Stevenson*, a case holding the manufacturer of bottled ginger beer containing a decomposed snail liable to the ultimate consumer.[37] Lord Atkin's opinion contained two propositions of law justifying the decision. The first was very general: 'A party must take reasonable care to avoid acts or omissions which he can reasonably foresee would be likely to injure persons ....closely and directly affected by his act.... The second was much more specific: A manufacturer of products, which he sells in such a form as to show that he intends them to reach the ultimnate consumer in the form of in which they left him with no reasonably possibility of intermediate examination....owes a duty to the consumer to take... reasonable care'.

In 1928 Goodhart's viewed the notion of *ratio decidendi* from the perspective of the classical theory. At one point Goodhart states that it is impossible to find a clear *ratio decidendi* in *Bridges v. Hawkesworth*, (1851) 15 Jur 1079, 21 LJQB 75.[38] Then, Goodhart wrote his famous article

33 Goodhart (1959), supra note 2134, p. 119.

34 Scofield (2005), supra note 2564, p. 312, referring to Cross & Harris (1991), supra note 2125, p. 72.

35 Lucke (1989), supra note 2577, p. 39. See [1901] AC 495, 506.

36 Ibid. See [1901] AC 495, 506.

37 Branting (1993), supra note 2143, p. 6, referring to Rupert Cross (1979), 'Precedent in English Law', third edition, (Oxford: Oxford University Press, 1979).

38 Scofield (2005), supra note 2583, p. 312. See A.L. Goodhart, "Three Cases on Possession", in 3 Cambridge Law Journal (1928), p. 195. This article also appears in Goodhart, 'Essays in Jurisprudence and the Common Law', (Cambridge

'Determining the *Ratio Decidendi* of a Case' in 1930. His theory is that the *ratio* consists of the facts the judge in the precedent case believed were material, and the judge's decision based on those facts.[39] The 'rule' for which the decision is binding is not the precedent court's ruling, but something narrower – the 'material facts' that were 'necessary' for the result of the case.[40] According to Goodhart, the authoritative *ratio decidendi* of a case is the proposition or propositions required to reach the result in that case given the facts as seen by the judge.[41] Goodhart stated, 'The judge, therefore, reaches a conclusion upon the facts as he sees them. It is on these facts that he bases his judgment, and not on any others. It follows from our task in analyzing a case is not to state the facts and the conclusion, but to state the material facts as seen by the judge and his conclusion based on them. It is by his choice of the material facts that the judge creates law'.[42] Goodhart agrees with Francis' claim that the *ratio decidendi* is not necessarily found in a judge's statement of the law, but he then adds: 'This, however, does not in any way conflict with my view that, in determining the principle of a case, we are bound by the judge's statement of the material facts on which he has based his judgment'.[43] For Goodhart, what judges say about what they consider to be the material facts of the cases they decide is important.[44] When it comes to facts, according to Goodhart, the judge actively 'chooses those which he considers material and rejects those which are immaterial, and then bases his conclusion upon the material ones'.[45] It would be odd not to be able to find a *ratio decidendi* under the Goodhart theory.[46] It would be something like: Fact I: Someone dropped his or her bank notes at D's premises. Fact II: P found the bank notes while doing business at D's premises. Fact III: The owner of the bank notes cannot be found. Conclusion: The court must give title to the bank notes to P.

University Press, 1931), p. 197.

39 Ibid., referring to Goodhart (1930a), supra note 2143, p. 161. This article also appears in Goodhart (1931), Ibid., pp. 1-26.

40 Lamond (2006), supra note 2580, p. 10. See Goodhart (1930a), Ibid.; Goodhart (1959), supra note 2582; Burton (1995), supra note 2134, pp. 25-58, 60-5 on 'case-specific facts'; Eisenberg (1988), supra note 2340, pp. 51-54, on 'minimalist' and 'result-centred' techniques.

41 Thurmon 1992, supra note 2581, p. 424, referring to Goodhart (1930a), Ibid., p. 169.

42 Goodhart (1930b), supra note 2144, p. 119; Lucke (1989), supra note 2584, p. 49, see Mirehouse v. Rennell (1832) 8 Bing 490, 515.

43 Scofield (2005), supra note 2587, p. 321, referring to Goodhart (1930a), supra note 2590, p. 166. N.20.

44 Ibid., p. 322, referring to Goodhart (1930a), Ibid., p. 169.

45 Ibid., referring to Goodhart (1930a), Ibid., p. 169.

46 Ibid., p. 313.

Providing a carefully worded formulation of the *ratio*, what matters is the substance of the factors considered in reaching the decision, not the particular language in which they are couched.[47] Although the idea of the *ratio decidendi* is a staple of legal practice, it is notable that it is a construct from a precedent rather than an explicit feature of most legal judgments. Judgments are highly discursive texts and very rarely identify their own *rationes*. What is more, even if a court chooses to explicitly formulate the *ratio* of its decision, this precise formulation is not itself regarded as binding on later courts.[48] What the *ratio* provides is a statement of the factors which the court regarded as providing the reasons that were crucial for reaching its result. So the *ratio* represents the view of the court that those facts spoke in favor of the outcome, and that they were not defeated by any combination of the other factors present in the case.[49] MacCormick holds the *ratio* is the ruling which is expressly or implied in judicial decision.[50] This approach makes use of the fact that decisions do not provide canonical formulations of the *ratio* to argue that the *ratio* is not to be identified with the court's stated ruling on the issue. The effect of such an approach is to narrow what is regarded as binding in the case to those facts which were crucial to the actual outcome, rather than the stated ruling applied to those facts. It goes against general legal practice, which usually does identify the *ratio* with the ruling made by the precedent court.[51] Edmund Morgan also argues that the *ratio* is the ruling in judicial decision.[52]

Cross (1979) indicates the *ratio* should be incorporated with the facts of the case; Gardner (1987, at 47) holds that the representation of the facts and the outcome are important in judicial decision. Gardner argues

---

47 Lamond (2006), supra note 2589, p. 14.

48 Ibid., p. 8. See S. Perry, 'Judicial Obligation, Precedent and the Common Law', in Oxford Journal of Legal Studies 7 (1987), pp. 215-257 (p. 235-237); Schauer (1989), supra note 1296, p. 455; A.W.B. Simpson, 'The Common Law and Legal Theory' (1973), reprinted in Legal Theory and Legal History: Essays on the Common Law, (Oxford: Hambledon Press, 1987), p. 372; M. Moore, 'Precedent, Induction, and Ethical Generalization', in Goldstein 1987, pp. 185-186; J. Stone, 'Precedent and Law: Dynamics of Common Law Growth', (Sydney: Butterworths, 1985), pp. 123-129.

49 Ibid., p. 13.

50 Hinchy (2006), supra note 2418, p. 189 (fn.14).

51 Lamond (2006), supra note 2596, pp. 10-11. See A.W.B. Simpson, 'The Ratio Decidendi of a Case and Doctrine of Precedent', in A.G. Gust (ed.), Oxford Essays in Jurisprudence, (Oxford: Oxford University Press, 1961), pp. 168-169; MacCormick (1978), supra note 2580, pp. 82-83 & MacCormick (1987a), supra note 2571, pp. 157-158; Raz (1979), supra note 2580, p. 184; Eisenberg (1988), supra note 2589, pp. 51-61.

52 Branting (1993), supra note 2586, p. 5, referring to Edmund M. Morgan, 'Introduction to the Study of Law', Chicago, 1948, second edition.

that cases should be studied not so much for their doctrinal statements as for ..their 'operative facts', and Gilmore's statement is that one should never quote general language from an opinion, divorced from the factual context in which the language was delivered.[53] Lucke concludes that the *ratio decidendi*, correctly understood, incorporates the actual facts of the precedent case rather than some generalized version of those facts.[54] Following the definitions in *Quinn*, by Goodhart, Cross, Gardner, Lucke, and Gilmore, the understanding of the *ratio* should take the facts into account. The *ratio decidendi* should be grounded on the specific facts of the case. Typical expressions of the centrality of precedents' specific facts include: (1) [I]t is the facts, and not the general rules of law found in precedents ...which serve as the foundation of the decisional process;[55] (2) Judgments must be read in light of the facts of the case in which they are delivered;[56] and (3) It is clear that the most important part of a representation for cases is the representation of the facts and the outcome.

As already mentioned, Goodhart has pointed out that it is necessary to distinguish between the general principle of a case, which constitutes the *ratio decidendi*, and the concrete decision.[57] The concrete decision is binding between the parties to it, but it is the abstract *ratio decidendi* which alone has to be followed by later cases.[58] A distinction must be drawn between the legal principle for which the reasoning in a decision stands and the binding force of the order made in the case (*Ruddock v. Taylor* (2005) 79 ALJR 1534, per Kirby J at [169]-[172]).[59]

Ratio decidendi is to be understood as the facts plus decision of a case [or the principle], as the legal insight of a case, [and as justified

---

53 Ibid., pp. 7-8, referring to A. Gardner, 'An Artificial Intelligence Approach in Legal Reasoning', (Cambridge, MA: Bradford Books/MIT Press, 1987), p. 47, citing Cross (1979), supra note 2586; L.K. Branting & B.W. Porter, 'Rules and precedents as complementary warrants,' in Proceedings of Ninth National Conference on Artificial Intelligence, (Anaheim: AAAI Press/MIT Press, 1991); J.C. Cueto-Rua, 'Judicial Methods of Interpretation of the Law', (The Publications Institute, Paul M. Hebert Law Center, Lousiana State University, 1981), p. 56; Cross (1979), Ibid., p. 44.

54 Lucke (1989), supra note 2584, p. 51. See [1932] AC 599 [accompanying text, see supra note 2334].

55 Branting (1993), supra note 2601, pp. 7-8, citing Cueto-Rua (1981), supra note 2602, p. 56.

56 Ibid., p. 8, referring to Cross (1979), supra note 2602, p. 44.

57 Goodhart (1959), supra note 2582, p. 118, referring to Goodhart (1931), supra note 2587.

58 Lucke (1989), supra note 2603, p. 38, referring to Paton (1946), supra note 2578, p. 159; Salmond (1924), supra note 2578, p. 201.

59 Kirby (2006), supra note 2552, pp. 3-4.

members of a rule category as a coherent set, as viewed in this book]. The *ratio* has its effect on the case at hand [even if the *ratio* has been overruled], and has its authority [if not having been overruled] as a legal rule to be followed in later cases, through the principle of *stare decisis* in Common law jurisdiction and through the principle of *jurisprudence constante* in Civil law jurisdiction, particularly in the EU law or the ECJ case-law.

V.1.3. DICTA

Obiter dicta represents other statements and views expressed in the judgment, and *obiter dicta* are not binding on later cases.[60] An *obiter dictum*, in the language of the law, is a gratuitous or given opinion, an individual impertinence, which, whether it be wise or foolish, right or wrong, bindeth none-not even the lips that utter it.[61] *Obiter dicta* can be influential even in the absence of a real decision. US Supreme Court Justice Morrison Waite, in 1886, made some remarks prior to verbal arguments in a case. His remarks were captured and included in the case's transcript, and have since become the bases for the legal doctrine that 'juristic person' – that is, non-human legal entities like corporations and partnerships – are entitled to the protections of the US Constitution's 14th Amendment.[62] When a court has multiple members and a dissent is issued, the dissent itself also has the status of *obiter dicta* because it is a statement issued by the court that does not have official legal weight. Although they do not carry any legal weight in and of themselves, *obiter dicta* are sometimes cited in later opinions and decisions, whether they are identified as such or not. While they do not carry official legal weight, *obiter dicta* can be influential. For instance, a judge, in imposing sentence, might point to specific elements of the crime or the convict's history that justifies a harsh or lenient sentence. These statements are not generally necessary for the imposition of sentence, and are thus *obiter dicta*, but will be thoroughly reviewed both by the prosecutors and defense attorneys presenting cases before judges in the future. Another example of the significance of *obiter dicta*, as shown by Dale Marshall, is cases where courts decline to accept a case because of lack of jurisdiction.[63] Having declined to rule on the merits, courts sometimes remark on the merits of the case. These remarks have no official standing but still significant as official utterances of the court.

---

60 Lamond (2006), supra note 2600, p. 7.

61 Fordham Law Review, Volume 7 / Issue 2, Article 9, 1938, Obiter Dicta, citing Birrel (1885), 'Obiter Dicta', title page.

62 Dale Marshall, 'What Is Obiter Dicta?', edited by Kriten Osborne, Last Modified March 10, 2014 (Conjecture Corporation, 2003-2014).

63 Ibid.

There are two types of *dicta*, however: *judicial dicta* and *obiter dicta*. The former carry greater authority than what are commonly referred to as *mere dicta*; the latter are *mere dicta*. The failure of some judges to understand the distinction between *judicial dicta* and *obiter dicta* has led to some confusion in case law. *Obiter dicta* are 'by the way' statements.[64] Since courts usually do not give as serious consideration to the statements they make in passing, the statements do not constitute the binding part of a judicial precedent.[65] But *judicial dicta*, as observed by Robert Scofield, are the product of a comprehensive discussion of legal issues and therefore should be granted greater weight than *obiter dicta*.[66] *Judicial dicta* should be followed unless they are erroneous or there are particularly strong reasons for not doing so.

An example of *judicial dicta* eventually becoming a *ratio decidendi* occurred in the cases of *In re Prewitt*, 8 Cal. 3rd 470 (1972) and *In re Oslon*, 37 Cal. App. 3rd 783 (1974).[67] These *judicial dicta* in *Prewitt* were to become a holding in *Oslon* (see *In re Oslon*, 37 Cal App. 3rd 783, 790 (1974). The *Oslon* court stated that 'the rationale of *Prewitt*' is that a policy of not giving documents to inmates is unfair because an inmate cannot prepare his or her case or challenge false or inaccurate information unless the inmate learns what information prison officials are considering in determining the length of incarceration or whether to grant parole (*In re Oslon*, 37 Cal App. 3rd , p. 789). The *Oslon* court stated: "We are disposed to accept the foregoing rationale of *Prewitt* as applicable to the present case even though the statements alluded to do not possess the force of a square holding. They are persuasive and were concurred in by the whole court after careful consideration. Accordingly, they are entitled to great weight (*In re Oslon*, 37 Cal App. 3rd at 789 – emphasis added)".[68]

In Australia, a review of the case law reveals that in most of the cases decided prior to the decision of *Farah Constructions Pty Ltd v. Say-Dee Pty Ltd*, handed down in 2007, in which the precedential effect of High Court *dicta* was discussed, lower courts tended to refer to High Court *dicta* as potentially highly persuasive, but insisted on their freedom to depart from such *dicta*. In what follows, we call this the 'traditional' or 'orthodox' view on account of its consistency with the traditional understanding of the rule of *stare decisis* as a rule that attaches only to the *rationes decidendi* of previous decisions. The traditional view was endorsed in the High Court

64 Robert G. Scofield, 'The Distinction between Judicial Dicta and Obiter Dicta', practice tip, in LOS ANGELES LAWYER / OCTOBER 2002, p. 17. See Cross & Harris (1991), supra note 2583, p. 41.

65 Ibid. See Cross & Harris (1991), Ibid., pp. 40-41.

66 Ibid. [accompanying text omitted].

67 Ibid., p. 18.

68 Ibid.

as early as 1909 in *The Federated Saw Mill, Timber Yard and General Woodworkers Employees' Association of Australasia; James Moore and Sons Pty Ltd*, ([1909] 8 CLR 465, 485), where Griffith CJ noted that in respect of 'question ...of an abstract character' or 'hypothetical... questions of law', [a]ny opinions expressed by the [High] Court ...can only be *obiter dicta* of more or less weight, but having no binding authority. More recently, in *Garcia v. National Australia Bank Ltd* ([1998] 194 CLR 395, 418), Kirby J reiterated the traditional view, stating that 'courts are not bound in law by ...*obiter dicta* or analysis that is not essential to the holding of the Court sustaining its order'.[69] An analysis of cases decided in lower courts since *Farah* reveals that lower courts appear more reluctant than before to adhere to the traditional view of the precedential effect of High Court *dicta* because they believe that in *Farah* the High Court has told them that they have a duty of obedience to its *dicta*, at least in certain circumstances. Turning first to post-*Farah* cases in which lower courts have regarded themselves as bound, obligated or required to follow High Court *dicta*, none are clearer than *Zotti v. Australian Associated Motor Insurers Ltd* ([2009] 54MVR 111), a decision of the NSW Court of Appeal - 2009. The case turned on whether an injury that the appellant had incurred as a result of a bicycle accident was sustained 'during....a collision' within the meaning of the *Motor Accidents Compensation Act 1999* (NSW). In the case of *Allianz Australia Insurance Ltd v. GSF Australia Pty Ltd* ([2005] 221 CLR 568), a majority of the High Court had issued *dicta* touching on the question. According to Spigelman CJ, *Farah* stood for the proposition that 'this court is obliged to follow ...the clearly expressed *dicta* of the High Court even if not part of the *ratio decidendi*' (*Zotti* [2009] 54 MVR 111, 116). Allsop P agreed. Allsop P would have preferred to decide the case in accordance with principles at odds with the *dicta* issued in *Allianz*. However, he did not regard himself as free to decide the case '[u]nconstrained by authority', and therefore followed the *dicta* in question (*Zotti* [2009] 54 MVR 119). And Campbell JA took a similar view, indicating that his preference would have been to depart from the *dicta* from *Allianz*, '[h]ad we been unconstrained by authority' (*Zotti* [2009] 54 MVR 129). The fact that the three judges who considered whether or not to follow the *dicta* from *Allianz* felt duty-bound, in light of *Farah*, to defer High Court *dicta* with which they expressed misgivings in the circumstances of the case is strong evidence of the effect that *Farah* is having on lower courts. That the judges deferred to the *dicta* from *Allianz* invoking the language of 'obligation', 'constraint'

69 Mathew Harding and Ian Malkin, 'The High Court of Australia's Obiter Dicta and Decision-Making in Lower Courts', in Sydney Law Review, Vol. 34:239, 2012, p. 243. See (1909) 8 CLR 465, 485 and (1998) 194 CLR 395, 418.

and 'authority' reinforces this point.[70] Mathew Harding and Ian Malkin[71] conclude that *Farah Constructions Pty Ltd v. Say-Dee Pty Ltd* has brought about the 'profound shift' that Justice Keith Mason, President of the New South Wales Court of Appeal, referred to in his retirement speech. The case law reveals that Mason's assessment of the impact of *Farah* was prescient. Most notably, in the pre-*Farah* cases, lower courts tended to take the view that they ought to treat High Court *dicta* with the utmost respect, but that they had no duty of obedience to such *dicta*; in the post-*Farah* world, the tendency appears to be to accept that a duty of obedience to High Court *dicta* arises, at least in some circumstances.

V.1.4. DISTINCTION AND PROCEDURAL DIMENSION OF COURT JUDGMENT

***

Broadly speaking, judgments will either be final or interlocutory. Interlocutory judgments are not entitled to preclusive effect unless they are final and 'on the merits'. Typically, such judgments are not considered as such, but this is not always the case.[72] Finality and a decision 'on the merits' are prerequisites for preclusion; hence interlocutory judgments will not be entitled to preclusive effects. Within these broad categories are several types of judgments that may be entitled to preclusive effects: (1) default judgments; (2) consent/confessed judgments; (3) summary judgments; (4) declaratory judgments; (5) constitutive judgments; (6) court decision regarding its own competence; and (7) motions to dismiss with prejudice. The following judgments are not capable of having preclusive effects; (1) motions to dismiss without prejudice, and (2) voluntary discontinuances.[73]

70 Ibid., p. 247. See (2009) 54 MVR 111, 116, 119, 129; and (2005) 221 CLR 568.

71 Ibid., p. 242. See (1909) 8 CLR 465, 485; (1998) 194 CLR 395, 418; (2009) 54 MVR 111, 116, 119, 129; (2005) 221 CLR 568.

72 Justine N. Stefanelli, 'Report – The Effect in the European Community of Judgments in Civil and Commercial Matters: Recognition, Res Judicata and Abuse of Process – United States', in British Institute of International and Comparative Law, Project Reference: JLS/2006/FPC/21 – 30-CE-00914760055, p. 10.

73 Ibid., p. 11. Note, however, that under FRCP (n 21) 41(a)(1)(B), if the Claimant has previously dismissed a state or federal action based on or including the same claim, the Claimant's second voluntary dismissal will act as an adjudication

A default judgment is a judgment rendered in consequence of the non-appearance of the defendant (*Beard v. Sovereign Lodge*, W.O.W, 184 N.C. 154, 113 S.E 661; *In re Smith*, 38 Idaho, 746, 225 P. 495, 496; *Brame v. Nolen*, 139 Va. 413, 124 S.E 299, 301).[74] Due to a party's failure to 'plead or otherwise defend', the entry of a judgment under rule 55 [75] is based solely on the assumption that the facts asserted in the opposing party's well-pleaded complaint are true.[76] Rule 55(a) provides that the clerk shall

---

on the merits that will have preclusive effect.

74 Henry Campbell Black, Black's Law Dictionary, fourth edition, (The Publisher Editorial Staff, St. Paul, MINN, 1957), p. 978.

75 Peter H. Bresnan and James P. Cornelio, 'Relief from Default Judgments Under Rule 60(b) – A Study of Federal Case Law', in Fordham Law Review, Volume 49 / Issue 6, Article 3, 1981, p. 956. Fed. R. Civ P. 55 provides: (a) Entry. When a party against whom a judgment for affirmative relief is sought has failed to plead or otherwise defend as provided by these rules and that fact is made to appear by affidavit or otherwise, the clerk shall enter his default. (b) Judgment. Judgment by default may be entered as follows: (1) By the Clerk. When the plaintiff's claim against a defendant is for a sum certain or for a sum which can by computation be made certain, the clerk upon request of the plaintiff and upon affidavit of the amount due shall enter judgment for that amount and costs against the defendant, if he has been defaulted for failure to appear and if he is not an infant or incompetent person. (2) By the Court. In all other cases the party entitled to a judgment by default shall apply to the court therefor: but no judgment by default shall be entered against an infant or incompetent person unless represented in the action by a general guardian, committee, conservator, or other such representative who has appeared therein. If the party against whom judgment by default is sought has appeared in the action, he (or, if appearing by representative, his representative) shall be served with written notice of the application for judgment at least 3 days prior to the hearing on such application. If, in order to enable the court to enter judgment or to carry it into effect, it is necessary to take an account or to determine the amount of damages or to establish the truth of any averment by evidence or to make an investigation of any other matter, the court may conduct such hearings or order such references as it deems necessary and proper and shall accord a right of trial by jury to the parties when and as required by any statute of the United States. (c) Setting Aside Default. For good cause shown the court may set aside an entry of default and, if a judgment by default has been entered, may likewise set it aside in accordance with Rule 60(b). (d) Plaintiffs, Counterclaims, Cross-Claimants. The provisions of this rule apply whether the party entitled to the judgment by default is a plaintiff, a third-party plaintiff, or a party who has pleaded a cross-claim or counterclaim. In all cases a judgment by default is subject to the limitations of Rule 54(c). (e) Judgment Against the United States. No judgment by default shall be entered against the United States or an officer or agency thereof unless the claimant establishes his claim or right to relief by evidence satisfactory to the court.

76 Ibid., pp. 956-957. See Thomson v. Wooster, 114 U.S. 104, 113 (1885); Nishimatsu Constr. Co., v. Houston Nat'l Bank, 515 F.2d 1200, 1206 (5th Cir. 1975); Trans World Airlines, Inc. v. Hughes, 449 F. 2d 51, 63-64, 69-70 (2d Cir. 1971), rev'd on other grounds sub. nom. Hughes Tool Co. v. Trans World Airlines,

enter the default of any 'party against whom ...affirmative relief is sought [and who] has failed to plead or otherwise defend as provided by these rules".[77] The effect of a default judgment, however, varies slightly from that of a final judgment rendered after a fully litigated trial on the merits. While the doctrine of *res judicata* applies to default judgments,[78] the majority of courts agree that collateral estoppel is inapplicable.[79] In New York, a default judgment is considered to be one which results from the defendant's conduct (or lack thereof) that most commonly takes the form of a failure to appear due to lack of timely response to judicial summons.[80]

Inc., 409 U.S. 363 (1973); Clifton v. Tomb, 21 F. 2d 893, 897 (4th Cir. 1927).

77 Ibid., p. 958, referring to Fed. R. Civ. P. 55(a). Although this procedure will normally be handled by the clerk, rule 55(a) does not limit the court's power to enter a party's default. Fisher v. Taylor, 1 F.R.D. 448, 448 (E.D. Tenn. 1940); United States v. Jackson, 25 F. Supp. 79, 79-80 (D. Or. 1938); see 6 J. Moore, Federal Practice 55.03[1] (2d cd. 1976); 10 C. Wright & A. Miller, § 2682. Although the court may enter a party's default, application to the court instead of the clerk is not advisable. In both Fisher and Jackson, the courts stated that the procedure should be handled by the clerk. 1 F.R.D. p. 448; 25 F. Supp. p. 79. Moreover, the Jackson court warned that it would not entertain such applications in the future. 25 F. Supp., p. 80.

78 Ibid., p. 963. See Morris v. Jones, 329 US 545, 550-51 (1947) ("judgment of a court having jurisdiction of the parties and of the subject matter operates as res judicata, in the absence of fraud or collusion, even if obtained upon a default " (citation omitted)); Moyer v. Mathas, 458 F.2d 431, 434 (5th Cir. 1972) ("judgment is no less res judicata because it was obtained by default, absent any proof of fraud, collusion, or lack of jurisdiction"); United States v. Martin, 395 F. Supp. 954, 959 (S.D.N.Y. 1975) ("the rule of res judicata is rendered no less inexorable by the fact that the judgment may have been taken by default"); see 1B J. Moore, Federal Practice 0.409[4], pp. 1024-1025 (2d ed. 1980).

79 Ibid. Compare Cromwell v. County of Sac, 94 U.S. 351, 356 (1976) (default judgment does not make allegations of complaint evidence in action on different claim) and United States v. Martin, 395 F. Supp. 954, 959-60 (S.D.N.Y. 1975) (default judgment has no collateral estoppels effect because nothing was actually litigated) with Last Chance Mining Co v. Tyler Mining Co., 157 U.S. 683, 695 (1895) (default judgment binding as to all facts by estoppels). Professor Moore argues that the predominant and better view is that a default judgment has no collateral estoppels effect. 1B J. Moore, Federal Practice 0.444[2], p. 4006 (2d ed. 1980). But cf. I.T.S. Rubber Co. v. Essex Rubber Co., 25 F.2d 180, 185 (D. Mass. 1922) (doctrines of res judicata and collateral estoppel do not apply to interlocutory act of entry of default): 6 J. Moore, Federal Practice 55.03[2], pp. 55-33 (2d ed. 1976) (same).

80 Stefanelli (2006), supra note 2621, p. 11. CPLR (n 5) 3215(a) reads: "When a defendant has failed to appear, plead or proceed to trial of an action reached and called for trial, or when the court orders a dismissal for any other neglect to proceed, the plaintiff may seek a default against him".

The plaintiff may also be guilty of a default, e.g., failure to appear at trial.[81] If federal collateral estoppel law is applied, then a pure default judgment is insufficient to have a preclusive effect.[82] However, the 'actually litigated' requirement may be satisfied where a default judgment is entered as a sanction against a party who substantially participated in the prior case. As discussed in *Balfour*, where a party has substantially participated in a prior action but engages in attempts to frustrate the effort to bring the action to judgment, it is not an abuse of discretion for a later court to give collateral estoppel effect to the default judgment to prevent further litigation of the issues involved in the prior action.[83] However, if the prior judgment was rendered by a state court, then the state collateral estoppel law applies with respect to the judgment's preclusive effect.[84] *Res judicata* and collateral estoppel will again be sketched out in Chapter V.2.

A consent or confessed judgment is most often used in the context of a contractual dispute, although it is available in tort cases as well. Such judgments mitigates the need for adversarial proceedings by allowing the creditor to file a judgment to which the debtor has voluntarily confessed.[85] These judgments are to be treated the same way as default judgments.[86] Consent or confessed judgments are similarly denied preclusive effect as the issues are not deemed to have been actually litigated.[87]

***

Upon motion, a court is permitted to grant summary judgment for a part after it has reviewed the 'pleadings and other available proof, such as depositions and written admissions' and determined that there is no substantial issue of fact on which to base a claim.[88] In New York, the courts

---

81 Ibid. CPLR (n 5) 3215(a) goes on to read: "When a plaintiff has failed to proceed to trial of an action reached and called for trial, or when the court orders a dismissal for any other neglect to proceed, the defendant may make application to the clerk within one year after the default and the clerk, upon submission of the requisite proof, shall enter judgment for costs".

82 Bush v. Balfour Beatty Bahamas, Ltd., 62 F.3d 1323 (11th Cir. 1998) (Tab 8).

83 Ibid.

84 In re Itzler, 247 B.R. 546, 548 (Bankr. S.D. Fla. 2000) (Tab 10) (citing St. Laurent II v. Ambrose (In re St. Laurent, II), 991 F.2d 672, 676 (11th Cir. 1993).

85 Stefanelli (2006), supra note 2629, p. 12. See DD Siegel (n 8) s 299, CPLR (n 5) 3218(a).

86 Ibid. See DD Siegel (n 8) s 451: this includes the applicability of issue preclusive effects.

87 Ibid., p. 10.

88 Ibid., p. 12. CPLR (n 5) 3212(b) reads: "A motion for summary judgment

will not award summary judgment if there is any doubt as to whether there is a triable issue.[89] If there is a dispute as to a material fact or if there are undisputed facts but the potential for different reasonable interpretations exists, the court must not award summary judgment.[90] It is a device used to decide whether issues of fact exist, not to resolve issues.[91] A summary judgment is considered to be a judgment on the merits which is entitled to preclusive effects.[92] The preclusive effects of the summary judgment will only apply insofar as the matter upon which such judgment has been granted. For example, if the defendant makes a motion for summary judgment based on lack of subject matter jurisdiction and is successful, such a judgment will not preclude a later action in which jurisdiction is available.

The standard formulation of the summary judgment procedure is simple. In Maryland under rule 610, for example, any party to an action may at any time make a motion for summary judgment in his favor...on the ground that there is no genuine dispute as to any material fact and that he is entitled to judgment as a matter of law.[93] The summary judgment

---

shall be supported by affidavit, by a copy of the pleadings and by other available proof, such as depositions and written admissions. The affidavit shall be by a person having knowledge of the facts; it shall recite all the material facts; and it shall show that there is no defense to the cause of action or that the cause of action or defense has no merit. The motion shall be granted if, upon all the papers and proof submitted, the cause of action or defense shall be established sufficiently to warrant the court as a matter of law in directing judgment in favor of any party".

89 Ibid. See Moskowitz v. Garlock 23 AD2d 943, 259 NYS2d 1003 (3d Dep't 1965).

90 Ibid. See Gerard v. Inglese 11 AD2d 981, 206NYS2d 879 (2d Dep't 1960): "Defendant has made no attempt to explain her failure to control the operation of her automobile, contending that the question whether the accident was caused by negligence on her part may only be determined on trial by a jury. Defendant's position is tenable only if there is a real issue to be tried. If such is the case defendant undoubtedly has a constitutional right to a jury trial. However, the court is not obliged to wait until a jury has been empanelled to decide whether a real issue exists. It may decide that question on motion and, without violation of a litigant's constitutional rights, it may refuse to try an issue when it is fictitious and sham" [citation omitted], see also Rapaport v. Scars, Roebuck and Co 28 AD3d 449, 812 N.Y.S. 2d 642 (2d Dep't 2006): "The competing expert opinions presented an issue of credibility for the trier of fact to determine. Accordingly, summary judgment should have been denied" [citation omitted].

91 Ibid. See DD Siegel (n 8) s 278.

92 Ibid. See Eidelberg v. Zellermeyer 5 AD2d 658, 174 NYS2d 300 (1* Dep't 1958): "On this history it is clear that the prior judgment is res judicata as to the present cause of action. A motion granting summary judgment is on the merits".

93 C. Christopher Brown, 'Summary Judgment in Maryland', in Maryland Law Review, Volume 38 / Issue 2, Article 3, 1978, p. 188. See MD R.P. 610(a)(1).

procedure provides a mechanism by which it can be ascertained if a factual dispute exists which will necessitate a trial.[94] If no genuine issue as to any material fact exists, the court may then resolve the case upon the issues of law. Thus, if "reasonable minds could reach but one conclusion from the uncontroverted facts, those questions of fact are for the Court to decide as a matter of law.[95] Summary judgment can also be used to induce a prompt settlement in a case. A plaintiff who can persuasively present his claim as having no factual dispute may obtain a quick settlement through the effective use of summary judgment.[96] Summary judgments are however deemed to be on the merits and are therefore entitled to preclusive effect.[97]

Lord Woolf and Jeremy Woolf, in The Declaratory Judgment 1 (Sweet & Maxwell 3d ed 2002), said 'declaratory judgment' is contrasted with 'executor[y], in other words coercive, judgment'. Edwin Brochard, in 'Declaratory Judgment' (Banks-Baldwin 2d ed 1941), contrasted 'declaratory judgment' with 'executor[y] judgment'.[98] Brochard defines a constitutive or investitive judgment as a judgment that 'creates a new legal relationship' and suggests that this type of judgment might also be 'divestitive' where it will 'terminate an existing status'.[99] A declaratory judgment is a non-coercive judgment that seeks merely to declare the rights of the parties with respect to the controversy. The Uniform Declaratory Act, which has been widely adopted across the United States, grants courts the power to 'declare rights, status and other legal relations whether or not further relief is or could be claimed'. Such declaration may be either affirmative or negative in form and effect and such declaration shall have the force and effect of a final judgment or decree.[100] All the courts do is to declare how the law applies [preventive adjudication]. Preventive adjudication complements remedial adjudication. Generally speaking, in remedial adjudication, a plaintiff seeks damages or an injunction to correct *past* harm; in preventive adjudication, a plaintiff seeks only a

---

94 Ibid., p. 194. E.g., Lipscomb v. Hess, 255 Md. 109, 118, 257 A.2d 178, 182-83 (1969).

95 Ibid. See Brady v. State Farm Mut. Auto Ins. Co., 254 Md. 598, 604, 255 A.2d 427, 430 (1969). Accord, Owen v. Simon, 245 Md. 404, 409, 226, A.2d 548, 551 (1967).

96 Ibid., p. 223.

97 Stefanelli (2006), supra note 2634, p. 10.

98 Samuel L. Bray, Article – 'Preventive Adjudication ', in The University of Chicago Law Review, Volume 77, Number 3, Summer 2010, n.12..

99 Ibid., n.13, referring to Brochard, 'Judicial Relief for Peril and Insecurity', in 45 HARV. L. REV. 793 (1932), p. 800 & n 17.

100 Stefanelli (2006), supra note 2646, p. 12. See Uniform Declaratory Judgment Act (1922) s 1.

declaration and does so to avoid *future* harm. Preventive adjudication is intuitively appealing – it helps people avoid harm and provides clarity in the law, and harm reduction and legal clarity are usually good things.

Preventive adjudication is only declaratory. This lack of a command to the parties has been roundly misunderstood. Some early critics of the declaratory judgment thought that this form of relief was meaningless because of the absence of a command. In 1920, the Michigan Supreme Court struck down a declaratory judgment statute,[101] relying on an opinion by Chief Justice Roger Taney in *Gordon v. United States,*[102] which maintained that an 'award of execution' is 'an essential part of every judgment passed by a court exercising judicial power'.[103] A court, Taney said, may not give 'merely an opinion'.[104] Taney and the Michigan Supreme Court were wrong, at least as a descriptive matter. For centuries English and American courts had exercised the power of issuing opinions without a command to the parties. Actions to remove clouds on titles or to quiet title were well established,[105] as a court's power in equity to do no more than 'decree what and where the boundary of a farm, a manor, province, or state, is and shall be'.[106] When Taney wrote his opinion in *Gordon*, English courts had been

---

101 Bray (2010), supra note 2647, pp. 1282-1283. See Anway v. Grand Rapids Railway Co., 179 NW 350, 361 (Mich 1920) (voiding a declaratory judgment statute for exceeding the "power of the Legislature ....to require [of courts] the performance of functions not judicial in character").

102 Ibid., p. 1283. See 117 U.S 697 (1864).

103 Ibid. See 117 U.S 702 (1864).

104 Ibid. See 117 U.S 702 (1864). Chief Justice Taney's opinion has a highly irregular history. Taney wrote the opinion for the Court but died before argument, and the Court resolved the case summarily. See Gordon v United States, 69 US (2Wall) 561, 561 (1864). Taney's opinion was mislaid for twenty years and then published with a note that "the surviving members of the court" recalled "carefully consider[ing]" it "in reaching the[ir] conclusion". Gordon, 117 US, p. 697. See also United States v. Jones, 119 US 477, 477-78 (1886) (noting that Taney died before the decision in Gordon, and that the published opinion "must have been prepared by him before the decision was actually made"); David P. Currie, 'The Constitution in Congress" Democrats and Whigs', 1829-1861 199 n 94, 200 n 103 (Chicago 2005) (noting that Taney's mislaid opinion was a draft opinion and that the Court's actual decision "took a narrower ground").

105 Ibid. See, for example, Ward v. Chamberlain, 67 US (2 Black) 430, 445 (1862) ("Jurisdiction in equity to remove a cloud from the title of the complainant is fully maintained by the modern decisions of the Courts, and so generally is the principle acknowledged, that all doubt upon the subject may be considered as put at rest."). See also David P. Currie, 'Federal Courts: Cases and Materials' 63 n 4 (West 4th ed 1990) (criticizing Taney's objection as making "little sense in light of the established jurisdiction to remove clouds from and to quiet titles to land, and to resolve interstate boundary disputes").

106 Id. See Rhode Island v. Massachusetts, 37 US (12 Pet) 657, 734 (1838). In

issuing declaratory judgments pursuant to statute for more than a decade, and Scottish courts had been hearing "declaratory" actions for three centuries. In 1927, the United States Supreme Court corrected Taney's mistaken pronouncement about the necessity of an 'award of execution',[107] and in 1930 the Michigan Supreme Court reversed and upheld a state statute authorizing declaratory judgments. Since 1930s, it has been well settled that courts in the United States may decide cases involving only declaratory relief.[108] In preventive adjudication, therefore, a plaintiff seeks an opinion that (1) is not accompanied by a command to the parties, (2) is prospective with respect to harm, and (3) resolves an indeterminacy in the application of law.[109] Nor is every case involving a declaratory judgment an instance of preventive adjudication. A plaintiff sometimes asks for a declaratory judgment *and* for damages or an injunction.[110] Sometimes a plaintiff seeks a declaratory judgment but the defendant counterclaims for monetary or injunctive relief,[111] or vice versa.[112] And sometimes a declaratory judgment

---

this case, almost thirty years before before Gordon, Chief Justice Taney dissented on grounds that were consistent with, but did not necessitate, his later conclusion that opinions without an "award of execution" were invalid. Ibid., p. 752 (Taney dissenting). For a discussion of state-boundary cases in the Supreme Court, see Charles Warren, 'The Supreme Court and Disputes between States, Address at the College of William and Mary, 34 Wm & Mary Bull 3,13-14 (June 1940) (noting that Rhode Island v Massachusetts was the third such case – there were more than thirty by 1940).

107 Ibid., pp. 1283-4. See Fidelity National Bank and Trust Co v. Swope, 274 US 123, 132 (1927) ("While ordinarily a case or judicial controversy results in a judgment requiring award of process of execution to carry it into effect, such relief is not an indispensable adjunct to the exercise of the judicial function"). In Swope, the Court listed examples of adjudications without an award of execution: [n]aturalization proceedings", "suits to determine a matrimonial or other status", "suits for instructions to a truste or for the construction of a will," "bills of interpleader", and "bills to quiet title where the plaintiff rests his claim on adverse possession", Ibid. Some of these are preventive adjudication and some constitutive adjudication.

108 Ibid., p. 1284. See, for example, Aetna Life Insurance Co v. Moore, 300 US 227, 240 (1937); San Luis Power and Water Co v Trujillo, 26 P2d 537, 540 (Colo 1933); Edwin M. Brochard, 'Judicial Relief for Peril and Insecurity', in 45 HARV L REV, p. 799 (arguing that it is the determination of legal relations, rather than the ability to compel parties to obey commands or orders, that "is the essence of judicial power").

109 Ibid., p. 1296.

110 Ibid., p. 1281. In Medlmmune, for example, the complaint included antitrust and unfair competition claims. 2004 WL 3770589, p. *1.

111 Ibid., pp. 1281-1282. See, for example, Snyder v. Bock, 204 P2d 1010, 1011 (Idaho 1949).

112 Ibid., p. 1282. See, for example, Altvater v. Freeman, 319 US 359, 360-61 (1943).

action is not prospective, because the plaintiff seeks a declaratory about past conduct, perhaps to set up a later suit for damages.[113] Declaratory judgments are similarly deemed to have claim and issue preclusive effect.[114] Brochard argues that the declaratory judgment is a form of practical relief that should be employed whenever it will promote expediency, increase clarity, decrease uncertainty, or serve additional useful purposes.[115]

In remedial adjudication, a court is concerned with an injury that has already happened (or will happen imminently), and it is asked to redress the injury, usually by awarding damages, issuing an injunction, or sentencing a criminal defendant to a term of imprisonment.[116] In remedial adjudication, the court gives the successful plaintiff something more: a command to the defendant, either to pay damages or adhere to an injunction.[117] The most common judgment is that of the money judgment. The amount of damages and interest awarded is usually included in judgments.[118]

***

In *Catlin v. United States*, the US Supreme Court set forth the concept of finality as ending the litigation and leaving 'nothing for the court to do but execute the judgment'.[119] The concept of finality means different things depending on whether the party seeks to invoke claim or issue preclusion. In claim preclusion, finality indicates that the court has concluded, all regular proceedings on the claim, other than award of costs and enforcement of judgments.[120] The final judgment rule requiring that judgments, decrees, and decisions of state and federal district courts be 'final' in order to be reviewable has long been an important requisite to the exercise of federal appellate jurisdiction.[121] In determining what constitutes final judgments,

---

113 Ibid. See Note, Declaratory Judgment and Matured Causes of Action, in 53 Colum L. Rev. 1130 (1953), p. 1143.

114 Stefanelli (2006), supra note 2649, p. 10.

115 Bray (2010), supra note 2650, p. 1277, referring to Edwin Brochard, 'Declaratory Judgment', 2d ed., (Banks-Baldwin, 1941), p. 299-307..

116 Ibid., pp. 1279-1280.

117 Ibid., p. 1282.

118 Stefanelli (2006), supra note 2663, p. 5.

119 Ibid., p. 8. See 324 US 229, 233.

120 Ibid. See Casad and Clermont (n 38), 51.

121 DUKE LAW JOURNAL, Vol. 1963: 754, CIVIL PROCEDURE: FINAL JUDGMENT RULE: STATE COURT VENUE DETERMINATION CONSIDERED FINAL FOR PURPOSES OF APPEAL ["DUKE L.J. 1963/754"], p. 754. Final judgments or decrees rendered by the highest court of a State in which a decision

the federal appellate courts, in reviewing district court decisions, and the Supreme Court, in reviewing the judgments of state courts, apply the same criteria.[122] These criteria have been defined by the Supreme Court in the following language: to be reviewable the judgment must be final and complete, as to the entire subject matter and all the causes of action;[123] it must effectively determine the litigation on the merits,[124] and not merely interlocutory or intermediate steps therein;[125] and it must fully determine the rights of the parties so that nothing remains to be done by the trial court except to enter the judgment which the appellate court has directed.[126] However, the courts have recognized that some flexibility is needed in order to prevent the undue harshness that would result from a rigid application

---

could be had, may be reviewed by the Supreme Court as follows: .... (2) By appeal, where is drawn in question the validity of a statute of any state on the ground of its being repugnant to the Constitution, treaties or laws of the United States, and the decision is in favor of its validity." 28 U.S.C § 1257 (1958). "The courts of appeals shall have jurisdiction of appeals from all final decisions of the district courts of the United States ....except where a direct review may be had in the Supreme Court." (Emphasis added.) 28 U.S.C. § 1291 (1958). The rule was incorporated in the original Judiciary Act of 1789, ch. 20, §§ 21, 22, 25, 1 Stat. 73. See generally, 1 BARRON & HOLTZOFF, 'FEDERAL PRACTICE AND PROCEDURE', § 57 (1960, Supp. 1962); 3A BARRON & HOLTZOFF, Ibid., § 1552; 6 MOORE, FEDERAL PRACTICE' 54.11-.14 (2d ed. 1953, Supp. 1962); Note, Appealability in the Federal Courts, in 75 HARV. L. REV. (1961), p. 351.

122 Ibid., p. 756. Although appellate jurisdiction in the two instances is derived from different statutory sources, [note omitted], the cases do not appear to distinguish between the judgments of state courts and those of federal district courts in determining whether such judgments are final. See e.g., the language used by the Supreme Court in the following cases: Parr v. United States, 351 U.S. 513, 518 (1956); Gospel Army v. Los Angeles, 331 U.S. 543, 546 (1947); Market St. Ry. v. Railroad Comm'n, 324 U.S. 548, 551 (1945); R.H. Arnold Co. v. Guimarin & Co., 263 U.S. 427, 434 (1923). Moreover, the courts cite state and federal interchangeably. See e.g., Brown Shoe Co. v. United States, 370 U.S. 294, 306 (1962). In Ex parte Tiffany, 252 U.S. 32, 36 (1920), the Court, speaking of the terms later used in 28 U.S.C. §§ 1257, 1291 (1958), said that "final decisions" means the same thing as "final judgments and decrees".

123 Ibid. See R.H. Arnold Co. v. Guimarin & Co., 263 U.S. 427, 434 (1923) (federal court of appeals decision affirming merits but remanding case for jury determination of damages held not final). But see FED. R. CIV. P. 54(b) which provides for entry of a final judgment upon one or more but less than all the claims in a multiple claim action, thus making such judgment appealable.

124 Ibid. See Parr v. United States, 351 U.S. 513, 518 (1956) (federal district court decision granting motion to dismiss held not final).

125 Ibid. See Market St. Ry. v. Railroad Comm'n, 324 U.S. 548, 551 (1945) (state court judgment affirming order of state commission held final).

126 Ibid. See Gospel Army v. Los Angeles, 331 U.S. 543, 546 (1947) (state court judgment remanding case for new trial held not final).

of the finality rule. Therefore the rule has been made subject to certain exceptions.[127] Congress and the Supreme Court have crafted exceptions to the finality rule to afford relief to parties whose rights may be harmed irreparably by orders that become effectively unreviewable if not appealed immediately.[128] For example, one federal statute grants appellate courts jurisdiction to hear appeals from interlocutory orders issued by district courts that grant, continue, modify, refuse, or dissolve injunctions.[129] The Supreme Court has created another exception to the final judgment rule, known as the collateral order doctrine.[130] Under this doctrine, a party may appeal immediately an order that finally determines important rights yet is too independent of the cause of action itself to defer appellate review until the whole case has been decided.[131] These exceptions ensure that the final judgment rule, by delaying appeal of certain preliminary or collateral orders, does not unfairly restrict a party's rights.[132] Consistent with this policy, courts have continued to construe the finality requirement

---

127 Ibid.

128 Richard Crummins, 'Judgment on the Merits Leaving Attorney's Fees Issues Undecided: A Final Judgment', in 56 Fordham L. Rev. (1987), p. 487. See DiBella v. United States, 369 U.S. 121, 124-25 (1962) (reviewing various exceptions to the finality rule).

129 Ibid. [footnote and accompanying text omitted].

130 Ibid., pp. 491-492. See Cohen v. Beneficial Indus. Loan Corp., 337 U.S. 541, 546-47 (1949); accord Stringfellow v Concerned Neighbors in Action, 107S. Ct.1177, 1181-82 (1987).

131 Ibid., p. 492. See Cohen, 337 U.S. pp. 546-547; see e.g., Mitchell v. Forsyth, 472 U.S 511, 530 (1985) (order denying claim of qualified immunity appealable as a collateral order); Lynk v. LaPorte Superior Ct. No. 2, 789 F.2d 554, 561 (7th Cir. 1986) (order granting or denying writ of hebeas corpus ad testificandum appealable under collateral order doctrine).

132 Ibid. See DiBela v. United States, 369 U.S. 121, 125-6 (1962). Federal Rule of Civil Procedure 54(b) provides another exception to the final judgment rule. Rule 54(b) allows for appeal from a judgment against one or more, but fewer than all, the claims or parties in circumstances where the judge certifies "that there is no just reason for delay". Ibid. The Rule was intended to afford relief to parties involved in litigation that includes multiple claims relating to separate and distinct rights of many persons. See 6 J. Moore, W. Taggart & J. Wicker, Moore's Federal Practice 54.15[1], pp. 191-94 (2d ed. 1988). "[I]f all these determinations had to await an appeal from a decree finally terminating the proceeding, rights of many persons would either be irreparably lost or seriously impaired ... " Ibid., p. 191; see also Sears, Roebuck & Co. v. Mackey, 351 U.S. 427, 428-29 (1956) (multiple claim action in which district court's judgment for defendant as to two, but not all, claims for relief deemed appealable under Rule 54(b)); Allis-Chalmers Corp. v. Philadelphia Elec. Co., 521 F.2d 360, 366-67 (3d Cir. 1975) (grant of summary judgment before adjudication of defendant's counterclaim not properly certifiable under Rule 54(b)). For a discussion of factors considered by courts in determining whether a given order is appealable under Rule 54(b), see Ibid., p. 364.

practically, rather than technically, in an effort to avoid an overemphasis on formalism.[133] Final judgments generally obtain preclusive effect, subject to specific exception.[134] Finality and a decision 'on the merits' are prerequisites for preclusion.[135]

***

The Civil Procedure Rules 1998 of the United Kingdom, Part 40, Rule 40.1 (1) says: "This Part sets out rules about judgment and orders which apply except where any other of these Rules makes a different provision in relation to the judgment or order in question". According to Rule 12.1 of the Civil Procedure, 'Default judgment' means judgment without trial where a defendant –(a) had failed to file an acknowledgement of service; or (b) has failed to file a defence. A claimant may obtain a default judgment –(a) on a claim for delivery of goods subject to an agreement regulated by the Consumer Credit Act 1974(1); (b) where he uses the procedure set out in Part 8 (alternative procedure for claims); or (c) in any other case where a practice direction provides that the claimant may not obtain default judgment [Rule 12.2]. The claimant may obtain judgment in default of an acknowledgement of service only if – (a) the defendant has not filed an acknowledgement of service or a defence to the claim or any part of the claim); and (b) the relevant time for doing so has expired [Rule 12.3(1)]. The claimant may obtain judgment in default of defence only if – (a) the defendant has filed an acknowledgement of service but has not filed a defence; and (b) the relevant time for doing so has expired [Rule 12.3(2)]. The claimant may obtain a default judgment if – (a) the defendant has applied for summary judgment under Part 24, and that application has not been disposed of; (b) the defendant has satisfied the whole claim (including

133 Ibid. See Coopers & Lybrand v. Livesay, 437 U.S. 463, 471 (1978) (rigidity would sometimes conflict with purpose of § 1291); Dibella v. United States, 369 U.S. 121, 125-26 (1962) (overly rigid insistence on finality defeats rule's purpose where appealed orders are collateral); Frank, 'Requiem for the Final Judgment Rule,' 45 Texas L. Rev. 295 (noting Court's preference for practical construction of the finality rule); see also Dickinson v. Petroleum Conversion Corp., 338 U.S. 507, 517-18 (1950) (Black, J., dissenting) (advocating flexible approach to finality requirement such that appellate courts review all cases where question of finality is close and can be answered either way by equally persuasive arguments).

134 Stefanelli (2006), supra note 2667, p. 10.

135 Ibid., p. 11. Note, however, that under FRCP (n 21) 41(a)(1)(B), if the Claimant has previously dismissed a state or federal action based on or including the same claim, the Claimant's second voluntary dismissal will act as an adjudication on the merits that will have preclusive effect.

any claim for costs) on which the claimant is seeking judgment; or (c)(i) the claimant is seeking judgment on a claim for money; and (ii) the defendant has filed or served on the claimant an admission under rule 14.4 or 14.7 (admission of liability to pay all of the money claimed) together with a request for time to pay [Rule 12.3(3)].

The claimant must make an application in accordance with Part 23 if he wishes to obtain a default judgment – (a) on a claim which consists of or includes a claim for any other remedy; or (b) where rule 12.9 or rule 12.10 provides [Rule 12.4(2)]. Subject to Rule 12.4(2), a claimant may obtain a default judgment by filing a request in the relevant practice form where the claim is for – (a) a specified amount of money; (b) an amount of money to be decided by the court; (c) delivery of goods where the claim form gives the defendant the alternative of paying their value; or (d) any combination of these remedies [Rule 12.4(1)]. Where a claimant – (a) claims any other remedy in his claim form in addition to those specified in paragraph (1); but (b) abandons that claim in his request for judgment, he may still obtain a default judgment by filing a request under paragraph (1).

Summary judgment is a judgment of a claim or a particular issue without trial [Part 24, Rule 24.1 of The Civil Procedure Rules 1998 of the United Kingdom]. The court may give summary judgment against a claimant or defendant on the whole of a claim or on a particular issue if – (a) it considers that – (i) that claim has no real prospect of succeeding on the claim or issue; or (ii) that defendant has no real prospect of successfully defending the claim or issue; and there is no other reason why the case or issue should be disposed of at a trial [Rule 24.2]. The Court may give summary judgment against a claimant in any type of proceedings (Rule 24.3(1). The court may give summary judgment against the defendant in any type of proceedings except – (a) proceedings for possession of residential premises against a tenant, a mortgagor or a person holding over after the end of his tenancy; and (b) proceedings for an admirality claim in rem [Rule 24.3(2)].

***

German law distinguishes three forms of judicial decisions, *Urteil* (judgments, § 313 ZPO), *Beschlusse* (orders, § 329 ZPO) and *Verfugungen* (procedural directions/dispositions, § 329 ZPO) [see § 160 (1) No. 6 ZPO].[136]

---

136 Christian A. Heinze, 'Report on The Effect in the European Community of Judgments in Civil and Commercial Matters: Recognition, Res Judicata and Abuse of Process in Germany', in BRITISH INSTITUTE OF INTERNATIONAL

The followings are other distinctions of judgments to be found in German law and doctrine. A distinction is made between condemnatory judgments, ordering a defendant to do or not to do something, e.g., pay a certain amount of money or refrain from certain acts of unfair competition (*Leistungsurteil*); declaratory judgments (*Feststellungsurteil*, § 256 ZPO), pronouncing the existence or non-existence of a legal relationship; and constitutive judgments which create, change or end legal rights or relationships / status, e.g., divorce, dissolution of a company (*Gestaltungsurteil*). All these judgments are judgments on the merits capable of having *res judicata* effect, but they differ in the operative parts (*Tenor*) depending on the remedy sought.[137] Judgments/substantive judgments on the merits (*Sachurteil*) is distinguished from procedural judgments which just contain decisions on procedural questions, e.g., dismissing the claim as inadmissible for lack of jurisdiction (*Prozessurteil*).[138] Another distinction is made between contradictory judgments based on contentious proceedings (*streitiges Urteil*) and non-contradictory judgments (*nichtstreitiges Urteil*) such as judgments by default (*Versaumnisurteil*, § 330 ZPO), judgments by admission/defendant's acceptance of the claim (*Anerkenntnisurteil*, § 307 ZPO), and judgment by waiver of the plaintiff/plaintiff's withdrawal (*Verzichtsurteil*, § 306 ZPO). All of these judgments are capable of having *res judicata* effect.[139]

Final judgments (*Endurteil*, § 300 ZPO) are distinguished from interlocutory or preliminary judgments (*Zwischenurteil*, §§ 280, 303, 304 ZPO). Interlocutory judgments may concern the cause of action (*Zwischenurteil uber den Grund*, § 304 ZPO) or incidental procedural questions between the parties (§ 303 ZPO, see also §§ 71, 238(1), 268, 387 ZPO) including the procedural admissibility (*Zulassigkeit*) of the action (§ 280 ZPO). Final judgments bring the proceedings to an end. Interlocutory judgments decide only incidental or preliminary matters, consequently, interlocutory judgments do not bring the proceedings to an end, but rather contain a ruling on a preliminary point which is binding on the court which has issued it (§ 318 ZPO) and may be appealed, usually only together with the final judgment (§ 512 ZPO), exceptionally also separately (§§ 280, 304 ZPO).[140] There is also a distinction between partial final judgments

---

AND COMPARATIVE LAW, Project Reference: JLS/2006/FPC/21-30-CE-00914760055, p. 5. The basic distinction between an Urteil and a Beschlusse is the fact that an Urteil normally (for exceptions § 128(2) ZPO) requires an oral hearing whereas a Beschlusse (normally) does not (§ 128(4) ZPO).

137 Ibid., p. 9, referring to Koch/Diedrich, 'Civil Procedure in Germany, (1998), No. 123.

138 Ibid.

139 Ibid.

140 Ibid., referring to Koch/Diedrich (1998), supra note 2686, No.126.

(*Teilurteil*, § 301 ZPO) and full final judgment (*Vollendurteil*, § 300 ZPO). Partial final judgments may be issued if part of the matter in controversy is ready for decision and the partial decision does not affect the latter decision on the rest of the matter (§ 301 ZPO).[141] In addition, there is also what is called 'judgments with reservation' (*Vorbehaltsurteile*, §§ 302, 599, 602, 605a ZPO). These judgments normally come into play if the plaintiff sues in summary proceedings relying entirely on documentary evidence or on a bill of exchange (*Urkunden- und Wechselprozess*, §§ 592 seq. ZPO).[142] ZPO (*Zivilprozessordnung*) § 300(1) unambiguously provides that 'the court *must* render final judgment' where the case is ripe (emphasis supplied).[143] It is tempting to conclude that a final decision in this sense and, consequently, a final judgment, is a decision which disposes of all the issues in controversy between all the parties to a particular case.[144] Immediately following the basic rule of section 300(1) which mandates a final judgment where a controversy is ripe for final decision, the Code provides in section 300(2) that, if cases were consolidated by the court for the purpose of simultaneous trial and decision, and only one is ripe for final decision, the court must render a final judgment.[145]

In Sweden, civil and criminal procedures are included in the Swedish Code of Judicial Procedure Ds. 1998:000. Chapter 17, section 1 of the Code provides that a court's determination on the merit of the matter at issue in an action is made in a judgment. Section 2 says that if a main hearing has been held, the judgment *shall* be based upon material presented at that hearing. If a new main hearing has been held, the judgment *shall* be based upon material presented at that hearing. In cases subject to Chapter 43 Section 14, second sentence, the judgment may also be based upon material presented after the main hearing. When a case is adjudicated without a main hearing, the judgment *shall* be based on the contents of the documents and what otherwise emerged in the case (SFS 1987: 747). Olivecrona points out that although many different formulae are used in declaratory judgments, they all have a directive function in that they indicate the correct behavior of the parties on the point in dispute.[146] Olivecrona makes a distinction

141 Ibid., p. 9.

142 Ibid., pp. 9-10, referring to Stein/Jonas (-Leipold), ZPO (1998) fn. 21, volume 4/1, § 322 No.56.

143 Herbert Bernstein, 'The Finality of A Judgment as A Requirement for Civil Appeals in Germany', in LAW AND CONTEMPORARY PROBLEMS, Vol. 47: No. 3, Page 35: Summer 1984, p. 44, n.89. see ZPO § 300(1).

144 Ibid., p. 44.

145 Ibid. see ZPO § 300(2).

146 Spaak (2009a), supra note 2556, p. 2, referring to Olivecrona (1971), supra note 2554, p. 210. The imperative aspect of the directive function identified by Olivecrona is rather weak.

between *executory* judgments which order the defendant to do something, *declaratory* judgments which declare the existence of a certain legal relation, and *constitutive* judgments which create a legal relation where there previously was none or dissolve an existing legal relation.[147] Declaratory judgments, according to Olivecrona, have a directive function, stating the correct behavior of the parti[es] on the issue in dispute, notwithstanding many different formulae used therein.[148] In issuing an adoption order or divorce decree, dissolving a business partnership, terminating parental rights, or granting a certificate of naturalization, courts render constitutive judgments. In these cases, courts 'do not declare the existence of a legal relationship but create a new one'.[149]

***

The French Code of Civil Procedure, Article 455 states that the judgment must set forth succinctly the respective claims of the parties and their grounds. Such presentation may take the form of a reference to the pleadings of the parties with the indication of their date. The judgment must be reasoned. It pronounces the decision in the form of operative part. The judgment which decides in its operative part the whole or part of the main issue, or one which rules upon the procedural plea, a plea seeking a plea of non-admissibility or any other interlocutory application, will, from the time of its pronouncement, become *res judicata* with regard to the dispute which it determines. The main issue means the subject-matter of the litigation as specified under Article 4 [Article 480]. The judgment, since its pronouncement, puts an end to the judge's jurisdiction over the dispute that he has determined. However, the judge has the power to withdraw his decision in case of a motion to set aside or a third party proceedings or an application for judicial review.

As to default judgment, Article 471 of the French Code of Civil Procedure provides that the defendant who does not appear may, on the initiative of the plaintiff or on a decision taken *sua sponte* by the judge, be invited to appear again where the citation has not been served on him

147 Ibid., p. 1, referring to Olivecrona (1971), Ibid., pp. 200-201. Examples of executory judgments include judgments that order a person to pay somebody else a sum of money; examples of declaratory judgments include judgments declaring that a certain person is the lawful owner of a certain object; and examples of constitutive judgments include judgments that dissolve a marriage or a company.

148 Ibid., p. 2, referring to Olivecrona (1971), Ibid., p. 210.

149 Bray (2010), supra note 2664, n.13, referring to Lord Woolf and Jeremy Woolf, 'The Declaratory Judgment', 1 (Sweet & Maxwell 3d. Ed. 2002), p. 2.

personally. The citation will, subject to special rules applicable to certain courts, be reissued in the same form as the first one. The judge may order that this must be done by a process served by a bailiff where the first citation was done by a clerk of the court. The judge may also inform the interested party, by ordinary letter, of the consequences of his failure to appear. If the defendant fails to appear, a ruling will nevertheless be made on the merits of the case. The judge will uphold the claim only to the extent that he considers it valid, admissible and well-founded [Article 472]. Where the defendant does not appear, the judgment will be rendered by default if the decision is of final instance and where the citation has not been served in person. The judgment will be regarded as a judgment after trial where the decision is subject to appeal or where the citation has been served personally on the defendant [Article 473].

V.1.5. CRIMINAL SENTENCING / IMPLEMENTATION OF SANCTION

In Criminal law, verdicts are followed by sentencing in criminal proceedings. A sentence is the penalty ordered by the court. Sentencing is primarily with the goal for punishment, deterrence, incapacitation and rehabilitation.[150] Sentencing practices vary across countries. Certain conduct may be criminal in one country, but it may be partially or totally decriminalized in another; jurisdictions classify similar crimes in different ways, exposing offenders to different sanctions. In Germany, crimes are divided into two categories, *Vergehen*, which are minor crimes, and *Verbrechen*, which are more serious crimes punishable by a minimum term of one year. The former is sometimes translated in the United States to mean a 'misdemeanor', this is not accurate because it includes many crimes of moderate-to-high severity that would be considered felonies in the United States (such as burglary, forgery, extortion, aggravated assult and many drug crimes).[151]

In the United States, prior to the 1980s, judges were allowed to impose sentences totally at their discretion in judicial decision-making. Sentencing disparities consequently happened, and very different sentences

150 West's Encyclopedia of American Law, edition 2. Copyright 2008 The Gale Group Inc. on Sentencing.

151 Ram Subramanian and Alison Shames, 'Sentencing and Prison Practices in Germany and the Netherlands: Implications for the United States, 50 years of Innovation 1961-2011', in VERA Institute of Justice, October 2013, referring to Richard Frase, 'Sentencing in Germany and the United States: Comparing Apfel with Apples', (Freiburg, Germany: Max Plank Institute for Foreign and International Criminal Law, July 2001), pp. 5-6.

are imposed upon different wrong-doers for the same crime. In a bi-partisan reform effort, Congress passed the Comprehensive Crime Control Act of 1984, which included provisions that make up the Sentencing Reform Act (SRA). Congress set up the United States Sentencing Commission (USSC) to produce federal sentencing guidelines, prescribing specific sentence minimum and maximum for specific federal crimes. The prescribed sentences take into account the particular criminal conduct and whether the convicted defendant had any previous criminal history. The sentencing guidelines require federal judges to ensure that the sentence reflects the gravity of the crime, that the punishment furthers the goal of deterrence, that the sentence protects the public from further crimes by the criminal, and that the criminal receives any necessary treatment, medical care or education to further the goal of rehabilitation.[152] The Federal Sentencing Guidelines produced by the USSC under the SRA came into effect on November 1, 1987 (28 U.S.C.A. § 994 [1988 & Supp. V 1993]). The guidelines changed its focus in sentencing from the offender to the offense. According to the guidelines, criminal offenses are to be categorized, and the sentence required upon conviction is then to be identifed. Only if there is a very good explanation and if the judges clearly state the reasons on the record, they may increase or decrease sentences or depart from the guidelines.[153]

The U.S Supreme Court upheld the constitutionality of the USSC and its system in *Mistretta v. United States*, 488 U.S. 361, 109 S.Ct. 647, 102 L. Ed. 2d 714 (1989), in which the Supreme Court held that the guidelines had not violated the Separation of Powers doctrine and were not an excessive delegation of legislative power. Before the *Mistretta* many federal judges refused to recognize the guidelines.[154] The sentencing guidelines used by twenty-two states and the federal government require judges to calculate criminal sentences using a mathematical formula. The defendant's offenses, prior criminal records and other factors are all to be calculated in order to come to a sentence to be computed. There is very little room for judges to depart from the sentence mandated by the guidelines.[155]

Critics who are mostly defense attorneys and judges have attacked the sentencing guidelines and argued that the guidelines give prosecutors too much power in the criminal justice system and give too little discretion to judges to shape a sentence to fit the individual defendants. Critics of the federal guidelines attack that the guidelines have in practice created another arbitrary system of sentencing. There has been a shift in power from the judge to the federal prosecutor; prosecutorial discretion has replaced

152 West's Encyclopedia of American Law 2008, supra note 2699.

153 Ibid.

154 Ibid.

155 Ibid.

judicial discretion. A prosecutor's charging decision becomes the most important in the case, since the criminal charge will trigger, upon conviction, a particular sentence in the guidelines. A prosecutor can determine whether a defendant's time in prison is short or long by manipulating the charges and a case's extenuating circumstances. Defendants with less effective counsels receive longer sentences because such counsels are not knowledgeable in the working of the guidelines to negotiate plea agreements which reduce the charges and jail time. Judges are forced to hand out the sentence dictated by the guidelines and are forced to ignore the particular circumstances of the case and the individual. Another criticism is that the guidelines reflect political concerns more than penological ones. Congress has imposed severe penalties which are out of proportion to the nature of some of the offenses.[156] Proponents of the sentencing guidelines argue that the guidelines eliminate 'judge shopping' and the arbitrary and disparate sentencing practices. Such proponents believe that the guidelines guarantee harsher punishment for federal felons, many of whom are convicted for selling illegal narcotics. Before the guidelines were created, defendants tried to avoid judges who handed down tough sentences and to find judges who would be lenient. The sentencing guidelines have, therefore, according to such proponents, reduced the arbitrary dispensation of punishment. Such proponents contend that the guidelines serve as a deterrent to crime since they provide predictable sentences. Criminals no longer can play the angles in the criminal justice system to their advantage but must face a defined punishment. The guidelines also provide an efficient means of delivering a criminal sentence that conforms to public policy goals set out by Congress and the guidelines commission.[157]

Because incapacitation and retribution are primary goals of sentencing in the U.S., incarceration is used frequently and for longer periods of time. In 2000, 70 percent of convicted offenders in the U.S. received a sentence that included a prison term, while only 30 percent received a probationary sentence (though some of these may have been split into prison and probationary sentences).[158] For the past four decades, Subramanian and Shames have noted that crime control policies in the United States centered heavily on the increase use of prisons.[159] Fueled by a belief that only incapacitation and punitive sanctions could protect public safety, these policies included the introduction of mandatory minimum sentences, habitual offenders legislation, parole release restrictions, truth-

---

156 Ibid.

157 Ibid.

158 Subramanian & Shames (2013), supra note 2700. See Pew Center of the States, Time Served: The High Cost, Low Return of Longer Prison Terms, (Washington, DC: The Pew Charitible Trusts, 2012), 13.

159 Ibid.

in-sentencing laws, and an overall increase in the number and length of custodial sanctions.

***

In Europe, sentencing theory as elaborated in the 1960s and 1970s strongly advocated the need for a wide range of penalty options to facilitate matching particular sentence to particular offenders. Putting the focus on individualization in sentencing partially reflected rehabilitation theory but was in particular called for by the pursuit of justice and the assumption that personal and individual guilt as expressed in criminal offending could be best accounted for by various sentencing options tailored to the individual case. The 1970s and 1980s also saw new concern for the role of the community in the system of criminal sanctions and their implementation. Community participation has been welcome not only for its potential in contributing to cost-effective reintegration and rehabilitation of offenders, but also because it expresses recognition of the community's responsibility for effective (informal) crime control.[160] With criminal policies turning away from the offender and towards the victim and the public, another change becomes visible. Sentencing theory, once strongly expressing the goal of fitting punishment to the individual offender, moves toward fitting punishment to the crime and the impact the crime has (on victims and society).[161] For selected groups of offenders, security and incapacitation become focal concerns. In particular for sex offenders, a punishment regime is established which is based on risk assessment, indeterminate detention and incapacitation.[162] In general, these changes are consistent with a move in criminology away from empirical theories and toward normative theories of crime and criminal justice. It is evidently punishment theories and practices emerging during the last decades which emphasize exclusion and security rather than fundamental individual rights, inclusion and re-integration. These changes have resulted in switching the goals of community sanctions to tight supervision, credibility and cost-effectiveness.[163] Hans-Jorg Albrecht describes that the argument brought forward in favor of

160 Albrecht (1987), supra note 1742, p. 28.

161 Ibid., p. 47. See e.g., Home Office: Making Punishment Work, Report of a Review of the Sentencing Framework for England and Wales, London, July 2001: White Paper on Criminal Justice: Justice for All. Home Office, London 2002, p. 86.

162 Ibid., referring to S. Walther, 'Umgang mit Sexualstraftatern: Amerika, Quo Vadis? Vergewisserungen uber aktuelle Grundfragen an das (deutsche) Strafrecht', MschrKrim 80(1997), S.199-221.

163 Ibid.

preventive detention is based on a logic of guilt-dependent criminal punishment, restricting not only the imposition of a criminal sentence, but also the length of a prison sentence.[164] A system of sentencing strictly guided and limited by individual guilt – according to this logic – prevents inflation of prison sentences by sidelining incapacitation and the pursuit of security in the decision-making on criminal punishment in the courts.

The political & social framework and the constitutional arrangements define the relationship between the judiciary, the public and the political system.[165] Explanations have been sought in differences in the welfare orientation expressed in penal systems.[166] In fact, retention of welfare policies seems to be correlated with vertical trust (trust in state institutions), less punitive attitudes of the public, and, ultimately, less use of imprisonment and more stable patterns of imprisonment.[167] However, France, Greece, Belgium and Spain have political agendas embracing the welfare state but display punitive patterns in the development of criminal penalties and prison populations.[168] In fact, sentencing theory as developed by the judiciary and its essential elements confirmed in legal doctrine provide for an effective path to restricting sentencing discretion and creating commitment to sentencing standards among the judiciary. The judiciary has generated mechanisms that stabilize sentencing outcomes through a strong attachment to traditional and established tariffs. Sentencing research has confirmed that professional socialization of judges (and public prosecutors) includes learning patterns that feed almost exclusively on (1) sentencing information passed and communicated through informal channels (within the judiciary), (2) documents containing information on past sentences (prior records accessible for prosecutors and judges before the sentencing decision), and (3) trial arrangements that provide for sentencing proposals of the public prosecutor and defense council before the judicial decision is made.[169] In addition, an effective system of self-control within the judiciary

164 Albrecht (2013), supra note 1745, p. 213.

165 Ibid., p. 229. See e.g., Michael Cavadino & James Dignan, 'Penal Systems: A Comparative Approach', (2006).

166 Ibid., referring to DAVID GARLAND, 'PUNISHMENT AND WELFARE: A HISTORY OF PENAL STRATEGIES', (1985); Tapio Lappi-Seppala, 'Penal Policy in Scandinavia', in 36 CRIME & JUST. 217 (2007), pp. 233-244.

167 Ibid., p. 230, referring to Helmut Hirtenlehner and Dina Hummelsheim, 'Schutzt soziale Sicherheit vor Kriminalitatsfurcht? Eine empirische Untersuchung zum Einfluss wohlfahrtsstaatlicher Sicherungspolitik auf das kriminalitatsbezogene Sicherheitsbefinden', 94 MONATSSCHRIFT FUR KRIMINOLOGIE UND STRAFRECHTSREFORM 178 (2011); Lappi-Seppala (2007), Ibid., pp. 373-377.

168 Ibid.

169 Ibid., p. 231, referring to Hans-Jorg Albrecht, 'Sentencing and Disparity – A Comparative Study', in 2 EUR. J. ON CRIM. POL'Y & RES. (1994), p. 98.

has been developed that reduces opportunities and incentives to deviate from established sentencing patterns.[170]

Criminal law and doctrine do not provide for guidance and structure beyond the statement that personal guilt must be the basis of a sentencing decision. Individual guilt in this respect has two functions: it determines the imputation of criminal responsibility (rationale of punishment) and it determines the sentencing decision and the size of the penalty (limitation or restriction of punishent). The judiciary has developed a model of joining various functions of criminal punishment: (1) The limiting function of guilt does not allow deviation from criminal punishment commensurate with guilt (BGH Apr. 10, 1987, 34 BGHST 345); (2) Deterrence and rehabilitative purposes may only be considered within a range of sentences that is commensurate with individual guilt.[171] Albrecht is of the opinion that normative discourses on sentencing center around the question of the relationship between personal guilt and positive general prevention, questions of proportionate sentencing and the range of admissible aggravating and mitigating circumstances, the weight to be attached to certain circumstances, and how such weight might be expressed.[172] These discourses fail, however, to make a distinction between the presentation of a sentencing decision and the making of a criminal sentence. Making the sentence refers to the decision-making process that results in imposing a concrete criminal penalty. The sentencing decision then has to be presented in writing and elaborated on all relevant factors that have been considered in determining the penalty. With respect to making a sentencing decision, most important are those rules that determine placement of an individual case on the applicable scale (or range) of penalties.

The German system, like the Dutch system, is organized around the central tenets of resocialization and rehabilititation. According to Germany's Prison Act, the sole aim of incarceration is to enable prisoners to lead a life of social responsibility free of crime upon release, requiring that prison life be as similar as possible to life in the community (sometimes referred to as 'the principle of normalization') and organized in such a way as to facilitate reintegration into society.[173] These principles of rehabilitation and normalization inform the sentencing practices as well as the conditions of confinement of the German criminal justice system [similar to the Dutch system]. Because the rehabilitation principle favors intermediate, non-custodial sanctions, prison is used sparingly. With

---

170 Ibid.

171 Ibid.

172 Ibid., p. 232.

173 Subramanian & Shames (2013), supra note 2707. See the Prison Act (Strafvollzugsgesetz) of 1977 § 2 and 3.

offender rehabilitation and resocialization the primary goals of corrections, conditions of confinement – in particular, treatment and disciplinary approaches – are less punitive and more goal-oreinted.[174] In Germany [like in the Netherlands], incarceration is used less frequently and for shorter periods of time. Germany, as Frieder Dunkel has observed, relies heavily on non-custodial sanctions and diversion, and only a small percentage of convicted offenders are sentenced to prison.

The system of sentencing and criminal sanctions implemented in Germany includes substantive and procedural elements. The substantive elements are found in the criminal penalties [provided in the criminal code], their minimum and maximum ranges, criminal offense statutes carrying each a minimum and maximum penalty, statutory prescriptions as regards the choice between different criminal sanctions such as day fines and prison sentences. The basic rule on sentencing mentions personal guilt as the decisive factor in determining the sentence, but concedes that the impact of the sentence on the offender should be taken into account.[175] Moreover, a non-exhaustive list of offenses and offender-related elements must be considered when it comes to determining the sentence.[176] The code gives explicit consideration to the victim and victim-offender reconciliation, allowing for mitigation in cases of seriously attempted or completely achieved reconciliation.[177] Recently, a crown-witness provision was introduced that provides for a sentencing discount, too.[178] Particular rules address sentencing of multiple offenses;[179] they demand a cumulative sentence (separate and consecutively enforceable sentences may not be imposed) and result in mandatory sentencing discounts.[180] In cases of statutory defined mitigating circumstances (most importantly, diminished responsibility, participation in the form of aiding and abetting, and attempt), minimum penalties are lowered significantly.[181] A mandatory and general statutory minimum for recidivist was abolished in 1986 (the minimum

174 Ibid. See Frieder Dunkel, 'The Sentencing System, Probation and Re-entry of Prisoners in Germany', (presented at the European-American Prison Project conference at Waldeck Prison, Dummerstorf, Mecklenburg-Western Pomerania, Germany, February 18, 2013); for the Netherlands, see Mariette Horstink, "The Custodial Institutions Agency" (presented at the European-American Prison Project conference at the Ministry of the Interior, The Hague, The Netherlands, February 21, 2013).

175 Albrecht (2013), supra note 2713, p. 214. See STGB, Nov. 13,1998, BGBL I, p. 3322, § 46.

176 Ibid. See STGB, Nov. 13, 1998, BGBL I p. 3322, § 46.

177 Ibid. See STGB, Nov. 13, 1998, BGBL I p. 3322, § 46a.

178 Ibid. See STGB, Nov. 13, 1998, BGBL I p. 3322, § 46b.

179 Ibid. See STGB, Nov. 13, 1998, BGBL I p. 3322, § 52-55.

180 Ibid. See STGB, Nov. 13, 1998, BGBL I p. 3322, § 54.

181 Ibid. See STGB, Nov. 13, 1998, BGBL I p. 3322, § 49.

had previously been raised to six months but was considered to have no practical relevance), but recidivism as an aggravating factor was introduced specifically for sexual abuse offenders in a 2003 criminal amendment.[182] Under the provisions of STRAFPROZESSORDNUNG [STOP] [CODE OF CRIMINAL PROCEDURE],[183] the procedural elements affecting sentencing refer to simplified criminal proceedings that – if applied – severely restrict the range of penalties available (day fines and suspended prison sentences up to one year may be imposed) (§ 407), and to the recently introduced formal rules on sentence bargaining; further procedural elements concern the duty to give detailed reasons in writing (§ 267) and the rules that allow for a review of sentencing decisions by the High Court or Federal Court of Justice. The duty to give detailed reasons in writing is suspended if both prosecutor and defense waive the right to appeal, resulting in the verdict becoming immediately final (§ 267).

The sentencing theory of 'margins' (*Spielraumtheorie*), as adopted by the German Court of Justice[184] and widely supported by penal scholars, assumes that a single sentence length exists, corresponding exactly to individual guilt as expressed in the criminal offense.[185] However, it is also assumed that it is not possible to determine this sentence with precision because of general limitations in decision-making under conditions of uncertainty and limited access to the truth.[186] Theory of margins simply says that a sentence corresponding to personal guilt may be chosen from a (narrow) range of sentences determined within the range of penalties carried by the offense statute. Minimum and maximum sentences of this narrow range must still be justified by guilt.[187] Within this assumed range of guilt-commensurate sentences, however, preventive functions of the penalty may be considered. Sentencing falling within the range are considered to be legally acceptable penalties. The consequence of the theory of margin, therefore, is not the generation of an effective tool for determining the size of a criminal penalty, but the theory contributes to opening a normative discourse on which arguments should influence the

182 Ibid., p. 215, referring to Hans-Jorg Albrecht, 'Sexualstrafrecht – Reformen und Ergebnisse', in 59 RECHT DER JUGEND UND DES BILDUNGSWESENS 148, 154 (2011).

183 Ibid. See STRAFPROZESSORDNUNG [STOP] [CODE OF CRIMINAL PROCUDURE], Apr. 7, 1987, BGBL. I, p. 1074, § 407 and § 267.

184 Ibid., p. 231. See BGH Nov. 10,1954, 7 BGHST 29 (32); BGH Aug. 4, 1965, 20 BGHST 264 (267); BGH Oct. 27, 1970, 24 BGHST 132 (133).

185 Ibid., referring to BERND-DIETER METER, 'STRAFRECHTLICHE SANKTIONEN' 115 (3d. ed. 2009); FRANZ STRENG, 'STRAFRECHTLICHE SANKTIONEN: DIE STRAFZUMESSUNG UND IHRE GRUNDLAGEN' 252 (2002).

186 Ibid.

187 Ibid.

limits of a guilt-commensurate criminal penalty.[188] However, the German normative framework of sentencing provides an opportunity to satisfy the obvious need to discuss all factors relevant for individualized sentencing and to achieve a decision that is carried primarily by those factors that establish the 'typical case' (or establish deviations from it).[189] The German Federal Court of Justice could identify several areas along the decision-making process where mistakes in law may occur when deciding on a criminal sentence.[190] First, the court identifies inconsistency in reasoning, which has obtained the status of a legal mistake, and which is directly related to the demand for complexity in reasoning about a criminal sentence.[191] Second, flawed assessment of sentencing facts (either mitigating or aggravating) has received the court's attention,[192] as has, third, deviation from the 'usual' penalty (or tariff) *in sentencing*.[193] As Albrecht has noted, although sentencing once was considered to be fully at the discretion of the trial judge, today a sentencing decision is considered to be, in its essential parts, the application of law, [rather than discretion].

***

In Sweden, so called 'penalty scales' are attched to the provisions on the specific crimes in the Code or elsewhere, with a particular maximum and a particular minimum sentence. Ocassionally the minimum has to be deduced from general rules on minimum sentence. What is important is that the maximum sentence and the minimum sentence in these penalty scales are always expressed using some of the two punishments, i.e., fines or imprisonment or a combination of these two punishments. Although the aforementioned sanctions (conditional sentence, probation and committal for special care) are not included in the penal scale for the crimes, they may be imposed instead of punishment in accordance with separately formulated provisions.[194] The court may, instead of imposing a punishment by way of fines or punishments, choose *another sanction for a crime.* Such sanctions are conditional sentence, probation or surrender to special care. The court may also use different combinations of punishment and

188 Ibid., p. 232.
189 Ibid., p. 233.
190 Ibid., p. 234, referring to STRENG (2002), supra note 2734, p. 265.
191 Ibid. See BGH Jan. 9, 1961, 17 BGHST 35.
192 Ibid.
193 Ibid., p. 235. See BGH Feb 27, 1992, 1992, 12 NSTZ 381.
194 Traskman (2003), supra note 1737, p. 186.

sanctions for a crime.[195] A principal rule on the choice of sanctions (Chapter 30, Section 4 of the Penal Code) stipulates, as written by Per Ole Traskman, that in choosing a sanction, the court *shall* pay special attention to any circumstance or circumstances that argue for *the imposition of a less severe punishment than imprisonment*.[196] In choosing a sanction, the court *shall* consider, as a motive for imposing a *conditional sentence*, whether there is an absence of reason to fear that the accused will be guilty of continued criminality. As a special reason for imposing a conditional sentence instead of imprisonment, the court may consider that the sentence *shall* be combined with a condition of *community service* if the accused is willing to accept such a condition, and that such a condition is appropriate having regard to the accused person and the circumstances in general (Chapter 30, Section 7 of the Penal Code).

A key concept is the concept of '*penal value*'. According to the principal rule on the measurement of punishment in Chapter 29, Section 1 of the Penal Code, the punishment *shall* be imposed within the statutory limits according to the penal value of the crime or crimes, and the interest of uniformity in sentencing *shall* be taken into consideration.[197] The penal value is determined with special regard to the harm, offence, or risk which the conduct involved, what the accused realized or should have realized about it, and the intentions and motives of the accused. In the code some aggravating circumstances (Section 2) and some mitigating circumstances (Section 3) are explicitly mentioned. In assessing the penal value, the following *aggravating circumstances,* as stated under Section 2, should be given special considerations in addition to what is applicable to each and every type of crime: (1) whether the accused intended that the crime should have markedly more serious consequences that it in fact had; (2) whether the accused manifested especial ruthlessness; (3) whether the accused exploited some other person's vulnerable position or that person's special difficulties in protecting himself; (4) whether the accused grossly exploited his position or otherwise abused a special confidence or trust; (5) whether the accused induced another person to take part in the crime by coercion, deceit or misuse of that person's youthfulness, lack of understanding or dependent status; or (6) whether the crime was part of a criminal activity which was especially carefully planned or carried out on a large scale and which the accused had a significant role; or (7) whether a motive for the crime was to aggrieve a person, ethnic group or some other similar group of people by reason of race, color, national or ethnic origin, religious belief or other similar circumstance. In assessing penal value, the following *mitigating circumstances* under Section 3 should be given special considerations in

195 Ibid., p. 187.
196 Ibid., p. 193.
197 Ibid., p. 190.

addition to what is prescribed elsewhere, if, in a particuar case: (1) the crime was occasioned by the grossly offensive behavior of some other person; (2) the accused, in consequence of a mental disturbance or emotional excitement, or for some other cause, had a markedly diminished capacity to control his actions; (3) the actions of the accused were connected with his manifestly deficient development, experience or capacity for judgment; (4) the crime was occasioned by strong human compassion; or (5) the act, without being free from criminal responsibility, was such as is covered by Chapter 24 [containing provisions on general grounds for exemption from criminal responsibility]. The sentence imposed may be less severe than that prescribed for the crime in question if this is called for having regard to the penal value of the crime.

Previous criminality may influence ('to a reasonable extent') the severity of punishment if it has not been taken 'appropriately into account in the choice of sanction or revocation of parole'. In determining the appropriate punishment the court, if sufficient consideration cannot be given to the circumstances through choice of sanction or forfeiture of conditionally granted liberty, *shall*, besides the penal value of the crime, take reasonable account of whether the accused has previously been guilty of crime. In this connection, special considerations *shall* be given to the extent of any previous criminality, to the time that has elapsed between the crimes, and whether the previous and the new criminality are similar in nature or whether in both cases they are of an especially serious character.[198] The rules on the measurement of punishment[199] contain a special provision concerning *equity mitigation*: In determining the appropriate punishment, the court *shall*, besides the penal value of the crime, give reasonable consideration to: (1) whether the accused has suffered severe bodily harm as a result of the crime; (2) whether the accused to the best of his ability has attempted to prevent, remedy or limit the harmful consequences of the crime; (3) whether the accused gave himself up; (4) whether the accused would suffer harm through expulsion by reason of the crime from the Realm; (5) whether the accused, as a result of the crime, has suffered, or there is good reason to suppose that he will suffer dismissal from, or termination of employment, or will encounter any other obstacle or special difficulty in the pursuit of his occupation or business; (6) whether the accused, in consequence of advanced age or ill health, would suffer unreasonable hardship by a punishment imposed in accordance with the penal value of the crime; (7) whether, having regard to the nature of the crime, an unusually long time has elapsed since its commission; or (8) whether there exists any other circumstance that calls for a lesser punishment warranted by the penal value of the crime.

198 Ibid., p. 191.

199 Ibid., pp. 191-192.

The core aim of the Netherlands 1998 Penitentiary Act is the re-socialization of prisoners in which incarceration is carried out with as few restriction as possible through the principle of association (both within prison and between prisoners and the community), and not separation.[200] The general, very low, minimum principal penalties are characteristics of the Dutch system of criminal sanctions. Therefore, a big difference arises between the (general) minimum and the (specific) maximum penalty that can be imposed for an offence. Because of the general minimum penalties, this difference becomes bigger in grave offences of which the seriousness is expressed in a higher maximum penalty. In each case, the criminal judge has the power to impose a sentence of which the ultimate limits are drawn between the special maximum and the general minimum. In the Dutch system of criminal law the judge has a great margin of discretion to determine the appropriate sanction, considering the gravity of the offence and the person of the suspect.[201] The absence of mandatory rules for imposing a penalty may contribute to a mild penal climate but may also result in great disparity in sentencing in the Netherlands, says Tijs Kooijmans.[202] The Courts of Appeal or the Supreme Court can undo extreme unjust sentences. But neither appellate courts nor the Supreme Court can never realize full equality in sentencing by lower courts. Various proposals have been discussed to improve the equality in sentencing without restricting too much the judges' power to individualize the sentence. Those proposals ranged from the establishment of a special Sentencing Court, or a data bank on sentences, to sentencing checklists or drawing up sentences guidelines for courts but none of those proposals led to a viable solution to the problem of disparity in imposing penalties.

The Dutch criminal judge, according to Kooijmans, is allowed to take into consideration, when he determines the penalty (the limit of which is bound by the concrete criminal provision), the criminal record of the suspect, including the crimes committed abroad, and other personal circumstances concerning the suspect.[203] This criminal record may convince the judge that another service penalty is not going to keep the suspect from committing another crime and, for that reason, a custodial sentence is appropriate. Dutch law does not contain a provision which prescribes that a previous foreign conviction should be an aggrevating circumstances for determining the penalty.

---

200 Subramanian & Shames (2013), supra note 2722, referring to Penitentiary Principles Act (1998), Art. 2; Rutger Krabbendam, "Prison System Modernisation Program" (presented at the European-American Prison Project conference at the Ministry of the Interior, The Hague, The Netherlands, February 21, 2013).

201 Kooijmans (2003), supra note 1754, pp. 204-205.

202 Ibid., p. 205.

203 Ibid., p. 213.

V.1.6. COURT'S CONCRETE DECISION AS "PERFORMANCE OF LAW"

***

The judicial decision is the pulse of legal life, and it is here that the analysis of the legal sources comes into play. A source of law, then, means the general factors (motive components) which guide the judge when fixing and making concrete the legal content in judicial decision.[204] As already mentioned, in judicial decision, Goodhart says *ratio decidendi* must be distinguished from court concrete decision or court order. Judicial order is one which involves exercise of judicial discretion and effects final result of litigation (*Happy Coal Co. v. Brashear*, 263 Ky. 257, 92 S.W.2d 23, 27).[205] Final order is one which either terminates the action itself, or decides some matter litigated by the parties, or operates to divest some right; or one which completely disposes of the subject-matter and the rights of the parties (*Salem King's Products Co. v. La Follette*, 100 Or. 11, 196 P. 416, 417; *Stockham v. Knollenberg*, 133 Md. 337, 105 A. 305, 307; *Marchant & Taylor v. Mathhews Country*, 139 Va. 723, 124 S.E. 420, 423). Charging order is the name bestowed, in English practice, upon an order allowed by St. 1 & 2 Vict. C.110, § 14, and 3 & 4 Vict. C. 82, to be granted to a judgment creditor, that the property of a judgment debtor in government stock, or in the stock of any public company in England, corporate or otherwise, *shall* (whether standing in his own name or in the name of any person in trust for him) stand charged with the payment of the amount for which judgment shall have been recovered, with interest (3 Steph. Comm. 587, 588).[206]

An order of the United States Supreme Court requires a person to do an act, and such an order must specify the file after service of the order, or some time, within which the act is to be done (Order 42, Rule 6 paragraph (1) of the Supreme Court of Judicature Act (Chapter 322) – Rules of Court, R 5 G.N. No.71/96 1997 Ed. (Revised Edition 2006 (1.4.2006). Orders also include orders to pay money to some other person, give possession of any immovable property or deliver any movable property [Order 42, Rule 6 paragraph (2)]. An order of the Court takes effect from the day it is pronounced, unless the Court orders it to be dated as of some other earlier or later day [Order 42, Rule 7 paragraph (1) and (2)].

---

204 Ross (1946), supra note 1079, p. 730, quoting Ross, 'A Texbook of International Law', (1947), p. 80.

205 Black (1957), supra note 2623, p. 986.

206 Ibid., p. 1247.

In *Isaiah Lester v. Allied Concrete Company and William Donald Sprouse*, Case No. CL08-150 and Case No. CL09-223, the Circuit Court of the City of Charlottesville, Virginia, issued its final order that: 1) The total of fees and expenses found to be payable to Defendants is $722,000, with the sum of $625,110 due Patton Boggs LLP and the sum of $96,890 due Zunka, Milnor & Carter, Ltd; 2) Of the grand total set forth above, Murray is obligated for, and is hereby ORDERED to remit to Defendants, the sum of $542,000; and 4) Of the grand total set forth above, Lester is obligated for, and hereby ORDERED to remit to Defendants, the sum of $ 180,000. In *Presidential Women's Center v. State of Florida*, Case No. CL-97-5796-AG, the Curcuit Court of the Fifteenth Judicial Circuit in and for Palm Beach County, Florida issued an order granting the Plantiff's Motion for Summary Judgment/Supplemental Motion for Summary Judgements, as follows: A permanent injunction is entered against any enforcement of Section 390.0111(3), as said Amended Statute is unconstitutional as a matter of law. DONE and ORDERED in Chambers, West Palm Beach, Palm Beach County, Florida this 13th day of September 2002.

In USCA Case #12-5117 the United States Court of Appeal for the District of Columbia Circuit ordered that the emergency motions for stay pending appeal be denied. Appellants have not satisfied the stringent requirements for a stay pending appeal. *See Washington Metropolitan Area Transit Commission v. Holiday Tours, Inc.*, 559 F.2d 841, 843 (D.C. Cir. 1977). The court further ordered that the appeal be expedited and calendared for oral argument on the first appropriate date in September 2012, following briefing. See 28 U.S.C. § 1657(a); D.C. Cir. Rule 47.2.[207]

The Federal Court of Australia in its judgment of April 7, 2014, Citation: Envestra Limited, in the matter of Envestra Limited [2014] FCA 395, issued an order, *inter alia*, that: Pursuant to section 411(1) of the Corporation Act 2001 (Cth) (Act) there be convened a meeting (Scheme Meeting) of holders of fully paid ordinary shares of the Plaintiff (other than Australian Pipeline Trust) (ARSN 091 678 778) (APT), APT Investment Trust (ARSN 115 585 441) (APTIT), Australian Pipeline Limited (CAN 091 344 704) (APL) and each of the entities controlled by APL in its capacity as responsible entity of APT and APTIT (Participating Envestra Shareholders), for the purpose of considering and, if thought fit, approving (with or without modification) the scheme of arrangement between persons who are Participating Envestra Shareholders on the Record Date (as defined in the Scheme) and the Plaintiff (Scheme), the terms of which are set out in Exhibit A in the proceeding (Scheme Booklet).

An order was issued by the Federal Court of Australia on April 8, 2014 in Case with Citation: Application of Sompo Japan Insurance Inc.,

207 USCA Case #12-5117, Document #1373694, File: 05/14/2012.

under the *Insurance Act 1973* (Cth) [2014] FCA 396, that in relation to the proposed scheme for the transfer of the insurance business carried on by Nipponkoa Insurance Company Limited (Nipponkoa) in Australia to Sompo Japan Insurance Inc., (the Scheme), the need for the Applicant to comply with s17C(2)(c) of the *Insurance Act 1973* (Cth) be dispensed with provided that the Applicant complies with the order below; that the Applicant cause a copy of the summary of the Scheme, approved by the Australian Prudential Regulation Authority, to be sent by pre-paid post to those policy holders of Nipponkoa; that the Applicant pay the costs of the Australian Prudential Regulation Authority of this application as taxed or agreed.

Under Section 313 of German Code of Civil Procedure as promulgated on December 5, 2005 (Federal Law Gazette I page 3202), (2006, page 431), as amended by Article 50 of the Act dated April 19, 2006 (Federal Law Gazette I page 866) (Act on Regulatory Reform of Federal Law in the Area of Responsibility of the Federal Ministry of Justice (Gesetz über die Bereingung von Bundesrecht im Zuständigkeitsbereich des Bundesministeriums der Justiz, BMJBergG 1) with effect per April 25, 2006, court's concrete order is termed 'the operative provisions of a judgment'. The operative provisions or the operative part is the basis of the enforcement by the execution organs. It must be sufficiently clear and precise to make it possible for the execution organs to enforce the judgment (e.g., identify without any doubt the objects of enforcement) without having recourse to the statement of the facts, the grounds for the decision, the court's file or the pleading. It is immediately clear from the operative part of judgment what the defendant must be required to do or not to do.[208] It is normally not permitted to extend the scope of the operative part of judgment by referring to the facts of the case or the reasoning of the court. Rather the parties *shall* be encouraged to state their demands as precisely as possible in their petitions to have the court rule on them and make it clear in the operative part of the judgment what the enforceable content of the decision *shall* be.[209]

In Germany, the order of the *Landgericht* that the defendant had to pay the plaintiff DM 8,000 as damages for pain and suffering was affirmed by the *Budesgerichtshof* in Case BGHZ35,363=NJW 1961,2059, September 19, 1961. In that case, the plaintiff claimed DM 10,000 as satisfaction for the harm done to him by the defendant company which was dealing in a tonic containing ginseng, because the plaintiff had suffered an unauthorized attack on his personality right by the advertisement that had given rise to the impression that he had, for payment, issued an opinion on a controversial topic in a department of knowledge not his own, and unprofessionally lent

208 Heinze (2006), supra note 2685, fn. 3, § 890 No.22.

209 Ibid., p. 10.

his name to advertising a doubtful product.[210] Another case in Germany was the '*CompuServe Case*' (*Somm Case*), File No : 8340 Ds 465 Js 173158/95, in which the Local Court (*Amtsgericht*) of Munich in its judgment on July 15, 1998 sentenced former CompuServe Germany managing director to 2 years' probation for the distribution of child pornography and other illegal materials that could be accessed via CompuServe's Internet access and its proprietary service (see Chapter IV.10.3, page 502-4).[211] The Austrian Supreme Court/*Oberster Gerichtshof* in Case: 7 Ob 302/05w, January 25, 2006[212] issued an order that the [Buyer] had to reimburse EUR 665.66 (including EUR 110.94 turnover taxes) for costs of the appellate response within 14 days, and according to this order the [Buyer] had to factually pay the sum of money as ordered.

The Dutch system of criminal law acknowledges the (general) possibility of a conviction under conditions. According to article 14a of the Criminal Code, where a penalty of not more than one year in jail or a penalty of detention, other than detention as a substitute penalty, a service penalty or a fine is imposed, the judge may order that these penalties should not be executed in whole or in part. Where a penalty of not less than one year in jail and not more than three years' imprisonment is imposed, the judge may order that part of the penalty, being not more than one third, should not be executed. The judge may in addition order that additional penalties imposed should not be executed in whole or in part. According to article 14b, the judge who orders that the sentence imposed by him should not be executed in whole or in part should at the same time determine a period of probation. The legal maximum of this probation period varies between two and three years.[213]

Court's concrete order is related to the discourse on law as fact in Chapter II.1.5 - page 222-3, touching performative language. There exist cause and consequence, which constitute the dimension of legal rule in the real world [time and space].[214] Olivecrona mentions that an example of executory judgement appears to be a judgment that orders a person to

210 Schlechtriem et al. (1999), supra note 2419.

211 Judgment of the Munich Court in the "CompuServe Case" (Somm Case), translation and comment by Christopher Kuner, http://www.kuner.com/data/reg/somm.html.

212 Case: 7Ob 302/05w, January 25, 2006, translation by Jan Henning Berg, edited by Institut fur auslanddisches und internationales Privat- und Wirtschaftsrecht der Universitat Heidelberg, Daniel Nagel, editor.

213 Kooijmans (2003), supra note 2750, p. 207. See article 14b (2) jo. article 14c (1) and (2), section 3 and d of Criminal Code.

214 Spaak (2009/2011), supra note 1476, pp. 39-40, citing Olivecrona (1971), supra note 2697, pp. 133-34.

pay somebody else a sum of money.[215] So, court's concrete decision (or court's order) is one that can be enforced or executed through real action. Olivecrona's imperative language of law is in line with Bentham's analysis of the language of law. Bentham seems to have thought of the meaning of a word in casual terms, as its capacity to act on a subject by raising an image of perceptible substance or emotions for which the word was a name. 'By these general terms or names, things and persons, acts, and so forth are brought to view'.[216] Words that do not bring to view such perceptible things have no meaning, on that view, except insofar as they can be expounded by 'paraphrases'.[217]

As to word and act, the 'John Searle sees something inside the head' just refers to something outside the head. That's the real magic, he says.[218] According to the theory of speech act by John L. Austin and John Searle, the act of discourse is constituted by a hierarchy of subordinate acts distributed on three levels: (1) the level of locutionary or propositional act, the act *of* saying; (2) the level of the illocutionary act (or force), what we do *in* saying; and (3) the level of the perlocutionary act, what we do *by the fact that* we speak.[219] If I tell you to close the door, I do three things. First, I relate the action predicate (to close) to two variables (you and the door): this is the act of saying. Second, I tell you this with the force of an order rather than a statement, wish or promise: this is the illocutionary act. Finally, I can provoke certain consequences, such as fear, by the fact that I give you an order; hence discourse is a sort of stimulus which produces certain results: this is the perlocutionary act.

Reporting what court orders really are is possible, and such reporting means to express the descriptivity of legal rules as we see in reality. A court's order, when executed or enforced, as 'speech act' is the law as it really is, the law we see in the real world. Such enforcement may be carried out voluntarily by the parties to the case as judicially settled, or by state's

---

215 Spaak (2009a), supra note 2695, n.1.

216 Timothy Endicott, 'Law and Language', in Standford Encyclopedia of Philosophy, first published Thursday, December 5, 2002, substantive revision Monday, August 9, 2010, § 1. See Jeremy Bentham, 'Of Laws in General' (1782), in H.L.A. Hart ed. (London: Athlone Press, 1970), p. 82; Jeremy Bentham, 'A Fragment on Government'(1776), in J.H. Burns and H.L.A. Hart ed., (Cambridge: Cambridge University Press, 1988), p. 28, 108n.

217 Ibid.

218 Marga Reimer and Eliot Michaelson, 'Reference', in Stanford Encyclopedia of Philosophy, 2014, § 2.1.

219 Thompson (1981), supra note 1865, pp. 134-35, referring to J.L. Austin, 'How to do Things with Words', (Oxford: Oxford University Press, 1962); John R. Searle,'Speech Act: An Essay in the Philosophy of Language', (Cambridge: Cambridge University Press, 1969).

officials in case of official enforcement. Court's orders as expressed in imperative language alone are already 'speech acts' (as elaborated by Austin and Searle), and such speech acts and the enforcement thereof constitute real acts. Speech act plus the enforcement thereof are performative, constituting the performance of law.

V.1.7. ADMINISTRATIVE ACTION / DECISION AS "PERFORMANCE OF LAW"

Administrative actions or decisions are made through administrative process. The judicial or administrative process by which sanctions, including license revocation or suspension and fines, are imposed is also important from a deterrence perspective because it has important implications for all three characteristics – swiftness, certainty, and severity – of penalties imposed. The administrative process requires only that the balance of evidence favor the conclusion that a sanction is merited. It is unconcerned with determining criminal guilt. The administrative process can thus be relatively swift and certain in applying sanctions, particularly license actions.[220] Under the administrative process, the regulator determines that a breach of regulatory legislation has occured and that an adiministrative penalty is imposed [payable to the regulator]. A recent survey of the use of administrative penalties in Canada observed that 'it is only relatively recently that they have become a favorite tool among regulators, but they have been increasingly used to engender compliance and cooperation from the regulated community, to secure environmental or consumer protection'. In most cases, administrative decisions are made on the imposition of administrative penalties on individuals and business that have been licensed to undertake regulated activities, and administrative penalties are used in these cases to enforce the terms of license. Because administrative penalties are imposed without a hearing in a court, and usually without any other formal hearing, other procedural protections must be in place to ensure that the process of administrative decision-making is fair, and is seen to be fair.[221] It has been observed that, because administrative penalties are imposed directly by the regulator, they 'are often thought of as being negotiated or imposed in the shadow of the formal legal system'.[222]

---

220 James L. Nichols and H. Laurence Ross, 'The Effectiveness of Legal Sanctions in Dealing with Drinking Drivers', in Judicial and Administrative Process – Background Paper, 1988, pp. 94-95, published in Alcohol Drugs and Driving, Vol. 8, Issue 2, dated April-June 1990, pp. 33-60, and, Journal of Safety Research 22(2): 117-117, June 1991.

221 Law Reform Commission of Saskatchewan (2012), supra note 1761.

222 Ibid., referring to Tait (2007), supra note 1763, p. 9 [footnote ommitted].

In Canada, Justice L'Heureux-Dube in *Baker v. Canada (Minister of Citizenship and Immigration)* [1999] 2 S.C.R. 817, holds: "Administrative law has traditionally approached the review of decisions classified as discretionary separately from those seen as involving the interpretation of rules of law. The rule has been that decisions classified as discretionary may only be reviewed on limited grounds such as the bad faith of the decision-makers, the exercise of discretion from an improper purpose, and the use of irrelevant considerations" [citations, including Wednesbury, omitted]. In my opinion, these doctrines incorporate two central ideas – that discretionary decisions, like all other administrative decisions, must be made within the bounds of the jurisdiction conferred by the statute [....] However, discretion must still be exercised in a manner that is within a reasonable interpretation of the margin of manoeuvre contemplated by the legislature [...]. The constitutionality of administrative penalties was addressed in 2004 by the Supreme Court of Canada in *Martineau v. MNR*, 2004 SCC 81, [2004] 3 S.C.R. 737 that administrative penalties are not objectionable in principle. The Court upheld provisions in the Customs Act allowing customs officials to declare property illegally imported into Canada forfiet without obtaining a court order. Although the provision in question was not an administrative penalty in the strict sense, it is analogous in allowing a regulatory sanction to be imposed without recourse to the courts. In *Martineau*, the Court assumed that the administrative regime met the minimum standards of natural justice, and that its purpose was truly regulatory rather than punitive. The Supreme Court in *Cardinal v. Kent Institution*, [1985] 2 SCR 643 at paragraph 14 has held: "[T]here is, as a general common law principle, a duty of procedural fairness lying on every public authority making an administrative decision which is not of a legislative nature and which affects the rights, privileges or interests of an individual".[223] A right to appeal an administrative action/decision, including imposition of an administrative penalty, exists only if it is specifically provided by statute. As Jones and de Villars say: "There is no legal or constitutional requirement that an appeal should exist from any decision made by a statutory delegate. It is possible to find numerous examples where legislation has made no provision for an appeal, whether to another step in the administrative hierarchy or to the court".[224] Recently, most administrative penalties in Canada provide for a right of review, although typically not before the penalty becomes enforceable.[225]

---

223 Ibid., n.16.

224 Ibid., referring to David Phillip Jones & Anne S de Villars, 'Principles of Administrative Law', fourth edition, (Scarborough, Ont: Carswell, 2004), p. 546.

225 Ibid., quoting Tait (2007), supra note 2771, p. 10.

The money penalty is only one of many sanctions available to administrative agencies for enforcing their regulations.[226] In the United States, six administrative agencies [the Immigration and Naturalization Service, the Occupational Safety and Health Administration, the Federal Home Loan Bank Board, the United States Postal Service, the Department of the Interior, and the Department of Labor] have the power to make decisions on the imposition of civil money penalties through a regulatory framework which does not provide for jury trial.[227] The Immigration and Naturalization Service has authority to assess civil money penalties against individuals who violate its regulations, 8 U.S.C. §§ 1221(d), 1223(d), 1227(b), 1229, 1253(c), 1281(d), 1284(a), 1285, 1286, 1287, 1321, 1322(a) and (b), 1323(b) (1970). The Supreme Court held that this assessment is subject only to limited judicial review. The Occupational Safety and Health Administration, 29 U.S.C. §§ 651 et seq. (1970), has authority to assess civil money penalties against individuals who violate its regulation, 29 U.S.C. § 666(a), (b), (c), (d) and (h) (1970. The Federal Home Loan Bank Board's authority to assess civil money penalties is based on 12 U.S.C. §§ 1425a(d), 1425b(b) (1970). The United States Postal Service may assess civil money penalties for violations of its regulation, 39 U.S.C. §§ 5206, 55603 (197)); 49 U.S.C. § 1471(a) (1970). The courts have ruled that this assessment is subject only to limited judicial review. In 1973, Congress enacted the Endangered Species Act, 16 U.S.C. §§ 1531-1543 (Supp. III, 1973), which authorizes the Secretary of Interior to assess civil money penalties subject only to limited judicial review, 16 U.S.C. § 1540(a) (Supp. III, 1973). In 1974, Congress enacted Fair Labor Standard Amendment, 29 U.S.C. §§ 202-16 (Supp. IV, 1974), amending 29 U.S.C. §§ 201-19 (1970), which authorizes the Secretary of Labor to assess civil money penalties against individuals for violations of the child labor regulations. Judicial review of this assessment is subject only to limited review, 29 U.S.C. § 216(e) (Supp. IV, 1974).[228]

Under the *Curtis-Pernell* test for Seventh Amendment applicability, the right to a jury trial depends upon the nature of the rights and remedies involved. Where the rights and remedies are legal in nature, as in the case of a civil money penalty, the Seventh Amendment guarantee applies. Where a civil money penalty has been administratively imposed, some courts have denied the jury trial right by unquestioning adherence to the general principle that the seventh amendment is inapplicable to administratively proceedings. However, that general doctrine is based upon precedent which has involved the adjudication of equitable matters and is inapplicable to civil money penalties, which are legal.[229] In England, Lord Greene, M.R. in

226 Hewit & Wallace (1976), supra note 1767, p. 719, n.2.

227 Ibid., p. 720.

228 Ibid., p. 720, 721, n.4.

229 Ibid., p. 744.

Associated Provincial Picture Houses Limited v. Wednesbury Corporation [1948] 1 K. B. 233, 234, holds that the discretion assigned to public authority will not be reviewed by the courts so long as all the things that ought to be considered have been taken into account and things which ought not to be considered have not been taken into account in the decision, and the decision is not unreasonable. Administrative decisions may be challenged before administrative courts in certain countries. Having been final (or not being challenged), administrative actions constitute *the law we see in reality*.

V.2. RES JUDICATA

Res judicata is a judicial policy which operates to preclude a matter which has once been adjudicated from being litigated a second time.[230] The long established doctrine of *res judicata*, according to the original Restatement of Judgments, is based on the "public policy of putting an end to litigation".[231] The draft of the Restatement of Judgments (Second) suggests reasons for this policy: 'fairness to the defendant, and sound judicial administration'.[232] In the words of James and Hazard, the policy is to 'bring an adjudication to a final conclusion with reasonable promptness and within reasonable limits of costs'.[233] To litigate the same matter twice or more would impose costs on the parties and the burdened and subsidized judicial system. Indeed, if a judgment were not conclusive as to what it actually determined, 'the adjudicative process would fail to serve its social function' of resolving disputes.

Modern developments in *res judicata* and due process have focused attention on the competing policies that underlie the doctrines: judicial economy and fairness to the litigants.[234] At first blush, the policies behind *res judicata* may appear to point toward not allowing the plaintiff to maintain a second suit. The public policy of putting an end to litigation

230 283 DUKE LAW JOURNAL (1966), RES JUDICATA ["DUKE L.J. 1966/283"] , n.1.

231 David P. Currie, 'Res Judicata: The Neglected Defense', in 45 University of Chicago Law Review 317 (1978), p. 325. See RESTATEMENT OF JUDGMENT § 1, Comment a (1942).

232 Ibid. See RESTATEMENT (SECOND) OF JUDGMENT § 48, Comment a, p. 36 (Tent. Draft No.1, 1973).

233 Ibid., referring to F. JAMES & G. HAZARD, 'CIVIL PROCEDURE', 530 (2d ed. 1977).

234 Glenn M. Gottlieb, 'Res Judicata and Collateral Estoppel Beneath the Corporate Veil', in 66 Cal. L. Rev. 1093 (1978), p. 1108.

is against the plaintiff.[235] The plaintiff has been given a day in court and, though successful, would normally not be allowed to bring a second action for further relief.[236] Moreover, the doctrine of *res judicata* is intended to protect the parties from the vexation and expense of repetitive litigation.[237] The decision whether to apply *res judicata* to issues not actually litigated should be made in light of the policies underlying that doctrine[238] the competing interests 'of the defendant and of the courts in bringing litigation to a close' and 'of the plaintiff in the vindication of a just claim'.[239] More specifically, the reason *res judicata* is given narrower scope when the second proceeding is on a different cause of action, otherwise a litigant might suffer unforeseeable effects on unrelated claims. Not only would this result be unfair, it might not serve the aim of judicial economy.[240] Under *res judicata*, 'a final judgment on the merits bars further claims by parties or their privies based on the same cause of action'.[241] *Res Judicata* prevents litigation of all grounds for, or defense to, recovery that were previously available to the parties, regardless of whether they were asserted or determined in the prior proceeding.[242] In *Brown v. Felsen*, *res judicata* thus encourages reliance on judicial decision, bars vexatious litigation, and frees the courts to resolve other disputes.[243] In determining whether the causes of action are the same, a court must compare the substance of the actions, not their form.[244] For purposes of *res judicata*, if the later case arises out of the same 'nucleus of operative facts', or is based upon the same factual predicate, as the former action, then the two cases are really the same claim or cause of action.[245] A

235 Ibid., p. 1099. See RESTATEMENT OF JUDGMENTS §1, Comment a; IB MOORE'S FEDERAL PRACTICE 0.405, p. 628; Polasky, 'Collateral Estoppel-Effects of Prior Litigation', in 39 IOWA L. REV. 217 (1954), p. 219.

236 Ibid. See RESTATEMENT OF JUDGMENTS § 1, Comment b.

237 Ibid. See IB MOORE'S FEDERAL PRACTICE 0.441 [1] [2]; Developments of the Law Res Judicata, 65 HARV. L. REV. 818 (1952), p. 820.

238 Currie (1978), supra note 2780, p. 340. See JAMES & HAZARD (1977), supra note 2782, p. 544.

239 Ibid. See RESTATEMENT (SECOND) OF JUDGMENTS § 61, Comment b, p. 81 (Tent. Draft No. 1, 1973).

240 Ibid.

241 F:\WORDWILL\ARTICLE\Res Judicata – September 2012 DOC. Brown v Felsen, 99 S.Ct. 2205, 2209 (1979) (Tab 1) (citing Montana v. United States, 440 U.S., 147, 153; 99 S.Ct. 970, 973, 59 L.Ed. 210 (1979).

242 Ibid. (citing Chicot County Drainage Dist. v. Baxter State Bank, 308 U.S. 371, 378; 60 S.Ct., 317, 320, 84, L.Ed. 329 (1940)).

243 Ibid.

244 Ibid. See Ragsdale v. Rubbermaid, Inc., 193 F.3d 1235 (11th Cir. 1999) (Tab 2) (citing Citibank, N.A. v. Data Lease Financial Corp., 904 F. 2d 1498, 1503 (11th Cir. 1990)).

245 Ibid.

transactional approach is followed in making this determination. Among the factors to be considered in determining whether the facts are so woven together as to constitute a single claim are their relatedness in time, space, origin, or motivation, and whether, taken together, they form a convenient unit for trial purposes. If there is substantial overlap with respect to the witnesses or proofs in the second action, the second action should ordinarily be precluded.[246] A court's task is to compare the factual issues explored in the first action with the factual issues to be resolved in the second.[247] The underlying core of facts must be the same in both proceedings.[248] Similar to *Ragsdale*, in *In re Brose*, a court looks to the substance of the actions, not the form they take, to determine whether the causes of actions are the same.[249] The elements of Federal claim preclusion are: (1) there must have been a final judgment on the merits; (2) the decision was rendered by a court of competent jurisdiction; (3) the prior action must have involved the same parties or their privies; and (4) the prior action must have involved the same claim.[250]

While *res judicata* will apply to proceedings in bankruptcy court if the elements are proven, the United States Supreme Court has recognized an exception to this general rule in the area of dischargeability actions.[251] In *Brown v Felsen*,[252] the debtor argued that since a prior state court collection action had not resulted in a finding of fraud, *res judicata* barred litigation of that issue in the context of a dischargeability action under § 17a(2) and 17a(4) of the Bankruptcy Act. The court rejected this argument, ruling that *res judicata* is inapplicable to dischargeability actions for the following reasons: (1) Considerations material to discharge are typically irrelevant to the ordinary collection proceeding. The creditor often simply sues on the instrument which created the debt. Even if an issue similar to those created by § 523 should arise, the state-law concept is likely to differ from that adopted in the federal statute; (2) If a state court should expressly rule on § 523 questions, then giving finality to those rulings would undercut

246 Ibid. Ragsdale v. Rubbermaid, Inc., supra note 2793, p. 1238 (citing RESTATEMENT (SECOND) OF JUDGMENTS § 24(2) CMT.B (1980)).

247 Ibid. In re Piper Aircraft Corporation, 244 F.3d 1289, 1302 (11th Cir. 2001) (Tab 3).

248 Ibid. In re Piper Aircraft Corporation, 244 F.3d (11th Cir. 2001) (Tab 3), Ibid., p. 1301.

249 Ibid. In re Brose, 242 B.R. 531, 533 n.7 (Bankr. M.D. Fla. 1999) (holding that a settlement agreement approved in a prior bankruptcy case of the debtor precluded relitigation of the issues settled therein under the doctrine of res judicata) (Tab 5).

250 Ibid. Ragsdale v. Rubbermaid, Inc., supra note 2795, p. 1235; MOORE'S FEDERAL PRACTICE § 131.01, p. 131-11.

251 Ibid.

252 Ibid. Brown v. Felsen, supra note 2790.

Congress's intention to commit § 523 issues to the jurisdiction of the bankruptcy court. Refusing to apply *res judicata* here would permit the bankruptcy court to make an accurate determination whether respondent in fact committed the deceit, fraud, and malicious conversion that petitioner alleges; (3) The facts relevant to the dischargeability of a debt are for the first time 'squarely in issue' when the bankruptcy is filed.[253] In *Howe v. Nelson*, 636 NW2d 687, 691-92 (Minn 1965), the court has concluded that '[t]he *res judicata* effect' of a declaratory judgment action 'is essentially no different from the *res judicata* effect of any other judgment'. In *Great Northern Railway Co v. Mustad*, 33 NW2d 436, 441 (ND 1948) the court has stated that a declaratory judgment 'carries the same weight as any other judgment under the principles of *res judicata'*. Shoben, Tabb and Janutis say "Declaratory judgments ....have *res judicata* effect".[254] Landes and Posner have observed that 'an important feature of anticipatory judgments is that they can be pleaded as *res judicata* in a subsequent case'. In *Allan Block Corp v. County Materials Corp*, Posner has explained that there is an 'exception to *res judicata* for cases in which the only relief sought in the first suit is a declaratory judgment'.

The strength of the policy underlying *res judicata* is greatest when an issue has actually been litigated and decided; only then is there the double expenditure of actual relitigation. But the *res judicata* principle is not limited. Even under the first Restatement of Judgments, the plaintiff who lost a lawsuit was not permitted to try again on the basis of new evidence,[255] or a different legal theory,[256] nor could a losing defendant try again on the basis of a defense he had failed to interpose the first time around.[257] Where the second action is based on the same cause of action as that upon which the first action was based, the judgment is conclusive as to all matters which were litigated or *might* have been litigated in the first action.[258] James and Hazard have concisely stated the reason: Wherever

253 Ibid. Brown v. Felsen, Ibid.

254 Bray (2010), supra note 2698, n.75, referring to Elaine W. Shoben, William Murray & Rachel M. Janutis, 'Remedies: Cases and Problems,' 982, Foundation 4th ed., 2007; Landes and Posner', in 23 J. Legal Stud., pp. 700-701. See also Allan Block Corp v. County Materials Corp, 512 F3d 912, 916 (7th Cir 2008).

255 Currie (1978), supra note 2787, p. 337. See RESTATEMENT OF JUDGMENTS § 48, Tilustration 1 (1942).

256 Ibid. See RESTATEMENT OF JUDGMENTS § 63 & ch. 3, Introductory Note, pp. 158-59.

257 Ibid. See RESTATEMENT OF JUDGMENTS, ch. 3, Introductory Note, pp. 158-59.

258 Ibid. See RESTATEMENT OF JUDGMENTS, ch. 3, Introductory Note, p. 159 (emphasis added). See JAMES & HAZARD (1977), supra note 2787, pp. 542-43. See also RESTATEMENT (SECOND) OF JUDGMENTS § 48 Comment a, p. 36 (Tent. Draft No.1, 1973): [F]airness to the defendant, and sound judicial

there will be a large overlap of issues or evidence if two trials are held, it is wasteful to society and harassing to the adversary to have more than one.

***

The doctrine of *collateral estoppel* balances the public policies in favor of judicial economy, avoidance of inconsistent verdicts, and protection of litigants from unnecessary expense[259] against the need for a full and fair litigation of each issue. Even though a court allows a second suit, there is no reason to burden the plaintiff, or the court, unnecessarily with proving issues that have already been determined in the plaintiff's favor.[260] In addition, the possibility of inconsistent outcomes that would result from a finding of no liability in the second suit has an adverse impact on the stability of society and the judicial system, and impairs the ability of individuals to plan future conduct.[261] When claim preclusion does not apply to bar an entire claim or set of claims, the doctrine of *collateral estoppel*, or issue preclusion, may still prevent the relitigation of particular issues that were actually litigated and decided in the prior suit.[262] *Collateral estoppel* has the two-fold purpose of protecting litigants from the burden of relitigating identical facts and issues with the same party and promoting judicial economy by preventing needless litigation.[263]

The elements of the federal *collateral estoppel* doctrine are: (1) the issue at stake must be identical to the one involved in the prior litigation; (2) the issue must have been actually litigated in the prior suit;

administration, require that at some point litigation over the particular controversy come to an end....even though the substantive issues have not been tried, especially if the plaintiff has failed to avail himself of opportunities to pursue his remedies in the first proceeding....

259 Gottlieb (1978), supra note 2783, p. 1102. See fenerally IB MOORE'S FEDERAL PRACTICE 0.441 [1]-[2], 0.444 [!]; Vestal, 'Res Judicata/Preclusion: Expansion,' 41 SO. CAL. L. REV., 357 (1974), p. 379; Developments in the Law-Res Judicata, 65 HARV. L. REV. 818 (1952), p. 820.

260 Ibid., p. 1102-1103. See IB MOORE'S FEDERAL PRACTICE 0.405; RESTATEMENT OF JUDGMENTS § 1, Comment a; Polasky (1954), 'Collateral Estoppel-Effects of Prior Litigation,' 39 Iowa L. Rev. (1954), pp. 219-220; Note, Collateral Estoppel of Nonparties, 87 HARV. L. REV. 1485 (1974), p. 1501.

261 Ibid., p. 1102, referring to Polasky (1954), Ibid., pp. 219-20; Note, Collateral Estoppel of Nonparties, 87 HARV. L. REV. 1501 (1974).

262 F:\WORDWILL\ARTICLE\Res Judicata – September 2012 DOC, supra note 2790. L.A. Durbin v. Jefferson Nat'l Bank, 793 F.2d 1541, 1549 (11th Cir. 1986) (Tab 7).

263 Ibid. Parklane Hosiery Co., Inc., v. Shore, 439 U.S. U.S. 322, 338 (1979).

(3) the determination of the issue in the prior litigation must have been a critical and necessary part of the judgment in that action; and (4) the party against whom the earlier decision is asserted must have had a full and fair opportunity to litigate the issue in the earlier proceeding.[264] The basic difference between claim preclusion (*res judicata*) and issue preclusion (*collateral estoppel*) is that claim preclusion applies to whole claims, whether litigated or not, whereas issue preclusion applies to particular issues that have been contested and resolved.[265] The Florida Supreme Court in *Avant v. Hammond Jones, Inc.* also stated as to what and how *res judicata* and *collateral estoppel* are.[266] In reference to Florida law, the Court stated: "*Res judicata* bar[s] a later suit between the same parties upon the same cause of action, the first adjudication being final as to matters that were or could have been presented, while *estoppel* by judgment [i.e., *collateral estoppel*] would be applied to prevent a party from re-litigating questions common to two causes of action when those questions were actually decided in the first".

***

The rule of mutuality, a traditional limitation on the doctrine of *res judicata*, has until relatively recent times[267] maintained a remarkably well-established position in the decisional law.[268] The rule requires that one who invokes the conclusive effect of a prior judgment must have been either a party or in privity with a party[269] to the action in which that judgment

264 Ibid. L.A. Durbin v Jefferson Nat'l Bank, supra note 2811, p. 1549.

265 DUKE L.J. 1963/754, supra note 2670. See MOORE'S FEDERAL PRACTICE § 131.01, pp. 131-25 (Tab 11).

266 F:\WORDWILL\ARTICLE\Res Judicata – September 2012 DOC, supra note 2811, Avant v. Hammond Jones, Inc., 79 So. 2d 423, 423-424 (Fla. 1955).

267 DUKE L. J. 1966/283, supra note 2779, p. 283. "For some of the earliest cases abandoning the mutuality requirement, see e.g., Coca-Cola v. Pepsi-Cola Co., 36 Del. 124, 172 Atl. 260 (1934); Liberty Mut. Ins. Co. v. George Colon & Co. 260 N.Y. 305, 183 N.E. 506 (1932); Eagle, Star & British Dominions Ins. Co. v Heller, 149 Va. 82, 140 S.E. 314 (1927).

268 Ibid. The mutuality rule is still applicable in numerous jurisdictions. E.g., Interstate Elec. Co. v. Fidelity & Deposit Co., 228 Ala. 210, 153 So. 427 (1934); Faber v. Van Zyl, 198 Iowa 1028, 200 N.W. 702 (1924); Wallace v. Goldberg, 72 Mont. 234, 231 Pac. 56 (1925); Taylor v. Baker, 70 Utah 534, 262 Pac. 266 (1927); Collins v. Treat, 108 W.Va. 443, 152 S.E. 205 (1930).

269 Ibid. The word 'privy' includes those who control an action although not parties to it (see § 84); those whose interests are represented by a party to the action (see §§ 85-88); successors in interests to those having derivative claims (see

was rendered.[270] The rule of mutuality has traditionally been applied in deciding which *persons* are bound by the adjudication of an issue once it is known that the issue was litigated and determined in a prior action.[271] Mutuality has been principally justified on the ground that it is dictated by the requirements of due process.[272] A fundamental principle of due process is the assurance that a person who has not had a fair opportunity to be heard on a question which affects his interests should not be bound by an adjudication of that question.[273] Within the context of due process, therefore, *collateral estoppel* should not be applied in such a way that the determination of an issue will bind a party to a subsequent litigation who was not a party to the action in which that determination was made.[274]

---

§§ 89-92)." RESTATEMENT, JUDGMENTS § 83, comment a (1942).

The notion of privity in this connection has not been without criticism: "The question of who is concluded by a judgment has been obscured by the use of the words 'privity' and 'privies,' which in their precise technical meaning in law, are scarcely determinative always of who is and who is not bound by a judgment. Courts have striven sometimes to give effect to the general doctrine that a judgment is only binding between parties and privies, by extending the significance of the word 'privies' to include relationships not originally embraced by it; whereas the true reason for holding the issue res judicata, does not necessarily depend on privity, but on the policy of law to end litigation....". Taylor v. Sartorious, 130 Mo. App. 23, 40, 108 S.W. 1089, 1094 (1998), quoted in Coca-Cola v. Pepsi-Cola Co., 36 Del. 124, 133, 172 Atl. 260, 263-64 (1934).

270 Ibid., pp. 283-284.

271 Ibid., p. 287. The term "mutuality" derives from the expression that the estoppel of a judgment must be mutual to be effective; that is, a party will not be bound by a prior judgment unless he would have been bound by it had it gone the other way. See Pittston Co. v. O'Hara, 191 Va. 886, 901, 63 S.E. 2d 34, 42, appeal dismissed sub nom. Winn v. Pittston Co., 342 U.S. 803 (1951).

272 Ibid. For a case discussion of due process requirements in res judicata, see Hedlund v. Miner, 395 III, 217, 230, 69 N.E.2d 862, 868 (1946). 89 U. PA. L. REV. 525 (1941); 27 VA. L. REV. 396 (1941).

273 Ibid. It is a principle of general application in Anglo-American jurisprudence that one is not bound by a judgment in personam in a litigation in which he is not designated as a party or to which he has not been made a party by service of process." Hansberry v. Lee, 311 U.S. 32, 40 (1940).

"An elementary and fundamental requirement of due process in any proceeding which is to be accorded finality is notice reasonably calculated, under all the circumstances, to apprise interested parties of the pendency of the action and afford them an opportunity to present their objections". Mullane v. Central Hanover Bank & Trust Co., 339 U.S. 306, 314 (1950).

274 Ibid. This does not mean, however, that everyone must in fact have a day in court, but only that the machinery must be provided so that a reasonable opportunity to be heard will be afforded under normal circumstances". Seavey, 'Res Judicata with Reference to Persons Neither Parties Nor Privies-Two California

The rule of mutuality effectuates the 'fairness' dictates of due process by requiring that unless *both* parties to the subsequent litigation were also parties to the former action, or in privity with such a party, the finality of the prior adjudication may not be asserted in the subsequent action.[275] Thus mutuality has been deemed requisite on the theory that since it is unfair to allow the prior determination of an issue to be asserted *against* one not a party to the prior proceeding, it is reciprocally unfair to allow the determination to be asserted *by* one not a party to the prior proceeding.[276]

Cases,' 57 HARV. L. REV. 98 (1943), p. 99.

275 Ibid. In order to keep the mutuality rule viable, the court developed certain exceptions in cases where its application would create an anomalous situation. Such a situation may occur when a party to one action is in a position of indemnity to a party in a subsequent action. Master-servant, principal-agent, employer-employee, and derivative liability relationships are subsumed under this category. For example, suppose that an indemnitor has recovered a judgment from a third party and that the third party then brings an action against the indemnitee. If the indemnitee is held liable to the third party, the court can either deny him his cause of action against the indemnitor or allow him to recover from the indemnitor who has already recovered a judgment in his favor. The first alternative is unjust; the second raises the anomaly that the indemnitor will be held liable on an issue on which he has already been adjudged free from fault. In order to avoid a choice between these undesirable alternatives, the courts have traditionally allowed the indemnitee to take advantage of the indemnitor's prior victory by a plea of res judicata. It is important to note, however, that the existence of the anomaly – the possibility of holding the indemnitor liable to the indemnitee on an issue which has already been decided in his favor – was the only reason for permitting the exceptions. Thus the indemnitee presumably should not be allowed to use offensively a prior judgment and the indemnitor should never be allowed to use a judgment obtained by the indemnitee, since in neither situation can the anomaly arise. See e.g., Good Health Dairy Products Corp. v. Emery, 275 N.Y. 14, 9 N.E.2d 758 (1937) (derivative liability exception); City of Richmond v. Davis, 135 Va. 319, 116 S.E. 492 (1923) (indemnitor indemnitee exception).

The Graves case itself, as the court noted, presents a situation where application of the employer-employee exception would be proper. It has been suggested, however, that to include the employer-employee relationship among the exceptions is slightly unrealistic since actions for indemnity by the employer against the employee are unlikely. "Perhaps a solution for this branch of the problem would be facilitated if the courts were to take candid account of the insurance factor". Currie, 'Mutuality of Collateral Estoppel: Limits of the Bernhard Doctrine,' 9 STAN. L. REV. 281 (1957), p. 306 n.58.

276 Ibid., p. 288. If the rule is a curious one, the reason given for it is even more so: - 'Nobody can take benefit by a verdict, who had not been prejudiced by it, had it gone contrary:" a maxim which one would suppose to have found its way from the gambling table to the bench. If a party be benefited by one throw of the dice he will, if the rules of fair play are observed, be prejudiced by another; but that the consequence should hold when applied to justice is not equally clear". 7

In order to assess the viability of the rule of mutuality, its status as a branch of the *res judicata* concept must be examined. The essence of the doctrine of *res judicata* is the judicially formulated proposition that a matter which has been adjudicated in a prior action cannot be litigated a second time.[277]

In *Sosna v Iowa* the state court suit was a divorce action by Mrs. Sosna against her husband. Her subsequent federal action was against the state and one of its officers. Had she won in the state court, her victory would not have bound the federal defendants, since they were not parties to the first action.[278] Once upon a time the rule of "mutuality" would have barred them from taking advantage of a decision against Mrs. Sosna as well.[279] The California Supreme Court abandoned the mutuality requirement in a perceptive 1942 opinion by Mr. Justice Traynor: 'The requirements of due process of law forbid the assertion of a plea of res judicata against a party unless he was ...a party thereto or in privity with a party thereto... There is no compelling reason, however, for requiring that the party asserting the plea of res judicata must have been a party, or in privity with a party, to the earlier litigation'.[280] The United States Supreme Court, noting a general trend away from the mutuality rule, agrees.[281] So does the draft of the new Restatement of Judgments.[282] The decisive consideration, as Judge Hastie said in a passage quoted approvingly by the Supreme Court, is that a party who has had one fair and full opportunity to prove a claim and has failed in that effort, should not be permitted to go to trial on the merits of that claim a second time.[283] It should therefore, according to Currie, be irrelevant that

---

WORKS OF JEREMY BENTHAM 171 (Browing ed. 1843), quoted in 35 YALE L. J. 607 (1926), p. 609 n. II.

277 Ibid., p. 285. The doctrine is, of course, tempered by the requirement that justice be done in the individual case. Thus it has been held not to apply where there are overriding competing policies. Spilker v. Hankin, ISS F.2d 35 (D.D.C. 1951) (preservation of attorney-client relationship); White v. Adler, 2S9 N.Y. 34, 43 N.E.2d 79S (1942) (individual's protection from official misfeasance).

278 Currie (1978), supra note 2804, p. 333. See RESTATEMENT OF JUDGMENTS § 93 (1942).

279 Ibid. See RESTATEMENT OF JUDGMENTS § 93 (1942).

280 Ibid., p. 334. See Bernhard v. Bank of America Nat'l Trust & Sav. Ass'n, 19 Cal..2d 807, 812, 122 P. 2d 892, 894 (1942) (emphasis added).

281 Ibid. See Blonder-Tongue Laboratories v. University of Ill. Foundation, 402 U.S. 313 (1971). Though the Court purported to limit its decision to the patent context before it, there is no reason to doubt the Court will follow the same rule elsewhere.

282 Ibid. See RESTATEMENT (SECOND) OF JUDGMENTS § 88 (Tent. Draft No. 2, 1975).

283 Ibid. See Bruszewski v. United States, 181 F.2d 419, 421 (3d Cir.), cert. denied, 340 U.S. 865 (1950) (quoting in Blonder-Tongue Laboratories, Inc. v. University of Ill. Foundation, 402 U.S. 313, 324 (1971).

the parties who would have benefited from *res judicata* in *Sosna* were not parties to the state court action.

The state court judgments in *Wooley v. Maynard* were criminal convictions, and the 'traditional' view, said to represent 'the preponderance of authority' as recently as 1969, is that criminal convictions are not entitled to *res judicata* effect in later civil actions.[284] The only reasons commonly given for this position are quite unpersuasive. That the parties may not be identical[285] is the discredited mutuality argument discussed above. It has no greater force in this context, and it has no application to *Wooley*, where the state or its officers was a party to all cases. The second reason is based on the difference in burden of proof between criminal and civil cases.[286] But while the demanding beyond a reasonable doubt standard of proof in criminal cases means that an acquittal generally does not establish the absence of civil liability,[287] which is governed by a preponderance of the evidence standard, the disparate burdens of proof cannot justify a court sitting in a civil action in declining to give a prior criminal conviction *res judicata* effect.[288] As Vestal convincingly argues, so long as the convicted party has had every opportunity and incentive to litigate the issue of his guilt,[289] the traditional rule should not be followed. The Supreme Court has noted with evident favor a general trend toward acceptance of this view.[290] The Court has itself given a federal conviction *res judicata* effect in a later civil action by the United States,[291] and in another context it has abandoned the mutuality rule.[292] The Supreme Court, making the same observation

284 Ibid. See A. VESTAL, RES JUDICATA/PRECLUSION 5-12 (1969), p. 373.

285 Ibid. See e.g., Moore v. Young, 260 N.C. 654, 657, 133 S.E.2d 51 0, 513 (1963); 2 A. FREEMAN, JUDGMENT § 654 (5th ed. 1925).

286 Ibid. See A. FREEMAN, JUDGMENT § 654 (5th ed. 1925).

287 Ibid. See Tennessee Odin Ins. Co. v. Dickey, 190 Tenn. 96, 99, 228 S.W.2d 73, 74 (1950); State v. Benavidez, 365 S.W. 2d 638, 640 (Tex. 1963); VESTAL (1969), supra note 2833, p. 369.

288 Ibid., pp. 334-335. See e.g., Eagle Star & British Dominions Ins. Co. v. Heller, 149 Va. 82, 88-89, 140 S.E. 314, 323 (1927); A. FREEMAN (1925), supra note 2835, §§ 656-57.

289 Ibid., p. 335, referring to VESTAL (1969), supra note 2836, p. 382.

290 Ibid. See Blonder-Tongue Laboratories, Inc. v. University of Ill. Foundation, 402 U.S. 313, 327 (1971).

291 Ibid. Local 167, Int'l Bhd. of Teamsters v. United States, 291 U.S. 293, 298 (1934).

292 Ibid. See [i.a.,] Res judicata barred state defendants from suing under § 1983 in the Mastracchio, Thistlethwaite, Brown, Coogan, Blankner, and Metros cases; RESTATEMENT OF JUDGMENTS § 93 (1942); Bernhard v. Bank of America Nat'l Trust & Sav. Ass'n, 19 Cal..2d 807, 812, 122 P. 2d 892, 894 (1942) (emphasis added); Blonder-Tongue Laboratories v. University of Ill. Foundation, 402 U.S. 313 (1971). Though the Court purported to limit its decision to the patent

in support of its rejection of the mutuality rule, has pointed out: 'the abrogation of mutuality has been accompanied by other developments such as expansion of the definition of *claim* in bar and merger contexts and expansion of the preclusive effects afforded criminal judgments in civil litigation which enhance the capabilities of the courts to deal with some issues swiftly but fairly'.[293] Accordingly, under the revised Restatement of Judgments[294] a single *claim* (cause of action) for *res judicata* purposes includes all rights of the plaintiff to remedies against the defendant with respect to all or any part of the transaction, or series of connected transactions, out of which the action arose.

***

The Full Faith and Credit Act (28 U.S.C § 1738) provides that the Acts of the legislature of any State, Territory, or Possession of the United States, or copies thereof, *shall* be authenticated by affixing the seal of such State, Territory or Possession thereto. The records and judicial proceedings of any court of any State, Territory or Possession, or copies thereof, shall be proved or admitted in other courts within the United States and its Territories and Possessions by the attestation of the clerk and seal of the court annexed, if a seal exists, together with a certificate of a judge of the court that the said attestation is in proper form. Such Acts, records and judicial proceedings or copies thereof, so authenticated, *shall* have the same full faith and credit in every court within the United States and its Territories and Possessions as they have by law or usage in the courts of such State, Territory or Possession from which they are taken.[295] It is the command of Congress in section 1738 of Title 28: "The ...judicial proceedings of any court of any ...State, Territory, or Possessions ....*shall* have the same full faith and credit in every court within the United States and its Territories and Possessions as they have by law or usage in the courts of such State, Territory or Possession from which

context before it, there is no reason to doubt the Court will follow the same rule elsewhere; RESTATEMENT (SECOND) OF JUDGMENTS § 88 (Tent. Draft No. 2, 1975); and Bruszewski v. United States, 181 F.2d 419, 421 (3d Cir.), cert. denied, 340 U.S. 865 (1950) (quoting in Blonder-Tongue Laboratories, Inc. v. University of Ill. Foundation, 402 U.S. 313, 324 (1971).

293 Ibid., p. 341. See Blonder-Tongue Laboratories v. University of Ill. Foundation, 402 U.S. 313, 327 (1971).

294 Ibid. See RESTATEMENT (SECOND) OF JUDGMENTS § 61(1) (Tent. Draft No. 1, 1973).

295 F:\WORDWILL \ARTICLE\Res Judicata – September 2012 DOC, supra note 2811.

they are taken".[296] This statute commands that a federal court must accord a state court judgment the same preclusive effect it would be accorded by the rendering state.[297] The Eleventh Circuit in *In re St. Laurent*, 991 F.2d 672, 676 (11th Cir. 1993), has expressly stated that, "...[i]f the prior judgment was rendered by a state court, then the collateral estoppel law of the state must be applied to determine the judgment's preclusive effect".[298] Thus the first question a federal court must address in determining whether relitigation is appropriate is whether the claim would be precluded under state preclusion law.[299] The statute requires all federal courts to give preclusive effect to state court judgments whenever the courts of the state in which the judgments were rendered would do so.[300] If, however, the prior judgment was entered by a federal court, its preclusive effect is determined by applying federal law.[301] As in *Huron Holding Corp. v. Lincoln Mine Operation*,[302] 'Every court within the United States', as one would expect, has been construed to include federal courts.

The language of the Rules of Decision Act is comprehensive: "The laws of the several states, except where [federal law *shall*] otherwise require ......*shall* be regarded as rules of decision."[303] There are sources of federal laws besides the Rules of Decision Act and the full faith and credit statute, and the Enabling Act for that matter. The well-known provision concerning issue preclusion is in the Clayton Act.[304] All other federal preemptions of *res judicata* have been created by the courts on the premise that a mandate to that effect is to be found in some specific substantive federal statutes.[305]

296 Currie (1978), supra note 2827, p. 326. See 28 U.S.C. § 1738 (1970). That "full faith and credit" to "judicial proceedings" requires that one jurisdiction give res judicata effect to another's judgments has been established "from the beginning". See Magnolia Petroleum Co. v. Hunt, 320 U.S. 430 U.S. 430, 438 (1943).

297 F:\WORDWILL \ARTICLE\Res Judicata – September 2012 DOC, supra note 2844. In re Keene, 135 B.R. 162 (Bankr. S.D. Fla. 1991) (citing Marrese v American Acad. Of Orthopedic Surgean, 470 U.S. 373 (1985)); MOORE'S FEDERAL PRACTICE § 133, 30 [1], pp. 133-20.

298 Ibid. In re Itzler, 247 B.R. 546, 548 (Bankr. S.D. Fla. 2000).

299 Ibid. MOORE'S FEDERAL PRACTICE § 133.30[2], p. 133-22 (citing Allen v McCurry, 449 U.S. 90, 96 (1980)).

300 Ibid. Pelletier v. Zweifel, 921 F.2d 1465, 1501 (11th Cir. 1991), citing Allen v McCurry, 449 U.S. 90, 96, 101 (1980).

301 Ibid. In re Brose, 242 B.R. 531, 532 n.2 (Bankr. M.D. Fla. 1999).

302 Currie (1978) supra note 2845, p. 326. See Huron Holding Corp. v. Lincoln Mine Operation Co., 312 U.S. 183, 193 (1941); Davis v. Davis, 305 U.S. 32, 40 (1938).

303 Geoffrey C. Hazard, Jr., 'Reflection on the Substance of Finality', in 70 CORNELL L. REV. 642 (1985), p. 643. See 28 U.S.C. § 1652 (1982).

304 Ibid. See U.S.C. § 16 (1982).

305 Ibid. See e.g., Alexander v. Gardner-Denver Co., 415 U.S. 36, 55-59 (1974)

But there is of course another general source – the Constitution and the statutes creating the federal courts. To be sure, those texts do not expressly deal with the *res judicata* effect of federal judgments. The Constitution in particular does not even mention federal judgments; it merely authorizes, among other things, the creation of courts to administer justice and provides that federal law should be supreme in its sphere.[306] State law has the *res judicata* effect by reason of the full faith and credit statute.[307] It is common ground that the full faith and credit statute concerns state court judgments, not judgments of federal courts.[308] And of course it is correct that because the full faith and credit statute is inoperative on federal judgments, it does not follow that the Rules of Decision Act [calling generally for state law 'rules of decision' is also inoperative on them. So far so good.[309] Congress has never comprehensively regulated how the federal courts should administer justice. It dealt with the main elements of fairness in the Judiciary Act of 1789[310] and its sequelae, including the Enabling Act of 1934. In section 34 of the Judiciary Act,[311] Congress dealt with the substantive law to be applied in federal courts, but it left equity and admiralty in general and a host of procedural particulars to resolution by decisional law of the federal courts. Congress spoke to the *res judicata* effects of state court judgments in the full faith and credit statute; under the principle of *expressio unius*, that left the matter of federal judgments as one of those matters to be resolved by federal decisional law.[312] That two jurisdictions are involved does complicate the federal court's task, for the statute requires only that judgments be given "the same....credit ...as they have...in the courts" of the jurisdiction where they are rendered. A court in another jurisdiction therefore has 'as much leeway to disregard the judgment ....as does the State where it was rendered'.[313] Section 1738 thus does not mandate a uniform federal law of *res judicata* [314] ; but it does require that a claim or issue be precluded in federal court if the *res judicata* law of the state in which the judgment was rendered so indicates.

(affording preclusive effect to arbitration would be inconsistent with congressional intent for title VII enforcement).

306 Ibid.

307 Ibid., p. 642. See 28 U.S.C. § 1738 (1982).

308 Ibid. See also Degnan, 'Federalized Res Judicata', in 85 YALE L. J. 741 (1976).

309 Ibid.

310 Ibid., pp. 644-645. See Ch. 20, 1 Stat. 73 (1789).

311 Ibid., p. 645. See Ch. 20, 1 Stat. 73, 92 (current version codified at 28 U.S.C. § 1652 (1982) (Rules of Decision Act).

312 Ibid.

313 Currie (1978), supra note 2851, p. 326. See Halvey v. Halvey, 330 U.S. 610, 615 (1947).

314 Ibid.

In *Sosna v. Iowa,* 419 U.S. 399 (1975), *Huffman v. Pursue,* 420 U.S. 592 (1975), *Wooley v. Maynard,* 430 U.S. 705 (1977), and *Venda Co. v. Lektro-Vend Corp,* 97 S.Ct. 2881 (1977), the federal plaintiffs had a 'full and fair opportunity for judicial resolution' of their claims in state court. *Res judicata* probably should have barred a second round in federal court, as it did in *Williams v. Washington,* 554 F.2d 369 (9th Cir. 1977), and in *Grossgold v. Supreme Court,* 557 F.2d 122 (7th Cir. 1977).[315] In *Guaranty Trust Co. v. York,* 326 U.S. 99 (1945) - the Frankfurter thesis, it is said : "...a federal court adjudicating a State-created right ......is .....only another court of the State......" (326 U.S. 108 (1945).

***

In Germany, the distinction between the operative part (*Tenor*) of the judgment and the reasons is also important for the purposes of *res judicata.* According to § 322(1) ZPO, judgments are only capable of substantive *res judicata* (*materielle Rechtskraft*) to such extent as they decide the demand raised by the statement of claim or counterclaim. According to § 308 ZPO, the court may not award anything/everything (except costs of proceedings) which a party has not specifically demanded. In order to determine what the court has decided, it is necessary to read the *Urteilsformel/Tenor* because this is the place where the judge states clearly what she has decided.[316]

The scope of *res judicata* is thus limited to the extend that the court has decided on the demands asserted by the parties in their complaint or counterclaim. The demand (*Streitgegenstand*) is not explicitly defined in the ZPO. According to BGH, the demand is determined by the plaintiff's prayer for relief (*Antrag des Klagers,* e.g., defendant to be ordered to pay 5,000 Euro or, in the case of a counterclaim, the defendant's prayer for relief) and the facts on which the prayer for relief is based (e.g., payment of 5,000 Euro as repayment of a loan or as damages for breach of contract, etc.).[317] An effect (one of the effects) of a judgment is that it may become formal *res judicata* (*formelle Rechtskraft*). This is dealt with in § 705 ZPO. It requires that either there is no ordinary appeal possible (e.g., against judgments of the BGH) or that the time period for appeal has lapsed without any appeal filed or that the parties have waived their right to appeal. If a party files an inadmissible appeal, formal *res judicata* takes effect (according to majority opinion) after the appeal has been dismissed.[318] Once a judgment

315 Ibid., p. 325.

316 Heinze (2006), supra note 2757, p. 11.

317 Ibid. See BGHZ 117, 1 (5); BGHZ 123, 137 (140); BGHZ 124, 164 (166).

318 Ibid., p. 13. See GemS OGB BGHZ 88, 353 (357); Stein/Jonas (-Munzberg),

is formally binding, it can only be attacked by an action for nullification or restitution (*Wiederaufnahmeklage*, §§ 578-580 ZPO); and according to *Wiederaufnahme in den vorigen Stand*, §§ 233 seq. ZPO, such a judgment may also be attacked by a motion for restoration to one's original position.

V.3. ENFORCEMENT OF COURT ORDER

Execution of judgment is putting into effect of final judgment of court (*Tice v. Tice*, 208 Iowa 145, 224 N.W. 571, 572). Execution embraces all appropriate means to execution of judgment (*Buckley v. F.L. Rlley Mercantile Co.*, 155 Miss. 150, 124 So. 267). Execution means the last stage of a suit, whereby possession is obtained of anything. It is styled 'final process' and consists in putting the sentence of the law in force (3 Bl. Comm. 412). It is the carrying into effect of the sentence of judgment of a court (*U.S. v. Nourse*, 9 Pet. 28, 9 L. Ed. 31; *Griffith v. Fowler*, 18 Vt. 394; *Huributt v. Currier*, 68 N.H. 94, 38 A. 502). Writ of execution is a civil proceeding for enforcement of a judgment against property (*Lash v. Mann*, 141 Ohio St. 577, 49 N.E. 2d 689, 6910).[319] The sanction of civil execution consists in forcibly taking away from an individual person/entity a piece of property through auctioning off that piece of property.[320] Sometimes from the neglected parties, or some other cause, it became impossible to carry a decree into execution without the further decree of the court upon a bill filed for that purpose. This happened generally in cases where, parties having neglected to proceed upon the decree, their rights under it became so embarrassed by a variety of subsequent events that it was necessary to have the decree of the court to settle and ascertain them. Such a bill might also be brought to carry into execution the judgment of an inferior court of equity, if the jurisdiction of that court was not equal to the purpose: as in the case of a decree in Wales, which the defendant avoided by fleeing into England. This species of bill was generally partly an original bill, and partly a bill in the nature of an original bill, thought not strictly original (Story, Eq. P1 342; Daniel, Ch. Pr. 1429).[321]

To begin collecting a judgment, a judgment creditor should contact the judgment debtor either directly or through the debtor's attorney if the debtor was represented by an attorney, and request payment of the judgment amount. If the judgment debtor does not pay, the judgment creditor is entitled to begin collection efforts. These may include one or any combination of the following: a) garnishment of wages and or bank accounts;

ZPO (2004) n.22, § 705 No.12.

319 Black (1957), supra note 2754, p. 678.

320 Kelsen (1967), supra note 1877, p. 109.

321 Black (1957), supra note 2868, p. 678.

b) lien, seizure and/or sale of real property and/or personal property, including automobiles; c) suspension of motor vehicle registration, and/or driver's license, if the underlying claim is based on the judgment of debtor's ownership or operation of a motor vehicle; d) revocation, suspension, or denial of renewal of any applicable business license or permit; and e) investigation and prosecution by the State Attorney General for fraudulent or illegal business practices. After one has provided the enforcement officer with information on the judgment debtor's assets, he or she can serve a restraining notice on the bank, or on some other person or business that owes money to the judgment debtor, and eventually take the money. If the judgment debtor is an employee, the enforcement officer can garnish (take) a portion of his or her salary to satisfy the judgment.[322]

[In Ireland] in general, once the judgment creditor has a judgment order, the judgment can be enforced. Getting a judgment means the judgment creditor is now entitled to use various mechanisms to get the money from the judgment debtor. This is known as enforcing a judgment – the legal term is 'execution' of the judgment. There are a number of different ways of enforcing a judgment. The judgment creditor chooses the means and can use several different means at the same time. In Ireland, the judgment creditor has 12 years from the date of the judgment to look for enforcement orders. Once issued, enforcement orders are generally valid for a year and may then be renewed.[323] [In New York] in order to start enforcing a judgment, the judgment must be 'entered'. Entry occurs after the clerk of the court signs and files the judgment. If one appears in person (without an attorney) and he is the winner, he may ask the clerk to prepare and enter (record) a judgment in his favor. Once the judgment is entered and filed by the court, the judgment is enforceable for a period of twenty years for money. When a 'Transcript of Judgment' is filed with the County Clerk, the judgment is enforceable for ten years against real property and is renewable for an additional ten years.[324]

In Hawai, Rule 69 of the Civil Procedure on 'Execution' provides: 'Process to enforce a judgment for the payment of money *shall* be a writ of execution, unless the court directs otherwise. The procedure on execution, in proceedings supplementary to and in aid of a judgment, and in proceedings on and in aid of execution *shall* be in the manner provided by the law of the State. In aid of the judgment or execution, the judgment creditor or his successor in interest, when ......, may obtain discovery from any person, including the judgment debtor, in the manner provided in these rules for

322 NYCOURTS.GOV. New York State Unified Court System. New York City Civil Court. Collecting the Judgment.

323 Citizens Information Board, Ground Floor, George's Quay House, 43 Townsend St, Dublin 2.

324 NYCOURTS.GOV, supra note 2871.

taking depositions (Hawai'i Rules of Civil Procedure (SCRU-11-0000051), adopted and promulgated by the Supreme Court of the State of Hawai'i, as amended April 7, 1980, effective April 7, 1980, with Amendments as noted)'.

Under German Code of Civil Procedure, compulsory enforcement may be pursued based on final judgments that have become final and binding, or that have been declared provisionally enforceable (section 704). If a petition is filed for the restoration of the *status quo ante* or for proceedings to be reopened, or if an objection as provided for by section 321a is lodged, or if the legal dispute is continued following the pronouncement of a judgment subject to a reservation of rights, the court may direct, upon corresponding application being made, that compulsory enforcement be temporarily stayed, against or without provision of security, or that it be pursued only against the provision of security, and that the enforcement measures are to be revoked against provision of security. Compulsory enforcement may be discontinued without any security being provided only if it is demonstrated to the satisfaction of the court that the debtor is unable to provide security and that the enforcement would entail a disadvantage that it is impossible to compensate or remedy [section 707(1)]. The judgment for enforcement is to be delivered without a review being performed of the decision's legality [section 723(1)].

On the conditions for the commencement of enforcement, section 751(1) provides: 'Should the assertion of the claim be dependent on the occurrence of a calendar date, compulsory enforcement may not be commenced prior to midnight of that day of the calendar'. Section 751(2) states: 'Should the enforcement depend on the provision of security incumbent on the creditor, compulsory enforcement may only be commenced or continued if the provision of security has been proven by a public record or document, or a record or document that has been publicly certified, and if a copy of such record or document has already been served or is served concurrently. Unless the compulsory enforcement is assigned to the courts, it will be implemented by the court-appointed enforcement officers who are to effect it on behalf of the creditor [section 753(1)]'. The creditor may avail himself of the assistance of the court registry in charging an office with the task of compulsory enforcement. The court-appointed enforcement officer charged with the task by the court registry *shall* be deemed to have been charged by the creditor [section 753(2)]. The court-appointed enforcement officer is authorized to search the debtor's residence and any means of storage insofar as the purpose of the enforcement so requires [section 758(1)].

In Germany, criminal judgments *shall* not be enforceable before they have entered into force [section 449 of German Code of Criminal Procedure, published on April 7, 1987 (Federal Law Gazette / *Bundesgesetzblatt* Part I p. 1074, 1319), as amended by Article 5 subsection (4) of the Act of October 10, 2013 (Federal Law Gazette Part I p. 3799)]. If there are sufficient reasons for assuming that the suspension will be revoked, the court may, until the revocation order enters into force, take measures to ensure that the convicted person will not abscond, and, if necessary, issue a warrant of arrest under the prerequisites of Section 112 subsection (2), number 1 or 2, or if certain facts substantiate the risk that the convicted person will commit substantial significant offences [Section 453c, subsection (1)]. The detention served on the basis of a warrant of arrest pursuant to subsection (1) *shall* be credited against the sentence of imprisonment to be executed [Section 453c, subsection (2)].

Prison sentences and default imprisonment for failure to pay a fine should be executed consecutively [Section 454b]. A court decision *shall* be obtained if doubts arise concerning the interpretation of a criminal judgment or the calculation of the sentence imposed, or if objections are raised against the admissibility of executing the sentence [Section 458, subsection (1)]. The provisions of the Ordinance on Recovery of Claims of the Judicial Authorities *shall* apply to the execution of a fine unless otherwise provided under this statute [Section 459]. After the judgment has entered into force the executing authority *shall* decide whether to grant relaxation of conditions of payment of a fine [Section 459a, subsection (1)]. The executing authority may subsequently amend or revoke a decision concerning relaxation of payment conditions pursuant to subsection (1) or section 42 of the Criminal Code. Here it may deviate from a preceding decision to the convicted person's detriment only on the basis of new facts or evidence [subsection (2)]. Where relaxation in the form of payment in specified installments is revoked pursuant to section 42, second sentence, of the Criminal Code, this *shall* be noted in the files. The executing authority may grant relaxation of conditions of payment again [subsection (3)]. Default imprisonment *shall* be executed on the basis of an order made by the executing authority [Section 459c, subsection (1)]. The execution order *shall* be contingent on the fine not being recoverable or on execution being dispensed with pursuant to Section 459c [subsection (2)]. Execution of default imprisonment may not be ordered for part of a fine not corresponding to a full day of imprisonment [subsection (3)]. Default imprisonment *shall* not be executed to the extent that the fine is paid or recovered or execution is dispensed with pursuant to Section 459d [subsection (4)]. If there is an order for forfeiture, confiscation or the rendering unusable of an object, it shall be executed by taking the object away from the convicted person or from a person with an interest in the forfeiture or confiscation [Section 459g].

In France, the judgment, which is not subject to any review action staying its execution, will become *res judicata.* The judgment, which is subject to such a review action, will have the same authority on the expiration of the time-limit for such a review action if the review action has not been made within the time-limit [Article 500 of the French Code of Civil Procedure]. The judgment will be enforced, under the following conditions, as from the moment it becomes *res judicata*, save where the debtor enjoys the benefit of a period of grace or the creditor enjoys the benefit of a provisional enforcement [Article 501]. As to the general conditions for execution, a judgment or a deed may be enforced only upon the production of a certified copy imprinted with an order of enforcement, save where the law provides otherwise [Article 502]. Judgments may not be executed against the parties standing liable thereto unless they have been notified, save where the enforcement is voluntary [Article 503].

In French criminal law, the execution of criminal judgment takes place upon the application made by the public prosecutor after the decision has become final [Article 708 of French Code of Criminal Procedure]. The public prosecutor and the parties prosecute the execution of the decision to the extent that each of them is concerned. However, proceedings for the recovery of fines and confiscations are undertaken by the tax collector in the district prosecutor's name [Article 707]. The district prosecutor and public prosecutor have the right to directly request the assistance of police to ensure the execution of the sentence [Article 709].

In Australia, the judgment creditor can enforce a judgment through Writ for the Delivery of Goods, Writ for the Levy of Property, Garnishee Order, Examination Notice, Bankruptcy and Winding up a company. On a Writ for the Delivery of Goods, the judgment creditor can ask the court to authorize the sheriff to 'sieze' the judgment debtor's goods and return them to the judgment creditor. The sheriff can also take and sell other property of the judgment debtor to recover the value of the goods. A Writ for the Delivery of Goods can only be used in a recovery of goods claim. A Writ for the Delivery of Goods can only be used if the court ordered that the judgment creditor's goods be returned to the judgment creditor, or, if the court ordered that the judgment debtor pay the judgment creditor money equal to the value of the goods instead (for example, if the goods were lost or destroyed) or damages. On a Writ for the Levy of Property, the judgment creditor can ask the court to authorize the sheriff to seize property belonging to the judgment debtor to pay the debt. In many cases the arrival of the sheriff with a writ will encourage the judgment debtor to take steps to avoid the sale of their property. The judgment debtor may instead make an application to the court to pay by installments, or may contact the judgment creditor to try and come to some arrangement. By virtue of a Garnishee Order, the judgment creditor can get the judgment debtor's money from his bank account or wages [from employer] or from any third party who holds money on behalf of the judgment debtor. If the judgment creditor is unsure about the judgment debtor's financial position, the judgment creditor can ask the judgment debtor to provide him information about the judgment debtor's income and assets. This is done with an examination notice or an examination order. This information can help the judgment creditor decide whether to take further enforcement action and what action to take. If the judgment debt is more than $ 5000 the judgment creditor can have the judgment debtor declared bankrupt by applying to the Federal Circuit Court or the Federal Court.[325]

Pursuant to article 553 of the Dutch Code of Criminal Procedure, the execution of judicial decision is carried out by the Public Prosecutor or the Minister of Justice on the recommendation of the Public Prosecutor. According to the jurisprudence of the Dutch Supreme Court, this is a very important rule: the promise of the Public Prosecution to a crown witness that, if the crown witness would meet his commitments, the Public Prosecutor would not execute an imposed custodial sentence, led to a bar from the prosecution of the (own) criminal case of this crown witness because this was in conflict with article 553 and a denial of the legal system concerning the decision to prosecute, the imposition of sentences and the execution of sentences.[326] In the verdict in HR 1 June 1999, NJ 1999, 567 (*Karman*-case), the Supreme Court made clear that the criminal judge is responsible for the execution, without having the possibility of modifying the judicial decision without the consent of a judge.[327] Article 553 also makes clear that the actual interference of the member of the Public Prosecution with the actual execution can be small. The Public Prosecutor can leave the execution to the Minister of Justice. Furthermore, article 553 of the code points out that the execution of sanctions is in the hands of the Public Prosecutor (and the Minister of Justice).[328]

Another characteristic of the system of Dutch criminal sanction is the system of early release which has been incorporated in article 15 and 15a of the Criminal Code. A convicted person sentenced to a custodial sentence for a determinate period of which more than one year is to be executed *shall* be released when two thirds of that sentence have been served. A convicted person sentenced to a custodial sentence of which not more than one year is to be executed may be released when he has been deprived of his liberty for not less than six months and when one third

---

325 NSW Government, Justice-LawAcess, LawAssist.

326 Kooijmans (2003), supra note 2762, p. 206. See HR 1 June 1999, NJ 1999, 567 (Karman-case).

327 Ibid.

328 Ibid.

of the remaining term has been served.[329] According to article 22g of the Criminal Code, when the convicted person doesn't commence the service penalty or the Public Prosecutor's Office is of the opinion that the convicted person doesn't properly complete the penalty imposed, or has not properly completed the penalty imposed, the Public Prosecutor's Office may order the execution of the detention as a substitute penalty.[330]

V.4. ALTERNATIVE DISPUTE RESOLUTION AS "PERFORMANCE OF LAW"

Alternative dispute resolution (ADR) does not describe a single approach or method, but comprises many practices for settling disputes between parties.[331] ADR methods fall into two major categories: binding and consensual.[332] Binding methods result in outcomes that automatically bind the parties, whereas consensual methods allow the parties to help shape the agreements and require their joint approval to take effect.[333] Binding processes include arbitration and private judging; and consensual methods include mediation, advisory opinion and non-binding mock-trials.[334] The two basic categories of ADR are mediation, also referred to as conciliation, and arbitration. Negotiation is the term referring to the efforts of the parties themselves to resolve an area of contention before resorting to calling in a third party and, as such, naturally precedes ADR or litigation.[335]

---

329 Ibid., p. 209.

330 Ibid., p. 211.

331 Scott H. Blackman and Rebecca M. McNeill, 'Alternative Dispute Resolution in Commercial Intellectual Property Disputes', in 47 The American University Law Review, 1709 (1998), p. 1711. See CENTER FOR PUB. RESOURCES AND THE INT'L TRADEMARK ASSOC., ADR IN TRADEMARK AND UNFAIR COMPETITION DISPUTES: A PRACTITIONER'S GUIDE (William A. Finkelstein ed., 1994) ["Finkelstein (1994)"], p. II-1 (stating that the differing policies are not mutually exclusive in any particular conflict, but often are used in a customized combination).

332 Ibid. See Finkelstein (1994), Ibid., p.II-2 (explaining that binding and consensual methods often involve the presence of a third party).

333 Ibid. See Finkelstein (1994), Ibid. (observing that most court-based ADR processes produce non-binding outcomes).

334 Ibid. See Finkelstein (1994), Ibid. (noting that binding processes involve a third party who has the authority to impose a resolution); [other references omitted].

335 Carol Daugherty Rasnic, 'Alternative Dispute Resolution Rather Than Litigation? A Look at Current Irish and American Laws' in Judicial Studies Institute Journal 4:2 (2004), p. 183.

In Mnookin's explanation, negotiation does not require the participation of a neutral third-party with decisional authority.[336] Instead, the parties themselves have the responsibility for deciding the terms of any resolution. Negotiation is voluntary, in the sense that disputing parties are not ordinarily forced to negotiate with each other. The process of negotiation is informal and without defined procedures or rules governing the presentation of evidence or arguments. Because the goal of negotiation is a mutually acceptable resolution, the parties to a negotiation can shape that resolution to suit their own needs and interests, and are under no obligation to reach a principled outcome, much less one justified by a reasoned opinion applying formal legal norms. If resolution is reached, the settlement is not ordinarily subject to judicial review. The settlement agreement can subsequently be enforced as a contract.

Mediation introduces a neutral third party when negotiations have failed. The role of the mediator is not judgmental, nor does he/she take a position on behalf of one party or the other. The underlying principle is to permit the parties themselves to make the ultimate determination resolving the issue, with the mediator's conciliatory assistance. His role, then, is to facilitate, rather than to impose, a settlement. The process of mediation is not adversarial, so it does not resemble an actual trial. Parties are not afforded the protections afforded by rules of evidence and/or constitutional rights.[337] There is no right to counsel during mediation. Most states in the United States have adopted some form of the Uniform Mediation Act or the Revised Uniform Mediation Act.[338] Mediation is typically a voluntary process where the parties themselves may choose the person who will act as the outside facilitator. It is private and confidential, and not open to the public. Although the mediator is typically responsible for managing the mediation process, there are no standard procedures or fixed rules. The process by which the mediator facilitates negotiation is often informal and unstructured.[339] Mediation offers an option for clients involved in disputes. During mediation, a neutral third party assists the conflicting parties in crafting a settlement.[340] The mediator does not decide

336 Robert H. Mnookin, 'Alternative Dispute Resolution', March 4, 1998, www. law. Harvard. Edu/programs/olin-/pdf/232p, No. I.

337 Rasnic (2004), supra note 2884, p. 183. Significantly, unlike Ireland, where juries are available in civil trials only in defamation cases, American constitutional law assures the right to trial by jury in civil cases when the amount in controversy is at least twenty dollars ($20.00). Constitution of the United States, 1787, Amendment VII (1791).

338 Ibid., p. 184. The National Council of Courts maintains a website from which information on states that have enacted Model laws or Uniform Act might be accessed, www.nccusl.org.

339 Mnookin (1998), supra note 2885, paragraph I.

340 Blackman & McNeill (1998), supra note 2880, p. 1714. See INSTITUTE

the outcome, but merely facilitates resolution between the parties.[341] In this process, the parties themselves try to create a solution that will work.[342] At the conclusion of mediation, the parties can both claim ownership of the resolution.[343] For a successful non-binding mediation, both parties must have a genuine desire to resolve the matter reasonably.[344]

Zimmer says that trained and certified mediators assist the parties in the process of negotiating a settlement agreement that they voluntarily work together to achieve and jointly agree to implement.[345] Traditional mediation is primarily facilitative, however, it also can include evaluative elements where the facilitator is a judge, experienced legal professional, or technical expert with specialzed knowledge in the subject matter area of the dispute, and the parties request that the facilitator provide a professional assessment of their position on one or more of the issues in the dispute. A new form of mediation conceived in the mid-1990s is known as transformative mediation. It is an ADR process in which the parties proactively seek not only to preserve but to transform their existing relationship as they jointly resolve the dispute. In the transformative mediation process, each party strives to achieve a greater understanding and recognition of the other parties' values, needs, interests, and objectives. The motivation behind transformative mediation is that the parties must take the dispute-resolution initiative largely on their own. They rely less on the mediator as a facilitator and/or evaluator and more on themselves. The parties thereby empower each other to take responsibility for the dispute and to resolve it in a manner that, ideally, will diminish the likehood of future disputes and result in improved and more productive relationships

---

FOR DISPUTE RESOLUTION, CENTER FOR PUBLIC RESOURCES, INC., CPR MODEL ADR PROCEDURES AND PRACTICES: MEDIATION I-1, I-4 (1995) ["CPR MEDIATION"] (defining mediation as a process where a neutral third-party "actively assists" parties towards a settlement).

341 Ibid. See CPR MEDIATION, Ibid., (explaining that a mediator does not make binding decisions while an arbitrator has the power to bind the parties).

342 Ibid. See CPR MEDIATION, Ibid. This expresses the traditional facilitative mediation. Some mediators have developed an evaluative mediation style. In this less traditional style, the parties still ultimately agree on the solution, but the mediator evaluates their claims during the process, providing feedback on the parties' assertions. See ENDDISPUTE INC., ADR PROCESS 4-18 (1994) ["ADR PROCESS"], pp. 4-2 to 4-4.

343 Ibid. See CPR MEDIATION, Ibid., p. I-4 (characterizing mediation as a form of communication that reduces hostility and facilitates rational discussion).

344 Ibid. See CPR MEDIATION, Ibid. (stating that the principal precondition for a successful mediation is the mutual goal of resolution).

345 Markus Zimmer, 'Overview of Alternative Dispute Resolution: A Primer for Judges and Administrators', in International Journal For Court Administration, December 2011, Part Five.

between them. The role of the transformative mediator is to support this process of mutual acknowledgement, empowerment, and improved or transformed relationships. It requires a special level of commitment and, to that extent, has limited appeal to some parties.

Significant in U.S. federal courts are the Federal Rules of Civil Procedure (FRCP) under which there is a type of mediation, which is pre-trial settlement. A majority of states have adopted many of these federal rules for state civil litigation. FRCP 68 addresses pre-court settlement. Jacquelin Nolan-Hadley, expert on ADR in the United States, has written that the purpose of this rule is to encourage settlement of civil suits before they actually go to trial – possibly via mediation. The federal judiciary in the United States has taken a pro-active role in encouraging pre-trial settlements, and federal judges have made ample use of FRCP 16, which authorizes them to conduct pre-trial conferences. This enables the judge to control the litigation at an early stage. As a neutral, the court can thereby communicate to both parties the direction the case is taking. However, there has been some concern that some courts might overuse this power and coerce the parties (or one of them) to agree to a settlement during such a conference.[346]

Negotiation and mediation often appear as initial steps of dispute resolution. When sufficient understanding by disputing parties of the factual situations of each of the parties is acquired, dispute resolution via negotiation and/or mediation might be the most effective and efficient method. Dispute resolutions achieved through negotiation and/or mediation, if implemented or voluntarily enforced, are the law we see in reality, constituting the "performance" of law as referred to in this writing.

Arbitration is the most formal of ADR methods, although there is no right to the American-style jury in civil trials. Additionally, rules of evidence are not applicable, so in this respect, it is somewhat of a hybrid between mediation and litigation. The Federal Arbitration Act, (1925) 9 U.S.C., sections 1-16, give parties the right to counsel. Significantly, this statute also empowers the arbitrator to compel witnesses to testify and to compel production of documents.[347] The Federal Arbitration Act, (1925) 9 U.S.C., sections 1-16, allow stays of litigation proceedings when an issue has been referred to arbitration and for orders compelling arbitration if a party has not complied with an earlier agreement to use this resolution procedure in the event of dispute.[348] Arbitration serves as one of the most popular and well-known forms of ADR.[349] In arbitration, the parties may

346 Rasnic (2004), supra note 2886, p. 186.

347 Ibid., p. 184. See (1925) 9 U.S.C., sections 6 and 7.

348 Ibid., p. 189. See (1925) 9 U.S.C., sections 2, 3 and 4.

349 Blackman & McNeill (1998), supra note 2889, p. 1712.

select one private arbitrator or a panel of three private arbitrators, who often possess a particular expertise in the area of the conflict.[350] General rules and regulations on arbitration have been promulgated by various organizations, however, parties may agree to tailor the regulations to fit their individual situations.[351] Depending on the structure the parties have selected, the arbitration itself can offer the parties limited discovery, freedom from some or all of the rules of evidence, an opportunity to examine and cross-examine witnesses, and the opinion to use briefs and oral arguments.[352] Arbitration, in Zimmer's view, is the form of ADR that most closely approaches the court adjudication function in which a judge (i) permits each party to present its arguments and evidence, then (ii) prepares a judgment that describes which of the parties prevailed, why that party prevailed, and what the consequences are for the other parties.[353] In arbitration, a similar model is followed with a professional arbitrator listening to each party, then preparing an arbitral judgment. In the arbitration process, the strict rules that govern court processes are relaxed somewhat, but arbitration remains one of the most formal of the ADR processes. The parties do not actively participate in evaluating their respective positions, nor do they participate in crafting the judgment. Those functions rest with the arbitrator. Where arbitration does differ from formal court adjudication is that the parties jointly select who will serve as their arbitrator, and most programs permit the parties to work with the arbitrator to negotiate what rules and procedures will be applicable to the process.

A dispute that might otherwise go to court becomes subject to binding arbitration only by the agreement of the parties. In this sense, arbitration is a creature of contract, and the terms of the parties' particular arbitration

350 Ibid., p. 1713. See ADR PROCESSES, supra note 2891, pp. 4-15 (stating that parties often select a neutral party with particular expertise or experience); Mnookin (1998), supra note 2888.

351 Ibid., p. 1718. See e.g., INSTITUTE FOR DISPUTE RESOLUTION, CENTER FOR PUBLIC RESOURCES, INC., CPR MODEL ADR PROCEDURES AND PRACTICES: ARBITRATION (1995) ["CPR ARBITRATION"], pp. I-5 to I-18 (discussing how parties can use CPR's non-administered arbitration rules and commentary as a procedural basis to settle disputes); AMERICAN ARBITRATION ASS'N, PATENT ARBITRATION RULES 6 (1993) (describing the procedure used to administer arbitration by the American Arbitration Association).

352 Ibid. See Finkelstein (1994), supra note 2880, pp. VIII-10, VIII-24 to VIII-25 (explaining that parties may adopt or reject certain rules of evidence depending on their situations); Gregg A. Paradise, 'Arbitration of Patent Infringement Disputes: Encouraging the Use of Arbitration Throughout Evidence Rules Reform,' in 64 FORDHAM L. REV. (1995), pp. 247, 270-278 (discussing how the lack of evidence rules for patent infringement arbitration is a double-edged sword and allows for the admission of certain forms of hearsay evidence).

353 Zimmer (2011), supra note 2894, Part Five.

agreement are generally controlling. Binding arbitration in lieu of judicial adjudication is voluntary in the sense that it is only by agreement that one is required to arbitrate; but once there is an agreement it is involuntary in the sense that courts will enforce it against a reluctant party by refusing to adjudicate disputes which are within the scope of the arbitration agreement and thus require arbitration.[354] As noted by Zimmer that binding arbitration more closely approximates court-based adjudication.[355] When two or more parties agree to participate in binding arbitration, they commit to abide by the judgment issued by the arbitrator whether or not it is in their favor. Parties which seek binding arbitration do so with the expectation that the resulting judgment will have legal status in the domicile where it is issued, that it will be enforceable under the authority of that domicile, and that the judicial authority in that domicile will not countermand, modify, or otherwise interfere with or intervene in the enforcement of the terms of the judgment.

Much like American law, the loser in an arbitration hearing in Ireland has no right to appeal except for similar circumstances – i.e., fraud, misconduct of arbitrator, or fundamental legal error. Also similar is the right to obtain judicial enforcement of an arbitration award. The Arbitration Act, 1954 provides by leave of the High Court for enforcement, the same as for a court order or judgment.[356] The procedure is via special summons.[357] Both Ireland and the United States have subscribed to the 1958 New York Convention on the Recognition and Enforcement of Foreign Awards. This applies to parties in all countries that are signatories to this treaty, and it is applicable not only to court judgments, but also to arbitration awards where they are enforceable by the courts (such as in Ireland and the United States).[358] Internationally, under the United Nations Commission on International Trade Model Law-U.N.Doc. A/57/17 (2002) – (UNCITRAL), there are two provisions which cannot be changed. The provisions state that (i) in resolving international disputes under the Model Law, the law must be interpreted in light of its international origin in order to promote uniformity and good faith, and (ii) parties must adhere to the procedurally fair treatment principle. Signifinactly, this document applies only to commercial issues.[359]

---

354 Mnookin (1998), supra note 2888.

355 Zimmer (2011), supra note 2902, Part Five.

356 Rasnic (2004), supra note 2895, p. 193. See Section 41 of the Arbitration Act, 1954.

357 Ibid. See Rule 4 of order 56 of the Rules of the Superior Courts (Statutory Instrument No. 15 of 1986).

358 Ibid., pp. 194-195.

359 Ibid., p. 195. A good summary of the Model Law can be found in J. Sekoles and M.B. Gerry, 'The UMA and UNCITRAL Model Law; An Emerging International

Arbitral awards can be implemented by the parties thereto voluntarily, or, can be enforced [executed] by the court in accordance with the prevailing law provisions. Such enforcement by the court is similar to the enforcement of court judgment in accordance with the formal procedural civil law provisions. Being implemented [or executed] voluntarily or being enforced [executed] officially, any arbitral awards are the law we see in reality, and they constitute the 'performance' of law as referred to in this writing.

Other ADR methods are mock-trial and private judging. Both mock-trial (non-binding and consensual) and private judging (binding) allow parties to take advantage of several facets of the traditional legal system, such as oral argument and the examination and cross-examination of witnesses.[360] Both of these options may also include using private juries composed of experts, able to digest information in a technology-intensive dispute. The two options, however, may offer very different outcomes.[361] In a non-binding mock-trial, decision-making individuals for each side typically observe opening and closing arguments by their attorneys and opposing counsel, as well as the examination and cross-examination of key witnesses.[362] This process educates corporate executives on both sides, allowing them to 'stand back' and make another, often more realistic, assessment of their case. Such a process typically promotes additional flexibility and allows the parties to negotiate a settlement with a greater chance of success.[363] The judge or jury, if present, may offer conclusions

---

Consensus on Mediation and Conciliation" (Summer, 2003) Dispute Resolution Magazine, 17.

360 Blackman & McNeill (1998), supra note 2898, p. 1714. See Expert Jurors Spur Accord at High-Tech Private Trial, CPRS ALTERNATIVE TO THE HIGH COST OF LITIGATION, Dec. 1987, reprinted in CENTER FOR PUBLIC RESOURCES INSTITUTE FOR DISPUTE RESOLUTION, CPR MODEL ADR PROCEDURES AND PRACTICES: TECHNOLOGY DISPUTES (1994) ["CPR TECHNOLOGY DISPUTE 1994"], p.III-28 (describing the procedures of a private trial involving witnesses, evidentiary rules, and motions); see also CPR TECHNOLOGY DISPUTE, Ibid., p. I-25 (explaining that a mini-trial is synonymous with a mock-trial).

361 Ibid., pp. 1714-1715. See Expert Jurors Spur Accord, Ibid., p.III-28.

362 Ibid., p. 1715. See CPR TECHNOLOGY DISPUTES (1994), supra note 2909, p.I-25 (describing consensual ADR where management representatives with a command of the disputed subject matter participate in the mock-trial).

363 Ibid. See CPR TECHNOLOGY DISPUTES (1994), Ibid., pp.I-9 to I-10 (explaining that a mock-trial encourages settlement because it gives both sides a balanced view of the case and a glimpse at the possible outcome). See generally Ibid, at IV (providing a sample negotiation clause for a negotiation between executives). For example, after a non-binding arbitration of a patent dispute concluded that the device in question did indeed infringe the patent, the parties settled. See Stenograph Corp. v. Fulkerson, 972 F.2d 726, 727 (7th Cir. 1992).

for consideration by the parties, but such a conclusion will not be binding on the parties.[364] Private judging, if established by the jurisdiction, creates a decision with the force of law and, unlike other ADR options, brings with it rights of appeal. Many states in the United States, including California, Connecticut, Nebraska, New Hampshire, New York, Ohio, Oklahoma, Oregon, Rhode Island, South Carolina, Texas, and Washington offer this option.[365] Private judging can be distinguished from arbitration because, in private judging, the parties do not typically select the rules of evidence or civil procedure, but follow jurisdictional rules.[366] The private judge is the functional equivalent of a public judge, except the private judge lacks the power of contempt.[367] Dispute resolution achieved through mock-trial or private judging, if implemented or enforced [executed], are the law we see in reality, constituting the 'performance' of law as referred to in this book.

V.5. CUSTOMARY PRACTICE AND UNDISPUTED PRACTICE AS "PERFORMANCE OF LAW"

***

In *Philosophical Investigation* (PI) (ready for printing in 1946, but rescinded from the publisher by Wittgenstein), one of the issues most associated with the later Wittgenstein is that of rule-following. In the former Wittgenstein, it was his stance that a rule is an abstract entity – transcending all of its particular applications; knowing the rule involves grasping that abstract entity and thereby knowing how to use it. The later Wittgenstein is different, and he begins his exposition by introducing an example: ".. we get [a] pupil to continue a series (say '+2') beyond 1000

364 Ibid. See CPR TECHNOLOGY DISPUTES (1994), Ibid., at IV (providing a sample negotiation allowing for both a jury mini-trial or a mediation presided over by a judge).

365 Ibid. See CPR TECHNOLOGY DISPUTES (1994), Ibid., p.I-18; see also Note, The California Rent-A-Judge Experiment: Constitutional and Policy Considerations of Pay-As-You-Go-Courts, in 94 HARVARD L. REV. 1592 (1981), p. 1600 (discussing the private judge process in California and how it allows for appeals to a trial court judge either by a motion to set aside the referee's findings or by a motion for a new trial).

366 Ibid. See ADR PROCESS, supra note 2891, p. 4-18 (noting that certain jurisdictions such as California have generally reference statutes which govern private judging).

367 Ibid. See ADR PROCESS, Ibid.

--- and he writes 1000, 1004, 1008, 1012 (*PI* 185). What do we do, and what does it mean, when the student, upon being corrected, answers *But I did go on in the same way*?" Wittgenstein proceeds (mainly in *PI* 185-243, but also elsewhere) to dismantle the cluster of attendant questions: How do we learn rules: How do we follow them? Wherefrom the standards which decide if a rule is followed correctly? Are they in the mind, along with a mental representation of the rule? Do we appeal to intuition in their application? Are they socially and publicly taught and enforced? In typical Wittgensteinian fashion, the answers are not pursued positively; rather, the very formulation of the question as legitimate questions with coherent content is put to the test. For indeed, it is both the Platonic and mentalistic pictures which underlie asking questions of this type, and Wittgenstein is intent on freeing us from these assumptions. Such liberation involves elimination of the need to posit any sort of external or internal authority beyond the actual application of the rule.[368]

The climax of the issue as often considered in *PI* 201: "This was our paradox: no course of action could be determined by a rule, because every course of action can be made out to accord with the rule. The answer was: if everything can be made out to accord with the rule, then it can also be made out to conflict with it. And so there would be neither accord nor conflict here".[369] Wittgensteins refers to human daily practice in accordance with the rules. People in their ordinary practice do things through established ['rigid'] intuition without deliberation or even without having a bit 'thought' on what they do. What they do are in accordance with the rules in their societies since they do the things in day to day life through habitual social upbringing.

***

Customary laws are the laws of certain communities. *In re* Estate of Apachee, 4 Nav. R. 178, 180 (W.R. Dist. Ct. Oct. 11, 1983) the Court quoted William Blackstone on the Law of England to define common or customary law: 'The lex non scripta, or unwritten law, includes not only general customs, or the common law property so called; but also the particular customs of certain parts of the kingdom; and likewise those particular laws, that are by custom observed only in certain courts and jurisdictions'.[370] In

368 Anat Biletzki and Anat Matar, 'Ludwig Wittgenstein', in Stanford Encyclopedia of Philosophy, first published Friday, November 8, 2002, substantive revision Monday, March 3, 2014, § 3.5.

369 Ibid.

370 Ezra Rosser, 'Customary Law: The Way Things Were, Codified', in the new

defining 'custom', the Navajo Court cites John Chipman Gray's *The Nature and Sources of Law* for the proposition that 'custom is what men do, not what they think'.[371] In Indonesia, the customary law, called the *'Adat'* law, consists of various customary practices that have long been existing in a number of traditional community rings in the Archipelago. In Vanuatu the term *'kastom'* encompasses customary law. *Kastom* is widely employed to describe traditional practices and indigenous ways of doing things. Margaret Jolly observed that: 'Increasingly the restricted notion of *kastom* as certain owned aspects of local knowledge and ritual creations has expanded to a notion of *kastom* as a whole way of life, a culture distinctive of a local group, or a generic indigenous culture'.[372] In *Waiwo v. Waiwo and Banga*, the Senior Magistrate (now Chief Justice) Lunabek stated: "... in Tanna like other islands of the Archipelago, custom plays an important role in day to day life of their inhabitants".[373] Applying lessons of the past to solve problems of the present and future is a basic part of human practical reason.[374] In day to day life we often consider precedent, or what we have done in the past, to help us make decisions and create rules, whether we do so consciously or unconsciously. We strive to bring some consistency to our actions in dealing with our coworkers, students, children and friends so that we will be fair in our dealings with others and will be recognized as such.[375]

In business world, many parties hire transaction lawyers to secure their business transactions. Such practice is growing more spreading in central business districts around the world. Transaction lawyers' decisions give rise to more foreseeable effects. Such decisions as existing due to legal reasoning process may be more explicit and visible, in the sense that such decisions have direct effects [due to formal reasons].[376] In daily practice, when

---

edition of Getches, Wilkinson, and Williams, Federal Indian Law (5th ed., 2004), in Tribal Law Journal Vol. 8, p. 19.

371 Ibid., pp. 19-20.

372 Miranda Forsyth,'Beyond Case Law: Kastom and Courts in Vanuatu', in 35 VUWLR (2004), p. 429, referring to Margaret Jolly, 'Custom and the Way of the Land: Past and Present in Vanuatu and Fiji', in 62 Oceania 330 (1992), p. 341.

373 Ibid., p. 434. Waiwo v. Waiwo and Banga (12 February 1996) Senior Magistrate Court, Vanuatu, Civ. Cas' 324/1995, <,http://www.paclii.org/vu/cases/ VUMC/ 1996/1.html> (last accessed 17 June 2004).

374 Algero (2005), supra note 2524, p. 782. See Interpreting Precedents: A Comparative Study 1 (D. Neil MacCormick & Robert S. Summers eds., 1997), p. 1. See also William Thomas Tete, 'The Code, Custom and the Courts: Notes Toward a Louisiana Theory of Precedent', in 48 Tul. L. Rev. 1 (1973), p. 6, ("If someone else has already considered a similar problem, it is only logical to look to the prior reasoning").

375 Ibid. See Schauer (1987), supra note 2149, pp. 57-73.

376 Wahlgren (2009), supra note 2573, p. 203.

one pays the price of a product and then gets the product upon payment, she and the seller perform what the sales contract law says. When one drives a car on the right path as usual, she performs what the traffic law provides. When one hires a cab and pays the taxy fare, she and the taxy driver perform what the hire contract law prescribes. Practices in accordance with the law by members of a certain legal community based on established intuition, or, the intuition of rigidity through habitual social upbringing, and/or, customary business practices in certain communities any where on earth in accordance with the customary laws of the communities, and/or customary practices other than business practice and habitual practice - which are all undisputed,- are the law we see in the real world, and such [undisputed] practices constitute the performance of law as referred to in this writing.

CHAPTER VI

Conclusion

***

The underlying notions of this book are performance, competence, descriptivity, prescriptivity, generativity and transformativity. A distinction, similar to Chomsky's (1965:5) distinction between *competence* and *performance* in linguistics, in which *competence* designates the presumed internalized grammar and *performance* refers to all the other factors that affects linguistic intuition and the ways in which language is used, is existent in law. It has been proposed in Chapters III and V of this book that, in law, *competence* of law refers to the law in our mind [the law we understand], and *performance* of law refers to the law we really see. The law we really see is in legal determinations, including judicial decisions, administrative actions/ decisions, arbitral awards, negotiation/mediation settlements, customary practice and undisputed legal practice, whereas the law in our mind [the law we understand] includes rule of law and principle of law.

As to the notions of descriptivity and prescriptivity, there is a theory that prescriptivity fills the gap between descriptivity and normativity,[1] therefore, in connection with this theory, addressing descriptivity and prescriptivity and their relationship should necessarily be involving the discussion on normativity. Harre and Gillet relate normativity to attitude and emotion, whereas Brandom focuses on inferentialsm within Hegelian philosophy. From Brandom's inferentialism, it can be concluded that normativity includes deontic and score changing endorsement from observation of discursiveness, commitment to such endorsement, and practical-reasonably implementation thereof with responsibility.[2] The upshot of this story that living the life of a Homo sapien, i.e., having experiences with conceptual content, is a matter of being committed to playing the game of giving and asking for reasons. Commitments are normative statuses, which are attitudes to conceptual contents one acknowledges, attributes and undertakes in an essentially social context. Harre and Gillet hold that attitudes and emotions come into existence in the performance of actions, and the report of a memory is not reproduction of a representation but instead a socio-culturally located event.[3] So, memories, judgments and emotional displays do not emerge *de novo* every time without constraints. Cultural context and discursive practices as well as individuals' physical and mental states provide *resources* that people

1 Pitz & Sachs (1984), supra note 528, p. 140.

2 Bransen (2000), supra note 264, p. 12.

3 Wortham (1997), supra note 254 [footnote omitted].

use to accomplish their judgments, displays and other actions. Therefore, it can also be concluded that normativity might mean constraint on attitude, emotion and action within socio-cultural context. If normativity is considered to totally overlap prescriptivity, normativity then includes prescriptivity or vice versa. If normativity is considered as separated to some certain extent from prescriptivity, then the notion of prescriptivity being separated [and different] from normativity fills the gap between normativity and descriptivity, as already identified through cognitive science, epistemology and philosphy, as described in Chapter I.2.

***

Prescriptive epistemology (Cartesian) seeks to find a set of rules which can be used to determine whether a given belief is justified or not, by reducing the belief in question to foundational beliefs, and, attempts to show that a given belief is in fact justified because it does meet the condition that it can be deduced from some foundational justified beliefs.[4] In another perspective, true descriptive theory can be empirically ascertained; it is verified if it corresponds with reality (the facts); falsified if it does not correspond with reality.[5] Descriptive approach assumes (overtly or covertly) that the problem of knowledge is not whether we have it or not, but rather what the knowledge that we do have is like.[6] Quine says that the central concern of epistemology is the theory-evidence relationship; if the foundationalist story about this relationship is a failure, then that leaves only one story worth telling about this relationship, namely, the story told by a purely descriptive, causal-nomological science of human cognition.[7]

Descriptive epistemology might be seen as complementary to traditional epistemology (Campbell's view). On this analysis, the function of the evolutionary approach is to provide a descriptive account of knowing mechanisms while leaving the prescriptive aspects of epistemology to more traditional approach.[8] This has also been outlined in Chapter I.2.

***

Generative grammar purports to describe the issue of competence. A

4 O'Niel (2004), supra note 524.
5 Nandi (1986), supra note 504, § 3.2.3 [accompanying text omitted].
6 Tabarrok (1994), supra note 334, pp. 146-147.
7 Leiter (1997), supra note 304, p. 292 [footnote omitted].
8 Bradie & Harms (2016), supra note 298, § 1.3.

generative grammar must be a system of rule that can iterate to generate an indefinitely large number of structures. In generative grammar, the means for modeling these procedures is through a set of formal grammatical rules. These rules tell us the order in which to put our words. This is the kind of information encoded in generative rules. These rules are thought to generate the sentences of a language, hence the name is *generative* grammar.[9] [Being] generative means specifying the rules, or more clearly, making the hidden linguistic rules in the mind explicit. The generativity capacity, according to Pelletier, includes relations between deep structure (*competence*) and surface structure (*performance*).[10] Deep structure (*competence*) transforms itself to surface structure (*performance*), and this is diagrammatic representation of linguistic competence. This indicates that generativity and transformativity occur simultaneously (Chomsky 1981:4).

Generativity in general has been outlined in Chapter I.3. Generative processes help pick up the features critical for the similarity comparison.[11] Similarity judgments are inferences about generative process, and two objects appear similar when they are likely to have been generated by the same process.[12] Generativity may also occur through analogy. Hesse's theory of material analogy[13] has shown that analogy generates the insight of the target situation by matching the similarities between the source situation and the target situation, based on the already known insight of the source situation. Analogies are widely recognized as playing an important *heuristic* role, as aids to discovery. They have been employed, in a wide variety of settings and with considerable success, to generate insight and to formulate possible solutions to problems.[14] A conclusion can be drawn that analogy is generative.

Similarity and generativity are inter-correlated. The generative framework of Kemp, Bernstein and Tanenbaum help to explain how similarity judgments are guided by intuitive theories.[15] They develop a formal theory of similarity and compare it to the featural account[16] which suggests that the similarity of two objects is a function of their common and distinctive features, and the transformational account which suggests that similarity depends on the number of operations required to transform one object into the other. According to Harré, scientific explanation

9 Carnie (2013), supra note 24, p. 6.
10 Pelletier (1980), supra note 43, p. 26.
11 Kemp et.al (2005), supra note 837.
12 Ibid.
13 Bartha (2013), supra note 2352, § 3.3 [footnote omitted].
14 Ibid., p. 2.
15 Kemp et al, (2005), supra note 2936 [footnote omitted].
16 Ibid. [footnote omitted].

consists in finding or imagining plausible generative mechanism for the patterns amongst events, for the structures of things, for the generation, growth, decay, or extinction of things and materials, for changes within persisting things and materials.[17] Hahn, Chater and Richardson [also] conclude that similarity is as transformation.[18] So, similarity is generative-transformational, and analogy through similarity matching is too. Then, having addressed similarity and analogy we come to the notion of generative-transformation.

Another component of generative-transformation is coherence, for which consistency is required.[19] As to consistency, Tennenbaum (1968) summarized the position as follows, 'The reasoning behind [the consistent position] relates to the organism's presumed need to apprehend and comprehend things and events about him. In monitoring, processing and interpreting information from the environment, some degree of consistency and equilibrium is seen as essential for reasons of parsimony and economy of effort, as well as to allow for the predictability of, and hence adaptability to, subsequent encounters......most assume a universal value for the organism in his having a stable predictable view of his environment'.[20] Consistency is a condition for coherence. In relation to the notion of coherence, coherence sets appear in discussion. A coherent set has its justified members. A coherent set, according to Lehrer and Sellars, is one which is consistent, complete and mutually explanatory, so the idea here will be that, as the set increases in size, we can hope that each member of it is better explained by the rest, explanations can improve in quality; this accounts for the growth of justifiction. And the notion of mutual explanation is clearly symmetrical, in the required sense.[21] A belief-set with reasonable coherence will make each of its members justified.[22] Generativity and transformativity might exist within a coherent set. The generative model assumes that objects will be considered good members of a category of a coherent set.[23] So each category or coherence set has its good or justified members.

When generative process happens through analogy, transformational process also occurs simultaneously there. Generative and transformational processes might exist within a coherent set. Transformational process in this book means transformation within a category as a coherent set. The

17 Losee (1972,1980), supra note 835, p. 145 [footnote omitted].

18 Hahn et al (2003), supra note 821.

19 Dancy (1985), supra note 756, p. 110.

20 Simon & Holyoak (2002), supra note 840, p. 285 [footnote omitted].

21 Dancy (1985), supra note 2944, p. 111 [footnote omitted].

22 Ibid., p. 116.

23 Rehder & Kim (2010), supra note 850, p. 1176.

process refers to transformation from one member to another member (or to other consequent members) of the same category [the same coherence set].

***

In light of the notions of descriptivity and prescriptivity as already described in Chapter I.2, descriptive and prescriptive jurisprudence in legal doctrine are viewed in this book. In jurisprudence, to be able to give a descriptive account of the 'nature' of law the philosopher must give an account that will cover only those things that are laws. If she includes within her 'sample' things that are not laws or excludes some things that are laws, the account will be incorrect. So before we begin considering what features laws have, we must make sure that what we examine are laws and only laws. But how we can know what counts as a law?[24] Austin argues that the true essence of law is the command of the sovereign by sanction. Law was simply that which was in the lawbooks or otherwise ordered by the government.[25] Kelsen identified two significant features of law: (1) these 'objects' are systems of norms for human behavior (i.e., 'social orders'); and (2) they are coercive.[26] Hart says that the description of law may include the description of prescriptions in law. Law is as approximately the acceptance by the people of the soverign and thus of the rules promulgated by that sovereign.[27] Alexy contends that law has in its structure both ideal and real dimensions, viewed from participant's viewpoint.[28] Ihering defines law as a means to mediate various interests, and the law functions a means to solve social problems. [29] Weber's definition of law is that an order will be called *law* if it is externally guaranteed by the probability that coercion (physical or psychological) to bring about conformity or to avenge violation, will be applied by a *staff* of people holding themselves specially ready for that purpose.[30] Pound views that law is as a tool for promoting social welfare[31] through discovery of values particularly important for the law to protect[32]

24 Priel (2007), supra note 2517, p. 146.

25 Aubert (1983), supra note 1074, p. 9 [footnote omitted].

26 Nance (1985), supra note 1636, pp. 13-14 [footnote omitted].

27 Miller (1985/1986), supra note 1350, p. 9 [footnote omitted].

28 Finnis (2014), supra note 1508, p. 1, 3 [footnote omitted].

29 Aubert (1983), supra note 2950, p. 375.

30 Nance (1985), supra note 2951, n.163 [footnote omitted].

31 Melton (1990a), supra note 1000, p. 256 [accompanying text and footnote omitted].

32 Ibid. [accompanying text and footnote omitted].

and experimentation to identify ways that the law might more fully achieve its purposes.[33]

As to what law really is, the core of Realism is, indeed, a certain sort of descriptive claim about how judges decide cases, according to which judges rationalize, after the fact, decisions reached on other grounds.[34] Holmes holds that the law was *just a prediction* of what courts would do in the future, because there were no timeless qualities in rules.[35] Llewellyn[36] wrote: "We require to study the behavior of the subject-matter of control, men in groups.. [T]he legal feature of this age remains, not the persistence among all men of an interest in general security, but the emergence of diverse and specialized groups with a need for specialized control.. for private interests seem to have been the influential factors in law's major changes in the past". Ross clearly delimits legal science to the realm of the 'is' – that is, in his case, the realm of psycho-physical facts – since valuations concerning the shape that the law ought to take are not within the realm of scientific investigation.[37] Any attempt by legal science to confuse the investigation of the factual reality of law and the normative evaluation of the contents of the law derails legal science towards metaphysics again, insofar as that would mean considering that there is any way to discuss values in objective terms.[38]

Morris Cohen has concluded the brief discussion of his legal philosophy that law, and even the ethical ideal itself, may certainly be viewed as the historic resultant of various social forces. Yet the old problem of natural law, the problem as to what under given conditions the law ought to be, remains. Realism in the law can be combined with genuine idealism in the doctrine of the inherent limitations of legal idealism due to the conditions of human nature, habits, the legal machinery, and the limitations of man's desire for the moral good.[39] Science does not deal only with what actually is. The actual has meaning for science only when judged in the light of some ideal or possible alternatives.[40] Dworkin argues that legal theory is prescriptive, which rests on at least one prior descriptive claim: that law is a member of a special category of social practices, interpretive practices, that can only bear prescriptive

33 Ibid. [footnote omitted].

34 Kreitner (2010), supra note 1028, p. 784 [footnote omitted].

35 Miller (1985), supra note 2952, p. 389 [footnote omitted].

36 Kreitner (2010), supra note 2959, pp. 783-784 [footnote omitted].

37 Escorihuela (2003), supra note 1103, p. 723 [accompanying text and footnote omitted].

38 Ibid.

39 Reid (1971), supra note 1629, p. 245 [footnote omitted].

40 Ibid., p. 254 [footnote omitted].

theorizing.[41] Dyzenhaus's argument from authoritarianism tells us his contention that jurisprudence is prescriptive. His argument from irrelevance tells us that Dyzenhaus considers prescriptive theory to be aimed at judges and intended to influence decisions in hard cases. And in his argument from vacuity, Dyzenhaus supposes that the only kinds of arguments that these prescriptivism can embody are normative political arguments.[42] Dyzenhaus says judges endorse a moral duty to obey the law, whatever its content, direct their decisions accordingly and 'adopt a very conservative view of their role'.[43]

Underhill Moore is of the opinion that the study of law lies within the field of behavioristic psychology, echoing Quine's naturalized epistemology, so the theory of adjudication is 'naturalized' because it falls into place as a chapter of psychology (or anthropology or sociology).[44] In Brian Leiter's words on natural legal philosophy, what is required for a 'naturalized' jurisprudence: we seek methodological continuity with the natural and social sciences.[45] Folk theories plainly satisfy this demand: they seek causal explanations for these decisions, inasmuch as they understand 'reasons' as 'causes'; and the look for regular, law-like-ideally lawful-patterns of decision. That lawyers posses workable, if informal, folk theories of judicial decision serves to vindicate and instantiate Realism's naturalistic program.[46]

Analogous to descriptive and prescriptive epistemology in cognitive science and philosophy, descriptive and prescriptive jurisprudence illuminate the existence of descriptivity and prescriptivity of law, as already discussed in Chapter II. This picture enables us to identify the law as 'the ought prescribes actions', including individual person's actions, entity's action, group's actions, judicial actions and administrative actions. Descriptive jurisprudence shows us the law as it is, prescriptive jurisprudence shows the law as it ought to be. This book takes both descriptive jurisprudence and prescriptive jurisprudence into account in order to show generative transformational notion in law. If in Chomskyan theory, *competence* prescribes *performance*, in jurisprudence the rule of law [and/or principle of law] prescribes legal determinations or lawful actions. So *competence* which is prescriptive and *performance* which is

41 Tucker (2013), supra note 1218, pp. 92-93 [footnote omitted].

42 Ibid., pp. 91-92.

43 Ibid., p. 84 [footnote omitted].

44 Torben Spaak, 'Naturalism in Scandinavian and American Realism; Similarities and Differences,' Department. of Law, Uppsala University, Sweden, 2009 ["2009b"], p. 23 [footnote omitted].

45 Spaak (2009/2011), supra note 2763, p. 12 [footnote omitted].

46 Leiter (1997), supra note 2932, p. 313.

descriptive are both existent in law; and legal prescriptivity directs legal descriptivity.

***

Legal prescriptivity and constraint have also to do with the protection of rights. Rights and/or interests are what the law protects. In order to safeguard legal rule and principle, there is the concept of legal sanction in jurisprudence. A sanction is 'as a detriment imposed for doing what is forbidden'.[47] Sanctions embrace formally denominated penalties and any constitutional authorized action by a constitutionally established institution that visits unpleasant consequences on another official or institution on the ground that he, she, or it has violated legal norms.[48] Sanctions can be authorized and administered either to promote wise policies or to enforce constitutional norms.[49] Legal constraint and legal prescriptivity do overlap to some certain extent in terms of concepts. In accordance with the prescriptivity theory as already discussed in Chapter I, prescripitivity may include ethical and methodological prescriptions. In line with this, Chapter III.4 has sketched out prescriptivity in law. Moral, value and justice are quoted in ethical prescription as contained in legal rules and principles. Utilitarianist prescription is also cited, since social benefits or advantages are often referred to in legal cases. There are also prescriptions from legal doctrine itself and from other disciplines, such as sociology, politics, economics, environment science, and the use of resources. When the law provides for economic concepts and activities, the law follows the prescriptions from economics. The same is when the law regulates facts and concepts in sociology, politics, environment science and the making use of natural and human resourses.

With respect to legal rule as the *competence* of law as proposed in this book, the term '*competence'* here is not the same as the term 'legal competence' in legal doctrinal writings. The term '*competence'* of law as proposed in this book is similar to the *deep structure* in Chomskyan linguistic theory as already mentioned above. If, the *deep structure* or *competence* in linguistics refers to what is understood in language use, being prescriptive of the real use of language, the *competence* of law in this book specifically refers to *ratio decidendi*. The *rationes decidendi* of precedents prescribe how similar future cases are to be determined. This does not mean that statutory law is set aside. It is the rule of law and principle of law which

47 Fallon (2009), supra note 2114, n.104 [footnote omitted].

48 Ibid., p. 999 [footnote omitted].

49 Ibid.

have been proposed as the *competence* of law in Chapter III of this book. As the *competence* of law, principle of law primarily refers to specific principle rather than general principle; and specific principle of law is substantive in nature. As the *competence* of law, rule of law includes substantive rule and formal rule. Substantive legal rule refers to the *ratio decidendi* of precedent as followed through the doctrines of *stare decisis* and *jurisprudence constante*, whereas formal rule refers much to statutory rule.

Common law rules –those developed by earlier court decisions – are sometimes overruled directly, and sometimes radically altered by further development. In case, the court is to determine an unprecedented case, the rule of law to be applied may be statute laws [or principle of law]. Statutory rules are subjected to interpretation and reinterpretation. And in the event there is no statute law to be applied, the principle of law should apply.[50] When a previous legal decision is overruled, the *ratio decidendi* of that decision will no longer be binding later similar cases. However, this does not affect the validity and effect of the concrete orders and judgment in the case whose *ratio decidendi* has been overruled.

Nominalists believe that timeless rules as concepts await discovery by judges for resolving particular situations. Such rules are the concepts through mechanism as applied within a certain authority frame.[51] The historical school of law believed that the lesson of history and societal customs should, in large part, shape the texture of the law. History could teach what basic principles should foremost be included in the legal system.[52] F.C.von Savigny's historical jurisprudence has structured the law in terms of autonomous concepts. Positive legal materials were transcended through structure-giving concepts such as *state, sovereignty* or *individual rights in public law* (as autonomous concepts) through historical or philosophical reflection.

Statutes are formal and written rules of law, passed by federal, state, city or county legislative bodies, with the constitutional power to exercise the legislative function in its jurisdiction. Being written rules of law to proscribe future conduct, statutes are written in very general and often vague language. A legislative 'enabling statute' grants the power to certain administrative bodies to enact administrative regulations. There is a hierarchy of statutory law, and the United States Constitution sits at the apex.[53] Statutes or legislated legal rules other than civil codes, are basic to both the Civil and Common laws. Statutory law is of the same paramountcy in Common law and Civil law. However, statutes differ in function in both

50 Dworkin (1967), supra note 1408, p. 37, 38 [footnote omitted].

51 Ibid., p. 16.

52 Miller (1985/1986), supra note 2966, p. 375 [footnote omitted].

53 Connelly, supra note 2341, paragrapgh II. A.

law traditions. In Civil law jurisdictions, general principles of law are systematically and exhaustively exposed in codes,[54] and the codes provide the core of the law. Particular statutes have their function to complete the codes. In Common law jurisdictions, statutes complete precedents, which later contains the core of the law. Precedents as the core of the law are specific rules applying to specific facts.[55] Civil law rules are suppletive, the parties are deemed to know the law and hence to be aware of those rules; while Common law rules are presumptive of the intention of the parties when relevant facts are present.[56]

***

The focus of this book is on the identification of generative-transformational process in legal reasoning, as addressed in Chapter IV. Legal reasoning includes fact-findings, rule identification and legal interpretation or law application. Fact-finding concerns with the facts to be tried, and rule identification with legal rule to be applied. Since it is facts that are to be tried, fact-finding is the first thing to do in legal reasoning. The procees of fact-findings is sometimes described as the process of establishing 'historical facts'.[57] Matters of fact and the truth of evidence constitute the area of fact-findings. In fact-finding, the facts to be tried, according to Thayer, are distinguished between the primary facts, what may be called the raw material of the case, and the secondary or ultimate facts. Thayer argued that the right inference or conclusion [from these primary facts], in point of fact, is itself [a] matter of fact.[58] Thayer says that questions of fact mean questions of 'ultimate fact', the facts 'in issue to be decided by the jury'.[59] Roy Stone proposes fact categories: *alpha* facts and *aleph* facts. *Alpha* facts were the facts determined by direct observation; *aleph* facts were the facts determined by reflection after all the evidence is in. [60] Descriptive doctrinal writers, such as Alchourron and Bulygin, say that judicial decisions are descriptive of empirical facts (not from the control of empirical truth) and of legal rules. [The absorbing of factual truth into legal truth as argued by Kelsen is not acceptable, since] 'empirical truth is only one and only upon it the judicial decision must be based'. Truthfulness is a

54 Tetley (1999/2000), supra note 2000, para. V. 7 [footnote omitted].

55 Ibid.

56 Ibid., para V.12 [footnote omitted].

57 Christie (1992), supra note 1839, p. 38 [footnote omitted].

58 Ibid., p. 41, n.123 [footnote omitted].

59 Ibid., p. 37, n.112 [footnote omitted].

60 Ibid., p. 38 [footnote omitted].

necessary condition of justice in judicial decision. Judicial truth is empirical truth of science itself.[61] Goodhart proposes the notion of material facts as established by judges in judicial decision-making. He suggests that the principle of each case could be found by determining the facts treated by the judge as material facts[62]

When facts are already found, it is often said that rule identification follows, though fact identification and rule identification actually happen at the same time. The objective of rule identification is to find a *complete legal rule* that matches the current case, not only an isolated legal description. The relationship between elements of such a legal rule must be identified. A description of antecedent or consequence must be established. The corresponding antecedent or consequence have to be found in order to get something out of the description of such a legal rule.[63] In relation to the application of law, Chapter IV.10 has addressed the issue of generativity in legal reasoning. As to this, a practice of precedent in law has a number of advantages due to the fact that it may make institutional decision *replicable*,[64] whose coinage it is.[65] Replicability means that decisions are more predictable than if they were made *de novo* each time. In legal reasoning, if coherence and consistency in thinking are sought, judges may well select legal rules and sources consistent with the legal rules and sources they have retrieved, and ignored those that would make coherence more difficult.[66] The canons belonging to legal constructivism is conceptual-formalistic, and conceptualism in the Continent of Europe was reacted by a non-mechanical conception of judicial procees in France, such as by Francois Geny in his theory of 'free scientific research', and later by Portalis.[67] Ledru-Rollin has written that case law has risen from the law; and the case law, little by little, does impress itself within equity and reflects the moral, ideals and new discoveries.[68]

In law application, intution is the largely-practically manner of how the law is applied. Judges and other law professionals have their structural professional knowledge, and the knowledge is used in problem solving to determine legal disputes or problems. *Stare decisis* follows intuition method in law application.[69] In Civil law jurisdiction, cognitive

61 Viola (1995), supra note 1820, p. 255 [footnote omitted].
62 Branting (1993), supra note 2604, p. 9 [footnote omitted].
63 Wahlgren (2009), supra note 2925, pp. 228-229 [footnote omitted].
64 Lamond (2006), supra note 2609, p. 19 [footnote omitted].
65 Ibid. [footnote omitted].
66 Spellman & Schauer (2012), supra note 2326, p. 14 [footnote omitted].
67 Dennis (1993), supra note 2572, pp. 6-7 [footnote omitted].
68 Germain (2003), supra note 2156, p. 197 [footnote omitted].
69 Black (1957), supra note 2870, p. 1577.

instrumental mechanicism or subsumption of fact to rule is largely employed in law application. According to Kant, to create rules which connect recognition and action by applying general sentences to concrete situations is impossible, since doing so will always need additional rules stating whether such general sentences fit concrete cases or not – and this leads to infinite recursion. At this point, only some technical or pragmatic rules are possible. In order to make subsumption possible, all pragmatic jurisprudence therefore can be understood just in a technical pragmatic way, at least as long as the model of application moulds jurisprudence, not understood as regard to recognition of rules having found its best example in customary law.[70] However, in Civil law jurisdisction the principle of *jurisprudence constante* is also followed. In France in 1970s, a legislative reform took place, where the exegetic or expositional method and use of legislative histories enjoyed a resurgence of interests. The doctrine of *jurisprudence constante* has been followed; when a series of decisions do/does form a constant stream of uniform and homogenous rulings having the same reasoning, the doctrine grants the cases considerable persuasive authority and justifies, without requiring, the court in abstaining from new inquiry because of its faith in the precedents.[71] Now the European Court of Justice (ECJ) much follows case-law principle in judicial decision-making.

Chapters IV.5 and IV.6 have described the principle of *stare decisis* and *jurisprudence constante* in which similarity-mapping and analogy are employed, and coherence based on consistency is taken into account. In Common law jurisdiction, when cases were brought before the Common law courts, judges sought precedents for their decisions in the principles [*ratio*] that had been laid down in earlier cases. This doctrine of *stare decisis* bound judges to apply similar principles in analogous cases. However, this development of the Common law, Hayek noted, did not entail that it remained static and unchanging. The law did indeed change, through its application to new circumstances and through variations in interpretation that emerged in specific legal decisions. Common law thus evolved over time as judge-made law. Like language, Common law formed a spontaneously generated arrangement, the product of human action but not of human design (Hayek 1973: SI).[72] As to *Jurisprudence constante,* as exemplified by the French practice, Lambert in an article published in the Yale Law Journal[73] has said that in France, the practice of the courts does not become a source of the law until it is definitely fixed by the repetition of precedents which are in agreement on a single point. Decided cases,

70 Ruckert (2006), supra note 2299, para 3.7 [footnote omitted].

71 Dennis (1993), supra note 2992, p. 15 [footnote omitted].

72 Ronald Hamoway, 'F.A. HAYEK AND THE COMMON LAW', in Cato Journal Vol. 23, No. 2 (Fall 2003), p. 243 [footnote omitted].

73 Goodhart (1930b), supra note 2591, p. 173.

therefore, only affect the law in so far as they create practice or body of doctrine.[74]

This book follows that deduction from general rule to legal determination including judicial decision is to be done if there is no precedent or if a case is in such a situation where following precedent is not possible or will cause unfairness. However, some writers say that deduction may also take place from event to event, not always from general concept to particular. Following this, in the event that a precedent is already in existence, deduction can then be made from precedent [existing substantive legal rule] to a new similar substantive legal rule. This is in line with the substantive behaviorist theory that epistemological account of explanation is deduction from observed events, as stated by Amundson.[75] It is possible to think that such deduction may overlap the notion of analogy. In this respect, deduction and analogy might seem a matter of degree in continuum. In most doctrinal writings, the term 'analogy' is chosen [rather than 'deduction' as such] in legal reasoning, consequently analogical logic is seen as widely used in legal reasoning.

***

The transformational process in law in this book is in the sense that legal determination may vary in its surface structural forms but those various surface structural forms belong to one single rule of law. The same may happen to administrative action/decision and alternative dispute resolution, such as arbitral award and negotiation/mediation settlement. Possible opinion may also be made that customary and undisputed practices are also generated from legal rules, and variations of a legal rule do transform in terms of similarity in the employment of analogy through habitual upbringing [professionally or in daily life]. This transformation has been identified in Chapter IV.10 in light of Chapter I.3.

As to analogy and coherence in legal reasoning, legal decision-making is on strongest justification for analogy that lies in the values of replicability for the sake of 'coherence in the law.[76] Writers observe there is a tendency of thin global coherence and of thicker local coherence as shown in the doctrine of law. Legal doctrinal writers, e.g., Dworkin, MacCormick, Raz, Sunstein and Peczenik, have addressed coherence in law, globally and locally. MacCormick contends that in deciding a case according to law, courts

---

74 Ibid., p. 174 [accompanying text omitted].
75 Amundson (1981), supra note 525, Part III.
76 Lamond (2006), supra note 2989, p. 25 [footnote omitted].

should first of all interpret the existing law in order to establish a coherent view of some branch of the law, and they should do this by showing how that branch of law is justified according to some coherent set of principles or values which underlie it. The court should then use this view of the law in order to justify its decision in a new case which comes before it.[77] Coherence based on consistency is taken into account in legal reasoning through the principles of *stare decisis* and *jurisprudence constante.* Many writers say that consistency is a condition for coherence, and consistency guarantees predictability and certainty. In jurisprudence it is held that the law is a purposeful enterprise that it displays structural constancies which the legal theorist can discover and treat as uniformities in the factually given.[78] In fact, the claim that coherence and the dominant conception of precedent lead to the linear ordering problem is true because precedent serves as a principle of conservation in coherence theories of law.[79] Coherence theories is simply one particularly favored way of spelling out what has been called the dominant conception of precedent.[80] Legal coherence in this book focuses specifically on the scope of legal reasoning only. Chapter IV.10.2 has already discussed about coherence in legal reasoning.

Coherence in legal reasoning focuses on each rule of law as a coherent set or a [rule] category. The focus is on *rationes decidendi* as justified members of a certain legal rule category. The legal coherence is coherence of justification, in which coherent effect is considered through similarity-mapping between a precedent and the case at hand. In Chapters IV.10.2 and IV.11, it has been identified that such coherence in legal reasoning is generative-transformational. This is analogous to and in light of what has been identified in Chapters I.3.3 and I.3.4 on coherence theory in cognitive science, epistemology and philosophy. In addition, analogy and coherence in cases have also been presented in Chapter IV.10.3 to show that generative-transformational process through the employment of analogy and the consideration of coherence exists in legal reasoning. In other words, Chapter IV has revealed that similarity, analogy, coherence, consistency, predictability, certainty, *stare decisis*, and *jurisprudence constante* have caused generative-transformational legal reasoning.

It has been identified in Chapter I.3 that similarity, analogy, coherence based on consistency in cognitive science, epistemology and philosophy are generative-transformational. In other words, similarity, analogy and coherence are the components of transformational generative process. In jurisprudence the generative transformational process has been

---

77 Dickson (2010), supra note 2555, p. 18 [footnote omitted].

78 Nance (1985), supra note 2955, p. 25 [footnote omitted].

79 Kress (1984), supra note 2547, p. 401 [accompanying text omitted].

80 Ibid., pp. 401-402.

identified as existent in legal reasoning, as already addressed in Chapters V.10. There, it has also been identified that analogy and coherence generate and transform legal determinations [including judicial decisions] from rule of law or principle of law. Described briefly, analogy and coherence are generative-transformational. The generation and transformation of gramatical sentences from grammar in linguistics is analogous to the generation and transformation of legal determinations from the rule of law [and the principle of law] in jurisprudence. So, it is undeniable that generative-transformational process exists in legal reasoning.

***

Legal determinations including judicial decisions are where the *performance* of law is suited. Judicial decisions constitute substantive legal rules that are directly enforceable or executed in reality. What to be enforced or executed in reality include court orders and/or court sentence orders. These are all enforced or executed through legal procedures [including voluntary enforcement/execution] in order to make the rules of law [and/or principles of law] explicit in order to be the law we really see. The notion of law *performance* has been addressed in Chapter V in which various court judgments, *ratio decidendi* of the case at hand, court concrete orders, criminal sentencing and *res iudicata* have been discussed. It is the enforcement or execution of court concrete order or sentence orders which are among those as proposed as the *performance* of law in this book, being analogous to *performance* in Chomskyan theory.

Any dispute settlements being alternative to judicial decision, when enforced, also constitute the law in action or the law in reality as the *performance* of law. This has already been elaborated in Chapter V.4. Arbitration, negotiation, mediation, private-judging, mock-trial, and any customary or undisputed law practices have been described as the *performance* of law, when enforced. Customary and undisputed practices are also the *peformance of law*. Undisputed law practice may be quite practical without deliberation or may be deliberate. Customary and undisputed practices as the *performance* of law have been addressed in Chapter V.5. When people buy commodities, they pay the prices and get the commodities. When people borrow things from others, they return the things to lenders. When people walk on the streets, they walk on the right path. When people sit in cafes, they sit properly. When all these events happen without dispute, they are examples of customary or undisputed practice without deliberation. When two companies make a contract, they make it with deliberation with or without hiring transactional lawyers.

When someone buys a big property, he may do it deliberately and lawfully without dispute. When these transactions happen without dispute, they are examples of undisputed practice with deliberation. These undisputed practices may constitute the *performance* of law if viewed from legal prespective. Within this context, there is direction from legal prescriptivity which underlies those practices, having been acquired by people through habitual social upbringing, legal consciousness and custom. So, there are real living laws other than concrete court orders. Those other real living laws may be any customary or undisputed deals or actions which are factually and voluntarily carried out by actors in social life.

***

The structuralist approach attempts to explain the text in terms of its internal relations, a type which comes from the field of language. It is the intention of language that is to say something about something. Language has both an ideal sense, to say something, and a real reference, to say it about something. [81] Paul Ricouer argues that the reader may seek, not something hidden behind the text, but something disclosed in front of it; not the internal constitution of the text, but that which points towards a possible world. To understand a text at this level is to move from its sense to its reference, from that which it says to that which it says it about. In Ricouer's theory, with the mediation of structural analysis, it seems possible to situate explanation and interpretation along a unique *hermeneutical arc* and to integrate the opposite attitudes of explanation and understanding within an overall conception of reading as the recovery of meaning.[82]

Seen as a kind of *reductio ad absurdum* the Wittgensteinian challenge indicates that we have gone off the right path in our understanding of how rule operate. Such theorists seek to avoid linguistic indeterminacy and think there is no gap interpretation that should bridge between grasping a rule and understanding the actions which it requires, so interpretation is not the fundamental determinant of meaning.[83] This may mean that in majority cases in reality, people do follow rules without interpretation [or without deliberate consideration], and such is acquired through habitual upbringing.

If in Chomskyan theory, grammar generates grammatical sentences, analogously in jurisprudence the law generates legal determinations or

81 Thompson (1981), supra note 2768, p. 9.

82 Ibid., p. 5 [footnote omitted].

83 Dickson (2010), supra note 3002, p. 11, 12 [footnote omitted].

lawful actions. If grammar generates structural description of sentence, analogously the law generates legal determinations, in which court concrete orders, or sentence orders, administrative decisions, customary practice and undisputed legal practice are included. The notions of descriptivity and prescriptivity in Chomskyan theory and in cognitive science, epistemology and philosophy lead us to view descriptive jurisprudence, [normative jurisprudence] and prescriptive jurisprudence, illuminating what we call the law we really see in real world [the *performance* of law as proposed in this book] and the law in our mind [the law we understand] constituting rule of law or principle of law as the *competence* of law. As has been discussed above, similarity-matching and analogy are employed, and coherence and consistency are taken into account in legal reasoning. Since similarity, analogy, coherence and consistency have been proven generative-transformational, legal reasoning process is undeniably *generative-transformational* or *transformational-generative*. Legal reasoning generates the *ratio decidendi* of the case at hand through similarity-matching between the facts of the precedent and those of the case at hand by employing analogy and taking coherenece into account, based on the already known *ratio decidendi* of the precedent, therefore the *ratio* of the case at hand and *that* of the precedent constitute justified members of the same rule of law as a coherence set or a rule category on one particualr issue in this sense, where both of the *rationes* are similar in terms of legal understanding. This process also shows transformation of the *ratio* of the precedent into *that* of the case at hand [and further into the *rationes decidendi* of consequent similar cases], and each of the *rationes* remains *justified* members of the same rule of law as a category. From the observation and identification above, it may be concluded that legal reasoning is *generative-transformational* or *transformational-generative*.

The observations, examinations, descriptions and identifications in this book amount to the conclusion that there is generative-transformational process in legal reasoning through the notions of similarity, analogy, coherence and consistency for the sake of predictability, certainty and fairness, therefore generative-transformational or transformational- generative law is undeniable. It is a sort of legal generative transformationalism. Legal generative transformationalism seems to be a matching point between Common law and Civil law traditions, due to the existence of transformational generative feature in legal reasoning in both traditions. Legal generative transformationalism also views the law on evolutionary dimension. This is in line with Nicholas Rescher's position[84] on the principle of simplicity and generality. He has gone a long way toward grounding epistemological principles in the nature of finite

84 Tabarrok (1994), supra note 2931, p. 151 [footnote omitted].

knowers rather than on metaphysical considerations, he does not go far enough, eventually trying to ground them in an evolutionary tale : ....To be sure, this methodological/procedural tale is not the whole story. There is also, in the final analysis, a substantive aspect to the matter of induction's justification. Our intellectual tastes (for simplicity, elegance, etc. as we naturally construe these ideas) are, like our physical tastes (palatability), the products of evolutionary pressure to prioritize those things that work – that prove effective and are thus survival conducive. The question of the seemingly pre-established harmony coordinating of.. theoretically disparate factors of convenience and effectiveness is ultimately resolved on the basis of evolutionary considerations in the order of rational selection (102, 107). He argues that evolution selects brains which have found effective theories to be simple, convenient, and elegant as well.

BIBLIOGRAPHY

Albrecht, Hans-Jorg, 'Sanction Policies and Alternative Measures to Incarceration: European Experiences with Intermediate and Alternative Criminal Penalties', in *Resource Material Series No. 80,UNAFEI, Tokyo (1987).*

Albrecht, Hans-Jorg, 'Sentencing in Germany: Explaining Long-Term Stability in the Structure of Criminal Sanctions and Sentencing', in *Law and Contemporary Problems, Vol. 76:211(2013).*

Alces, P. A., 'The Unruliness of Rules', Faculty Publication, in *Michigan Law Review, Vol. 101:2037, May 2003*, n.26.

Aldisert, R. J., Clowney, S., and Peterson, J.D., 'Logic For Law Students: How To Think Like A Lawyer', in *University of Pittsburgh Law Review Vol. 69:1 (2007).*

Algero, M. G., 'The Sources of Law and the Value of Precedent: A Comparative and Empirical Study of a Civil Law State in a Common Law Nation', in *Louisiana Law Review,Vol. 65, 2005.*

Alpa, Guido, 'Articles - General Principles of Law', (1994), produced by The Berkeley Electronic Press, http // digitalcommons law.edu/ annlsurvey/ vol1/issl/2.

Amundson, R., 'The Epistemological Status of a Naturalized Epistemology', Research supported by the NEH during the summer of 1981 and by the University of Hawaii Office of Research Administration, in *Inquiry 26*, 333-44, Part I.

Anderson, J. R., 'The Adaptive Nature of Human Categorization,' in *Psychological Review 1991,Vol.98, No.3,409-429.*

Anderson, R. A., Fox, I. And Twomey, D.P., *Business Law, UCC Comprehensive Volume*, twelfth edition, (Cincinnati; West Chicago, ILL; Dallas; Pelham Manor, N.Y; Palo Alto, Calif.: South-Western Publishing Co.,1984).

Aoun, Y. and Sportiche, D., 'Transformational Generative Grammar and the Study of Language', (MIT Cambridge, Mass, June 1980), in *GLOW Newsletter 5, September 1980.*

Ashby, F. G. and Perrin, N. A., 'Toward a Unified Theory of Similarity and Recognition', in *Psychological Review 1988,Vol.95,No.1, pp. 124-150.*

Aston, B., 'How does Community Law Affect National Soverignty?', Politics of Governance: The European Union,' 25.02.04. benaston.com.

Aubert, V., *In Search of Law, Sociological Approaches to Law*, (Oxford: Martin Robertson, 1983).

Aucher, G., Boella, G., and Van der Torre, L., 'Prescriptive and Descriptive Obligations in Dynamic Epistemic Deontic Logic', 2009, (Berlin Heidelberg: Springer Verlag, 2010), in *LNAI 6237, pp. 150-161, 2010.*

The Australasian Legal Information Institute (AustLII) – Free, comprehensive and independent access to Australasian law – a joint facility of UTS and UNSW Faculties of Law, last update 28 August 2018.

Ayer, A. J., *The Problem of Knowledge*, (Edinburgh: Penguin, 1956).

Balkin, J. M., 'Understanding Legal Understanding: The Legal Subject and the Problem of Legal Coherence', in *Yale L. J.* (1993) 103.

Balkin, J. M and Levinson, S., 'Law and the Humanities: An Uneasy Relationship-Essay', in *Yale Journal of Law and the Humanities*,Vol. 18: 155, 2006.

Barak, Aharon, 'Comparative Law, Originalism and the Role of a Judge in a Democracy: A Reply to Justice Scalia' – the Fullbright Convention, January 29, 2006.

Bartha, P., 'Analogy and Analogical Reasoning', in Stanford Encyclopedia of Philosophy,' first published Tuesday, June 25, 2013.

Bernstein, H., 'The Finality of A Judgment as A Requirement for Civil Appeals in Germany', in *LAW AND CONTEMPORARY PROBLEMS*,Vol. 47:No.3, Page 35: Summer 1984.

Biddle, C., 'Ayn Rand's Theory of Rights: The Moral Foundation of a Free Society', in *TOS* Vol. 6, No.3, Fall 2011.

Biletzki, A and Matar, A., 'Ludwig Wittgenstein', in Stanford Encyclopedia of Philosophy, first published Friday, November 8, 2002, substantive revision Monday, March 3, 2014. .

Bishop, M. B and Trout, J. D., 'The Pathologies of Standard Analytic Epistemology', (Blackwell Publishing Inc., 2005), in *NOUS* 39.4 (2005), pp. 696-714.

Black, H. C., *Black's Law Dictionary*, fourth edition, (The Publisher Editorial Staff, St. Paul, MINN, 1957).

Blackman, S.H and McNeill, R.M., 'Alternative Dispute Resolution in Commercial Intellectual Property Disputes', in 47 *The American University Law Review*, 1709 (1998).

Bodenheimer, E., 'A Decade of Jurispridence in the United States of America: 1946-1959', in *Natural Law Forum 1958*, Paper 27, [brought by Notre Dame Law School Scholarship].

Bogdandy, A., 'Founding Principles of EU Law: A Theoretical and Doctrinal Sketch', (Oxford, UK & MA, USA: Blackwell Publishing Ltd, 2010), in *European Law Journal*, Vol.16, No. 2, March 2010, pp. 95-111.

Boon, M., 'Tales of Experimentation, Book Review of Rom Harre, Pavlov's Dogs and Schrodinger's Cat: Scenes from the living laboratory', (Oxford: Oxford University Press, 2009), in *Metascience*, 20:159-163.

Bradie, M. and Harms, W., 'Evolutionary Epistemology', in Stanford Encyclopedia of Philosophy, first published Thursday, January 11, 2001, substantive revision Thursday, January 5, 2012.

Bradley, C. A. and Morrison, T. W., 'Presidential Power, Historical Practice, and Legal Constraint', Essay, in *Columbia Law Review*, Vol.113:1097, 2013.

Braman, E., 'Constraint in Legal Decision Making', prepared for the Workshop on Exploring the Judicial Mind, University of Virginia, March 30-31, 2007.

Bransen, Jan, 'Normativity as the Key to Objectivity – An exploration of Robert Brandom's Articulating Reasons', in *Inquiry*, Vol. 45(3), 2000, 373-392.

Branting, L. K., 'A Computional Model of Ratio Decidendi', in *Artificial Intelligence and Law*, March 1993,Vol.2, Issue 1, pp. 1-31.

Bray, S. L., 'Article – Preventive Adjudication', in *The University of Chicago Law Review*, Volume 77, Number 3, Summer 2010.

Bresnan, P. H. and Cornelio, J. P., 'Relief from Default Judgments Under Rule 60(b) – A Study of Federal Case Law', in *Fordham Law Review*, Volume 49 / Issue 6, Article 3, 1981.

Brewer, S., 'Exemplary Reasoning: Semantics, Pragmatics and Rational Force of Legal Argument by Analogy', in 109 HARV .L. REV, 923, 972 (1966).

Briggs, R., 'Normative Theories of Rational Choice: Expected Utility', in *Stanford Encyclopedia of Philosophy*, first published Friday, August 8, 2014.

Brown, C. C., 'Summary Judgment in Maryland', in Maryland Law Review, Volume 38 / Issue 2, Article 3, 1978.

Brush, M., 'Comments – The Swedish Penal Code of 1965', in 67 *Duke Law Journal* (1968).

Cahill, M. T., 'Retributive Justice in the Real World', in (2007) *Washington University Law Review*, Vol. 85:815.

Carnie, A., *Syntax – A Generative Introduction – Part 1 : Preliminaries : Generative Grammar,* third edition, (Chichester, UK: Wiley – Blackwell, A John Wiley & Sons, Ltd., 2013).

Catholic Encyclopedia, 'Intuition', APA citation, George Sauvage (1910), New York: Robert Appleton Company, Retrieved January 15, 2013, from New Advent; http://www.newadvent.org/cathen/ 08082b.ht.

Catholic Encyclopedia, 'Justice', APA citation, Slater, T., (1910), New York: Robert

Appleton Company, Retrieved January 19, 2013 from New Advent:http:///www.newadvent.org/cathen/08571c.htm.

Chaffee, E, 'Always Do the Right Thing: Ethical Intuitionism and Legal Compliance', March 10, 2008, in *Washington University Law Review, Commentaries,* Vol. 89:6.

Chomsky, Noam, *Syntactic Structure,* (The Hague: Mouton Publishers, 1957).

Chomsky, Noam, *Aspects of the Theory of Syntax,* (MIT Press, 1965).

Christie, G. C., 'Articles – Judicial Review of Findings of Fact', 1992, in *Northwestern University Law Review* Vol. 87, No.1.

Clermont, K. M., 'Jurisdictional Fact', in Cornell Law Review Vol. 91 - A Digital Repository, Cornell Law Faculty Publication, 7-24, 2006.

Connelly, Allison, 'Legal Reasoning: Analyzing Cases and Statutes', the College's Legal Clinic, University of Kentucky, Lexington, available at www. law. uky.edu /files/docs/clinic/legal_analysis. pdf. [A. Connelly has been the Head of the College Legal Clinic as of 1998].

Crummins, Richard S., 'Judgment on the Merits Leaving Attorney's Fees Issues Undecided: A Final Judgment?,' in *56 Fordham L. Rev.* 487 (1987).

Currie, D. P., 'Res Judicata: The Neglected Defense', in *45 University of Chicago* Law Review 317 (1978).

D'Amato, A., 'Legal Uncertainty', in 71 California Law Review 1-55 (1983) - Repository Citation: Faculty Working Paper 108, Northwestern University School of Law, 2010.

Dalberg-Larsen, J., *Alf Ross and the Sociology of Law,* Stockholm Institute for Scandinavian Law, 1957-2010.

Dancy, J., An Introduction to Contemporary Epistemology, Justification, Coherence Theories, (Basil Blackwell, 1985).

Dancy, J., 'Harold Arthur Prichard', in Stanford Encyclopedia of Philosophy, first published Monday, January 26, 2009, substantive revision Friday, Jan. 31, 2014.

Davison, R. M., 'An Action Research Perspective of Group Support Systems: How to Improve Meetings in Hong Kong - Chapter Three: Research Methodology', Ph.D. Dissertation, City University of Hong Kong, 1998, available at www. is.cityu.edu.hk/staff/isrobert/phd/ch.3.pdf

Del Vecchio, Giorgio, *The Concept of Nature and the Principles of Law,* 1908), in "The Formal Basis of Law" (Boston: Boston Printing Co., 1914, reprinted by Fred B. Rothman & Sons, 1969), *Modern Legal Philosophy Series, Vol. 10.

Dennis, J. L., 'Interpretation and Application of the Civil Code and the Evaluation of Judicial Precedent', in 54 *Lousiana Law Review* 1993.

Dession, G.H., 'Sanctions, Law and Public Order', in HeinOnline - 1 Vanderbilt Law Review 14 1947-1948 - Yale Law School, Yale Law School Legal Scholarship Repository, Faculty of Scholarship Series - Yale Law School Faculty Scholarship, 1-1-1947.

Dickson, J., 'Interpretation and Coherence in Legal Reasoning', in Stanford Encyclopedia of Philosophy, first published Tuesday, May 29, 2001, substantive revision Wednesday, Feb.10, 2010.

Dixon, M. H., 'Normative Ethical Theories, A Closer Examination', Ohio Northern University, available at www2.onu.edu/~m~dixon/handouts/ethicaltheories.html

Dorsey, D., 'A Coherence Theory of Truth in Ethics', in *Philosophical Studies* (2006) 127:493-523.

Driver, J., 'The History of Utilitarianism', in Stanford Encyclopedia of Philosophy, The History of Utilitarianism, first published Friday, March 27, 2009, substantive revision Monday, September 22, 2014.

Dryer, Matthew S., 'Descriptive Theories, Explanatory Theories, and Basic Linguistic Theory', in Felix Ameka, Alan Dench & Nicholas Evans (eds), (Berlin: Mouton de Gruyter, 2006), in *Catching Language: Issues in Grammar Writing*.

Dworkin, R. M., 'The Model of Rules', in The University of Chicago Law Review, Vol 35, 1967 - Yale Law School Legal Scholarship Repository, 1-1-1967.

Dyzenhaus, D., 'The Rule of Law as the Rule of Liberal Principle', University of Toronto, St. George, in *Arthur Ripstein, 'Ronald Dworkin', (Cambridge University Press 2007).*

Endicott, T. A. O., 'Law and Language', in Standford Encyclopedia of Philosophy, first published Thursday, December 5, 2002, substantive revision Monday, August 9, 2010.

Endicott, T. A. O., 'Legal Interpretation', in A. Marmor (ed.), 'Routledge Companion to Philosophy of Law', Legal Research Paper Series – Paper No. 39/2011, June 2011, (Routledge, 2012).

Escorihuela, A. L., 'Alf Ross: Towards a Realist Critique and Reconstruction of International Law', in *EJIL* (2003), Vol. 14 No. 4, 703-766.

Fallon, Richard H. Jr, 'Constitutional Constraints', in 97 [No.4] *California Law Review* (2009).

Fennelly, N., 'Legal Interpretation at the European Court of Justice', in *Fordham International Law Journal*, Volume 20, Issue 3, Article 4, 1996.

Feteris, E. and Kloosterhuis, H., 'The Analysis and Evaluation of Legal Argumentation: Approaches from Legal Theory and Argumentation Theory', in *Studies in Logic, Grammar and Rethoric* 16 (29) 2009.

Finnis, J., 'Law as Fact and as Reason for Action: A Response to Robert Alexy's on Law's Ideal Dimension', in American Journal of Jurisprudence 59 (2014) - Oxford Legal Studies Research Paper No. 21/2014 - Notre Dame Law School Legal Studies Research Paper No.1418.

Fodor, E. M., 'General Principles of Administrative Sanctions in the Romanian Law', in *Fiat Justitia*, nr.1/2007.

Foley, R., *The Theory of Epistemic Rationality*, (Cambridge, MA: Harvard University Press, 2009).

Ford, A., 'Robust Coherence: An Approach to Multi-agent Experience-based Planning', 2009, U.S. Air Force Research Laboratory, 525 Brooks Road, Rome NY, 13441, Association for the Advancement of Artificial Intelligence (www aaai.org).

Forsyth, M., 'Beyond Case Law: Kastom and Courts in Vanuatu', in (2004) 35 *VUWLR*.

Fredriksen, H. H., 'The Troubled Relationship between the Supreme Court of Norway and the EFTA Court – Recent Developments', University of Bergen, Norway, in *Bergen Open Research Archive* (2014).

Frickey, P. P., 'Revisiting the Revival of Theory in Statutory Interpretation: A Lecture in Honor of Irving Younger', in 84 *Minn. L. Rev.* 199 (1999).

Fordham Law Review, Volume 7 / Issue 2, Article 9,1938, Obiter Dicta, citing Birrel (1885), 'Obiter Dicta.'

Gab, O., Koppenhagen, N., Bregel, H., Madche, A. and Muller, B., 'Anatomy of Knowledge Bases used in Design Science Research', A Literature Review, (Berlin Heidelberg: Springer-Verlag, 2011), in *adfa*, 2011.

Garcia, I. M., 'Enforcement of Penalty Clauses in Civil and Common Law: A Puzzle to be Solved by the Contracting Parties', in *European Journal of Legal Studies*, Volume 5, Issue 1 (Spring/Summer 2012).

Garret, J., 'A Simple and Usable (Although Incomplete) Ethical Theory Based on the Ethics of W.D. Ross', Last Revision: August 10, 2004, in *Ted Lockhart's academic web page on W.D. Ross*, http://www.wku.edu/~jan.garrett/ethics/rossethc.htm

Gattis, M., 'Mapping relational structure in spatial reasoning', in *Cognitive Science* 28 (2004) 589-610, Elsevier.

Gentner, D. and Markman A. B., 'Analogy – Watershed or Waterloo? Structural alignment and the development of connectionist models of analogy', (1993), Department of Psychology, Northwestern University, Evanston, IL. - a research sponsored by ONR grant BNS-87-20301, (1987-2018 Neural Information Processing Systems Foundation/NIPS, Inc.).

Germain, C. M., 'Approach to Statutory Interpretation and Legislative History in France', in *Duke Journal of Comparative & International Law*, Vol. 13:195, Special Issue 2003.

Golding, M. P., 'Rights, Performatives, and Promises in Karl Olivecrona's Legal Theory', in *Ratio Juris* Vol. 18 No.1, March 2005 (16-29).

Goldman, A, 'What is Justified Belief?', in *Justification and Knowledge*, ed. George Pappas, pp. 1-23 (Doredrecht: Reidel, 1979).

Goldkuhl, G., 'The grounding of usable knowledge: An inquiry in the epistemology of action knowledge', paper accepted to *HSS99 (Högskolor och Samhälle i Samverkan)*, Falun, March 16-18, 1999.

Goodhart, A. L., 'Case Law in England and America', in *Cornell Law Review*, Volume XV, Number 2, February 1930.

Goodhart, A. L., 'The Ratio Decidendi of A Case', in *Modern Law Review*, Vol.22, No.2, March 1959.

Graham, G., *Philosophy of Mind, an introduction*, second edition (Malden, MA, USA & Oxford, UK: Blackwell Publisher, 1998).

Green, Jamal, 'The Rule of Law as a Law of Standards', in Justice Stevens's Law of Standard, in 99 *Georgetown Law Journal* 1289-1299 (2011).

Greenwald, A. G., Rudman, L.A., Nosek, B.A., Banaji, M.R., Farnham, S.D and Mellot, D.S., 'A Unified Theory of Implicit Attitudes, Stereotypes, Self-Esteem, and Self-Concept', in *Psychological Review*, 2002, Vol. 109, No.1, 3-25.

Grossman, L. A., 'From Savigny through Sir Henry Maine': Roscoe Pound's Flawed Portrait of James Coolidge Carter's Historical Jurisprudence', in *WCL* Research Paper No. 2009-21.

Hage, J., 'A Theory of Legal Reasoning and a Logic to Match', in *Artificial Intelligence and Law* 4 (3-4): 199-273 (1996).

Hage, J., 'Three Kinds of Coherentism', Michal Araszkiewics & Jaromir Savelka (eds), in *Coherence: Insights from Philosophy, Jurisprudence and Artificial Intelligence* (Dodrecht: Springer, 2003), pp. 1-3.

Hale, Lady, 'UK Constitutionalism on the March?', a keynote address to the Constitutional and Administrative Law Bar Association on Conference 2014, July 12, 2014.

Hamoway, R., 'F.A. Hayek and the Common Law', in *Cato Journal* Vol. 23, No. 2 (Fall 2003).

Hanley, R. F., 'Brush Up Your Aristotle', in 3 *J. Ass'n Legal Writing Directors* (2006).

Harding M. and Malkin, I., 'The High Court of Australia's Obiter Dicta and Decision-Making in Lower Courts', in *Sydney Law Review*, Vol.34:239, 2012.

Harré, Rom, *The Philosophy of Science*, second edition, (Oxford and New York: Oxford University Press, 1985).

Harré, Rom, 'Psychology's Recovery of its Proper Projects and Methods – Editorial', in *Europe's Journal of Psychology*, 2012, Vol. 8(3), 315-320.

Hartman, S. and Bovens, L., 'A Probabilistic Theory of the Coherence of an Information Set', a research supported by a grant of the National Science Foundation, Science and Technology Studies (SES 00-80580) and grants of the Transcoop Program and of the Feodor Lynen Program of the Alexander von Humboldt Foundation, Hartman & Bovens – 2001- sas-space.sas.ac.uk.

Hazard, G. C. Jr, 'Reflection on the Substance of Finality, in *70 Cornell L. Rev.*, 642 (1985).

Hazard, G. C. Jr, 'Law, Morals, and Ethics,' in (1995) Faculty Scholarship Series, Paper 2372 - Yale Law School Legal Scholarship Repository.

Heinze, C. A., 'Report on The Effect in the European Community of Judgments in Civil and Commercial Matters: Recognition, Res Judicata and Abuse of Process in Germany', in *British Institute of International and Comparative Law,* Project Reference: JLS/2006/FPC/21-30-CE-00914760055.

Herz, M., 'Choosing Between Normative and Descriptive Versions of the Judicial Role', in *Marquette Law Review* Vol. 75, No. 4, 1992, n.171.

Hesselink, M. W., 'The General Principles of Civil Law: Their Nature, Roles and Legitimacy', in Amsterdam Law School Legal Studies Research Paper No. 2011-35 - Centre for the Study of European Contract Law Working Paper No.2011-14.

Hewit, R. L and Wallace, W. P., Jr, 'Administrative Civil Money Penalties and the Right to Jury Trial - Notes & Comments', in *Washington and Lee Law Review* Vol. XXXIII 1976.

Hill, R. A., 'Compensatory Justice: Over Time and Between Groups', in *The Journal of Political Philosophy*, Volume 10, Number 4, 2002, pp. 392-415.

Hinchy, R., 'Judicial Method and Advocates' Immunity in the High Court of Australia and the House of Lords,' in *Murdoch University Electronic Law Journal*, 12 1 (2006), pp. 187-208.

Hruschka, J., 'The Greatest Happiness Principle and Other Early German Anticipations of Utilitarian Theory,' in 1991 *Utilitas*, 3 : 165 – 77.

Hull, N. E. H., 'Reconstructing the Origins of Realistic Jurisprudence: A Prequel to the Llewellyn-Pound Exchange over Legal Realism,' in *Duke Law Journal,* Vol. 1989:1302.

Hulme, D. & Toye, J., 'The case for cross-disciplinary social science research on poverty, inequality and well-being,' in *The Journal of Develpoment Studies*, 2006 .

Isenman, L. D., 'Toward An Understanding of Intuition and Its Importance in Scientific Endeavor', in *Perspective in Biology and Medicine,* 40, 3 Spring 1997.

Ives, W., 'European Union Law,' in Civitas 01/2006, last update: Lucy Hatton, 07/2011 - CIVITAS Institute for the Study of Civil Society 2006.

Iwanov, I., 'SIL Electronic Book Review 2011-003: "Linguistics and the formal sciences: The origins of generative grammar" by Marcus Tomalin, in *Cambridge Studies in Linguistics*, (Cambridge: Cambridge University Press 2006).

Jackendoff, Ray, 'Précis of Foundations of Language: Brain, Meaning, Grammar, Evolution,' in *Behavioral and Brain Science* (2003) 26, 651-70.

Janda, R., 'Toward Cosmopolitan Law,' in (2005) 50 McGill Law Journal / Revue de Droit de McGill.

Jaworska, A and Tennenbaum, J., 'The Ground of Moral Status,' in Stanford Encyclopedia of Philosohy, first published Thursday, March 14, 2013.

Johnson, K., *Introduction to Transformational Grammar*, University of Massachusetts at Amherst, Fall 2004.

Johnstone, Q., 'An Evaluation of the Rules of Statutory Interpretation,' (1954), in *Kansas Law Review*, Vol 3.

Keller, L. R., 'The role of generalized utility theories in descriptive, prescriptive, and normative decision analysis,' in *North-Holland Information and Decision Technologies* 15 (1989) 259 – 271.

Keller, M and Edelstein, W, 'The Development of Socio-Moral Meaning Making: Domains, Categories, and Perspective-Taking,' in W.M. Kurtines & J.L. Gewirtz (Eds.) (Hillsdale, NJ: Erlbaum, 1991), in *Handbook of moral behavior and development: Vol. 2, Research (pp. 89-114).*

Kelsen, Hans, *What is Justice*?- Justice, Law, and Politics in the Mirror of Science, collected Essays by Hans Kelsen, (Berkeley and Los Angeles: University of California Press, 1957).

Kelsen, Hans,'*General Theory of Law and State*,' 20th Century Legal Philosophy Series Vol. I (Anders Wedberg trans.), (New York: Russel & Russel, 1961).

Kelsen, Hans, *Pure Theory of Law*, translation from the Second (Revised and Enlarged) German Edition by Max Knight, (Berkeley, Los Angeles and London: University of California Press, 1967).

Kemp, C., Bernstein, A and Tenenbaum, J.B., 'A Generative Theory of Similarity', in Proceedings of the Twenty-Seventh Annual Conference of the Cognitive Science Sociey 27(27), 2005 - cloudfront.escholarship.org.

Kennedy, W.B., 'A Review of Legal Realism,' in 9 *Fordhan Law Review* 362 (1940).

Kennedy, D., 'Form and Substance in Private Law Adjudication,' in 89 *Harvard Law Review* 1685 (1976).

Kennedy, D., 'Freedom and Constraint in Adjudication: A Critical Phenomenology, Critical Legal Studies, Critical Phenomenology of Judging,' in 36 *Journal of Legal Education* (1986).

Kerr, Lord, 'Clifford Chance Lecture, 25 January 2012', The UK Supreme Court, The modest underworker of Strasbourg?; Judgments – In re P and others (AP) (Appellants) (Northern Ireland), in *Parliament home page > Parliament business > Publications and Records > Lords Publications > Judgment Index > Judgment.*

Kirby, M., 'Precedent-Report on Australia,' International Academy of Comparative Law Conference, Utrecht, The Netherlands, July 17, 2006.

Kirby, M., 'Statutory Interpretation: The Meaning of Meaning', School of Accounting and Law Symposium on Statutory Interpretation, Chapter House, St. Paul's Cathedral, RMIT University, Melbourne, August 13, 2009.

Klein, G. and Baxter, H. C., 'Interservice/Industry Training, and education Conference', in Paper No. 2500, (I/ITSEC), 2006, Klein Associates, A Division of Applied Research Associates, Inc., Fairborn, OH 45324-6362.

Kloepfer, S., 'Book Review: Legal Reasoning and Legal Theory, by Neil MacCormick', in *Osgoode Hall Law Journal* 18.4 (1980): 674-682.

Kloosterhuis, H., 'Toward a Typology of Argumentation based on Legal Principles', Hacia una tipologia de argumentacion basada en principios legale, in *COGENCY* Vol.3, No.2 (67-80), Summer 2011.

Kock, C., 'Michael Hoppmann' Argumentative Verteidiguing: Grundlegung zu einer modernen Statuslehre. Neue. 5', (Berlin: Weidler, 2008), Department of Media, Cognition, and Communication, University of Copenhagen.

Kohen, Ari, 'The Problem of Secular Sacredness: Ronald Dworkin, Machiel Perry, and Human Rights Foundationalism,' in *Faculty Publications: Political Science, Journal of Human Rights* 5 (2006), pp. 235-256.

Kolitch, Shawn., 'Constitutional Fact Finding and the Appropriateness of Empirical Data in Constitutional Law', in *Lewis & Clark Law Review*, Vol. 10:3, 2006.

Kooijmans, Tijs, 'Harmonisation Des Sanction Penales – Constant : The Netherland', in a report edited by M. Delmas-Marty (2003), the Scientific Bureau of the Supreme Court of the Netherlands and Law School of the Erasmus University, Rotterdam.

Kraut, R., 'Aristotle's Ethics,' in Stanford Encyclopedia of Philosophy, first published Tuesday, May 1, 2001; substantive revision Monday, March 29, 2010 (2014).

Kreitner, Roy, 'Biographing Realist Jurisprudence,' in Law & Social Inquiry, Vol.35, Issue 3, 765-791, Summer 2010.

Kress, K. J., 'Legal Reasoning and Coherence Theories: Dworkin's Rights Thesis, Retroactivity, and the Linear Order of Decisions,' in 72 *Cal. L. Rev.* 369 (1984).

Krishan, M., 'Review of Symmetry, Causality, Mind, Michael Leyton: Cambridge, Massachusetts: MIT Press, 1992, 630 pages,' Action editor: Stefan Wermter, in *Book review/Cognitive Systems Research* 8 (2007) 131-133.

Kruschke, J. K and Fragassi, M. M, 'The perception of causality: Feature binding in interacting objects', Department of Psychology, Indiana University, Bloomington, IN, supported in part by NIMH FIRST Award 1-R29-MH51572-01 to Kruschke, and by an Indiana University Cognitive Science Program Summer Research Fellowship to Fragassi - access to the lab at U.C. Berkely for this research in 1986-87.

Lamond, Grant, 'Precedent and Analogy in Legal Reasoning,' in Stanford Encyclopedia of Philosophy, first published Tuesday, June 20, 2006.

Lamont, J. and Favor, C., 'Distributive Justice,' in Stanford Encyclopedia of Philosophy, first published Sunday, September 22, 1996; substantive revision Wednesday, January 2, 2013.

Langlinais, A and Leiter, B., 'The Methodology of Legal Philosophy,' to appear in T. Gendler et al. (eds.),The Oxford Handbook of Philosophical Methodology, draft of October 26, 2012.

Law Reform Commission of Saskatchewan, 'Administrative Penalties, Final Report', University of Saskatchewan, Saskatoon, SK S7N 5A6, March 2012.

LeBar, M. and Slote, M., 'Justice as A Virtue,' in Stanford Encyclopedia of

Philosophy, first published Friday, March 8, 2002;substantive revision Wednesday, September 8, 2010 (2016).

Legal Definition of Statute, from the 'Lectric Law Library's Lexicon *Statute, http://www.Lectlaw.com/def2/s071.htm, 1995 – 2013 The 'Lectric Law Library.

Leiter, B., 'Rethinking Legal Realism: Toward a Naturalized Jurisprudence,' in 76 *Texas Law Review* 267 (1997).

Lenaerts, K and Gutiérrez-Fons, J.A., 'To Say What the Law of the EU Is: Methods of Interpretation and the European Court of Justice,' in *EUI Working Paper AEL 2013/9*, European University Institute, Academy of European Law.

Lin, Dekang, 'An Information-Theoric Definition of Similarity, Department of Computer Science, University of Manitoba, Winnipeg, Manitoba, Canada R3T 2N2, a work partially supported by NSERC Research Grant OGP121338, lcml, 1998.,

Lipton, P. (reviewer), 'Philosophy of Science Today, Oxford University Press, 2003', in Peter Clark and Katherine Hawley (eds.). Cambridge University, 2015, in *Notre Dame Philosophical Reviews.*

Locating The Law, A Handbook for Non-Law Librarians, Fifth Edition, Revised 2011, Southern California Association of Law Libraries (SCALL, Public Access to Legal Information Committee, edited by June Kim, © 2009, 2011 SCALL. www.aallnet.org/chapter/scall/locating/ch1.pdf

Losee, J., *A Historical Introduction to the Philosophy of Scince*, second edition, (Oxford and New York: Oxford University Press, 1972/1980).

Lovett, A., Sagi, E., and Gentner, D., 'Analogy as a mechanism of comparison', in *the Spatial Intelligence and Learning Center (SILC)*, Conference Paper 2007.

Lucke, H. K., 'Ratio Decidendi: Adjudicative Rationale and Source of Law', in *Bond Law Review*, Vol.1 [1989], Iss.1, Art.2.

Maduro, M. P., 'Interpreting European Law: Judicial Adjudication in a Context of Constitutional Pluralism,' in *Vol.1* EJLS No.2 (2007).

Marshall, Dale., 'What Is Obiter Dicta?', edited by K. Osborne, Last Modified March 10, 2014, Conjecture Corporation, 2003-2014.

Mayrhofer, Ralf and Rothe, Anselm, 'Causal Status meets Coherence: The Explanatory Role of Causal Models in Categorization', in N. Miyake, D. Peebles & R.P.Cooper (eds.), in *Proceedings of the 34th Annual Conference of Cognitive Science Society (pp. 743-748)-2012 - Cognitive Science Society, Austin, TX.*

McCuskey, D. and Conaway, W. J., 'The Interdisciplinary Approach', in Educational Leadership, Spring Conference, Region III ASCD, The Woodner Hotel, Washington, D.C., April 23, 1995.

McMahan, Jeff, 'Moral Intuition', Chapter 5 in *The Blackwell Guide to Ethical Theory*', second edition, edited by Hugh LaFollette and Ingmar Persson, (Blackwell Publishing Ltd., 2013).

McNaughton, D., 'Michael Huemer, Ethical Intuitionism, Palgrave Macmillan, 2006', in *Notre Dame Philosophical Review,* 2016.

Medne, Kristine and Muravska, Tatjana, 'Interdisciplinary: Dilemas within the Theory, Methodology and Practice,' Tatjana Muravska & Zaneta Ozolina eds., (Univ. of Latvia Press, 2011), in *Interdisciplinary in Social Sciences: Does It Provide Answers to Current Challenges in Higher Education and Research?*

Melenyzer, Lisa, 'Double Jeopardy Protection from Civil Sanctions after Hudson v. Uniteed States,' in 89 *J. Crim. L & Criminology* 1007 (1998-1999). .

Melton, G. B., 'Realism in Psychology and Humanism in Law: Psycholegal Studies at Nebraska,' in *Nebraska Law Review*, Vol.69:251, 1990.

Merkel, Adolf, ' *Appendix I - Rudolf von Ihering Law as A Means to An End'*, translated from the German by Isaac Husik, translated and reprinted from Ihering's "Jahrbucher fur Dogmatik des heutigen Romische' und Deutschen Privatrechts,' Bd. Xxxii, N.F. xx (Jena, Gustav Fisher, 1893).

Miller, J. M., 'The Science of Law: The Maturing of Jurisprudence into Fundamental Principles in Fairness', 1985, in *Western State University Law Review*, Volume 13, Spring 1986, Number 2.

Miller, R. C., 'Varieties of Interdisciplinary Approaches in the Social Science: A 1981 Overview', in *Issues in Intergrative Studies* No.1, pp. 1-37 (1982).

Mnookin, R. H., 'Alternative Dispute Resolution,' March 4, 1998, www. law. Harvard. Edu/programs/olin-/pdf/232p, No. I.

Mokyr, Joel., 'The Knowledge Society: Theoretical and Historical Underpinnings', Department of Economics and History, Northwestern University, presented to the Ad Hoc Expert Group on Knowledge Systems, United Nations, New York, Sept. 4-5, in part of Joel Mokyr's The Gift of Athena: Historical Origins of the Knowledge Economy (Princetown: Princetwon University Press, 2002).

Nance, Dale A., 'Legal Theory and the Pivotal Role of the Concept of Coercion', in *University of Colorado Law Review*, Volume 57, Number 1, Fall 1985.

Nandi, V., Model of Neutral-Inclusivity – Book of Instruments – About What is, can and should be, Nonpropositional and Propositional Reality, The

Normativeness of "Purely Descriptive" Theorizing, (Amsterdam: Stichting Foundation, 1986).

Neuhaus, P. H., 'Legal Certainty Versus Equity in the Conflict of Law', Law and Contemporary Problem', in 28 Law and Contemporary Problems, pp. 795-807 (Fall 1963) - *Duke Law Scholarship Repository Journal* LCP. Vol. 28, No.4 (1963).

Nevin, B. E., 'More Concerning the Roots of Transformational Generative Grammar', in *Historiographia Linguistics xxxvi:2/3 (2009), pp. 461-481.*

Nichols, J. L. and Ross, H. L., 'The Effectiveness of Legal Sanctions in Dealing with Drinking Drivers', in Judicial and Administrative Process – Background Paper, 1988 – in Alcohol Drugs and Driving Vol. 6, Issue 2, dated (April – June 1990), pp. 33-60, and, Journal of Safety Research 22(2):117-117, June 1991.

Nolan, P. S., 'Double Jeopardy's Multipunishment Protection and Regulation of Civil Sanctions after United States v. Ursery', in 80 *Marquette Law Review* (1997).

Nolfi, Kate, 'Why Is Epistemic Evaluation Prescriptive?', in Susanna Siegel ed., Special Issue on the Nature of Belief, in *Inquiry: An Interdisciplinary Journal of Philosophy* 57 (1): 97-121 (2014).

Noonan, J. T., 'The Concept of Law. By H.L.A. Hart. Oxford: Oxford University Press, 1961', in *Natural Law Forum.*

Nuzzo, Angelica., 'Reflective Judgment, Determinative Judgment, and the Problem of Particularity', in *Washington University Jurisprudence Review*, Volume 6 / Issue 1, 2013.

Olsson, Erik. J., 'Coherentist Theories of Epistemic Justification', in Stanford Encyclopedia of Philosophy, first published on Tuesday, November 11, 2003; substantive revision on Thursday, November 15, 2012.

O'Niel, Aidan, 'How the CJEU uses the Charter of Fundamental Rights', in eutopialaw, EU Law:Comment and Analysis, posted on April 3, 2012 by eutopialaw.

O'Niel, Shawn, 'Quine's Naturalization and Kim's Response', in PL370, 3-5, Fall 2004.

Ott, Claus and Schafer, Hans-Bernd., 'The Dichotomy Between Property Rules and Liability Rules: Experiences from German Law', in *Erasmus Law Review,* Volume 01 Issue 04, 2008.

Palmer, B. W and Giles, J. W., 'Philosophy of Law. Giorgio del Vecchio', translated by Thomas Owen Martin from the Eighth Edition, forward by Brendan F.

Brown, - The Art of Advocacy. Llyod Paul Stryker,' in *Cath. U.L. Rev.* 147 (1954).

Papageorgiou, Elena, 'The European Court of Justice and the Supremacy of EC Law', Law Office of Community Law, the Law Office of the Republic of Cyprus, www.law.gov.cy>law>lawoffice.

Pasnau, R., 'Epistemology Idealized', in *Mind*, Vol. 122, Issue 488, 1 October 2013, pp. 987-1021, (advanced access publication 12 February 2014).

Patterson, E. W., *Law in Scientific Age,* (New York and London: Columbia University Press, 1963).

Paunio, Elina, 'Beyond Predictability – Reflection on Legal Certainty and the Discourse Theory of Law in the EU Legal Order', in *German Law Journal,* Vol. 10 No. 11, 2009.

Pelletier, F. J., 'The generative power of rule orderings in formal grammars', in *Linguistics* 18 (1980), 017-072.

Peters, P. S, Jr and Ritchie, R. W., 'On the Generative Power of Transformational Grammars', 1965, 1968, (American Elsevier Publishing Company, Inc., 1973), in *Information Sciences* 6, 49-83 (1973).

Pitz, Gordon F and Sachs, Natalie J., 'Judgment and Decision: Theory and Application', in *Ann Rev. Psychol,* 1984, 35:139-63.

Plantinga, A., "Justification in the 20th Century," in Enrique Villandeva ed., (Atascadero, Calif.: Ridgeview Publishing Co.,1992), pp. 43-78, in *Philosophical Issues 2, Rationality in Epistemology.*

Polinsky, A. M and Shavell, S., 'The Fairness of Sanctions: Some Implications for Optimal Enforcement Policy', in *American Law and Economics Review* V2 N2 2000 (223-237).

Pollicino, Oreste, 'Legal Reasoning of the Court of Justice in the Context of the Principle of Equality Between Judicial Activism and Self-restraint', in *German Law Journal* Vol. 05, No. 03, 2004.

Popova, Maria, *The Science of "intuition",* (New York: Brain Pickings, 2012),' http:// www. Brainpickings.org/index.php/2012/11/08/the-science-of-intuition.

Priel, D., 'Evaluating Descriptive Jurisprudence', in American Journal of Jurisprudence: Vol.52: Iss.1, Article 6 (2007).

Priel, D., 'Two Models of General Jurisprudence', in Comparative Research in Law & Political Economy, Research Paper No.39/2013.

Priel, D, 'The Boundaries of Law and the Purpose of Legal Philosophy', in *Law and Philosophy*, 2008/09.

Protevi, J., 'Alexandre Lefebvre, The Image of law: Deleuze, Bergson,

Spinoza' Stanford University Press, 2008, 305+xxii pages, ISBN-13: 9780804759854, Chap 3', in *Cont Philos Rev DOI 10.1007/s11007-009-9106-0, Book Review'*, (Springer Science+Business Media B.B. 2009, Published online: May 26, 2009).

Pust, Joel., 'Intuition,' in Stanford Encyclopedia of Philosophy, first published Tuesday, December 4, 2012.

Quesada, J., 'Human Similarity theories for the semantic web', Similarity theories, (1987), proceedings of the First International Conference 2008-137.226.34.227, in *CEUR Workshop* Vol 419, paper 7, pdf., CEUR Workshop Organization.

Raban, Ofer, 'The Fallacy of Legal Certainty: Why Vague Legal Standards May Be Better For Capitalism and Liberalism', in *Public Interest Law Journal* Vol. 19: 175 (2010).

Raban, Ofer, 'Real and Imagined Threats to the Rule of Law: On Brian Tamanaha's Law As A Means To An End', 2007, in *Virginia Journal of Social Policy and the Law*, Vol.15, 2008.

Rasnic, Carol Daugherty, 'Alternative Dispute Resolution Rather Than Litigation? A Look at Current Irish and American Laws', in *Judicial Studies Institute Journal* 4:2 (2004).

Rawls, John, *A Theory of Justice*, (Cambridge, MA: The Belknap Press of Harvard University Press, 1971).

Rehder, Bob, 'Categorization as causal reasoning', in *Cognitive Science* 27 (2003) 709-748, Elsevier.

Rehder, Bob and Kim, Shin Woo, 'The Role of Coherence in Causal-Based Categorization', 2008, Department of Psychology, New York University, 6 Washington Place, New York, NY 10003 USA.

Rehder, Bob and Martin, Jay B., 'Towards A Generative Model of Causal Cycles', In: Kokinov,B., Karmiloff-Smith, A., Nersessian N.J., (eds.), (New Bulgarian Univ. Press, 2011), in *European Perspectives on Cognitive Science.*

Rehder, Bob and Kim, Shin Woo Kim, 'Causal Status and Coherence in Causal-Based Categorization,' in *Journal of Experimental Psychology: Learning, Memory, and Cognition* 2010, Vol.36, No.5, 1171-1206.

Reid, Herbert G. 'A Philosopher's Perspective on Law: A Study of Morris R. Cohen', in *American Journal of Jurisprudence,* Vol. 16: Iss. 1, Article 10 (1971).

Reimer, Marga and Michaelson, 'Reference', in *Stanford Encyclopedia of Philosophy*, 2014.

Reufels, M. and Molle, K., 'Labour Law within the Recent Jurisprudence of the European Court of Human Rights', in *Jurisprudencija / Jurisprudence*, 2012, 19(4):1567-1583.

Reynolds, R, 'Full Text of Ruling of the Dutch Supreme Court', in *RuneScape – Dutch Supreme Court's Decision, LIN: BQ9251, Supreme J, 10/00101*, IVPN Administration, February 1, 2010, (the base translation by Google Translate with amendment and formatting by R. Reynolds), under sub-heading III: Satisfy the other condition for criminal liability under Article 310 of the Penal Code – item 333

Robinson, P. H and Darley, J. M., 'Intuitions of Justice: Implications for Criminal Law and Justice Policy', in 81 *S. Cal. L. Rev.* 1, 3 (2007).

Robinson, P. H and Kurzban, R., 'Concordance & Conflict in Intuitions of Justice', in 91 *Minn. L. Rev.* 1829, 1854-55 (2007).

Robinson, P. H., Kurzban, R and Jones, O.D., 'The Origins of Shared Intuitions of Justice', in *Vanderbilt Law Review*, Volume 60, Number 6, November 2007.

Rodes, Robert E. Jr, 'On the Historical School of Jurisprudence', in 49 The American Journal of Jurisprudence 2004, Notre Dame Law School – Legal Studies Research Paper No. 06-31.

Rosenkrantz, Carlos, 'A Compensatory Conception of Corrective Justice Revisited', in *Diritto & questioni pubbliche,* Vol. 12 (2012):109-135, Palermo.

Rosser, Ezra., 'Customary Law: The Way Things Were, Codified', in the new edition of Getches, Wilkinson, and Williams, Federal Indian Law (5th ed., 2004), in *Tribal Law Journal* Vol. 8.

Ruckert, Joachim, 'Friedrich Carl von Savigny, the Legal Method, and the Modernity of Law', in *Juridica International* XI/2006, pp. 55-67.

Sage, Yves-Louis, 'Reinforcing the Rights of the Victim in the French Law on Civil Liability', in (1998) 28 *VUWLR*.

Salachova, Bohumila and Vitek, Bohumil., 'Interpretation of European Law, Selected Issues', in Acta Universitatis Agriculturae et Silviculturae Mendelianae Brunensis, Volume LXI, Number 2, 2013.

Schwartz, B. D., 'On explicit and negative data effecting and affecting competence and linguistic behavior,' in *Studies in Second Language Acquisition*, 15, 147-163 (1993).

Schwed, Menashe, 'Descriptive theories of argumentation as part of Quine's project of naturalized" epistemology', (May 17, 2001), in *OSSA Conference Archieve, Paper 104, University of Windsor Scholarship – OSSA Conference Archive – OSSA 4.*

Scofield, R. G., 'The Distinction between Judicial Dicta and Obiter Dicta', in *Los Angeles Lawyer*, October 2002.

Scofield, R. G., 'Goodhart's Concession: Defending Ratio Decidendi From Logical Positivism and Legal Realism in the First Half of the Twentieth Century', in (2005) 16 *The King's College Law Journal.*

Schlechtriem, P., Markesinis, B and Lorenz, S., 'Decisions of the Federal Court of Justice (Bundesgerichtshof),' Bundesgerichtshof (Sixth Civil Division), 19 September 1961 BGHZ 35, 362 = NJW 1961,' 2059 (with approving notes by W. Rotelmann NJW 1962, 736 and H. Hubmann = *VersR* 1962, 350, 562), in t*he German Law Archive courtesy of: Translated German Cases and Materials* [under the direction of P. Schlechtriem, B. Markesinis and S. Lorenz], translated by F.H. Lawson and B.S. Markesinis, HTLM edition by Lawrence Schafe.

Schubert, Maximilian (Rechtsreferent) and Clark, Birgit (Rechtsanwaltin), 'Wintersteiger' – Austrian Supreme Court refers jurisdiction question in AdWord cases to the ECJ', in *Journal of Intellectual Property Law & Practice*, 2011, Vol. 6, No.5.

Siegel, Charles, *Ethics, What We Still Know After a Skeptical Age*, (Berkeley, California: Preservation Institute, 2009).

Simon, D and Holyoak, K. J., 'Structural Dynamics of Cognition: From Consistency Theories to Constraint Satisfaction', in *Personality and Social Psychology Review*, 2002, Vol. 6, 283-294.

Simon, D., 'A Third View of the Black Box: Cognitive Coherence in Legal Decision Making', in *The University of Chicago Law Review* (2004) 71:511.

Simons, K. W., 'The Crime/Tort Distinction: Legal Doctrine and Normative Perspectives', in *Widener Law Journal*, Vol. 17, 2008.

Sinclair, K. Jr, 'Legal Reasoning: In Search of an Adequate Theory of Argument', in 59 *Cal. L. Rev.* 821 (1971).

Sinnot-Armstrong, Walter, '*R.M. Hare (1919 - ,'The Language of Moral*' (Oxford: Clarendon Press, 1952).

Shanahan, C. F., 'Significant Entangelments: A Framework for the Civil Consequences of Criminal Convictions', in 49 *American Criminal Law Review* 2012.

Skelton, A., 'William David Ross', in Stanford Encyclopedia of Philosophy, first published Tuesday, August 12, 2010, substantive revision Tuesday, June 19, 2012.

Spaak, Torben, 'Karl Olivecrona's Legal Philosophy: a Critical Appraisal', De Lege, Uppsala – Minnesota Colloquium: Law, Culture and Values, Mattias Dahlberg (ed), pp. 33-83, (Uppsala: lustus forlag, 2009), in *Ratio Juris* 24 (2): 156-193 (2011).

Spaak, Torben, 'Karl Olivecrona on Judicial Law-Making', in *Ratio Juris,* 2009, Vol. 22, Issue 4 : pp. 483-498.

Spaak, Torben, 'Naturalism in Scandinavian and American Realism; Similarities and Differences,' Department of Law, Uppsala University, Sweden, 2009.

Spellman, B and Schauer, F., 'Legal Reasoning', in Public Law and Legal Theory Working Paper Series 2012-09 - University of Virginia School of Law, February 2012.

Stănescu, Lucian-Sorin, 'The Teleological Interpretation and the Discovery of the Constitution's Efficiency Meanings', in *Fiat Iustitia* No.1/2014.

Stavropoulos, Nicos, 'Interpretivist Theories of Law', in Stanford Encyclopedia of Philosophy, first published Tuesday, October 14, 2003.

Stefanelli, Justine N., 'Report – The Effect in the European Community of Judgments in Civil and Commercial Matters: Recognition, Res Judicata and Abuse of Process – United States', in *British Institute of International and Comparative Law, Project Reference: JLS/2006/FPC/21 – 30-CE-00914760055.*

Stemplewska-Zakowics, K., Kobylinska, D., Suszek, H. and Szymczyk, B., 'Exploration in the Discursive Mind: Theoretical Model', in *International Journal for Dialogical Science*, Fall, 2010, Vol. 4, pp. 81-94.

Stelken, U., 'Administrative Law and State Liability', University of Speyer, in Lehrstuhl fur Offentliches Recht, insbesondere deutsches und europaisches Verwaltungsrecht, DHV - Deutsche Hochschule fur Verwaltungswissenschaften Speyer, § 3 Sources of Administrative Law.

Stratton-Lake, P., 'Intuitionism in Ethics,' in Stanford Encyclopedia of Philosophy, first published Monday, December 15, 2014.

Stuhlmuller, A., Tenenbaum, J.B and Goodman, N.D, 'Learning Structured Generative Concepts,' in Proceedings the Annual Meeting of the Cognitive Science Society, 32(32)-2010, cloudfront.escholarship.org

Subramanian, Ram and Shames, Alison., 'Sentencing and Prison Practices in Germany and the Netherlands: Implications for the United States, 50 years of Innovation 1961-2011', in *VERA Institute of Justice*, October 2013.

Suszek, H., Kobylinska, D., Stemplewska-Zakowics, K and Szymczyk, B., 'Exploration in the Discursive Mind: Research', in *International Journal for Dialogical Science*, Fall, 2010, Vol. 4, pp. 95-122.

Svennerlind, Christer, 'Philosophical Motives For the Swedish Criminal Code of 1965', in *Philosophical Communication,* Web Series, No.52, 2009,

Swisher, P. N., 'Teaching Legal Reasoning in Law School', in *74 Lib. J. 534 (1981).*

Tabarrok, Alexander, 'If You're So Rich.... The Economic Approach to Epistemology', in A Journal of Interdisciplinary Normative Study, Reason Papers, Issue No. 19,l Fall 1994, pp. 146-159.

Tamanaha, B.Z., 'Understanding Legal Pluralism: Past to Present, Local to Global,' in *Sydney Law Review*, Vol. 30: 375, 2008.

Tamanaha, B.Z., 'The Primary of Society and Failures of Law and Development', in *Cornell International Law Journal*, Vol. 44, 2011.

Tanner, J., 'The Naturalistic Fallacy', University of Durham, in *Richmond Journal of Philosophy* 13 (Autumn 2006).

Tarnas, R., The Passion of the Western Mind, Understanding the Ideas That Have Shaped Our World View, (New York: Ballantine Books, 1993).

Tetley, William , Q.C., 'Mixed Jurisdictions: Common Law vs Civil Law (Codified and Uncodified', in *60 La. L.Rev.(2000)* and *La. L. Rev.* 1999.

Thompson, J.B., *Paul Ricouer Hermeneutics and the human sciences*, essays on language, action and interpretation, editions de la Maison des Sciences de l'Homme – Paris, (Cambridge University Press, 1981).

Thurmon, M.A., 'When the Court Divides: Reconsidering the Precedential Value of Supreme Court Plurality Decisions', in *Duke Law Journal* Vol. 42:419 (1992).

Tiberius, Valerie and Hall, Alicia., 'Normative theory and psychological research: Hedonism, eudaimonism and why it matters,' Author Posting, (Taylor & Francis, 2010), in *The Journal of Positive Psychology*, Volume 5 Issue 3, May 2010.

Tomalin, Marcus, 'Goodman, Quine, and Chomsky: from a grammatical point of view', in *Lingua* 113 (2003) 1223-1253.

Traskman, Per Ole,'Harmonisation des Sanctions Penales – Constant: Sweden', in M. Delmas-Marty edition, (2003), in *DC3595CH14-RAPPORTS-NATIONAUX*'.

Trevino, A. Javier, 'The Influence of Sociology on American Jurisprudence: From Oliver Wendell Holmes to Critical Legal Studies', in *Mid-American Review of Sociology*, 1994, Vol XVIII, No. 1 & 2: 23-46.

Tsoutsanis, Alexander, 'Finding Vredo (pat.pending): The Dutch Supreme Court Decision of 'Escitalopram' in Lundbeck v. Tiefenbacher et al.,' in *Journal of Intellectual Property Law & Practice* 2014, 41-45.

Tucker, Adam, 'The Politics of Legal Positivism: A Reply to David Dyzenhaus', in (2013)38 *Australian Journal of Legal Philosophy*, 74-101.

Tversky, Amos and Kahneman, Daniel, 'Rational Choice and Framing Decision', in *The Journal of Business*, Vol.59, No.4, Part 2: The Behavioral Foundations of Economic Theory (Oct. 1986), S251-S278.

Velasquez, M., Andre, C., Shanks, T.S.J and Meyer, M.J., 'Justice and Fairness', in *Ethics* V# N2 (Spring 1990).

Viola, Francesco, 'Judicial Truth', in *Persona y Derecho,* 32, 1995.

Wachtel, T and McCold, P., 'In Pursuit of Paradigm: A Theory of Restorative Justice,' in Paper presented at the XIII World Congress of Criminology, 10-15 August 2003, Rio de Janeiro (International Institute for Restorative Practices, Bethlehem, Pennsylvania, USA, 2003).

Wahlgren, P., 'Legal Reasoning, A Jurisprudential Model', (Stockholm Institute for Scandinavian Law, 1957-2009).

Waldman, M. R., 'Neurath's ship: The constitutive relation between normative and descriptive theories of rationality', in *Behavioral and Brain Sciences* (2011) 34:5.

Walker, Vern R., 'Discovering the Logic of the Legal Reasoning', in WALKER. PRD2 - Hofstra University School of Law, Hempstead, New York, USA, 11/6/2007.

Warren, I.H and Aronstam, B.R., 'Delaware's Business Judgment Rule and Varying Standards of Judicial Review for Assessing Director Conduct in M&A Transactions,' Weil, Gotshal & Manges LLP – New York, NY, (the Canadian Institute – November 2007).

Wenar, Leif, 'Rights', in Stanford Encyclopedia of Philosophy, first published Monday, December 19, 2005; substantive revision Saturday, July 2, 2011.

Wendel, W.B, 'Legal Ethics Is About the Law, Not Morality or Justice: A Reply to Critics', Wendel.A3Edit, 1 February 1993, Major Reference Books – Wiley Online Library, in *International Encyclopedia of Ethics, 2013 – Wiley Online Library.*

West's Encyclopedia of American Law, edition 2. Copyright 2008 The Gale Group Inc. on Sentencing.

Winston, P.H., Binford, Th.O., Katz, B and Lowry, M., 'Learning Physical Descriptions from Functional Definitions, Examples and Precedents', 1983, in *AAAI-83 Proceedings - AAAI (www.aaai.org).*

Wortham, Stanton, 'Reviews of Rom Harre and Grant Gillet, The Discursive Mind, and James P. Gee, The Social Mind', in *GSE Publications, 6-1-1997,* reprinted from *Theory and Psychology*, Volume 7, Issue 3 June 1997, 422-424.

Yopchick, Jennelle E and Kim, Nancy S., 'The influence of causal information on judgments of treatment efficacy', (The Psychonomic Society Inc., 2009), in *Memory & Cognition 2009,* 37 (1), 29-41.

Young, J. O., 'The Coherence Theory of Truth', in Stanford Encyclopedia of Philosophy, first published Tuesday, September 3, 1996; substantive revision Wednesday, March 27, 2013.

Zimmer, Markus, 'Overview of Alternative Dispute Resolution: A Primer for Judges and Administrators', in *International Journal For Court Administration,* December 2011.

Zimring, Franklin E., 'The Multiple Middlegrounds Between Civil and Criminal Law', in 101 The Yale Law Journal 1901 (1992) - Berkeley Law – Berkeley Law Scholarship Repository, Faculty Scholarship.

Zinnecker, T. R., 'Syllogism, Enthymemes, and Fallacies: Mastering Secured Transactions Through Deductive Reasoning', in 56 *Wayne L. Rev.* 1581 (2010).

www.ingramcontent.com/pod-product-compliance
Lightning Source LLC
LaVergne TN
LVHW011854200926
848484LV00002B/452
* 9 7 8 1 9 1 2 1 4 2 2 5 5 *